MEN, WOMEN, AND CHANGE

A SOCIOLOGY OF MARRIAGE AND FAMILY

MEN, WOMEN, AND CHANGE

A SOCIOLOGY OF MARRIAGE AND FAMILY

Second Edition

Letha Dawson Scanzoni

John Scanzoni
University of North Carolina

McGRAW-HILL BOOK COMPANY

*New York   St. Louis   San Francisco   Auckland   Bogotá   Hamburg
Johannesburg   London   Madrid   Mexico   Montreal   New Delhi
Panama   Paris   São Paulo   Singapore   Sydney   Tokyo   Toronto*

For our sons
Steve and Dave

This book was set in Palatino by Black Dot, Inc. (ECU)
The editors were Alison Meersschaert and David Dunham;
the designer was Joan E. O'Connor;
the production supervisor was Leroy A. Young.
The photo editor was Inge King.
New Drawings were done by J & R Services, Inc.
R. R. Donnelley & Sons Company was printer and binder.

MEN, WOMEN, AND CHANGE
A Sociology of Marriage and Family

2 3 4 5 6 7 8 9 0 D O D O 8 9 8 7 6 5 4 3 2 1

See Acknowledgments on page A1-A3.
Copyrights included on this page by reference.

Cover photograph: Louise Nevelson, *America—Dawn*, collection of The Art Institute of Chicago. Photograph by Allan Mitchell.

Library of Congress Cataloging in Publication Data

Scanzoni, Letha.
    Men, women and change.

    Bibliography: p.
    Includes index.
    1. Marriage. 2. Family. 3. Sex role. 4. Socialization. I. Scanzoni, John H., date   joint author.
II. Title.
HQ734.S3766 1981   306.8   80-21105
ISBN 0-07-055054-9

CONTENTS

PREFACE

We hope this second edition of *Men, Women, and Change* will, like its predecessor, appeal to both the student and the professional. Again we've endeavored to keep it on the cutting edge of sociological theory. And again we've tried to treat topics systematically and scientifically, yet always humanely. Our emphasis is on the concerns of real people who live in the real world—not on impersonal numbers or abstract theories far removed from everyday life.

The combination of a professional writer who specializes in the study and communication of sociology (Letha Dawson Scanzoni) working with a sociologist who is involved daily in sociological research, teaching, and theory-building (John Scanzoni) helps sociological notions to come alive in an intellectually stimulating manner with maximum personal involvement on the part of the reader. Sociology isn't something unconnected to life—though it has sometimes *seemed* that way because of the dull, ponderous way it has often been presented (at least as viewed from the vantage point of many students!).

We're convinced that a sociology of marriage and family can and should be where students are. And this book shows what we mean by that. We've tried to present concepts like conflict, social exchange, power, gender-role socialization, and decision-making in a lively, interesting way, interwoven with up-to-date statistics which "tell a story" rather than appearing as cold, impersonal numbers. As in the first edition, we've used numerous case studies, photos, drawings, tables, and figures to capture attention and provide further information. And this time, we've added boxed inserts to underscore and illustrate how the text material relates to life all around us.

Our aim has been to present research and *explain* it—especially through cost/reward theory, but through other approaches as well—and to do this in such a way that students see sociology as far more than facts and figures. It's the stuff of daily living. It's about human beings in relationship with other human beings—or in conflict with other human beings—whether in conventional marriage and family arrangements or in alternative life-styles. Students should find the material presented provocative to thought and practical—both for individual decision-making and for choices related to social policy.

Incidentally, when we use the word *family*, we don't consider it synonymous with "white, middle-class, nuclear family." The information and theory presented in this book is applicable to all families. Material on marriages and families which vary by socioeconomic status and race is given thorough coverage but is not treated in isolated fashion as has often been the custom. Such information—for example, on black families—is woven throughout the book rather than being bunched in separate sections.

We've done our best to see that material in this text is current. And we've given special attention to the numerous new questions about marriage and family that have been raised in recent years and the new patterns that have emerged: living together outside marriage, gay relationships, communal arrangements, singleness and single parenthood, intentional childlessness, changes in divorce laws and custody arrangements, and other innovations. But at the same time, *Men, Women, and Change* doesn't center around fads. It centers around the most significant and profound phenomenon that touches marriage and family: the fact that female and male roles are being altered and becoming more interchangeable over time—a long-range pattern that can't help but affect the relationships of all persons to one another.

WHAT'S DIFFERENT IN THE SECOND EDITION?

It shouldn't be surprising that a book with *change* as a major theme would be open to changes in a new edition! In the preface to the first edition (1976), anticipating a constant flow of new data on sex roles, marriage, and family, we wrote the following:

> Because of the approach we've taken throughout this textbook, such incoming new information will only underscore our main thrust: change is taking place, and the explanation has to do primarily with increasing autonomy among women. The book keeps pace with all that is happening because its emphasis is on this very dynamic—change, motion, and process. In other words, the systematic integration of material into an overall theoretical framework of rewards and costs, conflict, exchanges and interchanges means that the book should remain right on top of any new developments that take place, explaining them, organizing them, making sense of them, and generating additional predictions regarding the future.

This new edition spells out some of the changes that are taking place, while continuing to utilize the best in recent sociological theory to illuminate and explain them. And the book has been extensively revised and expanded, with about two-thirds of the material either new or rewritten for even greater clarity and student appeal than characterized the enthusiastically received first edition. The word *revise* comes from a Latin word meaning "to come back," "to revisit." What new ideas and material did we bring as we "came back" to "revisit" *Men, Women, and Change?* Below is a brief overview.

As was true of the first edition, the social roles assigned to females and males and the questioning and challenging of those roles today continue to be a major focus throughout the book. But now we also have an entire separate unit on sex roles, where we not only discuss *sex-role socialization* (along with material on general childhood socialization as well), but in addition examine the *male-female equality question* in historical and cross-cultural perspective, including a look at some questions about whether biological factors influence sex roles.

The discussion on premarital sex now constitutes two chapters, one dealing with the question "What's been happening?" and the other with "What do the changes mean?" Most of the material from the first edition has been retained, with updated statistics. Considerable new material has also been added, including material on premarital contraceptive usage, premarital pregnancy, and related issues, providing not only information but *explanation* of the processes of contraceptive risk-taking and decision-making.

Chapter 6 expands the first edition's discussion of dating and mate selection with an enlarged section on dating and more material on *love* in connection with mate selection. Chapter 7, "His Family, Her Family: The Kin," is entirely new in this edition. It provides a thorough understanding of what *kinship* is all about in our culture and is related to the students' lives in their present and future families. The special extended family patterns of blacks and Chicanos are also described.

In order to provide a more thorough discussion of alternatives to traditional marriage and family in this edition, we've included two greatly expanded chapters to replace the one chapter on this topic in the original edition. Chapter 8, "The Cohabitation and Gay Marriage Alternatives," is made up of about 80 percent new material dealing with two widely discussed subjects: homosexual relationships and cohabitation arrangements. The two are examined separately and compared in relation to societal definitions of marriage and laws about marriage. By analyzing these topics in this way, students are encouraged to think through the question "What *is* marriage?" In addition, the practical everyday lives of persons in these two alternative life-styles are discussed in light of the most recent research. Then, in Chapter 9, the discussion of alternative life-styles continues with a focus on single-ness, single parenthood, communes, and other group arrangements. The discussion on legitimacy status now includes material on unwed fathers as well as unwed mothers. Much of the material in this chapter is new, and statistics are brought up to date.

The fifth part of the book, "Structure and Process in Marriage," contains what many instructors tell us they regard as the core of the book. It explains both the structure and the process, or dynamics, of marriage through the use of a uniquely developed typology of four patterns of marriage and what goes on in each. Students find this extremely helpful in analyzing the marriages of parents, friends, relatives, and others, as well as their own present and future marriages. In the first edition, this unit had three chapters. It has now been expanded to five. Essential material from the first edition remains, and much new material has been added, including new material on marital sex among working-class couples, extra-marital sex, two-location marriage (commuter couples), vestiges of traditional views of women in marriage laws, and an expanded treatment of family violence.

Moving to the final section of the book, "Continuing Processes of the Family Experience," the chapter on decisions about whether or not to have children includes all essential material from the first edition, expanded and updated. But the chapter "Socializing Children for Achievement" in the first edition has been replaced by a new chapter titled "The Years of Childrearing." This new chapter is a more extensive treatment of parenting, much broader than the chapter in the first edition, though including some of the same material. A new discussion of child abuse is also included.

Chapter 17, "The Middle and Later Years of Marriage," is new, as is Chapter 18, "Divorce and Remarriage." Because of space limitation in the first edition, these topics were dealt with only briefly and lumped together in one final chapter with other subjects. Here they are discussed at length and in connection with numerous subtopics much in today's news and of great interest to students and instructors.

Finally, the Epilogue brings together the latest statistics available as we went to press and discusses them in view of the fears some persons have expressed about the "death of the family." Our conclusion is that the family is not dying. But it's changing.

And that's what this book is about—men, women, and *change*. We send out this edition with the same hope with which we launched the first edition—a hope that it will not only inform students but will challenge them to think analytically and theoretically about what is happening and what the changes mean for themselves and for society as a whole. We want the book to enable readers not only to know *what* but also to know *why*.

As before, special thanks to our McGraw-Hill editor Alison Meersschaert who has been with us through both editions and whose encouragement and friendship have cheered us on. Thanks also to David Dunham, our development editor, for his personal interest in the project and for his careful attention to details during the production stage.

We are also grateful to those instructors and students who have graciously commented on the first edition of the book and whose suggestions have been incorporated in this second edition. Their letters and words of appreciation during our travels have been a real source of encouragement. We are likewise grateful to those reviewers who read the manuscript for this new edition and made helpful suggestions and comments. And, as with the first edition, special thanks go out to those undergraduate and graduate students and colleagues with whom we have interacted over the years and whose questions, challenges, observations, and insights on male-female roles and relationships have stimulated and prodded our thinking and research all the more, making it possible for this book to come about in the first place.

Letha Dawson Scanzoni
John Scanzoni

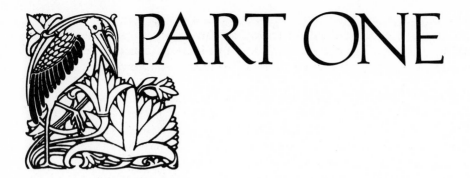

PART ONE

INTRODUCTION

CHAPTER 1

(Charles Gatewood)

A BRIEF INTRODUCTION TO STUDYING MARRIAGE AND FAMILY

M ost of us live out a large share of our lives in some form of family or another. And we can easily see that families can't be ignored if we want to understand the societal patterns and processes all around us. Why? Because the social relationships called *family* are such an important part of society. In fact, no society has ever existed without some sort of social arrangements that may be labeled "kinship" or "familial."

What people do in their families makes a difference in the larger society. For example, if people have large families, crowded schools may be a problem. On the other hand, what happens in the larger society can have considerable impact on families. The occupational world is especially important in this regard. As one illustration, we might think of those husbands who feel powerless in their jobs and who try to compensate by exercising power over their wives and children—sometimes even to the point of violence. The world of the family and the broader world beyond the home are interacting constantly.

A SOCIOLOGICAL APPROACH IS A SCIENTIFIC APPROACH

Since families are so much a part of our lives, it may at first seem strange to stand back and look at them in the way sociologists do. Won't something of the wonder and "mystery" of love, marriage, and family be lost if we try to analyze them? Not really—no more than the wonder of plant life is lost through the studies of biologists. And no more than our marvel at the vastness of the universe is lost through the efforts of astronomers. In fact, the work of such scientists *enhances* our experience and appreciation of plants and the universe by increasing our understanding of them. And so it is with the study of marriage and family.

From the time of its origin in the nineteenth century, modern sociology has rested on the notion that the basic principles and methods of science can be applied to the study of human societies in much the same way that they are applied to the biological and physical sciences. Science is a way of thinking, a way of discovering why things happen as they do, how things work, and what can be used for humanity's benefit as a result of such knowledge.

Sociologists, in their particular area of scientific study, focus on *associations*—that is, two or more persons in some kind of relationship to one another, whether it be a marriage, a labor union, or an entire society. They are looking for answers to four basic questions: (1) How did this association come into being? (2) What holds it together? (3) How and why does it change? (4) How and why does such an association break up?

The U.S. Bureau of the Census (1977, *Current Population Reports*, Series P-20, No. 311, p. 158) defines the term *family* as "a group of two persons or

In studying the family, sociologists seek to understand how families form, why they stay together, how they change, and why some break apart. (Burk Uzzle/Magnum)

more related by blood, marriage, or adoption and residing together." Such a definition of family is limited only to those of an immediate household and doesn't take into account the *extended family* of relatives that we'll be discussing in Chapter 7; nor does it fit some of the "quasi-kin" and alternative family forms discussed in Chapters 8 and 9. Nevertheless, we can take the Census Bureau's definition as a starting point and can see how the above four sociological questions apply. A sociological study of the family simply means that sociologists seek to understand how families form, why they stay together, how families change, and why some families break apart. Such study can have practical implications and applications in our own personal lives.

HOW SOCIOLOGISTS STUDY THE FAMILY

An important aspect of the scientific method is the measurement of concepts. A concept is a general idea or notion about something which is arrived at by mentally combining its various particulars into one overall picture. Education is a concept, as is fertility. When we begin using some measure, concepts are also known as *variables*. The emphasis is on how something varies.

For example, counting the number of years spent in school is a way to measure education. Years in school could *vary* anywhere from zero to ten or twelve or more. Thus, we may speak of education (number of years in school) as a variable. Or to take another example, the number of children born to a woman is a way to measure fertility. Again, that too could vary—anywhere from zero to six to twenty.

Scientists are vitally interested in the relationships between variables. Therefore, they often make use of statistics to examine relationships. Here, for instance, it has been found that the more years of schooling a woman has completed, the fewer children she is likely to have. In other words, there is an *inverse relationship* between education and fertility. As education goes up, fertility goes down.

The procedure of selecting concepts, measuring them, and examining their interrelationships is part of theory building. *Theory* involves explanation; it is an effort to help us understand the *why* of things. By seeking answers to "why" questions, we can better understand what marriage and family are all about. While sociological research provides facts (for example, statistics on births out of wedlock, data on marriages and divorces, and so on), facts don't always speak for themselves. The vast store of information on marriage and family needs to be analyzed, compared, and explained; this procedure, too, is part of sociological research and is essential not only for present understanding but for predicting future trends as well. We'll be seeing how this works throughout this book.

KEY CONCEPTS IN STUDYING MARRIAGE AND FAMILY

As part of their scientific study of marriage and family, including theory building, sociologists have tended to organize their thinking around three key

Nuclear family *is the term sociologists use for the basic unit of a husband and wife and their children (Erika Stone/Peter Arnold, Inc.)*

concepts: time, structure, and interaction. Some sociologists stress one or another of these primarily; others stress all three to some degree.

TIME

With the passage of time, one generation follows another and one family leads to the formation of another family. Children grow up under their parents' care in one *nuclear family* (the term sociologists use for the basic unit of a husband and wife and their children, since this unit forms the nucleus or core grouping for what is meant by the term *family*). This first nuclear family is a child's *family of orientation*, the family from which he or she originates. The word *orientation* comes from a Latin root meaning "the east" or "sunrise." Sometimes the family of orientation is spoken of as the *family of origin*. Upon reaching adulthood, persons continue to remain members of their families of orientation; but they are also likely to become members of other families as well—the new families that come into being when these persons marry and have children of their own. Such a nuclear family, in which a person is a spouse and parent rather than a daughter or son, is called the *family of procreation*.

In that family of procreation, changes also take place with the passage of time. We see a cycle in which a person goes from being single, to being one of

A Family Album

My family are the people I live with in time; the people whose lives prepare for mine, whose lives parallel mine. . . .

My family, whose existence in Germany has been traced back to the 14th century, emigrated to this country—driven by Hitler—shortly after I was born. I grew up knowing almost nothing about that other, European existence; they rarely spoke of it.

When I was a child and my parents would tell me stories from their childhoods, I never really believed them; I couldn't quite comprehend how anyone could have lived before I was alive. And even as adults, we tend to think of the people around us as having always been the way we know them in the present.

When I found these photographs, they were a revelation to me. I had discovered a life that has completely disappeared, but whose myths and ethics have been continued into my generation, shaping the strengths and conflicts in my person. . . .

The question is: how do you renounce the misconstructions of the past without cutting off your roots? The solution to that problem must be different for each person, but these photographs have given me some clues toward my own solution. I see that the structure that causes conflicts is established by people, real personalities, rather than by mystical, unchallengeable forces. And if it is established by people, then it can be changed by people—in this case, myself. The more I look at and study these photographs, the more I understand how my life has led from my family and will lead into my family; that my person and what I have learned from the mistakes of the past will help me to help shape my future.

SOURCE: Catherine Hanf Noren, "My Family Album: The Past as Prologue," *Ms.*, 2 (June, 1974), pp. 54, 62. Copyright 1974, Catherine Hanf Noren.

a pair (through marriage), to being one of a group (as children join the family), then back to being one of a pair (as children leave home), and finally to a single existence once again (after the death of a spouse). This sequence in which a family first expands and then contracts is often called the *family life cycle* (Duvall, 1962). Some sociologists prefer the term *family career* and have various ways of dividing up its stages (Hill, 1964; Rodgers, 1964, 1973; Hill and Rodgers, 1964).

A focus on these cycles and the changes in relationships and patterns that occur in families with the passage of time is often referred to as the *developmental* approach to studying families. Responsibilities attached to different stages of the family career are called *developmental tasks* and range from toddlers' learning to feed themselves to aging persons' adjustments to retirement (Havighurst, 1953; Rodgers, 1973; Duvall, 1962; Aldous, 1978).

Of course, everyone doesn't fit neatly into the conventional family life cycle pattern. Some persons never marry; others marry but never have children. Some marry but become divorced or widowed at any stage in the family life cycle. Some remarry, while others do not. Some persons rear children as single parents (never-married, divorced, or widowed). And some persons marry for the first time in old age. Thus, a number of sociologists and others with an interest in family research have sounded a call for "recycling" or "updating" the traditional life-cycle concept to accommodate today's reality (Feldman and Feldman, 1975; Glick, 1977; Nock, 1979; Aldous, 1978; Rodgers, 1973; Spanier and Sauer, 1979; Murphy and Staples, 1979).

Not everyone fits neatly into the conventional family life-cycle pattern. Some persons never marry; others may marry in old age. (David Strickler/Monkmeyer)

An alternative perspective is provided by sociologist Glen Elder, Jr. (1975) whose preferred term is the "life course" (p. 165). Elder sees three different time dimensions involved in the course of our lives. First, there is *individual time*—a person's own life span from birth to death. Second, there is *social time*—the timetable marked by important social events and transitions, such as marriage, becoming a parent, or entering retirement. And third, there is *historical time*—the era in which a person lives. Sociologists need to take all three into account.

For example, by emphasizing the need to look at historical time as well as individual and social time, Elder is alerting us to the differing life chances and experiences that characterize persons born in a particular year or decade as compared with persons born at some other point in time. An individual's life course and a family's life cycle are affected by changing social conditions. A war or changing economic conditions, for instance, could affect age at marriage, the number of children a couple chooses to have, when children will be born, where the family will live, what life-style they'll be able to attain or maintain, whether the children will go to college, and so on.

To take another example: a person born during a year when the birthrate was especially high can expect more crowded schools and more limited occupational opportunities. That person may therefore settle into a particular job or family pattern that might have been quite different had she or he been born at another time with a less competitive job market.

A group of persons who experience a specific event at the same point in time is called a *cohort*. The word comes from a Latin term for a certain Roman military unit. A *birth cohort* consists of persons born in a particular year (or other designated period of time), a *marriage cohort* consists of persons married at the same point in time, a *graduation cohort* would be a group that graduated from high school or college during a certain year, and so on. Elder (1975) especially urges more sociological studies of birth cohorts so that the life course of a group of persons born at one point in time can be compared with the life course of another group born at a different point. Such research can yield a great deal of knowledge about social change, including social change within the specific areas of marriage and family.

STRUCTURE

In addition to focusing on time and the changes time brings, sociologists like to look at how a certain social arrangement is put together—in other words, how is it *structured*, what are its various parts, and how do they work together? To think of structure this way leads us to the idea of social systems. Dictionaries define the word *system* as a combination of parts that work together to form a complex, unified whole. We're all familiar with terms like transportation system, heating system, reproductive system, system of government, and so on.

Sociologists who utilize what is called the *structural-functional* approach emphasize that the family is a system. They sometimes borrow from the biological sciences and view the family as an organism with a structural

As a structure, the family is characterized by persons in various positions whose behavior affects one another because the parts are interdependent. (Erika Stone/Peter Arnold, Inc.)

arrangement of interdependent parts, each having a function to perform, just as is true of the human body. They also point out the functions performed by the family in relation to the larger society: replacing society's members through bringing children into the world, socializing children, producing and consuming goods and services, maintaining the physical and emotional well-being of its members, and performing specified tasks within the home and community.

As a structure, the family is characterized by persons in various positions (spouse, parent, child, sibling) whose behavior affects one another because the parts are interdependent. The system works best when all parts are functioning properly. From the structural-functional point of view in sociology, anything that would be considered unfavorable to the smooth working of the system is termed *dysfunctional*. The emphasis is on *order* or keeping the system "in equilibrium" (Parsons, 1951; Abrahamson, 1978).

INTERACTION

In addition to time and structure, sociologists place great importance on a third key concept—the process of human interaction. Put very simply, interaction is the back and forth interplay that goes on between persons, whether in society as a whole or in a group within society (such as a family). On another level, what goes on inside our minds is also important because various thought processes constitute a kind of "interaction with oneself" (Meltzer et al., 1975:vii). This inner interaction both affects and is affected by our outer interaction with people. For example, a young couple may be trying to decide whether or not to continue their relationship. Each looks at what is liked about the other (what seems rewarding in the relationship) and weighs that against what isn't liked (what seems costly in the relationship). The way the relationship goes is affected by such thought processes; but on the other hand, such thought processes are being affected by how the relationship goes!

Some sociologists emphasize a *symbolic interaction* approach, pointing out that humans interact with one another through symbols (words, gestures, or pictures that stand for something else). And we must be able to interpret the symbols (a smile, a clenched fist, a traffic sign, a spoken word) or meaningful communication and interaction can't take place effectively. Symbolic interactionists stress that *shared meanings* are what hold society together (Meltzer et al., 1975:50).

Human beings interact with one another through symbols which have shared meanings. (Seghers/Monkmeyer)

As applied to the sociology of marriage and family, a symbolic interactional perspective gives special attention to communication processes through observing "the world of everyday experience" and developing theory out of that experience (Stryker, 1964: 135–136). Furthermore, it isn't only important to observe what family members *do*; our understanding is incomplete unless we try to find out how they *feel* about what they do and why.

Furthermore, how we feel or what we do depends to a great extent upon how we define a particular situation (Thomas, 1923). The key word is *define*. It's not what a situation is in any objective sense, but what persons perceive it to be that matters. If persons "define situations as real, they are real in their consequences," said one of the early pioneers in symbolic interaction theory, W. I. Thomas (1928; quoted in Truzzi, 1971:275). Thomas's notion of the *definition of the situation* is important to keep in mind in understanding human interaction.

To Georg Simmel, a turn-of-the-century pioneer in sociological theory, *reciprocity* was the stuff of everyday life. He observed how people give to each other, receive from each other, and take from each other. One person acts, the other reacts; and the actions and attitudes of each affect the other. Sociologists who have devoted much attention to Simmel's insights point out that he was hammering home one central idea—namely, that "all human interactions should be viewed as kinds of exchanges" (Levine et al., 1976:823). He thus laid the groundwork for the sociological approach that has come to be known as *exchange theory* (Simmel, 1950).

Exchanges both cost us and reward us. That's why we may just as easily speak of exchange theory as *cost/reward* (or *reward/cost) theory*. When in the process of human interaction we are *giving*, it costs us something—time, energy, money or material goods, comfort and convenience, or perhaps something else, depending upon the situation. And when we *receive*, somebody else is experiencing cost so that we may receive the reward or benefit that comes to us through the particular interaction.

Simmel (1955) makes another important point by stressing that both conflict and cooperation are ways human beings relate to each other. And that statement applies to male-female relationships and family relationships as well as to other kinds of social interaction. To say that cooperation is the essence of human relationship and that conflict means the absence of relationship is, according to Simmel, nothing short of erroneous.

In other words, Simmel saw conflict as nothing more nor less than a form of human interaction—a kind of exchange in itself. There couldn't *be* a conflict without at least two persons, Simmel stressed; so why not admit that conflict is a form of exchanging something between the parties involved? If it takes two to tango, it also takes two (or more) to engage in conflict; and when parties are involved directly in something of concern to both sides, some kind of interchange is occurring. True, the exchange may be of grievances, punishments, force, or resistance—quite a contrast from the exchange of favors and benefits most persons think about in connection with the idea of reciprocity. But it's an exchange nevertheless.

*(Drawing by Koren; © 1978
The New Yorker Magazine,
Inc.)*

In speaking of interaction, then, as a key sociological concept, we're thinking about *symbols* and *shared meanings* in communication, *how situations are defined* by the individuals involved, and all that is involved in *exchange processes*—including both *cooperation* and *conflict*. Especially important is an emphasis on *rewards* (things people share in considering desirable) and *costs* (things people share in wanting to avoid), because this emphasis is receiving widespread attention in all the social sciences today. In fact, it is becoming an increasingly dominant way of thinking about society. Thus, when we speak in this book about the weighing of rewards and costs as a way to help explain what is happening in marriage and family, we're applying an approach that more and more social scientists find intriguing in explaining social phenomena. But all of the other key concepts relating to time, structure, and interaction have important parts to play as well.

CHAPTER HIGHLIGHTS

What happens in families affects the larger society, and what happens in the larger society affects families. That's why a sociological study of marriage and family is so important. Sociology utilizes the basic principles and methods of science in studying human societies, focusing especially on *associations*—how and why they form, change, hold together, and break apart. Families are associations that may be studied in this way. As part of their scientific study of marriage and family, sociologists conduct research, measure and compare variables, seek explanations of findings through theory-building, and tend to organize their thinking around three key concepts: time, structure, and interaction.

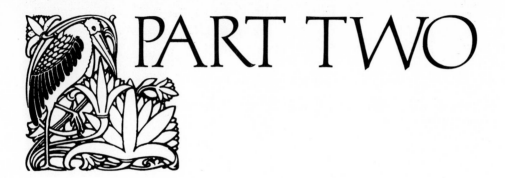

PART TWO

SEX ROLES

CHAPTER 2

(© Mark Chester/Editorial Photocolor Archives)

BECOMING WOMEN AND MEN

A baby boy survived a highway crash in which both his parents died. The baby's aunt, an unmarried middle-aged woman, took the child to rear. This was the theme of a strange and eerie television drama that unwittingly presented a lesson in *role socialization* (how a person is trained to play a particular part in society).

The infant's aunt was obsessed with an intense hatred of men. Unable to bear the thought that this tiny baby would grow to be a noisy, irksome boy, she determined to rear him as a girl. Moving to a remote area where her situation would not be known, she gave the boy a girl's name, kept him isolated and virtually housebound, and dressed him in frilly clothes. The child contentedly played with dolls and in other ways acted as girls were expected to act, never suspecting he was a male. Only after several years when an outsider happened upon the scene was the shocking secret discovered.

Farfetched? Perhaps. The drama was, after all, fiction. Yet John Money and Anke Ehrhardt, authorities on psychohormonal research, report the real-life case of a baby boy who through a tragic accident lost his penis. The misfortune took place during the performance of a circumcision by means of electrocautery. A sudden surge of too-powerful electrical current burned the penis so severely it sloughed off not long afterward. The distraught parents sought help for many months and were eventually directed to the Johns Hopkins Hospital and School of Medicine. There, they were counseled to rear the child as a girl; and, with the help of further surgery and hormonal treatment, this is being done quite successfully (Money and Ehrhardt, 1972, chap. 7; Money and Tucker, 1975, chap. 4).

Money and Ehrhardt tell of similar child-rearing stories in cases of *hermaphroditism*—a congenital condition in which a baby's sexual anatomy is not clearly differentiated. The infant may appear as neither distinctly male nor distinctly female. And in some cases, the baby appears to be of the opposite sex from what she or he actually is.

In one such case, the parents thought they had a son when in reality they had a daughter. As puberty approached, the "boy" loved motor-bike racing with male companions, had a girl friend, enjoyed hunting and fishing with his father, and in general followed a traditional masculine behavior pattern. Imagine his dismay when breasts began to develop! If more time had elapsed, he would have begun menstruating as well. However, after expert counseling, a decision was made that he should continue through life as a male. His female reproductive organs were surgically removed, and he was given hormones which would make possible the development of secondary sexual characteristics such as a deepened voice and facial hair (Money and Ehrhardt, 1972, chaps. 8 and 10).

Such stories are unusual and may seem strange to us. Most of us take the ideas of masculinity and femininity for granted. We tend to think that what we *are by birth* (either male or female) will determine what we *become* (either masculine or feminine). Don't boys grow up to be "masculine" (defined as active, courageous, assertive, and rational), while girls grow up to be "feminine" (defined as passive, dependent, emotional, and nurturant)? How then can we explain what happened in the stories we examined?

In both the fictional and true-life stories, what mattered was not the infant's biological sexual makeup, but rather how the child was brought up by adults. That's why Money and Ehrhardt (1972, chap. 8) stress the importance of what they call the "sex of assignment." In the case of the circumcision accident, for example, the sex *assigned* to the baby boy was female. In other words, gender identity (self-awareness of oneself as being either male or female) is more dependent upon social learning than upon genetic makeup.

Of course, for most persons, the biological sexual makeup (chromosomal pattern, sex glands, and internal and external sex organs) and the sex of assignment are one and the same. A male child is reared as a boy, a female child as a girl. But we're talking about social learning nevertheless. To be reared as a boy means *learning* to act as males are expected to act in our society. To be reared as a girl means *learning* to act as females are expected to act in our society. When a girl is told to "act like a lady," it's expected that she has in mind some image of how a "lady" is expected to act—an image learned from others. And when a boy is encouraged to be a "man's man," he is expected to have learned what that expression means and to act accordingly.

UNDERSTANDING SEX ROLES

Those expectations of how a person should act because she is female or he is male are called *gender-related norms*. Norms are the "supposed to's" of life—the behaviors our society lays down for us and expects us to carry out. Certain norms are attached to various social positions. For example, attached to the social position of parent is the norm that parents should take care of their children. If we think of the *whole cluster of norms attached to a social position*, we have what sociologists call a *role*. We're accustomed to the theater's usage of the term. An actor takes a certain part and then speaks and conducts himself or herself according to a prewritten script, thus "playing the role" of, for instance, Macbeth or Lady Macbeth.

Sex roles or *gender roles* are the parts society assigns us to play in the drama of life, according to whether we entered this life as a baby girl or a baby boy. To state it another way, a sex role consists of the cluster of shared norms attached to the differing social positions of male and female. Figure 2-1 shows how we carry these roles around with us—although in reality, of course, we carry the norms in our heads, not in a suitcase!

The norms for each sex relate to both *temperaments* (what females and males are supposed to be like) and *tasks* (what males and females are supposed to do). But by no means is there universal agreement on how each sex is expected to act or on how labor should be shared or divided up between men and women. Sex roles vary considerably among different cultures.

Take the matter of temperament, for example. In Margaret Mead's (1935)

FIGURE 2-1   Sex roles: The "packages" of social expectations carried around by males and females.

anthropological study of New Guinea tribes, she found that one group considered a gentle temperament the ideal for both sexes. But in another tribe, an aggressive temperament was the ideal for both sexes. In yet another tribe, the cultural ideal was aggressiveness for women and gentleness and sensitivity for men. In the familiar pattern of our own culture, we have the reverse of this third tribe.

Besides such variations in ideal *temperaments* encouraged for each sex, there are also variations in the *tasks* that are labeled "men's work" or "women's work" in different societies. Such variations (as illustrated by Table 2-A) seem to show that sex roles do not spring from natural, biological traits or "instincts" which cause men the world over to "act like men" and women to "act like women." What it means to "act like a woman" or "act like a man" depends mainly upon the expectations of one's society.

THE SOCIALIZATION PROCESS

We learn our society's expectations and requirements through a process called *socialization*. In other words, we are taught to be social beings. How? Think of it this way: We're born into a particular social world. That social world—or

*Sex roles vary considerably
among different cultures. This
Senoufu tribe weaver in Ivory
Coast, Africa, is performing a
task often assigned to women in
other cultures. (© Marc and
Evelyne Bernheim/Woodfin
Camp & Assoc.)*

culture—is already there when we arrive on the scene. It consists of customs,
values, and rules that need to be transmitted to us so that we can fit into that
world and become a part of it.

Our parents are usually (but not always) the first "transmittors" or
"agents of socialization." But as time goes by, many others also play a part in
the process—for example, brothers and sisters, friends, teachers, and
religious leaders. Reading materials, radio, television, and movies may also
play an important part in our socialization.

At the root of all this is the sense of *self* we are developing. In other
words, while various influences are acting upon a child from the outside,
something is happening inside as well. That was an important point stressed
by George Herbert Mead (1863–1931), one of the early theorists in the
symbolic interactionist school of thought described in Chapter 1.

MEAD'S "SOCIAL SELF" AND "GENERALIZED OTHER"

What does Mead have in mind in saying that each human being has a *self*?
"Mead simply means that such an individual may act socially toward himself,
just as toward others," writes sociologist Bernard Meltzer (1967). "He may
praise, blame, or encourage himself; he may become disgusted with himself,
may seek to punish himself, and so forth. Thus the human being may become
the object of his own actions" (pp. 9–10).

TABLE 2-A   *Cross-cultural data from 224 societies on division of labor by sex*

ACTIVITY	NUMBER OF SOCIETIES IN WHICH ACTIVITY IS PERFORMED BY				
	MEN ALWAYS	MEN USUALLY	EITHER SEX	WOMEN USUALLY	WOMEN ALWAYS
SUBSISTENCE ACTIVITIES					
Pursuit of sea mammals	34	1	0	0	0
Hunting	166	13	0	0	0
Trapping small animals	128	13	4	1	2
Herding	38	8	4	0	5
Fishing	98	34	19	3	4
Clearing land for agriculture	73	22	17	5	13
Dairy operations	17	4	3	1	13
Preparing and planting soil	31	23	33	20	37
Erecting and dismantling shelter	14	2	5	6	22
Tending fowl and small animals	21	4	8	1	39
Tending and harvesting crops	10	15	35	39	44
Gathering shellfish	9	4	8	7	25
Making and tending fires	18	6	25	22	62
Bearing burdens	12	6	35	20	57
Preparing drinks and narcotics	20	1	13	8	57
Gathering fruits, berries, nuts	12	3	15	13	63
Gathering fuel	22	1	10	19	89
Preservation of meat and fish	8	2	10	14	74
Gathering herbs, roots, seeds	8	1	11	7	74
Cooking	5	1	9	28	158
Carrying water	7	0	5	7	119
Grinding grain	2	4	5	13	114
MANUFACTURE OF OBJECTS					
Metalworking	78	0	0	0	0
Weapon making	121	1	0	0	0
Boatbuilding	91	4	4	0	1
Manufacture of musical instruments	45	2	0	0	1
Work in wood and bark	113	9	5	1	1
Work in stone	68	3	2	0	2
Work in bone, horn, shell	67	4	3	0	3
Manufacture of ceremonial objects	37	1	13	0	1
House building	86	32	25	3	14
Net making	44	6	4	2	11
Manufacture of ornaments	24	3	40	6	18
Manufacture of leather products	29	3	9	3	32
Hide preparation	31	2	4	4	49
Manufacture of nontextile fabrics	14	0	9	2	32
Manufacture of thread and cordage	23	2	11	10	73
Basket making	25	3	10	6	82
Mat making	16	2	6	4	61

TABLE 2-A *Cross-cultural data from 224 societies on division of labor by sex (Continued)*

	NUMBER OF SOCIETIES IN WHICH ACTIVITY IS PERFORMED BY				
ACTIVITY	MEN ALWAYS	MEN USUALLY	EITHER SEX	WOMEN USUALLY	WOMEN ALWAYS
SUBSISTENCE ACTIVITIES					
Weaving	19	2	2	6	67
Pottery making	13	2	6	8	77
Manufacture and repair of clothing	12	3	8	9	95

SOURCE: D'Andrade, 1966, pp. 177–178.

Yet, if the self *is* "us," how can we stand back and see the self as something separate—as though it were an object out there somewhere? Why is it that we can say, "I comforted my*self*," "I put my*self* in my friend's shoes," or "I was angry at my*self*"? It's almost as though we're thinking of our *self* as another person! Such thoughts also intrigued Mead and led him to say that "it is impossible to conceive of self arising outside of social experience" (in Strauss, 1956:217). We become social beings—human beings—through interaction with other persons.

Imitation Stage   It starts, claimed Mead, when we are tiny children and mimic the actions of others. We're trying to be like some adult, in a sense putting ourselves in that person's place by behaving like him or her. Of course, at this early stage, we don't understand what we're doing. For example, a toddler sees her mother writing a letter. The little girl picks up a crayon or pencil or even a stick and begins moving it across a piece of paper "just like Mommy."

Role-Playing Stage   After the imitation stage, according to Mead, children next move on to a role-playing stage. One day the child is a father or mother, another day a teacher, another day a mail carrier delivering make-believe letters to family members, another day a fire fighter or dentist or "animal doctor."

What is especially significant is not only that the child learns to take someone else's part and act out a different role, but the child is also learning to act back toward *himself* or *herself* in certain roles. Timmy may pretend he is Daddy scolding Timmy (himself) for spilling his milk. Julie may pretend she is the nursery school teacher showing the children how to use the finger paints. In the role of the teacher, Julie may praise herself: "That's a lovely painting, Julie." As Julie-the-student, she may in turn ask the teacher (the other part she is playing) to answer a question. Mead called this "the simplest form of being another to one's self." It is therefore possible to have a dialogue with oneself. "The child says something in one character and responds in another character, and then his responding in another character is a stimulus to himself in the first character, and so the conversation goes" (in Strauss, 1956:228). These two experiences—what Mead called "taking the role of the

Socialization begins with imitation—at first without complete understanding. (© Alice Kandell/Rapho/Photo Researchers, Inc.)

other," and carrying on a dialogue with oneself—were considered crucial steps in the development of a self.

Game Stage The third step in the development of a self, said Mead, takes place when children are involved in organized activities involving a number of persons and rules of the game. He used the example of a baseball game. There, it's not enough to take one single "role of the other" as in make-believe, where the child is a doctor one moment and a storekeeper the next. In a baseball game, the child has to take on the role of many others all at once, keeping in mind what the other players are doing or might do. In addition, there are the rules of the game to keep in mind. The child begins thinking of all the *roles* (pitcher, batter, first baseman, right fielder, umpire) and all the *rules* together. They form an organized whole in his or her mind, and they affect the child's actions in response.

Whereas earlier, when a child took "the role of the other" the other was a *person*, a different kind of "other" is involved in the baseball game. Mead called it *the generalized other* and defined it as "an organization of the attitudes of those involved in the same process." In other words, it's all the roles and rules of the game put together, with each player keeping them in mind. And moving beyond childhood games, Mead emphasized that "the attitude of the generalized other is the attitude of the whole community" (in Strauss, 1956:232).

We are being affected by the generalized other when we make statements like these: "I know what people will think," or "If I do that, I'll be the talk of the town!" or "I did it simply because I knew that was what was expected of me." Mead pointed out that, through the generalized other, the community exercises control over its members. It's as though we're carrying the community around in our heads!

THEORIES OF CHILDHOOD SEX-ROLE LEARNING

While it is useful to speak of developing a general sense of self— a self in interaction with others and therefore a *social* self—we may wonder what all this has to do with developing a "boy" self or a "girl" self. Again, the two factors of imitation and recognizing societal "rules of the game" have important parts to play. But not only does an abstract "generalized other" influence sex roles; *specific* others are also involved—people such as parents and teachers who reinforce behaviors that are considered appropriate for one's sex.

Psychologists Eleanor Maccoby and Carol Jacklin (1974:1) have examined in detail the many behavioral science studies that have been undertaken in attempts to understand why females and males behave differently. Maccoby and Jacklin conclude that theories set forth to explain sex differences fall into three basic categories: (1) those stressing imitation, (2) those that focus on "self-socialization," and (3) those emphasizing reinforcement.

Imitation *Imitation theories* are concerned with a child's early identification with the same-sex parent. The idea is that the child models himself or herself after the parent and other persons of the same sex. We've already seen Mead's stress on the importance of mimicking adults during a child's early years. Mead was talking about the general development of a social self. In imitation theories of sexual differentiation, the spotlight is specifically on imitation of a society's notions of masculinity and femininity.

"Self-Socialization" The category that Maccoby and Jacklin label "self-socialization" refers especially to the work of *cognitive developmental* theorists such as Lawrence Kohlberg (1966). Such theorists focus on a child's development of a gender-related self-concept ("I'm a girl," or "I'm a boy"). But in addition to a self-concept, the child is developing an understanding of what behavior is appropriate for each sex. ("I'm a girl and girls do this." "Girls don't do that! That's what boys do!" "I'm a boy, and this is how boys act.") In other words, the child is learning sex roles. It's a process that is part of the child's overall growing awareness of how the world is organized and how people fit into it. As part of childhood development, the girl or boy is grasping some sense of societal rules of the game and what that means for her or him personally. We might think again of Mead's baseball game and how the requirements of the "generalized other" are internalized, becoming part of us.

Reinforcement   The third general category of theories of sexual differentiation are *reinforcement theories*. Here the emphasis is on the part parents and other adults play through the use of rewards and punishments to encourage children to behave in ways considered appropriate for their particular sex.

Norwegian sociologist Harriet Holter (1970) contrasts cognitive development and reinforcement theories by pointing out the different sequence of a child's experience in the two. In cognitive development theory, the pattern seems to be this: "I am a boy, therefore I want to do boy things, therefore the opportunity to do boy things (and to gain approval for doing them) is rewarding." However, says Holter, in reinforcement theory the pattern is more like this: "I want rewards, I am rewarded for doing boy things, therefore I want to be a boy" (p. 191). The same would hold true of a girl who might reason similarly about being rewarded for doing "girl things."

Imitation, self-socialization, and reinforcement theories all support the idea that sex roles are learned, not innate, and that they are learned at a very young age. Furthermore, explains Holter, children are learning much more than the fact that two social categories—women and men—exist. Children are also learning "social evaluations" of those categories. Even during their preschool years, they begin to realize that "males are defined as power-holders, women as the opposite" (p. 196).

THE HOW AND WHY OF SEX-ROLE SOCIALIZATION

We've been looking at what is taking place *within* the child during the socialization process. We now need to turn attention to influences from the outside.

The stage is set with the announcement: "It's a girl!" or "You have a son!" Studies have shown that adults describe a baby differently according to whether they have been told the baby is a girl or a boy. If they think a baby is a girl, they describe her as cuddly. But the very same baby will be described as active and aggressive if they think the baby is a boy (Meyer and Sobieszek, 1972; see also Chafetz, 1978, chap. 3).

Parents, of course, know whether they have a boy or a girl. And that makes a difference in how they treat their infant. The tradition of dressing girls in pink and boys in blue has been one way of making a distinction between the sexes—although such rigid color coding is less common today. Parents also interact differently with baby girls and baby boys. They tend to talk more to their infant daughter. But if they have an infant son, they are more likely to pick him up often and enjoy playing roughly with him. Barbara Lusk Forisha (1978:323–324), a specialist in the study of sex roles, has summarized much of the research on adult-infant interaction. She points out that parents evidently expect boys to be more active and girls to be more gentle and verbal and thus interact with their infant children accordingly. Without realizing it, they are probably helping bring about the very behaviors they expected! This brings us to a more detailed look at the matter of *reinforcement* mentioned above.

Sanctions Animal trainers elicit desired behaviors by offering rewards. A porpoise learns that jumping through the hoop will bring a tasty morsel of food, but failing to follow the trainer's instructions will mean that the choice prize will be withheld. The porpoise who chooses to misbehave and not cooperate at all may be taken out of the game and set aside for a while. Through the use of sanctions, both positive ones and negative ones, the creature is learning to act as the trainer wishes.

As human beings interact with each other, sanctions also come into the picture. This is particularly true in sex-role socialization. *Positive* sanctions are the rewards people give us for behavior that they consider appropriate for persons of our gender. *Negative* sanctions are punishments for behavior considered inappropriate.

For example, if a little girl announces that she wants to be a nurse when she grows up, adults may pat her on the head and smile approvingly. Parents will buy her a toy nursing kit and cap and encourage her to practice on her dolls. But if the girl says she plans to be a brain surgeon, adult encouragement may not be so quickly forthcoming. She is likely to feel that she isn't being taken seriously. "What? A pretty little girl like you? Brain surgeons have to work long, hard hours. Don't you want to be a mommy? You wait and see; some handsome young man will come along someday and want to take care of you, and you can forget about such ideas. Let *him* be the brain surgeon, not you!"

But suppose a small boy were to announce he plans to be a nurse when he grows up. With few exceptions, adults would voice disapproval and would tell him his aspirations are "too low" or that nursing is "woman's work" and not at all a man's job. His parents would buy him a little doctor's kit, not a nurse's kit. Even the pictures on the toy boxes would reinforce the stereotype of male physicians and female nurses.

Sanctions are related to the power parents hold in controlling resources that a child needs or desires. Some of these resources are tangible and include money spent or withheld for certain toys or hobbies, or for education, enrichment programs, travel opportunities, and the like. But beyond such obvious material aspects of parental power, there are intangible aspects which exert a tremendous influence. The desire of children to know that their parents approve of their conduct, feel warmly toward them, and are proud of them makes children very conscious of any sanctions—whether positive or negative.

In such a social exchange process, the attitude and actions of parents seem to be saying, "If you give me what I want from you, I'll give you what you'd like to have from me. But if you don't act the way I want you to, you'll be sorry. I'll show my displeasure, and I'll withhold the rewards you want. Or

Positive sanctions are given to little girls for behavior considered appropriate to their sex. (Mimi Forsyth/Monkmeyer)

there will be penalties of some other sort. Then you'll learn how important it is that you shape up to my expectations." Of course, this is never stated in such bald terms! But it provides a description of the underlying dynamics taking place between parents and children.

During the early years, children have few resources of their own that could make it possible for them to challenge their parents' power. However, the power of one person over another decreases when the second person finds alternative sources or rewards. Thus, as children are increasingly exposed to influences beyond those of their parents, they may not respond quite so readily to parental sanctions. Outside sources may provide the benefits once largely sought from parents alone. Pleasing one's peers may become more important than pleasing one's parents on certain issues. New ideas learned in school or through the media may cause children to challenge their parents' views on politics, religion, or social customs. Also, as children grow older, they become more aware of their own part in the exchange process between them and their parents. Children obtain more bargaining leverage as they awaken to the potential power they have through being able to give or withhold the positive reinforcement desired by their parents. If children feel they are not being rewarded for certain behaviors for which they feel they deserve to be rewarded, they may in turn not reward their parents with the approval and role-model identification that matters so much to the parents.

Adolescents in particular may identify with role models who provide benefits they consider more worthwhile than those provided by their parents. These alternative role models may markedly influence the gender-role norms the young person chooses to follow. For example, Bill's father may be a truck driver, part-time auto racer, and have little interest in the world of ideas. His hobbies may be mechanics and hunting. Bill's interests may lie in books and music. Of a gentle, sensitive temperament, he cringes at the thought of killing animals for sport and refuses to accompany his father on hunting trips. Bill prefers to attend the nature-study club sponsored by the public library. He likes to write poetry and play the piano. Bill's father worries about his son and fears he is a "sissy," not living up to the father's stereotyped notions of masculinity. But Bill has found a friend in Mr. Peterson, the English teacher at Bill's junior high school. Mr. Peterson provides Bill with books and articles to read, gives him the encouragement and approval the boy yearns for, and provides Bill with a sounding board for the discussion of his ideas and poetry. Already Bill is planning to major in literature in college and someday to be a teacher like Mr. Peterson.

Similarly, an adolescent girl might be influenced by the example of a woman by whom she is employed during the summer. Even though the girl's parents may have reinforced traditional gender-role patterns, she begins admiring other qualities in her employer— assertiveness, independence, strength, and leadership. Realizing that such qualities are necessary for advancement in the business or professional world, and impressed with her employer's exciting life, the adolescent begins to reject her mother's tradition-al life as an example of what a woman should be and chooses to follow her employer as a role model instead. The rewards offered in this setting appear far more compelling than anything provided at home, regardless of the positive and negative sanctions the girl's parents have been using.

Concerns of Parents   It is said that imitation is the sincerest form of flattery. It means a great deal to any one of us to know that somebody looks up to us and wants to be like us. And parents especially, having had the primary task of molding their children from infancy, desire to have their task rewarded by producing human beings who admire them enough to want to identify with them. When children don't identify with their parents and reject them as role models, the parents feel punished—not only by their children's repudiation of their example but also by the disapproval of the parents' peers (their reference group). The parents then are experiencing *costs* rather than rewards in the process of social exchange, and the sense of "net profit" in the parent-child relationship is diminished.

Let's take some hypothetical examples to see how this works. Alice Grey has two daughters and a son. The son is established in a business and is happily married to a young woman who reminds Alice of herself as a young bride years ago. The daughter-in-law holds traditional sex-role norms and regards her greatest responsibility and joy in life to lie in "being a good wife and mother." This outlook on life is precisely that which Alice has always

Parents desire the gratification that comes with having their children identify with them and look up to them. (Sybil Shackman/Monkmeyer)

held. She and her husband feel rewarded not only in that their son followed the pattern of his father in developing qualities suited to achievement in the business world, but also in his choice of a wife who fulfills the sex-role norms his parents held up for females during his childhood socialization. Alice's younger daughter's aspirations also are rewarding to Alice and make her feel a success in having socialized her for an appropriate role in adult life. The young woman is presently working as a secretary but hopes to marry and settle down to raising a family soon.

It's the older daughter Susan who worries Alice. Susan is working on a Ph.D. in marine biology and is not at all concerned about marriage. If she does marry at some point in life, she tells Alice, the marriage will be egalitarian and there will be no sacrifice of career commitment on Susan's part. Furthermore, Susan has no desire to have children and says that if she were to marry, either she or her husband would have sterilization surgery. Alice cannot understand Susan and feels she is rejecting all that Alice has lived for and held dear. Susan has no desire to be the kind of woman her mother is; in fact, Susan thinks of her mother as a *negative* role model—an example of what she doesn't want to be, a pattern of the kind of life she doesn't want to lead. By not identifying with her mother, Susan is calling into

(Erika Stone/Peter Arnold)

question her mother's own self-identity and the values her mother upholds. This is threatening to Alice Grey and hurts her deeply. Her daughter has failed to reward her and, in fact, is punishing her.

In another case, the hard-driving businessman who lives for money and buries himself in his work may find that his son turns completely away from such a life-style. Instead, the son devotes himself to some humanitarian project and calls into question his father's materialistic values, shattering his father's dreams for him.

Of course, children may also take *non*traditional parents as negative role models. Instead of following their parents' way of life, they follow the conventional societal patterns that their parents have rejected. For example, a mother who has emphasized intellectual excellence, independence, achievement, mastery, and career commitment for her daughter and has provided her with a living example of professional accomplishment will likely experience deep disappointment if the daughter organizes her life around traditional sex-role norms. It's as though the daughter is saying, "I want to be just the opposite of what you are." One mother who went to medical school when her youngest daughter was four years old could not understand why, ten years later, the girl refused to share the mother's joy upon opening a new clinic. The girl talked only about becoming a full-time housewife and expressed no interest in either college or career.

In so many words, parents themselves are seeking reinforcement in the gender-role norms they have chosen to follow. They desire the gratification that comes with having their children identify with them and look up to them as role models. They want to be rewarded by their children's choice of them as living examples of what it means to be a man or woman, and therefore they reward their children in ways that will reinforce such sex-role identification.

Companionship, as well as identification, may be another concern of parents—especially in many mother-daughter relationships. Social psychologist Ralph Turner (1970) points out that in homes where sex roles are traditional, deep comradeship between a mother and daughter is most likely to occur if "the daughter forms a somewhat traditional self-conception. The common interest in domestic activities permits a collaboration that can continue into adulthood, so long as the daughter's self-conception does not move toward a repudiation of traditional feminine activity" (p. 387). Mothers who socialize their daughters to delight in work traditionally considered "women's work" in our society (sewing, decorating, cooking, making beds, washing dishes, doing laundry, and so on) are essentially working to build a lifelong friendship based on shared interests—a friendship that mothers anticipate as being very rewarding. Daughters who choose not to follow such a pattern may also wish for a close relationship with their mothers but may have little hope that it will be experienced. Poet Adrienne Rich (1976) explains: "The woman activist or artist born of a family-centered mother may in any case feel that her mother cannot understand or sympathize with the imperatives of her life; or that her mother has preferred and valued a more conventional daughter, or a son" (Chap. 9).

In contrast to mother-daughter comradeship built around "task bonds," according to Turner, father-son collaboration has been made more difficult through traditional sex-role norms which assign fathers the breadwinning responsibility. Thus, while during their growing-up years boys may experience comradeship and task bonding through working together with their fathers in certain household chores, hobbies, and sports, sons are not actually involved in a father's occupational career in the way that daughters are involved in the mother's major activity, homemaking. What sons learn from this arrangement, says Turner (1970), is that "the work that is crucial to the male identity is usually removed from the home" (p. 388).

Other concerns of parents in socializing their children may relate to *religious beliefs,* a concern for *societal order,* and a concern for what parents believe to be their *children's best interests.*

Some parents believe that traditional sex roles have been ordained by God and are not open to questioning. Thus, sons are to be socialized for a strong leadership role and daughters for a supportive, subordinate role. Other parents, however, may be equally religious but may view matters quite differently. Such persons may see the teachings of their faith as upholding female-male equality—especially when those teachings are understood in the light of current theological studies (Driver, 1976:434–442).

Many parents may give little thought to the "why" behind their child-rearing practices, since traditional gender-role patterns have had such strong support in the larger society outside the home. Such parents may simply accept traditional gender roles as the given order of things ("that's just the way life is."). The sanctions they use to reinforce those roles are seen as being in their children's best interests—a way of fitting sons and daughters into the parts society expects them to play in adulthood, including sex-role specialization in marriage.

Such a view has been common in the structural-functional approach to a sociology of marriage and family. The emphasis is on keeping a system in equilibrium. One sociologist from this school of thought, Talcott Parsons (1955), has been quite explicit in claiming that sex-role specialization benefits the nuclear family by functioning to maintain that system. The roles of the spouses are viewed as *complementary* from Parsons' vantage point. If the husband attends to his occupation and the wife attends to her role as the family's center of nurturance, there is less chance for competitiveness to develop between husband and wife—a rivalry that could lead to marital dissolution. Such a functionalist perspective suggests that serious conflict and system disruption could occur if a woman chose to be as active and achievement-oriented as her husband in pursuing an occupation. Therefore, the functionalist might argue, parents socialize their children in traditional sex roles so that such system disruption can be avoided.

On the other hand, writers who think in *conflict* terms tend to view such a functionalist perspective as a freezing of the status quo. Those who take a Marxist position and look upon male-female relations as an illustration of class struggle would say that present socialization practices simply reflect the domination of women by men (Engels, 1884; Rowbotham, 1972; Mitchell, 1971). Some would argue that, out of self-interest, men want to limit the participation of women in the occupational opportunity system. In this way, one-half the population can be kept from its rewards so that the other half might have them for itself. One method of accomplishing this would be to socialize boys for such access to the opportunity system but to socialize girls to behave in precisely the opposite manner necessary to achieve society's economic and power benefits.

Other sociologists who take a *different* conflict perspective from that taken by Marxist theorists also disagree with the functionalist emphasis on sex-role specialization in the family. These sociologists would point out that persons in a relationship can work out a *negotiated* arrangement of "who does what" in a way that is agreeable to each and which does not produce feelings of rivalry. Furthermore, from this perspective, conflict can be healthy for a husband-wife relationship and strengthen it rather than lead to dissolution.

Parents, of course, are not usually rearing their children with such sociological analyses in mind! Rather, they are trying to prepare their children for life as they, the parents, see it. They want what they think will be good for their children. Included in their concern may be a desire to protect their children from societal criticism and pressures that are sometimes directed toward those who don't fit the conventional mold for their gender. For example, we spoke earlier of a little girl who would like to be a brain surgeon and of a little boy who would like to be a nurse. Because of sex-role stereotyping, persons in both situations are likely to encounter problems directly associated with their being nontraditional—even in spite of changes in recent years which have meant more men in nursing schools and more women in medical schools (Schoenmaker and Radosevich, 1976; Fitzpatrick, 1977; Bourne and Wikler, 1976).

Studies have shown that, for a male nurse, both his professional identity and other persons' perceptions of his sexual identity become problems (Etzkowitz, 1971). He is constantly mistaken for either an orderly (lower status) or a physician (higher status). And because of another kind of stereotyping, his sexual orientation is sometimes called into question: "There is a set of mental equations which go: Female + Nursing role = Nurse; Male + Nursing role = homosexual" (p. 432).

Sociologists Patricia Bourne and Norma Wikler (1976) write likewise of "double binds" of women in medical school: "When women do demonstrate the characteristics and traits of the 'ideal' professional, they violate the expectations of the female role. This role violation tends to engender anger and hostility from others. . . . But if [the female physician] exhibits traits appropriate to her role as female, she will jeopardize her standing in her role as professional."

RAISING QUESTIONS ABOUT SEX ROLES

Many persons believe that traditional sex roles are *not* in children's best interests—not if they keep both males and females from realizing their full human potential by forcing them to be something they don't wish to be or to do something they don't wish to do. An increasing number of persons are convinced that traditional sex roles need to be critically examined and many childhood socialization practices changed.

For example, various researchers have called attention to the way sex-role stereotypes are reinforced through the design, display, and promotion of toys (Chafetz, 1978:80–85; Kutner and Levinson, 1976). And some studies suggest that differences in girls' and boys' childhood games may prevent girls from developing certain skills, attitudes, and work styles that are so important later on for achievement in the business world (Hennig and Jardim, 1977 edition, chap. 2; Lever, 1978).

Even traditional differences in dress have affected the relative freedom of the sexes (Chafetz, 1978:88). In the Victorian period, women's activities were curtailed through such encumbrances as tightly laced corsets and long, heavy skirts. The freedom of movement offered by more realistic garments seemed exhilarating. One ecstatic woman wrote in 1894 of the "delightful sense of independence and power" she experienced when she put on a pair of knickers to ride her bicycle (Roberts, 1977). And in our own day, say social scientists Marcia Guttentag and Helen Bray (1977), "teachers have reported that recent changes in dress codes which allow girls to wear slacks are the most important factors in erasing distinctions in activities, since the elementary school girls can now climb and jump and run as fast as the boys without the hindrance of a skirt" (p. 397).

Just as traditional sex-role socialization practices can limit the options and opportunities of females, such practices can also have negative consequences for males. Psychologist Herb Goldberg was so concerned about this that he entitled his book, *The Hazards of Being Male* (1976). He points out the countless ways males are socialized to hold back their feelings and to deny needs—and the toll this takes on mental and physical health. "Though [a boy] too has needs for dependency," writes Goldberg, "he learns that it is unmasculine to act in a dependent way. It is also unmasculine to be frightened ('scared'), to want to be held, stroked, and kissed, to cry, etc. While all of these expressions of self are acceptable in a girl they are incompatible with the boy's sought after image of being tough and in control" (Chap. 12).

Why do we need sex roles at all? some persons are asking. Such a point was raised in a short story by Lois Gould (1972, 1978) that appeared first in *Ms.* magazine and later grew into a book. "X: A Fabulous Child's Story" told of a fictitious scientific experiment in which a couple agreed to rear their child completely apart from gender roles. They told no one else their child's sex—friends and relatives found it infuriating to be told only, "It's an X"—and reared the child according to the Official Instruction Manual for Project Baby X. There, they read that their infant should receive "plenty of bouncing and plenty of cuddling, *both.* X ought to be strong and sweet and active. Forget about *dainty* altogether." The child was given both "girl toys" and "boy toys," including "a boy doll that made pee-pee and cried, 'Pa-Pa,' and a girl doll that talked in three languages and said, 'I am the Pres-i-dent of Gen-er-al Motors.'" The child's hairstyle and clothing were suited to both sexes and didn't give away X's secret. And the guidebook instructed the parents never to make little X feel embarrassed or ashamed about any play activities. If X got dirty, they were not to say, "Nice little Xes don't get dirty climbing rocks." Or "If X falls down and cries," said the book, "never say, 'brave little Xes don't cry.' Because, of course, nice little Xes *do* get dirty, and brave little Xes *do* cry. No matter how dirty X gets, or how hard it cries, don't worry. It's all part of the Xperiment." The story goes on to tell of the joys, problems, and challenges associated with X's entrance into school with all its gender-related rules and customs and the expectations of teachers, other children, and their parents.

Some behavioral scientists point out the greater flexibility that characterizes persons not bound by traditional gender roles (Forisha, 1978). One of the leading researchers in this area is psychology professor Sandra Bem (1975, 1976). Her special interest has been in a combining of qualities traditionally viewed as "masculine" or "feminine" and thus closed off to one or the other sex. She speaks instead of "psychological androgyny," which gets its name from the Greek words for male (*andros*) and female (*gyne*). Bem (1977) explains that psychological androgyny "allows men and women to be *both* independent and tender, *both* assertive and yielding, *both* masculine and feminine. In other words, psychological androgyny expands the range of behaviors available to everyone" (p. 319).

Some behavioral scientists prefer to go beyond the concept of androgyny. They would rather not think in terms of a combination of so-called "masculine" and "feminine" qualities, since such terminology could still suggest that various traits are *gender*-related. Instead, they propose transcending sex roles altogether so that "the expression of specific traits is situationally determined and not sex linked" and suggest reformulating masculinity/femininity measurement scales in research and theory (summarized in Harrison, 1978, p. 328). In other words, a person who displays a high degree of nurturance would not be said to rank high in "femininity" but simply would be characterized by warmth and caring—qualities which either sex can display and which don't need to be labeled "feminine." And if that same person also displays a high degree of assertiveness, that doesn't mean he or she is showing his or her "masculine" side. The problem is in the terminology. In this regard, our discussion of the sociological terms *expressive* and *instrumental* at the beginning of Chapter 3 may be helpful.

"My daughter Patience."

(Drawing by Drucker; ©
1978, The New Yorker
Magazine, Inc.)

While many people view a movement away from traditional sex roles as being expansive, liberating, and more fully in accord with human potential, many other people find the idea threatening. They fear that "unisex" tendencies are emerging which will blur virtually all sex differences. Some persons fear that homosexuality will increase—although there is no evidence of a causal connection between sex-role preference and *sexual* (erotic) orientation. Furthermore, many homosexual persons are very traditional in terms of sex roles ("macho" men and "feminine" women). Gender roles, whether traditional or nontraditional, do not make people either homosexual or heterosexual.

An overlapping fear is that children will become confused about their own gender identities and will grow up not knowing what is expected of them as women and men. These various fears were probably behind the decision of television censors to turn down a proposed television dramatization of the story of Baby X described earlier (*Newsday* syndicated report, *The Greensboro (NC) Record*, August 2, 1978).

Professors Money and Ehrhardt (1972, chap. 1) offer the reassurance that a growing child can recognize that there are two distinguishable sexes no matter how much culturally prescribed behaviors may overlap at any given time or place. Why? Because "nature herself supplies the basic irreducible elements of sex difference which no culture can eradicate, at least not on a large scale." These basic elements of sex difference include the differing sexual organs and the fact that women menstruate, have babies, and produce milk for their infants. Men cannot do these things but can produce sperm and impregnate. Other reminders that the bodies of the two sexes differ are seen in such secondary sexual characteristics as differences in voice pitch and in the presence or absence of facial hair. What is really important, say Money and Ehrhardt, is that a child grow up "to know that sex differences are primarily defined by the reproductive capacity of the sex organs, and to have a positive feeling of pride in his or her own genitalia and their ultimate reproductive use." If such is the case, it doesn't matter how interchangeable activities may be between mother and father. In fact, they emphasize, "it does not even matter if mother is a bus driver and daddy a cook."

However, throughout history, societies all over the world have tended to add to the obvious physical distinctions and have insisted upon other kinds of differences between the sexes— differences that are socially created. In Chapter 3, we'll look at some of these differences and what they have meant in various times and places.

CHAPTER HIGHLIGHTS

In this chapter, we have considered how males are trained (socialized) to be "masculine" and females are trained to be "feminine" according to their particular society's definitions of those terms. Sex roles encompass both *temperaments* (what males and females are expected to be like) and *tasks* (what females and males are expected to do). In sex-role socialization, *positive sanctions* are the rewards people give us for behavior they consider appropriate for persons of our sex; and *negative sanctions* are the punishments and disapproval directed our way when our behavior is considered inappropriate for our sex. Many persons today are questioning the wisdom in rearing children according to sex-role stereotypes. Some behavioral scientists point out that greater flexibility characterizes persons not bound by traditional gender roles. Such persons feel they have more options and opportunities and can simply be themselves rather than feeling they must conform to societal expectations of "masculinity" or "femininity." *Psychological androgyny* is the combination in one person (of either sex) of those qualities that have usually been associated with masculinity (strength, rationality, independence) and those qualities that have usually been associated with femininity (tenderness, intuitiveness, dependence). Some behavioral scientists suggest getting away from the terms *masculine* and *feminine* altogether.

CHAPTER 3

(Susan Berkowitz)

THE MALE -
FEMALE
EQUALITY
QUESTION

I don't want to do that. That's *boys'* work!" a middle-aged woman remembers telling her mother years ago. The mother quickly saw through the child's chore-avoidance strategy and replied simply, "Work doesn't know whether a boy or girl is doing it. Now get busy!"

Perhaps work doesn't know, but societies do. And as we saw in Chapter 2, males and females have been expected to fulfill different societal roles which include both work activities and personal characteristics. "Boys' work" has been geared toward keeping the world running, "girls' work" toward keeping the home running. Why should this pattern be so widespread? And why has greater prestige generally been associated with the male role?

TWO DIMENSIONS OF LIFE: EXPRESSIVE AND INSTRUMENTAL

In searching for an answer to the riddle of male-female social inequality, it may help to begin by thinking of life as having two basic dimensions or sides. There is the "people" side of life (called *expressive* by sociologists) and the "work and activities" side (which sociologists call *instrumental*).

Behaviors associated with the *expressive* dimension of life include nurturance, tenderness, warmth, caring, empathy, showing affection through words and gestures, and everything else concerned with interpersonal relationships. Behaviors associated with the *instrumental* dimension of life, on the other hand, include such qualities as autonomy, activity, creativity, drive, ambition, courage, assertiveness, leadership abilities, mastery—qualities associated with getting a job done. Instrumental behaviors are task-oriented, whereas expressive behaviors are person-oriented.

Some people are quick to label expressive behaviors "feminine." However, caring about other human beings and putting forth effort to establish and maintain human relationships is as appropriate for males as for females. Similarly, instrumental behaviors aren't "masculine." A woman who achieves is not trying to be—or performing—"like a man," as is sometimes asserted. The word *instrumental* is derived from a Latin word meaning "equipment." Instrumental qualities such as drive, assertiveness, mastery, and self-sufficiency are nothing more nor less than tools or equipment necessary for obtaining society's economic benefits; and they can be utilized by persons of either sex.

Careful observation of the society around us should alert us to an important realization: the economic-opportunity system bestows its rewards of prestige, power, and material gain not on those who perform expressively but on those who perform instrumentally. (The term *economic-opportunity system* can serve as a kind of shorthand to sum up all that is involved in the network of means and ends associated with work and achievement.) And it is this unequal reward distribution that provides a key to understanding the male-female inequality we see in most societies. Chapter 2 provided ample evidence that female socialization has concentrated more on the expressive side of life than on the instrumental, thereby putting women at a disadvantage with respect to the economic-opportunity system. We now need to explore this topic further.

IS BIOLOGY DESTINY?

Some persons argue that women are just naturally less endowed with instrumental qualities; and if that means they are thereby cut off from equal achievement opportunities, no one is to blame except nature. Such a thesis is expressed, for example, even in the title of anthropologist Steven Goldberg's book, *The Inevitability of Patriarchy* (1974), and is summed up in a statement on the book jacket: "Why the biological difference between men and women always produces male domination." Goldberg (1974: 210–212) sees a "biologically based male superiority" that includes aggression and dominance and extends to reasoning abilities and achievements in the arts and sciences. Ignoring the societal constraints that have limited opportunities for women, and arguing chiefly from a biological base centered in male hormones, Goldberg attempts to prove his point by claiming that "there is not a single woman whose genius has approached that of any number of men in philosophy, mathematics, composing, theorizing of any kind, or even painting."

HORMONES AND SEX ROLES

One person who has reacted strongly to such assumptions about male and female potential is Estelle Ramey, a professor of physiology and biophysics who specializes in hormonal research. Referring to an old religious dictum that asserts that "the devil can quote Scripture for his own purposes," Ramey (1973) charges that "the Devil can quote endocrinology as well as Scripture" (p. 237). She is disturbed that some persons have attempted to "keep woman in her place" by referring to hormonal studies without taking into account the complexity of the topic. She compares such efforts to the way in which the "anatomy is destiny" ideas of Sigmund Freud were once used. In the society of his day, says Ramey, "Freud's distorted view of female psychology" was the most easily received of all his theories. Why? "Because it appeared to give a physiological basis to the prevailing theological and cultural attitudes toward women."

Ramey doesn't deny that hormones have a part to play in certain sex-related differences. Some of her own research, for example, indicates that females might be better suited physiologically than males to serve as astronauts. And her concern about the shorter life span of males has prompted her to study the part hormones may play in the development of heart disease (Kolbenschlag, 1976).

However, she cautions against reading *too much* into certain research findings—especially about the effects of prenatal hormones on the developing brain and any influence on later behavior. She refers to one study which compared a control group with fifteen girls who had been exposed before birth to excess androgens (sometimes called "male hormones," since males produce androgens in greater amounts than females do). The "masculinized" girls were characterized by more "tomboyism," higher energy levels, more career interest, and less interest in babies and motherhood (Ehrhardt, Epstein, and Money, 1968). Ramey (1973:240–41) points out that a close look at the data should forestall any conclusion that hormones themselve *cause* females to be either traditional or nontraditional in sex roles. The parents of the masculinized girls knew their daughters were different in certain respects; in fact, some of the girls were thought to be boys at birth. Ramey wonders if parents in such cases might not treat their children differently, and she cautions that certain other environmental factors need to be taken into account as well.

Other researchers, including Money and Ehrhardt themselves (1972) likewise call for a measure of caution in the conclusions drawn from such studies (Weitz, 1977). Research psychologist Anke Ehrhardt (1977), who was one of the investigators in this particular study, suggests that the influence of hormones versus environmental factors might not be a matter of either/or but rather both/and—in other words, an interaction between the two. One possibility she raises is that exposure to excessive androgen before birth may *predispose* such girls to be more energetic and less maternal, but that a certain environment is required in order for that predisposition to show up in actual behavior patterns.

At the same time, sociologist Alice Rossi (1977), who is a feminist and by no means interested in "keeping women in their place," has come to the position that social scientists need to take the human biological heritage more seriously. This would include not dismissing out of hand the possibility that hormonal factors actually may enter into differing male and female attitudes and behaviors concerning parenthood. She calls for a "biosocial perspective on parenting" that would stress "the influence of physiological factors on women as a consequence of hormonal cyclicity, pregnancy, and birth" (p. 24).

The problem is that so many complexities surround this topic (Gross et al., 1979). Take the matter of testosterone, for example. Testosterone is produced in much greater amounts in male bodies than in female bodies and is therefore considered one of the "male" hormones. Yet, Estelle Ramey (1973:242) points out that when researcher A. E. Fisher injected testosterone into one part of the brain of both male and female rats, the rats of both sexes acted like mothers! When Fisher injected it into another part of the brain, both sexes began showing male sexual behavior. Commenting on this same research, Money and Ehrhardt (1972) write:

Fisher's experiment clearly demonstrates not only that testosterone might release parental behavior of the type usually designated as maternal [such as nest-building and grooming the young], but also that males carry in their brains the capacity for this behavior. Maternalism should, therefore, more accurately be designated parentalism. (p. 268)

Ramey (1973:243) also shows that it is overly simplistic to call testosterone the "take charge" hormone, while ignoring social factors. She is aware of research that has shown an association between high testosterone levels and aggressiveness and leadership, but she points out that the *situation* might affect the amount of testosterone produced rather than the other way around. She tells of an experiment in which a monkey was considered top monkey in his social world; and, along with his high position, he was found to have a high level of testosterone. But, when he was placed in a lower position on the social ladder of the monkey world, his testosterone level dropped along with his status! Thus, one cannot make the assumption that greater levels of testosterone mean greater leadership abilities and that therefore men are more likely to be leaders than women. It doesn't work out quite so neatly.

Perhaps the only thing that can be said about hormones and sex differences is that, while hormonal factors both before and after birth cannot be ignored, they should not be viewed as a basis for a fatalistic determinism that seals the destinies of females and males. We must pay attention to the social environment and how human beings of both sexes respond to that environment. And we must keep in mind a point emphasized by Ramey, namely, that the differences that may be seen between one man and another man or one woman and another woman are as great as any differences that may be seen between women as a group and men as a group. In other words, it's a matter of *individual* differences between human beings for the most part, as well as different life circumstances. Ramey's (1973) conclusion (written at a time when both Israel and India had female prime ministers) is worth quoting:

> In all this miasma of claims and counter claims about the role of sex hormones in determining human behavior, there are no data to show that males as a group are more intelligent than females, or that there is any area of psychic response unique to either sex. For those who would use animal and human data to suggest that subtle but important contributions to behavior are made by the sex hormones, there can be no definitive proof to the contrary. Males are different biologically from females. They are also different sociologically. Men become United States Presidents and women do not. But then women do become Premiers of Israel and India and Ceylon. Endocrinologists have nothing to contribute to the explanation of these national differences. . . . To the question: Which has the best hormonal basis for leadership and achievement, man or woman? The meaningful answer can only be: Which man and which woman? (p. 244)

Just as Ramey cautions against drawing unwarranted conclusions from hormone research, other scientists warn against overgeneralizing from animal studies to human beings.

Psychology professor Annette Ehrlich, who specializes in the study of primates, emphasizes that even those primates most closely related to human beings show great variation in social organization, roles, traditions, and rituals. Some social patterns fit with stereotypical male-female behavioral differences in humans, others are opposite, and still others show amazing flexibility. Attempts to prove that any particular kind of human behavior stems directly from our primate ancestry are nothing more than "an interesting form of game playing" that provide no help in solving social problems such as sex discrimination, Ehrlich (1976) asserts. She elaborates further:

> The behavior of each species needs to be viewed in relation to its own environment. Thus, if we want to resolve specifically human problems such as war, then we have to look closely at such specifically human environmental factors as the military-industrial complex, nationalism, poverty, and racism— none of which has any counterpart among the nonhuman primates. (p. 30)

To resolve specifically human problems such as war, we have to look closely at specifically human environmental factors which have no counterpart among the nonhuman primates. (Hugh Rogers/Monkmeyer)

Psychologist Naomi Weisstein (1971) points out another problem related to claims that certain sex-role patterns are rooted in the very fabric of nature. Writers who make such claims tend to be very selective in the studies they cite. They ignore examples from among certain primates where female aggressiveness and competitive behaviors exceed those of males, just as they ignore studies of those primates where males are greatly involved in parenting. "In marmosets, for instance, the male carries the infant at all times except when the infant is feeding," writes Weisstein (p. 154). "In summary," she goes on, "primate arguments can tell us very little about our 'innate' sex-role behavior; if they tell us anything at all, they tell us that there is no one biologically 'natural' female or male behavior, and that sex-role behavior in non-human primates is much more varied than has previously been thought" (p. 156; see also Stack et al., 1975).

SEX ROLES IN PRELITERATE AND DEVELOPING SOCIETIES

Having seen that neither hormonal studies nor animal studies provide answers to the *sex-stratification system* we see among humans, we next turn our attention to other societies. Are men ranked higher than women everywhere in terms of prestige, power, and wealth? And if so, why?

PRELITERATE SOCIETIES

In trying to answer these questions, anthropologists, social theorists and others have taken three basic positions. Some have said, "In the beginning, women ranked higher than men." Others have argued, "In the beginning, women and men were equal to each other." And still others have asserted, "In the beginning and ever since, men have always outranked women." Let's briefly examine each of these viewpoints.

Idea Number One: "In the Beginning, Women Ranked Higher Than Men"   During the nineteenth century, drawing upon ancient myths and folklore, various persons proposed that in early evolutionary stages women held the power. Friedrich Engels was one of the supporters of this view (Tavris and Offir, 1977:16–17). Interest in the idea of a matriarchal era was revived in recent years by some spokespersons in the women's movement (for example, Davis, 1971).

However, unable to find convincing evidence for such matriarchal systems, whether of the past or present, most anthropologists tend to doubt their existence. "We now know," writes anthropologist Ernestine Friedl (1975), "that even in societies with matrilineal descent-reckoning, that is, those in which eligibility for marriage, the holding of property, inheritance, and succession to office all depend on a person's kin relationships through females . . . , it is the men who hold the most prized offices and exercise basic control over resources" (p. 4). Although matrilineal systems *do* provide certain advantages for women, they assuredly do not put women in the top position. Take the Iroquois, for example. Women of this group could exercise considerable power. But, say social scientists Carol Tavris and Carole Offir (1977), "even Iroquois women, who played an important role in village politics and lineage, could not join the Council of Elders, the ruling body" (p. 17).

For some scholars, a major problem in relying on legends to prove a former era of female dominance is that "the link which would explain how the rule of men succeeded that of women has always been missing" (Sullerot, 1971, p. 20). At the same time, certain other scholars specializing in the history of women's status—including some anthropologists—have endeavored to supply theories to answer that riddle. Some scholars are persuaded that, if not matriarchy, then at least a kind of "primitive egalitarianism" existed in the beginning; and their theories have generated considerable discussion and debate among both supporters and those who disagree (Reed, 1975; Leacock, 1976; Rohrlich-Leavitt, 1976; Friedlander, 1976; Whitehead, 1976a, 1976b). These debates lead us to the next point.

Idea Number Two: "In the Beginning, Women and Men Were Equal" Many Marxists today believe that women started out not *above* men but rather as men's equals. However, that equality was eroded as class societies developed, along with private property and the nuclear family system. Likewise, colonial conquests played a part in destroying the original equality. The model is one of oppression and conflict. Eleanor Leacock (1977:497) is one anthropologist who believes such ideas make sense. She points out that in simple societies childbearing and childrearing did not keep women from making other contributions to society as well; women provided food supplies for their families and enjoyed autonomy. Yet, she asserts, the situation changed with the coming of conquerors, missionaries, traders, and colonial officials. In view of this change, Leacock wonders why women's role *in reproduction* should be considered the reason for their subordination when that was not true at the beginning.

In hunting and gathering societies, the simplest societies of all, groups move about seeking food rather than remaining in one location and cultivating it. Both men and women work together in finding food; they are *co-providers*. And the more the sexes work together in subsistence endeavors, the greater the measure of equality between them (Friedl, 1975). An awareness of this pattern no doubt lies behind sociologist Joyce McCarl Nielsen's (1978) assertion that "all evidence suggests that at the very beginning of human civilization, women and men were roughly equal in status; at least the status gap between them was not as great as it is in more technologically developed societies. . . . women's status, relative to men's, seems to be decreasing over time" (pp. 22, 39).

Friedl (1975), on the other hand, is convinced that some degree of male dominance may be found in all societies. By male dominance, she means that, although men may not always have *exclusive* rights, they do have "highly preferential access . . . to those activities to which the society accords the greatest value"—activities which give them some measure of power or control over others. And that brings us to the third point of our discussion on the relative ranking of the sexes.

Idea Number Three: "Men Have Always Outranked Women in Status" Most hunting and gathering societies divide up labor in a certain way between males and females (Friedl, 1975:12–16; Nielsen, 1978:24–25). Men usually do the hunting or fishing, while women gather small plants, certain small land creatures, and some small creatures of the sea, such as clams or mussels. However, the prestige food is meat; and since men bring home the meat, men have the greater prestige. Still, women's contributions are highly valued, too; and women are viewed as nearly—though not necessarily fully—equal partners.

On the other hand, male dominance is greatest where the food supply is entirely dependent upon hunting—as is true among the Eskimos. If obtaining and controlling the distribution of meat gives men power and prestige even where meat makes up only a small part of the diet, it isn't surprising that such prestige and power are magnified enormously when meat becomes the whole diet! Friedl emphasizes a point we shall see again and again in attempting to understand the differing roles of the sexes, namely, that "the generous

Male dominance is greatest where the food supply is entirely dependent upon hunting, as has been the tradition among the Eskimos. (Georg Gerster/Rapho/Photo Researchers, Inc.)

distribution of scarce or irregularly available resources is a source of power, and that men and women differ with respect to their opportunities" (p. 32) in this regard.

But why do "men and women differ with respect to their opportunities"? Peggy Sanday (1973), another anthropologist interested in sex roles, suggests that human survival requires an investment of energy in three basic tasks: reproduction, defense, and subsistence. Reproduction has been assigned to women through biology. And the demands associated with bearing and rearing children may limit the energy and attention a woman can give to the other two tasks. Even if a woman makes a major contribution to subsistence in hunting and gathering societies, which is what Leacock referred to previously, she is often carrying an infant within her body or else outside nursing at her breasts. Thus, she is not free to engage in the prestige activity of hunting, which requires traveling unencumbered by burdens while tracking down animals (Friedl, 1975:16–18). And just as a "male monopoly" on hunting exists among the simple societies of hunters and gatherers, a "male monopoly" on the clearing and allocation of land exists among the more technologically advanced societies of *horticultural peoples*—those using hoes and digging sticks to cultivate food (Friedl, 1975). Friedl emphasizes that by controlling land allocation and warfare, men in such societies "are more deeply involved than women in economic and political alliances which are extradomestic" (p. 135)—alliances that are maintained through an exchange of goods and services.

It becomes clear at this point that the differing statuses of the sexes may somehow be related to economic factors, even in simple societies. It's an idea worth examining more fully.

Factors Affecting the Status of Women and Men Some anthropologists suggest that the key to explaining male-female differences in prestige and power is quite simple: traditionally women have been assigned to the *domestic* sphere of life, whereas men have been assigned to the *public* sphere (Rosaldo, 1974). And it is the public sphere that seems to count in terms of prestige and power (Lamphere, 1977:626).

For example, in a hunter-gatherer society, women may play an important part in providing for their families through the fruits and vegetables they gather. But the products of their labors are not for distribution and exchange outside their own families—in contrast to the male hunters who control the distribution of big game to the entire community. Friedl (1975) stresses that greater value is attached to that which is produced for extradomestic exchanges rather than for immediate household use. A similar principle seems to be at work in urban, industrialized societies where the work of homemakers is seldom granted the same social value as paid employment in the public world.

Marx and Engels argued that, as long as women were restricted to work within private households and excluded from a society's productive labor, the sexes could never be equal (Sanday, 1973:1685). Therefore, some social scientists assert that the movement away from hunting and gathering societies toward horticultural and agricultural societies, and later industrialization, has meant a gradual decrease in women's status over time. In this view, technological advances such as the invention of the plow—and thousands of years later, the industrial revolution—have resulted in a greater separation between men in the public world, engaged in market-value work, and women in the private world, engaged in care and maintenance work for their families (Nielsen, 1978:9–10).

May we assume, then, that the more that women contribute to subsistence through their productive labor, the higher will be their status in a particular society? Sanday (1973) sought an answer to this question by examining data from 748 societies. Surprisingly, she found that, although it was *necessary* for women to be engaged in productive labor in order to have higher status, productive labor in itself did not *guarantee* higher status. Other factors entered in.

Sanday defined female status in terms of "the number of economic and political rights which accrue to women" (p. 1682). She found societies in which such rights were extremely few even though women contributed as much as 75 percent of what such societies required in order to survive! Why should this be? "In many societies," explains Sanday, "it appears that females are used as slave labor and are rigidly prohibited from access to control over what they produce" (p. 1697). If a woman is considered her husband's property, both she and the fruits of her labor are under his control—which is one reason some anthropologists say that we must study marriage exchange customs in relation to women's subordinate position (Lamphere, 1977:621).

Not only must a woman *control* what she produces if she is to have higher status, says Sanday, but her product must be something that has a *high prestige or market value*. Rosaldo (1974:19), for example, speaks of parts of New Guinea where women grow sweet potatoes for daily consumption. But men grow yams. And yams are the food distributed at the special feasts of the society, which means yams have the greater prestige value, just as was true of the socially distributed meat of the hunter-gatherer societies.

In some societies, male power stems from contributing to the society something considered of high value; however in other societies, power is simply *ascribed* to men not because of what they do, but because of what they are—men. They are considered to have a right to control on the basis of beliefs associated with religion or magic. How women may gain power in these two different situations is described by Sanday (1973):

> In societies where control and production are linked and a competitive market exists, female power is likely to develop *if* females are actively engaged in producing valued market goods. In societies where control is based on a magical or religious title, female power is unlikely to develop unless some exogenous influence (such as the introduction of cash cropping, famine, etc.) creates a new demand or results in a revaluation of female produce. (p. 1695)

Developing societies are those societies in which vast changes are taking place through technological advances in agriculture and a movement toward industrialization and urbanization. Whether such changes raise or lower the status of women has been a matter of some dispute. No doubt, depending on the particular situation, women's status can move in either direction.

Greater Opportunities for Female Independence Sanday spoke of outside influences creating new demands for what women can produce. The Afikpo Ibo women of Nigeria illustrate her point well.

Before European contact, these women made and traded pottery (although their mobility was hindered because of frequent warfare) and also cultivated crops. But the control of income was in the hands of the men, who also carried on such prestige activities as yam cultivation. With the cessation of war, women began traveling more freely, which meant increased trade opportunities. Contact with the outside world also had an impact on the farming activities of the women, because the cassava plant (the source of tapioca and other food products) was introduced.

The Afikpo Ibo men treated the cassava plant with contempt. *They* would stick with their ritually esteemed yams. However, they said, the women could

Women in West Africa have been market vendors for generations and have, with their earnings, supported their entire families. (Marc and Evelyne Bernheim/Woodfin Camp & Assoc.)

Productive labor by women does not in itself guarantee higher status. Here a Middle Eastern young woman works at the fine art of carpet weaving. (Diane Rawson/Photo Researchers, Inc.)

grow cassava in between the men's heaps of yams if they wished. And any profits the women earned could be kept by the women. The crop proved to be successful beyond everyone's wildest dreams, making it possible for the women to become quite self-sufficient. They were now capable of providing both for themselves and their children. As a result, "Afikpo husbands have found it increasingly difficult to keep their wives at home in their formerly subordinate position" (Levine, 1970:178, as quoted in Sanday, 1973:1696).

Decreased Opportunities for Female Independence Contact with other cultures and movement toward modernization, while increasing opportunities for women in some cases, can reduce them in others. For example, the demand for their small handicrafts may diminish as manufactured goods become more available. Or work loads for women may increase without compensation, as in cases where men migrate to urban centers to find work while their wives remain behind to cultivate crops. Only rarely do the women share in the wages their husbands earn, although the men may invest a considerable portion of those earnings in purchasing more farm land which the women are expected to work. Such work is considered a woman's duty and is not regarded as productive labor with cash value (Boulding, 1976:104).

One sociologist (Papanek, 1977) faults governments for insensitivity and wrong assumptions. "As long as women are considered the dependents of men, in the economic and legal sense," she writes, "it will be difficult to consider women's needs *directly* in development planning" (p. 16). She is critical of the way official government records list women in the statistical category of "unpaid family worker," as though men are supporting their families rather than recognizing that women and men are doing so together. To illustrate, she cites the women who work as carpet weavers in the Middle East. The product is marketed by male family members, but the women who make the carpets receive no monetary payment, only food, shelter, and clothing.

Problems of Both Sexes in Developing Societies   Living and working in societies undergoing change is sometimes painful for men as well as for women. For example, one writer from a University in Kenya provides examples of men who, under colonialism, left their African villages expecting great gain by working as soldiers or plantation workers. But pay was low, and they returned to find themselves "no better off than their wives, who had to till the land to feed their children" (Pala, 1977, p. 11).

Anthropologist Ann Stoler (1977) speaks of the "Green Revolution" in Indonesia, where "as in other countries, the introduction of new high-yielding rice varieties, hulling machines, expensive pesticides, and fertilizers to increase agricultural production has primarily benefited the already secure members of rural society and has increased rural income inequalities" (p. 87). Women from poor families who once relied on daily employment as rice pounders now find their work done by hulling machines. Even so, they are better off than their male counterparts, because the women have a tradition of alternative ways to earn income, such as through handicraft and small-scale trade. For the men, the options are more limited. In some societies, the solution is thought to lie in leaving rural areas and seeking employment in urban centers. In such cases, men usually find better employment opportunities than do migrant women, a large portion of whom can find no employment in the cities except domestic service at low pay (de Miranda, 1977; Arizpe, 1977).

At this point, it should be clear that the impact of modernization on women's and men's roles in developing societies is complex and varies greatly by economic conditions, social class, and other factors (Chinchilla, 1977). For example, religious beliefs about the roles of the sexes may have to undergo change in some societies. One sociologist (Mernissi, 1975) who specializes in a study of Muslim societies points out the tension between a tradition that segregates the sexes on the one hand and a recognition on the other hand that full economic development and national advancement will mean using all the talent available— including the talent of women—in the production process. "But to achieve that aim," Mernissa writes, "Muslim society would have to grant the women . . . all the other rights which have until now been male privileges" (p. viii), which would mean vast changes throughout all areas of social life.

Summing up the general impact of the development process in Third

World countries, economist Ester Boserup (1977) reports that, although some societal groups gain and other groups lose through the replacement of their goods or services by something new, women are especially likely to find themselves among the losers. She explains:

> Although both men and women may become victims of development, it is more difficult for women to adapt to new conditions, because (1) family obligations make them less mobile than men, (2) their occupational choice is more narrowly limited by custom, (3) they usually have less education and training, and (4) even without these handicaps they often face sex discrimination in recruitment. (p. vii)

She also stresses that the work force of these developing countries has a higher percentage of females than of males who are "engaged in traditional occupations, which are precisely those gradually replaced by modern enterprises in economic development."

SEX ROLES IN INDUSTRIALIZED SOCIETIES

Sociologist Michael Gordon (1978:71–92) has shown how industrialization separates the home from the place of work and transforms the family from a "unit of production" (making and growing things) to a "unit of consumption" (buying things with money earned outside the home rather than manufacturing items directly). Having already examined sex roles in societies that are beginning to industrialize, we now turn to several societies that have already achieved a significant degree of industrialization.

THE UNITED STATES

In the United States, as well as in England, the early stages of industrialization were characterized by the employment of whole families together in the mills and factories—much as whole families had once worked together on the farm or in family-run cottage industries (Kanter, 1977:10; Gordon, 1978:76). But over the course of the nineteenth century, a variety of factors combined to edge women out of the labor force. The emergence of a middle class made it possible for married women to enjoy the "luxury" of remaining at home, supported by their husbands who were now expected to carry the entire breadwinning burden alone. A spate of "female culture" books were published, admonishing women to be dependent, pious, domestic, and entirely centered in home and family (Welter, 1966). At the same time, industrialization was also producing an urban working class whose life-style was quite different out of necessity. Many of its members were immigrants. Both single and married working-class women found that the stay-at-home cultural ideal was impossible for them to attain. Their families couldn't live on the husband's paycheck alone; they needed any earnings wives and children could bring in, too.

The early stages of industrialization were characterized by the employment of whole families together in the mills and factories much as families had once worked together on the farm or in family-run cottage industries. (The Granger Collection)

Social Status and Sex-Role Socialization   *Social stratification* is an important concept to sociologists because class position bears upon how persons think and act with regard to most matters—including sex roles.

Just as a geologist examines various layers or strata of rock that make up a cliff, so the sociologist notes the characteristics of different strata of society. It may bother us at first to think of human beings as though they were rock deposits, with one layer above, another layer beneath. Such an idea may seem to imply that certain groups of people are somehow "better" than others. And that goes against Western democratic ideals that stress the worth and dignity of all persons and emphasize equal rights and opportunities for all. However, we need to keep in mind that, when sociologists speak of higher and lower statuses, they aren't saying that one group of persons is *better* than another group. But they are saying that one group is *better off* than another group. One group holds a more advantageous position than another in relation to the economic-opportunity system, and that makes a big difference in a society that values persons according to where they fit into that system.

The United States Census Bureau measures social status by looking at three indicators: education, occupation, and income. Since occupation and income depend to a great extent upon education, many sociologists consider education itself to be a good indicator of social status.

With regard to sex-role socialization, research shows that the less education parents have, the more likely they are to encourage sex-typed behaviors on the part of their children. Males in the family are treated one way, females another. Parents with more education, on the other hand, tend not to be quite so traditional in the sex-role training they give their children. In other words, the lower the social status, the greater the gender differentiation; and the higher the social status, the less the gender differentiation (Scanzoni, 1975b).

Education involves questioning the status quo. It means exposing oneself to new ideas, gaining new information, and bringing about change. Persons who have had limited educational opportunities are less likely to raise questions about traditional values and customs. They tend to accept *what is* as the natural order of things or the will of God or at least something beyond their control—and let it go at that. Therefore, they're less open to the possibility of change.

The realistic conditions under which working-class persons live affect how they look at life. For example, the restrictive natures of their jobs usually permit little creative thought and independent judgment. "The essence of lower class position is the belief that one is at the mercy of forces and people beyond one's control," writes sociologist Melvin Kohn (1969). In contrast, he suggests, "the essence of higher class position is the expectation that one's decisions and actions can be consequential" (p. 189). Because of differing expectations related to both educational and occupational opportunities, persons of higher status are more likely to be characterized by *self-direction;* they are accustomed to acting on the basis of their own judgment. But persons of lower status, having had limited educational opportunities, tend to be characterized by *conformity.* They are concerned with obedience, not rocking the boat, following the dictates of authority. Such behavior is required of them on the job (innovation on the assembly line would not be welcome!); and so they socialize their children accordingly, thus perpetuating the pattern.

Conformity to what is expected of one can even bring a sense of security. One sociologist suggests that lower-status persons, having been unable to attain a high *achieved* status through education and accomplishments, tend to attach great importance to *ascribed* status (a status assigned by others so that one fits into what is considered one's "proper" place in life). Sex roles are in the "ascribed" category. Thus, a lower-status person's feelings of "anxious vulnerability" seem to be "soothed by rigidly defined social relationships" (McKinley, 1964).

For such persons, who feel so little control over the circumstances that govern their lives, clearly spelled out sex roles may seem one way of providing some sense of order, predictability, and certainty. "And you knew who you were then," sang the blue-collar Bunkers of television's "All in the Family." What was it in those bygone days that made you know "who you were then"? Archie regularly crooned out the answer: "Girls were girls and men were men."

Earlier, we spoke of instrumental (task-oriented) behaviors and expressive (person-oriented) behaviors, pointing out that instrumentality has traditionally been emphasized in the socialization of boys and expressiveness in the socialization of girls. However, the degree to which either expressiveness or instrumentality is stressed for either sex varies by social class. Middle-class parents, more than blue-collar parents, are interested in seeing their children develop to some extent along *both* instrumental and expressive lines. Working-class parents, on the other hand, are more interested in seeing their sons develop instrumental qualities and their daughters expressive qualities.

Both middle-class and working-class parents socialize their sons to be active, aggressive, competitive, independent, adventuresome, strong, and courageous. But there is a difference in the degree of *expressiveness* emphasized at these different status levels. Middle-class parents tend to strive for more nurturance and tenderness in their sons than is true of blue-collar parents (Komarovsky, 1962; Balswick and Peek, 1971). And, although both classes stress instrumental behaviors, there are differences in what instrumentality *means* among boys at different status levels, one indication being a lower regard for scholastic achievement among adolescent boys at lower status levels (Chafetz, 1978:92–93). In contrast, in homes where the parents have higher levels of education, instrumentality does not mean great emphasis on physical strength and demonstrations of "macho," but rather on mastery, competency, aspirations for academic excellence, and working toward achievement within higher-status occupations.

When it comes to daughters, middle-class parents encourage behaviors considered traditionally "feminine," such as nurturance and gentleness; but at the same time, they want their daughters to develop a considerable degree of independence and assertiveness. In other words, middle-class parents desire that their daughters be somewhat instrumental as well as expressive—though not quite so instrumental as their sons. Working-class parents, for their part, tend to consider instrumental behaviors "masculine" and don't encourage such behaviors in their daughters. As a result, girls from these homes are likely to be more passive and subordinate than girls at higher status levels. This is true in spite of the likelihood that the circumstances of life will make it necessary for many of these girls to enter the labor force when they reach adulthood, and thus they could have benefited from more emphasis on developing instrumental skills.

Race and Sex-Role Socialization   The purpose of gender-role socialization is to prepare persons for their adult functioning in relation to the economic-opportunity system. Historically in the United States, white males have been socialized for direct participation in that system, while white females have been socialized primarily for indirect participation, the expectation being that the economic-opportunity system's rewards would come to them through their husbands' accomplishments.

Of course, history shows that not all persons had equal access to economic opportunity—either directly or indirectly. Numerous men were disappointed to find that despite the rags-to-riches theme of the Horatio Alger stories, hard work did not always bring wealth and success. And numerous women were very much involved in providing for their families, working side by side with the men in carving out the wilderness, running family farms, and laboring for long, hard hours in factories. They were anything but the weak, passive, dependent, genteel ladies of leisure held up in the female advice books. Yet, for both white women and white men, as evasive as financial success might have seemed at times, there was still the American Dream to drive them onward. There was still hope.

For black persons, the story was different. Even when socialized to *want* the American Dream and to aspire toward it, they were hindered constantly by obstacles placed in their way by the dominant white society. The door to opportunity might appear open, but as soon as blacks ran up to it, they would find it slammed in their faces. Black men and black women had to develop together strength, perseverance, and resiliency in order to survive.

Cut off from the economic opportunities open to whites, black males found that socialization for mastery, achievement, and competition counted for nothing if a person was going to be judged on the basis of skin color rather than ability. Both under slavery and later during the period of Jim Crow (when segregation was legal and encouraged), the black male's self-concept was dealt heavy blows. He was told both directly and indirectly that he was inferior because he was black. But at the same time, he was a man. And societal gender norms stressed proving one's manhood through achievement. Yet the white-controlled occupational structure blocked his chances for the very thing societal norms demanded! It was a no win situation. First, there had been the degradation of slavery; later, there was the degradation of being given only the lowest-paying, unskilled service jobs—or no jobs at all. For some black males in the agricultural South, sharecropping opportunities opened up so that husbands, wives, and children could work together on farms under former slave owners. But conditions were far from ideal.

Often black males couldn't find any work, and their families had to rely on the efforts of their wives, sometimes being forced to depend on incomes that meant bare subsistence (Lerner, 1972). Under slavery, black females had learned from earliest childhood that being female did not mean being docile, weak, passive, and dependent. Black women worked right alongside men— cutting wood, building fences, driving ox carts, and working in the fields in the blazing heat. Gender made no difference.

Sojourner Truth, a tall black woman with no formal education who traveled around speaking and singing for the antislavery cause, underscored that point. At the second National Woman's Suffrage Convention held in Akron, Ohio, in 1852, a group of clergymen had invaded the gathering and monopolized the convention floor with endless discourses on woman's supposed "inferior nature" and "proper place in life." When one speaker stressed that woman was innately helpless and dependent, Sojourner Truth could stand it no longer. She rose and dramatically put such myths to rest by

"I have plowed and planted and gathered into barns and no man could head me. And ain't I a woman?"—Sojourner Truth (Library of Congress)

recounting her days as a slave. It took strength to bear the lash. It took strength to keep going and not be utterly crushed in spirit as one by one her children were sold. And it took strength to perform the hard work imposed on her. What was all this foolish talk about woman's need to be treated as a fragile object? Nobody had ever helped *her* into carriages or lifted *her* over mud puddles! And nobody had ever given *her* the best place, Sojourner Truth declared. "And ain't I a woman?" she asked. Holding up her strong arm, she told the audience to look at it as she continued: "I have plowed and planted and gathered into barns, and no man could head me! And ain't I a woman?" (Quoted in Brawley, 1921). Sojourner Truth provided the delegates with a living example of the way black women refused to be confined to the sex-role stereotypes held up by white society. Circumstances had forced them to be active, assertive, and independent in spirit.

After slavery ended, black women frequently found it easier than black men to find employment. According to anthropologist Diane K. Lewis (1977), the laws that segregated blacks and whites and limited black opportunities were mainly concerned with defining the black *man's* place and making sure he stayed in it. "Since slavery coexisted with male dominance in the wider society," says Lewis, "black men, as men, constituted a potential threat to the established order of white superiority. Laws were formulated that specifically denied black men normal adult prerogatives" (p. 341). She refers to the powerlessness black males were made to feel in view of lynchings and the sexual exploitation of black women by whites—acts which were "covertly sanctioned" by the dominant society. And for nearly a century after slavery, Lewis continues, "stringent institutionalized barriers" blocked black men from membership in trade unions (and thus from the job market), prevented full participation in the political process, and undermined their status as husbands and fathers, such as through certain welfare laws.

Although racial discrimination was experienced by women and men alike, black women had certain limited access to the opportunity structure. They could usually find employment in domestic and service occupations, working as maids, cooks, laundresses, or day laborers—occupations where there was little competition from whites. Factory jobs, except for the most menial tasks, however, were usually closed off from black persons of both sexes (Lerner, 1972).

For all these reasons, over the course of American history, socialization patterns for blacks were in some ways similar and in some ways different from those of whites. Black males learned the dominant society's values with regard to achievement but found they were blocked from economic opportunities in adulthood. Young black women learned that having been born female did not destine them to fulfill the dominant society's sex-role stereotypes. By force of circumstance, black women found themselves participating directly in the economic system and bringing home the meager rewards that system permitted to persons with black skin.

Contrary to myths about the black family, the majority of husbands and wives put great effort into keeping their families together— often against incredible odds (Genovese, 1974; Gutman, 1976). In spite of the difficulties placed in their paths, both partners did everything they could to help one another and their children. "We read of exhausted black men tending plots of land and going hunting and fishing to obtain food for their families," writes Lewis (1978), "just as we read of overburdened women having to cook and sew after a full day's work in the fields" (p.737).

The widespread employment of black women which resulted from whites' determination to keep black men out of the labor force had an unintended consequence that continues today: less rigid gender roles for black children (Noble, 1966; Steinmann, Fox, and Farkas, 1968; Scanzoni, 1977). Black daughters tend to be socialized in ways that emphasize strength, drive, mastery, individualism, and independence. And black sons, living in a subculture where female employment has been a long tradition, tend to grow up to be husbands who, more than white men, are likely to hold egalitarian sex-role norms (Scanzoni, 1975a, 1975b; Lewis, 1975, 1977, 1978).

Again contrary to myths about the black family, census data indicate that in the majority of black families, both parents are present. However, as Lewis (1975) points out, the research on child rearing in these families is limited. But what research does exist has led Lewis to conclude that there may exist a distinctive Afro-American cultural heritage that helps de-emphasize the gender polarity found in white culture. For example, a small black child of either sex learns to fondle and care for babies and toddlers—the child's

A small black child of either sex learns to fondle and care for babies and toddlers—the child's younger siblings—and these nurturant behaviors carry over into adult life. (Suzanne Szasz/Photo Researchers, Inc.)

younger siblings. And these nurturance behaviors carry over into adult life. In other words, not only do both women and men in black culture display "behavior considered appropriate for males in white culture," comments Lewis (1975), "but behavior which is associated with females in white culture is characteristic of both men and women in black culture."

Although her emphasis is on gender-role egalitarianism among blacks, Lewis (1977:345) is not unaware of problems that arise in certain situations— particularly where male unemployment is high. Some black men, having been severely beaten down by white injustices in the economic system, may sometimes react to the breadwinning role and aspirations of black women with bitterness rather than appreciation. And the resentment may show up in efforts to dominate women (Wallace, 1979). The feeling seems to be that the degree of autonomy that black women have gained by earning necessary income has actually come about because of racist policies that have kept down black men from slavery onward—thus keeping them from the leadership role society says males should enjoy. Not feeling that they could strike back at the society and the structural conditions that caused the problem, some angry black men have reacted against black women. A number of black women have written of the harm done to *both* black women and black men by the unquestioning acceptance of the stereotype of "domineering matriarchs" out to "emasculate" and dominate men, instead of recognizing that black women were often *forced* into taking primary responsibility for their families and did so out of concern for the entire family's well-being (Lerner, 1972, chap. 10).

SOCIALIST SOCIETIES

Because Marx and Engels deplored the social system in which men dominated women, the socialist and communist countries represent a special case of trying to promote equality for women and men in their social roles (Holter, 1970; Sedugin, 1973). We shall, at various points throughout this book, be examining some of these efforts to see how successful they have been in certain aspects of life. Here we want to look briefly at general attitudes toward sex roles in several societies.

Eastern European Countries Observers have pointed out that sex-role emancipation is considerably more advanced in East Germany than in West Germany (Katzenstein, 1970). Both in East Germany and in the Soviet Union, women are much more actively involved in occupational achievements than in the United States (Geiger, 1968; Field and Flynn, 1970).

Nevertheless, studies show that Soviet women remain responsible for maintaining the home, no matter how heavily involved they are in occupational achievements (Field and Flynn, 1970). And that means that the role models Eastern European children see continue to demonstrate certain aspects of gender-based specialization. Children learn that, whatever else women do, they are still the persons who do the housework.

Some leaders of the Communist party have expressed concern. They are aware of the chidings of Lenin, who once wrote: "So few men—even among the proletariat—realize how much effort and trouble they could save women, even quite do away with, if they were to lend a hand in 'women's work.' But no. . . . They want their peace and comfort" (Zetken, 1934). A journal of the Communist Party, U.S.A., has called attention to the problem in several articles, suggesting collective child-care arrangements and the socialization of housework as possible solutions. In the meantime, writes Alva Buxenbaum (1973), "we have had to take into our account the fact that the double burden of house and job (or in the case of housewives with young children, being tied down to the household) is a major obstacle to their consistent participation in activity. . . .   A sharing of household chores by conscious Communist husbands and wives can free Communist Women for political activity."

Hilda Scott (1974), in dealing with the question raised in the title of her book, *Does Socialism Liberate Women?* points up similar problems in Czechoslovakia, where household and child-care responsibilities fall to women disproportionately and where men have greater work opportunities and receive higher pay in spite of the socialist ideology of equality of the sexes. Sex-role stereotypes continue, and the weight of tradition hinders change.

People's Republic of China Mainland China is of particular interest in this regard, because, up to the time of the 1949 Revolution, traditional male-female roles were deeply imbedded within the rigid norms of Confucianism. Yet the Chinese Communist party has determined to accomplish a blurring of sex-role differences.

Long before the Communists came to power, certain voices had been raised against a number of practices that severely oppressed women: foot binding, female infanticide, the sale of young girls, prostitution, concubinage, the expectation that widows and betrothed women who had lost fiancés should commit suicide, and various cruel marriage and divorce customs. However, the Communists led an all-out campaign to elevate the status of women—although, as psychologist Joyce Jennings Walstedt (1978) observes, the intensity and seriousness of that campaign had its ups and downs over the years. Even so, says Walstedt (1978), "given that all factions in the Chinese struggle grew up in a country that was one of the least advanced in terms of sexual equality, the extent of change in 28 years is without precedent in modern times." Whereas only a few decades ago the position of women in the Chinese family was one of "virtual serfdom," it is now "one of economic independence in relatively egalitarian marriage relationships" (pp. 379–80).

At the same time, enough remnants of older thought patterns have remained to cause Walstedt to conclude that "despite gains made under socialism, the revolution has fallen short of its goal of a classless society in which women have coequality" (p. 379). Many of the same problems exist in the People's Republic of China as in the Soviet Union or Czechoslovakia. Service work, traditionally viewed as "women's work," is downgraded whether done in or out of the home. And a certain amount of job discrimination that favors men and limits women is still present. Furthermore, women continue to have the greater responsibility for child care, although, says Walstedt, "women are not as overburdened by their parenting role as they are in some countries" (p. 390), because the whole community helps in the rearing of children. However, the custom of assigning to women such chores as cooking, cleaning, mending, shopping, and laundering persists—even though women are also actively engaged in the labor force as full-time workers. Such practices occur in spite of the fact that official propaganda associated with the new Marriage Law of 1950 stresses the importance of husbands and wives sharing household tasks together (Kristeva, 1975:61).

Irene Eber, a specialist in Asian studies, shows how the literature of the Chinese people also reveals more than a trace of traditional values and outlooks regardless of the official commitment to male-female equality. Although recent literature in the People's Republic emphasizes such themes as free choice in marriage partners, equal work and educational opportunities for both sexes, and economic independence for women, the stories are honest about the struggles involved. Such tensions show that change doesn't come easily or instantly.

Traditional "feminine" virtues—such as tact, resourcefulness, gentleness, and modesty—are extolled in women. But at the same time, women are expected to be strong and independent, capable of making wise decisions on their own. "Women's difficulty in working with men derives in large part from the latter's fear of losing face and being humiliated," writes Eber (1976). "Thus women must be unobtrusively competent, firm, but not aggressive—a difficult situation when one is the only woman among men" (p. 34).

Eber illustrates by citing a 1973 story in which the only woman on board ship is second in command to the captain. Knowing of the captain's displeasure in working with women, the woman modestly declines opportunities to display her skills—until an emergency forces her to take over the ship. Even in her heroism, it is made clear in the story that she must continue to "behave modestly and tactfully throughout, in order not to embarrass the captain" (p. 34).

In another story recounted by Eber, three boys and a girl are coworkers at a hydroelectric station construction site. When the boys' hand-sewn shoes wear out, they decide to place them by the side of the road, hoping that the girl will notice them and mend them. Exceeding their expectations, the girl instead sews *new* pairs of shoes for each boy and at the same time keeps up her occupational endeavors.

And in yet another story, a wife prides herself on her contributions as a behind-the-scenes helpmate to her husband. She says that, because he works in the collective all day, she is serving the people best indirectly, by helping her husband so that he can perform his work better. She views this as a more important duty than concentrating on her own achievements. Eber explains why Chinese fiction presents such ideas:

> Women's increased role in production and their insistence that they be allowed to perform other than traditional women's work clearly produced uncomfortable visions of competition between the sexes. Because the prospect of wives abandoning housework and children as well as their submissive role was not easily accepted, a number of stories show women fulfilling their various roles with equal competency—and dutifully taking second place to men. (p. 30)

Some observers believe the yin-yang philosophy of old China may foster what Walstedt calls "nonconscious sexism." Yin is the passive "feminine principle" believed to exist throughout the universe, and yang is the active "masculine principle." The two are viewed as complementary opposites in all of nature. Thus, it is possible that some persons are fearful of upsetting an assumed natural balance by the introduction of drastic changes in sex roles; and so they resist (Walstedt, 1978:389; Hong, 1976).

Israeli Kibbutzim   The Israeli kibbutzim (plural for *kibbutz*) represent perhaps the most dramatic attempt anywhere to experiment with alternative life-styles and variations in family forms. A kibbutz is an agricultural commune. Strictly speaking, a discussion of such communes does not fit with our focus on industrialized societies. Yet, such a discussion is appropriate at this point in line with our consideration of socialist experiments, because the kibbutzim

In the kibbutz, the infants are housed with other infants in a "baby house" separate from the parents. (Ken Heyman)

were based on Engels' notion that all social differences between the sexes should be done away with.

How can this be done? The conventional pattern based on the original ideology has involved taking rather elaborate steps to assure that children of the kibbutz may learn undifferentiated sex roles from their earliest days. The process begins at birth by housing the infant with other infants in a "baby house" (*crèche*) separate from the parents. From birth to nine months, infants interact progressively less with their biological parents. At nine months, contacts are restricted to two or three hours daily after the parents complete their workday, with longer periods permitted on holidays. Until children are eighteen years old, virtually all their socialization is transmitted by a *metapelet*, the caretaker (usually female) who is in charge of each small group of children, as well as by schoolteachers and peers (Rabin, 1970:292–95).

When parents and children get together during this period, parents reinforce what the children learn from their other role models. The entire system was designed to eliminate traditional sex-role images among kibbutz children and has had a record of working relatively well over the years. When kibbutz and American children of ten years of age were compared, kibbutz children were found to be much less aware of sex differences in social roles

(Rabin, 1970:294). Summarizing a number of studies, including their own, psychologists Benjamin Beit-Hallahmi and Albert Rabin (1977) report no negative clinical or psychological effects stemming from kibbutz child-rearing patterns. Follow-up studies are now being carried out, and the available findings thus far show kibbutz-born young adults "to be remarkably effective, productive, and well-adjusted" in their overall functioning (Beit-Hallahmi and Rabin, 1977).

However, something has been happening in the kibbutzim in recent years. Certain changes have begun showing up which indicate a return to some degree of sex-role traditionalism— the very thing the founders of the kibbutzim had worked so hard to abandon (Schlesinger, 1977). In view of that early commitment to sexual equality, such a turn of events has been surprising. It has even caused some persons to claim that the renewed emphasis on the nuclear family and a more stereotypical division of labor proves that a woman's "natural bent" is toward domestic concerns after all.

But as sociologist Helen Mayer Hacker stresses, what has happened in some kibbutzim isn't really "a female retreat from equality," but rather "a retreat from the ideal of women's doing 'masculine' work." And there are structural reasons for this which are associated with how the kibbutz is set up. Hacker (1975) points out that total commitment to role *interchangeability* never existed. "Rather," she writes, "the emphasis was on changing women's roles without any corresponding change in men's roles" (p. 189).

ROLE INTERCHANGEABILITY

Hacker's point has come up again and again in discussing sex roles throughout the world. Most efforts at change have been in one direction only. But, to be effective, change must move in two directions: men will need to share in domestic and childrearing tasks, even as women will need to share in the world of work (Rosaldo and Lamphere, 1974:14). Sociologist Elise Boulding (1976) suggests that this is something "Marxist analysis failed to put its finger on," assuming that state-supported services would solve the problem. In Boulding's opinion, "there is no way out for men but to confront parenthood, and no way out for women but to confront sharing their centuries-old monopoly on the breeder-feeder role" (p. 116). Rosaldo (1974) makes the same point when she asserts that "the most egalitarian societies are not those in which male and female are opposed or are even competitors, but those in which men value and participate in the domestic life of the home. Correspondingly, they are societies in which women can readily participate in important public events" (p. 41).

LOVE

Boulding (1976) suggests another element that Marxist analysis has failed to take into account—love. "By failing to deal in theoretical terms with the special role of love and tenderness that enhances all other social interactions when present, and diminishes them when absent," she writes, "Marx left love as women's work by default. It simply could not be taken over by the state" (p.116).

And why is love so important? Because it modifies dominance relations, says Boulding. She is not speaking of "love" in an empty sentimental sense but rather in the sense of justice (no oppression), genuine caring, and reciprocity between the sexes.

MEN'S LIBERATION

Much of the current discussion of changing sex roles has focused on women, but Boulding (1976) suggests that "the men's liberation movement, in setting out to destroy both the image and the reality of sex-linked dominance behavior, may in the end be the most significant social movement of the twentieth century." As socialization practices emphasize tenderness and the development of expressiveness as well as instrumentality for men, the stage is set for "a new kind of involvement of men with children" (p. 117), as well as moving traditional male-female relationships toward total equality. (See also Pleck and Sawyer, 1974; Pleck, 1976; Scanzoni, 1979a.)

CHAPTER HIGHLIGHTS

Two basic dimensions of life are the "people" side (called *expressive* by sociologists) and the "work and activities" side (called *instrumental*). Traditionally, males have been socialized to concentrate on the instrumental side and females on the expressive. Some persons have ignored societal factors and argued that biology determines the relative status of the sexes. However, the part hormones may play in certain behavioral differences between females and males is extremely complex. Also, animal studies indicate great variation in male-female behaviors in the primate world so that no particular pattern can be assumed to be "naturally" male or "naturally" female. Some anthropologists suggest that the assignment of women to the domestic sphere and men to the public sphere explains male-female differences in prestige and power. At the same time, cross-cultural studies indicate that the amount of labor a woman does won't in itself enhance her status unless she has *control* over what she produces and thus has some degree of economic independence. In addition, what she produces must rank high in prestige or market value. Historically in the United States, white males have been socialized for direct, and white females for indirect, participation in the economic-opportunity system. Widespread employment of black women that resulted from whites' determination to keep black men out of the labor force has had unintended consequences: less rigid gender roles for black children; a tradition of strength, independence, and occupational endeavors on the part of black women; and a willingness on the part of black men to hold egalitarian sex-role norms.

Among industrialized nations, the communist and socialist countries have made special attempts to eliminate inequalities between the sexes; yet vestiges of traditional sex-role patterns remain. Some social scientists are persuaded that efforts toward full equality for women and men are doomed to failure unless men develop expressive qualities and share in domestic and child-care responsibilities at the same time that women develop instrumental qualities and aim toward achievement in the economic-opportunity system. Thus, all of life would be shared by both sexes, without disproportionate loads or privileges assigned to either.

PART THREE

BEFORE MARRIAGE

CHAPTER 4

(© H. Cartier-Bresson/Magnum Photos Inc.)

SEX BEFORE MARRIAGE: WHAT'S BEEN HAPPENING?

I f a virgin happens to walk by, the statue of the pioneer mother over there will rise up in surprise!" So goes the campus folklore at one university. Other colleges have similar legends. Maybe a cannon will spontaneously fire or the stone lions will roar. Of course, no one expects this to happen. After all, there aren't any virgins any more. Or are there?

Most people seem to have opinions about the incidence of premarital sexual intercourse today, but all too often such opinions are poorly informed. Yet there is no reason to rely on hearsay. There are reliable sociological studies that can help us understand what is going on today. And information from history can help us understand what went on yesterday as well. What about tomorrow? We can observe trends, formulate theories about what is happening, and then speculate about the future of sex without marriage.

The gender-role definitions discussed in the preceding unit carry over into sexuality. Part of traditional masculinity has been the assumption that sex has different meanings for men and women. Men have assumed that they have stronger physiological cravings than women—that they have boundless sex drives that can only be satisfied by "having a woman" however and whenever they want her. Traditional femininity, on the other hand, has included the idea that women have milder physiological inclinations toward sex—that for them sexual desire is less compelling and overpowering.

Therefore, many Americans were understandably shocked by the revelations of the 1953 Kinsey volume. Dr. Alfred Kinsey (1953, chap. 8) and his associates at the Institute for Sex Research at Indiana University had found that, of the married women in their sample born after 1900, nearly 50 percent had engaged in sex before marriage.

Americans who were accustomed to the double standard that maintained that boys-will-be-boys-but-girls-will-be-angels found it a bit easier to accept the Kinsey findings on *male* sexual behavior. Among men with a high school education in Kinsey's sample, 85 percent had experienced sexual intercourse before marriage; and among men with some college, the figure was 68 percent.

One thing became clear. If the norms for sexual behavior decreed abstinence before marriage, they were being flouted or ignored by large numbers of people. In many books and movies, religious teachings, and marriage manuals, the wedding night was portrayed as a mysterious rite in which two nervous, inexperienced virgins shyly gave themselves to one another in the marital embrace. But for over half the population, this vision was mythical. (For others, of course, the traditional ideas about the wedding night were close to reality, with one or both partners never having experienced sex relations prior to marriage.)

Although, at first, many questions were raised about the reliability of the Kinsey studies because of sampling procedures, studies by others verified his findings. Sociologist Ira Reiss (1960a, chap. 3) points out that the studies of

Terman (published in 1938), Burgess and Wallin (1953), and Kinsey (1948 and 1953) included couples from California, Chicago, and the Northeast, yet the results were strikingly similar. Each of these major studies indicated that about 50 percent of the women born in this century were not virgins at the time of marriage. "Considering the geographical and time spans that separate these studies and their respondents," says Reiss, "such findings are indicative of high validity."

Another point of agreement in these studies was the finding that women tended to link sex with love and affection. Their premarital sexual activity did not necessarily indicate "promiscuity," in the sense of having engaged in sex with a variety of partners. The Terman, Burgess and Wallin, and Kinsey studies taken together showed that, of the women studied who reported having had premarital intercourse, from one-half to two-thirds reported that their only partner was the man they later married.

Until fairly recently, many sociologists had maintained that premarital sexual behavior remained much as Kinsey found it, particularly with regard to rates of premarital intercourse (Reiss, 1960a; Bell, 1966; Ehrmann, 1959; Gagnon and Simon, 1970). Reiss pointed out, for example, that there seemed to be little room for change in male rates of nonvirginity, because, for generations, from 85 to 90 percent of men have experienced sexual relations before marriage (Reiss, 1972:179). And among women born in the present century, the 50-percent figure seemed to be holding steady until the late 1960s.

To be sure, many people *believed* that rates of premarital intercourse were soaring, and the popular press kept referring to a "sexual revolution." However, the word *revolution* implies an abrupt and radical change; and scholars could find no evidence that any such thing had occurred since the period around World War I. At that time, it was true that there was a sudden upsurge in rates of premarital sex, as shown in Kinsey's finding that only 25 percent of women born before 1900 entered marriage nonvirginal in contrast to 50 percent of the women born between 1900 and 1910 (Kinsey et al., 1953, chap. 8). This doubling of the rate of nonvirginity among women in just one decade could be called with some justification a sexual revolution. But since that time, any changes have been gradual and the continuation of a trend rather than something abrupt. Some scholars have suggested that it might be more accurate to speak of an *evolution* in sexual permissiveness rather than a revolution.

CHANGING ATTITUDES

According to Reiss (1972, p. 169) and other researchers, the kinds of changes that occurred after the 1920s had to do mainly with *attitudes* toward premarital sexuality rather than a lowering of the proportion of virginal males and females. People began feeling more free to discuss sex openly. Regrets and guilt feelings about premarital sex—particularly in a stable, affectionate

The evolution of bathing suit styles from 1900 to 1920 reflects the changes in sex attitudes and behavior during that same period. (The Bettmann Archive, Inc.)

relationship—were reduced. Other changes related to both the timing of premarital sex (nearness to marriage being less important than was once the case) and the meaning of premarital sex (a move toward what Reiss calls person-centered sex rather than body-centered sex).

PETTING

Another significant change that took place had to do with petting. Kinsey and associates used the term *petting* to refer to "physical contacts which involve a deliberate attempt to effect erotic arousal," that is, sexual contacts that do not involve an actual union of the male and female genitals. Petting might involve manual or oral stimulation of the breasts and genitals, or it might include the placing of the genitals close together without any effort toward penetration. Sometimes petting is a prelude to actual sexual union, but in other cases, petting (especially to the point of orgasm) is an end in itself—a substitute for sexual intercourse. Kinsey (1953, chap. 7) pointed out that, although premarital petting certainly existed among Americans in earlier decades and centuries, the practice became more widespread among those born after 1900 and its incidence had increased steadily down to the time of his studies.

Robert R. Bell (1966) spoke of this increase in premarital petting as "the greatest behavioral change in premarital sexual experience since the 1920s" (p. 58), a point that had also been stressed by Winston Ehrmann (1957). In a similar vein, Reiss (1960a, chap. 10) found in his research on sexual attitudes that, among those who believed in abstinence from sexual intercourse before marriage, there was nevertheless a great increase in the number who felt petting was permissible. Petting provided a way to engage in considerable sexual intimacies while at the same time preserving one's virginity since actual *coitus* (sexual intercourse) did not occur.

REISS'S CATEGORIES OF PREMARITAL SEXUAL STANDARDS

The publications of Ira Reiss have added significantly to the body of sociological studies on premarital sex. One of his most important contributions has been his differentiating and labeling four main categories of premarital sexual attitudes or standards which are held in the United States today. His research showed that during the years between 1920 and 1965, "young people increasingly came to see the selection of a sexual code and sexual behavior itself as a private choice similar to that made in politics and religion" (1973).

Attitudes toward premarital sex, according to Reiss (1960a), fall into these four categories: abstinence, the double standard, permissiveness with affection, and permissiveness without affection. Persons who hold the *abstinence standard* believe that sexual intercourse before marriage is wrong for both males and females. The *double standard*, on the other hand, is in essence two standards—one for males and one for females. Persons who hold the double standard believe that males have the right to engage in sexual intercourse before marriage but that premarital sexual intercourse is not permissible for females. Traditionally, the abstinence standard and the double standard have existed side by side, with abstinence being viewed as almost a kind of "official" standard while covertly the double standard was widely practiced.

Reiss found that young men and women were no longer willing to limit their notions about premarital sex to choice between these two standards alone. They added to abstinence and the double standard two new standards, both of which were basically equalitarian. Reiss labeled these *permissiveness with affection* and *permissiveness without affection*. Persons who hold the permissiveness-with-affection standard believe that a man and woman who are in a stable relationship such as engagement or who love each other or have strong affection for one another have the right to express their feelings through coitus. In other words, premarital sex is not wrong for either males or females if deep affection is present.

The remaining standard, permissiveness without affection, also makes no distinctions between male and female privileges. Those who hold this standard believe that both women and men may engage in premarital sexual intercourse regardless of how stable the relationship is or how much affection the partners feel toward each other. Sex is viewed as primarily a giving and receiving of sexual pleasure, a part of the good time two persons may have in going out together. It's sex for fun—casual, hedonistic, without any feeling that love is necessary to justify it.

Two other researchers found evidence of a fifth standard which they call *non-exploitive permission without affection* (Jurich and Jurich, 1974). The emphasis is on an agreed-upon meaning before sexual intercourse takes place so that exploitation will not occur. According to this standard, "if one party desires both sex and commitment and the other wants just sex, any sexuality would be exploitive and is, therefore, immoral" (pp. 736–37).

BELIEFS AND BEHAVIOR

Sociologists are interested both in what people believe and in how people behave. Reiss concentrated on beliefs or attitudes. Although he predicted in 1960 that attitudes allowing for greater sexual freedom would eventually result in behavioral changes in the same direction, he himself remained skeptical that such a change was actually taking place until more than ten years later, when the data from several studies by others convinced him that a rise in female nonvirginity rates was indeed taking place (1972:180; 1973)—a topic to be explored in greater detail later in this chapter.

HISTORICAL BACKGROUND

Most of the so-called sex revolution or evolution has centered around female autonomy. *Autonomy* has to do with self-government, independence, being free to carry out one's own will and being responsible for one's own actions, in contrast to being under the control of another. Traditionally, women have been under the control of men—first their fathers, later their husbands. This means that female sexuality has usually been subject to stricter regulations than has been true of men, who throughout history have been given freedom by parents and the larger society to "sow their wild oats" with prostitutes or women of low social position.

Sexual intercourse before marriage is not a new phenomenon. If one takes a historical perspective, it must be remembered that prior to modernization and the rise of the dominant Puritan ethic regarding sex, most Western societies consisted largely of lower-class, uneducated masses, with the remainder being upper-class aristocrats and gentry. Literature of the times indicates that premarital sex was very widespread among the masses and among much of the upper strata as well. However, with the rise of the middle classes and the influences of Lutheranism and especially Calvinism (in which both the Protestant work ethic and the Puritan sex ethic are rooted), sexual permissiveness came to be less acceptable.

PURITAN INFLUENCE

Puritan theology took seriously biblical warnings against both pre- and extramarital sex. Sanctions against sex outside of marriage were rigidly enforced, as is clearly seen both in the Puritans' own writings and in such fictionalized accounts as Hawthorne's *The Scarlet Letter*. Both men and women were expected to be chaste, abstaining from coitus until after wedding vows had been exchanged and remaining completely faithful to each other from that time forward.

Rationality and self-discipline were important virtues in Puritan thinking, and they were expected to be demonstrated in sexual conduct as well as in affairs of business. Over time, rational control meant financial and occupational success as the Protestant work ethic took root and blossomed into the middle-class life-style. And to be "of good character" meant steering clear of irrational and irresponsible sexual behavior that might disgrace the family, bring about an unwise "forced" marriage or dishonor one's reputation through the birth of an illegitimate child. Because women were the child-bearers, it was they who faced greater restrictions and tighter controls.

REVIVALISM

The great eighteenth-century Wesleyan revivals in England and similar movements in America converted large numbers of the lower-class masses into lives that involved frugality, hard work, and respectability. Historians have pointed out that, although revivalism did not fully accept the Calvinistic theology of the Puritans, the movement was in thorough agreement with "the Puritan concern for a rigorous public and private moral code" (Gaer and Siegel, 1964:190; see also Cowing, 1968:641–42). Any indication of sexual permissiveness was attacked in the interests of protecting the sanctity of marriage and the home. The religious groups that grew out of revivalism as well as those that descended from Puritanism greatly influenced the moral tone of the United States. One reflection of this was in the materials people read. As Joseph Gaer and Ben Siegel (1964), authorities on religion and literature, have pointed out, "So successfully did evangelical Protestantism impose its views on literature that nineteenth-century American fiction was almost totally devoid of illicit love at a time when Europe's romantic writers were making it a central theme" (p. 190).

Historian Edmund S. Morgan (1966) cautions, however, against the popular assumption that the Puritans were ascetics or prudes. They viewed human sexuality in a positive way as a creation of God to be enjoyed within marriage according to God's law. But they urged watchfulness so that human love would not be permitted to assume greater importance than divine love. And although one result of the later revivalistic movements was increasingly strict control over sexuality—especially female sexuality—there was no attempt to desexualize women totally. It was left to nineteenth century Victorianism to try something like that.

THE VICTORIAN PERIOD

During the Victorian period, women were taught that no decent woman had sexual desires; only "loose" women enjoyed sex. Married women were expected to tolerate coitus as a wifely duty and a necessary indulgence of their husbands' "animal nature." As much as possible, respectable women were protected from all that might add to their knowledge of sex; they were to be kept innocent. Newspapers in some cases refused to publish news of births (though marriages and deaths were published), and pregnant women were ashamed to be seen publicly in what was euphemistically called "a delicate condition." Female physicians were rare, and many women delayed essential medical examinations and treatment rather than endure the embarrassment of having their bodies seen and touched by a male. Some doctors tried to help the situation by having dummies in their offices so that a woman could point to the corresponding areas that were troubling her in her own body" (Graham-Murray, 1966:153).

Women in their roles as angel-of-the-house and guardian-of-virtue were to be characterized by refined speech. References to anything related to sex or parts of the human body must be expurgated from vocabularies or spoken of in euphemisms. For example, respectable women substituted such words as *lower extremities* or *limbs* in speaking of legs—even if they were referring to table legs or the legs of a piano. The word *breast* was also taboo; in the presence of ladies, it was proper to refer to a *bosom* of chicken at the dinner table. Both the clothing styles and furniture styles of the period showed a desire to cover up any hint of nakedness, with even the "limbs" of furniture often wearing ruffles and skirts.

Censors abounded. Eager to save society, such crusaders even sought to remove all earthy or sexual references from great works of art. Noah Webster in 1833 issued a special edition of the Bible in which offensive words (such as *womb*, *belly*, or *teat*) were removed or changed and all sexual references were blurred and made as inexplicit as possible. For example, the testicles were referred to as "peculiar members" or "secrets." Thomas Bowdler's nineteenth-century *Family Shakespeare* was another attempt to take great writings and make them tame and decent enough for women and children. With abandonment, he mutilated the great plays of Shakespeare, cutting out all that in Bowdler's opinion was offensive and coarse (Rugoff, 1971).

There seemed no end to prudery. The first museum in the United States endeavored to protect modesty by having separate visiting days for ladies, so that they would be spared the embarrassment of viewing nude statues and paintings in the presence of men. And in England, Lady Gough in her 1863 *Etiquette* wrote that the perfect hostess should make sure that "the works of male and female authors be properly separated on her bookshelves." It was considered indecent for books by male and female authors to rest side by side unless the authors happened to be married to each other (Rugoff, 1971:61, 111).

However, scholars are quick to point out that the notion of Victorian prudery was nothing but a myth if one considers society as a *whole*. The congested conditions of the cities in the wake of the industrial revolution, in which working-class families were crowded together in deplorable, subhuman conditions, constantly threw persons of both sexes together in such a way that sexual relations were difficult to avoid. James Graham-Murray in his book *A History of Morals* refers to the communal dormitories of nineteenth-century England in which there was no segregation by sex. Men, women, boys, and girls who worked together in the factories also slept together at night on piles of dirty straw in hovels called "padding kens." Graham-Murray also points out that it was legal at that time to have intercourse with any girl over twelve years of age. With large numbers of young girls and women laboring for meager wages in their factories, factory owners and managers took full advantage of the situation. Prostitution flourished. "During the Victorian age the supply of prostitutes in proportion to the size of the population was greater than ever before or since," writes Graham-Murray (1966:149,152). Pornographic materials were also widely distributed in Victorian England, especially pornography that featured bizarre acts and torture.

How could all this occur in a society so obsessed with sexual morality and prudery? The Victorian middle and upper classes were concerned about one aspect of sexual morality only— female chastity. Perhaps never in history did the double standard enjoy wider acceptance. Wives tolerated their husbands' extramarital affairs and visits to prostitutes as a necessary evil in view of men's supposedly greater sexual needs and stronger passions. For unmarried men, prostitution was even considered a positive good; it provided a means

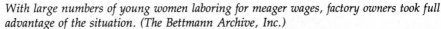

With large numbers of young women laboring for meager wages, factory owners took full advantage of the situation. (The Bettmann Archive, Inc.)

of sexual outlet. Single young men could thereby satisfy their sexual urges without degrading respectable women who were in the pool of eligible marriage prospects. At the same time, there were cases of moralists who advised men to "test the virtue" of young women they courted; and if a woman responded to amorous advances, she was to be spurned as unworthy (Rugoff, 1971:49).

CHANGES IN FEMALE SEXUAL BEHAVIOR

In view of this historical perspective, particularly with respect to the century prior to our own, it is easy to see that the major place for change (whether in the "sex revolution" around the 1920s or the "sex evolution" afterward) would likely be in the area of female sexuality. And this is exactly what various sociological studies have shown. We are not saying that changes have not also occurred among males; because there *are* certain changes, one illustration of which is a lowering in the percentage of males who have their first experience of sexual intercourse with a prostitute. However, the greatest changes in premarital sexual behavior have been changes among females.

Sociological studies that focus on such changes have *not* been attempts to "count virgins" in order to demonstrate that things are getting either better or worse (depending on one's personal value position). Nor are such studies indicative of a biased male perspective colored by a Victorian-like obsession with female virginity or nonvirginity. Rather, sociologists are interested in studying current social phenomena, contrasting them with the past and then trying to find out *why* changes occur and what they *mean*.

PREMARITAL SEX TODAY

Some sociologists have suggested that the term *premarital* implies sexual intercourse between two persons who will eventually be wed to one another or at least that they will marry someone eventually. They suggest that the more general notion of sexual behavior outside of marriage might be better described as "nonmarital sex." However, since most studies of the sex behavior of nonmarried persons use the term *premarital* without assuming that all such behavior is oriented toward marriage or that a marriage is in everybody's future, we will use the same terminology as we examine some of these studies.

SIGNS OF CHANGE DURING THE 1960s

In 1971, two professors from Johns Hopkins University conducted a massive research project to learn about the sexual experience of young unmarried women in the United States. John Kantner and Melvin Zelnik are authorities on the dynamics of population growth and change, and they wanted to find information on females aged fifteen to nineteen years. Were young unmarried women having sexual intercourse? Did they understand the basic facts of conception? Of contraception?

Kantner and Zelnik (1972) carefully drew a large national sample and conducted interviews with over four thousand young women who had never been married. Among the data they collected was the finding that 46 percent were no longer virgins at age nineteen. In contrast, Kinsey's 1953 volume had indicated that 20 percent of the women in his sample had experienced sexual intercourse by age twenty.

Other sociologists had also begun noticing changes taking place in the mid-1960s. As we saw earlier, in the interval after World War I through the 1950s, the sexual scene remained much the same insofar as rates of premarital intercourse were concerned. But now something was beginning to happen. Why? And what did it mean?

The evidence kept coming in. Two sociologists who had conducted a study among female university students in 1958 decided to return to the same university with the same questionnaire ten years later. They found that, not only had there been an increase in the percentage of women who reported having sexual intercourse during engagement, but even more significantly, there were indications that women in 1968 were less likely to think engagement was necessary before sexual intercourse was permissible (Bell and Chaskes, 1970).

Two other sociologists repeated in 1968 a study of college students which they had originally conducted in 1958. Harold Christensen and Christina Gregg (1970) compared a sample of students from the Mormon culture of the Intermountain region of the Western states with a sample of students from the Midwest. Male rates of premarital sexual intercourse among both groups remained roughly the same over the ten-year period. But there was a significant jump in female rates. In the Intermountain group, for example, the percentage of women who had experienced sexual intercourse more than tripled. (See Table 4-A.)

Not only was the incidence of premarital sexual intercourse increasing, but the age at which persons experienced it was decreasing. Whereas 3 percent of the women in Kinsey's (1953, chap. 8) sample had experienced premarital coitus by age fifteen, the figure had increased to 14 percent in the Kantner and Zelnik (1972) sample nearly two decades later. A marked reduction in the age of first coitus was also found in a study of West German adolescents, with a particularly big jump in the percentage of both male and female sixteen-year-olds who experienced sexual intercourse. (See Tables 4-B and 4-C.)

Especially striking to German sociologists Gunter Schmidt and Volkmar Sigusch (1972) were the parallel changes in sexual behavior in the United States and Germany during both the 1920s and the 1960s. Furthermore, there was a corresponding rise in premarital coitus during those two decades in other industrialized countries, such as England and France (Schmidt and Sigusch, 1972; Chesser, 1957; French Institute of Public Opinion, 1961). Were these happenings mere coincidences, or do they show us something?

TABLE 4-A *Percentage of college students with premarital coital experience: Changes during the 1960s*

	REGION							
	INTERMOUNTAIN				MIDWESTERN			
YEARS	MALES %	TOTAL NUMBER IN SAMPLE	FEMALES %	TOTAL NUMBER IN SAMPLE	MALES %	TOTAL NUMBER IN SAMPLE	FEMALES %	TOTAL NUMBER IN SAMPLE
1958	39	(94)	10	(74)	51	(213)	21	(142)
1968	37	(115)	32	(105)	50	(245)	34	(238)

SOURCE: Adapted from Christensen and Gregg, 1970, p. 621.

TABLE 4-B *Cumulative incidence: Age at first coitus (high educational level) by year of birth (West Germany)*

AGE (YRS.)	1966 STUDY				1970 STUDY
	BORN 1936-1940	BORN 1941-1942	BORN 1943-1944	BORN 1945-1946	BORN 1953-1954
	MALES (%)				
	(n = 649)	(n = 881)	(n = 838)	(n = 395)	(n = 108)
13	2	1	1	1	1
14	3	3	2	2	2
15	5	4	4	4	10
16	9	7	7	6	38
17	14	11	11	12	
18	21	18	20	21	
	FEMALES (%)				
	(n = 92)	(n = 208)	(n = 266)	(n = 212)	(n = 108)
13	0	0	1	1	1
14	0	0	1	1	1
15	1	1	2	1	7
16	1	1	3	3	26
17	2	4	7	7	
18	4	12	11	14	

SOURCE: Schmidt and Sigusch, 1972, p.35.

A number of sociologists suggest that these kinds of patterns do indeed have something to say to us. They can help us to see that *social* factors are involved even in such personal matters as sexual intercourse. The times and places in which we live and the persons with whom we associate have much to do with how we think about premarital sex and what we do about it. It is not simply an individual, private decision.

TABLE 4-C   *Cumulative incidence: age at first coitus (low educational level)*
by year of birth (West Germany)

	MALES (%)		FEMALES (%)	
AGE (YRS.)	1968 STUDY BORN 1947-1948 (*n* = 150)	1970 STUDY BORN 1953-1954 (n = 94)	1968 STUDY BORN 1947-1948 (*n* = 150)	1970 STUDY BORN 1953-1954 (n = 89)
13	4	3	5	0
14	9	10	5	7
15	15	18	7	16
16	25	40	19	25
17	44		33	
18	60		53	

SOURCE: Schmidt and Sigusch, 1972, p. 36.

COMPARING TWO PERIODS OF SIGNIFICANT CHANGE

There is some debate about the exact time when the first period of increased freedom in premarital sex began, with some sociologists saying the 1920s and others suggesting several years earlier (Smith, 1973), but there is general agreement that it occurred sometime around World War I. Ira Reiss (1973) singles out the period of 1915–1920 to be compared with the years 1965–1970. Both five-year periods were times of rapid social change.

World War I marked the end of one era and the beginning of another. As Reiss points out, "Historically, this period appeared as a culmination of trends toward making the United States a modern, industrial nation," adding that the increase in female nonvirginity at this time "seemingly was part and parcel of an overall societal change occurring in all major social institutions." Similarly, in the mid-1960s, the United States was again involved in another major war, Vietnam, and in addition was undergoing another change into a different kind of society, a post industrial society. Reiss writes: "the post industrial society is usually distinguished by its concern for the equitable distribution of rights and privileges whereas the industrial society is primarily concerned with the production of goods and services." During both the 1915–1920 and the 1965–1970 periods, doubts and questions were raised about society, its values, and its morals. Some sociologists viewed this as a rebellion on the part of youth and a rejection of norms imposed upon them by adults, including sexual norms. It was a movement away from the traditional roles assigned to youth as "dependent and inexperienced learners," with emphasis instead on a new self-definition in which young people came to view themselves as a social and political force in their own right. "The result was a radical rejection of the societal infantilization of youth and an emphasis on a new autonomy," write Schmidt and Sigusch (1972:42–43).

They suggest that, at least in West Germany, there were probably two reasons that sexuality played such a key role in this process: (1) the conflict between restrictive sexual norms and the strong sexual desires of youth, and (2) a feeling that sexual prohibitions are demonstrative and symbolic of overall "societal tendencies toward the infantilization of youth." To demand *sexual* freedom is a way of demanding the right to other freedoms as well. Schmidt and Sigusch write: "A society which denies legal sexuality to those of its members who have the strongest sexual desire creates the preconditions for making sexuality the central problem in generation conflict and for instrumentalizing sexuality as a weapon and provocative challenge in the conflict."

At the same time, from the vantage point of the United States, Ira Reiss (1973) suggests that what may appear to be rebellion against adult values is in reality "an actualization of rather traditional American values . . . equalitarianism, openness, honesty, legitimation of choice, autonomy, happiness, pleasure, love, affection, and experimentation." These values, including attempts to implement them in the sexual realm, have deep roots in the past. Historian William O'Neill (1967), for example, has suggested that the late-nineteenth-century debates over divorce and the victory of the pro-divorce forces in the early years of the present century meant a triumph for an individualistic approach to marriage. This triumph was on the cutting edge of a new outlook on morality.

In comparing the commonly called "sexual revolutions" of the two time periods under discussion (around the time of World War I and in the latter half of the sixties), we should keep in mind that there have been other periods with a high incidence of premarital sexual activity and there will doubtless be others, with periods of lower incidence in between. This raises the possibility of a cyclical pattern over history (with highs and lows of premarital sexual intercourse) rather than a linear pattern (a continually increasing incidence of premarital sexual intercourse over time).

Daniel Scott Smith, a social historian, provides evidence of a cyclical pattern in comparing proportions of American women who were pregnant at the time of marriage during different historical periods. (See Table 4-D.) He did not rely on this information alone, but on other data and considerations as well (such as contraceptive usage, ability to bear children, and induced abortions which could also affect premarital pregnancy rates). All the information taken together, however, presents "a coherent and plausible pattern," according to Smith. The peak period of premarital pregnancy in America prior to this century occurred in the late eighteenth century, with lows occurring in the mid-seventeenth and mid-nineteenth centuries. With certain variations, there was a similar cycle in Western European premarital pregnancy and illegitimacy data (Smith, 1973).

Much more research needs to be done to explain what the probable upsurge in premarital sex meant during certain earlier periods; but, for the two time periods in our century to which we have been giving attention, the desire for *autonomy*—for control over one's own sexual destiny—stands out as a major factor.

TABLE 4-D   *Long-term historical variation in white American premarital pregnancy*

PERIOD	PERCENTAGE OF FIRST BIRTHS WITHIN NINE MONTHS OF MARRIAGE		DESCRIPTION OF SAMPLE
	MARRIAGES	AREAS	
Before 1701*	*11.1%*	*9.9%*	*1,113 marriages in nine areas (8 in New England)*
1701–1760*	*23.3*	*19.4*	*1,311 marriages in nine areas (6 in New England)*
1761–1800*	*33.7*	*34.0*	*1,011 marriages in six areas (5 in New England)*
1801–1840*	*25.1*	*28.3*	*573 marriages in two areas (1 in New England)*
1841–1880*	*15.5*	*16.9*	*555 marriages in two areas (both in New England)*
1960–1964†	*22.5*		
1964–1966‡	*19.5*		

*Daniel Scott Smith and Michael S. Hindus, "Premarital Pregnancy in America, 1640–1966: An Overview and Interpretation." (Paper presented at the annual meeting of the American Historical Association, New York City, December 1971.)
†Wilson H. Grabill and Maria Davidson, "Marriage, Fertility and Childspacing: June 1965," U.S. Bureau of the Census, Current Population Reports, series p-20, no. 186 (Washington, 1969), table 17, p. 39. This measure includes births from eight months and zero days to nine months and thirty days after marriage but excludes those born before marriage; the denominator includes all births after forty-eight months of marriage.
‡U.S. Department of Health, Education and Welfare, Public Health Service, "Interval between first marriage and legitimate first birth, United States, 1964–66," Monthly Vital Statistics Report, vol. 18, no. 12 (March 27, 1970): 2, table 2. Proportion of first births under eight months of marriage.
SOURCE: Smith, 1973, p. 323.

MOVING AWAY FROM THE DOUBLE STANDARD

Already we have focused on the quest for autonomy among youth, both around the time of World War I and again in the 1960s, but we cannot pass over that other segment of the population which also made new demands for autonomy during these two time periods—women.

Women began to insist on their right to control their own lives rather than being dependent upon and subordinate to men. The feminist movement of the early decades of the twentieth century and the women's movement which received much of its impetus from the publication of Betty Friedan's book *The Feminine Mystique* in 1963 coincide with the two periods of a greater incidence of premarital sexual intercourse. In saying this, we are not implying that feminism "causes" premarital sexual activity to increase, nor that conversely an increase in premarital sex will "cause" feminism to emerge. The link between feminism and sexual freedom is simply that cluster of values mentioned earlier, particularly the quest for autonomy (the right to individual choice and self-direction for all persons) and equalitarianism, which insists that women and men deserve equal treatment and which therefore demolishes the arguments for the old double standard.

Why is the double standard under attack? "Not because of any decline in the rate of abstinence but because of its inherent contradiction and hypocrisy," write three sociologists who studied changing sexual attitudes and behavior during the 1970s (King, Balswick, and Robinson, 1977). "Young people have persistently attempted to identify and attack contradictory and hypocritical aspects of societal structure" (p. 458).

A movement toward a single standard does not *necessarily* mean a movement toward greater sexual permissiveness. It simply means that women and men are expected to hold the same standard, whether that standard is total abstinence, total permissiveness, or something in between.

However, during the 1970s, the movement already evident during the 1960s continued in the same direction: greater permissiveness for women. The gap between the sexes grew smaller both in terms of attitudes and behavior, as may be seen in Tables 4-E and 4-F, which show the results of studies of students at a southern university between 1965 and 1975. In 1965, 70 percent of the female students in the sample believed premarital sexual intercourse was immoral, as compared to 33 percent of male students; but by 1975 only about 20 percent of both sexes viewed premarital sexual intercourse as immoral. And although the percentage of males who had engaged in sexual intercourse showed an increase from 65 percent to 74 percent over the ten-year period, the percentage of females engaging in premarital sex doubled. By 1975, 57 percent of women in that student sample reported having experienced sexual intercourse, as compared to 29 percent in 1965 (King, Balswick, and Robinson, 1977).

Another 1975 study of adolescents from four communities found that among sixteen- and seventeen-year-olds, 67 percent of males and 45 percent of females reported engaging in premarital sexual intercourse (Brown, Lieberman, and Miller, as reported in Baldwin, 1976:14). However, many sociological studies have focused primarily upon changes in female behavior—which is, of course, the area where the greatest changes are taking place. (See Figure 4-1.)

Zelnik and Kantner (1977), for example, who had conducted the 1971 study mentioned earlier, drew another national probability sample of fifteen- to nineteen-year-old women in 1976. Whereas 27 percent of unmarried young women in this age range in 1971 reported having had sexual intercourse, the figure rose to 35 percent for a comparable group in 1976—a 30 percent increase over the five-year period. As of 1976, 55 percent of unmarried women nineteen years old had experienced sexual intercourse.

Among other interesting findings of Zelnik and Kantner (1977:61) are these: Unmarried women are having sexual intercourse at earlier ages, with 18 percent of fifteen-year-olds having had such experience. By age sixteen, one out of every four young women is no longer a virgin. (See Figure 4-2.) However, young women in the fifteen- to nineteen-year age range are *not* having sex more frequently than did the 1971 sample; but they are having

TABLE 4-E *Percentages of 1965, 1970, and 1975 college students strongly agreeing with certain statements regarding the morality of premarital sexual relationships*

	MALES		FEMALES	
STATEMENT	%	NUMBER	%	NUMBER
1. *I feel that premarital sexual intercourse is immoral.*				
1965	33	(n = 129)	70	(n = 115)
1970	14	(n = 137)	34	(n = 158)
1975	19.5	(n = 133)	20.7	(n = 295)
2. *A man who has had sexual intercourse with a great many women is immoral.*				
1965	35	(n = 127)	56	(n = 114)
1970	15	(n = 137)	22	(n = 157)
1975	19.5	(n = 138)	30.1	(n = 296)
3. *A woman who has had sexual intercourse with a great many men is immoral.*				
1965	42	(n = 118)	91	(n = 114)
1970	33	(n = 137)	54	(n = 157)
1975	28.5	(n = 130)	41	(n = 295)
4. *A man who has had sexual intercourse with a great many women is sinful.*				
1965	41	(n = 128)	50	(n = 114)
1970	24	(n = 136)	26	(n = 156)
1975	30.5	(n = 131)	33.6	(n = 298)
5. *A woman who has had sexual intercourse with a great many men is sinful.*				
1965	58	(n = 137)	70	(n = 113)
1970	32	(n = 136)	47	(n = 157)
1975	33.6	(n = 131)	37.2	(n = 298)

SOURCE: Adapted from King, Balswick, and Robinson, 1977.

TABLE 4-F *Percentage of 1965, 1970, and 1975 college students having premarital intercourse*

	MALES	FEMALES
	%	%
1965	65.1 (n = 129)	28.7 (n = 115)
1970	65.0 (n = 136)	37.3 (n = 158)
1975	73.9 (n = 115)	57.1 (n = 275)

SOURCE: Adapted from King, Balswick, and Robinson, 1977.

intercourse with *more partners* than was the case earlier, as may be seen in Figure 4-3.

Contrary to what many parents and other adults believe about the association of adolescent sexual activity with automobile usage, Zelnik and

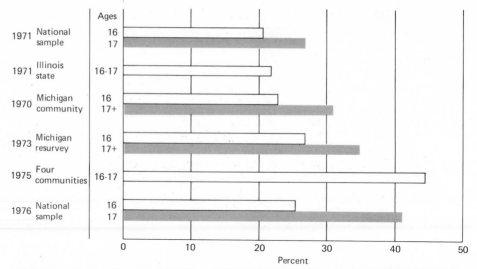

FIGURE 4-1 *Percent of unmarried teenage women who have had sexual relations: Various recent United States surveys. (Adapted from Baldwin, 1976, and based upon these sources: National survey: Melvin Zelnik and John F. Kantner, "Sexuality, Contraception and Pregnancy among Young Unwed Females in the United States,"* in Research Reports, *vol. 1, Commission on Population Growth and the American Future (U.S. Government Printing Office, 1972) Table 1; Illinois: Patricia Y. Miller and William Simon, "Adolescent Sexual Behavior: Context and Change,"* Social Problems, *vol. 22, no. 1 (October 1974), p. 62; Michigan: Arthur M. Vener and Cyrus S. Stewart, "Adolescent Sexual Behavior in Middle America Revisited: 1970–1973,"* Journal of Marriage and the Family, *vol. 36, no. 4 (November 1974) Table 5, p. 732; Four communities: Sarah S. Brown, E. James Lieberman, and Warren B. Miller, "Young Adults as Partners and Planners," presented at the Scientific Session of the 103rd Annual Meeting, American Public Health Association, Chicago, November 1975, p. 5, Zelnik and Kantner, 1977.)*

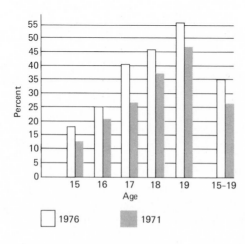

FIGURE 4-2 *Percent of never-married women aged 15-19 who have ever had intercourse, by age, 1976 and 1971. (Source: Zelnik and Kantner, 1977.)*

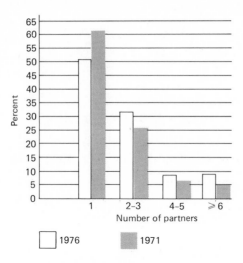

FIGURE 4-3   *Percent of sexually experienced never-married women aged 15-19, by number of partners ever, 1976 and 1971. (Source: Zelnik and Kantner, 1977.)*

Kantner (1977) found that "more than three out of four white and black respondents report that they have had intercourse in their own or their partner's home, or in the home of a friend or relative, regardless of whether it was the first, most recent, or only time that they have had intercourse" (p. 60). If the sexual activity took place outside a home, it was for blacks most likely to have occurred in a hotel or motel; for whites, automobiles and out-ot-doors were other favorite spots. First intercourse was most likely to occur in the summer.

PREMARITAL SEX, CONTRACEPTION, AND PREGNANCY

The Zelnik and Kantner (1977) national study of unmarried young women also revealed that "more of the sexually active are using contraception, they are using the more effective methods, and they are using all methods with greater regularity" than was true in their 1971 study. However, these social scientists also raise a note of caution:

> Although the increasing use of the pill and the IUD among teenagers should help prevent undesired pregnancy, questions may also be raised about the desirability of early and continued use of these contraceptives because of known and suspected increased risk of serious side effects. (p. 71)

Over against the risk of side effects is the risk of pregnancy. Approximately 780,000 premarital pregnancies occurred among fifteen- to nineteen-year-olds in 1976. But, if none of the sexually active adolescents had used contraception, according to Zelnik and Kantner (1978), 680,000 *additional* premarital pregnancies would have taken place in this age group. "These additional unwanted teenage pregnancies would have had to be resolved

Teenage Pregnancy

Despite an increased use of contraceptives, the number of teenage pregnancies continues to be high. (Mary Ellen Mark/Magnum Photos, Inc.)

More than one million adolescents are still getting pregnant each year. This is because the proportion of sexually active unwed teenagers has continued to increase; many doctors and clinics are still hesitant about serving teenagers, especially if they are under 18 and do not have parental consent; and sex education programs in schools, churches and youth organizations seldom provide information to teenagers on how they can prevent pregnancy or tell them where they can go to get contraceptive help. The result is that most adolescents present themselves for services six months to a year after they begin sexual activity.

SOURCE: Tenth anniversary summary report in *Family Planning Perspectives* 11 (January/February 1979), p. 3.

through more abortions, more out-of-wedlock births and more shotgun marriages" (p. 142) say these researchers, pointing out the psychological, social, and economic consequences of such pregnancies.

Even more premarital pregnancies could have been prevented if greater numbers of sexually active young persons had utilized contraception consistently. However, although a higher percentage of sexually experienced fifteen- to nineteen-year-old unmarried women in 1976 reported *always* using contraception (30 percent as compared to 18 percent in 1971), the percentage of those who reported *never* using contraception was also higher (25 percent

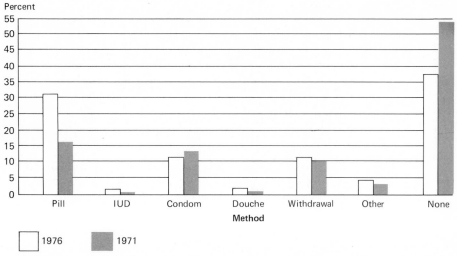

FIGURE 4-4   *Percent of sexually experienced never-married women aged 15-19, according to method used at last intercourse, 1976 and 1971. (Source: Zelnik and Kantner, 1977.)*

in 1976 as compared to 17 percent in 1971). Many others reported using contraception "sometimes." Figure 4-4 shows whether contraception was practiced at the time of the last intercourse before the respondents were interviewed; and, if so, what method was used.

DECIDING ABOUT CONTRACEPTION

If an unmarried woman can view herself as a sexual being—if she can *accept* her sexuality—she is more likely to use contraception, according to three sociologists who studied a sample of university women (Reiss, Banwart, and Foreman, 1975:628). They found that young women who sought contraceptive advice were likely to be those who (1) believed in the right of sexual choice; (2) felt assured they could make such a choice; and (3) were involved in a relationship with some degree of serious commitment. In this model, the starting point is one's own mental attitude (acceptance of sexuality) which is *then* applied to sexual behavior with a dating partner.

Sociologist Prudence Rains (1971) suggests a different sequence in which the relationship itself is the starting point, and this in turn shapes attitudes and behavior. Rains also recognizes the part "moral ambivalence" plays in the decision to use or not to use contraception. In studying a sample of unwed mothers, she found that those young women who engage in premarital intercourse even though such behavior goes against their moral convictions are the ones tending not to use contraception or to use it only inconsistently. Thus, this model, like that of Reiss and his colleagues, emphasizes the part played by an *acceptance* of sexual activity and one's own sexuality. However, Rains suggests a pattern that with some variation seems to go like this: In the first stage, the young woman experiences feelings of love for someone which "provides a rationale for sexual intimacy" (Delamater and Maccorquodale, 1978:235). Second, she enters an exclusive dating relationship. Third, she begins rethinking her sexual standards to the point of concluding that sexual intercourse with her partner would be right for her. And fourth, she accepts the possibility of sexual involvement in future relationships. When her thinking reaches this fourth stage, according to Rains, the woman is most likely to become a consistent user of contraceptives.

On the basis of their own study of sexually active young women, sociologists John Delamater and Patricia Maccorquodale (1978) found moderate support for the Rains model with its emphasis on how a young woman reformulates her sexual standards to line up with her experience. They found somewhat less support for the other model (Reiss et al., 1975) with its focus on the way prior-held sexual standards influence sexual activity and contraception. Yet, since, neither model appears to tell the whole story, Delamater and Maccorquodale conclude that further research is likely to show that "premarital contraceptive use is influenced by both of the types of factors emphasized in the two models," namely, one's own personal *attitudes* about sexuality and premarital sexual activity as well as one's actual *experience* with a partner.

Premarital contraceptive use is influenced by two factors: personal attitudes about sexuality and premarital sexual activity, and one's own experience with a partner. (Erika Stone/Peter Arnold, Inc.)

It's certainly possible to accept oneself positively as a sexual being and yet, for religious or moral reasons, refrain from premarital sexual activity. It's quite a different matter, however, to be unwilling to admit even to oneself one's own sexual feelings and the fact that one is engaging in premarital sexual intercourse when such is actually the case (G. Fox, 1974). Yet, such ambivalence and denial are not unusual, especially among young women, because of the different "sexual scripts" males and females tend to follow as a result of divergent socialization (Laws and Schwartz, 1977).

Sociologist Greer Litton Fox (1977a), for example, points out how society's idealization of the "nice girl" can influence a sexually active young woman not to use contraceptives. She explains:

> Regular use of contraception requires preparedness and preplanning, acknowledgement prior to coitus of the probability of coitus, and a willingness to take responsibility for sexual behavior. But the only excuses a young woman may give for sexual intercourse prior to marriage and still claim some vestige of niceness to herself are coercion (rape) and, more importantly here, to be so uncontrollably in love as to be virtually swept away by the spontaneous and unrestrainable passions of the particular moment. Obviously, to be prepared for coitus with contraceptives would give lie to the rationale that each act of intercourse was unanticipated and unplanned, merely a temporary and transitory lapse of virtue. In short, in order to be responsible to her "virtue" or "niceness," the nice girl construct requires that a woman be irresponsible sexually with regard to contraceptive use. (p. 816)

Such a young woman faces a dilemma. Because a "nice girl" doesn't engage in sex before marriage, to use contraceptives is to declare to herself, her partner, and the physician, clinic, or drugstore where she obtains the contraceptives that she *is* engaging in sexual intercourse and is therefore *not* a "nice girl." Yet, if she neglects to use contraceptives, she may find herself announcing to the world in another way that she is not a "nice girl"—by becoming premaritally pregnant.

RISKING PREGNANCY: COSTS AND REWARDS

In her book, *Taking Chances*, sociologist Kristin Luker (1975) describes contraceptive risk-taking as "a weighing process between a series of fairly well-defined costs and benefits" (p. 36). The process she calls *decision-making theory* is in many respects similar to what we describe as *exchange (or cost-reward) theory* in Chapter 1 of this book. The basic presupposition is that humans are goal-seeking creatures who wish to gain benefits while keeping costs low. Luker's focus is on the internal processes taking place as a person sorts out factors that appear costly and those that appear rewarding.

"In making decisions about contraception [women] try to attain many goals, only one of which is not getting pregnant," asserts Luker in discussing her study of women who had visited an abortion clinic to have their pregnancies terminated. She points out that, although bearing a child might seem a cost to be avoided, there are also costs in ending a pregnancy through abortion or preventing it through contraception. At the time of her study, costs associated with abortion included financial costs, social disapproval, being required to go through psychiatric testing, and being labeled "disturbed" or "having personality disorders."

When it comes to using contraception to prevent pregnancy in the first place, costs are again perceived by many women. Some costs listed by Luker are (1) the costs of acknowledging one is engaging in sexual intercourse, even being known as "sexually available"; (2) the costs to romantic spontaneity; (3) the difficulties often encountered in trying to obtain and then maintain effective contraception; (4) the costs of facing male attitudes that may include indifference, lack of cooperation, trickery (telling a woman she doesn't need contraception because the man has had a vasectomy), opposition to the use of contraception, and male insistence on dominance in the relationship; and (5) biological and medical costs, such as experiencing the side effects of some contraceptive methods.

On the other hand, Luker (1975, chap. 4) found that, at the time of taking a contraceptive risk, some women saw not costs but rather *potential benefits* in becoming pregnant—even though later they changed their minds and sought abortions. Since it is generally believed that a premarital pregnancy can be nothing but costly, the fact that some women anticipated such an event as possibly rewarding may seem surprising. What benefits could they expect? Some women were convinced that "being pregnant proves that you are a woman." As Luker explains, "To be pregnant is to be at the core of the traditional definition of the female role, and it is one way of dealing with the new and sometimes frightening roles that society is demanding of women" (p. 66). Similarly, some women felt that becoming a mother would signify their worth as persons and saw pregnancy as a path to enhanced self-esteem, as well as providing someone (a baby) to need them and love them. Some took risks in an attempt to find out if they were fertile, especially if they had some reason to believe they might not be. "Fertility is like money in the bank," writes Luker, "it is nice to know it is there, even if there are no immediate plans to use it" (p. 69).

Some of the women in Luker's study anticipated rewards in their relationships with other people as a result of pregnancy. Some believed a pregnancy might force the male partner to define his commitment to the relationship and possibly marry the woman. Others thought of pregnancy as a way to punish their parents or to force them to pay attention to their daughter or recognize her as an independent adult. For some, becoming pregnant was a way of crying out for help from social agencies—a cry that was not likely to be ignored. Lastly, Luker found a few women who viewed taking chances as being rewarding in itself, believing that "the risk of pregnancy brings an excitement of its own to the sexual act or enlivens an otherwise dull existence" (p. 76).

Luker concludes that in contraceptive risk-taking, women are "tacitly bargaining with themselves . . . to determine the costs and benefits of contraception, the costs and benefits of pregnancy, and the likelihood that pregnancy will occur" (p. 85).

MALES AND CONTRACEPTION

"Who should be responsible for contraception?" When sociologist Greer Litton Fox (1974) asked this question in a pilot study of 275 college students, nearly three-fourths replied that responsibility should be shared by both the male and female partners. However, when Fox looked closely at answers *female* students gave in a second pilot study which asked some related questions, she found that although the *ideal* of shared responsibility was so widely held, the reality was quite different. A high proportion of women felt that contraceptive responsibility falls primarily to the female. Some explained in pragmatic terms: "She's the one who could become pregnant—not *him*." Some felt males didn't take contraception seriously. Some felt that male methods were less effective anyway but believed that males could at least share the responsibility by helping their female partners obtain and pay for contraceptives.

At the same time that these college women recognized the reality of the situation, they indicated both ambivalence about their own part in contraception (the "nice girl" construct once again) and considerable resentment over having the burden of contraception placed disproportionately on their shoulders while men could go comparatively free. Fox tapped into this when she asked the women why many college men don't use contraceptives. "The respondents suggested first of all that men consider contraceptives a female responsibility," she writes, "second, that men won't use contraceptives because they get in the way of their own pleasure, and third, that men don't care enough about what happens to the girl to bother with contraceptives" (p. 19).

Fox concludes that the use of contraceptives is perceived as having different meanings for the sexes. Young women tend to view their own part in contraception negatively, feeling that the need for them to take the responsibility means their male partners don't really care about them and that, furthermore, there is some "vague moral taint" involved in obtaining contraceptives. However, in contrast, the women in Fox's study tended to attach positive meanings to male contraceptive use. She explains:

> The male's use of contraceptives or his sharing in their use is taken as a sign of extra caring, a proof of his commitment and love for his partner. Because the male partner himself loses little by not using contraception ("*he* is not stuck with a

pregnancy") and indeed may actually stand to gain from not using them (thereby increasing his "pleasurable sensations"), when the male *does* use them he does so *gratis*, almost as a sacrifice. (p. 20)

In another study, Fox (1977b) found that, among sexually experienced unmarried young women, those most likely to be effective users of contraception were those who held nontraditional sex-role attitudes along with a belief that they could control their own lives rather than being at the mercy of external forces or "luck." However, she found that neither variable (nontraditional sex-role attitudes and sense of control) separately or jointly explained the contraceptive behavior of males. Fox emphasizes that "clearly, the male contraceptor needs more attention from researchers."

One study of over four hundred white, black, and Hispanic male high school students in a large northeastern city indicated that the majority had not used contraception at last intercourse, or else had either practiced withdrawal or relied on their partner's douching (Finkel and Finkel, 1975). Although two-thirds of the young men in this sample realized that douching was not a good method of contraception, less than one-third realized that pregnancy was possible even though withdrawal was practiced. (See Table 4-G.)

Of the 72 percent of sexually active respondents who said they had not used a condom during their most recent sexual experience, about one-fourth said they didn't feel contraception was important, another quarter said they believed their partner was using some method of contraception, 32 percent reported they hadn't had a condom with them at the time, and a final 16 percent said they had believed their partner could not get pregnant at that particular time (Finkel and Finkel, 1975:259).

CONTRACEPTIVE NEGOTIATION

"Contraceptive practice, it must be emphasized, is an ongoing, two-party affair," writes psychiatry professor Warren B. Miller (1973), "and in the beginning of every sexual relationship (every stable relationship in particular), there are important negotiations that take place " (p. 200).

However, whether such negotiations actually take place seems to be problematic, judging from some of the materials just examined. At the same time, a study by sociologists Linda Thompson and Graham Spanier (1978) indicates that a partner's influence is a "strong contributor to contraceptive use in young adult men and women" (p. 490). According to Thompson and Spanier, "discussion with the sexual partner about contraception and sharing knowledge about contraception with the partner foster effective use of birth control."

If communication never begins or breaks down later, problems in the area of contraception are likely. After several years of observing women who sought prenatal care or abortions at the Stanford University Medical Center, Miller (1973) concluded that at a number of stages in a woman's sexual career

TABLE 4-G   *Number and percent of correct responses to statements on reproduction and contraception: high school study*

STATEMENT	NO.	%
A douche (female washing herself after sexual intercourse) is a good method to prevent pregnancies. (F)	272	66.3
A male's sperm lives less than one day inside a woman. (F)	278	67.8
Rubbers (scumbags, condoms, bags) help prevent unwanted pregnancies. (T)	376	90.2
A female can most easily get pregnant just before her period begins. (F)	192	46.4
Rubbers (scumbags, condoms, bags) help prevent VD. (T)	313	75.4
During sexual intercourse, if a male takes out his penis before coming, his partner may get pregnant anyway. (T)	133	31.9

SOURCE: Adapted from Finkel and Finkel, 1975.

she is most vulnerable to an unintended pregnancy. One such time for unmarried women is during the early stages of a relationship when a couple become sexually involved before a "contraceptive pattern" has been worked out through negotiation. Another vulnerable time is during a crisis in the relationship. "Even though two partners may have developed a working pattern of communication and cooperation regarding contraception," Miller points out, "either one may forget or simply abandon this previously established routine under the stress of a serious argument." Some women may at such times entertain a conscious or unconscious desire to become pregnant as a means of preventing the relationship from ending.

Another period of vulnerability is after a breakup between the partners. At such a time, for example, a woman might stop using oral contraceptives. "A surprise weekend or late effort to repair the broken relationship may find the woman contraceptively unprepared," writes Miller (p. 201).

ACCESS TO INFORMATION AND CONTRACEPTIVES

In spite of the increases in sexual activity among unmarried young persons and in spite of the large numbers of premarital pregnancies that occur each year, many persons oppose efforts to provide contraceptive information through sex education programs or efforts to make contraceptives more readily available. Even advertising (including emphasis on the condom's use for preventing venereal disease as well as for contraception) has been restricted (Redford et al., 1974).

"If a daughter confides to her mother that she is shoplifting to support a drug habit, would you then advise the mother to instruct her daughter on how to shoplift without getting caught?" This question was addressed to the syndicated advice columnist "Dear Abby" (Van Buren, 1978) and expresses the reasoning of many adults who wish to limit the availability of contraception in the hopes that, by so doing, unmarried persons will be less likely to engage in sexual relations out of fear of the consequences. However, as sociologist Phillips Cutright (1972a) has pointed out, denial of access to contraception has *not* discouraged sexual activity among unmarried adolescents, and there is no reason to believe that "access to effective medically supervised contraception and abortion" will increase such activity. But such access could make a great difference in the numbers of premarital pregnancies occurring among adolescent young women.

CHAPTER HIGHLIGHTS

Some sociologists suggest that the abrupt changes that occurred around World War I might justifiably be called a "sexual revolution," but that gradual changes in the direction of sexual permissiveness since than may be better termed an "evolution." Reiss has pointed out four primary sexual standards related to premarital sex: abstinence, the double standard, permissiveness with affection, and permissiveness without affection. Most of the changes associated with the so-called sex revolution and later evolution have centered around female autonomy and a movement away from the double standard. Beginning sometime in the mid-1960s, two significant changes occurred: an increase in the incidence of premarital sexual intercourse among young women and a lowering of the age at which persons of both sexes first experienced sexual intercourse. The changes evident in the 1960s continued during the 1970s. A 1976 study by Zelnik and Kantner showed that 55 percent of unmarried women nineteen years of age had already experienced sexual intercourse, and 1 out of 4 young women was no longer a virgin by age sixteen. The 1976 study showed that although more unmarried women always use contraception, the percentage of those reporting that they *never* use contraception had also increased. Factors involved in a decision to use contraception before marriage include a woman's attitudes toward her sexuality, sexual activity, and sex roles; a sense of control over her own life; involvement in a relationship with a male; communication with her sex partner; and the sorting out of costs and rewards related to both contraception and pregnancy. And even though both males and females speak of contraception as a shared responsibility, females indicate that in reality the major burden falls to them.

CHAPTER 5

(Susan Berkowitz)

SEX BEFORE MARRIAGE: WHAT DO THE CHANGES MEAN?

Is the rise in the incidence of premarital sexual intercourse related to changes in gender roles? A proposition stated by sociologist Richard F. Tomasson (1970) suggests that "where females have greater equality and are subject to less occupational and social differentiation, the premarital sex codes will be more permissive than where the female's status is completely or primarily dependent on the status of her husband" (p. 180).

To illustrate, he cites the greater emphasis on gender-role equality in the Scandinavian countries, which are also known for their greater acceptance of premarital sexual permissiveness. And he suggests that differences in black and white premarital sex codes within the United States may also provide an example of his point by referring to an explanation offered by sociologist James Coleman (1966). Where women are more independent and egalitarian, as in the case of blacks, we can expect that "the sex codes will be less rigid," argues Coleman (p. 127).

SEX AND SOCIALIST EXPERIMENTS

It would seem that, if Tomasson and Coleman are correct, the most likely nations to have a high degree of premarital sexual permissiveness would be socialist countries, because the equality of the sexes is an important part of socialist ideology. Such an ideology leaves no room for the double standard which gives premarital sexual privileges to males but not to females.

However, an egalitarian ideology could mean either that *both* males and females should be free to engage in premarital coitus or else that *neither* males nor females should be free to engage in premarital coitus. Several socialist experiments give evidence of a struggle between these two positions—total sexual permissiveness on the one hand, and total sexual abstinence before marriage on the other. In some cases, a position between the two polar extremes has become the prevailing norm, namely, the standard that Ira Reiss has named "permissiveness with affection."

SOVIET UNION

Freedom in sexual matters, or discipline in sexual matters? This was the question Russia struggled with repeatedly. In the early years after the 1917 Revolution, the Communist Party followed the thinking of Marx and Engels in making it clear that sex belonged to the private sphere of individual freedom rather than to the public sphere subject to regulation by the State. At the same time, the institution of the family was devalued and expected to wither away in the years ahead, along with other social institutions considered no longer necessary. As a result of all this, Russia had its own version of the "roaring twenties." A 1920 party journal carried an article asserting that "an unimaginable bacchanalia is going on . . . the best people are interpreting free love as free debauchery" (Geiger, 1968, p. 64).

There are many ideas about how sexual freedom fitted into the Revolution and Marxist philosophy. Sociologist H. Kent Geiger (1968:66–71) points out that the peasants in particular simply accepted the new sexual freedom as "a gift of the Revolution," a "pleasure to be enjoyed to the full." Others followed what came to be known as the "glass of water theory," a more sophisticated view in which the significance of sex was akin to swallowing a drink of water to quench physical thirst. And some suggested that "sexual property" should be held in common and shared along with all other kinds of property. Closely linked to the drink-of-water theory was what Geiger calls the "elemental nature" view. Here sex was treated merely as an instinct to be satisfied and was rationalized on the basis of writings of Marx and Engels which emphasized "natural man."

Many persons viewed sexual permissiveness as a symbolic defiance of the entire old order, a patriotic means of opposing bourgeois morality. Others found still different ways to link sexual freedom with the communist cause. Some said they needed alternative outlets for sex drives because their devotion to the Revolution left no time for settling down with a family. Others said a permanent union involved too much risk since the spouse might later turn out to be uncommitted to the cause. Still others suggested that poverty justifies promiscuity, because the poor can't maintain a family.

The notion of "free love" in the writings of Marx and Engels actually emphasized "freeing" love from economic concerns so that a man and woman could form a union based on deep feeling for one another rather than on other considerations. But the term *free* was widely misinterpreted, as was the idea of "love." Among the students, there arose the opinion that the way to enter into love was through sex. If good Marxists were to love, then they must realize that sexual attraction formed the base on which love could be built. If the sexual foundation didn't work out, the whole superstructure would topple.

Such rationalizations and the accompanying behavior troubled the older generation of Marxists. For one thing, it soon became clear that, even in a social order that promised the equality of the sexes, women were the least likely to benefit from the sexual anarchism being advocated by some. Through mockery and ridicule, young Communists used a new "male line" as they tried to persuade young women to grant sexual favors. They told women they were not true comrades if they still followed bourgeois prejudices about sex outside of marriage. Lunacharski indignantly remarked, "The frightened girl thinks she is acting like a marxist, like a leninist, if she denies no one" (Quoted in Geiger, 1968:63).

However, the old values were still strong among the majority of the population, and many persons were genuinely concerned about the sexual excesses that seemed to follow in the wake of the overturned social order. Yet how could the young be trained? It was hard to come up with convincing reasons for sexual restraint in view of the way many young theorists had begun to interpret Marxist thought. Men, even party leaders, were engaging in sexual adventures that left helpless women pregnant and abandoned while the men went on their merry way enjoying still more of the new freedoms. As Geiger points out, this problem caused deep distress among those who took Marxist thought seriously and therefore decried the exploitation of the weak by the strong.

One female writer suggested that a possible solution might lie in freeing women from enslavement to certain ideas, such as the quest for love and identity through attachment to men. The aim of Alexandra Kollontai was to "teach women not to put all their hearts and souls into the love for a man, but into the essential thing, creative work. . . . Love must not crush the woman's individuality, not bind her wings" (Rowbotham, 1972, chap. 6). She didn't deny that sex and love could or even should go hand in hand, but she wanted people to view them as separate feelings. In Kollontai's thought, a sexual union could be either prolonged or transient and still express love, totally apart from institutional forms. She argued that women had the right to enjoy sexual gratifications with a number of men, just as men felt they had such rights with regard to women (Geiger, 1968:62ff.; Rowbotham, 1972, chap. 6).

The new sexual freedom brought other problems besides the exploitation of women. Kollontai, drawing on Marx and Engels, looked forward to a new order in which the self-absorption of traditional romantic love where the sexual partners focused only on themselves and each other would give way to "solidarity love." This higher love would embrace the whole of the new society in "sympathetic bonds." But until that time, male-female relationships would present problems. In Kollontai's words, "Contemporary love always sins in that, absorbing the thoughts and feelings of 'the two loving hearts' it at the same time isolates, separates off the loving pair from the collective" (Quoted in Geiger 1968:63).

There was also the very real problem of energies deflected from the task of building the new society. An ascetic wing of the party had emphasized this all along. Lenin (quoted in Geiger, 1968), among others argued that the Revolution "cannot tolerate orgiastic conditions . . . no weakening, no waste, no destruction of forces. Self-control, self-discipline, is not slavery, not even in love." He argued against the glass-of-water theory of sex as being contrary to the true meaning of "free" love in communist thought, which emphasized a union based on deep feeling and comradeship. His own opinion was that a normal man wouldn't drink out of a gutter nor out of a glass "with the rim greasy from many lips" (p. 84).

Others selectively used Freudian ideas to emphasize sublimation, arguing that a common pool of energy could express itself either in sexual activity or in socially constructive activity. Energy expended on sex was considered to be stolen and diverted from uses more beneficial to society. Young people must channel their sexual drives, redirecting energies into the service of the Revolution. They were now told that preoccupation with sex was characteristic of capitalism and bourgeois society and not at all in keeping with the rigorous discipline needed to build communism. If, under capitalism, religion served as opium to deaden the sensitivities of the masses, sex served in a similar capacity and likewise produced a narcotic effect (a statement of Zalkind, quoted in Geiger, 1968:85).

Thus, the pendulum began to swing the other way. During the 1920s, the cry was for human liberation and noninterference in sex as a private matter. But by the end of the twenties, the emphasis was on "social usefulness," with interference and regulation justified on the basis of Lenin's contention that sexual promiscuity was not a private and personal matter at all but rather of social concern because of the possibility of pregnancy (Geiger, 1968:84).

PEOPLE'S REPUBLIC OF CHINA

In China, the cultural revolution seems to have skipped the early stages of total sexual freedom that at first characterized the Soviet experience. Instead, the People's Republic has from the outset upheld a stringent standard of premarital sexual abstinence for both sexes, along with faithfulness after marriage. Prostitution was abolished, and new jobs were provided for the prostitutes (Sidel, 1972, chap. 3). Women concerned with emancipation and equal rights were not interested in freedom to engage in premarital coitus. Quite the contrary. Chinese women wanted to escape the sexual slavery to

Chinese women want to assert themselves as persons and workers, not sex objects. (Rene Burri/Magnum Photos, Inc.)

men that had bound them for centuries. They wanted to assert themselves as persons and workers, not sex objects (Rowbotham, 1972, chap. 7).

The Maoists have encouraged late marriages for both sexes, because love affairs and family concerns are thought to divert energies from educational and career pursuits and from service to the revolution. As part of the propaganda campaign of the early 1960s, young women were warned that early marriage and childbearing would severely damage their health and that of their offspring. Young men under twenty-five were told that "unrestrained indulgence of the sexual impulse" would hinder their sleep and exercise after work, that it would dissipate bodily fluid, bring about nervous disorders, and cause such ailments as headaches, dizziness, tension, memory decline, mental and physical pain, impotence, and premature old age (Aird, 1972). Such warnings are similar to those that were spread in the nineteenth-century United States through advice books addressed to young men. The emphasis was upon the supposed conservation of energy by restraining from masturbation and sexual intercourse in order to redirect energies into occupational success. One historian has called this view of sexuality "the spermatic economy" (Barker-Benfield, 1972). It is interesting to observe its revival in China as late as the 1960s.

ISRAELI KIBBUTZIM

In the early revolutionary phase, the young pioneers of the kibbutz, like their counterparts in the Soviet Union and China, attempted to build a society free of sex-role differentiation. At the same time, this new society would discourage the bonding of women and men into small, isolated family units. Part of this was in reaction to anything "bourgeois," as traditional marriage was considered (Spiro, 1970, chap. 5). For one thing, conventional marriage kept women in a lower status socially, economically, and legally. But another strain that was just as strong in the antifamilistic tendencies of these collectives was the realization that the internal ties of small family units would bind the individuals within them to one another more than to the community as a whole. "Families may easily become competing foci of emotional involvement that can infringe on loyalty to the collective," explains sociologist Yonina Talmon (1972:4). We saw earlier that similar concerns were voiced at one time in the Soviet Union.

Quite naturally questions began to arise about handling sexuality in the kibbutz. If conventional marriage were abolished, would it mean total sexual freedom? Could anyone have sex relations with anyone he or she desired? The kibbutz had no clear-cut ideology, so things had to work themselves out by trial and error. There were experiments with polygamy, for example, and a rejection of "bourgeois" standards such as premarital chastity and lifelong fidelity (Spiro, 1970). At the same time, there were efforts toward de-eroticizing the sexes, with emphasis on how alike men and women were. Women adopted male dress and discontinued concern with cosmetics and beauty care. Dormitory rooms were shared by men and women in groups in casual, nonsexual roommate arrangements. A mixed shower was instituted but was soon abandoned because the persons involved felt their previous training was too strong and inhibiting.

Sexual relations were themselves considered a personal matter, and premarital intercourse met with no disapproval on the part of the community. Promiscuity (in the sense of casual sex with a variety of partners) was discouraged, but if a man and woman *both* desired coitus out of love for each other and deep emotional attachment, they felt free to engage in intercourse. At the same time the exclusiveness of romantic love presented problems for the collective in the way it set couples apart. Thus, it became customary for couples to try to keep secret the special ties between them.

This secrecy and restraint in public demonstration of "coupleness," was one of several counterbalances that Talmon (1972:8–10) suggests were operative in keeping in check the liberal "emphasis on personal autonomy and erotic gratification." Other counterbalances were the sexual modesty and reticence the young people brought from their Jewish upbringing, and the rigorous way of life in the kibbutz, with its emphasis on deferred gratification, commitment to the task at hand, and strict self-discipline.

As a result of the strong counterbalances to the earlier free love notions, there arose a comparatively conservative attitude toward sex in the kibbutz. Group activities are encouraged rather than couple activities, and children and adolescents are encouraged to view one another in nonsexual ways, that is, to simply see one another as persons (Spiro, 1965:327). Sexual relations during high school days have been discouraged primarily because they are considered distracting and would hinder young people in their work and studies. After high school graduation, however, young men and women are considered fullfledged members of the kibbutz and may freely engage in sexual relations. The community regards this as a private matter of concern only to the man and woman involved until a couple wishes to marry. Traditionally, at the time of marriage the couple would apply for a common room and this gesture would be the only ceremony required (Spiro, 1970:113). However, in recent years, there has been a move toward having a wedding as a meaningful and memorable event (Talmon, 1972:21).

There have been other changes in recent years. Talmon has pointed out trends away from asceticism and austerity and a working out of new compromise patterns. She sees evidence that the sense of social mission that once imbued the kibbutz community is declining. Other sociologists have shown that this "laxist tendency" has had an effect in the sexual sphere (Rabkin and Spiro in Spiro, 1970, chap. 9). The traditional sexual code, with its stress on restraint, is still the official standard; but there is more pairing off among high school students. Sexual relations sometimes occur among these couples, and abortions have been arranged for some of the teenage pregnancies that have resulted. Some girls begin dating as early as the eighth grade, and they usually date upperclassmen. High school girls are more apt to be sexually experienced than are boys, because many girls of high school age have older boyfriends from among soldiers or young men of the kibbutz

(Rabkin and Spiro, 1970). At the same time, sexual promiscuity continues to be frowned upon, and premarital sexual intercourse is most acceptable in a relationship likely to lead to marriage.

As we saw in Chapter 3, the kibbutz in recent years has been characterized by a growing differentiation of sex roles, with women being allotted more traditionally feminine tasks in the work of the collective. Women have also begun showing more concern about dress, including jewelry and makeup. Even a hairdresser may now be found in the kibbutz. Attractiveness to males and an emphasis on marriage and children seem to be taking on an importance to kibbutz women that was unknown in the early days of the movement. In this context, the permissiveness-with-affection standard appears to be widely accepted.

SOCIALIST DEMOCRACY OF SWEDEN

When Tomasson formulated his proposition regarding an association between female equality and greater permissiveness in premarital sex, he had in mind primarily the Scandinavian countries— particularly Sweden, which was the focus of his sociological study. He refers to research which indicates that "the majority of young Swedes have premarital intercourse and that they begin at an early age." For example, a 1968 study showed that over 95 percent of the married persons in the sample had experienced premarital coitus. A study of military draftees in 1964 indicated that 83 percent of the men had experienced sexual intercourse before marriage (Tomasson, 1970, chap. 6). Studies of college students conducted in 1960 and 1965 yielded the information that within the five-year period, the percentage of boys who had experienced premarital coitus rose from 72 percent to 81 percent. For girls, the percentage rose from 40 percent to 65 percent. And in another 1965 study designed to investigate the sexual habits and knowledge of teenagers, it was found that 57 percent of the boys and 46 percent of the girls had experienced coitus by their late teens. For boys, the median age for their first experience was 16; for girls, it was 17 (Linner, 1967, chap. 2).

Birgitta Linner, a Swedish authority in family counseling, has pointed out that sex surveys were woefully few in Sweden until rather recently, since Swedish sociologists tended to rely on studies done in the United States. Because of this, we have no record of a jump in nonvirginity in the 1920s that might be compared with what was happening elsewhere in the world—such as the United States, England, France, and Germany—during that time of rapid social change.

However, an event did take place in Sweden in 1920 that laid the groundwork for vast changes in the years to follow. In that year, Sweden passed the first democratic family laws anywhere in the world (Linner, 1967, chap. 1). Husband and wife, according to the new Marriage Code, were to have equal roles and rights and mutual responsibilities within the family— including the assumption of financial obligations for one another and their children, with housework being considered as a financial contribution to the household. Other laws followed in the decades ahead—laws affecting divorce, women's rights, the care of children, benefits for unwed mothers, financial allowances, and so on. Both official government policy and the general social climate were moving in the direction of full equality for both sexes and away from the old double standard in any of its forms.

Sex education has been required in all school grades for more than a decade. This has included efforts to socialize children to look upon their roles in the family and society as being equal and interchangeable rather than linked to gender. Contraceptive information is also considered important and is disseminated through sex education in the schools and through public service advertisements. Although there are moral debates over the issue, the feeling is rather strong in Sweden and other Scandinavian countries that young people should be able to act upon their sexual urges responsibly, using birth control (rather than being told they must refrain from sex until marriage which some feel results in unwise early marriages, just as lack of contraceptive information can result in unplanned pregnancies before marriage).

Even so, from one-third to one-half of Swedish brides are pregnant on their wedding day (Linner, 1967, chap. 3; Tomasson, 1970:184). This does not reflect a high proportion of "forced marriages" so much as it indicates the norm of sexual intercourse during engagement. It also tells us something about the social acceptance of premaritally conceived children and their parents in Swedish society. Unmarried pregnant women are not encouraged to marry just to "give the child a name" or protect themselves and their children from the cruel taunts of society. In Sweden, large numbers of unmarried women elect to keep their children born out of wedlock, and the laws and social policy provide generous and humane support (Linner, 1967, chap. 3; Linner, 1966). Overall, the emphasis in Sweden is more on the permissiveness-with-affection standard rather than casual sex with a variety of partners. At the same time, there is enough "casual sex" to cause what Linner refers to as the one "pessimistic aspect of sex in Swedish society," the rising frequency of venereal disease.

It should be kept in mind that premarital sexual experience is not a new thing in the Scandinavian countries. As sociologist Harold T. Christensen (1969) points out, "In Denmark . . . sexual intercourse during engagement is a tradition at least three or four centuries old," and it was not at all unusual for couples to wait until pregnancy occurred before going ahead with the wedding. Linner (1966 and 1967) likewise refers to the agricultural roots and peasant culture that are part of Sweden's history; and in this setting sex relations before marriage and premaritally conceived children were not at all unusual. In fact, the number of children born out of wedlock is lower now than in the nineteenth century. Nevertheless, the older generation has had some difficulty in accepting the newer attitudes toward sex in Sweden, no doubt because of greater openness in discussing the subject and the replacement of double-standard thinking with a norm of sexual equality for both sexes.

Tomasson (1970, chap. 6) has written that "a permissive sex ethic, which is essentially a premarital sex ethic that gives females the same rights and privileges that men tacitly enjoy in other more sexually restrictive societies, is only an aspect of the general status of women in a society." He describes the requisite "general status of women" in terms of four characteristics: a high level of equality with males, minimization of sexual differentiation in roles, relative economic independence from males, and status determined by individualistic achievements rather than by the status of husbands.

These four characteristics are descriptive of Sweden, and Tomasson's proposition fits. The premarital sex ethic in Sweden is permissive. However, these four characteristics are also descriptive of Communist China, and there the premarital sex ethic is restrictive. Both countries have in common the renunciation of the double standard. But while Sweden has moved toward equality in *permissiveness*, the People's Republic of China has moved toward equality in *abstinence*. Even socialist experiments have no "one and only" answer to the question of premarital sex.

EXPLAINING THE DYNAMICS OF PREMARITAL SEX

We have seen that throughout history and in various cultures, males have been more sexually permissive before marriage than have females. Table 5-A illustrates this not only by showing higher overall male rates of nonvirginity, but also through presenting the different percentages for men and women during each year of college. The data came from a 1967 national sample of nearly 1,200 undergraduates from twelve colleges and universities in the United States and may be compared to some of the studies cited earlier in this chapter.

Not only is the percentage of males who experience premarital sexual intercourse higher than that of females, there is also evidence that more males

TABLE 5-A   *Gender, year in college, and sexual status (virgin or nonvirgin)*

| | SEXUAL STATUS (% NONVIRGIN) | |
YEAR IN COLLEGE	MALE	FEMALE
Freshman	*36*	*19*
Sophomore	*63*	*30*
Junior	*60*	*37*
Senior	*68*	*44*
Total from entire sample, all years of school combined	*56*	*32*
Number of students in sample (n)	*(593)*	*(584)*

SOURCE: Adapted from Simon, Berger, and Gagnon, 1972, p. 208.

than females engage in other forms of sexual expression outside of marriage as well. For example, sociologist Donald Carns (1969:57) found in this same sample of college students that 93 percent of the males had masturbated in comparison to 49 percent of the females. And in an international sample of college and university students, two sociologists, Eleanore Luckey and Gilbert Nass (1969), found that "women subjects in general reported less participation in all categories of sexual behavior than men did."

Traditionally, males and females have differed in *attitudes* as well as behavior, with males accepting higher levels of sexual permissiveness as right for themselves than females are apt to feel would be right for *them*selves. However, the research of sociologist Ira Reiss (1960a, 1967b) showed that females were more likely to have permissive attitudes toward premarital sexual behavior if *love* was involved. Moving from attitudes to actual experience, sociologists William Simon, Alan Berger, and John Gagnon (1972:216–17) point out that in the 1967 study of college students cited above, "women almost universally had at least emotional ties to their first coital partner and that 59 percent planned to marry him." They contrast this finding with the experience of males, only 14 percent of whom reported that their first experience of sexual intercourse was with the woman they planned to marry.

SEXUAL LEARNING AND GENDER-ROLE SOCIALIZATION

The attitudinal and behavioral differences in women and men with regard to premarital sex do not indicate that males are biologically more "highly sexed"

Traditionally, males and females have differed in their attitudes about sex. (Barbara Pfeffer/Peter Arnold, Inc.)

than females. It is true that at one time people believed that men had stronger sex desires, drives, and needs than women, who were considered uninterested in sex; but modern scientific research has shown such beliefs to be in error. William H. Masters, a professor of obstetrics and gynecology, and his associate, Virginia Johnson, have conducted careful scientific studies of human sexuality which show that physiologically what happens during sexual orgasm is much the same for both men and women—that is, both males and females go through four basic stages of arousal and sexual climax: a time of excitement, then a "plateau" of pleasurable sensations, followed by the explosive sexual climax (orgasm), and then the phase called "resolution" (a return to the normal preexcitement state). Men and women are not so different sexually as was once thought. Women are capable of sexual response and enjoyment to the same degree as men—perhaps even more so. In fact, the Masters/Johnson (1966) research showed that women have the capability for more sexual orgasms in a shorter space of time than is usually true of men. The reason for this is that women do not go through a "refractory period" between the orgasm and resolution stages, as men do. Two authorities on human sexuality explain: "During this period, regardless of the nature and intensity of sexual stimulation, the male will not respond. He cannot achieve full erection and another orgasm" (Katchadourian and Lunde, 1975, p. 67). A certain amount of time must elapse first.

Responses to Sexually Explicit Materials   West German sociologists Gunter Schmidt and Volkmar Sigusch (1970, 1973; Schmidt, Sigusch, and Schafer, 1973) also found that women can be aroused and react just as strongly as men through viewing erotic films and slides or reading sexually explicit stories. Through carefully conducted, controlled, and measured laboratory experiments in which persons reported on their sexual behavior and sexual reactions in the twenty-four hours before and twenty-four hours after exposure to sexually explicit materials, Schmidt and Sigusch (1970, 1973) found that 87 percent of the men and 72 percent of the women observed some sort of physiosexual reaction (usually a full or partial erection in the men and genital sensations and vaginal lubrication in the women), and that furthermore, "psychosexual stimulation leads to an increase of masturbation to the same extent in both men and women." However, although there were similarities in physical reaction, the emotional reaction of the women to the films was somewhat more pronounced than was true of men, particularly in the degree to which they reported shock, irritation, or disgust.

These findings differed greatly from the Kinsey studies two decades earlier, which had seemed to indicate that women are not generally aroused by observing portrayals of sexual action in pictures and films or by reading erotic novels and stories. Kinsey (1953, chap. 16) suggested the likelihood that "most females are indifferent or antagonistic to the existence of such material because it means nothing to them erotically." Women, said Kinsey, indicated more interest in "more general situations, affectional relationships, and love."

Schmidt, Sigusch, and Schafer (1973) attempted to discover if sexually explicit stories in the context of affectionate expression would be more erotically stimulating to females than to males, and also whether the introduction of the affection element would cause a greater response in women than would a sexual situation separated from affection. On the basis of their research, these social scientists concluded that "the stories with and without affection do not have a significantly differing effect on men or women." They went on to say:

> Affection is not a necessary precondition for women to react sexually to sexual stimuli in the same manner as men. Even for stories which describe sexual relations in detail excluding and avoiding any expressions of tenderness and affection . . . sexual arousal and sexual activation among females are as great as among males. This finding tends to refute the claim that female sexuality is basically more dependent on affection than male sexuality. (p. 198)

Commenting on these findings, Paul Gebhard (1973), who became director of the Institute for Sex Research upon Kinsey's death, suggests that the discrepancies with the earlier Kinsey findings may be explained by the wording of the Kinsey question (which depended upon respondents' recall of earlier feelings) and which did not take into account the different cultural conditioning males and females have received. Gebhard points out that women in our culture are trained to be cautious about sex, whereas males "do not receive this defensive conditioning." Thus, when women are suddenly presented with a picture of sexual activity, they may react negatively; whereas, when presented with such materials gradually, as in a motion picture, they are likely to experience sexual arousal. The Kinsey research uncovered indications of this tendency, but it was not taken into account when male and female responsiveness were compared. Gebhard reaches the same conclusion as did the West German researchers. He points out that both Masters and Johnson and the Institute for Sex Research have shown "the essential equality of males and females in response to tactile stimuli," that is, the capabilities of both sexes to react when the sense of touch is involved (as in petting, masturbation, or coitus). And he suspects that, if culturally produced variables are taken into account, research will show males and females to be "very similar, if not identical, in their inherent capacity to respond sexually to visual stimuli," as well.

Gender-typed Approaches to Sexuality Gebhard's reference to cultural conditioning on top of the studies that show that males and females are not *biologically* different with respect to sexual arousal and response brings us once again to the matter of *socialization*, the training that persons receive to fit them for their roles in society. In Chapters 2 and 3, we saw that males and females are socialized differently from one another. These differences may be seen even in the learning and experience of sexuality.

Mary Walshok, a sociologist who has conducted research on the relationship between gender-role typing and sexuality, states that males are typically more "instrumental" in their sexual attitudes and behavior, while females tend to be more "expressive." "On the whole," writes Walshok (1973), "male patterns are characterized by a capacity to treat sexuality as an end in itself, whereas female patterns are less directly sexual and more typically an outgrowth or expression of some more encompassing emotional or social commitment" (p. 2). Earlier, we saw that the degree to which persons are either instrumental (task-centered and goal-oriented) or expressive (person-oriented) is a matter of social learning.

At the very beginning of sexual awareness, gender-typed differences show up. Almost twice as many males as females experience sexual orgasm through masturbation during adolescence; and among females who have experienced orgasm through masturbation, about half do so only after having first experienced orgasm through a sexual experience with a male (Gagnon and Simon, 1973:181). The male peer group encourages boys to experiment with sex, talk about it, joke about it, and so on. Adolescent boys more than adolescent girls come in contact with pornographic materials and similarly are more likely to report sexual arousal through sexual fantasies and daydreams. When adolescent girls daydream, they are more likely to be thinking about a situation of romantic love rather than about sex as an end in itself. Sociologists John Gagnon and William Simon (1973:181–82) report that for females "opportunities for learning and performing sexual activity are not provided" so that "an interest in sexuality for its own sake or for the sake of pleasure" is not developed to the extent it is in males during this period of life.

Gagnon and Simon (1973:12, 73) point out that, in the unwritten script usually followed during adolescent petting, "the description is one of male as subject (active, controlling) and female as object (passive, controlled). Males . . . do, females react or gate keep." Less awakened to her sexual self, the female is concentrating on preventing too much access to her body at the same time that the more erotically aware and experienced male is attempting sexual activity which is clearly goal-directed.

Sexual Language: Male-Female Differences   Even the graffiti found on the walls of public rest rooms gives evidence of gender-typed approaches to sexuality. The Kinsey researchers found that 86 percent of male toilet wall inscriptions were sexual in nature, both in words and pictures. Females were much less likely to make any sorts of inscriptions; but when they did, they tended to draw pictures of hearts or to write in lipstick phrases such as "Bill and Sue" or "Kathy loves Jeff." Kinsey and his associates (1953, chap. 16) viewed this comparison of the female and male inscriptions as indicative of "some of the most basic sexual differences between females and males." For males, sexual interest appeared to be genital-centered, while for females it was relationship-centered.

More than twenty years after this finding by Kinsey, sociologists Nancy Kutner and Donna Brogan (1974) studied the sex-slang knowledge of three groups of students at a southern university (male and female undergraduate students and female graduate students in nursing). These researchers found that "male undergraduates listed a significantly larger number of sex-related slang expressions on the average than did the two female groups studied." When asked to list slang expressions for the words *woman* and *man*, males listed considerably more slang expressions for *woman* than they did for *man*. Females, on the other hand, listed similar numbers of slang expressions for both *woman* and *man*. Furthermore, "males much more frequently than females listed slang expressions for 'woman' which denoted woman as a sexual object," Kutner and Brogan report. And on the topic of sexual intercourse, males listed sixty-three distinct slang terms, a large number of which indicated male dominance over the female. Females, for their part, listed twenty-nine slang expressions for sexual intercourse. And although they included some of the dominating-male terms, they tended more than males to list such euphemisms as "making love," "going to bed," "having relations," and "sleeping together" (pp. 482–83).

Kutner and Brogan had hypothesized that as women became less traditional in their gender-role attitudes, their awareness of sex slang would increase. The researchers found that indeed, among females, "the extensiveness of sex-related slang vocabulary does tend to increase as nontraditional sex-role orientation increases." But another part of their hypothesis was not borne out: males with traditional sex-role attitudes did not list more sex slang expressions than did males who were nontraditional and thus more egalitarian in gender roles. According to Kutner and Brogan, "it appears that participation in the male subculture with its shared terminology generally overrides the influence of differing sex-role ideologies" (p. 483).

Peer Pressure   Sociologist Lester Kirkendall (1968) has written of the problems of male virgins, calling attention to the pressures peer groups place upon males who are relatively sexually inexperienced. If a male has not yet tried sexual intercourse, he is sometimes made to feel that something must be wrong with him and that he is not demonstrating masculinity. Such pressures toward sexual performance may be felt in high school, college, the military, or in work situations with older males who tease about sexual intercourse.

Gagnon and Simon (1973:68-81) make the observation that the adolescent male world is a *homosocial* (not to be confused with homosexual) world, with a great concern for the approval of those of the same gender. Sexual contacts with females, then, become ways of establishing and confirming social status among males. Males talk together about "scoring," "how far one can get," "making bases or hitting a home run," and so on. The emphasis is on the "degree of sexual access achieved," write Gagnon and Simon, contrasting these male conversations with female conversations where young women describe relationships in terms of the "level of affection offered." Females have traditionally spoken less about sex and more about perceived or hoped-for feelings of fondness or love on the part of the male.

It has been observed that the adolescent male world is a homosocial world, with a great concern for the approval of those of the same gender. (© Shelly Rusten)

The First Time Sociologist Donald Carns (1973), using data from the 1967 national sample of college students, found gender differences even in the management of the first coital experience. Males tended to talk about the experience sooner and to more people and more often met with approval on the part of those to whom the event was reported than was true of females. Among males who had experienced sexual intercourse, more than half reported that five or more college friends knew about it. Among the sexually experienced females, less than one-fourth indicated that five or more college friends knew about their premarital coitus, and 27 percent had told no one at all. Twenty-nine percent of the women had talked about the event with only one or two friends. Among sexually experienced men, nearly 18 percent told no one, and only 14 percent reported the event to as few as one or two friends.

A difference also showed up in *when* persons told their friends, with 30 percent of the males reporting that they told someone immediately after the event, in contrast to 14 percent of the females. Among the sexually experienced males, 86 percent reported that the first person told about the event reacted approvingly. Sixty-seven percent of the females met with such approval, with the remainder meeting with mixed reactions or disapproval. Carns concluded that the evidence points to "a pattern of male 'ego-sex' [which] emerges within the context of the so-called 'male bond' (male peers as audiences for sexual prowess)." This is in sharp contrast to the female's management of the first experience of sexual intercourse.

In explaining why he focused on the first event of sexual intercourse, Carns described it as "pivotal behavior, one which creates either problems or prospects," because in our society the first coitus is "decidedly an irreversible event. One possesses one sexual status before the act—'virgin'—and another afterwards." A person's management of the event and its public presentation would therefore seem to tell us a great deal about that person's conception of his or her identity as a sexual being.

Different Perceptions of One's Sexual Being Traditionally, females and males have had different perceptions of themselves as sexual beings. But why? At this point, some insights from John Gagnon and William Simon (1973:12, 73) are helpful. They take issue with psychoanalytic theories that view adolescent and adult sexuality as a reenactment of sexual predispositions developed during infancy and suggest instead that sexual behavior is *learned* behavior. "The development of the sexual comes relatively late in character development," they write, "and rather than being the engine of change, it takes its meaning primarily from other sources of personality development." They point out that part of the legacy of Freud is our ability to seek out a sexual

Traditionally, females and males have had different perceptions of themselves as sexual beings. (Ken Heyman)

ingredient in nonsexual behavior and symbolism. But it may be erroneous to begin with sex and see how other areas of life are affected by sexuality. Perhaps the order should be *reversed*. Perhaps we need to ask how sexual behavior might "express and serve nonsexual motives" (Simon and Gagnon, 1969:736, 750).

In viewing sexual attitudes and behavior as resulting from social learning, Gagnon and Simon draw attention to the part played by gender-role *socialization* specifically. Training for society's assigned roles, masculine and feminine, produces two different approaches to sexuality (rather than being the other way around). Whereas males learn sexuality "prior to profound linkages with the rest of life," females act out their sexuality "later and in response to the demands of males and within the framework of societal expectations." Gagnon and Simon (1973) write: "For the female, sexual activity does not occur for its own sake, but for the sake of children, family, and love. Thus sexuality for the female has less autonomy than it has for the male, and the body (either of the self or of others) is not seen by women as an instrument of self-pleasure. This vision of sexuality as a form of service to others is continuous with the rest of female socialization" (pp. 181–82).

HOW CERTAIN SOCIOLOGICAL THEORIES APPLY

In accounting for the learned differences in male and female sexuality, sociologists have taken different approaches. Some, arguing from the structural-functional vantage point, would say that the gender-role learning which emphasizes female sexuality in the context of love and commitment is necessary for a woman's fulfillment of her traditional family-centered role (wifehood, motherhood, and serving the interests of others as the expressive hub of the home).

Others would question this approach, raising the objections that males, too, could be socialized to view sex in a context of love, commitment, marriage, and family; or that females could be socialized to have more autonomy in sex and learn to appreciate it for its own sake in the way males are trained to. One sociologist has spelled out a detailed analysis of what he calls "sexual stratification" in terms of conflict theory and social exchange. Randall Collins (1971) asserts that historically and cross-culturally men have usually been the "sexual aggressors" and women the "sexual prizes for men." The model is one of coercion, with a dominant group (males) having control over a subordinate group (females). In some societies, females are clearly viewed as sexual property, taken as booty in war, used by fathers in economic bargaining, considered to be owned by husbands, and so on. Collins argues that the root of male dominance has lain in the physical strength, size, and aggressiveness of the male sex, while female vulnerability stemmed not only from their generally smaller size but also from their role in bearing and caring for children.

Sexuality, Dominance, and Material Resources   Referring to the conflict model of stratification of the social theorist Max Weber, Collins shows how it applies to the male-female sexual situation in various types of societies. The first point is that "persons struggle for as much dominance as their resources permit." Thus males, by virtue of their physical strength, freedom from the biological limitations of menstruation and childbirth, and greater economic advantages, gained domination over women. The main resource of a female was considered to be her sexuality, to which a man acquired exclusive rights because of his greater resources. In some societies this exchange resulted from economic bargaining with the woman's father; and in such societies, women "are closely guarded so as not to lose their market value," which has given rise to customs such as wearing a veil, strict chaperonage, and so on. In ancient Hebrew society, for example, if a man seduced and had sexual intercourse with an unbetrothed virgin, he was required to take her as his wife and pay her father the bride price. If the father refused to give his daughter to him, the man still had to pay the father the bride price, since the loss of virginity made the woman of less worth on the marriage market (Exodus 22:16–17).

Collins' second point refers to Weber's belief that *ideals* are used as weapons in struggles for domination. In this case, the double standard with its emphasis on female chastity is illustrative.

The third factor is that changes in the structure of domination take place when there are shifts in resources. As certain political and economic changes occur, women gain a better bargaining position. No longer under the control of their fathers, they "become at least potentially free to negotiate their own sexual relationships," writes Collins, "but since their main resource is their sexuality, the emerging free marriage market is organized around male trades of economic and status resources for possession of a woman" (p. 13). Along with sexuality, female capabilities in homemaking and in providing emotional support for males also came to be valued resources as the ideology of romantic love grew.

The Long Survival of the Double Standard   The situation described by Collins is a possible explanation for the survival of the double standard, since it helps explain the traditionally greater reticence of females to accept for themselves the sexual permissiveness that has characterized males. Collins suggests that "the most favorable female strategy, in a situation where men control the economic world, is to maximize her bargaining power by appearing both as attractive and as inaccessible as possible." Overt sexuality may not be used to attract the male but only hinted at indirectly as a sort of grand prize or ultimate reward, because "sexuality must be reserved as a bargaining resource for the male wealth and income that can only be stably acquired through a marriage contract." Because men and women are bargaining with "unequal goods," femininity and female chastity are idealized, and woman is placed on a pedestal so that "an element of sexual repression is thus built into the situation."

The greatest bargaining power of all for women comes with increasing employment opportunities. Freed from economic dependence upon males, the sexual bargains struck by women can be less concerned with marriage and more concerned about other kinds of exchanges. Collins suggests that in a situation where women have their own economic resources, "dating can go on as a form of short-run bargaining, in which both men and women trade on their own attractiveness or capacity to entertain in return for sexual favors and/or being entertained."

Collins began with a picture of coercion in which one socially dominant group oppresses or exploits the other (conflict theory), but he moved on to a situation described in terms of a "free market," "bargaining," trading sexual resources for status and security (in other words, exchange theory). Persons give and receive in sexual relationships, and the exchange may be a fair one or it may be one in which one person has a greater advantage and receives the higher profits (Libby and Carlson, 1973).

Referring to traditional male-female dating relationships in a society where males dominate, Gagnon and Simon (1973) point out that "the physical exchanges are surrounded by other exchanges of words and gifts that affirm the increasing accessibility of the female's body" (p. 76). Males in particular may use as resources words (assuring females of affection so that intimacy is legitimated from the female perspective) and gifts (paying for the dinners, movies, and so on, indicating an investment that is expected to result in varying degrees of sexual payoffs).

On the other hand, in societies where gender-role differentiation is not emphasized and females and males are in a more equal position by virtue of equal opportunities in the economic system, there is not the same kind of game playing in dating relationships. In Sweden, for example, dating is more casual, with little emphasis on playing the roles of feminine charmer, using sexual attractiveness as bait, or masculine pursuer on a mission of conquest. Friendship and equality are emphasized, with females feeling free to take the initiative in establishing relationships and to pay their own way on dates. It is conventional for dating partners to meet at the place of their date rather than an arrangement whereby the boy calls for the girl. In the early stages of relationship in Sweden, there is actually less emphasis on sex than is true in the United States, where kissing and petting are often introduced very early in a dating relationship. Swedish young people tend to take time to let intimacy develop slowly; but when intimacy in other aspects of the relationship has been developed, they tend to move on to the full sexual intimacy of coitus rather than leveling off at heavy petting and "technical virginity" (Tomasson, 1970:180–81). Females in Sweden, less concerned about guarding their sexuality as their chief bargaining resource, do not feel compelled to engage in intercourse because of the insistence of their boyfriends but rather do so because they themselves want to. "It even occasionally happens that boys agree to coitus because the girls want it," writes Swedish family-life authority Birgitta Linner (1967, chap. 2).

The term *technical virginity* has sometimes been used to describe the widespread practice of engaging in various sexual intimacies while still maintaining technically a state of virginity. Petting to orgasm through what is sometimes called "mutual masturbation," oral-genital stimulation, and placing the genitals together without proceeding to penetration are examples of such intimacies (Reiss, 1960a; Bell, 1966). It is widely believed that engaging in them will not make persons "nonvirginal."

SOCIAL MEANING OF VIRGINITY

Those who write and speak of virginity as a concept tend to think of it as a "given," something with an agreed-upon meaning so that "everybody knows what it is." Two sociologists, David Berger and Morton Wenger (1973), have raised questions about this idea. They have concluded that the concept of virginity is a "variable one, assigned different meanings in different social contexts," and that furthermore the lack of agreement on the meaning and norms surrounding virginity "is due to the long-term changes in the economic role of women in modern industrial society."

Speaking of female virginity, Berger and Wenger claim that the ideology has persisted because it has served both sexes: "[It] not only serves the interests of men as a class by giving them overall control of women as property, but it also serves women's interests as individuals in that they find society legitimizing their control (marginal though it may be) over the only scarce resource available to them, the sexual and ego-gratification of males" (p. 666). These sociologists further suggest that support of the concept of virginity as an ideal will decline with women's economic advancement.

Zulu Chief Orders Tests for Virginity

Agence France-Presse

PIETERMARITZBURG, South Africa—A Zulu chief at the tribal location of Mafunze near here is having every girl in his area subjected to compulsory virginity examinations in a bid to curb immorality, illegitimacy and prostitution.

Chief Valindaba Ngcobo this week rallied the elder women in various villages to present him with a list of virgins, and in July he will present a bull to the village which records the highest number of maidens.

Seven elderly women have been appointed in each region to examine the young girls in special huts provided for the purpose.

Young women found to be 'deflowered," as he put it, will have to pay the chief a fine of $11. Those who refuse to undergo the test at all, will find their parents facing a $45 fine. Any young man who accepts responsibility for seducing a girl will have to pay the chief an $11 fine and present the girl's parents with two animals—either sheep, goats or cows.

"One of the best ways to stamp out immorality, illegitimacy and prostitution among our young people is by having virginity tests," explained Chief Valindaba. "I started the tests because it is important for a girl to remain a virgin until she is married."

SOURCE: *Greensboro (NC) Daily News*, January 8, 1979.

In an attempt to find out if their ideas were on the right track, Berger and Wenger asked sociology students at two state-related Eastern colleges to complete a questionnaire designed to find out if the concepts of male virginity and female virginity are considered valid concepts, and if so, what does virginity mean? In answer to the question, "Does it make sense to say a woman (man) has lost her (his) virginity," 43 percent of their sample rejected the concept of virginity for both sexes, while 57 percent retained a belief that the notion of virginity as a *concept* has value.

Flexibility in Definitions   However, what is of particular interest is that even among those who think it makes sense to think in terms of "virginity" and "nonvirginity," there is considerable disagreement about exactly what constitutes virginity or its loss. The researchers asked a series of questions describing various types of sexual behavior and experiences for both males and females, and the respondents were asked to state whether or not each event constituted "loss of virginity." (See Table 5-B.)

Only about one-third of the respondents viewed the rupture of the hymen as meaning a female has lost her virginity, indicating that to most respondents the concept has another meaning than a physical state of being. But 81 percent considered the full penetration of a vagina by a penis to mean the loss of virginity for a female, which the researchers point out "is somewhat consistent with conventional notions of virginity." But they raise additional questions: "How, though, is the bringing of a male to climax consistent with this notion? Or the bringing of self to climax?" With regard to male virginity, slightly over half of the respondents considered the penetration of a woman's vagina, even without ejaculation, to constitute the loss of male virginity. A majority (around two-thirds or more in most cases) did not consider a male to have "lost his virginity" if he had intimate contact but did not ejaculate, or ejaculated by a woman's manipulations, or brought a woman to climax, or reached orgasm through masturbation.

Virginity and the Sexual Marketplace   From this data, Berger and Wenger conclude that a *variable* concept of virginity exists and that such a variable concept "is in the interests of both males and females in a society wherein there is considerable social stratification (economic and otherwise) by sex." According to these sociologists, the variable concept which allows a woman a certain amount of leeway in terms of the point where she crosses the line from virgin to nonvirgin permits her to have a degree of sexual gratification while still maintaining "her sexual value as an exclusive mate." Furthermore, it puts her in a position of advertising her product so that a man is enticed to become a captive "consumer market" at the same time that the woman has a socially sanctioned reason (the ideology of virginity) for not giving away the ultimate reward, thus keeping her market value high.

For males, the variable concept of female virginity also serves a purpose, claim Berger and Wenger. "It allows the buyer with low resources (poor, unattractive, powerless, etc.) to buy 'used goods' while providing the

TABLE 5-B   *Attitudes toward sexual events and/or behaviors constituting "loss of virginity"*

	YES, MEANS LOSS		NO, DOESN'T MEAN LOSS	
	%	NUMBER	%	NUMBER
Has a female lost her virginity if:				
She brings a male to climax?	16.3	(33)	67.8	(137)
Her vagina is penetrated other than by a penis?	16.8	(34)	66.5	(135)
Her vagina is fully penetrated by a penis?	81.3	(165)	4.9	(10)
Her hymen is ruptured?	32.7	(66)	51.5	(104)
She brings herself to climax?	40.9	(83)	40.4	(82)
Her vagina is partially penetrated by other than a penis?	6.4	(13)	74.9	(152)
A male brings her to climax?	21.7	(44)	61.1	(124)

("No responses" account for missing percentages.)

	YES, MEANS LOSS		NO, DOESN'T MEAN LOSS	
Has a male lost his virginity if:				
He has a wet dream?	0.0	(0)	76.7	(128)
Penetrates a woman's vagina, but doesn't ejaculate?	53.3	(89)	22.8	(38)
He has intimate sexual contact, but doesn't ejaculate?	6.6	(11)	69.3	(115)
He ejaculates by a woman's manipulations?	5.4	(9)	68.7	(114)
Only if he brings a woman to climax?	12.7	(21)	62.7	(104)
He ejaculates by self-manipulation?	1.8	(3)	73.0	(119)

("No responses" account for missing percentages.)

SOURCE: Berger and Wenger, 1973, p. 672.

ego-maintaining illusion that he has bought a new product." They are of course using the term *used goods* from the standpoint of the traditional ideology of virginity with its emphasis on being "untouched" and reserved for the exclusive possession of one man. It was also found that persons who had already engaged in sexual intercourse were less likely to feel that there was any validity in the notion of virginity as a concept. The researchers explain this too in terms of a market analogy by saying that the coitally experienced have "lost their market value along a certain commodity dimension, and therefore may wish to maximize their status along it by denying its existence." Those who had engaged only in petting were less apt to deny that virginity is a valid concept.

One point that Berger and Wenger emphasize is that an effective ideology cannot be too specific about what constitutes its violation. Therefore, certain female conduct is viewed as acceptable because it does not deprive women of their one scarce resource (total sexual access), although, as Table 5-B makes clear, there is considerable disagreement about just what conduct does cause a female to pass over the invisible line between virginity and nonvirginity.

Males and Virginity   As regards male virginity, the only response showing considerable agreement about what constitutes its loss was the item about vaginal penetration. In fact, there is some indication that male loss of virginity is not viewed as a loss at all but rather as a gain. Acts indicating physical maturity (for example, ejaculation through "wet dreams" or masturbation) are not thought to change one's sexual status. Rather, according to Berger and Wenger, "it is possession (use) of a woman's unique resource (to be blunt, her vagina) that for males constitutes movement to the status of 'sexually experienced,' i.e., 'powerful' or 'wealthy.'" Having borrowed from exchange theory and conflict theory, these sociologists reach this conclusion: "Virginity, rather than seen as a 'state of being' in society, is viewed as a social-relational concept having to do with the state of conflict between two parties contending for scarce rewards in society, and in which conflict the contenders bring to bear those resources most available to them" (p. 675).

As we have seen repeatedly, the ideology of female virginity is particularly strong in cultures with high male dominance. When varieties of sexual activity short of actual intercourse are practiced in such settings, the

Woman Wins Award in Virginity Suit

MOUNT CLEMENS, Mich. (AP)—A jury has awarded $250,000 to a woman who sued her husband because he accused her of not being a virgin on their wedding night.

Anna Biundo Ruffino, 25, received the award of damages Friday in Macomb County Circuit Court. She had sued her husband, Salvatore, a carpenter, in June 1977, shortly after their marriage.

The couple's marriage ended within one week and an annulment is pending.

Both Ruffino and his wife emigrated from western Sicily. He grew up in the Detroit area and she grew up in Santa Clara, Calif.

Mrs. Ruffino argued in her suit that her husband's accusation caused gossip to spread from Sicily to California. Bridal chastity is a tradition among many Sicilians, according to testimony at the trial.

Mrs. Ruffino testified she was a virgin on the day of her wedding and that she never spent time alone with a man before her wedding night. She said her husband deserted her five days after the wedding.

Ruffino, 32, did not deny accusing his wife of not being a virgin, but his lawyer argued there was no damage to her reputation and that she was not entitled to damages, and that there would be an appeal.

SOURCE: *Greensboro Daily News*, June 17, 1979.

unwritten rules may be stricter than in the bargaining context of cultures where women have more autonomy. Political scientist Evelyn Stevens (1973:97) writes of the double-standard situation in Latin America where a young woman usually engages in intimate forms of noncoital sexual activity only with her fiancé and then only as a means of holding his interest in her until they are married. If he is quite certain that she has not engaged in such behavior with any other man, and if she provides him with the assurance that she is not enjoying the behavior, the Latin American male "may encourage or even insist on her 'obliging' him in this way." However, the permissiveness-with-affection standard appears to be gaining acceptance in Latin America to some degree, which may mean a gradual decline in the rigid double standard. One professor at a Colombian university found that among female students in a human sexuality class, not only was there a high incidence of such noncoital sexual activities as oral-genital contact reported, but one-third reported having engaged in actual sexual intercourse. Of these, two-thirds said their first coital experience had been with their *novio* (sweetheart or fiancé). These findings were contrasted with the less than 2 percent nonvirginity rate among young Colombian women in a 1969 study (Alzate, 1978).

PREMARITAL SEX IN SOCIAL CONTEXT

Sociologist Ira Reiss (1967a; 1967b) has demonstrated that many different sociocultural factors enter into a person's attitudes and behavior with respect to premarital sex. Just as no other behavior develops in a social vacuum, so it is with sex. A basic theory of Reiss is that "the degree of premarital sexual permissiveness which is acceptable among courting individuals varies directly with the degree of autonomy in the courtship roles and with the degree of premarital sexual permissiveness accepted in the social and cultural setting of those individuals." Increased autonomy for women usually is a factor in increasing courtship autonomy (for example, by eliminating the chaperonage system, lessening or doing away with parental control of mate selection, and making possible greater individualistic bargaining power). However, the second part of Reiss's proposition also comes into play. We saw this demonstrated in our examination of premarital sex in communist countries such as the Soviet Union and the People's Republic of China. The prevailing social norms discourage premarital sexual permissiveness in spite of the emphasis on female autonomy.

Some of the social factors in the United States which are most associated with different outlooks on premarital sex are religion, socioeconomic status, and race.

RELIGION

Research has shown that religion *does* make a difference in sexual attitudes and behavior. The particular religious faith doesn't seem to matter so much as

Research has shown that religion does make a difference in sexual attitudes and behavior. (Hugh Rogers/Monkmeyer)

does a person's commitment to that faith. A religiously devout person is less likely to engage in premarital sexual intercourse than a person who is less devout.

But how can sociologists measure devoutness or degree of religious commitment? One way is to measure the frequency with which persons attend religious services. Admittedly, this method has its shortcomings and measures devoutness in terms of involvement in institutional religion; yet it is helpful in tapping the degree of an individual's commitment.

When Kantner and Zelnik (1972) studied the data from their 1971 national sample of fifteen- to nineteen-year-old females, they found that the likelihood of a young woman's having engaged in premarital sexual intercourse went down as her church attendance went up. The highest rates of premarital sexual intercourse were found among those young women who reported they subscribed to no religion. This was true of both blacks and whites.

Traditionally, the teachings of Catholicism, Protestantism, and Judaism have emphasized that sexual intercourse should be reserved for marriage.

Sociologist Donald Carns (1969), in analyzing data from a national survey of college students, also found that religiosity acts as a brake and has a powerful effect on the degree of premarital sexual involvement. Carns measured religiosity two ways: in terms of *attendance* (including not only worship services but all types of religious functions, such as Sunday school, choir rehearsals, church-sponsored youth groups, and so on) and in terms of *religious self-image*. That is, respondents were asked how religious they personally perceived themselves to be, regardless of their degree of involvement in institutional religion.

Carns found that the more religious students were (whether rated by their own self-perception or by frequency of attendance at religious functions), the less likely they were to engage in premarital sexual activities. This was true for both males and females. It was also found that the higher persons rate in terms of religiosity, the more likely they are to cite "the wrongness or immorality of premarital coitus" as the reason they abstain. In addition to moral reasons for not engaging in premarital sexual intercourse, highly religious persons also tend to cite social reasons—namely, that their reputations would likely be damaged if they were to have sex relations before marriage. They are particularly concerned about their reputations among other religious persons—what sociologists would call their "reference group," the group of "significant others" by whose standards they measure themselves and whose approval is highly desired.

SOCIOECONOMIC STATUS

The Kantner/Zelnik (1972) data from their national probability sample of fifteen- to nineteen-year-old females showed that "the higher the socioeconomic status—whether measured by poverty status, family income or parental or guardian education—the lower, generally, are the proportions with coital experience."

Other studies indicate that the *meaning* of premarital sex also seems to vary according to social class. Whereas among middle-class young people there has been a move away from the double standard toward what Reiss calls "person-centered" sex, lower-class persons continue to think in terms of the double standard. Lee Rainwater (1966a) points out that this is particularly true of white males in lower-status groups. Such males take pride in their sexual conquests, boast of their ability to have sexual intercourse with a large number of girls, and categorize girls according to their accessibility for sexual relations. Highest in value are virgins, and lowest are the "easy lays," with "one-man girls" ranking somewhere in between. Rainwater points out that among blacks there are not such clear-cut differences in the amount of sexual activity viewed as permissible for males and females.

Even so, a study of lower-class boys from among three ethnic groups showed that the double standard is very much alive regardless of race. Bernard Lander interviewed Puerto Ricans living in New York, Appalachian whites living in Chicago, and blacks from Washington, D.C., with regard to sex attitudes and conduct. The double standard was particularly observable in the Chicago and Washington samples (cited in Rosenberg and Bensman, 1968).

Commenting on Lander's study, Bernard Rosenberg and Joseph Bensman (1968) point out that middle-class values of personalized sex have little relevance among impoverished groups in urban ghettos. Sex and love are not viewed in terms of emotional or material responsibility, nor on the other hand is there much evidence of "pure joy in unrestrained sexuality," which is sometimes thought to characterize lower-class persons. Rather, premarital sex is often considered to be sheer physical release, "the 'friction of two membranes'—in which the female is the necessary but unequal partner." Sex is also considered a way of winning prestige in peer-group competition and thereby proving one's masculinity. Rosenberg and Bensman write, "Since [sex] is a competitive game, the boy who plays cannot expect to earn points for scoring over an easy mark, a 'pig.' Victory consists in overcoming the largest possible number of inaccessible girls. The conversion of females into trophies reduces them to nonpersons."

It isn't hard to see the connection between sex-role socialization and sexual attitudes and behavior later on. In Chapter 3, we talked about the greater rigidity in sex roles that characterizes persons of lower social status. Boys are taught to be "masculine"— strong, dominant over women, emotionally cool and tough. Girls are taught to be "feminine"—dependent on men and submissive to them, emotionally warm and tender. Adults and peers encourage boys in their sexual pursuits, but at the same time daughters are usually shielded from even the basic facts about sex in the hope that such guarding will keep them innocent, pure, "good girls" in contrast to those who are promiscuous (Rainwater, 1966a). Being sexually restrained, in turn, is believed to win the greater respect and admiration of boys. Thus, when one of Lander's sample of Chicago whites from Appalachia was asked if he still considered a girl "decent" if she went to bed with him, the boy replied, "It's a matter of how hard I have to work. If I have to work real hard I think a lot of them. If they give it to me right off I think they're pigs."

Before leaving the general subject of social-class differences with regard to sexual permissiveness, it might be well to mention a conclusion reached by Ira Reiss. It will be recalled that Reiss concentrated in his research on *attitudes* toward premarital sex rather than on actual behavior, but he has suggested that a change is occurring which now makes questionable the idea (though rooted in historical fact) that the lower classes are more permissive in both attitudes and behavior. Reiss (1972:176–77) refers to his national sample of 1963 which did not show the expected differences by class as far as attitudes are concerned.

"After very elaborate computer checks," he wrote, "we discovered that there were, in relation to sexual orientation at least, two radically different social class systems." He was referring to whether persons at all class levels were either *liberal* or *conservative* in views on politics, education, and religion. He found that out of a group of conservatives, lower-status persons among them were the most permissive sexually. But in a group of liberals, the most permissive sexually turn out to be those of the higher classes (college-educated people). Reiss says it is not really surprising that this new permissiveness shows up among persons with college backgrounds, pointing out that this new sexual orientation "emphasizes control of pregnancy and venereal disease and stresses person-centered sexual encounters." "In short," writes Reiss, "it differs from the older, lower-class permissiveness which had an economic base and a fatalistic philosophy."

RACE

Because of the lack of privacy and crowded conditions of the ghetto, children of the black underclass (below the poverty line) are exposed to sex at a very early age. In the words of one black mother, "I can't hide the facts of life from them because they can see them every day on any stairway, hall, or elevator in the project" (Hammond and Ladner, 1969:43–44). Parents may attempt to protect girls more than boys because of fears of such consequences as pregnancy, but at the same time, parents know that a great deal of sexual experimentation is likely to go on.

Although lower-class black girls are not stigmatized in quite the same way as is true of lower-class white girls who engage in premarital sex, there are still some elements of an unequal power distribution between males and females in the sexual realm. A sexually experienced eight-year-old girl told researchers, "I don't like any of the boys around here cause they 'do it' with you and then they 'do it' with somebody else and they act like yourself ain't yourself." Already, this young female seemed to long to be "special" to a male rather than serving as one of his many sexual conquests. "In the later adolescent years, however, sex for girls takes on the important function of being a form of exchange," write sociologists Boone Hammond and Joyce Ladner (1969), "primarily for material goods and services (gifts, money, etc.). Some economically and emotionally deprived girls are able to gain access to certain necessities from boy friends through their participation in sexual activities" (p. 49).

In their 1971 national sample of black and white teenage girls at all social levels, Kantner and Zelnik (1972) found that, for both races, the higher the family income, the lower were the rates of premarital sex. Also, the higher the education of the male parent or guardian, the lower were the rates of premarital intercourse among these fifteen- to nineteen-year-olds. However, at all socioeconomic levels, a higher percentage of black young women had experienced sexual intercourse than was true of white young women. The 1976 study (Zelnik and Kantner, 1977) yielded a similar finding, although the relative differences in percentages of sexually experienced blacks and whites had grown smaller. Another difference between the races that showed up in both the 1971 and 1976 studies related to the age at which sexual intercourse begins, with sexually experienced blacks having begun coitus earlier than whites. (See Table 5-C.)

TABLE
5-C *Percent of never-married women aged 15-19 who have ever had intercourse, by age and race, 1976 and 1971*

AGE	STUDY YEAR AND RACE														
	1976						1971						% INCREASE 1971-1976		
	ALL	WHITE		BLACK			ALL	WHITE		BLACK			ALL	WHITE	BLACK
		%	N	%	N			%	N	%	N				
15-19	**34.9**	**30.8**	**1,232**	**62.7**	**654**		**26.8**	**21.4**	**2,633**	**51.2**	**1,339**		**30.2**	**43.9**	**22.5**
15	18.0	13.8	276	38.4	133		13.8	10.9	642	30.5	344		30.4	26.6	25.9
16	25.4	22.6	301	52.6	135		21.2	16.9	662	46.2	320		19.8	33.7	13.9
17	40.9	36.1	277	68.4	139		26.6	21.8	646	58.8	296		53.8	65.6	16.3
18	45.2	43.6	220	74.1	143		36.8	32.3	396	62.7	228		22.8	35.0	18.2
19	55.2	48.7	158	83.6	104		46.8	39.4	287	76.2	151		17.9	23.6	9.7

SOURCE: Zelnik and Kantner, 1977, p. 56.

One way to account for these differences is to think in terms of social exchange and the resources that are brought into the bargaining in such an exchange. Almost inevitably, additional elements beyond sex itself enter into the sexual bargaining process. If blacks are shown to be more sexually active than whites, it has nothing to do with the old myth that blacks are more "sexy" and have higher sex drives than whites. Rather, the explanation may lie in the fact that white racism has caused blacks to have been relatively blocked in their achievement aspirations at every class level.

Because among blacks there is likely to be less optimism about future educational and job opportunities, many young black women may feel that sexual favors are the only bargaining elements they have in their relationships with men. Thus physical gratifications and the approval and attention they bring may seem to be the only kinds of rewards they can reasonably expect. Hammond and Ladner (1969) for example, tell of girls who engage in sexual intercourse in exchange for a movie date or even a ride in a car. One fifteen-year-old from a background of deprivation told the interviewers that sex relations provided a way of escape from her feelings of poverty. "[Sexual intercourse] makes you forget that you don't have the kinds of things you need for school," she said, "the money to buy your lunch and clothes to wear and stuff like that. I play hooky sometimes because I don't have those things but then I 'do it' and have a good time and I don't have to worry about those things" (p. 50).

It is the absence of viable alternatives, then, that makes young black women (particularly in the underclass) more likely to seek sexual gratifications. Along with this comes increased vulnerability to exploitation. This is true even though blacks tend to hold more egalitarian sex roles than whites. The aspiration to be autonomous rather than merely dependent must be coupled with education and economic resources that make such autonomy possible. Many young black women from economically deprived backgrounds lack the resources which would enable them to fulfill their individualistic aspirations. There is evidence that young blacks are keenly aware of the systematic deprivation of economic rewards that their parents experience and that they will later face as adults (Lott and Lott, 1963; Scanzoni, 1977). Because of this deprivation, they may therefore be more likely than whites to turn elsewhere for meaningful rewards and gratifications. The sexual arena is one such source of rewards that are attainable.

In examining the differences between the sexual experience of white and black young women, it is useful to think in terms of *absolute* and *relative* comparisons. Absolutely, higher-educated blacks have more economic rewards than less-educated blacks; therefore, girls in these families have less reason to pursue alternative rewards (such as physical, social, and material rewards associated with sexual activities). The rate of premarital intercourse thus goes down among blacks as the socioeconomic status rises. Relatively, however, when blacks are compared to whites with the same education, there is deprivation. Blacks, even with college and professional training, get fewer economic rewards than their white counterparts. This relative deprivation helps explain why young persons in higher-status black families nonetheless have higher rates of premarital sex than whites at the same income level. Dollar wise, they are actually not at the same level as whites with similar training; they are blocked from the full achievement and its accompanying benefits that their education would seem to promise. Thus, alternative gratifications such as sex are apt to be sought after to a greater degree than would otherwise be the case.

However, another explanation is possible. Although it is true that greater premarital sexual activity among black females below the poverty line may indicate a quest for pleasures that are open to them when they are blocked from other gratifications, there may be another explanation for greater sexual permissiveness among black females at higher status levels. Recall Coleman's thesis that greater female autonomy means less rigidity in premarital sex codes—a thesis that seems to be borne out in Sweden. Coleman reiterates a point we made in Chapter 3 namely that female autonomy among blacks is greater than among whites for both historical and occupational reasons. Where females are dependent upon males, the principal good-in-exchange of females (sexual access) must be closely guarded and carefully conserved in order to retain its value; but when female status is not so dependent upon a relationship to males, females can be less cautious. Sexual activity may then be engaged in for its own sake, as a source of pleasure, rather than as a means of bargaining to obtain status through a marriage contract. Coleman (1966) writes of the autonomous woman: "Her sexual activity is not so much a commodity by which she establishes her ultimate social position, and she need no longer withhold it for exchange purposes. She becomes more like the male in this regard, having less reason to maintain her sexual activity as a scarce good in a market, more reason to consume it for its direct enjoyment" (p. 217).

TRENDS

The question may be raised: Will the greater autonomy that women are gaining through greater opportunities in the economic sphere inevitably mean greater premarital sexual permissiveness in attitudes and behavior? The answer is not clear-cut. Sociologist Mary Walshok (1973) has concluded from her research that women with high occupational aspirations are likely to be unconventional with regard to gender roles. Possessing a more "masculine" view of roles as segmented and distinct so that "work is work, play is play, and sex is sex," such women "can take a less contextual and romantic view of sexuality."

On the other hand, psychologist Judith Bardwick (1973) points out that women are in a transitional era and that there is much pain and tension since women have internalized older values even though they may now view such values as injurious. They are not sure as yet of the sexual life-style they would like to put in place of the older view, which incorporated sex into love, commitment, marriage, and motherhood, and which provided "justification"

"Before I respond to that, are we discussing women the sex
or women the movement?"

(Drawing by Lorenz; © 1977
The New Yorker Magazine,
Inc.)

for sexual pleasure. Sex in itself has not been able to fill an empty void of self-esteem and identity among many women who expected to find a new sense of meaning through sexual liberation, says Bardwick.

Various spokeswomen for feminism have made a similar point, showing also how men have taken advantage of the so-called sexual revolution by further using women as sex objects (Mitchell, 1971; Firestone, 1970). One writer for the women's movement, Shulamith Firestone (1970, chap. 6), has written: "By convincing women that the usual female games and demands were despicable, unfair, prudish, old-fashioned, puritanical, and self-destructive, a new reservoir of available females was created to expand the tight supply of goods available for traditional sexual exploitation, disarming women of even the little protection they had so painfully acquired."

Perhaps at this stage of change, the problem lies in the different ways males and females view the sexual autonomy of women. Females may think of it as freedom to be "consumers" rather than "sellers," enjoying their "scarce resource" in a direct manner rather than conserving it for bargaining purposes to obtain other kinds of benefits. Many males, on the other hand, accustomed to the traditional male outlook on sex, may find it hard to understand female desires and capacities to enjoy sex as males have done. Such males may simply consider the "scarce resource" to have become more plentiful. Furthermore, its "market value" may be seen as lower due to an increased supply, with the result that men may bargain with fewer rewards in the exchange, thus increasing the exploitation of women.

However, at the same time, there are indications of change among males. Donald Carns (1973) suggests that two trends may be occurring simultaneously and at their own pace, with males moving away from concerns about performance, conquest, the adolescent male bond, and preoccupation with sex isolated from other factors. Women, on their part, having been awakened to a new awareness and appreciation of their sexuality, may be moving toward a pleasure-centered approach. "One would hope," says Carns, "that if indeed these trends are occurring, the genders do not pass each other in the night." Although women may be heading in the direction of "seeking genital expression so long denied them by a sexually repressive culture," Carns suggests, men are "looking for situations of affection and tenderness unalloyed by the performance principle forced upon them by the restrictions of hypermasculinity" (p. 687). In a broader context than sexuality, according to sociologist Alice Rossi (1973) male college students in recent years have begun to indicate that they expect to find major gratifications less in their occupations and more in their family relationships.

Actually, it is not likely that the two sexes will "pass as ships in the night." Rather, they may very well find themselves in the same harbor. Sexual exchange isolated from other rewards is exceedingly difficult to maintain. The parties involved (male or female) are likely to find they want something more—love, attention, a meaningful relationship, a sense of belonging and "being special" to one another as total persons. This may account for the popularity of the permissiveness-with-affection standard which appears to be the most widely accepted standard today, not only in the United States but in other nations such as West Germany and Sweden as well (Tomasson, 1970; Linner, 1967; Reiss, 1960a, 1967b, 1973; Schmidt and Sigusch, 1972).

CHAPTER HIGHLIGHTS

Some sociologists see an association between less rigid gender roles and less rigid premarital sex codes. An egalitarian ideology of premarital sex can mean either of two polar extremes. Either *both* males and females should be free to engage in premarital sexual intercourse, or else *neither* males nor females should be free to do so. Several socialist experiments give evidence of a struggle between these two poles, in some cases settling on a standard somewhere in between (especially "permissiveness with affection"). Traditionally, males have been socialized to think of sex in "instrumental" terms, while females have been socialized to think of sex in "expressive" terms. Collins utilizes conflict and exchange theories to explain "sexual stratification," a historical pattern in which men have been the dominant group and "sexual aggressors" and females have been the subordinate group and "sexual prizes for men." Increasing employment opportunities for women can mean increased bargaining power in their relationships with men, because women are thereby freed from economic dependence upon men and also from the idea that a woman's bargaining resource is her sexuality. Overall, a person's attitudes and behavior with respect to premarital sex are affected by many different sociocultural factors, including religion, social class, and race. Carns has suggested that two trends seem to be occurring simultaneously, as men show some evidence of now wanting sex to mean more than performance and conquest, while women are indicating a new concern for pleasure and an appreciation of their sexuality for its own sake.

CHAPTER 6

(© Christa Armstrong/Photo Researchers, Inc.)

DATING AND
MATE SELECTION

A 1968 study commission on marriage and divorce in Kenya concluded that the elimination of the custom of the bride price would be impractical. Young African males immediately protested. How could they afford to marry if the bride price kept going up? The average price of $550 seemed exorbitant. Yet, to parents of daughters, the amount requested in the transferral of a young woman from one family to another seemed only reasonable. The increased costs of rearing daughters and paying for their schooling had to be taken into consideration since educational opportunities had opened up for females (Lord, 1970:57).

Sometimes called the bride wealth, the bride price may consist of money, livestock, or other goods paid by the groom (usually with the assistance of his relatives) which signify a compensation to the woman's parents for the loss of her domestic service. It also symbolizes a linkage between the family of the bride and the family of the groom. In some societies, the family of the bride also contributes a dowry (money, goods, or other property) to the marriage. Such customs draw attention both to kin involvement and the extent to which economic factors may play a part in marriage.

In China, one of the first orders of business after the 1949 communist revolution was to draw up legislation changing traditional Chinese marriage customs. The 1950 law gave young people the right to choose their own

A YOUNG LADY'S DOWER HER WEIGHT IN PINE TREE SHILLINGS

Economic factors, such as dowries (money, goods, or property contributed by the bride's family), were important in seventeenth-century marriage bargaining. (New York Public Library Picture Collection)

mates, have full equality in marriage, and have the right to divorce. The law came about partly through the efforts of a woman lawyer who, while a political prisoner, met two women who had opposed the feudal marriage laws. One woman was serving a life sentence, and the other was sentenced to death.

KIN CONTROL AND BARGAINING

The women just described faced such stringent penalties because they had opposed Chinese village marriages based on bargaining between two sets of parents and which often involved an intermediary who negotiated the bride price. Many of the marriages were "blind marriages," so named because the man and woman had never seen each other before the wedding. In some cases, parents arranged the marriages of their offspring while the boy and girl were yet small children, although the couple would not live together as husband and wife until they were older. The Chinese elders claimed that the old god in the moon bound together the feet of males and females destined for each other, and parents and intermediaries merely acted as instruments to carry out his will (Macciocchi, 1972:356–357).

Religious concerns likewise played an important part in marriage negotiations among the Puritans in seventeenth-century New England. Parents considered it their duty before God not only to make sure that their children found their "particular calling" with regard to a life's work, but also to make certain that their children were settled in a proper marriage. However, the wishes of the couple were not overlooked. Ministers admonished parents not to impose their wills on their children, pointing out that "we know by long Experience that forc'd Matches any way seldome do well." Historian Edmund Morgan (1966) writes that usually "the Puritan fathers must have confined the exercise of their power to haggling over the financial agreement after the children had chosen for themselves— provided of course that they had chosen within the proper economic and religious limitations" (p. 85).

Deciding on financial agreements involved a great deal of bickering and bargaining between the two sets of parents, although the normal ratio was for the woman's parents to furnish half as much as was furnished by the man's parents. Sometimes the settlements included lands and other times money; but in any case, once the bargaining ended, a legal contract was drawn up binding the parties to the financial agreement. Only then could the marriage take place.

Japan is another country where tradition decreed that parents must participate in bargaining arrangements about the marriages of their offspring. The young people were not involved with one another or with the marriage plans until their two families had made the contract which would be sealed at the betrothal ceremony. Sociologist Robert O. Blood (1967) points out that "Concern on both sides created a bargaining situation in which each party exaggerated its assets and hid its liabilities, worrying lest the antagonist succeed in doing the same" (p. 5). To avoid the problems and feuds this might cause and to save face in cases where offers were rejected, families engaged the services of a matchmaker who acted as a go-between to work out negotiations between the two families.

FREE CHOICE IN MATE SELECTION

It's easy to see that bargaining in mate selection has been known throughout history all over the world. Because marriage was usually thought of in terms of linking two families rather than simply two individuals, the kin considered it a right and duty to make marital choices for young men and women. And economic factors, such as bride prices, dowries, inheritances, and so on, played a crucial part in the decisions.

However, for the most part, the right to choose one's own mate has been a freedom taken for granted throughout the history of the United States. The early immigrants often left behind parents and other relatives (the extended kin), with the result that finding a marriage partner was up to the individual rather than to his or her family. The fact that a *woman* had such free choice in finding a marriage partner seemed surprising to a French traveler who visited America in the mid-nineteenth century. "While still quite young," he wrote, "ignorant of herself, life not yet a lesson, when circumstances the most frivolous, appearances the most deceptive, and errors of judgment may blind her reason—she makes the most important decision of her life" (Carlier, 1867:33–34).

We saw that even among the Puritans free choice in mate selection was not discouraged, although parents supervised and gave advice. The bargaining between families was rooted in a concern that the newlyweds would have sufficient goods to set up housekeeping rather than springing from a concern that the families might make a profit or strike a good deal in uniting two kinship lines. "What shall these young beginners do for household stuff?" asked one worried Puritan father who had given a sum of money toward his daughter's marriage but realized the father of her future husband had given only a tract of land. On the advice of a third party, both fathers agreed to add more money so that the young couple could purchase needed supplies for their new home (Morgan, 1966:82).

Such illustrations from the past or from other cultures may strike most people as interesting; but at the same time, they seem remote from life today. After all, goes the reasoning, modern young people no longer dicker and negotiate and bargain in choosing a marriage partner; they simply fall in love. Yet the idea of marriage as a marketplace is more entrenched in our minds and vocabulary than we realize. People shake their heads in pity as they observe the sufferings of the wife of an alcoholic or compulsive gambler. "She certainly got a rotten deal in marrying him," they say. "That man deserved better," they say of another marriage. "He really struck a poor bargain when he married that woman." Of a woman recently divorced or widowed, people

Courtship in the Zulu Social System

Poverty and enforced migratory labor among the indigenous peoples of South Africa are part of an ideology of apartheid. . . . This paper is about those women who live in the countryside while their husbands work in the city as migrant laborers.

The Zulu social system is organized on patrilineal lines; descent is through males organized into lineages—the most important group being a lineage segment whose members trace descent to a common grandfather. In order to perpetuate these lineages and maintain continuity while the men, the most important members of the corporate group, are away, women have devised various ways of coping with the men's absenteeism. For instance, young men now find it very difficult to meet and court young women. Courtship in my society is, by tradition, quite different from the Western manner of courtship. A Zulu young man makes no dates but, instead, surprises a young woman by waiting for her at a waterhole, on the road to a store, or wherever she is likely to be on her own, away from her parents. On these occasions, using the best phrases and oratory he can master, he tells her of his love for her. The woman responds by ignoring or deprecating him. To demonstrate his sincerity, he persists by trying to get further opportunities to speak to her and to win her heart. Only after several attempts, if it becomes obvious that all his efforts are futile, does he give up. Now that young men do not find time to pursue a girl in this way, their sisters often take over and woo other girls on their behalf, while the brothers always put in an appearance whenever they have an opportunity to return to the countryside. Thus a young woman finds herself acting the role of her brother while simultaneously seeking for herself a suitable husband, who is most of the time represented by his sister.

On marriage a woman joins her husband's family. Marriage in Zulu is not a contractual union between the spouses. A Zulu woman goes on a long journey (enda); *a man receives her into his patrilineage* (thatha), *where she is expected to continue the descent line of her husband. She gradually becomes incorporated into her husband's group, and in her old age she is a full member. As an ancestress she is considered the mother of her descendants rather than a daughter of her parents in the spirit world. Conceptually she has indeed made a long journey—from her natal family to full membership in her family of procreation.*

SOURCE: Harriet Sibisi, "Migrants and Women Who Wait: How African Women Cope with Migrant Labor in South Africa," *Signs: Journal of Women in Culture and Society* 3 (Autumn 1977), pp. 167–168.

may remark, "I think she's in the market for another husband, but she'll probably take some time to shop around first." In another case, we hear, "He's trying to talk her into marrying him. You should hear his sales pitch!" All of these terms, of course, are borrowed from the world of business and trade.

DATING

Bargaining in the marriage market begins with the custom conventionally known as dating. For a time, the term *dating* was largely discarded, since many young persons felt it was too formal to describe the kind of social interaction taking place between the sexes—especially the pattern that characterized the mid-1960s through much of the 1970s: informal get-togethers, group activities, and spur-of-the-moment mutual decisions to go out for a pizza. To a great extent, this more relaxed style replaced the older pattern in which a man phoned a woman days or even weeks in advance to arrange to take her to a special dance or movie on some specific evening (hence, the term *date*—in the calendar sense of a set-apart time).

With the newer pattern that emerged in the sixties and seventies, terms like "getting together" and "going out" came to be preferred (Hoult, Henze, and Hudson, 1978:114–120). By the late 1970s, however, there was some indication of a return to the term *dating*, broadening it to include both the formal sense and the more casual arrangements. Some sociologists have suggested the coexistence of "two separate streams . . . one closely allied with the pattern of formal dates typical of the 1950s and early 1960s, and the other characterized by a spirit of 'comradeship' and more continuous interaction with no formal dates" (Krain, Cannon, and Bagford, 1977:664).

RATING AND DATING, AND DATING AND RATING

The late sociologist Willard Waller (1937) was probably the first to study seriously the phenomenon of dating. He viewed it as an end in itself—something distinct from traditional courtship, which had marriage as its aim. Waller's research focused on the dating system among fraternity and sorority members at Penn State during the 1929–1930 school year. The picture that emerged at that time was one that some sociologists have called "an almost ruthless competition for dates" (Krain, Cannon, and Bagford, 1977:665). The persons one dated and the frequency of dates could enhance or hinder one's own social status, and that's what all the competition was about. Waller called this status-seeking process the "rating-dating complex."

Students in Waller's sample were found to fit into one of several "prestige" categories, the most desirable dates being rated Class A. Men in Class A were those who belonged to the more prestigious fraternities, had ample spending money, had access to a car, were well-dressed, and were known for their participation in campus activities. They were also known to have a "good line." These were the men who "rated" because of the abundant resources they had to offer; thus they dated the highest status women.

Women who were rated Class A were those whose bargaining power sprang not only from belonging to the best sororities but also from their ability to dance, their physical attractiveness (with special emphasis on good clothes), and their "smooth line." However, what really mattered was their ability to gain a reputation for popularity. In Waller's words (1937, as quoted in Krain et al., 1977): "The girl's prestige depends upon dating more than anything else; here as nowhere else nothing succeeds like success. Therefore, the clever coed continues to give the impression of being much sought after even if she is not" (p. 665). And that meant not being seen too often with the same person. The more dates she had with different desirable men, the greater was a woman's prestige. Of course, women and men who didn't have dates or who dated less prestigious persons could find themselves lower on the prestige hierarchy. The social pressures were intense. Persons who *rated* dated; and persons who *dated* rated.

UPDATE ON THE "RATING-DATING COMPLEX"

Forty years after Waller's study was published, researchers Mark Krain, Drew Cannon, and Jeffery Bagford (1977) studied fraternity and sorority members at the University of Iowa. Although they found that Greek organizations were still ranked by prestige, just as had been the case on the campus Waller studied, and although students continued to date persons at the same prestige level as themselves, Waller's rating-dating complex did not hold in other respects. The researchers took this finding, along with some other studies by other sociologists, as indicative of a trend toward a "more relaxed

Recently the trend has been toward a more relaxed and humanistic pattern of dating, replacing the more competitive and materialistic aspects of the "rating-dating complex." (Paul S. Conklin/Monkmeyer)

and humanistic pattern of dating" which had been gradually replacing "the more competitive and materialistic aspects of dating" that Waller had observed.

"GAME PLAYING" AND DATING AMONG BLACKS

However, sociologist Robert Staples (1978) states that "because of the differential socialization of men and women in our society, dating is often laden with conflict. Once dating ceased to be a means to marriage, it became more exploitative." As a result, says Staples, there has arisen "a dating game in which individuals attempt to maximize their gains while minimizing their efforts" (p. 59). While pointing out that game playing goes on among both blacks and whites, Staples has given special attention to what he calls "the black dating game."

Staples (1973) cites a number of problems reported by black single adults: the insensitivity some women have shown in declining date invitations and the resultant hostility and ego deflation many men feel, differing expectations between dating partners as to the place and meaning of sex in dating, and the failure of dating partners (either sex) to show up for agreed upon dates.

The main complaint of black women according to Staples is that they feel it's unfair for a man to insist that a woman refrain from dating anyone but him at the same time that he sees no need for such exclusiveness on his own part. Women in such situations feel they are considered a man's property. "The Black male's justification for his behavior," writes Staples, "is that he will lose face if his main woman is known to be dating other men." Black men, for their part, often complain that many black women are "gold diggers," trading sex for economic and material rewards. Staples describes the feelings of some men who charge that some black women are actively "looking for men with money and then helping them spend all of it as soon as possible." "Sex for such purposes, however," he comments, "leads Black men to view women as enemies and allows them to justify their own exploitative behavior."

Speaking as a black himself, Staples (1978) has voiced concern over such problems. "Black people cannot afford such internal tensions. We have to accept responsibility for eliminating the sources of these male-female conflicts," he asserts, "and, the best place to begin is at home" (pp. 66–67). At the same time, Staples emphasizes that there exist regional, historical, and social class variations in black dating practices, and "lack of information limits the generalizations that we can make" about such practices. What *is* clear is that certain problems related to bargaining and "game playing" exist among black men and women.

MALE-FEMALE DATING TRADE-OFFS

Similar patterns can be observed among whites as well. Whether we're talking about "rating and dating" or dating "games," at the root of such practices are traditional assumptions about male-female inequality and the very real differential bargaining resources of the sexes.

One sociological study that tapped into this was Judith Richman's participant-observation study of a New York City dating service conducted in 1972. Although caution must be exercised with regard to generalizing from findings based on such a select group—those persons who decide to phone a dating service to arrange for a dating partner—the study nevertheless provides some interesting information. Richman's small sample consisted of twenty-seven women (median age: mid-thirties) and thirty-two men (median age: mid-twenties). "The responses of the majority of males and females in this sample were consistent with the sociological conceptualization of the traditional bargaining relationship between the sexes, "writes Richman (1977). When respondents were asked to describe the "ideal date" and tell what qualities in a man or woman were most important to them, "the majority of women consistently cited and placed greatest emphasis on the achieved occupational-economic statuses of men, while the majority of men placed greatest emphasis on the ascribed physical qualities of women" (p. 162).

However, when Richman endeavored to find out if respondents' attitudes toward sex roles made any difference in qualities desired in a dating partner, as well as respondents' own self image, she found the following: Females holding traditional attitudes toward sex roles wanted to date males who were up to fifteen years older than they themselves were. Females who were more open to feminism, on the other hand, stated that the age of their dating partners was unimportant or that they assumed they would date men their own age. Some stated a willingness to date men younger than themselves. Males open to feminism also felt age was unimportant in a dating partner or preferred to date females the same age as themselves. (None, however, indicated a willingness to date women older than themselves.) Traditionalist males, for their part, preferred to date females younger than themselves.

On the matter of *self-identity*, traditionalist women thought of themselves chiefly in terms of physical attributes and expressive qualities (such as being friendly and understanding). More feminist-minded women saw their identity as encompassing their own "achievements, interests, and intelligence in addition to physical and expressive characteristics" (p. 164). The self-concepts of traditionalist males in Richman's sample centered almost totally around their achieved statuses (education, income, career accomplishments and prospects), whereas men more favorable to feminist ideology stressed other factors as well, including their own physical and expressive qualities.

What did traditionalist males look for in a dating partner? Richman found they placed "great emphasis on physical characteristics and secondarily on expressive qualities." Some men emphasized a permissive attitude toward sex as well. Men more open to equality in sex roles "were generally the individuals seeking intellectual and expressive qualities in women rather than focusing chiefly on physical qualities or sexual behavior" (p. 161). Women who supported the goals of the women's movement also were nontraditional in what they looked for in a dating partner, just as was true of their male counterparts. These women "desired to meet men with certain expressive qualities or similar interests instead of those of high-class statuses" (p. 160). In contrast, traditionalist women were those most concerned about the achievement and social status of their potential dates and were only secondarily concerned about their expressive and intellectual characteristics.

Richman concludes that traditional expectations about male-female trade-offs in dating will continue so long as women are primarily defined in terms of their wife-mother roles and men are defined through their occupational roles. "When the economy ceases to discriminate between the sexes," she asserts, "we may also see the beginning of a bargaining situation in the dating institution that is not differentiated by sex" (p. 165).

DATING: A RECENT AMERICAN CUSTOM

If a woman and man are going to get married, they first have to meet each other. And if they're going to meet and get to know each other, they *have to date*. Right? Wrong. At least if we think in historical, cross-cultural terms.

Dating is taken for granted in modern America, but actually the custom is relatively new. Prior to around the time of World War I, a young woman and man could only plan on seeing one another on a regular basis if they had marriage in mind—and then only under the watchful eyes of their elders. In 1913, a newspaper editorial sounded an alarm: "Sex o'clock" had struck in America. Young men and women were enjoying one another's company as they tried out the newest dances and went off on other "dangerous" recreational pursuits such as unchaperoned swimming, buggy rides, and picnics (Feline, 1975, chap. 3). Complaints of this sort were not entirely new in our country, however. Historian Ray Hiner (1975 as quoted in Gordon, 1978) refers to a worried social commentator who in 1718 expressed similar distress:

> When children and young people are suffered to haunt the taverns, get into vile company, rabble up and down in the evening, when they should be at home to attend family worship; in the dark and silent night, when they should be in their beds, when they are let alone to take other sinful courses without check or restraint, they are then on the high road to ruin. (p. 171)

But by the early part of the twentieth century, the impact of industrialization was being felt as young men and women left the farms and small towns and moved to the cities. Two things were happening: parental control over male-female relationships was lessening, and young people were getting together for recreational times (dates) without necessarily having marriage in mind.

PURPOSES OF DATING

So far we've referred to at least two purposes for dating. Dating provides a way of finding and getting to know a potential mate. And dating can be a

By the early part of the twentieth century, young people were getting together for recreational times without necessarily having marriage in mind. (Photo by Alice E. Austen/The Staten Island Historical Society)

recreational end in itself—a way of having a good time. Sociologists James Skipper and Gilbert Nass (1966) suggest that, along with these purposes, dating can be a way of *status-seeking*; and it can also have a *socialization* function. In other words, dating can be a way of socializing persons into the "how" of getting along with persons of the other sex—a way of learning and trying out social skills.

Sometimes one partner may have one motivation in mind, whereas the other partner may have an altogether different reason for dating. Skipper and Nass provide several illustrations. For example, a woman may date a wealthy sports car owner in order to impress her friends as she rides around with him (status seeking on her part). However, the man she is dating may be interested in learning to feel more at ease with women (socialization purposes on his part). "In another case," write Skipper and Nass, "a boy may date an attractive girl because he desires a sexual experience with her (recreation). The girl may be dating the boy because she views him as a potential husband (courtship)" (p. 413).

Skipper and Nass studied some of the problems that may occur when dating partners have differing dating motivations in mind instead of a consensus—especially when one partner is thinking in terms of a serious commitment leading to marriage, while the other partner cares only about a good time or is looking for a sexual experience. Assuming only the four basic motivations for dating that these sociologists list—*courtship* (mate selection), *recreation, socialization,* and *status seeking*—Skipper and Nass suggest that future research could examine ten possible dating motivation combinations: "courtship-courtship, courtship-recreation, courtship—status seeking, courtship-socialization, recreation-recreation, recreation—status seeking, recreation-socialization, status seeking—status seeking, status seeking—socialization, and socialization-socialization" (p. 420). Such research, according to these sociologists, might also show variations in the importance attached to certain motivations and also how motivations might change over the course of dating.

TRENDS

During the 1978 Christmas season, a television advertisement showed a young woman calling up a male friend and asking if it would be convenient for her to visit his apartment that evening to drop off the Christmas gift she had for him. Holding up the advertised product (her gift to him), the woman turns to the television audience and speaks about "how times have changed." Whereas once she wouldn't have felt free to phone a man, much less invite herself to his apartment, she can now discard sex-role stereotypes and expectations and instead have a more casual, relaxed attitude toward male friends without being thought "bold" or in poor taste.

Movement away from rigid sex roles in dating also shows up in such matters as asking for dates and paying for dates (either sex may do either, or the costs may be shared) and in uncertainty about some aspects of dating etiquette (opening doors, putting on coats, handling the check at a restaurant, and so on). Some of these matters are now being discussed in books and articles; meanwhile, dating partners have been making their own rules.

Sociologist Michael Gordon points out that friendship and companionship are what many persons are now seeking in the dating experience. Commenting on the decline of the older rating and dating pattern and the emergence of the "going steady" pattern of dating that became especially noticeable in the years after World War II, Gordon (1978:183) explains that steady dating patterns could mean *convenience* as well as commitment, depending on the particular relationship. Furthermore, exclusive dating provided relief from the competition and stress associated with rating and dating. Under that older pattern, writes Gordon, "one was essentially putting oneself and one's self image on the auction block and continually being fed messages concerning self-worth. For those who did not rate high, the psychic costs of such a system must have been very high indeed."

Emerging patterns, however, may make their own demands. "It is obvious that today's mate-selection is no longer a period of determining the best bargain and sealing that bargain in marriage," writes sociologist Michal McCall (1966:197). Marriage is not necessarily considered for life and may be but one of many involvements with a person of the opposite sex. Speaking in terms of weighing costs and rewards and making a worthwhile exchange in the mate-selection marketplace, McCall asserts that the modern "courtship" system serves as a training school in bargaining. "In other words, 'courtship' teaches the individual how to bargain—how to form, maintain, and leave relationships," says McCall. "The emphasis in modern life is on keeping up one's bargaining skills, for one never entirely leaves the market."

McCall uses quotation marks around the word *courtship* because she is trying to show that the "contemporary pattern" differs from the mate-selection patterns of two other historical periods. In what she calls the "traditional pattern," parents and kin groups did the marriage bargaining. In the "intermediary pattern," both the parents and the young persons themselves were involved; and it was under this pattern that true *courtship* took place. One courted or was courted by a prospective mate, a person selected from among many other suitors or young women. This person was believed to be the one "for whom one was destined," the "one true love," the "one and only with whom one would go through life." Having found one another and having sought parental approval, the woman and man made a "permanent contract of exchange"—the marriage contract. From the time the marriage vows were spoken until "death did them part," these persons were expected to exchange their personal resources *only* with each other. "This contract," says McCall, "was a bargain to end any further cross-sex bargaining" (p. 196).

However, McCall observes a different bargaining system taking place in what she terms the "contemporary pattern." Under the traditional and intermediary patterns, the bargaining (whether conducted by the kin or the courting couple primarily) concentrated on *marriage* as the end goal. That was what the bargaining was all about; with marriage, the bargaining was over for all practical purposes. In the contemporary pattern, on the other hand, it is not unusual for a person to enter many close relationships in succession, with each involvement supposed to be appreciated for its own uniqueness. Individuals are expected to be deeply committed to the current serious relationship—whether the relationship is an exclusive dating partnership, a living together arrangement, or a socially recognized marriage. Bargaining takes place within these relationships and can be a training ground for further relationships, but it is not necessarily bargaining directly aimed toward marriage.

According to McCall, no longer is the emphasis on finding the "one and only" for a lifetime, because few people any longer believe in a "one and only" for whom each person is destined. Persons have the potential of relating to many other persons. Furthermore, relationships break up, even after marriage, and new relationships are formed—or at least *can* be—throughout life. That is why McCall, drawing upon the "permanent availability model" of sociologist Bernard Farber (1964, chaps. 4–5), claims that individuals are never out of the marriage market. The whole modern dating system therefore is "*set up* to give individuals training and experience in 'getting along with others' in intimate relationships."

McCall explains further:

[In the sense of the contemporary pattern], involvements (including the marriage involvement) are not contracts but restrictive trade agreements. The two individuals agree to exchange only with one another, at least until such time as the balance of trade becomes unfavorable in terms of broader market considerations. They agree to exchange exclusively for so long as the rewards in *this* involvement exceed the costs of continuing it in the face of chances for other rewards elsewhere. The individual, by forming numerous such exclusive and reciprocal trade agreements at various times, gets some idea of his [or her] overall worth as a product and of the market conditions, as well as learning bargaining skills, as mentioned above. (pp. 197–198)

SELECTING A MARRIAGE PARTNER

Although McCall claims that "marriage is merely one kind (though perhaps a more stable and lasting kind) of involvement" (p. 198), it would appear that in the minds of most people marriage is looked upon as a *unique* relationship.

WHAT IS MARRIAGE?

In recent years there has been a great deal of discussion about when a "relationship" becomes a "marriage." Some have argued that the whole idea of legal marriage should be discarded because legal bonds suffocate freedom and spontaneity, causing persons to stay together because they "ought to" or "must" rather than because they want to. Such critics suggest that the relationship of a man and woman should be regarded as a private matter, concerning only the individuals involved. They see no need for the regulations and forms set up by society. "How can a piece of paper or reciting some words make us married?" some have asked. "We feel we're already married in our own hearts—perhaps even in the eyes of God. We can't see why some sort of ceremony is necessary."

But even though such persons may feel married, are they really? What *does* make people married? Is it sex? Are two persons married who have coitus with each other twice a week? What if, in addition, each has sexual intercourse with another person? Does a group marriage then exist? Few people would be willing to define marriage on the basis of sex relations alone. Could it be the license then that makes a marriage? No, not really. However, there have been cases of poorly informed and often illiterate persons who have mistakenly thought that obtaining the license was all that was required of them, only to find out after many years of living together that they were never legally married.

If it isn't sex and it isn't a license that makes a couple married, then it must be the wedding ceremony—right? Not really. There isn't anything magic in the words themselves that transports two people from one state (singleness) into another state (marriage). Furthermore, there is a wide variation in wedding ceremonies in various cultures. In ancient biblical times,

Isaac and Rebekah's wedding ceremony consisted of nothing more than an exchange of gifts and entering a tent together (Genesis 24); but in our culture, a man and woman who entered a house together after a gift exchange could hardly argue that these acts made them married.

Or to take another example, anthropologists have written of the marriage ritual practiced by the Kwoma of New Guinea. A prospective bride is brought to live with a young man's family for a time of observation by his mother. If the mother feels the young woman is a suitable future daughter-in-law, she asks her to cook some food for the young man. Unsuspectingly, he eats it, without realizing it has been cooked by his future wife. At that moment, the mother announces that the young man is now married, because he is eating food prepared by his betrothed. Upon hearing this announcement, the new husband is supposed to rush out shouting that the food tastes awful. This is the public declaration to the tribe that the couple is now considered to be married (Stephens, 1963:221–222). Needless to say, no man in our society could consider himself married because he ate dinner at a woman friend's apartment and then told his friends that she is a terrible cook. It is not the ceremony itself that makes a marriage but rather what it signifies in a particular culture.

What we need is a definition of marriage that is applicable historically and cross-culturally, but yet is able to fit new varieties of marriage patterns that are emerging. Anthropologist George Murdock (1949) provides us with the basis of just such a definition. From his studies, he concludes that there are two essential dimensions to marriage—the economic and the sexual. When a man and woman are interdependent both economically and sexually, they may be said to be married.

We can broaden the scope of the definition and say that marriage exists when two (or more) persons maintain ongoing instrumental and expressive exchanges. The *expressive* or person-oriented dimension includes sexual gratification, but it may also include other elements such as companionship (someone to do things with, joint participation in leisure activities) and empathy (someone to listen and talk to, someone who understands and cares). The *instrumental* or task-oriented dimension of marriage includes economic behaviors (earning and spending income) and the performance of necessary household tasks.

Furthermore, for marriage to be valid from a societal point of view, there must be some sort of public disclosure. Therefore, societies require rituals, ceremonies, licenses, and the like, to symbolize that a legal bond between a particular man and woman exists, a bond recognized by the society in which they live. The arrangement of mutual sexual access and economic sharing between the two persons is of concern not only to the individuals but to others as well (parents and other relatives, friends, and society as a whole).

If we ask *why* people get married, the answer now becomes clear. People enter marriage because they believe it to be a rewarding situation both in terms of the instrumental and expressive sides of life. And that's where bargaining comes in. Before marriage and afterward as well, the processes of

Societies require rituals, ceremonies, and licenses to symbolize that a legal bond exists between a particular man and woman, a bond recognized by the society in which they live. (© Chester Higgins, Jr./Rapho/Photo Researchers, Inc.)

social exchange go on as each partner endeavors to find ways of giving and receiving both expressively and instrumentally to the satisfaction of each one and for the overall benefit of the relationship.

WHO MARRIES WHOM?

Anthropologists and sociologists use the term *endogamy* to describe marriages between persons within the same social group. When a person marries someone outside his or her own social group, the practice is called *exogamy*. (The terms are easily remembered by thinking of their roots. The ending comes from the Greek *gamia*, meaning "act of marrying." *Endo* means "within," and *ex* means "out of.") Thus, endogamy occurs when blacks marry blacks. Exogamy occurs when blacks marry whites. Jews who marry fellow Jews are marrying endogamously, whereas exogamy occurs when Jews marry Gentiles.

Another commonly used term is *homogamy* (from the Greek term *homos*, meaning "the same"), which refers to the tendency of persons to marry persons with characteristics similar to their own—particularly in terms of age, intelligence, education, and social background. The physician's daughter marries the lawyer's son. The college graduate marries a fellow college graduate. The waitress marries the factory worker—and so on.

However, if a woman marries someone of quite different educational and social background, she is said to have married either up or down. The physician's daughter who completes four years of college and then marries the factory worker who is a high school dropout illustrates the principle of *hypogamy* or marrying down. On the other hand, if a waitress (with only a high school education or less) were to marry a lawyer or physician, she would serve as an example of *hypergamy* or marrying up. Again, you can avoid confusing these terms by recalling their roots. *Hypo* derives from the Greek for "under" or "below" and is used in such words as hypodermic needle, a needle which injects material under the skin. *Hyper* means "over" or "above" and is familiar to us from such terms as hyperacidity or references to a child's hyperactivity.) In speaking of hypogamy and hypergamy, it is customary for social scientists to take the woman as the reference point. That is, it is the *wife* who is considered to have married either beneath or above her social status, no doubt because in *traditional* social-class measurements women have been considered to take on the social status of their husbands rather than having an independent status of their own—something that, as we'll see later, is now being questioned.

Education One area where the principle of homogamy is clearly at work is education. Most people marry those whose amount of education is similar to their own. "Similar" may be defined as the same educational level or one level removed. (See Table 6-A.)

Education is a resource persons may offer in marriage bargaining, and it is also an indication of social status. Persons with the same or similar education levels are more likely to perceive the marriage bargain to be a just and fair one than would usually be true of spouses having vast differences in education (where there would be an imbalance in resources brought to the

TABLE 6-A *Marriages by levels of education*

IN 1970, OUT OF EVERY 100 MARRIED COUPLES (ALL RACES COMBINED):
39 *husbands and wives were at the same educational level;**
19 *husbands were one level** *higher than their wives;*
18 *wives were one level** *higher than their husbands;*
12 *husbands were two or more levels** *higher than their wives;*
12 *wives were two or more levels** *higher than their husbands.*

*EDUCATIONAL LEVELS:

0–4 years elementary school
5–7 years elementary school
8 years elementary school
1–3 years high school
4 years high school
1–3 years college
4 years college
5 or more years college

SOURCE: Based on data from the 1970 census. U.S. Bureau of the Census, 1972, PC(2)-4C, p. 269.

marriage). And of course, it goes without saying that persons with similar education are likely to hold similar values, goals, and outlooks on life, and thus have more in common than is generally true where wide gaps exist in educational background. Thus, nearly two-thirds of husbands with four years of college have wives with at least some college. And four out of five wives with four years of college are married to husbands who have also attended college. (See Tables 6-B and 6-C.)

Age Just as wide gaps in education are rare, so too are wide age differences between persons who marry each other. In 1977, among 59 percent of all couples in the United States, the ages of both spouses were either the same or the difference between them was no more than four years. Only one in five couples had a husband between five and nine years older than the wife, and among only 7 percent of all couples was the husband ten or more years older than the wife (Rawlings, 1978:4).

It is more common for the husband to be older than the wife than for the wife to be older than the husband. Similarly, persons tend to expect that the husband will be the taller, more educated, and have the better occupation of the pair. All of this is symbolic of a phenomenon sociologists call the *marriage gradient* (Bernard, 1972, chap. 3), the expectation that the male partner will have slightly superior status as compared to the female partner when marriage choices are made. This pattern stems from traditional notions of sex roles in which men are considered leaders and protectors and women followers who look up to men. Earlier we saw Richman's study of dating

TABLE 6-B   *Education of husband, by education of wife: March 1977*

EDUCATION OF HUSBAND	TOTAL		ELEMEN-TARY	HIGH SCHOOL			COLLEGE		
	NUMBER (THOU-SANDS)	PERCENT	0 TO 8 YEARS	1 TO 3 YEARS	4 YEARS	1 TO 3 YEARS	4 YEARS	5 YEARS OR MORE
All husbands	48,002	100.0	13.4	16.0	45.1	13.8	8.2	3.5
Elementary:								
0 to years	8,725	100.0	49.3	22.9	23.5	3.2	0.8	0.3
High School:								
1 to 3 years	7,063	100.0	13.6	37.3	42.0	5.3	1.4	0.3
4 years	16,468	100.0	5.4	14.5	65.2	10.5	3.2	1.0
College:								
1 to 3 years	6,938	100.0	3.0	7.0	49.8	28.9	8.6	2.7
4 years	4,787	100.0	0.9	2.4	33.5	27.4	28.9	6.8
5 years or more	4,022	100.0	0.8	1.5	20.8	22.8	31.0	23.1

SOURCE: Stephen Rawlings, "Perspectives on American Husbands and Wives," *Current Population Reports: Special Studies*, Series P-23, No. 77 (United States Bureau of the Census, 1978), p. 13.

TABLE 6-C   *Education of wife, by education of husband: March 1977*

	TOTAL		EDUCATION OF HUSBAND					
			ELEMEN-TARY	HIGH SCHOOL		COLLEGE		
EDUCATION OF WIFE	NUMBER (THOU-SANDS)	PERCENT	0 TO 8 YEARS	1 TO 3 YEARS	4 YEARS	1 TO 3 YEARS	4 YEARS	5 YEARS OR MORE
All wives	48,002	100.0	18.2	14.7	34.3	14.5	10.0	8.4
Elementary:								
0 to 8 years	6,438	100.0	66.8	15.0	13.9	3.2	0.7	0.5
High school:								
1 to 3 years	7,690	100.0	26.0	34.3	31.1	6.4	1.5	0.8
4 years	21,653	100.0	9.5	13.7	49.6	15.9	7.4	3.9
College:								
1 to 3 years	6,616	100.0	4.2	5.7	26.2	30.3	19.9	13.8
4 years	3,933	100.0	1.9	2.5	13.6	15.2	35.2	31.7
5 years or more	1,671	100.0	1.8	1.4	10.3	11.4	19.4	55.7

SOURCE: Stephen Rawlings, "Perspectives on American Husbands and Wives," *Current Population Reports: Special Studies*, Series P–23, No. 77 (United States Bureau of the Census, 1978), p. 13.

which showed that persons who held more egalitarian gender-role norms were less likely to hold traditional attitudes about male-female age differences.

Among all couples in the United States in 1977, the wife was the older of the pair in 14 percent of the cases. One out of every four wives over age sixty-five had a husband younger than herself. "Since women generally live longer than men," explains sociologist Stephen Rawlings (1978), "one would expect that widows who remarry would tend to choose a man younger than themselves" (p. 4).

Religion   Data on religious intermarriage is not as complete as social scientists would like it to be—one reason being that questions on religious identification are not included in the census or on many other public registrations. However, the limited data on trends in interfaith marriages seem to indicate an increase in such marriages (Barron, 1972; Mueller, 1971). Particularly among Roman Catholics and Protestants, a great deal of exogamy occurs. The religious climate of greater openness, tolerance, and cooperation between Catholics and Protestants since Vatican II may be one explanation for more persons feeling free to marry outside their particular church group (Mueller, 1971:21; Besanceney, 1970:162–167).

Exogamy is rarest of all among the third major religious grouping, Jews, where persons are strongly encouraged to select mates from within their own group. Loyal Jews are expected by parents and religious leaders alike to marry endogamously. Such a stance has been taken by the Jewish community throughout their history. The popular musical *Fiddler on the Roof* made clear

First Anniversary

(Wide World Photos)

"It's been one exciting year," Mark Goodman, 21, says of his year-old marriage to his 78-year-old stepgrandmother, Ray. And he said his parents are coming to accept the situation.

A year ago Monday, Goodman married Ray Goodman—a former chorus girl and his father's widowed stepmother.

The couple then lived in England, where the law forbade a marriage between a man and his grandfather's widow. The two came to Los Angeles and married in private.

His parents, who live in this area, did not attend the wedding but Goodman says they are getting used to the idea now and visit frequently.

"I think they are learning to accept the situation," he said. "Time did a lot of things and we get along fine now. Mother and father are friendly."

Goodman likes to play down the importance of age in their relationship. "We love each other. We're happy. That's what counts, isn't it?"

SOURCE: *Greensboro* (NC) *Daily News*, January 30, 1979.

the agony that Jewish parents have traditionally undergone when one of their offspring marries a Gentile. The Hebrew Scriptures provide warnings against marriages between Jews and non-Jews. The prophet Ezra, for example,

81-Year-Old Father Back into Diaper Routine

BIRMINGHAM, Ala. (AP)—It's been 29 years since Willie Williams has had to change diapers on a child of his own, but he'll soon be getting back into the routine.

Williams and his wife, whom he married last year, recently became the proud parents of a 6-pound, 14-ounce girl.

They have known each other "all our lives." That might not seem so unusual, until you consider that Williams is 81, and his wife, Geraldine, is 31.

"I've got five children and the baby," Williams said. "The new one looks just like me."

SOURCE: *Greensboro* (NC) *Daily News*, March 15, 1979.

---

counseled his people to divorce their foreign wives. On the other hand, the two Old Testament books named after women both contain stories of Jewish-Gentile marriages. Esther, a Jew, by her influence as the wife of a Persian king, saved her people from destruction. And the Gentile Ruth had Jewish husbands in both her first and second marriages. Ruth, however, was willing to say, "Thy people shall be my people, and thy God my God" (Ruth 1:16). Such conversion to Judaism by a non-Jew has traditionally been the one way in which he or she becomes acceptable as a potential marriage partner for a Jew (Gordon, 1964).

At the same time, as journalist Kenneth Briggs (1976) points out in a report on an American Jewish Committee study of intermarriage, "religious law forbids conversion solely for the purpose of marriage. It must be based on personal, religious grounds." But he goes on to say that "even some Orthodox rabbis are re-examining their attitudes toward this practice to make it easier for the non-Jewish person to be taken into the faith." It is the Orthodox branch of Judaism that traditionally has been most opposed to religious intermarriage, whereas the Conservative and Reform branches have become somewhat more accepting. "Much of this reassessment seems to reflect a conviction that condemning intermarriage or declaring the Jewish partner 'dead' in the eyes of his religion have been counterproductive," writes Briggs. He refers to a comment by one of the researchers involved in the Committee's study: "If there is going to be intermarriage, what is the most creative way of responding to make sure that there is no loss of Jewishness by the Jewish partner?"

And evidently there *is* going to be intermarriage. Despite the long traditions and negative sanctions relating to marriages between Jews and non-Jews, several studies indicate an upsurge in such marriages in recent years (Mueller, 1971; Gordon, 1964; Briggs, 1976). Rabbi Albert I. Gordon (1964), a social anthropologist, explains why many rabbis view this upsurge with alarm: "Intermarriage is generally regarded by American Jewish leaders as a symptom of the weakening of Jewish religious ties and the lack of empathy for their own people that has characterized Jews in the past" (p.

213). On the other hand, among Gentiles, there seems to be a growing acceptance of Gentile-Jewish marriage unions (Stember, 1966:104–107).

Race With rare exceptions, people tend to marry within their own racial grouping. In other words, racial endogamy seems to be the strongest of all.

In 1977, barely 1 percent of the 48 million married couples in the United States were in interracial marriages—marriages between blacks and whites, whites and other races, or blacks and other races (Rawlings, 1978:7). (In reporting data, the term "other races" is used in reference to those whose national origin is Japanese, Chinese, Filipino, American Indian, and so on.) In black-white and black-other marriages, the black partner is more often the husband. In white-other marriages, the white partner is more apt to be the husband; but in white-black marriages, the white partner is more likely to be the wife. (See Table 6-D.)

Some states had laws against interracial marriage up until the 1967 United States Supreme Court decision which declared such laws unconstitutional. As Table 6-D shows, the number of interracial marriages of all kinds has been growing in recent years, with black-white marriages increasing from 65,000 in 1970 to 125,000 in 1977—a 92 percent increase. (See Figure 6-1.)

A number of sociologists have pointed out that much more research must be done in the area of interracial marriage before we can clearly ascertain trends and understand their meaning (Monahan, 1973; Aldridge, 1973; Heer, 1974). Past explanations for the low incidence of white-black marriages have focused on evidence that in a color-caste society the dominant group rates the characteristics of the less-dominant group as being of less worth than the

TABLE 6-D   *Interracial married couples: 1977 and 1970*

(NUMBERS IN THOUSANDS)

RACE	1977	1970	CHANGE, 1970 TO 1977
Total married couples	48,002	44,597	3,405
Total interracial married couples	421	310	111
All black-white married couples	125	65	60
Husband black, wife white	95	41	54
Wife black, husband white	30	24	6
Other interracial married couples	296	245	51
Husband black	20	8	12
Wife black	2	4	−2
Husband white	177	139	38
Wife white	97	94	3

SOURCE: Stephen Rawlings, "Perspectives on American Husbands and Wives," *Current Population Reports: Special Studies*, Series P-23, No. 77 (United States Bureau of the Census, 1978), p. 10.

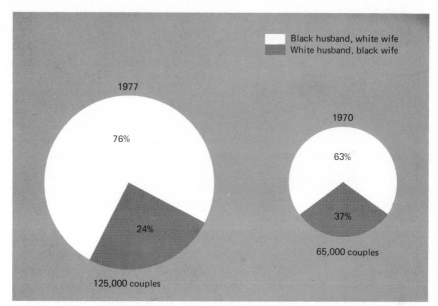

FIGURE 6-1 *Interracial (black/white) couples, 1977 and 1970. (Source: Stephen Rawlings, "Perspectives on American Husbands and Wives,"* Current Population Reports: Special Studies, *Series P-23, no. 77, U.S. Bureau of the Census, 1978, p. 8.)*

characteristics of the dominant group (Washington, 1970; Sickels, 1972; Barron, 1972; Gordon, 1964). Thus, in a white-dominated society, whites have defined blackness as of less value than whiteness and therefore have tended not to strike a marriage bargain that seemed unfavorable. Not only did the exchange of rewards in interracial marriage seem unequal according to this line of reasoning, but there were also costs to consider. Whites who marry blacks have traditionally suffered severe disapproval from other whites, with especially negative sanctions from relatives and close friends.

Blacks, too, may negatively sanction those of their number who marry outside their race. Many feel strongly against such marriages for reasons similar to the traditional views of Jews cited earlier. Pride in one's own group and loyalty to that group are expected to be reinforced by endogamy. Convinced that black is beautiful, many blacks look upon marriage to a white person as not only undesirable but almost as an act of treason against the black race and black culture. To enter such a marriage is viewed by some as acquiescence to a society that has held blacks down, an alliance with the oppressor. One survey, however, indicates a greater willingness on the part of black parents to accept a daughter's marriage to someone of another race than is true of white parents. (See Table 6-E.)

One way sociologists have attempted to explain what happens in black-white marriages has been in terms of a theory of *racial*-caste hypogamy coupled with *social*-class hypergamy. First suggested by sociologists Kingsley Davis (1941) and Robert Merton (1941), the theory states that a woman from a

TABLE 6-E *Parents' reactions to their daughter's marrying someone of another race*

	WOULD FIND IT ACCEPTABLE (%)	WOULD ACCEPT BUT BE UNHAPPY ABOUT IT (%)	NOT ACCEPT IT, HAVE STRAINED RELATIONSHIP (%)	DON'T KNOW (%)
Black women	33	29	16	21
Black men	36	33	6	25
White women	14	38	44	5
White men	16	32	47	5

SOURCE: The Virginia Slims American Women's Opinion Poll, conducted by the Roper Organization, Inc. for the Virginia Slims company, 1975. Adapted from a report in *Ebony* magazine, September, 1975. Reprinted in *Readings in Marriage and Family 76/77: Annual Editions* (Sluice Dock, Guilford, CT: The Dushkin Publishing Group, Inc., 1976), pp. 65-68.

higher racial caste is willing to marry a man from a lower racial caste in a situation where to do so will raise her from a lower social class to one of higher status. What is "marrying down" on the one hand (hypogamy) is "marrying up" on the other (hypergamy). David Heer (1974), a sociologist who has given much attention to the study of black-white marriages, suggests caution with regard to such an explanation, although he points out that the theory may have some validity if other considerations are taken into account.

The Merton-Davis theory has been widely accepted because of evidence from government studies which show a tendency for black men who marry white women to have a higher level of education than is true of black men who marry black women. White women who marry black men have tended to have a lower level of education than white women who marry white men (Carter and Glick 1970:126–129). Sociologist Zick Rubin (1973) sums up what has sometimes been called the "compensation principle" in terms of exchange theory. He writes: "These interracial marriages can be seen as exchanges on the interpersonal marketplace, in which the higher educational status of the black husband (and the earning power that may go along with it) is exchanged for the higher social status of the white wife (which accrues to her simply by virtue of her skin color)" (p. 196).

However, Jessie Bernard (1966), another sociologist, has taken issue with this notion. Bernard's analysis of the 1960 census data did not show a tendency for wives of black men to have relatively lower education if white rather than black. The idea that interracial marriage involves an exchange of status based on skin color for status based on educational and occupational achievement may be increasingly questionable (Monahan, 1973).

Perhaps what may be occurring is a tendency for marriages between blacks and whites to involve other kinds of exchanges, with persons being attracted to one another on the basis of rewards which make the consideration of racial differences less important than was once the case. Education, exposure to persons of other races in travel, work, and school, and ideological concerns based on humanistic and religious values may all play a part in de-emphasizing skin color as a basis for evaluating persons.

Among highly educated persons with a common universe of values, for example, partners in *cross-national* marriages have been known to consider themselves as belonging to a kind of international community or life-style that transcends national boundaries. In one study of Western nationals who married persons from India, it was found that spouses considered the culture they shared in common (for example, the scientific community) to be far more important than the cultures of their countries of origin. As one Indian respondent summed it up: "I would have so little in common with a parochial Indian." Sociologist Ann Baker Cottrell (1973) concludes that such Indian-Western marriages are inaccurately called "mixed marriages." Perhaps a similar statement might be made about many black-white marriages as well.

In the United States, marriages in which one partner is of Spanish origin are more common than marriages where the spouses are of different races. "In 1977, there were 762,000 couples in which one spouse was of Spanish origin and one was not," writes social demographer Stephen Rawlings (1978:7). This figure compares with the 421,000 couples who were in interracial marriages. Nearly a third (31 percent) of the 2.4 million married couples with a husband or wife of Spanish origin were couples where the other partner was *not* of Spanish origin. Even so, such couples comprise less than 2 percent of all married couples in the United States.

The Incest Taboo The question may arise: If persons tend to marry within their own group (e.g., the same race or religion), why don't persons marry within the most basic group of all—their own family? Wouldn't that be endogamy of the purest type? This brings us to the matter of *incest* or sexual intercourse between persons who are closely related. The incest taboo is an institutionalized norm found almost universally which prohibits sex relations between parents and their children, between brothers and sisters, and (with some variations in the degree of kinship) between members of the nuclear family and relatives outside the nuclear family (for example, with in-laws, aunts and uncles, cousins, etc.).

There have been many attempts to explain the existence of the incest taboo, and the usual rationale for its existence today is related to genetics,

Pink Is from Mama

"Daddy is brown and Mama is pink," says my young son Ricky. "I get my dimple and curly hair from Daddy and my pink from Mama."

We are an interracial family with three sons. . . .

Some people may feel that Kermit and I have denied our sons an identity, a sense of stability in a particular community or race. But I think that in the future people will have to overcome the narrow boundaries of race and nationality if true harmony among the world's peoples is ever to achieved. . . . [Our sons] have a race to belong to—the human race.

SOURCE: Marion Booker, "A Young Mother's Story: Pink Is from Mama," *Redbook* (October, 1969), p. 12.

namely, a concern that marriages between closely related persons might increase the likelihood of defective offspring (since both spouses might be carriers of the same inherited genetic weakness). However, although this rationale has provided support for the incest taboo, it does not explain its *origin,* since there is no evidence that a concern about genetic abnormalities guided the ancients in forming their prohibitions. Nor does the genetic explanation always seem logical even today (for example, in cases where elderly first cousins, long past the age of childbearing, are forbidden to marry by certain state laws). (See also Chapter 7, p. 188.)

One way we might attempt to explain the original basis for prohibitions against incest, as well as exceptions such as the brother-sister marriages in ancient Egypt, is to think again in terms of exchange theory.

Anthropologist Claude Lévi-Strauss (1956) has written of the way the incest taboo reinforces the interdependency of families. "For incest-prohibition simply states that families (however they should be defined) can only marry between each other and that they cannot marry inside themselves." Furthermore, "the prohibition of incest is a rule of reciprocity. It means: I will only give up my daughter or my sister if my neighbor will give up his also. . . . The fact that I can obtain a wife is, in the last analysis, the consequence of the fact that a brother or a father has given up a woman" (Lévi-Strauss, 1949).

Couple Speak Out on Their Forbidden Love

A brother and sister talked for the first time today of their forbidden love for each other and their battle with the law since they married.

"You know it's weird because they want to put you in jail for being in love. Like love's against the law," said Vicki Pittorino, 23, who married her younger brother in Andover, Mass. last month.

The bride's distraught mother notified police when she learned of her daughter's marriage to David Goddu, 22, and the siblings now face 20 years in jail under Massachusetts law.

Goddu, who met his natural sister for the first time a few months ago, said, "We set our minds to do it [separate], but we can't do it.

Miss Pittorino said she spent four years searching for her brother.

"We found that the only reason that incest was against the law was because of children," Miss Pittorino said. "And we decided before we got married . . . that we would not have children . . . and Dave would get a vasectomy."

Both sets of adoptive parents are distraught over the marriage. Goddu said his parents, James and Eileen Goddu, were "100 per cent embarassed."

And he seems to understand his parents' feelings. "My father asked me why I didn't tell him, and I said, 'Dad, how could I tell you that I married my sister.'

The siblings said they agreed to discuss their marriage because "we don't want people to think we need help, that we need a pyschiatrist. The only way people were going to understand was for us to tell it ourselves."

SOURCE: Sam Rosensohn, *New York Post,* June 20, 1979, as reprinted in *Sex and the Law,* September, 1979, p. 5.

The emphasis in these statements is upon an exchange of women, and we are again reminded of the customs surrounding the bride wealth or bride price in many cultures and of the economic gains and social linkages which are associated with marriage. Building upon the ideas of Lévi-Strauss, we might suggest that the incest prohibition originally served as a means of ensuring an institutionalized pattern of gains through exchanges. Couples who married within their own families would only be sharing what they already possessed; it would be a closed arrangement with no bride prices, dowries, greater social linkages, and so on. But to marry *outside* one's family opened the way to bring other resources in.

Exceptions to keeping the incest taboo may be similarly explained. If persons married outside their families in order to bring in additional resources, there might also be cases where persons married inside their families in order to keep resources. Marrying out of the family could bring gains; but marrying in the family could prevent loss. This is likely the reason for the father-daughter and brother-sister marriages during the time of the Pharaohs. In fact, Egyptologists have uncovered evidence of brother-sister marriages in many periods of Egypt's history, not only within the royalty but also among the commoners. Sociologist Russell Middleton (1962) suggests that the most plausible explanation is that such unions "served to maintain the property of the family intact and to prevent the splintering of the estate through the operation of the laws of inheritance. Since daughters usually inherited a share of the estate, the device of brother-sister marriage would have served to preserve intact the material resources of the family as a unit." Often these were "marriages of convenience" so that property could be transmitted which would otherwise have fallen to the state.

WHY DO PEOPLE CHOOSE PARTICULAR MATES?

"I can't for the life of me figure out how those two got together!" "I wonder what she sees in *him*?" "That guy could have married any girl he pleased, and yet he picked her. I can't understand it."

We've all heard statements like these, and perhaps we've made similar remarks ourselves. Most people are interested in how particular persons got together and decided to form a marriage partnership. All sorts of questions arise: Why do persons tend to choose mates with similar social characteristics? How can we explain mate selection in terms of our earlier discussion about male-female exchanges prior to marriage? And what is the place of love in all of this?

FIELD OF POTENTIAL MATES

Men and women view each other through an initial screening or filtering process which is represented by a potential "field of eligibles." Screened out are persons not defined as eligible, perhaps because they are not within the same race, religion, educational level, or age group. We have seen, for

"In 1953, Horton was considered a real catch."

(Drawing by Henry Martin; ©
1978 The New Yorker
Magazine, Inc.)

example, that the percentage of black-white marriages is small. Or to take
another illustration, a devout Catholic is unlikely to consider an atheist as a
potential marriage partner. A woman with a Ph.D. in psychology is not likely
to marry the auto mechanic who services her car—no matter what movies and
soap operas may say. The thirty-year-old single woman who is introduced to
her friend's seventy-year-old bachelor uncle will in all probability think of him
as only an acquaintance and not as a possible marriage partner. There are, of
course, exceptions to all of these patterns; but in general, as we have seen
from the statistics, they hold true.

NARROWING THE CHOICE

When persons have passed through the filtering process and have been
defined as belonging to a category that makes a marriage bargain seem
equitable, the question of which one to marry still remains (Becker, 1973).
Obviously, no one can marry all of them; he or she is faced with the task of
selecting just one potential mate out of the total field of eligibles. How is that
selection made? And why do some people cross these lines to marry persons
from somewhat different backgrounds?

Again we see the part that exchange and bargaining play in the
mate-selection process. Clearly, there are numerous kinds of resources that
men and women can offer each other in addition to those benefits represented
by the broad categories of race, religion, and educational groupings.
Particularly important are those resources that cluster around sex-role
definitions.

The traditional form of marriage places the husband in the role of breadwinner and the wife in the role of nurturant sustainer of the home. Persons who want this form of marriage will gravitate toward those who hold similar views, and again it is a matter of reward seeking. Women who hold traditional gender-role patterns will be attracted to men who appear able to provide them with the status and material comfort they define as acceptable. Sociologist Willard Waller had this in mind when he wrote in 1938: "There is this difference between the man and the woman in the pattern of bourgeois family life; a man, when he marries, chooses a companion and perhaps a helpmate, but a woman chooses a companion and at the same time a standard of living. It is necessary for a woman to be mercenary" (Waller, 1938:243 as quoted in Rubin, 1973:205).

At the same time, men who hold traditional views of sex roles are attracted to women who feel the same way. Such men desire wives who will provide the nurturance, support, and respect that husbands have traditionally deemed essential in a good homemaker. They are looking for women who will center their lives around husbands and children and for whom all other interests are secondary.

Persons who hold modern, egalitarian notions of marriage also seek out like-minded partners. Women who are persuaded that they have the right to self-determination and an individual identity are certainly not interested in joining themselves in marriage to men who believe that females should be passive, dependent, and subordinate to male leadership. Instead such women are attracted to men who give promise of granting them the rewards of acceptance, recognition, free choice, affirmation of talents, and encouragement to achieve.

Similarly, some men highly value and admire achievement-oriented women and are drawn toward them, finding what they have to offer rewarding rather than threatening. In answer to the question often put to men married to successful women, "How does it feel to be the husband of . . .?" Bertrand B. Pogrebin (1972) writes, "In a word—terrific." Pogrebin, a lawyer, is married to the writer Letty Cottin Pogrebin. "I could go on at this point with all the superlatives that describe the pleasures of living with someone who likes what she is doing and is recognized for doing it well," he writes. "I could describe the people I've met and the places I've been because of her. Or the genuine interest and respect I have for her activities." Pogrebin is clearly speaking here in terms of rewards.

One study of college students showed that although both blacks and whites valued expressive qualities in a prospective mate, black males especially placed a high value on instrumental qualities such as a mate's having a good job, being willing to share financial responsibilities, and desiring to "move ahead" and improve economic status. "Black college males, influenced by the possibility of restricted economic opportunity, may be particularly sensitive to the economic demands of family life," write researchers Willie Melton and Darwin L. Thomas (1976). "Hence, qualities of a wife which make her agreeable to, and capable of, sharing with him the role of provider are highly valued" (p. 516).

Sex-role patterns are important parts of the exchange process prior to marriage because they set the stage for what is likely to occur later in marriage. The partners are either implicitly or explicitly anticipating their *future* roles.

WHAT PART DOES LOVE PLAY?

We say that persons "marry for love," but already we have seen that love isn't some mysterious force that strikes indiscriminately. Rather, love seems to be sparked among persons of similar social characteristics and resources. Whatever love is, it is clear that persons do not "fall in love" with just anybody; only certain ones will do.

ROMANTIC LOVE

Love has many meanings, but one of the first meanings that comes to mind in connection with man-woman relationships is the notion of romantic love. Such love has its roots in the Greek idea of *eros* or what the ancient Greeks saw as "diseased hysteria," an overwhelming force that irresistibly draws two persons together and makes them helpless under its power. All that matters is that the two are together, and all other considerations become secondary. Smitten, overcome, engulfed, the star-crossed lovers try to explain what has happened to them and conclude that it must have been moonglow or fate or the season or a magic potion of the gods or some other strange power which brought them straight to one another.

The idea is as recent as current love songs, and as ancient as the dramas of Euripides, whose Phaedra "groans in bitterness of heart and the goads of love prick her cruelly, and she is like to die." The goddess Aphrodite had stricken Phaedra with an uncontrollable seizure of desire for the chaste young man, Hippolytus, Phaedra's husband's illegitimate son. Aphrodite did this out of spite, desiring to punish Hippolytus for ignoring her, the goddess of love, and worshiping another goddess instead. Poor Phaedra in her suffering tries to fight off the lovesickness, believing she can conquer love "with discretion and good sense," but when that fails, she concludes that death is the only answer. Her faithful nurse provides comfort, telling Phaedra that it is futile to think that her puny swimming could provide an escape from the great sea of love into which she had fallen. "Give up your railing," counsels the old woman. "It's only insolent pride to wish to be superior to the gods. Endure your love. The gods have willed it so. You are sick" (Euripides, *Hippolytus*, Prologue, lines 395–400, 470–475).

The ballads of the twelfth-century troubadours with their themes of knights who pledged undying devotion to their ladies went a step further and exalted romantic love as the noblest emotion of which the human heart is capable. This courtly love of which the troubadours sang reinforces traditional male-female images. The man is the aggressive pursuer, and the woman is the pure, beautiful prize to be pursued. The gentleman is to *serve* his lady—to perform significant deeds for her that will make her justly proud of him. Now she is in his debt, and to repay him dances off to bed with him. Eight centuries later, though the dragons have all been slain, the pattern remains. The gentleman serves his lady by providing economic benefits for her both before and especially after marriage. She thus is in his debt, and he gains authority over her.

LOVE ISN'T ONLY A FEELING

The "diseased hysteria" and courtly "Amor" notions of romantic love do not exhaust the meanings of the word *love*. Denis de Rougemont (1940) distinguishes between "an obsession which is undergone and a destiny that we shoulder." *"To be in love,"* he writes, "is not necessarily *to love*. To be in love is a state; to love, an act. A state is suffered or undergone; but an act has to be decided upon."

Social psychologists Elaine Walster and G. William Walster (1978) put it another way:

> Love can appear in two very different forms: passionate love and companionate love. Passionate love is a wildly emotional state, a confusion of feelings: tenderness and sexuality, elation and pain, anxiety and relief, altruism and jealousy. Companionate love, on the other hand, is a lower-key emotion. It's friendly affection and deep attachment to someone. (p. 2)

DEVELOPING LOVE AFTER THE MATE-SELECTION PROCESS

Even where mates are selected by parents, the mates are expected to develop feelings of affection for each other (Goode, 1959; Rubin, 1973). The Bible speaks of Isaac who watched the arrival of a special camel caravan. It was bringing the bride whom he had never met but who had been chosen by his father's trusted servant. "Then Isaac brought her into the tent, and took Rebekah, and she became his wife; and he loved her" (Gen. 24:67). In such situations, factors other than love are considered the basis for marriage. "Love does not lead to marriage but marriage leads to love," goes a Korean saying, which continues rather cynically, "if such a thing as 'love' exists."

Sociologist Choong Soon Kim (1974) points out that many Korean young people are exposed to this and other teachings that de-emphasize the notion of love. For example: "I never knew what love was/I don't know what love is/I don't care what love is/ I don't intend to be told what love is." Through such teachings, parents—especially in rural villages—have sought to justify the practice of having their children's marriages arranged by a "go-between" in charge of matchmaking.

The old Korean custom of arranged marriages has been incorporated into the contemporary teachings of the Unification Church, a controversial

Phaedra pining for love of Hyppolytus. (Culver Pictures)

Courtly love. (Culver Pictures)

Contrary to ideas perpetuated in myths and love songs, love isn't some mysterious force that strikes indiscriminately. Rather, love seems to be sparked among persons of similar social characteristics and resources.

Romantic love. (Culver Pictures)

Love today. (Barbara Pfeffer/ Peter Arnold, Inc.)

What Makes Love Tick?

A few years ago Sen. William Proxmire, D-Wis., gave his Golden Fleece Award for government waste to a social psychologist who had received a federal grant to study love. Proxmire said love was on the top of the list of things that the American public doesn't want to know about; ever since, I have sadly kept my own "love scale," which I developed for my doctorate in social psychology a decade ago, in the back of my file cabinet buried under a pile of questionnaires and computer printouts. If Proxmire didn't think it a good idea to measure love scientifically, who was I to argue?

But, just as I was about to send out some Valentine's Day cards the other day, the subject of a "love scale" was brought up in a Los Angeles courtroom as a matter of evidence, when Michelle Triola Marvin's lawyer asked Lee Marvin whether he had ever loved Ms. Marvin "even a little bit." As we all know by now, Michelle Marvin lived with Lee Marvin without ever marrying for six years. He broke up with her, and she has now sued for a portion of the financial assets that he amassed during that time. It is a landmark case of great import to cohabiting couples everywhere, and now—Proxmire notwithstanding— it apparently all comes down to taking the measure of love.

To Michelle Marvin's lawyer's question, Lee Marvin countered, "What kind of love are you talking about?" The judge, sensing that some precedents were about to be set, suggested that Marvin provide his own definition.

Marvin was prepared. "Love is a matter of degrees," he said. "I think of a gas tank with the empty and full positions. There is young and frivolous love. There is childlike love. Then there is the other end of the scale, which could be the love between people—a deep regard for the other person, truthfulness, loyalty, fidelity and a tremendous sense of selflessness toward the other person. I did not have that kind of love."

The problem, of course, is that definitions of love are easy to come by. . . .

In my own attempt to solve this problem 10 years ago, I developed a "love scale." The scale's items tap what I regard as the three major components of love: attachment (the desire to be near the other person), caring (the concern for the other person's wellbeing) and intimacy (the desire for close and confidential communication). The more a person agrees with each of the items, the more he or she can be said to love the other person. One's love score can actually range from zero, which is no love at all, to 117, which is as much love as possible—something like Marvin's gas-gauge analogy.

Now, if Marvin had only been asked to fill out my "love scale" while he and Michelle Marvin were living together—an annual check is recommended—we wouldn't have to waste the court's time arguing about definitions or quibbling about "love letters" that may or may not have meant what they said.

I don't pretend that my love scale would provide the final word in the matter of Marvin vs. Marvin. During the past decade a number of other social scientists have been studying love, and their contributions would have to be reckoned with as well. . . .

While this approach might not settle all of the questions, either, at least it's scientific, and we social psychologists could get to be expert witnesses.

But there's something else that social scientists—and most of the rest of us—have learned about love that the lawyers and judge may have missed. At bottom, this case is not a matter of love but of commitment. Lee Marvin may, in fact, have loved Michelle Marvin a great deal. At one time he might even have had a full gas tank, or a score of 117 on my scale. But loving someone is not a commitment to love and support that person forever.

That's what marriage is for.

SOURCE: Zick Rubin, in the *Greensboro* (NC) *Daily News,* February 21, 1979. (Syndicated from the *Los Angeles Times.*)

religious sect founded by Sun Myung Moon. The group, which has alarmed some parents, is active in the United States and elsewhere. Surprisingly, a number of American young people who have joined the group are willing to have their mates chosen for them by Moon, even though arranged marriages are very out of keeping with the usual pattern of mate selection in the United States today.

Since the goal of Unificationists (or "Moonies") is the unification of humankind, marriages may be cross-racial and cross-cultural. Periodically, persons are selected to experience what is called "the blessing"; that is, they are matched by Moon and married in a mass ceremony. (See boxed insert.)

Some of the young Moonies have told us in personal interviews that they feel relief over having surrendered decisions about marriage into what they feel are wiser hands. They believe that after marriage they will grow to love the mate chosen for them. Meanwhile, they are glad, they say, to be rid of the pressures of dating customs and free to experience cross-sex friendships on a brother-sister basis within the group.

Most persons in contemporary American society, however, seem to prefer choosing for themselves the person they will marry. Furthermore, they want that person to be someone they loved prior to the wedding.

WHAT MAKES CERTAIN PERSONS LOVE EACH OTHER?

Attractions between persons may be either extrinsic or intrinsic. In an *extrinsic* relationship, the emphasis is on something outward and tangible. Some firms

Receiving "the Blessing." Couples matched by Sun Myung Moon, founder of the Unification Church, are united in a mass marriage ceremony.

"The matching began in the largest lecture hall about 3:00 P.M. The men and women sat at the opposite ends of the room. Starting with the physically oldest members first and moving through various categories of age, position, etc., Master began to match the couples. When he would pick two people, they would go into a small adjoining room to consult with one another. If they accepted, they came out and bowed to Master, and everyone applauded. If they found some difficulty, they could try again or express a preference. Sometimes Master accepted their preference, sometimes he advised against it. Invariably, we found that Master's judgment was the best.

"Many of the couples hardly knew or had never seen each other before. However, once they began to talk with one another after the engagement, after the blessing, in Tokyo and back in the United States visiting their parents, the real miracle became more and more apparent. . . .

"The most prevalent feeling was that God had been arranging the whole thing all along, that their mates had been created just for them. Master, knowing God's heart and will for each of them, had brought them together."

SOURCE: *New Hope News*, March 10, 1975, as reprinted in Frederick Sontag, *Sun Myung Moon and the Unification Church* (Nashville: Abingdon, 1977), pp. 165–167.

advertise very bluntly: "We want your business." But in an *intrinsic* relationship, the emphasis is on the inward and intangible. It is not a case of "wanting someone's business," but rather of wanting the *someone*—and wanting that person for his or her own sake. (The military may, of course, say, "We want *you!*" in their recruiting advertisements; but there the emphasis is on something extrinsic—the service a person can give.)

In an extrinsic relationship, one person treats the other as a means to some end. We might think of philosopher Martin Buber's (1958) description of an "I-it" relationship in which a subject is relating to an object. Thus, a sales representative takes a client out to dinner, hoping to make a sale. Their being together has only this end in view.

In contrast, the intrinsic relationship corresponds to Buber's notion of an "I-Thou" encounter, where the relationship is one of subject to subject rather than of subject to object. The two persons are attracted because of each other and because of the relationship itself. Friends or lovers go out for dinner simply because they enjoy each other and like to be together. There is an exchange of listening and speaking in which each person's self is revealed to the other. There are inputs on both sides which shape and mold the relationship itself. The two persons are associating with one another for their own sakes and not for the sake of some expected external benefit.

This does not mean, however, that no benefits are desired or expected at all. Throughout this book, we have observed the general sociological principle of reward-exchange in the formation and maintenance of associations. Love does not mean that a relationship is exempted from this principle (Blau, 1964:36, 76). But different dynamics are at work in a love relationship. In an extrinsic relationship (the sales representative with a client), the exchange of specific rewards is the very reason that the association exists; the rewards themselves are the aim. But in an intrinsic association, the supreme value is the *association* in and of itself, with the mutual exchange of rewards taking place *in order to sustain the relationship.*

Although we usually think of love in altruistic terms, Blau makes the point that "selfless devotion generally rests on an interest in maintaining the other's love." Persons in love furnish benefits to each other to show commitment to the partner and to their relationship and to induce the partner to enlarge his or her commitment and inputs as well. Love, therefore, is the extreme example of a deep, strong, intrinsic attraction between persons; yet it is based on the norm of reciprocity. To love is to expect love in return. Love unrequited becomes love unkindled. "Men and women who insist that they are capable of dispensing love with no thought of return are simply deceiving themselves," write Walster and Walster (1978). "Those who expect such selfless love from their partners most assuredly are" (p. 134).

DESIRE FOR EQUITY

The Walsters' comment is not based on mere opinion but comes out of their scientific research on the topic of love. In fact, Elaine Walster and another social psychologist, Ellen Berscheid, unexpectedly found themselves in the news when in 1975 Senator William Proxmire alerted taxpayers that the National Science Foundation had awarded these researchers an $84,000 grant for continuing work on passionate and companionate love. Proxmire was against such research because he felt no amount of money could provide an answer to the "why" of love. But there was another reason. "I'm also against it because I don't want the answer," he said in a press release. "I believe that 200 million other Americans want to leave some things in life a mystery, and right at the top of things we don't want to know is why a man falls in love with a woman and vice versa" (quoted in Walster and Walster, 1978, viii).

Columnist James Reston (*New York Times*, March 14, 1975) retorted that although it may be true that many persons prefer to leave love a mystery and "don't want the answer," "if the sociologists and psychologists can get even a suggestion of the answer to our pattern of romantic love, marriage, disillusion, divorce—and the children left behind—it could be the best investment of federal money since Jefferson made the Louisiana Purchase."

One way to understand what goes on in intimate relationships is to think in terms of what Walster, Walster, and Berscheid (1978) call "equity theory." They define intimate relationships as "relationships between loving persons whose lives are deeply intertwined" (p. 146). Among other characteristics of such relationships, persons have a deep liking or love for one another, expect the relationship to endure, and have the capability of highly rewarding each other. By the same token, they also have the capability of deeply hurting one another.

Equity theory deals with costs and rewards and combines exchange theory with a number of pyschological theories (Walster, Walster, and Berscheid, 1978:2). It is concerned with judgments about what is fair or unfair in a situation or relationship. One of the basic propositions of equity theory is stated and explained by Walster and Walster (1978):

> People feel most comfortable when they're getting exactly what they feel they deserve in a relationship. *Everyone* in an inequitable relationship feels uneasy. While it's not surprising that deprived partners (who are, after all, getting less than they deserve) should feel resentful and angry about their inequitable treatment, it's perhaps not so obvious why their *over*benefited mates (who are getting more than they deserve) feel uneasy too. But they do. They feel guilty and fearful of losing their favored position. (p. 135)

Walster and Walster (1978:135; Walster, Walster, and Berscheid, 1978) have observed that if two persons are in a relationship that turns out to be inequitable, they will experience *distress* and will try to relieve that distress in one of three ways: they may try to do something to restore equity to the relationship, or they may try to convince themselves that the relationship is equitable even though it isn't (so that equity exists in their heads if not in actuality). Or third, they may simply decide to break up.

"It appears, then," say the Walsters (1978), "that just falling in love is *not enough for most of us. . . . Implication: We all want a lot more out of our relationships than we think we do*" (p. 133; italics in the original).

But what do we want out of our relationships? For one thing, we want to be appreciated.

Gratitude   Some sociologists point out that gratitude is an important component in social bonding and can be a crucial factor in bringing and holding persons together (Nisbet, 1970). We're disappointed if our gifts and good deeds aren't recognized by those who benefit from them. Suppose, for example, we see someone drop an armload of books and papers. We rush to help, not even thinking about recognition or reward. However, if our efforts are met with only cold indifference or, worse yet, a brusque directive to get out of the way and mind our own business, we will feel disappointment. Even a simple "thank you" would have been enough. But as it is, a potential bond between two persons has been slashed.

If gratitude is so important in social bonding in general, it is especially important in the interactions associated with a love relationship. Such a point is being made by the wife who complains, "You just take me for granted. I never hear a word of thanks for all the things I do for you." Or the husband who laments, "Nag, nag, nag. That's all you ever do! Does it occur to you that a man might like to hear a word of appreciation once in awhile?" Interactions that call forth admiration, recognition, and gratitude go on before marriage as well—whether in the exchange of tangible gifts or of intangible benefits such as compliments and loving gestures.

Self-Disclosure   Of course, the development of love as an exchange involves more than gratitude. Social psychologists have been giving much attention to what they call the "social-penetration process," or how persons in a sense "get into" one another so that interpersonal relationships can develop (Taylor, 1968). If true intimacy is to come about, the interaction between persons must include self-disclosure. In other words, we reveal information about ourselves (our feelings, ambitions, fears, attitudes, anxieties, incidents from our past, and so on)—information that otherwise would not be known by the other person. The other person, in turn, looks on our intentional self-disclosure as a social reward. It shows that person that we like and trust her or him. And it also frees that person to make similar disclosures about herself or himself (Worthy, Gary, and Kahn, 1969; Taylor, Altman, and Sorrentino, 1969).

At the same time, an element of risk is always involved in self-disclosure. The person to whom we open up ourselves might react negatively to the information revealed and may lower his or her regard for us. Maybe that person will even use that information to hurt us in some way. These are some of the reasons that self-disclosure is difficult for many people (Rubin, 1973:160–162).

However, in a relationship involving commitment and love, a high degree of self-disclosure comes to be expected as an element of reward in the

Being loved by someone means you have a confidant to whom you can expose your innermost feelings. (Susan Meiselas/Magnum Photos, Inc.)

social exchange process. Being loved by someone means that person accepts you as you are—even when the secrets of your heart are laid bare. Thus you have a confidant to whom you can unload your heartaches and expose your innermost feelings. And loving someone in return means that likewise you are rewarded by that person's trust and confidence through self-disclosure on his or her part.

Reiss's "Wheel Theory" of Love Sociologist Ira Reiss (1960b) sees self-disclosure as a crucial second step in his "wheel theory" of love and its development. Reiss conceptualizes love as an ongoing cycle that begins with a sense of rapport between two individuals. This rapport then turns toward mutual self-revelation; and as the "wheel" turns further, the persons develop a mutual dependency on one another. Reiss notes that the more technical term for such mutual dependencies is "interdependent habit systems." He explains: "One becomes dependent on the other person to fulfill one's own habits: e.g., one needs the other person to tell one's ideas or feelings; . . . to joke with; . . . to fulfill one's sexual desires. When such habitual expectations are not fulfilled, loneliness and frustration are experienced. Thus, such habits tend to perpetuate a relationship." From mutual dependencies, the wheel turns to personality need fulfillment. The harmonious connection between the persons (rapport) is increased, the self-revelation continues, and so on, as the wheel keeps turning. (See Figure 6-2.)

At the same time, says Reiss, the wheel could hit a snare at some point

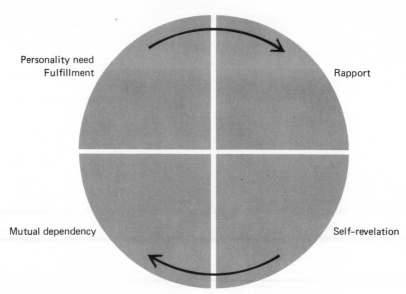

Personality need
Fulfillment

Rapport

Mutual dependency

Self-revelation

FIGURE 6-2   *Graphic presentation of the wheel theory of the development of love. (Source: Reiss, 1960b, p. 143.)*

and the relationship could begin to "unwind." An argument or competing interest might lessen rapport between the persons, which in turn would block the self-disclosure, disturb the "interdependent habit systems," and frustrate fulfillment of personality needs.

Reinforcement and Feelings of Self-Worth   Akin to the notion of mutual dependency is the emphasis two psychologists place on the part reinforcement plays in building self-esteem in persons who are loved. "Through reinforcement, lovers mutually enhance each other's self-concept," write Howard Miller and Paul Siegel (1972:14–22). Pointing out that in an ongoing love relationship, reinforcement efforts often need to be *intentional,* they write: "By 'conscious and deliberate' we mean that each partner can deliberately choose to help satisfy the other's needs, to bolster the other's feelings of self-worth and attractiveness. The fading of the original thrill of mutual discovery and infatuation can be replaced by consciously learning how to make the other person feel attractive, adequate, and simply good about himself. This can be as obvious as praise, or as subtle as paying attention at appropriate moments." However, unless this reinforcement springs from honesty, it has little value. When compliments and expressed interest are not genuine, "that person will lose his power to reward you."

Should Love Be Beyond Reward-Seeking?   Many people are reluctant to admit that an exchange of rewards occurs in love. They feel that such a notion somehow devalues the ideal of love as intrinsically selfless and sacrificial, without any expectation of anything in return. However, a little reflection on the kinds of rewards sought in a love relationship might make the notions of exchange, bargaining, and benefits a bit easier to accept. After all, why else would persons enter into love relationships and marriage than out of an expectation that they would gain something from such relationships?

We have already talked about two parts of marriage: the instrumental side being concerned with economic factors and task performance and the expressive side having to do with the affectionate-companionate dimension. To speak of love is to speak of the *expressive rewards* persons seek from a marriage partner— rewards such as *companionship* (someone to do things with, go places with, spend leisure hours with), *empathy* (someone to talk things over with, someone to bring reinforcement of one's self-concept, someone to understand and care), and *physical affection* (hugging, kissing, the squeeze of a hand, caressing, sexual gratifications). Prior to marriage, these same three elements in one degree or another are sought after as valued rewards in a developing relationship. Though it is often unconscious, a type of bargaining is going on between the partners as they reach out to receive these benefits from one another. The decision to continue the relationship and later to enter into marriage hinges in large part on this reward exchange.

Earlier, we quoted the Walsters' statement that "we all want a lot more out of our relationships than we think we do." That statement was based on a study they and their colleagues Jane Traupmann and Mary Utne conducted in which several hundred dating couples and married couples were asked what they expected to give and get in relationships (Walster and Walster, 1978: 130–133; Walster, Walster, and Berscheid, 1978:236–242). Among the assets considered "critically important in a date or mate" were the ability to be friendly and relaxed in social settings, being intelligent and informed, being physically attractive and practicing good health habits, showing and expressing love to the partner, understanding and responding to the partner's

"I got what I wanted, but it wasn't what I expected."

(Drawing by Wm. Hamilton; © 1978
The New Yorker Magazine, Inc.)

emotional needs and personal concerns, providing security in the relationship at the same time the partner's individuality and freedom are respected, a willingness to work on a mutually satisfying sexual relationship, sexual fidelity, sharing in day-to-day household and financial responsibilities, being a good companion, sharing the load of decision-making, remembering special occasions such as birthdays and anniversaries, and being appreciative. There's no denying that people want their most intimate associations to be nothing short of *rewarding*.

RATIONALITY AND LOVE

For years, critics have charged that romantic love by its very nature inhibits rational discussion of elements beyond the couple's relationship itself—elements such as finances, status, education, occupation, and life-style. The point becomes clear in a popular song of recent years which emphasized that it doesn't matter "if we don't have money" because "I'm still in love with you, honey." Critics of romantic love would be quick to say, "They'll find out! When the honeymoon is over and the bills have to be paid, they'll find how little they have to hold them together. Those ecstatic feelings are going to fade away fast when the rent is due and groceries have to be bought and all the rest."

Added to these older criticisms are the new challenges to romantic love that are beginning to emerge on several fronts. Essentially, the goal is to make the mate-selection process more rational so that persons become more aware of the realities (actual costs and rewards) involved.

GENDER ROLES, PREMARITAL SEX, AND CONTRACEPTION

Rationality in mate selection involves many things that have already been touched upon in this book: deciding about gender roles (particularly as they affect women who opt for nontraditional roles), having some idea about future aspirations, and determining how to handle the question of sexual gratification.

Similarly, the introduction of contraceptive usage in premarital sexual relations is based upon rational considerations. Through the efforts of organizations such as Planned Parenthood, sexually active unmarried men and women are urged to take precautions against conceiving children. Even some religious groups and spokespersons have suggested that, despite traditional teachings on the wrongness of sex outside marriage, a realistic approach should take into account that many persons do engage in premarital sex and need guidance in avoiding undesirable consequences such as pregnancy and venereal disease. One minister (Shedd, 1968) has suggested that an unmarried couple who are engaging in sexual intercourse should have a "deep-think" discussion, considering every angle of what they are doing, and if they feel they cannot quit, they should determine to use contraceptives.

"Since you can't be as good as you wish," he writes, "will you at least be as smart as you can?" (p. 78). The essence of the advice is rationality.

AGE AT FIRST MARRIAGE

Rationality—realistically assessing rewards and costs—can also enter into the timing of marriage. In fact, it isn't difficult to see important connections between sex roles, contraception, pregnancy, and the age at first marriage. A teenager who expects only to be a wife and mother some day, and who begins dating early, engages in premarital sex, does not use contraceptives, and who becomes pregnant before she finishes high school, quite likely will marry young. Moreover, age at marriage has important consequences for the future. The adolescent girl in the example just mentioned has a high chance of becoming divorced. If she and her husband remain married, they are likely to have a higher number of children than if they had married later. And their income can be expected to be lower than that of persons who marry later.

The longer one delays marriage, the longer one is deferring the kinds of gratifications that marriage supplies. But for a woman to be able to delay marital rewards, alternatives have to take their place. The 1970 census shows that the more education persons have, the older they are when they marry (U.S. Bureau of the Census, 1973, PC (2)-4D, p. 266). We have already seen the association between education and gender roles. The more a woman seeks individualistic rewards for herself, the greater her autonomy and independence as a person, the later she is likely to marry. Men who favor such female reward seeking are also likely to marry later, choosing women who have taken time to complete their education and perhaps already embarked on careers.

Women who are less educated marry younger because fewer alternative rewards are open to them. When such women become pregnant out of wedlock, their marriage age is often lowered still further. Regardless of class background, however, premarital conceptions tend to have a lowering effect on age at marriage.

Nationally, the median age at first marriage in the United States had been dropping from about 1890 to 1956. (See Table 6-F.) During that same period, the gap between the sexes at the age of first marriage began to narrow. In 1890, there was a four-year difference between the age at which women married and the age at which men married; but by 1956, that difference had shrunk to two and a half years.

Beginning in 1957, one of the trends began to reverse. While the ages of marital partners continued to move closer together, there was a new trend for both sexes to wait longer to marry. By 1979 (latest available figures), the median age for males at first marriage was 24.4 years. For females, it had risen to 22.1. Explanations for the phenomenon of later marriage today may be related to changes in gender-role norms and shifts in life-styles—a topic to be discussed more fully in Part 4.

TABLE 6-F *Median age at first marriage, by sex: 1890 to 1979*

YEAR	MALE	FEMALE	YEAR	MALE	FEMALE
1979	24.4	22.1	1959	22.5	20.2
1978	24.2	21.8	1958	22.6	20.2
1977	24.0	21.6	1957	22.6	20.3
1976	23.8	21.3	1956	22.5	20.1
1975	23.5	21.1	1955	22.6	20.2
1974	23.1	21.1	1954	23.0	20.3
1973	23.2	21.0	1953	22.8	20.2
1972	23.3	20.9	1952	23.0	20.2
1971	23.1	20.9	1951	22.9	20.4
1970	23.2	20.8	1950	22.8	20.3
1969	23.2	20.8	1949	22.7	20.3
1968	23.1	20.8	1948	23.3	20.4
1967	23.1	20.6			
1966	22.8	20.5			
			1947	23.7	20.5
1965	22.8	20.6	1940	24.3	21.5
1964	23.1	20.5	1930	24.3	21.3
1963	22.8	20.5	1920	24.6	21.2
1962	22.7	20.3	1910	25.1	21.6
1961	22.8	20.3	1900	25.9	21.9
1960	22.8	20.3	1890	26.1	22.0

SOURCE: *U.S. Bureau of the Census, Current Population Reports. Series P-20, No. 349, "Marital Status and Living Arrangements: March 1979" (Washington, D.C.: U.S. Government Printing Office, 1980), p. 1.*

ARE MATE SELECTION PATTERNS CHANGING?

Up to now, the great majority of marriages have started out on a traditional footing. Owing to earlier sex-role socialization and to the basic nature of predominant dating and courtship patterns in most modern societies, the husband is designated as the *unique provider*, and the marriage centers around his job demands and its rewards. Decisions about such matters as where to live, the wife's job or educational plans, the family's life-style, and the number and spacing of children are largely determined by the husband and his occupational role.

The woman, in this traditional pattern, is designated as the warm, nurturant, supportive companion—an adjunct to her husband who orders her life in terms of his. Sociologist Shirley Angrist (1969) speaks of the "contingency orientation" that is part of a young girl's socialization. Women grow up having learned to be flexible and malleable so they can be prepared to adapt to whatever contingencies life may bring their way. Long-range goals, mastery, and self-determination cannot hold a high place in the lives of persons who know that plans may be disrupted at any point. The first contingency is marriage, but at the same time, a young woman knows she

Marriage at 13

When the deposed Shah Mohammed Reza Pahlavi ruled Iran, he decreed that the minimum age for marriage was to be 18—for both sexes.

Under the new regime of Ayatollah Khomeini, however, Iran has lowered the age limits for marriage to 15 for boys and 13 for girls. This conforms to ancient Islamic tradition based on the Koran, which holds that girls are physically prepared for marriage at the age of 13 and boys at 15.

Many modern or semi-modern parents in Iran's largest cities may refuse to go along with Ayatollah Khomeini's change, but religious Moslems in the country's rural villages will no doubt revert to the Koranic custom.

SOURCE: *Parade* Magazine, June 17, 1979, p. 15.

must be prepared for an occupation—just in case she doesn't marry, or in case the marriage ends through divorce or the husband's death. Within the marriage, pregnancy and child care are further contingencies for which she must be prepared to adjust. And likewise, women who hold traditional gender roles are constantly prepared to adapt to their husbands. ("If he does this, I'll do that." "If it fits in with my husband's plans, maybe I can do thus and so.") As to the immediate future (the next decade or two), we may expect that for a large proportion of persons (especially the noncollege population), the processes of dating, courtship, and marriage formation will continue to follow these traditional patterns.

Yet, a major theme of this book is change; and certainly changes are occurring in the area of mate selection. Marriage patterns have not stood still for the past 200 years, and they are not standing still today. As never before, they are coming under close scrutiny, and frank questions are being asked. Upturns in the age at first marriage may in part be a reflection of this new posture. The basis of the scrutiny is a very simple one: What good is marriage? In other words, how rewarding is it? Trends in mate selection in the future will reflect how that question is being answered.

CHAPTER HIGHLIGHTS

Historically and cross-culturally, the kin have influenced or controlled the choice of a marital partner. However, for the most part, the right to choose one's own mate has been a freedom taken for granted in the United States. At the same time, *dating* (getting together for a good time, without intending the relationship to lead toward marriage) is a relatively new custom; and over the years, both the term *dating* and the patterns of social interaction between the sexes have undergone changes. When it comes to selecting a mate, men and women view each other through an initial screening or filtering process represented by a potential "field of eligibles." Persons tend at first to screen out those whose educational level, age, race, and religion are very different from their own—although there are, of course, exceptions in all these areas. In general, we may say that persons are attracted to each other and maintain a relationship on the basis of the rewards they give one another. To speak of love is to speak of the *expressive rewards* persons seek from a partner—companionship, empathy, and physical affection. When two (or more) persons maintain ongoing instrumental and expressive exchanges, we may say a marriage exists; the basic elements are *sexual and economic interdependency*. But to be valid from a societal point of view, some form of *public disclosure* is also necessary. Marriage patterns are coming under close scrutiny today, and there appears to be a move toward making the mate-selection process more rational (in contrast to romantic love notions of being helplessly "swept off one's feet"). Frank questions are being asked as persons become more aware of the realities of marriage—the costs and rewards—and are weighing decisions about whether, when, and whom to marry with those realities in mind. Crucial to the bargaining process taking place between a woman and man before marriage are *gender-role patterns*, because they set the stage for what is likely to occur later within the marriage.

CHAPTER 7

(Erika Stone/Peter Arnold, Inc.)

HIS FAMILY, HER FAMILY: THE KIN

"You don't marry a person, you marry a family!" So goes the conventional folk wisdom, neatly summing up a fact of life. Even the most starry-eyed couple looking forward to marriage soon realizes they have to face up to their relationship to their families of origin. After marriage, *her* family and *his* family will likely come to be considered jointly as "our folks." And over the years, this will mean a variety of decisions, ranging from which family to visit for Thanksgiving to caring for a widowed parent in old age.

VARIATIONS IN PARENTAL POWER

At the outset, like parents in other times and cultures, modern American parents are concerned about their children's marriages and do everything they can do to make sure their young people don't strike a poor bargain on the marriage market. Parents like to be able to boast, "Our daughter married well. We're so proud of her and her husband," or "Our son has made a really good marriage. He married a wonderful girl from a fine family." Parents influence their children's marriage choices by the way they socialize them in their growing-up years and by the neighborhoods to which they move, the people with whom they associate, the schools to which the children are sent,

Families include two categories of people: those related by blood and those related by marriage. (© Sepp Seitz/Woodfin Camp & Assoc.)

Extreme Example of Parental Control over Young Person's Love Life

---

LAMIA, Greece (AP)—A 47-year old Greek woman was held captive for 29 years in a basement dungeon because her family was scandalized by a love affair she had when she was a teen-ager, police said today.

The discovery was made after one of the villagers "could no longer bear the woman's screams and decided to speak," police said.

Police said an investigation was underway against local authorities because they knew of the captivity but pledged themselves to secrecy for the family's sake.

The woman, Helen Karioti, was hospitalized suffering from malnutrition, anemia, partial mental derangement and other ailments, police said.

Her brother and two sisters, who kept her captive, were arrested and charged with illegal detention.

They testified that Miss Karioti was kept in the dungeon on their parents' orders because she had fallen in love and had an affair with another teen-ager. The parents died two years ago.

"Because of the scandal in the village and the family dishonor, our parents decided to lock her up," the oldest brother, Efthimios 59, testifies.

Police said the woman was dressed in rags, slept on a mud floor, and was fed scraps through a grate. Her fingernails were several inches long, and she had not seen the light of day since her captivity.

The woman was held captive at the village of Kostalexi, just outside Lamia.

SOURCE: "Family Imprisons Woman 29 Years over Love Affair," *Greensboro Record*, November 8, 1978.

---

and so on. In the past, one function of sororities and fraternities was to serve in the parents' stead, making sure that young men and women away from home supervision would mix with the "right" persons on the university campus so that marriages outside one's social class, race, or religious group would be less likely to occur (Rubin, 1973:201–203; Scott, 1965).

Except in unusual cases of coercion (see adjoining boxed insert), the degree of kin control over marital choice simply reflects the level of resource-based power held by the kin. Sociologist Richard Emerson (1962) has spelled out ways resources and power are linked together. Perhaps it would be helpful to rephrase some of his basic principles and think of them in the following way:

"WHAT I CAN OFFER YOU GIVES ME POWER OVER YOU."

(See Figure 7-1.) When A gives more benefits to B than B gives to A, A has the greater power. B needs the resources of A more than A needs the resources that B has to offer. In the past, parents obviously had more resources to hold out to their offspring than vice versa, and thus parents could choose or else strongly influence the selection of mates. Parents could offer to pass on farms,

FIGURE 7-1   *Party A has high degree of power because of the resources*
A is able to hold out to party B.

lands, and family businesses to those offspring who conformed to their
wishes with regard to marriage and could threaten to withhold such benefits
from children who refused to comply.

"IF YOU CAN GET AS GOOD OR BETTER REWARDS ELSEWHERE, I LOSE POWER."

A's high degree of power decreases as B finds other sources of benefits. (See
Figure 7-2.) As societies modernize and business and industrial enterprises
develop, young persons have opportunities to obtain both tangible and
intangible benefits apart from their parents. Thus the power of parents over
their children is diminished, with subsequent loss of influence in mate
selection.

"IF YOU DON'T WANT WHAT I HAVE TO OFFER, I LOSE POWER."

Another way that A's power can be limited occurs if B *renounces* the rewards
that A can give. (See Figure 7-3.) Even in premodern times, if a young person
decided to become a priest or nun, for example, both the material benefits
offered by parents and the prospect of marriage benefits became meaningless.
Church power totally replaced parental power. Or to take another example of
renouncing rewards, a young person might be willing to finance his or her

FIGURE 7-2   *Party A has limited power because party B has alternative source of rewards.*

FIGURE 7-3   *Party A has limited power if party B renounces the kind of rewards party A can give.*

own college education rather than accept parental money known to have "strings attached" as to college choice and career and/or marriage decisions. Similarly, persons have been known to renounce family inheritances in order to marry someone their parents disapprove of, and with the renunciation of these financial rewards comes a freedom from the parents' control.

"IF YOU CAN GET ME TO CHANGE MY MIND, MY POWER DECREASES."

Finally, power is limited on the part of parents if their children have the capability to persuade them to change their minds about marital choice. The process of persuasion can take the form of discussion, a bargaining session, blackmail, or various types of coercion, including actual physical force. Young people might threaten to elope if their parents withhold consent to marry, or they might use a premarital pregnancy to force their parents to go along with their wishes. There has been speculation that such may have been the case with Lord and Lady Randolph Churchill, the parents of Winston. Both families had opposed the marriage, and there had been interminable negotiations about financial arrangements and legal matters. Yet, rather suddenly, a surprisingly small, simple wedding took place; and Randolph's parents did not even attend. These factors, combined with the birth of Winston Churchill seven months later, raised in some people's minds a question about whether the marriage may have been forced by the young couple (Martin, 1969, chap. 4).

POWER IS RELATED TO SOCIAL CLASS

The ability to persuade or bargain with one's parents so they will accept one's own choice of a mate depends in great measure on the outside resources a young person has access to *as compared to the parents' resources.* In an upper-class family, for example, a son or daughter knows that the wealth his or her parents have available for their offspring is vastly greater than any material resources the offspring could expect to find elsewhere. In such cases, young persons hesitate to run the risk of being cut off from the family assets. Thus, we may say that in a sense, upper-class youth have *least* freedom in mate selection, middle-class youth more, working class still more, and lower-class most freedom of all. (See Figure 7-4.) Overall, however, in the United States and in Western society generally, young persons have considerable power and autonomy in selecting whom they wish to marry—as we saw in Chapter 6.

But what about kin relations after the choice of a marriage partner has been made? Exactly who are the kin anyway?

THE EXTENDED KIN: WHO ARE THEY?

If we were to plan an old-fashioned family reunion, we would invite two categories of people: persons related to us by blood and persons related to us by marriage. Anthropologists and sociologists use the term *consanguinity* (derived from the Latin word for blood and blood relations) to refer to those persons who share a common descent or biological heritage— for example, grandparent, parent, sister, brother, aunt, uncle, and cousin.

The word *affinity*, on the other hand, is used to describe a relationship that exists because of marital ties. *Affines* (from the Latin *adfinis*, meaning "one who is connected by marriage") are such persons as stepparents, stepbrothers and stepsisters, in-laws, and spouses of aunts and uncles. The term *extended kin*, like a family reunion, includes both blood relations and those related by marriage—or what anthropologist David Schneider (1968) calls relationships "in nature" and relationships "in law."

RELATIONSHIPS "IN NATURE"

We are born into some relationships. "Two blood relatives are 'related' by the fact that they share in some degree the stuff of a particular heredity," writes

FIGURE 7-4   *Differences in parental influence on youth, by social class.*

Schneider (1968). "Each has a portion of the natural, genetic substance. Their kinship consists in this common possession" (p. 24).

Blood relationships are in one sense permanent. A common biogenetic makeup links together persons in such relationships, regardless of whether they want to recognize their interconnectedness or not. Two brothers may separate early in life and perhaps may never speak to one another again. A parent may disown a child. A daughter or son might sever all relations with a parent. But "in nature," the persons are still related; one has not become an ex-brother or ex-parent or ex-son or ex-daughter. To speak about blood

In a society based on kinship, "the kin group is the unit within which economic, political, educational, and religious interaction occurs." (© Ginger Chik/Peter Arnold, Inc.)

relations in this way, explains Schneider, is to speak about the "order of nature," which he then contrasts with the "order of law."

RELATIONSHIPS "IN LAW"

Schneider points out that whereas heredity or "blood" binds together relatives in nature, "relatives *in law* are bound only by law or custom, by the code for conduct, by the pattern for behavior" (p. 27). A sister gets married, and her husband becomes our relative, our brother-*in-law*. Or a parent remarries, and a child immediately has a new relative—a stepmother or stepfather, possibly stepsisters and stepbrothers. A relationship in law sets up a certain interconnectedness between persons that is not there "naturally."

By the term *law*, then, Schneider (1968:27–29) simply means social customs, rules, and expectations in contrast to biological givens. He thus speaks of three classifications of relatives: (1) those related *only in nature*—for example, the continuing "blood" tie between an unwed parent and her or his baby even after the child's placement with adoptive parents; (2) those related *only in law*, such as a husband and wife, stepsiblings, a spouse and his or her parents-in-law, or parents and an adopted child; and (3) those related *both by blood and by social declaration* (or "law")—the relationship between offspring and natural parents (with certain exceptions related to adoption and to issues of legitimacy and illegitimacy), sisters and brothers, grandparents and grandchildren, and so on.

Finding Identical Twin Brother Alive "Greatest Thing"

LIMA, Ohio (AP)—James Springer, brought up believing that his identical twin had died at birth, says meeting his brother face-to-face was "the greatest thing that ever happened to me."

Born in August 1939 in Piqua, Ohio, the brothers were adopted by different families when they were only weeks old. They say they don't know what happened to their biological parents nor why they were put up for adoption.

Originally both sets of adoptive parents—Jess and Lucille Lewis and Ernest and Sarah Springer—had been told the other twin had died at birth. But Mrs. Lewis learned the truth by accident when she returned to probate court to complete adoption procedures.

As years passed, Lewis wondered about his brother, but said he hesitated to try to find him because he was "afraid it might stir up problems."

Eventually, however, curiosity overcame Lewis, who works as a security guard at a steel company. The Miami County Probate Court located the Springers, who had remained in Piqua, and wrote them that Lewis had inquired about his brother.

Springer, who lives in Dayton and works as a records clerk for a utility firm, then contacted Lewis and drove to his brother's home in Lima earlier this month.

Besides having the same first name, the brothers each first married and later divorced women named Linda. They have taken vacations on the same beach in St. Petersburg, Fla.

Each twin is six feet tall and weighs about 180 pounds. Lewis wears his hair short and combed back, Springer longer and combed forward, but with a change of style, either could readily pass for the other.

SOURCE: *Greensboro* (NC) *Daily News*, February 20, 1979.

What Do You Call Your Parent-in-Law?

Some informants call their spouse's parents by parental terms; that is, spouse's mother is "mother," "ma," "mom," etc., while father is "father," "pa," "pop," "dad," etc. Some use a parental-plus-name form such as Mother Smith (Father Smith), Mother Jane (Father Jim), or Ma Perkins (Pa Perkins). First-naming is also used here, but informants are often quick to state that first-naming is not always the first name used. If they met as strangers there is a tendency toward Mr. and Mrs.-plus-last-name forms, and only later when the spouse's parent permits or invites it is the first-name form used. Informants are also quick to note the prevalence of no-naming here.* One informant in his mid-fifties, married for more than twenty years, claimed that he had never addressed his wife's mother by any form whatever! If it was absolutely necessary to get her attention he made coughing or throat-clearing noises, to which she had learned to respond.

*This is the zero form of address. It may sometimes be articulated as a throat clearing or "uh hum" sort of noise. Erving Goffman first suggested the term "no-naming" to me some years ago.

SOURCE: David Schneider, *American Kinship: A Cultural Account* (Englewood Cliffs, NJ: Prentice-Hall, 1968), pp. 84–85.

Changing ideas about such classifications show up in changes in family law over a period of time—especially with regard to inheritance laws, support laws, adoption laws, divorce laws, definitions of legitimacy and illegitimacy, and laws and definitions surrounding what constitutes incestuous marriage (Farber, 1973). For example, states vary not only in whether statutes permit or prohibit the marriage of certain blood relatives, such as first cousins, but they also vary in whether or not the marriage of affines (persons related only "in law") is considered incestuous and thus forbidden—for example, marriage between stepbrothers and stepsisters or marriage between in-laws. Under existing statutes in some states, marriages have been declared illegal in cases involving a man who married his uncle's widow, a woman who married her father-in-law, and persons who have married stepchildren or stepgrandchildren (Einbinder, 1973–74: 783–784).

Sociologist Bernard Farber (1973) traces the origin of such laws to certain interpretations of the Bible and to definitions of affinity which have placed the person related "in law" in the same position as if she or he were permanently related by blood to relatives acquired through marriage—a view that was linked to concerns about property and which governed estate regulations. According to Farber, a shift in how the family is defined brings about a shift in laws pertaining to affinal marriages. He sees evidence of such a shift occurring.

Michael Einbinder (1973–74:783–787), an authority on family law, is persuaded that "logic favors the limitation or elimination of affinity statutes," and that they have outlived any usefulness they may once have served. Already "in some instances," he writes, "the effect of affinity statutes has been eliminated by the holding that the relation of affinity between one spouse and the blood relatives of the other ceases on the death of either spouse."

MARRIAGE: A SPECIAL CASE

Schneider (1968) speaks of marriage as "the example of a relationship in law within kinship *par excellence*" (p. 96). Furthermore, marriage is *"the* relationship in law which is specifically restricted to mean a sexual relationship." In marriage, a husband and wife are not "natural" relatives by "blood." But in this particular relationship of choice (a choice either made by them or for them), the two are declared by society to have entered an intimate relationship above which none ranks higher. According to the Judeo-Christian tradition, for example, they are declared to be "one flesh."

Sex, marriage, and kinship are intricately bound up together, as the following quotation from sociologist Bernard Farber (1973) makes clear:

> The biological acts of sexual intercourse and birth have everywhere generated norms and values that deal with the relatedness of people. . . . the stabilization of sexual relationships provides the basis for defining reciprocities associated with the institution of marriage. These reciprocities involve not only the married

couple but also persons related to them. In addition, the act of birth creates the necessity of establishing rules for determining responsibility for children over their life cycle, i.e., as they mature into adulthood, marry, procreate, age, and die; these responsibilities reflect the individual's concern for those related to him by descent. The claims established through marriage and descent thereby create for each individual a reservoir of relatives from whom he can anticipate certain kinds of conduct associated with "family" or "kinship" in the society in which he lives. The extent and nature of these claims vary from one society to another. (p. 4)

ROOTS AND BRANCHES: THE FAMILY TREE

Farber's reference to descent reminds us that our kin include those who have come before us and who will come after us. "Within families, all the symbolic input of past generations, all the give and take of present generations, and all the potentials for future generations come into play," writes sociologist Marvin Koller (1974:8).

A great surge of interest in family genealogies accompanied the 1977 television dramatization of Alex Haley's book *Roots*, which traced his own family lineage from its origin in Africa, through slavery, and into recent times. Even earlier, as social historians were showing increasing interest in the everyday lives of ordinary people of the past, ordinary people of the present were being encouraged to record their own family's history. For instance, a 1976 three-day conference at Washington, D.C.'s Smithsonian Institution featured workshops, lectures, and films to help persons "dig at the the family tree" by searching through diaries, old letters, wills, scrapbooks, other records, and memories. One of the speakers, anthropologist Margaret Mead, urged the audience to interview their grandparents and also to write something down for grandchildren as a way of anchoring family members in both past and future. Another speaker, psychiatrist Murray Bowen, pointed out that each person is a mix of sixty-four families over a period of five generations. And in ten generations, we're a mixture of just over one thousand families (Shenker, 1976)!

In American society, persons are considered part of both their mother's and their father's family. Anthropologists would say we have a system of *bilateral* descent reckoning. Kin on both sides are recognized, and a person is related to both sides of the family equally. Some societies, however, have a *unilateral* system of descent reckoning. One is considered to belong in a special sense to only one side of the family. This is especially true where societies are organized around *kin groups;* and with certain exceptions, one is assigned membership in only one such group (Lee, 1977, chap. 6). In a society based upon kinship as the "basic organizing principle," writes sociologist Gary Lee (1977), "it is often the case that no other kinds of groups or social structures exist independently of the kinship structure. . . . the kin group is the unit within which economic, political, educational, and religious interaction occurs" (p. 152). In such societies, where it is common to have a unilateral descent system, descent may be traced through the father's line (*patrilineal* descent) or through the mother's line (*matrilineal* descent).

Persons in our own society, which is *not* built around kin groups, often give little thought to descent. Schneider (1968:68) points out that most Americans have trouble remembering if their great-grandparents even had brothers and sisters, much less whom they married or how many children they had. And when he conducted an anthropological study of kinship in Chicago and asked informants to "List for me all the people whom you consider to be your relatives," it was quite common for informants to pause somewhere in their listing and ask, "Do you want the dead ones too?" Persons seemed unsure about whether to consider as relatives persons who were no longer alive. "Further," says Schneider, "there seemed to be a clear tendency for the dead to be omitted entirely in the very early phases of the collection of the genealogy, and only to come to light during later enquiry, often in another connection" (pp. 69–70).

RELATIVES: CLOSE AND DISTANT

We may think of relatives in terms of *genealogical* closeness—a parent is closer than a second cousin, for example. Or we may think in terms of *social* and *emotional* closeness: we *feel* closer to Uncle Jack and Aunt Sue than to Aunt Ellen and her husband. We may also think in terms of *geographical* closeness or distance: Grandma and Grandpa Smith live across the street, while Grandma and Grandpa Robinson live across the country.

Sociologists make various classifications of kin. Bert Adams (1968:12) is thinking in terms of genealogical closeness when he makes the distinction between the "kin of orientation" (those from the same family of origin—one's parents, brothers, and sisters) and the "secondary kin" (aunts, uncles, cousins, grandparents, and so on). Another sociologist, Ralph Piddington (1965), seems to have in mind degrees of social and emotional closeness when he divides kin into the categories of "noneffective kin" and "effective kin." *Noneffective kin* are persons genealogically related to an individual but with whom social relationships are not maintained.

Piddington further divides the category of *effective kin* (those with whom social interaction is maintained) into two subcategories: *priority kin* (members of one's own nuclear family and those kinfolk most closely related to it, particularly the parents of each spouse, where there is a certain degree of "recognized moral obligation to enter into appropriate social relationships") and *chosen kin* (more remote kin with whom one is not duty-bound to enter social relationships, but with whom such relationships are entered just the same out of free choice). Most of us can probably think of relatives in our own lives who fit into these various categories.

What Piddington calls the noneffective kin would probably fall into a category Schneider (1968) refers to as "that limbo called wakes-and-weddings relatives, shirt-tail relations, or kissin' kin" (p. 74). Persons seen only at funerals and weddings or who are relatives of relatives (thus brought into the extended kin network on somebody else's shirt-tails) are persons with whom

An Interview on Kinship Conducted by a Cultural Anthropologist with an Informant in the United States

Informant: You want like my son-in-law's parents? No, I never see or hear of them. They're not related to me.

Anthropologist: Do you have to be close to someone to have them related to you?

I: Yes. You use the relationship. When it drifts away you are no more related. You see I went to one of my husband's cousin's bridal showers. It was for a first cousin's bride-to-be. You only meet all these people there. You meet them like at weddings or showers, or bar mitzvahs or funerals. For these things they call on you and I answer the roll call. [Shrugs her shoulders as if to say, "What could be more simple?"] You walk in and you meet them all and half of them are pregnant, so you say, "How nice that you are going to have a baby, congratulations on becoming a new mother," and they say, "But I got two at home already." So you see how it is.

A: So are these people related to you?

I: They are when you meet them like that, but when you leave them, they're not any more.

A: They are not related between weddings and funerals, but they are during them?

I: Yeah.

A: Have they ever been related to you except at things like weddings and funerals and bar mitzvahs?

I: Oh, sure, but they aren't now. You see this business of being related to someone has to do with sociability. There are social cousins.

A: Can you give me any kind of rule for the person who is related to you?

I: Well, they got to be sociable with you or they're not related.

A: All right, but some of the people you named are related to you by blood, right?

I: Yeah, you get them by accident. You can't do anything about them—and grandchildren are the bloodiest!

A: Then you have relatives by accident. Your father's sister had children, right?

I: Yeah.

A: So they are related to you by blood.

I: No, they're not related. They'd have to be social. They were at one time, they aren't now.

A: Do any of your female first cousins have husbands?

I: Yes.

A: Are they your cousins?

I: I never see them.

A: Are their children related to you?

I: No, because I never saw them.

A: Your father's sisters—were they married?

I: Yeah.

A: Were their husbands considered uncles?

I: No, I never saw them.

SOURCE: David M. Schneider, *American Kinship: A Cultural Account* (Englewood Cliffs, NJ: Prentice-Hall, 1968), pp. 64–65.

there is little direct contact. That's what makes it hard in many cases to think of them as actual relatives. Schneider points out that most of us tend to think of our relations *as persons to whom we relate*—persons with whom we have social interaction. (See accompanying insert.) That is one reason persons have difficulty deciding whether or not a list of relatives should include those who have died. The social relationship—the interaction, the communication—has ceased; yet the dead may continue to occupy an important place on the family tree and in the memories of those who loved them.

Interestingly, Schneider (p. 17) found some regional and religion-based variations in terms used for distant kin. Northerners (especially from the Midwest) tended to speak of "shirt-tail relations." Catholics more than non-Catholics referred to "wakes-and weddings relatives." And southerners were more likely to talk about "kissin' kin" or "kissin' cousins." One common explanation for this last-mentioned term is given by Schneider: "The kiss is the sign that no matter how distant, such persons are nevertheless relatives and therefore are entitled to that sign of being a relative, the kiss" (p. 70).

One exception to the tendency not to count as relatives those with whom social contact is extremely rare or nonexistent is in the case of a famous relative. "During the course of the field work," Schneider writes, "we not infrequently encountered the statement that So-and-So, a famous personage, was a relative. Sometimes the relationship was traceable, sometimes not. When it was traceable, it could clearly be seen that this was the only relative of such distance on the genealogy, whereas closer relatives were unknown or unheard of" (p. 67).

THE EXTENDED KIN: INTERACTION PATTERNS

Earlier we saw the important part played by the kin in various times and cultures, particularly in such matters as mate selection, inheritance rights, and economic sanctions. In modern industrial societies of the Western world, however, the kin network does not have power to influence persons to the extent that was once the case (and which remains the case in some cultures). Since the kin no longer control economic resources, they lack the authority that would accompany such control. Industrialization makes it possible for persons to achieve on their own. They are no longer dependent on kinship connections for lands, houses, farms, and businesses; and they are no longer tied to where relatives are—either geographically or occupationally.

Aware of such changes, many persons have concluded that something worthwhile and beneficial has disappeared from modern life. They speak of the isolation of the nuclear family, the depersonalization of urban and suburban living, the evaporation of a sense of belonging, sharing, and community in contemporary society.

But is it really true that the modern nuclear family is isolated from the wider kin network? Has urbanization weakened kinship ties, or do such ties persist despite residential and social mobility? Sociologists have given a great deal of study to these questions and have been forced to do some rethinking over the years.

ISOLATION OF THE KIN—FACT OR FICTION?

During the 1930s and 1940s, a great deal was written about what came to be known as "classical urban theory," one aspect of which concerned the kin. Certain influential sociologists suggested that people in urban society are characterized more by "secondary" (impersonal) contacts than by "primary" (more intimate) relationships with family and close friends as in rural societies. Health needs, help in trouble, education, recreation—these were things no longer provided by the kin but rather by other institutions and agencies set up for such purposes as part of urbanization. At marriage, it was assumed that couples broke away to form families which served as independent units of social life entirely separated from the extended kin (Wirth, 1938; Parsons, 1943; see also summaries in Adams, 1968, and in Sussman and Burchinal, 1962).

However, in the 1950s sociologists began taking another look at the widely held view that urban dwellers lived isolated lives and had few primary relationships. Studies of kinship and friendship patterns among city residents showed that such persons were *not* cut off from intimate, meaningful social contacts in general, nor were they cut off from the kin in particular. What was discovered was simply that urban dwellers have more secondary, impersonal, or segmental contacts than rural persons do. But these secondary relationships are not *replacements* for primary relationships; they exist right alongside them (Adams, 1968:3).

The question of *why* kinship ties persist in modern society is discussed by sociologist Marvin Sussman (1966), who bases his explanation on exchange theory. Persons perceive that they receive valued rewards from kinfolk, and the kinfolk likewise perceive that they, too, receive as well as give valued rewards. Thus reciprocity goes on, with closest ties being maintained with those relatives who are viewed as having the greatest rewards to offer. These rewards may be tangible (for instance, gifts of money or material goods) or intangible (simple enjoyment of one another's company, grandparents' affection and attention to small children, and the like). Sometimes the rewards are in the form of mutual aid and service, such as baby-sitting or looking after the house while the nuclear family is on vacation. Just keeping in touch is in itself perceived as rewarding, whether such communication and contact is maintained through visits, letters, or phone calls. The notion of reciprocity in kin relationships also includes some sense of duty and moral obligation—particularly with regard to one's aging parents.

WHATEVER BECAME OF THE MULTIPLE-GENERATION HOUSEHOLD?

Most of us have an image of a bygone era in which large families lived happily together under one roof—parents, children, grandparents, maybe even an aunt, uncle, or cousin or two. And then industrialization came along and changed all that. Research by modern social historians, however, indicates that such a picture is more mythical than real. Extended families often lived nearby, but living together in the same house was the exception rather than the rule.

After making detailed studies of household size spanning over three centuries, Peter Laslett and his colleagues from the Cambridge Group for the History of Population and Social Structure have concluded that "mean household size remained fully constant at 4.75 or a little under, from the earliest point for which we have found figures, until as late as 1901." Furthermore, writes Laslett (1972), "there is no sign of the large, extended coresidential family group of the traditional peasant world giving way to the small, nuclear, conjugal household of modern industrial society. In England in fact, . . . the large joint or extended family seems never to have existed as a common form of the domestic group at any point in time covered by known numerical records" (p. 126). According to Laslett, the nuclear or simple family household of parents and children has been and continues to be the basic domestic unit. (See Table 7-A.)

For the most part, variations in household size were not so much related to the presence or absence of kin members as to the number of children at home, boarders or other live-in persons, and especially servants. "Servants were simply children who had changed households, from the parental home to the household of the master," writes Laslett (1972:147). Thus, children sent to learn some craft or trade or simply for employment would swell the ranks of the second household while lowering the number in their original home. This practice would seem to account for Laslett's finding a direct relationship between household size and social status: the higher the status, the larger the household, according to statistics from one hundred English communities from 1574 to 1821. Persons of higher status were able to hire more live-in workers (servants).

It was also common in the United States to record servants as members of a household. Social historian John Demos (1972:561) found in his studies of the Plymouth Colony that the average household size was just under six persons, most commonly consisting of a husband and wife and their children, with perhaps a servant or two, and possibly one or (more rarely) two grandparents. Since life expectancy was lower than now, the likelihood of

TABLE 7-A *Multigenerational households in sixty-one English communities, 1574–1821.*

	OVERALL (%)
1. *Proportion of households of one generation*	23.8
2. *Proportion of households of two generations*	70.4
3. *Proportion of households of three generations*	5.8
4. *Proportion of households of four or more generations*	0.0

SOURCE: Adapted from Peter Laslett, "Mean Household Size in England Since the Sixteenth Century," in Peter Laslett, ed. (with the assistance of Richard Wall), *Household and Family in Past Time* (London and New York: Cambridge University Press, 1972), p. 153.

having elderly grandparents in the home for very long was not great. Infant mortality was also high. Thus, even parents with large numbers of children frequently did not see all of them reach adulthood. Furthermore, just as was true in Europe, many children in Colonial America left their parental homes early to take up residence as servants in other homes. Such servanthood is described by Historian Edmund Morgan (1966):

> Most of the inhabitants of seventeenth-century New England either were or had been "servants." Today the word "servant" usually means a domestic: the cook, the butler, the chambermaid. In the seventeenth century it meant anyone who worked for another in whatever capacity, in industry, commerce, or agriculture, as well as in what we now call domestic economy . . . slaves were also known as servants, and so were apprentices. Servants, then, might differ considerably in their economic and social status. (p. 109)

The findings of one other study of household structure in North America also deserve mention, because they too show much less change in multigenerational household living than has generally been supposed. When sociologist Edward Pryor, Jr. (1972:575, 580) examined Rhode Island census records for two time periods, he found that in 1875, 82 percent of households consisted of nuclear families (parents and children, with no extended kin present). In 1960, the figure was 85 percent. In other words, in 1960, 15 percent of Rhode Island residents had some relative living with them—actually not a great deal less than the 18 percent with extended kin living with them in 1875. As to the presence of grandparents and grandchildren in the home, only 8 percent of Rhode Island households were multigenerational (three or more generations) in 1875. In 1960, 5 percent were multigenerational.

EXTENDED FAMILY TIES AMONG BLACKS

Among black Americans, the "informal absorption of families and individuals by relatives" has been a tradition from slavery onward (Hill and Shackleford, 1975). This absorption may occur in a number of ways, as is shown by social scientist Andrew Billingsley (1968:16–21) who has worked out a *typology* of black family structures (a way of classifying black families by type).

Billingsley starts out with three basic types of families: the married couple (the "incipient nuclear family"), the married couple with their children living with them (the "simple nuclear family"), and the solo parent whose children live with him or her (the "attenuated nuclear family"). The terms aren't hard to remember if you keep their meanings in mind. The word *incipient* refers to the initial stage of something; and of course, the husband-wife union is the necessary foundation stage in order for a simple nuclear family to emerge. The word *attenuated*, on the other hand, comes from a Latin term meaning to reduce. Billingsley is using it to describe a "reduced" family—one headed by a single (never married), separated, deserted, divorced, or widowed parent, rather than by two parents.

If any of these categories of families takes in other relatives, a distinct type of extended family household will come into being. The childless married couple (or with children grown and gone) who take in relatives become an example of "the incipient extended family." The married couple with children at home (simple nuclear family) become a "simple extended family" when they take other relatives in. And when other relatives join the solo parent household, an "attenuated extended family" household comes into being. According to Billingsley, all of these patterns exist in appreciable numbers among black families, and "to know which of the subtypes of extended family is under consideration would help to clarify the generalizations which may be made." In other words, it's as erroneous to speak of *the* black family as it is to speak of *the* white family—as though only one kind existed.

Secondary Members These various kinds of extended family households may include relatives who come by themselves or who bring families with them. When a family takes into its household persons who are alone, the family is adding what Billingsley calls *secondary members*. They may be a brother or sister or parent of the wife or husband; or they may be aunts, uncles, cousins, grandparents, nephews, nieces, or grandchildren.

"The historic fortitude and self-reliance of the black elderly is vividly reflected in the fact that they are more likely to take others into their households than to be taken into the households of younger relatives." (Shelly Rusten)

"Most dependent secondary members of black extended families are grandchildren," assert Robert Hill and Lawrence Shackleford (1975) after an extensive examination of the literature and statistics on black extended families. They observe that two-thirds of black children under eighteen who are not living with either parent are living with either grandparents or great-grandparents, whereas about one-fifth live with aunts and uncles.

"The historic fortitude and self-reliance of the black elderly is vividly reflected in the fact that they are more likely to take others into their households than to be taken into the households of younger relatives," Hill and Shackleford write, pointing out that only 4 percent of black families (headed by husbands and wives or by women alone) have persons sixty-five years or older living with them. In contrast, half of black families headed by women aged sixty-five or older are rearing children under eighteen who are not their own.

Subfamilies   In addition to welcoming individuals, sometimes a family takes in another family unit. Billingsley (1968:20) refers to such families-within-families as *subfamilies*. They might be an "incipient subfamily" (husband-wife pair), a "simple nuclear subfamily" (parents and children), or an "attenuated subfamily" (a solo parent with her or his children) who have found themselves in circumstances that necessitated moving into a relative's household.

Only 6 percent of all black families are subfamilies. Three out of four such families are made up of a female solo parent (usually separated, divorced, or widowed) and her children. Most commonly they move in with the woman's parents or parents-in-law—or in some cases, with her sister (Hill and Shackleford, 1975).

Other Patterns   Billingsley (1968) also speaks of the *augmented family*, a family augmented or enlarged by the addition of one or more persons from outside the family—in other words, nonrelatives. As one illustration, we may think of those black children who live in family arrangements where neither of their own parents is present. Six percent of such children are living with persons not related to them (Hill and Shackleford, 1975).

Some students of black family patterns feel that Billingsley's useful typology should go further and incorporate certain other arrangements: for example, two sisters living together (Williams and Stockton, 1973) or one of the most prevalent patterns of all—"the informal adoption of individuals and subfamilies by relatives who live alone (e.g., widowed grandmothers or aunts)" (Hill and Shackleford, 1975).

Base Households and the Extended Family Network   Extended black family networks tend to have one central place that everyone considers "home"—no matter how far away they live. Social work professor Elmer Martin and educator Joanne Mitchell Martin (1978) call this place the *extended family base household*, pointing out that "family reunions, outings, vacations, celebrations, weddings, and other family activities take place there" (p. 6). This base household, the very center of the extended family network, is the residence of "the dominant family figure"—the woman or man considered the leader of the extended kin, the person (usually elderly) most revered and respected among all the relatives and recognized as crucial to the family network's continuing existence (Martin and Martin, 1978:17).

The dominant family figure keeps the kin network informed of family news, provides counsel and moral support, helps work out family conflicts, passes down family history to younger generations, and instructs the young about their black heritage (including telling stories of what it was like for black people during the dominant family figure's growing-up years, as well as providing instructions on matters ranging from the preparation of soul food to survival techniques for getting along in the world). This person who serves as the hub of the extended kin also lays great stress on developing a sense of family. "Fostering a sense of family involves encouraging family members to feel some obligation to their relatives," write Martin and Martin (p. 18). While pointing out the mutual aid system throughout the black kin network, the Martins write that "the first option for anyone in need of a place to stay is the family base. . . . It can consist of three family members one month and ten the next, one generation today and three tomorrow. It can accommodate one family member temporarily until he can find work as well as another for the rest of his life" (p. 39). Housing that allows for such flexibility is much harder to come by in urban areas than in rural areas and small towns (Martin and Martin, p. 85).

Martin and Martin (1978) conducted in-depth interviews with up to twenty persons per family out of each of the thirty extended black families on which they focused—extended families comprised of over a thousand persons in all. Their definition of such families is useful in understanding black extended family patterns:

> When we speak of a black extended family, we mean a multigenerational, interdependent kinship system which is welded together by a sense of obligation to relatives; is organized around a "family base" household; is generally guided by a "dominant family figure"; extends across geographical boundaries to connect family units to an extended family network; and has a built-in mutual aid system for the welfare of its members and the maintenance of the family as a whole. Our definition grew out of our personal membership in families of this nature and our observations of similar families. (p. 1)

EXTENDED FAMILY TIES AMONG MEXICAN-AMERICANS (CHICANOS)

Like black families, Chicano families also maintain strong ties among the kin. They know they can count on one another in times of trouble or need and tend to prefer their system of mutual aid over Anglo-controlled agencies (Mirandé, 1977). At the same time, the independent nuclear family unit is the preferred family form. "One may choose to live near parents and other relatives, or perhaps even with them, out of economic necessity," writes

Chicano families also maintain strong ties among the kin, but the independent nuclear family unit is the preferred family norm. (© Joel Gordon, 1979)

sociologist Alfredo Mirandé (1977), "but the norm is that the nuclear family remains autonomous and in a separate residence" (p. 753). Yet, the nuclear family reaches out to relatives on both the father's side and the mother's side, with special emphasis on good relationships with the mother's sisters (Queen and Habenstein, 1974:429). Grandparents are highly loved and respected, and they are viewed less as authority figures than as sources of warmth and nurturance (Mirandé, 1977).

In one study of children in an urban *barrio* in Houston, Texas, Chicano children named only relatives when asked to name persons they loved. In contrast, Anglo children and black children named both family and nonfamily members, indicating that in their view friends as well as relatives were persons one could love (Goodman and Beman, 1971, reported in Mirandé, 1977).

However, this finding may not only indicate the great importance of the kin in the life of the Chicano child; it may also show that the line of demarcation between close friends and relatives is less clear. "Not only are relatives included as friends, but friends are symbolically incorporated into the family," Mirandé (1977:752) points out. Especially noteworthy has been the custom of *compadrazgo* or ritual kinship in which persons are linked together as *compadres*, a close friendship tie that is comparable to a kin tie and which originally functioned to provide substitute parents (godparents) for children in the event their own parents died (Mirandé, 1977). "While the *compadrazgo* may take a number of forms, notably coparenthood," write social

Becoming Relatives by Special Ritual

Compadrazgo or co-godparenthood is the relationship between the parents and godparents of a child christened in church; through their participation in the ceremony, godfathers and godmothers, the parents of the child, and sometimes the priest who baptized the child, become ritually related. Having replaced the "pagan" institution of blood brotherhood, compadrazgo became common all over Europe and still exists in parts of Greece, Spain, Italy, Serbia, and Russia. In England co-godparents were known as god-sibs (that is, "siblings in God"); here, however, the relationship did not endure as an institution and went through the vicissitudes of social change which the etymology of the word—from godsib to gossip—indicates.

. . . In most cases it is the reciprocal relations between the parents of the child and the godparents which explain why this Christian institution flourishes in parts of Europe and South America today. The christening ritual sanctions a relationship between friends and neighbors, the child acting as a symbol—an expression and a guarantee of this friendship. . . .

These ritual relations between friends serve very practical purposes and at the same time offer a means of greater emotional fulfilment and an assurance that an individual does not stand alone. Compadres lend each other money; a woman will work in her friend's house when she is sick; they mourn the death of a relative. Compadres must be kind and friendly and a network of ties . . . helps maintain community order. . . . Throughout Latin America, for example, it is a friendly bond which may be used to forestall sexual aggressiveness; you can avoid trouble with a man who is determined to seduce your wife by making him your compadre! He cannot refuse the offer of friendship and once it is made the wife is henceforth sexually taboo.

SOURCE; Robert Brain, *Friends and Lovers* (New York: Basic Books, 1976), from Chapter 4.

scientists Stuart Queen and Robert Habenstein (1974), "by providing fictive kinship linkages, its effect is to generate social and interpersonal cohesion and thus to reduce the potential extrafamilial conflict that might arise in a highly family-centered society. Coparenthood, which is considered the most important, links two families through the baptismal ritual" (p. 429).

HOW IMPORTANT ARE THE KIN?

Of course, the relative importance attached to friendship and kinship pertains not only to Chicano society but to the larger society as well. For one thing, close relationships require an investment; and we are not likely to enter or maintain relationships in which our investment doesn't pay off. Sociologist Mark Granovetter (1973) suggests that "the strength of a tie is a . . . combination of the amount of time, the emotional intensity, the intimacy (mutual confiding), and the reciprocal services which characterize the tie" (p. 1361). However, since everyone has a limited supply of time and emotional energy (scarce resources), the extent to which we invest in any one relationship can affect the amount of resources left for other relationships (Shulman, 1975). Persons who invest their time and energy heavily in the extended kin network, for example, and are rewarded in reciprocal fashion, may attach less importance to outside friendship. The reverse could be true, also. Or time and effort poured into one's own nuclear family can cut down on time and effort put into extended kin relations (Robins and Tomanec, 1962).

Life Cycle Variations in Kin Interaction Various researchers have studied degrees of involvement with kin, friends, neighbors, and voluntary associations at different stages of life (Shulman, 1975; Mattessich, 1978). As sociologist Norman Shulman (1975) emphasizes, "at each stage people tend to establish and sustain networks of relationships geared to the needs and concerns of their particular stage of life" (p. 820).

Data from Shulman's sample of 347 urban respondents indicated that single young adults are least likely to name relatives among those persons closest to them; friends are considered of greater importance. Shulman explains this as resulting from "the nonfamilial nature of the major concerns of people at this stage of the life cycle," when interest centers on educational and career concerns, enjoying companionship, and seeking a mate—all of which contribute to a preference for interaction with persons of similar age and interests.

However, when persons enter marriage and especially as they become

For young, single urban dwellers, friends are considered more important than relatives. (© Ginger Chih, 1978)

parents, relatives take on a new importance. "Kin involvement peaks noticeably for individuals with one or more pre-school children," writes sociologist Paul Mattessich (1978). "Needs for advice, for help with child care, and for financial assistance act to push people at this stage toward kin, as does the simple desire to 'show off' the children. The interest of kin, especially grandparents, to see the children is probably higher at this stage than at any other" (p. 11).

Social anthropologist Elizabeth Bott (1957), after intensive interviews with a small number of English families, describes the common life cycle pattern as consisting of "several phases of expansion and contraction." Informants remembered childhood contact with grandparents, aunts, uncles, and cousins, in addition to involvement with their own parents and siblings. "However," writes Bott, "most people indicated that in late adolescence and early adulthood they had broken away from their parents and siblings to some extent, and contacts with extrafamilial kin were dropped or greatly reduced" (pp. 156–157). After this contraction phase, there came another expansion phase after marriage and children.

Calling on the Kin for Help   Regardless of the stage of the life cycle, interaction among kin is likely to be high during times of disasters, such as floods or tornadoes. For many people at such times, relatives provide a variety of services ranging from baby-sitting to offering temporary shelter, food, clothing, and even small loans (Drabek et al., 1975).

But what about the everyday problems and crises not related to major disasters? To whom do people turn? Sociologist Reuben Hill (1970) found differences associated with what stage of the life cycle persons happened to be in. His study focused on three generations of families: (1) a "grandparent" generation, with virtually all children launched; (2) a "parent" generation, contracting in size as children were being launched or were already gone from the home; and (3) a "married children" generation, just beginning its childbearing stage and thus expanding in size.

When respondents were asked to indicate preferred sources of help in times of crisis, the grandparent generation reported that they turned first to their children (the middle or "parent" generation). Second, they turned to friends among their own peer group, then to health and welfare agencies, then to private specialists, and last of all to their married grandchildren.

The parent generation preferred to turn first of all to their parents (that is, the grandparent generation) and next to their married children. Turning to friends was the third choice of this middle generation, then to private specialists, and last to their own brothers and sisters.

What about the "married children" generation? They reported that they turned first to their parents and second to private specialists. Their third choice was friends, followed by sisters and brothers, with help sought from grandparents their fifth choice (Hill, 1970:69).

Why Do the Kin Help?   Sociologist Alvin Gouldner (1960) has written on the "norm of reciprocity," which helps explain the stability of a social system.

Quite simply, reciprocity is the process that goes on as we give benefits to others (through what we do for them or give to them), which induces them to provide benefits for us in return.

Although Hill (1970:76–80) does not entirely disagree with those sociologists who explain intergenerational kin exchanges in terms of the norm of reciprocity, he attaches importance to two other norms that may be operative as well: "filial obligation," defined as "the norm of responsibility of children for their parents"; and *noblesse oblige*, the "sense of obligation of the more advantaged family to aid those perceived to be in less fortunate circumstances."

However, both filial obligation and *noblesse oblige* fall under Gouldner's explanation of how the norm of reciprocity works. The parents in their middle years who are giving to their own parents (the grandparent generation) may indeed feel a "filial obligation," but that sense of obligation stems from knowing that in the past their parents were the ones who gave to them. Gouldner (1960) emphasizes that reciprocity "tends to structure *each* role so as to include both rights and duties" (p. 169). Parents have rights, but they also have duties toward their children. And children have rights, but they also have duties toward their parents. To some extent, these reciprocities exist throughout life.

Gouldner also refers to a universal norm of *moral obligation* to reward those who have earlier rewarded us. This norm, part of what reciprocity is all about, seems more fitting than *noblesse oblige* in explaining expecially the pattern Hill found in which the grandparent generation may frequently find themselves "dependents," with their grown children (the parent generation) serving as "patrons" (p. 304).

Where relatives receive aid but are unable to give, they may develop a sense of dependency that is humiliating and embarrassing to them and results in less visiting with the kin or participating in kin activities (Hill, 1970: 76–77, 304). This lends support to the findings of numerous studies by social psychologists that show that "while reciprocal exchanges breed cooperation and good feelings, gifts that cannot be reciprocated breed discomfort, distress, and dislike" (Walster, Walster, and Berscheid, 1978:107).

DOES MOBILITY AFFECT KIN RELATIONS?

Three sociologists have described several different kinds of mobility: residential, personal, vertical, and ideational (Burgess, Locke, and Thomes, 1963:363–384). As applied to kin relations, we may say that persons may reside *geographically* close to or distant from kin. Similarly, persons may be close or distant in terms of the *personal experiences* they have had—trips, social contacts, life enrichment experiences that set them apart from others in their family, for example. Third, persons may be close to or distant from their kin in terms of *social status* because they or the kin have moved either up or down socioeconomically (vertical mobility). Last, persons may be close or distant from various kin members because of the way they have moved in terms of the *ideas* they hold and the *values* they espouse—for example, their religious beliefs and allegiance to some group may set them apart from the kin or may bring them closer.

Most studies of kinship and mobility have concentrated on either *geographical* (residential) mobility or on *socioeconomic status* (vertical) mobility. Little attention has been given to the other two areas mentioned above—except where changes in personal ideas, values, social contacts, and life experiences are related to changes in social status.

Geographical Mobility and Kin Interaction   Sociologists Lee Robins and Miroda Tomanec (1962) measured closeness of interaction with relatives in terms of "the number of avenues used for communication, performance of services, and fulfillment of obligations." As might be expected, they found that closeness decreases when relatives are geographically distant. At the same time, they write, "We do not know from our data whether geographic distance also makes relatives *feel* subjectively less close." Maintaining contact with geographically distant kin is costly—whether costs are measured in terms of financial outlay (costs of trips, phone calls, mailing gifts, and so on) or in terms of time and energy invested in writing letters, planning and making visits, entertaining relatives as houseguests, and the like.

In kin relationships that are considered rewarding, intimacy is maintained regardless of distance. Bott (1957) suggests that the crucial criteria for separating these relationships from other less intimate ones are "the amount of contact combined with the amount of effort people put into making special visits to the relative" (p. 121). Bott's study showed that persons may be "close" to some relatives even though they live far away. At the same time, they may be less close (in terms of social contacts and feelings of affection) to other relatives who live nearby (pp. 126–128).

Research by sociologist Bert Adams (1968:23–24) showed that unskilled and semiskilled blue-collar persons, persuaded they could find work as well in one industrial area as another, frequently relocated for the precise purpose of getting away from unsatisfactory kin relations. At the same time, good kin relations could keep blue-collar persons living in an area. Relationships matter more than job opportunities in determining where to live—a pattern that contrasts with that of white-collar persons, where "opportunity takes precedence over relationships," says Adams. White-collar repondents told him they would like to be able to see their kin more often but that occupational demands had meant moving away.

Status Mobility and Kin Interaction   What happens to kin relations when a working-class person moves into the middle class? Contrary to what we might expect, most available studies indicate that kin interaction isn't greatly affected by status mobility (Klatzky, 1972:40). For example, in a study of 305 black parents representing 178 family units, Harriette McAdoo (1978), a professor of social work, looked at four patterns of mobility. The highest percentage of her sample (62 percent) were newly middle class after two generations of working class; another 23 percent had grandparents in the lower class, parents in the working class, and were themselves middle class;

still others had parents who had been born into the working class but had moved to the middle class into which the respondents had been born (6 percent); and last, some respondents (9 percent) reported having been middle class for three generations.

What did McAdoo find? "The kin help system had been maintained before, during, and after mobility," she writes. "Parents did not have to cut themselves off from their families to become upwardly mobile. Eighty percent of the families indicated an intensive involvement in the kin exchange system. . . . No differences in kin help were found between those born middle class or working class, nor between the four mobility patterns." She did find, however, that "those newly mobile were more pressured to share with those of lower income than those who were born middle class."

Robins and Tomanec (1962), in interviewing 140 college students, found that although the students came from middle-class homes and expected careers in high-status occupations, "they showed no preference for white collar over blue collar relatives" at this point in life.

Of all relatives, contact with *parents* is especially maintained regardless of whether persons have moved up or down in status (Bott, 1957:148–149; Klatzky, 1972:38–41). The encouragement and support of parents is important to their upwardly mobile offspring (Adams, 1968:171), and the success of that son or daughter reflects positively on the parents (Bott, 1957:149). On the other hand, the downwardly mobile person may draw comfort and feel less of a failure through identifying with his or her parents who remain at a higher status level (Klatzky, 1972:40; Litwak, 1960).

SEX ROLES AND KIN INVOLVEMENT

Wives more than husbands tend to keep up kinship ties regardless of geographical distance. And they tend to keep in closer touch with their own side of the family than with the husband's side (Robins and Tomanec, 1962; Berardo, 1967; Farber, 1966:76–77; Bahr, 1976). The key role played by females in maintaining kin contacts is dramatically illustrated by sociologist Felix Berardo's (1967:553) finding that if a mother died, a family's interaction with the extended kin fell almost as low as if both parents had died. But if a father died, the frequency of kin contact was almost as high as if both parents were alive.

However, sociologist Howard Bahr (1976:77–78)points out that maintaining kin contact through letters, phone calls, and visits does not tell the whole story. "In fact," he writes, "the apparent female domination of the kinship role may stem largely from the husband's default or delegation of kinship tasks. He seems content for the wife to function as chief correspondent, executive secretary, or family clerk. But when the decision is whether to provide economic aid to relatives, or when there is overt disagreement [about the kin], he is likely to make the decision." Bahr's assertion is based on a study of over two hundred couples randomly selected from lists of parents whose children were in the third grade.

Some sociologists, thinking in terms of the traditional family where the wife is not employed, have suggested that a wife's fulfillment of kinship obligations is only to be expected. After all, she has more time available. Since Bahr found that employed mothers, as well as mothers with large families, were less involved in keeping up communication with the extended kin, he suggests the "available time" idea may have merit. But although this may be one explanation for the reduced kin contact of mothers with large families, it doesn't necessarily explain why full-time employed mothers were found to be "less likely to affirm obligations to kin and less likely to feel remiss in their interaction with them" (Bahr, 1976:75).

Perhaps we are seeing here what we see in the case of husbands: a concentration on the instrumental tasks of income-producing and achievement in the economic-opportunity system, with lesser importance attached to performing traditional expressive duties toward the extended kin. Interestingly, however, Bahr found that the women "most kin-oriented" in terms of feeling obligation and concern about meeting that obligation were not the full-time homemakers but rather the wives who were employed part-time.

That wives more than husbands have shown greater involvement with kin relations is not surprising in view of traditional socialization patterns. As we saw earlier in this book, females are taught to be nurturant and concerned about interpersonal relationships, while males learn early the importance of putting their energies into achievement. Thus, upon marriage, couples may find themselves dividing up tasks and responsibilities on the basis of traditional gender-role norms—which means that caring for the kin, like caring for the children, is assigned to the person trained for nurturance, namely, the female.

However, just as less rigidity in gender roles is associated with higher levels of education and higher status in general. Bahr (1976) found "an inverse relationship between socioeconomic status, as measured by income, education, or occupation, and the proportion of husbands who defined communicating with kindred as primarily a wife's responsibility" (p. 73). In other words, the more education and the higher the husband's income, the less he was likely to think his wife should be the one to keep in touch with relatives; and the more he was likely to feel he too was responsible for such contact.

CHAPTER HIGHLIGHTS

In general, the degree of kin control over marital choice simply reflects the level of resource-based power held by the kin, especially parents. The kin include both persons related by blood ("in nature") and by marriage ("in law"). The persistence of kin ties may be explained in terms of reciprocity; that is, kinfolk perceive their relationships rewarding as they give to and receive benefits from one another. A tradition of strong ties among the kin is especially pronounced among black and Chicano families. Generally speaking, for most persons, interaction with kin tends to vary according to the stage of life one happens to be in at any particular time. But regardless of the stage of the life cycle, interaction among kin is likely to be high during times of disaster. And if kin relationships are considered rewarding, intimacy is maintained regardless of geographical distance. However, mobility is not only a matter of geography. Persons may move closer to or farther from the kin in terms of personal experiences, ideas and values, and socioeconomic status as well. Yet, contrary to what we might expect, most studies have indicated that kin interaction isn't greatly affected by status mobility, especially when it comes to interaction with parents. Contact with parents is usually maintained regardless of whether persons have moved up or down in status. One indication of traditional sex-role socialization patterns with regard to kinship interaction shows up in findings that wives more than husbands keep in touch with relatives, expecially maintaining close ties with their own side of the family.

PART FOUR

ALTERNATIVES TO TRADITIONAL MARRIAGE AND FAMILY

CHAPTER 8

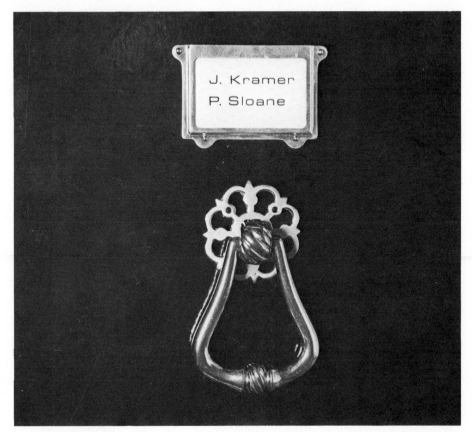

J. Kramer
P. Sloane

(Kenneth Karp)

THE COHABITATION AND GAY MARRIAGE ALTERNATIVES

At a conference on religion and social issues, a handsome bearded man in his thirties passes around a photograph of his family as he talks about his love for his spouse and children. The picture shows two men and two children, all smiling happily. The man is a partner in a gay marriage. His partner is the father of the children and has legal joint custody with his former wife, who is grateful for the loving devotion the two men give to the children. She tells her former husband's male spouse that he is part of the family. Often the three parents and the children get together for picnics, birthdays, and holiday celebrations.

In another section of the country, a leading feminist is being interviewed on a talk show. She is asked why she never married and how she feels about marriage as an institution. She replies that marriage as it presently exists is stifling to wives and prevents a woman from fulfilling her total potential. She announces that she has no interest in marrying unless present arrangements of marriage and the family are drastically changed. Until such a time, singleness is preferable.

On another TV talk show, a young unmarried couple tell why they have chosen to live together. The man speaks of the unhappiness of his own childhood and the heartbreak of his parents' divorce, and how this soured him on the institution of marriage. As he speaks, he cuddles the squirming infant on his lap. The woman tells of her concern for their child's well-being. She maintains that she and the baby's father are together because they want to be, not because they *have* to be, adding that their relationship is not dependent upon a contract signed in accordance with society's decrees. Like many other unmarried couples who have chosen to live together, this man and woman feel that marriage can be a trap, forcing people into roles and destroying the freedom and spontaneity they enjoy in their present arrangement.

Because such examples are given wide coverage in the mass media, there is much talk about the "death of the family" in modern society. However, many social scientists, including demographers, view the matter differently. Demographers are specialists in the study of population characteristics and are able to point out trends in births, deaths, marriages, divorces, and other areas of vital concern. "The family (in modified form) will go on," predicts Census Bureau demographer Paul C. Glick (1979:5), emphasizing that "the overwhelming majority of American people still live in nuclear families that include a married couple and/or a parent and one or more children."

At the same time, some persons are interested in different life-styles and new definitions of "family." Even Glick's description of the nuclear family is stretched to include solo parent situations. In this unit, we'll be examining some of these alternatives to conventional marriage and family, giving special attention to unmarried living together, homosexual marriage, singleness and single parenthood, communal living, and group marriage. This chapter will explore the first two of these, because both cohabitation and homosexual partnerships are examples of pair bonding that force us to re-examine definitions, customs, and laws pertaining to marriage.

COHABITATION—LIVING TOGETHER WITHOUT MARRIAGE

One of the most talked about emerging life-styles in recent years has been the phenomenon usually called *cohabitation*—an arrangement in which unmarried opposite sex partners set up a household together.

HOW WIDESPREAD IS COHABITATION?

Although we don't know exactly how many unmarried persons choose to live together in a marriagelike situation, a close but cautious look at statistics from the United States Bureau of the Census can provide some clue. In 1977, out of all people and all households in the United States, about 1 percent included an unmarried woman and man living together. But if instead of looking at the total population, we concentrate only on unmarried adults in the population, the percentage jumps to 3.6. That would mean that about one out of twenty-eight unmarried adults is living with someone to whom she or he is not married or otherwise related. If we start with another base, two-person

The mere fact that two unrelated adults share living quarters together tells us nothing about the nature of their relationship. (Joel Gordon)

Cohabitation Dispute Ends at Justice. Agreement Says Lifestyle No Longer a Factor in Hiring.

The Justice Department has agreed that it will no longer refuse to hire a job applicant solely because he or she is living out of wedlock with a member of the opposite sex.

The agreement, in the form of a consent order, signed by U.S. District Court Chief Judge William B. Bryant, ends four years of litigation over the tricky issue of the government agency's right to deny employment because of an applicant's personal living arrangements. . . .

The consent order applies only to the central offices of the Justice Department and not to affiliated agencies such as the FBI, the Drug Enforcement Administration, the Bureau of Prisons, the U.S. Marshals Service, the Immigration and Naturalization Service and the Law Enforcement Assistance Administration.

The order grew out of a lawsuit brought in 1975 by Kathleen Bishop, then a student of Catholic University law school, who was turned down for a summer law clerk job after she acknowledged under questioning that she was living with a man out of wedlock. . . .

The brief but carefully worded consent order says that the Justice Department agreed it "shall not find a person unsuitable for employment solely because that person resides with and/or engages in sexual intercourse with an unrelated member (or members) of the opposite sex." . . .

The consent order adds, however, that the department may find a job applicant unsuitable if his or her residence or sexual intercourse with another person "affects job fitness."

While the order does not specify what might adversely affect "job fitness" it suggests that such a judgment must be based on specific evidence, rather than "unsubstantiated conclusions."

SOURCE: Paul W. Valentine, the *Washington Post*, November 13, 1979, p. C1.

couple households, we find that 4.2 percent of such households consist of an unrelated man and woman (Glick and Norton, 1977:33). This figure is considerably lower than in Sweden, for example, where 12 percent of living-together male-female couples are unmarried (Trost, 1975:678).

In actual figures, in 1977 nearly two million adults in the United States were living with an unrelated adult of the opposite sex. Women who had unrelated men living with them in the woman's household numbered 351,000. And men who had unrelated women living in numbered 606,000 (Glick and Norton, 1977:32–33). At the same time, it's important to remember that the fact of two unrelated adults sharing living quarters together tells us nothing about the nature of their relationship. "Some of these persons had a landlady-tenant or landlord-tenant relationship," write Glick and Norton, "and some were paid employees of the householder." They continue:

Most of them, however, were either in the same age group or in an adjacent age group, and most of them probably lived as partners, roommates, companions, or friends. A detailed analysis of the data by age of the man and woman reveals that more unmarried couples now consist of a young man sharing living quarters with a young woman, whereas in 1960 [what the Census Bureau refers to as] unmarried couples included more middle-aged and elderly women with a young man as a tenant. (p. 32)

VARIED INTENTIONS

When a man and woman decide to move in together, even though they have not met licensing and ceremonial requirements, their intentions may vary. In some cases, they may be thinking in terms of a test run to see if they're suited to be marriage partners later on. Their living together before that time would be considered a *trial marriage*. In other cases, the couple might be interested in a do-it-yourself marriage without the bother of state requirements such as blood tests, obtaining a license, and so on. They think of themselves as married and present themselves to the world as such, even though they have never had a wedding ceremony performed. Their union would be considered a *common-law marriage* in states where such marriages are recognized. A third category of living-together arrangements is entered by couples who are not necessarily interested in either testing out future marriage possibilities or in considering themselves married in the common-law sense. They simply set up housekeeping together for companionship and convenience in an *ad hoc arrangement*.

COMMON-LAW MARRIAGE

Trial lawyer Barbara Hirsch (1976:3) defines common-law marriage as "the lawful union of man and woman by declaration, intention, and conduct, which in certain domiciliary states joins the parties in a relationship that may be severed only by death or divorce." Where common-law marriage is recognized, the legal rights and duties are the same as in any other marriage; and the children of such a union are considered legitimate. But "both parties must actually intend their relationship to be a marriage," Hirsch emphasizes. And of course the couple must be living in a state that recognizes common-law marriage at the time they establish their relationship. Only in such a case could a couple expect the courts to consider their marriage authentic.

Hirsch explains further what common-law marriage means:

They are Mr. and Mrs. They may file joint tax returns and in all other respects conduct themselves as married people. Having established that relationship, they are married. If they live in a common-law state and that state is their home, then they are married wherever they travel and wherever they later reside. The only way to end a marriage, ceremonial or common-law, is by death or divorce. Annulment doesn't count because that is a legal procedure which declares null and void only a purported marriage which was, in fact, no marriage at all. (p. 4)

The legal recognition of common-law marriage may be traced to the colonial period of American history when distance made it impractical if not impossible for some couples to travel to a marriage license office or to find an authorized officiant to perform a marriage ceremony. Currently, only thirteen states, the District of Columbia, and one territory (the Virgin Islands) permit couples to form common-law marriages (Kephart, 1977:336–337).

There seems to be a growing trend toward abolishing the institution of common-law marriage, mainly because of the many legal complications associated with it. Questions may arise over the legitimacy of offspring or the settlement of estates. Sociologist William Kephart (1964) refers to the costly court battles that are often necessary for a common-law wife after her husband dies. "Unless she can prove that a common-law marriage existed— seldom an easy task—neither she nor her children are entitled to the property rights or inheritance that normally are theirs" (p. 950). Sometimes upon the death of a wealthy bachelor, women who claim to have been common-law wives step forth hoping to gain an inheritance. And sometimes such claims are made even with regard to a married man. For example, after a 1974 air crash in which a honeymooning couple was killed, a woman filed suit with the airlines claiming she had lived as the groom's common-law wife and had several children by him. Second spouses of persons who have been in common-law marriages often run into particular difficulties with regard to estate settlements, because a common-law husband or wife may have had the mistaken notion that getting out of such a marriage is just as simple as getting into it, not knowing that certain state laws may require a formal divorce decree. The subsequent spouse in such cases may have entered in good faith what he or she thought was a legal marriage only to find that the courts consider it to have been an illicit cohabitation because of a former common-law marriage which was never formally ended (Sussman, Cates, and Smith, 1970:270).

For reasons such as these, some legal experts and social scientists believe that the institution of common-law marriage should be abolished and that the only unions considered valid should be those in which the man and woman have secured a license from the state, had a wedding ceremony of some sort, and have obtained a properly signed marriage certificate. Other authorities disagree, pointing out that this would condemn many children "to bastardy" and increase injustice and suffering in the world rather than alleviate it. "This is particularly true among those social and economic classes who have not accepted middle-class standards of marriage," says one professor of law. "Certainly American marriage law should tolerate this much cultural diversity" (Clark, 1968, as quoted in Krause, 1971:18).

Common-law marriage is not easy to define, since various states and even various courts tend to interpret it differently. For one thing, whether or not a union has been a valid marriage according to common law is something that is determined *after* the union has been entered. In the words of one law professor: "As a doctrine [common-law marriage] has little or no effect at the outset of the parties' relationship. It comes into play after the relationship has existed for some time, for the purpose of vindicating the parties' marital expectations" (Clark, 1968:58). Harry Krause (1971:17–18), another professor of law, refers to a threefold test for such a marriage. The union is regarded as a valid marriage "if the intending spouses have presently consented to be husband and wife, if the marriage has been consummated, and if the spouses have publicly held out each other as such." He explains that "the requirement of 'present consent' to marriage distinguishes the resulting relationship from an engagement to be married at a future time." It also distinguishes it from a trial marriage.

TRIAL MARRIAGE

Before purchasing a new car, it's only rational to take it out for a test-drive first. Some people have suggested that marriage should follow a similar pattern, allowing a test period of living together before making the final commitment. Such an arrangement usually goes by the name *trial marriage*. Some proponents suggest a structured form, others an unstructured.

Structured Trial Marriage Structured trial marriages would be institutionalized in some way, with regulations by society to legitimate the union. The idea in itself is not new, although new variations continue to be suggested from time to time. Maurice of Saxony was already suggesting trial marriage in the eighteenth century because he considered marriage for life "a betrayal of the self, an unnatural compulsion." His proposed solution was the formation of temporary marriages, with contracts acknowledged as being for a limited period of time (Berger, 1971).

A similar idea was proposed by one Judge Ben B. Lindsey. He called his concept "companionate marriage" and wrote up his ideas for *Redbook* magazine in 1926, only to meet with ostracism and severe criticism after the article's appearance. Shortly afterward, Bertrand Russell proposed a similar idea, suggesting it would be especially applicable to university students as a better way of channeling sexual desires than was the case with the "excitement of parties and drunken orgies" during the Prohibition Era. Russell was rewarded for his efforts by scandal, slander, and the loss of his teaching position at the City College of New York. Americans made it clear that they were not ready for a revision of marriage customs (Lindsey, 1926, 1927; Russell, 1929; Skolnick, 1973:248).

Forty years after its publication of Judge Lindsey's article, *Redbook* published another much-discussed article on trial marriage—this time by anthropologist Margaret Mead (1966). Mead proposed a two-step marriage arrangement, each step differing in commitments and responsibilities. The first (or trial) part would be called *individual marriage*. It would be entered by a simple ceremony, carry limited economic responsibilities, would not allow children, and would be easy to end. The second (or permanent) step would be called *parental marriage*. It would be entered only by those couples who, after the first step of individual marriage, desired to form a lifetime relationship and undertake the obligations of parenthood.

Responses to Dr. Mead's proposal varied from praise for its emphasis on responsible parenthood to criticism for suggesting the temporary arrangement of the "individual" marriage form (Mean, 1968). One woman wrote: "I still prefer God's one-step plan, which is *only* for mature couples, united for life, who are prepared for responsible parenthood." Other persons suggested that many couples already follow a similar plan through existing channels: they enter legal marriage, responsibly use contraceptives for a few years of getting to know one another sexually and socially, then embark on parenthood when they feel the time is right. If the marriage doesn't seem to be working, there is divorce. In view of this, they wondered, what would be the need for such a two-step plan?

Students especially seemed to reject the idea. They couldn't see any reason to go through a marriage ceremony in order to live together and have sex relations if no children were desired. Why have new laws for what many were already doing anyway? One student flatly accused Dr. Mead of wanting "to bottle up freedom, to hedge it with ceremony and publicly acknowledged responsibility." In the end, Margaret Mead (1968) concluded, "It now seems clear to me that neither elders nor young people want to make a change to two forms of marriage. They want to reserve the word 'marriage' for a commitment that they can feel is permanent and final, no matter how often the actual marriages may fail."

There have been other attempts to add a new dimension of rationality to marriage through structured trial unions, all of which would of course require changes in present marriage laws (Berger, 1971). One example was Virginia Satir's proposal at the 1967 convention of the American Psychological Association which suggested that marriage be made a statutory, five-year, renewable contract. This would provide a built-in mechanism for periodic review of the marriage so that a decision could be made either to go on with the relationship or to let it be terminated (Satir, 1967).

Unstructured Trial Marriage   The proposals for structured trial marriages just examined would involve licensing and regulation by society. Many couples see no need for such involvement by the state, preferring to view the man-woman relationship as a private matter (Greenwald, 1970). They see the rationality in the trial-marriage idea but prefer an unstructured form. They simply live together. If they get along well and want the relationship to continue on a permanent basis, they can become legally married. On the other hand, if their living together convinces them they're unsuited for each other, they can go their separate ways.

Again, it must be stressed that the basic idea behind trial marriages is the notion that the selection of a marriage partner should involve rationality. Persons in such arrangements do not hold to the idealism of folklore (such as, "They fell in love, got married, and lived happily ever after—because love conquers all"). A trial marriage is entered in the expectation that rewards and especially the costs of a particular male-female exchange will become apparent *before* a permanent decision about the relationship is made.

Earlier, we saw that mate selection is essentially a process of seeking to strike the best bargain possible. Sociologist George Homans (1961) uses the term *profit* to describe the ratio of rewards to costs as experienced by persons in social exchange. In a trial marriage, if the ratio is perceived as unfavorable (too many costs, not enough rewards), the partners are not encumbered by legal requirements to stay together. A "low profit" situation can easily be terminated. This does not mean that decisions to break up will be painless. Just as in actual divorce, if one partner perceives the reward/cost ratio to be favorable and wishes to continue the arrangement, he or she is the one likely to feel the more hurt and deprived when the relationship ends.

In sum, trial marriage serves as a prelude to marriage and not as a substitute for it. For those who engage in it, it's a kind of experiment—a way of determining whether or not to seek legal marriage with this particular partner or with some other partner (perhaps after another trial marriage) or never with anyone.

AD HOC ARRANGEMENTS

The Latin expression *ad hoc* means "for this [special purpose]." Some couples who choose to live together unmarried view their arrangement as simply an ad hoc situation, existing for its own sake. For them, living together is not viewed as an experiment, and the persons concerned do not think of it as a trial marriage (structured or unstructured) or any other kind of *marital* arrangement. They are not interested in entering legal marriage through licensing and ceremonies, nor are they interested in having their relationship declared a common-law marriage—even if they happen to be in a state where common-law marriages are recognized. They simply want to live together totally apart from the institution of marriage, and they don't want others to consider them "married" in any sense (White and Wells, 1973; Macklin, 1972). Some ad hoc arrangements are short-term; others are ongoing, lasting years.

However, two small-scale studies indicate that females more than males may think of their living together as a possible prelude to marriage and not simply as a substitute or end in itself (Arafat and Yorburg, 1973; Lyness, Lipetz, and Davis, 1972). In other words, while some males may be viewing their cohabitation arrangement as only ad hoc, their female partners may be considering it a trial marriage. This would reflect traditional socialization which encourages females to seek their identity and self-esteem in marriage and motherhood. In addition, any guilt feelings and fear of censure for engaging in sex outside of marriage are easier to deal with if a woman believes her sexual partner is her future spouse.

In sociologist Kristin Luker's study of women seeking an abortion (discussed earlier in Chapter 4), she too found that the women in her study tended to think of cohabitation as a trial marriage. This in turn often led to taking chances in birth control practices. Luker (1975:101) reports that particularly where couples were economically interdependent, "women in the study began to feel after some period of time spent in consensual unions that they were not only being taken advantage of, but that they would be wasting the best years of their lives should the relationship not end in marriage. The pressure to test commitment and to force a declaration of intentions is an ideal precondition for contraceptive risk-taking."

CONCEALED ARRANGEMENTS AND OPEN ARRANGEMENTS

It would be helpful at this point to try to sort out the relationship between cohabitation (living together outside of marriage) and legally recognized marriage (entered by fulfilling licensing and ceremonial requirements). This brings us back to the definition of marriage presented in Chapter 6.

Marriage, sociologically defined, consists of a relationship in which two or more persons maintain ongoing expressive (including sexual) and instrumental (including economic) exchanges. This definition is broad enough to encompass marriage in many forms—trial, legal, group, gay, traditional, modern, and so on. An important adjunct to this way of viewing marriage has to do with the *public nature* of the arrangement.

It is not likely that anyone would call an "affair" a marriage. Affairs are romantic attachments and regularized sexual liaisons usually carried out secretly and often considered to be of brief duration. While there are certain expressive interchanges and quite possibly a giving and receiving of material gifts, there is no expectation of the ongoing sexual and economic interdependency that characterizes marital arrangements. What is more, persons involved in affairs try to keep their relationship hidden. Public revelation is the last thing such lovers would want!

However, suppose two persons move in together and carry on both expressive and economic exchanges in much the same way as married persons. Yet, they carry on their relationship covertly, even though it is often difficult. Parents, peers, the postal service, the telephone company, insurance companies, the Internal Revenue Service, employers, and others who have an interest in them have no idea that this man and woman are sharing the same apartment. Even though their arrangement is a step closer to marriage than an affair would be, it still cannot be called a marriage—even in the sociological sense. Why? Because their relationship is clandestine and there is a deliberate avoidance of any public disclosure and social recognition.

If persons are secretive about their living together—covert instead of overt—it probably means that they fear punishments that could be imposed upon them by people they consider important in their lives, those whom sociologists call "significant others." Such people might apply negative sanctions so severe that they could disrupt the relationship entirely. If the relationship is that uncertain, tentative, and fragile, it cannot be called a marriage, since a marriage by definition is an *ongoing* exchange.

Two hypothetical couples serve as illustrations of the difference between covert and overt arrangements. Natalie and Kurt decide during college days to share a small apartment together. They don't hide the fact that they are living together, and their friends continue to accept them, visit them, and include them in invitations to various events and activities. Jean and Ed, on the other hand, don't want people to know about their similar living arrangement. They make it a point not to tell their friends out of fear that their friends would shun them if they knew. They are not prepared to accept such a cost, because they know it might undermine their attraction for each other. How? Because the cost of rejection by friends might prove to be more significant than the rewards Jean and Ed currently furnish each other. Their arrangement might not seem worth the suffering of social ostracism.

Natalie and Kurt seem to have much more going for them than is true of Jean and Ed. For one thing, the parents of both Natalie and Kurt know about their relationship and do not punish through the withholding of benefits. The parents continue to help with college expenses and also help pay for travel when the couple visits them. Both the financial aid and the willingness to visit with the couple, desiring to be with them rather than shunning them, are important rewards that the parents are not withholding. Their approval of the relationship helps sustain it.

Conversely, Jean and Ed perceive that their parents would cut off all financial assistance if they knew how they were living. Furthermore, the parents would probably be icy cold to them and perhaps even refuse to see them. This lack of approval plus the loss of economic benefits could also prove of greater significance than their own mutual benefits and thus threaten the ongoingness of their relationship.

Let's assume that several years pass. Natalie and Kurt have completed college and each enters a livelihood where their living-together arrangement is not likely to incur punishments from people who provide them money (and thus exercise a certain degree of control over them). All this time, Kurt and Natalie have simply continued to live together without legal sanctions, and they plan to continue their arrangement into the future. Can we say they are married? Yes and no. Sociologically speaking, they would appear to be clearly married; they are in an ongoing relationship, publicly declared, in which there is both full expressive and instrumental interdependency. If we look at Figure 8-1, we can see that their situation is different from trial marriage and

FIGURE 8-1 Continuum of relationships between the single state and married state

1. NONMARRIAGE		2. MARRIAGE			
		a. SOCIOLOGICAL DEFINITION		b. LEGAL DEFINITION	
The affair	Living together covertly	Living together overtly		Common-law marriage	Legitimized union
(Regularized sexual liaisons)		Trial marriage or Temporary ad hoc arrangement	Ongoing consensual union (not legally recognized)	(In states where legally recognized)	(Fulfilling state requirements for licensing and solemnization)

neither is it a temporary ad hoc situation. Yet it is not quite the same as a legal union. Their relationship may be called an "ongoing consensual union" (a long-standing situation of living together simply by mutual consent).

Figure 8-1 shows on one side a *state of nonmarriage* (point 1). This gradually fades into a *sociological* definition of marriage (point 2*a*) which occurs when there is an overt ongoing exchange of instrumental and expressive benefits. The key word here is *overt*; the relationship is publicly known. However, to be legitimate in terms of a *legal* definition of marriage, (point 2*b*) the relationship must be socially sanctioned by fulfilling state requirements for licensing and solemnization in the presence of witnesses. In between the stage in which a couple may be considered to be married in a sociological sense and the stage in which marriage exists in the legal sense, there is an intermediate stage considered legal in some states only, namely common-law marriage.

In other words, it's not enough to think simply in terms of two statuses, singleness and marriage. To understand the phenomenon of cohabitation, we need to envision marriage as a matter of degrees, with various cohabitation patterns fitting at different points along a continuum.

COHABITATION AND THE LAW

Marriage carries with it certain rights and duties. But since cohabitation (whether a trial marriage or a temporary or ongoing ad hoc arrangement) is not defined as legal marriage, questions have arisen about whether cohabitation similarly entails privileges and duties—especially in respect to property settlements. During the early 1970s, unmarried couples who separated occasionally went to court to determine which partner could keep the waterbed or other items from among the goods they had accumulated while sharing an apartment together. Both the number of such cases and the size of the requested property settlements have grown considerably over the years since then.

Widespread attention was especially focused on the $1.8 million suit filed against the actor Lee Marvin by his former live-in companion Michelle Triola Marvin (who had legally changed her surname although she had not married Marvin). Ms. Marvin had taken quite literally the actor's alleged remark early in their six-year cohabitation that "what I have is yours and what you have is mine," and the California Supreme Court ruled she had the right to sue for what she felt was her share of the amount the actor had earned during their time together. However, although the state supreme court had upheld Ms. Marvin's *right* to seek a property settlement just as though she had been a legal wife, the superior court judge who heard her case refused to grant her request for half of Lee Marvin's $3.6 million earned during their years of cohabitation. But the judge did rule that she was entitled to $104,000 for "rehabilitation purposes" so that she could learn or improve skills to aid in her employment, which prompted Ms. Marvin to remark triumphantly, "I am proud to have paved the way for other unmarried women" (*Greensboro* (NC) *Daily News*, April 19, 1979).

Some cohabiting couples have looked for ways to avoid possible legal problems in the future by drawing up a formal contract at the outset. In California, a company sprang up specifically to aid couples in formulating such agreements. Called UnMarriage Unlimited, the firm advertised a cut-rate contract for just under twenty-five dollars which included a waiver of claims for support as well as arrangements for dividing property and caring for any children born of the relationship (Jenkins, 1978).

In his book, *Oh Promise Me But Put It in Writing,* lawyer Paul Ashley (1978:69–77) suggests a number of legal approaches that can be used to develop contracts between persons in cohabitation arrangements: trust relationships, partnership agreements, cooperative enterprises, and joint-ownership plans. Such arrangements have to do only with property rights, property management, sharing in tangible profits and losses, and the like. They have nothing to do with the personal and sexual aspects of the relationship.

Indeed, a contract that sought to regulate the totality of a cohabiting couple's life together would probably not stand up in courts as a recognized legal contract. Why? Because such a contract "is intended to perpetuate consortium," explains lawyer Barbara Hirsch (1976:96). "It is therefore in derogation of the public policy favoring lawful marriage and legitimate offspring—and therefore unenforceable."

Hirsch points out other ways in which cohabitation practices may not only violate public policy but also may violate actual laws, including certain state laws against fornication (sexual intercourse between a man and a woman who are not married to each other) and certain sexual techniques. She writes:

> Whether, however, the statutes against fornication, sodomy, fellatio, cunnilingus, transportation across state lines, false registration into hotels, and so forth are actually going to ruin your plans for a skiing trip to Aspen is up to you. The actual risk of criminal prosecution is small, but the laws are there. (p. 39)

Sociologist D. Kelly Weisberg (1975:557) defines the central problem as "one of cultural lag." As more and more persons engage in behavior that is not legally sanctioned, the legal process may lag behind the social change that has already taken place. "The law thus penalizes participants of alternative families which fulfill the same needs and perform the same functions [as legally defined families]," says Weisberg. Traditional legal definitions have reserved the word *family* for persons descending from a common ancestor or who have entered a recognized relationship through formal adoption or marriage ceremonies, and legal rights and duties associated with family status are spelled out by the courts. Laws are designed to discourage the establishment of nontraditional family forms, Weisberg emphasizes, and therefore the judicial system grants to conventional families rights denied those persons who elect to live in other kinds of relationships.

At the same time, sociologist Lenore Weitzman and her colleagues (1978) point out that many of the "rights" attached to husband-wife status are actually disadvantageous for the individuals concerned. The traditional

Cohabitation—A Crime?

There is the potential of criminal indictment every time consorts take a vacation together. Nancy, who has an innocent face and hardly appears to be engaged in a life of crime, recounted the romantic beginning and sad ending to her consortium with Ted. Among the sensitive issues in their relationship was their travel arrangements. Ted did a lot of traveling in his business—that other people paid for. In each city, a hotel room was reserved for him in his name.

"Ted dropped me off near the hotel and I was supposed to—I did—walk around this strange downtown and look in store windows and walk up and down the aisles of the gift shop until enough time passed and I assumed he had checked in and was safely in his room. Then I'd phone him from the cigar stand, ask his room number, and go up. That's how we worked it. I never told him how infuriating this was. Sometimes, to get back at him, I'd kill time, stop for coffee, browse longer, before I called and came up."

Scott was matter-of-fact. Sure, he and Laura were living together, sure everyone knew about it. "If my boss doesn't like it, so what? I like it." But even Scott, when he and Laura went to Scottsdale, to that elegant resort hotel, checked in as "Mr. and Mrs." Traveling together is fraught with peril.

If you check into a hotel as Mr. and Mrs., or under assumed names, you are committing a crime. Most states impose criminal penalties for false registration at hotels. On the other hand, if you register in your own names, the hotel may not accept you. And that is not just because the hotel management is narrow-minded. It is because the management is subject to criminal penalty if it registers a single man and woman in the same room. The crime is "keeper of a disorderly house" and may mean license revocation, fine, or imprisonment. Then, to top it all, you can't legally register just one name and have your consort sneak in later, as Nancy did. You are also cheating the hotel out of its double-occupancy rate, adding dishonesty to the offense. The alternative is that each of you registers separately in a separate room, you pay the exorbitant two-room rate, and one sneaks into the other's room, subjecting you to criminal prosecution for fornication and to the hotel's rancor at being itself exposed to prosecution (the rancor is greatly quieted by the receipt of the extra rate, though).

When planning to travel together in Europe, remember that the hotelkeepers check and hold your passports. Whether you will succeed in staying in the same room depends on the country and the particular hotel. Best to check ahead.

SOURCE: Barbara B. Hirsch, *Living Together: A Guide to the Law for Unmarried Couples* (Boston: Houghton Mifflin, 1976), pp. 37–38.

definition of marriage and family that family laws are designed to promote and protect assumes four essential obligations: First, the husband is considered to be head of the household. Second, the husband is assigned responsibility for supporting the family. Third, the wife is assigned responsibility for domestic services. And fourth, the wife is assigned responsibility for child care (Weitzman et al., 1978:306–311). These authors suggest that carefully worded contracts drawn up by cohabiting, premarried, and married couples can allow for greater flexibility and more egalitarian relationships than the state-imposed legal marriage contract which assigns rights and responsibilities on the basis of sex. At the same time, Weitzman and her associates recognize that the question of the enforceability of such private contracts is not indisputably settled.

WHO COHABITS AND WHY?

Most studies of cohabitation have focused on college students. The living-together phenomenon has been especially popular among this segment of the population; and besides, students are a convenient and readily available group for researchers to study!

Campus Cohabitation Why the widespread acceptance of campus cohabitation? A number of ideas have been put forth, suggesting it might have something to do with greater sexual permissiveness in general and the popularity of the "permissiveness-with-affection" standard in particular; or perhaps it's related to changes in university regulations, such as the elimination of curfews and different hours for females and males and the availability of off-campus housing and twenty-four-hour visiting privileges in dormitories. Other suggestions put forth to explain cohabitation among college students include changes in the traditional status of women, availability of contraceptives and abortion to cut down pregnancy risks in such arrangements, disenchantment with conventional marriage, and a willingness to tolerate a variety of life-styles (Peterman, Ridley, and Anderson, 1974:344; Macklin, 1972:98).

But just how widespread is cohabitation among the student population? Because of certain sampling problems and because some studies have focused only on particular classes or particular universities, findings of several studies cannot be generalized to all students in the United States. Nevertheless, these studies provide some interesting data.

A questionnaire filled out by 1,100 students at Penn State indicated that one-third had lived with a member of the opposite sex for some period (Peterman, Ridley, and Anderson, 1974). A random sample drawn from the Arizona State student body showed that 29 percent of males and 18 percent of females had cohabited in the past or were currently in such a relationship (Henze and Hudson, 1974). And a nonrandom sample of students in marriage and family courses at fourteen state universities scattered across the nation turned up the finding that about one out of four of these students had cohabited at some time (Bower and Christopherson, 1977). In view of such findings, sociologist Charles Lee Cole (1977:76) suggests that census figures such as those cited earlier may be on the conservative side since they don't include a systematic representation of the college student population.

Beyond the College Population Moving beyond the campus, questions on cohabitation were included in two other large-scale research projects that were primarily designed to examine other topics.

In the first, sociologists Richard Clayton and Harwin Voss (1977) examined data from a study of nonmedical drug use. A nationwide random sample of twenty- to thirty-year-old men was drawn from Selective Service registration records between 1962 and 1972. Eighteen percent of the men reported they had at some time lived for six months or more with a woman outside marriage, but only one out of twenty were in cohabitation relationships at the time of the interview. "This suggests that cohabitation is *not* a permanent form of heterosexual union," write Clayton and Voss. "These relationships either terminate or the partners marry" (p. 277). They point out that the extent of current cohabitation (Are you *now* cohabiting?) will be "substantially lower than the lifetime prevalence of cohabitation" (Have you *ever* cohabited?).

In this sample of 2,510 men, Clayton and Voss also found variations by race (black men in the sample being somewhat more likely than the white men to have lived in cohabitation relationships) and by religiosity (as measured by attendance at religious services), with lower cohabitation rates among those who reported attending religious services once a week.

In another study, sociologist Kersti Alice Yllo (1978) examined data from a national area–probability sample of 2,143 women and men living with opposite sex partners (some married to their partners, some not). Although the 1976 survey was primarily concerned with family violence, the interview questionnaire was intentionally broad in scope and provided information on a variety of issues, including cohabitation. Unlike most other studies of cohabitation, Yllo's sample included an age range of from eighteen to seventy years.

Age and Cohabitation   Yllo found that just under 2 percent of her sample weren't married to the opposite sex partner with whom they lived. Sixty percent of these unmarried cohabitors hadn't yet reached their thirtieth birthday (as compared to 27 percent of the married couples in the survey)—which means that cohabitors tend to be young. But at the same time, Yllo takes pains to point out that these figures also mean that 40 percent of cohabitors are *over* age thirty. Yet, researchers have given them remarkably little attention.

Yllo's data showed that the percentage of persons in cohabitation relationships declined with each succeeding age bracket, with eighteen- to twenty-four-year-olds having the highest rates. Lowest rates were among those persons aged fifty-one to sixty. But above that age, the rates suddenly shot up. Yllo suggests that "this dramatically higher rate of cohabitation for the elderly provides evidence that social structural factors [factors outside the individual], in this case Social Security laws which prohibit [widowed persons] from remarrying and continuing survivor's benefits, can affect the rate at which individuals opt for a nontraditional lifestyle" (p. 43). If Yllo's explanation is correct, we should see a drop in the cohabitation rate for persons over sixty in the years ahead because of some major changes in the Social Security law. Effective January, 1979, beneficiaries were instructed, "If

The dramatically higher rate of cohabitation among the elderly has been attributed to Social Security laws which, until recently, prevented widowed persons from collecting survivor's benefits if they remarried. (Ginger Chih/Peter Arnold, Inc.)

you receive widow's or widower's benefits, your checks no longer will be stopped or reduced if you remarry at age 60 or later'' (U.S. Department of Health, Education, and Welfare, February, 1978:6).

Religious Factors Yllo suggests that social structural rather than personal factors may also enter into another finding, namely, an overrepresentation of Catholic women in the cohabitation grouping. Other researchers, in their more limited samples of college students, have noticed a similar pattern (Henze and Hudson, 1974; Peterman et al., 1974). The usual explanation has been based on the assumption that cohabitation is one way for a young Roman Catholic woman to break loose from parental and church restrictions. Such a woman "is perhaps reacting to the greater freedom in the campus setting by experimenting with new ideas and patterns of behavior," suggest Henze and Hudson (1974:726).

Yllo, however, offers a different explanation which may be more applicable to the broader population that her sample represents. She suggests that cohabitation may be a way of dealing with the Roman Catholic church's position on divorce and remarriage. "Young Catholic women may want to be more sure of their possible marriage partner since divorce is not viewed as an option for them later," writes Yllo. "Also, older Catholic women whose marriages have failed are denied the opportunity to divorce and remarry. Consequently, they may have to settle for a separation from their husband

and a cohabiting relationship with their new partner" (p. 45). She sees this as further indication of ways "social structural constraints may affect cohabitation rates."

Marital Breakup and Cohabitation   Though not necessarily related to religious considerations, cohabitation rates for divorced persons are higher than for never-married individuals. Various researchers have therefore speculated that an unsatisfactory marriage experience may lead some persons to avoid the risk of repeating such an experience by taking the cohabitation route instead. Census Bureau surveys have shown 5.4 percent of divorced men to be cohabiting (compared to 3.6 percent of unmarried adults in general); and among divorced men under age thirty-five, the cohabitation rate jumps to 8.3 percent (Glick and Norton, 1977:33–34). Clayton and Voss (1977:283) found in their sample that 21 percent of the men who had experienced marital disruption were cohabiting at the time they were interviewed, while only 8 percent of the never-married men were in such relationships. Yllo (1978:47) also found such differences in her data on married and unmarried couple relationships. Among cohabitors, 32.5 percent of males and 23.7 percent of females reported they were either divorced or separated from a spouse. Among the married persons in her sample, only slightly more than 11 percent had experienced an earlier marital breakup.

MAINTAINING A COHABITATION RELATIONSHIP

In her studies of cohabiting couples at Ohio State, sociologist Nancy Moore Clatworthy (1975:77) found that most persons reported living together "for convenience or economic reasons or simply because they liked or loved the person that they lived with." Other reasons cited were "companionship" and "security."

The formation of cohabitation relationships usually comes about gradually. Couples tend neither to jump into them nor to deliberate over them; rather, they just drift into such arrangements. One person stays at the other's place one night, and that makes it easier to stay overnight the next time, until one or the other partners eventually moves in fulltime (Macklin, 1972; Cole, 1977:70). In some cases, living together does not mean sexual involvement (Macklin, 1972).

According to Cole (1977), a shift in a couple's perception of their relationship occurs when they begin living together. He writes:

> At the point in the process when the partners move in together, the social reality of their relationship undergoes a significant change that calls for a new subjective assessment of that relationship. They must now redefine their social situation to account for the fact that they are cohabiting. This redefinition frequently is accompanied by a reassessment of their feelings toward their partner as well as their own self-concept. If the partners perceive that cohabiting provides them with a favorable reward-cost ratio, they will likely continue to live together. (p. 70)

(Note how Cole is here combining features of social exchange and symbolic interaction theory.)

Expectations and Commitment   Cole's ongoing research on cohabiting couples has shown only a small minority to be committed to marrying the partner or working hard toward making the relationship a lasting one. Rather, the majority report that they intend to stay in the relationship as long as the association is "mutually satisfying" or "personally enjoyable." "These data suggest that most cohabitants will invest time and energy in a relationship as long as the rewards (satisfactions and enjoyments) outweigh the costs (sacrifices)," Cole (1977:71) emphasizes. A cohabitation relationship is constantly being evaluated and reevaluated, as the participants weigh advantages against disadvantages (Macklin, 1972; Cole, 1977; Libby, 1977a).

Some Kinds of Cohabitation Relationships   Three specialists in family life have suggested that cohabiting relationships tend to fall into one of several categories: the "Linus blanket" type, the "emancipation" type, the "convenience" type, and the "testing" type (Ridley, Peterman, and Avery, 1978).

In the first type (named for the security blanket used by a character in the Peanuts cartoon strip), the relationship is built on "an overwhelming need for one member of the pair to have a relationship with *someone*, with little apparent regard for whom, or under what conditions. To have someone to be with, even though he or she may treat you badly, is better than not having anyone at all" (Ridley, Peterman, and Avery, 1978:130). According to these authors, such a relationship has emotional security as its aim and does not provide opportunities for developing communication and problem-solving skills. Ridley, Peterman, and Avery explain:

> Negative statements made to the insecure person (frequently in the form of criticisms) are often interpreted as a severe questioning of his or her self-worth. The result is that the more secure person perceives and/or acts as if the partner is

"I thought people had to be married for the magic to go out".

(Drawing by Mahood; © 1972 The New Yorker Magazine, Inc.)

fragile ("can't take criticism") and that they cannot "rock the boat" without hurting their partner and the relationship. (pp. 130–131)

What these authors term the "emancipation" type of cohabitation relationship is characterized by feelings of guilt, uneasiness, and "unfinished business" on the part of one of the individuals. A desire to break free of internalized past restrictions may push one toward cohabitation; but upon entering such a relationship, internal pressures and feelings of wrongdoing now cause the person to want out of the relationship, with the result that the cycle begins again. Such persons tend to remain in cohabitation arrangements only briefly.

The third type of cohabitation relationship described by Ridley and his colleagues is the "convenience" type which they say "is perhaps best exemplified in the short duration cohabiting relationship of freshmen or sophomore males." Such a situation "allows the male to have regularized sexual contact and the luxuries of domestic living without the responsibilities of a committed relationship." These authors state that "his major task is to keep the female interested in the relationship when it appears that she is putting more into the relationship than he is" (p. 131). They point out that females may also enter such relationships for "convenience" reasons; although the more common pattern is for males to seek such arrangements, knowing they can count on female socialization to have prepared the female partner to assume domestic tasks.

Last, Ridley, Peterman, and Avery list the "testing" type of cohabitation. The emphasis is on trying out interpersonal skills in a more complex male-female involvement; and at the same time, the partners are learning something else. Ridley and his associates explain:

> In a sense, the partners seem to use the relationship to get to know more about themselves—their likes and dislikes, and to learn more about how intimate relationships of this type apparently lead to a deeper level of self-understanding for both individuals. However, when the relationship solidifies too quickly—prior to the development of individual interests and preferences—the partners feel overinvolved and dependent on the relationship with the accompanying sense of loss of identity. (p. 132)

PARENTS AND COHABITATION.

In their sample of college students, Henze and Hudson (1974:724) found that while more than eight out of ten students would feel comfortable discussing their cohabitation relationship with their friends, only about one-third felt they could be comfortable discussing such a relationship with their parents. It is not difficult to guess the reason. Various studies have shown that students in cohabitation relationships know or expect their parents to be disapproving of such relationships (Macklin, 1972; Bower and Christopherson, 1977). Roughly between about one-fourth (Peterman, Ridley, and Anderson,

1974:348) and one-half (Macklin, 1972:100; Bower and Christopherson, 1977:449) of the parents of cohabitors are thought to be aware of the arrangement; the rest are thought not to know—although they may suspect. Macklin (1972:100) reports that problems with parents mentioned by respondents in her study of female cohabitors included not only real or anticipated disapproval of the male partner, but also "fear of discovery, guilt because they were deceiving or hurting their parents, rejection by or ultimatums from parents, and most frequently, sadness at not being able to share this important part of their lives with their parents."

SEX ROLES AND COHABITATION

Many people believe that choosing to live together apart from traditional marriage will also mean living apart from traditional marriage *roles*. But is cohabitation more egalitarian? Or do couples find themselves slipping into conventional husband-wife patterns?

In Clatworthy's sample of cohabitors in a college setting, 77 percent of the respondents reported that they shared food costs and rent; and 59 percent reported that they shared household chores such as laundry, cleaning, cooking, and shopping equally (1975:74–75). On the other hand, Cole (1977:72–73) summarizes seven studies that suggest that "cohabitation is not as equalitarian in the assignment of sex roles and/or household tasks as one might expect" and that furthermore males and females have different perceptions of their contributions within the household, with females believing that they have the greater work load and males believing that gender-role equality exists.

With regard to household decision-making, Cole reports that his own ongoing longitudinal research on cohabiting couples indicates that three-fourths of them practice "segmentalized decision meeting," that is, one partner more than the other is responsible for certain decisions according to that partner's expertise and interests. For instance, whoever owned the car before the cohabitation began tends to remain responsible for the car's upkeep. At the same time, many decisions are made jointly. Overall according to Cole, it appears that females are expected to make more household-related decisions than males. "It is unclear," he writes, "whether or not this greater female responsibility is indicative of traditional sex-role inequality where the woman is frequently relegated a disproportionate share of the responsibility for household tasks and decisions" (p. 72).

In her large random sample of married and unmarried couples from the general population, Yllo (1978:48–49) found no significant difference between cohabitors and marrieds with regard to decision-making; cohabiting relationships were not found to be more egalitarian on this dimension. Similarly, when the two groups were compared on household division of labor, the data showed that "cohabiting couples are fairly traditional in terms of dividing household tasks along sex lines." Men, whether they were in cohabitation relationships or marriage relationships, "differed in no significant ways as to the type and amount of work they do." And for their part, women in the two groups showed no differences from one another with regard to managing money and responsibility for social activities. But one difference did show up between the two categories of women. Whereas 70 percent of married women under age thirty reported having primary or total responsibility for cooking, cleaning, and repairing the house; only half of the *cohabiting* women in this age group reported such responsibility. On the other hand, approximately two-thirds of women over age thirty bore much or all responsibility for these chores—*regardless* of whether they were cohabiting or married. Since no significant differences showed up among the men, however, Yllo hesitates to conclude that even the younger cohabitors have an overall more egalitarian division of labor than do their married counterparts.

Three other sociologists studied matched samples of married and cohabiting college men and women in research designed specifically to test whether cohabiting couples share chores more equally (Stafford, Backman, and Dibona, 1977). Their conclusion? "Women of both groups are still taking most of the responsibility for, and performing most of, the household tasks" (p. 43). They attribute this finding to traditional sex-role ideology and the socialization and parental role models to which persons of both sexes have been exposed during their growing-up years. "Simply removing the institution of marriage and the traditional authority of the male that has accompanied it in Western society will not usher out traditional sex roles," write these researchers. "The nonconscious ideology that . . . keeps women and men in their places will gradually have to be eroded" (p. 55).

In an exploratory study that provides some indication of the impact of an egalitarian ideology, sociologist Lenore Weitzman (1978) and her associates at the Center for the Study of Law and Society at the University of California at Berkeley asked students to prepare their own marriage or living-together contracts. These contracts would be written as alternatives to the traditional legal marriage contract which assigns rights and responsibilities on the basis of sex.

Some of the students were already married so they prepared their contracts as "contracts within marriage." Other students were planning to be married but wanted to live together first in a trial union so they prepared contracts accordingly. The third and largest group were the cohabitors, most of whom "explicitly rejected legal marriage and wrote these contracts to establish a different structure for their relationships," say Weitzman and her colleagues (p. 323).

These researchers found that, in general, the personalized contracts written by the couples—whether married, premarried, or cohabiting—"*were more likely to structure intimate relationships as partnerships* and to provide for a more equal sharing of both rights and responsibilities" (p. 374) than is true of the traditional legal marriage contract. The *most* egalitarian contracts were written by the cohabiting couples, and the least egalitarian were written by the married couples. Couples planning on marriage were somewhere in between the two.

The major difference between the cohabitors' contracts and those of the married couples related to individualism and to the allocation of decision-making and responsibilities. Cohabitors tended to stress each partner's individuality (including self-support and separate finances), while the married persons emphasized togetherness (viewing property and support as "joint endeavors"). As to decision-making and division of labor, the cohabitors were "much more likely to contribute equally to decisions and to share equally responsibilities," in contrast to the married couples who were "more likely to assign decisions and responsibilities to a single person on a sex-related basis" (Weitzman et al., 1978:371).

Apparently, in ideology at least, some cohabitors are looking for something different from conventional marriage—a way in which a man and woman can structure their shared life by rewriting the rules of the traditional marriage contract with its sex-specific rights and duties. *Carrying out* the ideology may be another matter however, as several of the studies have shown. "Repeatedly, people see themselves slipping into stereotyped sex roles in running households," observes sociologist Robert Whitehurst (1974, as quoted in Stafford et al., 1977:46), pointing out that it's easier to philosophize about sex-role equality than to live it consistently because the impact of traditional socialization runs so deep. (See also Mainardi, 1970.)

In short, cohabitation as it is developing today shows both similarities to conventional marriage and profound differences. A woman and man are

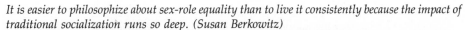

It is easier to philosophize about sex-role equality than to live it consistently because the impact of traditional socialization runs so deep. (Susan Berkowitz)

Anything but "My Better Half"

This piece will use names of two people: Pietro and Tess.

For three years Pietro and Tess lived together without marrying. Such an arrangement had ceased to be scandalous when they took it up, had even become fashionable. It expressed the partners' re-evaluation of the culture, or their liberation from tired old values, or something. It doesn't matter what. Pietro and Tess did it.

They were married a few weeks ago. "It had got to the point where it didn't matter," Tess explained at the reception. "For all practical purposes we were married anyhow, and very happily, but it was starting to go sour because we didn't have the marriage certificate."

The canker in the love nest was the English language. Though English is the world's most commodious tongue, it provided no word to define their relationship satisfactorily to strangers. When Tess took Pietro to meet her parents the problem became troublesome. Presenting Pietro, she said, "Mommy and Daddy, this is my lover, Pietro."

Pietro was not amused. "It made me sound like a sex object," he said. "What's more, Tess's dad kept taking me off alone and trying to pump me for tips about how to become a lover."

Pietro felt demeaned and cheapened. Afterwards he quarreled with Tess and accused her of not respecting him as a person who had a fine mind and was a first rate stockbroker. "Next time," Tess said, "I'll introduce you as my stockbroker." Pietro stormed out of the house.

A few weeks later they were invited to meet the President. Entering the reception line, Pietro was asked by the protocol officer for their names. "Pietro," he said, "And this is my mate."

As they came abreast of the President, the officer turned to Mr. Carter and said, "Pietro and his mate."

"I felt like the supporting actress in a Tarzan movie," said Tess. It took Pietro three nights of sleeping at the YMCA to repair the relationship.

"Why don't we call a spade a spade?" Tess suggested. Pietro pointed out that it was all very well to call a spade a spade, but it sounded ridiculous to call a relationship a relationship. Tess insisted they try it anyhow, so when Pietro bumped into Mayor Rizzo one day in Philadelphia, he said, "Frank, let me introduce you to my relationship, Tess." The mayor said he was delighted, but he looked more like a man who suspected somebody was trying to put one over on him and fled without wishing Tess a nice day.

"Let's get down to basics," Pietro told Tess. "I'm your man and you're my woman. Why don't we just come out and say so?" And so, when Pietro ran into Sammy Davis, Jr., at a party, he said, "Sammy, this is my woman, Tess." Whereupon Sammy seized Tess, whirled her into a fast fox trot and brought down the house by shouting, "Tess, you is my woman now."

Back to the drawing board, on which they kept the dictionary.

"This is my beloved," was no good. Sounded like a bad poem.

"This is my companion?" worse. Invalids, octogenarians, wealthy lunatics and kleptomaniacs had companions, but not persons who were young, enlightened and progressive enough to take turns washing the dishes. "Boyfriend" and "girlfriend" might have worked if they hadn't sounded so 1926. Pietro and Tess were 1976; yes, and 1977, too, and also 1978. For Pietro, this eliminated, "This is my chick, Tess," "This is my bird, Tess," and "This is my sweetie, Tess."

For Tess it eliminated "This is my beau, Pietro," as well as "This is the man in my life, Pietro." For a while they tried "my friend." One night at a glamorous party Pietro introduced Tess to a marrying millionaire with the words, "This is my friend, Tess." To which the marrying millionaire replied, "Let's jet down to the Caribbean, Tess, and tie the knot."

"You don't understand," said Pietro. "Tess is my friend."

"So don't you like seeing your friends headed for big alimony?" asked the marrying millionaire.

"She's not that kind of friend," said Pietro.

"I'm his friend," said Tess.

"Ah," said the matrimonialist, upon whom the dawn was slowly breaking, "Ah—your—friend."

As Tess explained at the wedding, they couldn't spend the rest of their lives rolling their eyeballs suggestively every time they said "friend." There was only one way out. "The simple thing," Pietro suggested "would be for me to introduce you as 'my wife.' "

"And for me," said Tess, "to say, 'This is my husband, Pietro.' "

And so they were wed, victims of a failure in anguish.

SOURCE Russell Baker, New York Times News Service (Syndicated), *Greensboro* (NC) *Daily News*, January 4, 1979.

sharing a life together—materially, emotionally, and sexually. Some social commentators therefore speak of cohabitation as a *quasi-marriage* relationship. (The term *quasi* derives from the Latin *quam*, "as," and *si*, "if." Thus, cohabitation is something resembling marriage if not marriage "for real." It's to live *as if* married.) Yet, cohabitation doesn't have the legal recognition and social support so necessary for actual marriage to exist in the fullest sense of that word (as defined in this book).

That brings us to another type of quasi-marriage relationship in which some persons are living in the face of even less social support and in the complete absence of legal recognition: same-sex marriage.

GAY MARRIAGE

Nearly two thousand years ago, the Roman poet Ovid wrote of a man who informed his pregnant wife that family financial conditions were such that only a boy could be afforded. Tearfully, he said that if a female were born, the baby must immediately be put to death. When the mother gave birth to a girl, she followed the counsel of a goddess in not telling the father, who thought he had a son. Only the mother and a faithful nurse knew the truth. The baby was dressed in male attire and given the name Iphis, a name used for both boys and girls.

When Iphis was thirteen, the father arranged a marriage between his handsome offspring and a beautiful girl named Ianthe. The two were the same age and had been educated together, so that a deep bond of love had grown between them. Ianthe's passion for Iphis grew and she longed for the wedding day, whereas Iphis, though equally in love, kept postponing it. Her desperate mother invented excuses of illnesses or visions interpreted as bad omens. Ovid describes the sense of hopelessness:

> Iphis loved a girl whom she despaired of ever being able to enjoy, and this very frustration increased her ardour. A girl herself, she was in love with one of her own kind, and could scarcely keep back her tears, as she said: "What is to be the end of this for me, caught as I am in the snare of a strange and unnatural kind of love, which none has known before? Cows do not burn with love for cows, nor mares for mares. It is the ram which excites the ewe, the hind follows the stag, birds too mate in the same way, and never among all the animals does one female fall in love with another. How I wish I had never been born! (Ovid's *Metamorphoses*, p. 223, Penguin edition.)

Iphis tried to talk herself out of her feelings. "Pull yourself together, Iphis, be firm, and shake off this foolish, useless emotion. . . . It is hope that conceives and nourishes desire: and your case denies you hope." Rebelliously, she reasoned that none of the usual obstacles kept her from her beloved's embrace; there was no guardian forbidding the marriage, no husband to whom she was bound, no stern father standing in the way of her happiness. It was all the fault of nature. She bemoaned: "My wedding day is at hand, and now Ianthe will be mine: yet she will not be. I shall thirst in the midst of waters." Crying out to the god and goddess of marriage, Iphis asked why they should even bother to "come to this ceremony, at which there is no bridegroom, where two brides are being wed."

The problem was solved through the intervention of the same goddess who had advised the girl's mother while awaiting Iphis's birth. A miracle was performed within the temple, and Iphis was changed into a young man—a suitable bridegroom for the happy Ianthe.

In mythology, such a gods-to-the-rescue ending might seem a reasonable device for solving the problems of the characters involved. But the solution is not so simple in real life. Persons interested in a same-sex marriage today would be quite unlikely to welcome the intervention of Iphis's goddess. It's true, of course, that some persons undergo sex reassignment surgery and hormonal treatment because they consider themselves women who are trapped in men's bodies or men who are trapped in women's bodies. But strictly speaking, such persons are *transsexual*, not homosexual. Their personal image of themselves as female or male doesn't match what their bodies tell them they are. Thus, they want their bodies changed to conform to what they feel is their true sex (Green, 1974, chap. 6).

In contrast, a homosexual male thinks of himself *as a male*—but as a male who is sexually attracted to persons who are likewise male. And a homosexual female thinks of herself *as a female*—but as a female who is sexually attracted to persons who, like her, are also female. Therefore, most persons interested in "gay marriage" haven't the remotest interest in undergoing a sex change. They want to be what they are and yet be able to be united in a socially recognized relationship to persons they love—even though the persons they love are not of the opposite sex.

WHAT IS HOMOSEXUALITY?

Paul Gebhard (1972), director of the Institute for Sex Research at Indiana University, defines homosexual behavior as "physical contact between two individuals of the same gender which both recognize as being sexual in nature and which ordinarily results in sexual arousal." He defines psychological homosexual response as "the desire for such physical contact and/or conscious sexual arousal from thinking of or seeing persons of the same gender." The term *homosexual* is derived from the Greek *homos,* meaning "one and the same," and it may be applied to either males or females who are sexually attracted to members of their own sex. Usually, however, homosexual women prefer to be called *lesbians,* a word derived from Lesbos, a Greek island where in ancient times a woman named Sappho directed a girls' school and addressed sensuous poems to her students.

It is beyond the scope of this book to discuss theories of why some persons are *homosexual* (sexually attracted to the same sex) and other persons are *heterosexual* (sexually attracted to the opposite sex), while still others are *ambisexual* (sexually attracted to and able to relate to both sexes equally— another term for this is *bisexual*). Actually, sex researchers have found that being heterosexual or homosexual isn't so much a simple matter of either/or as it is a matter of degrees along a continuum related to both feelings and behavior. (See Figure 8-2.) Some persons fall more on the heterosexual side of the scale, whereas others fall more on the homosexual side.

Gebhard estimates that between 4 and 5 percent of males and between 1 and 2 percent of females in the United States today could be classified as

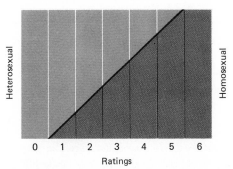

FIGURE 8-2   *The "Kinsey continuum" or heterosexual-homosexual rating scale. Definitions of the ratings are as follows: 0 = entirely heterosexual. 1 = largely heterosexual, but with incidental homosexual history. 2 = largely heterosexual, but with distinct homosexual history. 3 =equally heterosexual and homosexual. 4 = largely homosexual, but with distinct heterosexual history. 5 =largely homosexual, but with incidental heterosexual history. 6 = entirely homosexual.*

The categories on the heterosexual-homosexual scale may be defined as follows:

0   *Individuals are rated as 0's if all of their psychological responses and all of their overt sexual activities are directed toward persons of the opposite sex. Such individuals do not recognize*

any homosexual responses and do not engage in specifically homosexual activities. While more extensive analysis might show that all persons may on occasion respond to homosexual stimuli, or are capable of such responses, the individuals who are rated 0 are those who are ordinarily considered to be completely heterosexual.

1 *Individuals are rated as 1's if their psychosexual responses and/or overt experience are directed almost entirely toward individuals of the opposite sex, although they incidentally make psychosexual responses to their own sex, and/or have incidental sexual contacts with individuals of their own sex. The homosexual reactions and/or experiences are usually infrequent, or may mean little psychologically, or may be initiated quite accidentally. Such persons make few if any deliberate attempts to renew their homosexual contacts. Consequently the homosexual reactions and experience are far surpassed by the heterosexual reactions and/or experience in the history.*

2 *Individuals are rated as 2's if the preponderance of their psychosexual responses and/or overt experiences are heterosexual, although they respond rather definitely to homosexual stimuli and/or have more than incidental homosexual experience. Some of these individuals may have had only a small amount of homosexual experience, or they may have had a considerable amount of it, but the heterosexual element always predominates. Some of them may turn all their overt experience in one direction while their psychosexual responses turn largely in the opposite direction; but they are always erotically aroused by anticipating homosexual experience and/or in their physical contacts with individuals of their own sex.*

3 *Individuals are rated as 3's if they stand midway on the heterosexual-homosexual scale. They are about equally heterosexual and homosexual in their psychological responses and/or in their overt experience. They accept or equally enjoy both types of contact and have no strong preferences for the one or the other.*

4 *Individuals are rated as 4's if their psychological responses are more often directed toward other individuals of their own sex and/or if their sexual contacts are more often with their own sex. While they prefer contacts with their own sex, they, nevertheless, definitely respond toward and/or maintain a fair amount of overt contact with individuals of the opposite sex.*

5 *Individuals are rated as 5's if they are almost entirely homosexual in their psychological responses and/or their overt activities. They respond only incidentally to individuals of the opposite sex, and/or have only incidental overt experience with the opposite sex.*

6 *Individuals are rated as 6's if they are exclusively homosexual in their psychological responses, and in any overt experience in which they give any evidence of responding. Some individuals may be rated as 6's because of their psychological responses, even though they may never have overt homosexual contacts. None of these individuals, however, ever respond psychologically toward, or have overt sexual contacts in which they respond to, individuals of the opposite sex.*

X *Finally, individuals are rated as X's if they do not respond erotically to either heterosexual or homosexual stimuli, and do not have overt physical contacts with individuals of either sex in which there is evidence of any response. After early adolescence there are very few males in this classification, but a goodly number of females belong in this category in every age group. It is not impossible that further analyses of these individuals might show that they do sometimes respond to socio-sexual stimuli, but they are unresponsive and inexperienced as far as it is possible to determine by any ordinary means.*

(SOURCE: *Alfred C. Kinsey, Wardell B. Pomeroy, Clyde E. Martin, and Paul H. Gebhard,* Sexual Behavior in the Human Female *[Philadelphia: W. B. Saunders Co., 1953; New York: Pocket Books edition, pp. 470–472].)*

"predominantly homosexual," defined as a rating of 4–6 on the Kinsey scale (Gebhard, 1972; and in personal interview, February 10, 1978). Gebhard is speaking here of persons whose homosexuality is overt in terms of behavior, not persons who are psychologically predominately homosexual but who have seldom or never acted upon their feelings.

Being "Gay"   In recent years, the word *gay* has come into wide usage by homosexual persons of both sexes. Once serving as a sort of secret code word among homosexuals who wanted to avoid discovery, it has now become a term of pride. "Gay is good." "Gay is power." "Gay is angry; gay is proud." Psychotherapist George Weinberg (1972:70–71) distinguishes between being *homosexual* (having "erotic preferences for members of one's own sex") and being *gay*, which he defines as being free of the need for ongoing self-inquisition, and ridding oneself of guilt, shame, and regret over being a homosexual. "To be gay," writes Weinberg, "is to view one's sexuality as the healthy heterosexual views his." The emphasis is on self-acceptance.

Persons who regard themselves as gay in the sense described by Weinberg are not apt to be terrified in the way Iphis was by their attraction to members of the same sex. They do not view such attraction as loathsome or unnatural. Indeed, they would even call into question Iphis's observation about the animal world by pointing out that research has indicated that animals *do* sometimes engage in homosexual behavior—including the ram, which Iphis especially cited in her lament (Money and Ehrhardt, 1972:228). Unlike Iphis, the gay person does not wish to be changed, but proposes instead that society do the changing. The gay person would like to be accepted just as he or she is.

Gay Life-styles   "Too often homosexuals have been viewed simply with reference to their sexual interests and activity," write researchers Alan Bell and Martin Weinberg (1978:25) of the Institute for Sex Research. "Usually the

DOONESBURY   by Garry Trudeau

social context and psychological correlates of homosexual experience are largely ignored, making for a highly constricted image of the persons involved. . . . Both homosexuality and heterosexuality generate numerous life-styles, and future research may indicate that these are far more important indications of people's whereabouts than is sexual orientation per se."

Bell, a psychologist, and Weinberg, a sociologist, conducted in 1970 a comprehensive study of nearly one thousand homosexual persons of both sexes and a comparison group of nearly five hundred heterosexual persons of both sexes. But their study differed from other studies in that they were not trying to find out how homosexuals as a group differed from heterosexuals as a group. They were persuaded that a simplistic lumping together of all persons into one or the other of two groups based solely on sexual orientation would give a faulty picture. After all, we don't think in terms of only one *heterosexual* life-style. Why should we assume that only one *homosexual* life-style exists? We know that some heterosexuals are in long-term marriages; some opt for "open" marriages; some persons are sexually inactive; some are "swinging singles," and so on. Bell and Weinberg focused on the similar diversity that exists among homosexual persons. Their study makes it clear that there are vast differences among homosexual persons, and there is no *one* gay life-style. "An important lesson to be learned from our data," say these researchers, "is that homosexual men and women are best understood when

"Homosexual men and women are best understood when they are seen as whole human beings, not just in terms of what they do sexually." (Chie Nishio/Nancy Palmer)

they are seen as whole human beings, not just in terms of what they do sexually, despite the connection between sex and other aspects of their lives" (p. 218).

Bell and Weinberg found that five different types of homosexuals could be categorized from their investigation: (1) *close-coupleds*, persons living in monogamous homosexual relationships similar to heterosexual marriage; (2) *open-coupleds*, persons living with a special same-sex partner but who also seek some sexual and emotional satisfactions outside the relationship; (3) *functionals*, a group Bell and Weinberg compare to "'swinging singles" in the heterosexual world; (4) *dysfunctionals*, "troubled people whose lives offer them little gratification"; and (5) a group the researchers term *asexuals*, defined here as isolated, withdrawn persons whose "most prominent characteristic . . . is their lack of involvement with others" (Bell and Weinberg, 1978:217–228).

WHAT IS A GAY MARRIAGE?

We have pointed out that marriage exists when two (or more) persons maintain ongoing instrumental and expressive exchanges—that is, when they are both economically and sexually interdependent—and when the relationship is publicly known (at least to a circle of friends) so that it is more than an understanding between the parties concerned. Thus, from a sociological point of view, an overt ongoing relationship of two economically and sexually interdependent women, or of two economically and sexually interdependent men, could be called a marriage. In such cases, the persons involved share bed and board and regard themselves as spouses, mates, or lovers rather than as friends or roommates. Their situation may be compared to the heterosexual cohabitors discussed in the first part of this chapter: they are in an ongoing consensual union but without legal recognition.

Indeed, sociologist Donna Tanner (1978), in her study of lesbian couples, compares the development of such relationships to our continuum in Figure 8-1. First, there is the *trial phase* (much like the affair or regularized sexual liaison on the left side of the continuum), the beginning of the romantic attachment. Next, says Tanner, comes an *insulation* period of living together covertly, one function of which is to enable the lesbian couple "to focus their attention on developing a permanent commitment to each other." The third stage, *stabilization*, Tanner compares to the ongoing consensual union in our Figure 8-1, where a couple lives in an overt continuing relationship that is not legally recognized. "Similarly," she writes, "the lesbian dyad becomes accepted as a couple by their friends and is invited out socially as a social unit. The partners have by now begun to establish an economic, emotional, and sexual interdependency" (p. 91). It is at this stage that the relationship fits the sociological definition of marriage. Public acknowledgement of their bonding together as a pair is highly important. In Tanner's study, "one couple reflected that they didn't start thinking of themselves as a social unit until they were defined as such by their peers" (p. 78).

Although a gay marriage might be considered an actual marital union according to a *sociological* definition of marriage, it is not considered a valid marriage from a *legal* standpoint. A test case, *Baker v. Nelson,* occurred when two men appealed to the Minnesota Supreme Court in 1971 after a lower court ruled in favor of a county clerk who had refused to grant the men a marriage license. The homosexual couple contended that since there was no state law specifically prohibiting same-sex marriages, there was no reason to assume such marriages would be illegal.

Their case further relied on arguments based upon the United States Constitution, in particular the Fourteenth Amendment's guarantee that no state shall "deprive any person of life, liberty, or property, without due process of law; nor deny to any person within its jurisdiction the equal protection of the laws." The petitioners argued that the "due process" clause lay at the root of the United States Supreme Court's ruling on the unconstitutionality of a Connecticut law prohibiting the use of contraceptives by married

The 1971 wedding of James Michael McConnell and Jack Baker took place in Minneapolis, despite a court ruling against the legality of homosexual marriage. (United Press International)

couples, because such a law was in violation of the *privacy* inherent in the marital relationship.

Furthermore, according to the homosexual couple, the state was violating the "equal protection" clause by discriminating against them as a same-sex couple. Such patent discrimination could be compared to the racial discrimination in marriage laws which the United States Supreme Court had ruled unconstitutional. The case of *Loving v. Virginia* showed that it is in violation of the Fourteenth Amendment for states to make laws against interracial marriage. In that ruling, Chief Justice Warren had written:

> Marriage is one of the "basic civil rights of man," fundamental to our very existence and survival. To deny this fundamental freedom on so unsupportable a basis as the racial classifications embodied in these [antimiscegenation] statutes, classifications so directly subversive of the principle of equality at the heart of the Fourteenth Amendment, is surely to deprive all the State's citizens of liberty without due process of law. The Fourteenth Amendment requires that the freedom of choice to marry not be restricted by invidious racial discriminations. (Kanowitz, 1973:645–648)

The Supreme Court of Minnesota ruled against the homosexual couple, however, stating that these arguments did not apply to their case. While it was true that the state's statute with regard to marriage did not expressly forbid same-sex marriages, the wording was such, said the court, that heterosexual marriage was clearly the intent. Terms such as *husband and wife* and *bride and groom* were used, and the word *marriage* was employed "as one of common usage, meaning the state of union between persons of the opposite sex."

The court referred to definitions found in *Webster's Dictionary* and *Black's Law Dictionary,* each of which refers to distinctions of sex, and declared that it is unlikely that the original draftsmen of the marriage statutes had anything other than this in mind. The court went on to say that "the institution of marriage as a union of man and woman, uniquely involving the procreation and rearing of children within a family, is as old as the book of Genesis." Disregarded as not applicable was the argument of the homosexual couple that "the state does not impose upon heterosexual married couples a condition that they have a proved capacity or declared willingness to procreate."

The court further declared that the ruling that struck down the Connecticut law regarding contraceptive usage by married couples could not be relied on as a basis for arguing against *all* state interference in marriage. "The basic premise of that decision . . . was that the state, having authorized marriage, was without power to intrude upon the right of privacy inherent in the marital relationship," said the Minnesota Supreme Court justices, pointing out that the state's classification of persons authorized to marry does not violate the Fourteenth Amendment.

However, the court admitted that state restrictions on the right to marry are not entirely beyond the reach of that Amendment, as was shown in the United States Supreme Court's decision which struck down state laws forbidding interracial marriages. "But in commonsense and in a constitutional sense, there is a clear distinction between a marital restriction based merely upon race and one based upon the fundamental difference in sex" (Kanowitz, 1973:647–648). It was decided by the court that the two men did not have the right to marry one another.

"The *Baker* case presents many of the legal problems that arise whenever the government seeks to regulate fundamental societal institutions," writes legal scholar Arthur Silverstein (1972–73:607) in a discussion of the constitutional aspects of the right of homosexual persons to obtain a marriage license. "The states have surrounded the institution of marriage with a variety of legal benefits and restrictions. As part of this regulation, they have also sought to control entry into that institution."

A specialist in family law, Michael Einbinder (1973–74) describes another case that took place in 1973, *Jones v. Hallahan*. Two lesbians had been denied a marriage license, and the Kentucky Court of Appeals upheld the denial. The court did not draw upon constitutional arguments but based its decision solely on the traditional notion of marriage as a union between opposite sex persons. "In addition," says Einbinder, "the court said that even if a license had been issued and a ceremony performed, the resulting relationship would not constitute marriage" (pp. 785–786).

HOMOSEXUAL MARRIAGE AS AN ALTERNATIVE LIFE-STYLE

Despite the fact that gay marriages are not recognized as legal, many lesbians and male homosexuals *do* form lasting same-sex unions which they may think of and speak of as marriages. The ideals of permanence, faithfulness, and a shared life (both sexually and economically) are often held up, just as in the case of heterosexual marriages. Speaking from the standpoint of the homosexual, Del Martin and Paul Mariah (1972:126) ask how a limiting value can be placed upon the sexual expression of love, whether heterosexual or homosexual. "Is it polarity, the joining of male-female and penis-vagina that makes a 'marriage' whole and therefore 'holy'?" they ask. "Isn't it rather the mutual respect and the mutual love for one another, each to and for the other as a human being, that makes the difference? And isn't love 'socially desirable'?"

Some persons enter gay unions repeatedly, each time hoping that the ideal lover has been found. Others have a relationship that has endured for a very long time. Martin and Mariah refer to two men who are now in their seventies and have lived together in a homosexual marriage for more than fifty years, although at the same time they consent to one another's occasional seeking of extra sexual gratification outside their own relationship. (They would fit into Bell and Weinberg's (1978) "open-coupled" category described earlier.) Other long-term homosexual unions are exclusively monogamous—"close-coupled," to use Bell and Weinberg's term. Del Martin and Phyllis

Lyon (1972), founders of a lesbian organization, have written a book describing their many years together in a quasi-marriage and providing examples of other long-lasting lesbian unions. "It is not uncommon to find Lesbian couples who have been together for twenty years or more," say these authors (p. 111).

Many homosexual persons argue that there would be more long-lasting "gay marriages" if society would lend its support and approval. They attribute the high number of failures to society's pressures and the disdain they are subjected to rather than to any inherent weakness in the homosexual relationship itself. Recognizing the need for emotional support among gay persons, various gay organizations have sprung up in recent years, including religious ones. The Metropolitan Community Churches, a denomination founded primarily for gay people by the Rev. Troy Perry who is himself "married" to another male, has weddinglike ceremonies so that homosexual couples and lesbian couples can enter into what the group speaks of as "Holy Union," thereby giving the two persons some sense of a public declaration and formalization of their relationship. There also exist gay synogogues for Jewish homosexuals, and supportive—if not always officially recognized—organizations within both the Roman Catholic church and most Protestant groups. In addition, most religious groups have been giving serious study to the topic of homosexuality in recent years, including in some cases a reconsideration of traditional religious teachings (McNeill, 1976; Woods, 1978; Twiss, 1978; Jennings, 1977; Nelson, 1978; Scanzoni and Mollenkott, 1978; Batchelor, 1980).

But Why Marriage? The question may arise as to why homosexual persons can't simply live together without worrying about legal marriage. Of course, many do live together that way right now; it's the only way they can! But some reply to the question by citing both practical reasons and a need for psychic support. On the practical side, there is the matter of finding housing, because they are likely to encounter discrimination if they wish to let their relationship be known openly. Problems with regard to employment also cause difficulty. "Try telling your boss you can't move to a new job because of your lover," writes Dennis Altman (1971:29), a problem that would be understood if a heterosexual person were speaking of his or her spouse. Other practical problems cluster around insurance, tax laws, and inheritance rights (the homosexual "spouse" is not likely to receive a share of the estate of a partner who left no will, no matter how long the couple has lived together nor how estranged the deceased had been from his or her biological family). Even something so simple as a hospital visit can become a problem. Altman (1971:50) refers to a report in the London *Times* which told of a dying lesbian who was permitted only visits by her immediate family and denied the privilege of seeing her partner of twenty years. Some spokespersons for gay civil rights argue that such problems could be solved by the legalization of gay marriage.

Why the Term *Gay Marriage Matters to Some Gay Persons*

The basic dynamics and nature of a gay relationship based on permanence and fidelity are identical to those of a straight marriage. . . . Three years worth of comparing notes with a great many straight married couples leaves no doubt in my mind that our relationships are of the same order and the same nature. So again I ask, why all the concern about what we shall be allowed to label Gay unions?

I can perceive only one answer. . . . It's the old "the same, but different" evasion tactic that has raised its head as other groups have moved toward their liberation. "Yes, blacks are equal to whites BUT we'll give them their own waterfountains, their own places to sit and their own neighborhoods to live in. Separate but equal. Well . . . almost equal."

It used to be I didn't much care what people called Wayne's and my relationship: a marriage, a holy union, a covenant. I used to think it was best left to semantics—a trifling matter as long as people understood what the relationship was about. I don't think so any more. I had forgotten that what we call things (and people) is very important. Very important indeed.

Well, here it is world: Gay People Get Married. And they will continue to get married whether or not any government or church chooses to sanction their marriages. And it will continue to be hard (sometimes very hard, as has been the case in our marriage) for gay people to sustain their marriages without the social and religious structures and sanctions with which heterosexual people are presently graced. And that, my friends, is oppression.

SOURCE: John Fortunato-Schwandt, "Gay Marriage: A 'Confluence of Terms,' " *Integrity Forum* (May–June 1979), p. 17.

Some gay activists think differently. They refuse to refer to their couple relationships as "marriages"—even though such relationships may perform the functions of marriage as it is usually defined (Barnhart, 1975). Such persons are persuaded that the idea that gays should marry in a legal sense implies that heterosexual marriage is the norm for close social relationships. They suggest that gay couples instead invent new ways of relating that do not imitate conventional marriage. For some, such "new ways" center around sexual concerns and mean breaking free of the sexual exclusivity understood in the traditional marriage contract. For others, the concern doesn't center around sexual matters at all but rather around gender roles and the notion that marriage would almost certainly mean a strict division of labor and a dominance-subordination relationship. The argument is similar to that of some heterosexual cohabitors who reject legal marriage even though the option is open to them.

Sensitive to such feelings, Bell and Weinberg (1978) chose the term *Close-Coupleds* in reference to gay persons in partnerships that were both "close" and "closed." "We resisted the temptation to call this group 'happily married,' although some of its members described themselves that way," say these researchers, "because we did not want to imply that heterosexual relationships and marriage in particular are standards by which to judge people's adjustment'' (p. 219).

However, many homosexual persons are not particularly concerned about terminology. Rather, they are concerned about the psychic costs of being involved in a same-sex union in a society that doesn't recognize the relationship as valid. Altman (1971:66) points out that all the world loves a lover—as long as it's not a homosexual one. He decries the fact that homosexuals do not have the right to publicly express their love without encountering severe ridicule and disapproval. "It is impossible to know to what extent love is strengthened by being public," he writes, "yet . . . I suspect that after a time lovers have a real psychological need for the support that comes from being recognized as such."

Similar anguish was expressed in a letter to a San Francisco newspaper in which a young college-educated male, working his way up in a large corporation, said he could not really expect his career to progress beyond the lower end of middle management without marriage to a woman. The problem was that he already was "married"—but to another male who had come with him when he transferred from another city. His roommate's accompanying him in itself was difficult to explain; but beyond that, the letter writer was mentally tortured by having to pretend constantly that he was single, an eligible bachelor expected to flirt with the women at the office, take them out, and even to give his male colleagues the impression that he was having an affair with some female friend. He said he felt "trapped in a cage of

A Covenant of Commitment

"Of course, there have been mock marriages performed in the gay community, with a friend performing the ceremony, followed by a reception at a gay bar for the newly wedded couple. But there have also been genuine religious services held in a church. These aren't weddings, as heterosexuals know them, but covenant services, a recognition in the sight of God and the church of a bond between the two persons involved.

"We had occasion to witness such a 'Celebration of Commitment' at an Episcopal church when a friend, Joyce, invited us to a service for her and Madeline, which was to be performed by her pastor and with her parents in attendance. Joyce was jubilant when she broke the news to us. This tall, pensive, sensitive young brunette had been through years of struggle with her parents, her church and her psychiatrist. Finally she had received the blessings of all three to be herself.

"Dressed in a simple blue suit, her eyes brimming with joyful tears, she solemnly made her vow to Madeline, 'I give you this ring as a token of our covenant, vowing to live in close friendship, to strive for fuller knowledge of your being, and to care for you above all others. I pledge myself to realize your needs, encourage your full potential, and to love you even as I love myself. May God be between me and thee forever.'"

SOURCE: Del Martin and Phyllis Lyon, *Lesbian/Woman* (San Francisco: Glide Publications, 1972); Bantam Books edition, 1972), pp. 104–105.

pretending." "I am married!" he stated repeatedly. "I do not look one bit different from other respectable, aggressive, married young men." Yet society does not recognize his marriage, because it is a gay marriage. (Reported in Feldman and Thielbar, 1972:338–339).

"Our data indicate that a relatively steady relationship with a love partner is a very meaningful event in the life of a homosexual man or woman," write Bell and Weinberg (1978:102). Their research indicated that such relationships "involve an emotional exchange and commitment similar to the kinds that heterosexuals experience." Homosexual respondents spoke positively of such special relationships "and clearly were not content to limit their sexual contacts to impersonal sex."

Male-Female Differences in Sexual Behavior   We saw in Chapter 5 that different socialization has meant differences in how females and males perceive their sexuality. Males tend to think of sexuality in a more detached and "instrumental" manner, while females learn to view it in a more "expressive" sense, especially in the context of a loving relationship. These gender-related differences are also seen in homosexual behavior patterns.

Homosexual males, for example, are far more likely to engage in *cruising* (going out specifically to look for sexual contacts in such places as gay bars and nightclubs, gay baths, and so on) and to engage in impersonal sex with strangers (Bell and Weinberg, 1978:73–102; Weinberg and Williams, 1974, 1975). In Bell and Weinberg's (1978:299) San Francisco study, only 16 percent of the white homosexual males and 14 percent of the black homosexual males reported they had *not* engaged in cruising during the year before the interview was conducted. In contrast, 83 percent of both black and white lesbians had not cruised.

On a similar note, numerous studies have shown that homosexual males tend to have many more sexual partners over a lifetime than is true of homosexual females. Kinsey and his colleagues (1953:475) reported that among persons who reported having homosexual contact, only 29 percent of the women had engaged in such contact with more than one or two partners, whereas 49 percent of the men reported such a pattern, with many having had "scores or hundreds of sexual partners." In Bell and Weinberg's study, three-fourths of the white homosexual males reported having had one hundred sexual partners or more over the course of their lives. This was also true of 59 percent of the black homosexual males. In contrast, only 2 percent of white lesbians and 4 percent of black lesbians reported this many sexual partners. The majority of the women had had sexual relationships with fewer than ten women over the course of their lives. Some of them (3 percent of white lesbians and 5 percent of black lesbians) had only had one sexual partner ever. This was true of none of the men. (See Table 8-A.)

In a West German study of lesbians and homosexual males aged eighteen to thirty-five, Siegrid Schäfer (1977) of Hamburg University's Institute for Sex Research found that the median number of sexual partners since the first homosexual experience was 5 for women, but fifteen times that number (75)

TABLE 8-A. *Homosexual experience with different partners,*
San Francisco Study.

NUMBER OF HOMOSEXUAL PARTNERS EVER	WHM*	BHM*	WHF*	BHF*
	(N=574)	(N=111)	(N=227)	(N=64)
0: 1	0%	0%	3%	5%
1: 2	0	0	9	5
2: 3–4	1	2	15	14
3: 5–9	2	4	31	30
4: 10–14	3	5	16	9
5: 15–24	3	6	10	16
6: 25–49	8	6	8	11
7: 50–99	9	18	5	8
8: 100–249	15	15	1	2
9: 250–499	17	11	1	2
10: 500–999	15	14	0	0
11: 1000 or more	28	19	0	0

*WHM—White homosexual males; BHM—Black homosexual males; WHF—White homo-
sexual females; BHF—Black homosexual females
SOURCE: Adapted from Alan P. Bell and Martin S. Weinberg, *Homosexualities: A Study of
Diversity Among Men and Women* (New York: Simon and Schuster, 1978), p. 308.

for the men. Schäfer also compared both homosexual persons and heterosexual persons as to the number of sex partners they had had during the last year
before participating in one of several research studies. As Table 8-B shows,
more females (whether homosexual or heterosexual) reported having only
one partner than was true of males. But a distinct difference showed up
between homosexual and heterosexual males—both in the percentages
reporting no more than one sexual partner and in those who reported having
more than six.

Behavioral scientists have suggested that both the divergent socialization
patterns of males and females and the structural situation in certain parts of
the gay subculture may account for such differences. Schäfer emphasizes that
while females have been trained to view sex in a context of love, commitment,

TABLE 8–B. *Partner mobility in homosexual and heterosexual samples (West Germany)*

NUMBER OF SEX PARTNERS IN LAST 12 MONTHS (INTERCOURSE)	HOMOSEXUALS (THIS STUDY)		HETEROSEXUALS					
			STUDENTS (GLESE AND SCHMIDT, 1968)		WORKERS (SCHMIDT AND SIGUSCH, 1971)		ADOLESCENTS (SIGUSCH AND SCHMIDT, 1973)	
	FEMALES (N = 151)	MALES (N = 581)	FEMALES (N = 366)	MALES (N = 1400)	FEMALES (N = 106)	MALES (N = 106)	FEMALES (N = 86)	MALES (N = 105)
1	43%	5%	73%	63%	65%	33%	67%	44%
6 or more	8%	78%	4%	15%	2%	18%	5%	13%

SOURCE: Siegrid Schäfer, ''Sociosexual Behavior in Male and Female Homosexuals: A Study in Sex Differences,'' *Archives of Sexual
Behavior* 6 (September, 1977), p. 361.

and fidelity, both homosexual and heterosexual males have been socialized to regard their sexuality "as something in and of itself," with sexual needs separate from affectional needs. Yet heterosexual males have sexual partners (females) who were socialized to integrate sexuality and affection. Schäfer suggests the possibility that women, plus the institutions of marriage and family, may act as a brake on any tendency heterosexual men might have toward engaging in impersonal sexual contacts with many different partners such as is true of the majority of their homosexual counterparts. "These inhibiting conditions do not exist among homosexual males," writes Schäfer, adding that "this is of course compounded by the standards and norms of their subculture, in which sexual success is an important status symbol" (p. 362). Related to Schäfer's explanation are these comments by Bell and Weinberg (1978):

> Another important reason for homosexual men's large number of partners could be the fact that society provides them with little or no opportunity to meet on anything more than a sexual basis. Driven underground, segregated in what have been termed "sexual marketplaces," threatened but perhaps also stimulated by the danger of their enterprise, homosexual men would be expected to have an enormous number of fleeting sexual encounters. (p. 101)

In addition to differences in the way males and females are socialized and the structural conditions of that part of the male gay subculture that encourages impersonal sexual contacts and the measurement of self-worth in terms of sexual expression, Bell and Weinberg also suggest that the different ways females and males first experience their homosexuality may influence many of the differences between lesbians and gay males. Lesbians tend to have become involved with their partners in an emotional way after knowing them for some time, and only then do they begin expressing their love in a sexual way. Bell and Weinberg point out how different this pattern is from the situation of the gay male, "who is apt to have engaged in numerous sexual activities with other males at a relatively early age and whose model of homosexuality consists chiefly of men 'on the make,' of sex without commitment, of the excitement of sexual pursuit" (p. 102).

At the same time, it must be remembered that many homosexual males establish ongoing same-sex love relationships and live in quasi-marriage partnerships with the special person in their lives.

Everyday Life among Gay Couples   Bell and Weinberg (1978:346) found that 10 percent of the homosexual males in their sample and 28 percent of the homosexual females were living in homosexual couple relationships comparable to marriage. Comparing these "Close-Coupleds" with the other homosexual groups in their study, Bell and Weinberg write:

> They were the least likely to seek partners outside their special relationship, had the smallest amount of sexual problems, and were unlikely to regret being

homosexual. They tended to spend more evenings at home and less leisure time by themselves, and the men in this group seldom went to such popular cruising spots as bars or baths. . . . Both the men and the women were more self-accepting and less depressed or lonely than any of the others, and they were the happiest of all. (pp. 219–220)

In addition to the Close-Coupled, 18 percent of the male respondents and 17 percent of the female respondents were in Open-Coupled relationships. "They were not happy with their circumstances, however," write Bell and Weinberg, "and tended (despite spending a fair amount of time at home) to seek satisfactions with people outside their partnership" (p. 221).

The majority of homosexual couples reported that they shared housework equally and that they combined their incomes totally or in part, although there were certain household responsibilities that fell more to one partner than the other (Bell and Weinberg, 1978:91–101, 323–324).

"Coupled" homosexual persons, like "single" homosexual persons, tended to belong to friendship cliques or networks that served as the functional equivalent of the extended family (Bell and Weinberg, 1978:247–249). Research psychologist Evelyn Hooker (1965) has pointed out that this less visible part of the overall gay community must be recognized if we are to understand the whole. Such friendship groups may get together for spur of the moment dinners or may plan elaborate cocktail parties. Often they will celebrate someone's birthday or the anniversary of one of the homosexual couples.

In Tanner's (1978) study of lesbian couples, she found that often anniversaries are private affairs, "ranging from a bottle of wine at home to dinner at a favorite restaurant." One couple reported celebrating their anniversary every month during the first year, but yearly thereafter. Favorite leisure activities for the lesbian couples in Tanner's study included watching television together or attending movies, getting together with friends, and eating out. Some couples mentioned enjoying concerts and museums together; others told of shared hobbies ranging from camping to chess, from skiing to taking adult evening courses together. "Almost all the couples interviewed said they had dinner parties for friends, usually gay friends, at least once a month," writes Tanner. "This could include anything from ordering Kentucky Fried Chicken to a sit-down dinner with candles with two other couples" (pp. 83–84).

Of course, like their heterosexual counterparts, most homosexual couples spend the greater proportion of their time in occupational pursuits. For all these reasons, a comment by Bell and Weinberg (1978) is fitting:

It is little wonder that so many homosexual men and women reject the label "homosexual," in that it exaggerates the sexual component of their lives, and prefer such terms as "gay," "lesbian," or "homophile." These terms connote much more an entire life-style, a way of being in the world which only incidentally involves sexual activity with persons of the same sex. (p. 115)

In Bell and Weinberg's study, 20 percent of the white homosexual men and 13 percent of the black homosexual men reported that they had been married to women in the past. And among the lesbians in the sample, over one-third of the white women and nearly half of the black women had been married to men. Bell and Weinberg suggest that the greater incidence of cross-sex marriage among homosexual women may be related to *physiological* factors (women are physically able to participate in sexual intercourse apart from being sexually aroused) and to *social* factors (the expectation that females will grow up to marry and have children). These researchers also found that it is not unusual for some lesbians to be unaware of their homosexuality until after marriage to a male. These women's marriages tended not to last long, and the cause of the marital dissolution often related to their having formed a lesbian relationship with another woman or to their lack of interest in sexual intercourse with their husbands (Bell and Weinberg, 1978:160–170).

The homosexual males in this study tended to report that their marriages had been more satisfactory than was true of the lesbians, yet less happy than the comparison group of heterosexual males. Homosexual husbands "tended not to have told their wives about their homosexuality before marriage nor to have promised to do anything about it." A considerable number (more than half) of homosexual husbands reported that while engaging in sexual intercourse with their wives, they had sometimes or often fantasized that they were with a male partner instead. Most of these marriages broke up for reasons similar to those of the lesbians in the study: involvement in a homosexual relationship or lack of interest in sex with their spouses. Some reported that wives simply refused to tolerate the husband's homosexuality (p. 165).

In another study, sociologist Brian Miller (1978) classified thirty homosexual husbands into four basic categories. First, there are those who absolutely refuse to think of themselves as homosexual and who dismiss their secretive extramarital sex with other males as nothing more than physical release. They stay apart from the social aspects of the overt gay subculture, and their behavior "is characterized by clandestine, impersonal encounters in parks, tearooms [men's rooms], highway rest stops, and with hitchhikers or male hustlers" (p. 214). A second category consists of men who acknowledge themselves to be homosexual and don't try to fool themselves about their extramarital same-sex behavior. But they are less likely to look for impersonal sexual contacts in the same kinds of places as is true of the first category. They *are* like the first category, however, in that their conventional family life-style provides them with a cover, that is, a *public* identity that is heterosexual.

The third category of homosexual men observed by Miller were those who were separated or divorced from their wives and who were somewhat involved in the overt gay subculture's social networks and activities, while at the same time "passing" as heterosexual in certain other contexts—especially employment. The final category of homosexual men interviewed by Miller also were no longer living with their wives. But unlike the category just described, these men become *thoroughly* immersed in the gay world and are often self-employed (in many cases with a gay clientele) or work for an employer who does not see their overt homosexuality and gay activism as a problem.

Miller points out that some men may over a period of time move from one category to another to still another in an increasing acceptance of their homosexuality. This gradual process entails reformulating both personal and social identity and is often initiated by "falling in love with another man" (p. 228). Miller points out that the entire process of change in these men's self-images and their reconception of the outer world provides an example of adult resocialization. What had once been viewed as a stigmatized identity (homosexual), and thus not accepted as applicable to oneself, gradually comes to be viewed in positive terms. At some point, such a man begins to identify with gay subculture life and looks to persons in the gay community as his new reference group.

GAY PARENTHOOD

The men in Miller's first category were especially likely to rank their fatherhood role as central to their lives. One reported that his marriage was horrible but that the children were "the consolation prize." Another told the researcher, "My children are the only humans I have ever loved. . . . I need my kids; they're what keep me going" (p. 216). A homosexual husband in the second category reported that his children were the reason he had remained in an unsatisfactory marriage. Each year, he would consider divorce but decide to wait until the children were older. "Now that they are in college, I can't leave because they are my judges," he said. "They'd never forgive me for doing this all these years to their mother" (p. 217).

Do Gay Parents Want Their Children to Be Gay?

"Most thoughtful gay parents want their children to be who they are. Most of us realize that early in our own background our feelings were established, and most of us can recall being attracted to members of the same sex at a very early time—certainly before our 10th birthdays. At the same time, most gay parents would prefer that their children not be subjected to hostility and, therefore I suspect, would in one sense be more pleased if their children were heterosexual—not because of any aversion to homosexuality—but merely because of the ugly treatment they would not like to have their children endure. But that's a dangerous line of thinking, for it's as if blacks were to prefer that their children had been white or that parents had preferred that their daughters were sons. It's an ugly part of society which has to be changed."—Bruce Voeller, a gay father and Co-Executive Director of the National Gay Task Force, in reply to a question about whether gay parents worry that their children may be homosexual.

SOURCE: Bruce Voeller and James Walters (interviewer), "Gay Fathers," *The Family Coordinator* 27 (April 1978) p. 151.

In Bell and Weinberg's much larger sample, of the white homosexual males and white homosexual females who had been married heterosexually, 50 percent reported having children. An even higher proportion of the black homosexual formerly-marrieds were parents—71 percent of the men and 73 percent of the women (p. 391). The small number of homosexual parents who said they had children age twelve or older who knew about their homosexuality tended to report that the parent-child relationship had not suffered as a result of the children's awareness (see also Miller, 1979). Sociologist Mildred Pagelow (1976) reports that her research on lesbian mothers indicates it may be easier for these women to let children know than it is to acknowledge their homosexual life-style to other relatives, especially parental family members. She writes:

> It appears that the majority of Lesbian mothers prefers to be open with their children, especially when they share a home with their lovers; yet they often feel compelled to "pass" with their own parents. Techniques involve suppression of affectionate behavior, little or no physical contact while in the presence of parents, and frequently a rearrangement of clothing and bedroom furniture. (p. 7)

Lesbian Mothers

Sandra Schuster and Madeleine Isaacson are a lesbian couple who were granted custody of their six children in 1971—a decision that was contested by their former husbands and went through various stages of litigation, eventually reaching the Washington State Supreme Court. At first the women were given temporary custody, then later were told they could retain custody on the condition that the two of them wouldn't live together. They found apartments across the hall from each other and later petitioned the court for and were granted a modification of that order so that they could live together as a family unit. At the same time in 1974, their former husbands, having remarried, sought a reconsideration of the custody decision, arguing that their children would be better off in the heterosexual home environments the fathers could now provide. The Supreme Court of the state of Washington heard their case in 1976 and requested a rehearing which took place a year later. Still another year passed before a decision was handed down and then finalized February 28, 1979. Only two of the justices felt the women should retain custody and continue living together, while four others felt they should have custody but live separately as in the original decision. The three remaining justices were of the opinion that custody should be granted to the children's fathers instead. The ruling of the lower court stood because there was no consensus by a majority of five.

In a 1978 photo essay, Linda Reed has written:

> Sandy and Madeleine feel their daily activities are not much different than other families in what they describe as their "conservative" neighborhood. "We get up every day, brush our teeth, go to work. Our kids go to soccer, take music lessons and everything else."

(Picture—The Northwest Photo Magazine.)

Madeleine feels that "when people think of homosexuality, they think in terms of sex only. I have the idea that people think I spend all my time in bed. Do you know what it's like to have six kids? I'm lucky if I get to bed at all. We're a family, and ninety percent of our lives and problems are just like everybody else's."

SOURCE: Based on personal correspondence from Sandra Schuster and Madeleine Isaacson to the authors, March 1 and May 14, 1979; and Linda Reed, "Sandy, Madeleine & the Kids," *Picture* (December, 1978), pp. 6–9.

ROLES IN GAY COUPLE RELATIONSHIPS

Many people have the idea that homosexual couples pattern their lives after traditional heterosexual marriage, with one partner playing a "husband" role and the other partner playing a "wife" role in all aspects of life, ranging from how the courtship was conducted, through household division of labor, to sexual techniques employed by each person.

Some basis for such a stereotype existed in the past and has continued to a lesser extent into the present. In one unusual case, a San Diego superior court judge ordered a lesbian to pay $100 monthly support to her ex-partner who had given up her job in another city to be with the woman, the two having participated in a Holy Union ceremony at a Metropolitan Community Church and also having signed an agreement in which the one who had given up her job agreed to perform the duties of a housewife while the other agreed to be the breadwinner for both. When the relationship ended, the woman who had agreed to the "wife" role brought suit against the other woman for breach of contract. The judge saw the case as analogous to cohabitation situations where rulings on property and support agreements among unmarried heterosexual couples have been issued (the *Advocate*, San Francisco, July 12, 1978; Lewis, 1979:136).

Bell and Weinberg (1978) found only limited evidence of such stereotyped role playing in their San Francisco study. When homosexual males and homosexual females in same-sex coupled relationships were asked whether they or their partner did all the "feminine" or "masculine" tasks around the house, only a few of either sex reported such a domestic arrangement (pp. 93, 101, 325). Folk beliefs about a simplistic dichotomy of "active" and "passive" partners in *sexual* aspects of such relationships also were not supported. Bell and Weinberg's data showed that both homosexual men and lesbians "are apt to engage in many different forms of sexual contact with their partners and that a very strict adherence to a particular sexual role is quite uncommon" (p. 111). Sex researchers William Masters and Virginia Johnson (1979:213–215) speak of the "my-turn–your-turn" sexual interaction characteristic of homosexual relationships, with each partner having a turn as initiator and as responder, as both giver and receiver.

According to one sociologist, some evidence exists for continued stereotypically "masculine" role playing on the part of some lesbians ("butch" role) and stereotypically "feminine" role playing on the part of other lesbians ("femme" role) with whom they form attachments (Jensen, 1974).

One of the most famous lesbian relationships of all time was that of the writer Gertrude Stein and her companion of forty years, Alice B. Toklas. Their stereotypical role-playing is much less common in lesbian partnerships today. (Culver Pictures)

" 'I am a person acted upon, not a person who acts,' Alice told one of Gertrude's biographers; but she was certainly active when it came to managing their lives. She cooked, gardened, kept house, made travel arrangements, typed Gertrude's manuscripts—and even published them for a time under the imprint of Plain Edition. When guests showed up, Alice was called upon to entertain their wives. The ladies were, of course, 'second-class citizens,' [Allen] Tate recalled. It was a far cry from the lesbian salon of Natalie Barney a few streets away, where women danced in one another's arms and disappeared into bedrooms; but, then, Alice and Gertrude were a bourgeois couple, monogamous and proper. And Alice was—to use the contemporary word—'oppressed'; even 'The Autobiography of Alice B. Toklas' was written by Gertrude. Not until after Gertrude's death in 1946, when she continued to receive their old friends and wrote her famous cookbook, did she really come into her own."

SOURCE: James Atlas, "Alice Entertained the Wives," The *New York Times Book Review* (July 10, 1979), p. 15.

Role playing of this sort, however, "is characteristic of a minority of women in the lesbian subculture today," reports another sociologist, Barbara Ponse (1978:115). In her three-year study of that subculture, respondents who reported ever having engaged in role playing indicated that it was "a temporary pattern of behavior, engaged in either playfully or seriously in light of expectations they encountered in particular groups or relationships.

Thus, it was a passing phase of becoming socialized into the life of the lesbian world" (p. 121).

One reason role playing occurred to a greater degree in the past was explained by one woman who said that twenty years ago, many lesbians, particularly in small towns and rural areas, "didn't have any other models to follow so when they found themselves attracted to women, they really thought they must be like men." She concluded that "it's really meeting other lesbians and being in the community that teaches you that you don't have to be masculine to love another woman" (quoted in Ponse, 1978:120). Ponse points to the feminist movement and the widespread questioning of stereotypical gender roles, along with gay political activism and the greater visibility of the gay community as forces contributing toward the diminishing of role-playing expectations. Another study indicates that androgyny in gay couple relationships contributes to greater satisfaction, since both partners are displaying both instrumental and expressive qualities within the relationship (Ickes et al., 1979).

TYPES OF GAY MARRIAGES

Tanner (1978) divides the lesbian quasi-marriages in her study into three types. She then compares each one to a corresponding pattern in our own typology of heterosexual marriages (described in Chapters 10 and 11 of this book).

Tanner's *traditional-complementary* category of lesbian couples corresponds to our "head-complement" category—a marriage arrangement in which one partner is the dominant, unique breadwinner and the other is the dependent homemaker. Traditional gender roles are followed in the division of labor.

A second type of lesbian relationship observed by Tanner is the *flexible nurturing-caretaking* model. Such a relationship allows for more flexibility so that the division of labor is *not* along conventional gender role lines. However, in this type of relationship, one of the partners tends to be the caretaker, earning more money and also meeting the greater emotional needs of the partner (who in some cases may be a student). "The caretaking partner usually admits to enjoying the feeling of having someone dependent on her and likes the 'mother streak' it brings out in her," writes Tanner (p. 103). Where both partners are employed but the incomes are unequal, the bargaining power differential that results is comparable to the situation in our senior partner–junior partner model of marriage described in Chapter 11.

The final category described by Tanner is the *negotiated-egalitarian* type of lesbian union, which she compares to our equal partnership model. Role-interchangeability, equal authority in decision-making, and mutual interdependency and reciprocity characterize such relationships. Roles are negotiated and renegotiated as personal and situational changes arise; they are not arbitrarily assigned on the basis of stereotypical gender-role patterns or anything else.

259

THE COHABITATION
AND GAY
MARRIAGE
ALTERNATIVES

WHEN GAY RELATIONSHIPS END

Tanner's study was based on a sample of twelve lesbian couples. Although at the time of the interviews one of these marriagelike relationships had been in existence for twelve years, Tanner found the average length to be about two years. She collected her data between 1972 and 1975; and by the time her findings were published in 1978, only two of the lesbian partnerships were still intact. "A long-lasting dyadic relationship is rare," concludes Tanner (p. 107).

Breaking Up But why? No doubt the lack of social support is a major contributing factor. Whereas heterosexual couples are given every encouragement to stay together and establish a strong home life, homosexual couples are given no societal support at all. With rare exceptions, any support they have must come from other homosexual persons. Those couples who have enduring relationships are often envied by those who long to experience such a relationship, and there is much sadness in watching such a relationship come to an end. Jensen (1974) reports that after one gay marriage in her sample broke up, all of the other lesbians in the community endeavored to comfort the partner, who was considered to have been mistreated. But at the same time, they voiced fears "that dreams of a lasting homosexual union may only be illusory."

In the larger society, not only are homosexual couples *not* encouraged to remain together; they are positively encouraged to break off their relationships, because many persons—including their families, friends, employers, and religious leaders—consider such relationships to be immoral. Sociologist Norval Glenn (1979) found that data from seven different national samples during the mid-1970s indicated that attitudes toward homosexuality continue to be "highly restrictive" in contrast to the greater permissiveness in attitudes toward premarital sexual relations. Close to three-fourths of the respondents, in these samples of 1,500 each, answered that homosexual relations are "always wrong."

Tanner (1978:3) points out that not only must homosexual couples face the lack of social support and the absence of "scripts" or models to follow in establishing and sustaining a gay quasi-marriage relationship; they also face certain unique strains. For example, the two persons must often separate for holidays because relatives expect them to come to their respective parental homes, not knowing they are "coupled" and not likely to approve even if they did know. Then there are the usual problems and conflicts that any couple, whether homosexual or heterosexual, must work out in living together. Jealousy was often mentioned as a conflict area in Tanner's sample, as was money. "In all of the dyads where money was a point of contention one partner was earning considerably more than the other," Tanner explains, "and the quarrels concerned feelings of dependence or frustration about the inequitable ability of one person to make her financial contribution to the household" (p. 81). In Bell and Weinberg's sample, on the other hand, income disparity for the most part had no particular effect on the relationships of either male or female homosexual couples.

Bell and Weinberg (1978:315) found that the two major reasons lesbian couples tended to break up related to one partner's romantic involvement with another woman or else dissatisfaction with their own relationship. Homosexual male couples tended to report their breakups occurred for reasons beyond their control (for example, a partner's moving away because of employment, military service, or educational opportunities). Others reported that the relationship was unsatisfying to one or both partners. The percentage that broke up because one of the partners became romantically involved with someone else was considerably smaller than among their female counterparts.

The late Howard J. Brown (1976:141) wrote: "A homosexual trying to make his way in a long-term relationship is like a member of any minority group making an incursion on territory hitherto forbidden: He must be stronger, braver, and wiser than everyone else to avoid foundering." A highly respected physician, medical school professor, hospital administrator, and chief health officer of New York City under Mayor John Lindsay's administration, Brown had begun working to change societal attitudes toward homosexual persons and had announced his own homosexual orientation shortly before being stricken with a fatal heart attack in 1975 at the age of fifty-one.

Not only does the stigma attached to homosexual relationships and the absence of societal support mean that gay persons must work especially hard on their couple commitments; they may also find that these same factors mean that their interdependency is even greater than that of heterosexual couples. Thus, their breakups are especially painful, with the result that one or the other partners may even contemplate suicide at such a time. In pointing this out, Bell and Weinberg (1978:216) refer to data that indicate that failure to establish an ongoing relationship "may be even more consequential and problematic for most homosexual adults than whatever difficulties they might have in accepting their homosexuality." These behavioral scientists suggest that counselors work with *couples* as well as individuals in order to help homosexual persons in quasi-marital unions to strengthen their relationships and work out difficulties, or else "to make their eventual parting an occasion for personal growth instead of alienation."

Gay couples who have sought consecration of their commitment through a Holy Union ceremony in the Metropolitan Community Churches are expected to seek a special "divorce" or "annulment" through that denomination if the marriage ends. Only then are they considered free to enter a same-sex remarriage.

Separation by Death As is true of their heterosexual counterparts, not all homosexual marriages fall apart. Many endure to the very end, and the partners are separated only by one or the other's death.

One of television's "All in the Family" programs captured some of the pathos surrounding such circumstances. Edith Bunker's "spinster" cousin had died, and not until the time of the funeral did the Bunkers learn of her long-term quasi-marriage to her female apartment mate. While Archie pronounced God's wrath upon the relationship and fumed over the bereaved partner's request to keep a sentimentally valued silver tea set, his wife put aside her shock and quickly grasped the human element. She realized that the two women, both schoolteachers, most assuredly would have lost their jobs had their lesbian relationship been made known. With genuine warmth and caring, Edith recognized the depth of her cousin's partner's grief and spoke of how hard it must have been to love somebody so much and not be able to tell anyone about it.

The partners in some gay marriages prepare for the eventuality of death by naming one another as beneficiaries to life insurance policies or provide for each other in wills. In such relationships, however, even where there are wills, relatives sometimes contest them. The boxed insert on this page shows

Loss of a Homosexual Partner through Death

I know of a homosexual couple who had lived together for twenty-one years. One of the men died suddenly of pneumonia. A week after the funeral, his brothers appeared at the apartment; they had come to pack up and move out his furniture, paintings, tableware—everything. The two lovers had bought many of these things together over the years, but the apartment belonged to the deceased. The surviving partner told me that he believed that his lover's brothers had long suspected that theirs was a homosexual relationship and that now the brothers were, in effect, challenging him to defend his right to any of the belongings. He said nothing, and was left with nothing.

Forewarned, of course, homosexual couples can prevent this sort of thing (though I have known of cases where the family of the deceased contested his will, where, once again, the homosexual is caught in a vicious circle, for the law does not allow him to marry his partner, but at the same time it cannot assure him that his partner will inherit his estate because the two men were not married). What is almost impossible to avoid, until and unless society recognizes homosexual relationships, is the shock, the horror, and the utter loneliness of facing a bereavement without any of the traditional consolations. Relegated to the status of mere friend, the surviving partner must watch helplessly as members of his lover's family move in and establish their claim as next of kin, as they make funeral arrangements their own way, possibly shipping the body out of town. The fanfare surrounding death in our society is a tried and true way of protecting mourners from the first few weeks of grief, distracting them and at the same time acknowledging the importance of what they are going through. Not only must a homosexual face his grief without such support; he is also obliged, unless he is in an unusual situation, to completely hide what he is feeling. This sets up an unbearable emotional cul-de-sac. I have known men to be shattered by it.

SOURCE: Howard Brown, *Familiar Faces, Hidden Lives: The Story of Homosexual Men in America Today* (New York: Harcourt Brace Jovanovich, 1976), pp. 140–141.

some of the psychic pain experienced by the partner who is left alone. In any case, the desire to provide for the loved one after one's own death illustrates the expectation of permanence that characterizes many homosexual unions. For some, the intent is clearly "until death do us part"—even though society provides no legal recognition of gay marriages at this point in time.

CHAPTER HIGHLIGHTS

This chapter has focused on *cohabitation* (an arrangement in which unmarried opposite sex partners set up a household together) and *gay marriage* (a similar arrangement between homosexual partners).

Heterosexual couples who live together outside marriage may have in mind a *trial marriage* (to test whether or not they want to be married and to prepare for later marriage), a *common-law marriage* (considered a legal marriage in a small number of states), or an *ad hoc arrangement* in which the relationship exists for its own sake and as a substitute (not preparation) for marriage. Furthermore, the phenomenon of cohabitation forces us to see that it isn't enough to think in terms of two statuses: singleness and marriage. Rather, marriage is a matter of degrees along a continuum. Between nonmarriage and formal legal marriage exists a sociological definition of marriage as an ongoing, publicly declared relationship of sexual, emotional, and financial interdependency. Evidence thus far suggests that most cohabitation relationships either dissolve or the partners get married. To simply continue in an ongoing consensual union is not common. Couples usually drift into cohabitation arrangements gradually and maintain them so long as rewards exceed costs. In general, cohabitation rates for divorced persons are higher than for never-married persons. Cohabitation may be called a *quasi-* (or "as if") marriage in that a woman and man are sharing a life together materially, emotionally, and sexually; yet it lacks the legal recognition and social support necessary for marriage to exist in the fullest sense of the word.

Persons interested in another kind of quasi-marriage, *gay marriage,* want to be united in a socially recognized relationship to persons they love, even though the persons they love are of the same sex. A gay union can be considered a valid marriage in the *sociological* sense, but as yet it is not recognized in the legal sense. A sustained homosexual relationship is thus an *ongoing consensual union* as in the case of heterosexual cohabitors, but without the option of legal marriage. Those homosexual persons who would like to see gay marriage recognized in law are concerned both about the psychic costs of not having their coupled relationships validated publicly and about the costs in terms of legal privileges and financial benefits denied them. Many homosexual couples consider themselves married, even if society does not, and work to establish permanent relationships. Homosexual males usually have a much greater number of sexual partners over a lifetime than is true of lesbians, reflecting divergent socialization which stresses a more instrumental attitude toward sex for males in general and a more expressive attitude toward sex among females in general. Role playing similar to traditional stereotypical gender roles was at one time somewhat more common among homosexual persons than at present. The trend is away from role playing and toward egalitarian relationships.

CHAPTER 9

(Barbara Pfeffer/Peter Arnold, Inc.)

LIVING ALONE
AND IN GROUPS

I n the preceding chapter, we examined two alternatives to traditional marriage which were nevertheless based upon *couple* relationships. However, whether by choice or by circumstance, not everyone lives as part of a pair. Some people live alone. Others live with their children. And still others live in some sort of group arrangement.

SINGLENESS

In 1970, Roberta Hornig wrote an article for the *Washington Evening Star* entitled "See Aunt Debbie . . . First-Grade Symbol of Swinging Single," which presented the suggestion that grade school children not only needed to see women in roles other than that of homemaker; they needed also to gain a strong image of the unmarried career woman. To aid in this, first-grade reading books could introduce attractive, active, happy, fulfilled "Aunt Debbie," who could show Dick and Jane through her example that alternative life-styles exist for women. Not all women are wives and mothers. Children could learn that single women can lead interesting, exciting lives and work in occupations that bring great enjoyment (in Bernard, 1972, chap. 10).

SINGLENESS IN HISTORICAL PERSPECTIVE

Children in early America heard an altogether different message than that suggested by Hornig's proposal for a positive presentation of singleness. A North Carolina physician wrote in 1731: "[Girls] marry generally very young, some at thirteen or fourteen, and she that continues unmarried until twenty, is reckoned a stale maid, which is a very indifferent character in that country." In Puritan society, women were called "ancient maids" if they had not married by the time they reached their twenty-fifth birthday (Calhoun, vol. 1, 1919:67, 245). There were no sparkling, vivacious, ambitious, industrious Aunt Debbies around then. The single state received no encouragement whatsoever. In fact, it was positively discouraged.

Both social and economic sanctions were used to push people into marriage. Older single women were ridiculed, often despised, treated as life's failures, and assigned to unpaid drudge-work in the homes of married brothers and sisters. To make matters worse, there arose in literature the stereotype of the neurotic spinster, the meddling busybody, the sour, prim, and proper "old maid" of the children's card game (Watt, 1957, chap. 5).

Bachelors were mocked and treated with harsh disapproval, too. Early American society found it difficult to tolerate unattached persons of either sex. Arthur Calhoun (1919), a social historian, points out that bachelors virtually found themselves "in the class of suspected criminals." Rarely were

Origin of the Term "Spinster"

The denotation and connotation of the word "spinster" has changed greatly over time, paralleling the changing status of single women in their society and their own political consciousness. In the seventeenth century, the term was used generally to refer to the female sex. The task of spinning was part of every woman's daily routine. Late in the century, the word became a legal term for the unmarried woman. Spinning was the prime contribution made by these women to the domestic economy. In the eighteenth century, spinning schools were established by New England's communities to occupy and make socially productive its dependents—orphans, widows, and single women. With the industrial revolution, this socially and economically productive role was lost. The word "spinster" took on the negative connotations of extra, left-over, dried up, and grasping. By late in the nineteenth century, the single woman, particularly of a professional, reform, or intellectual cast, was branded in major medical texts as a "mannish maiden," an Hermaphrodite, no longer strictly female in sex. Yet among themselves, unmarried women used the term "productive spinster," harkening back to a time when the word was used with pride and designated a woman of valued and significant occupation.

SOURCE: Lee Chambers-Schiller, "The Single Woman: Family and Vocation among Nineteenth-Century Reformers," in Mary Kelley (ed.), *Woman's Being, Woman's Place: Female Identity and Vocation in American History* (Boston: G. K. Hall, 1979, p. 348).

single men permitted to live alone or even to decide *where* they should live; the courts decided that for them. Many of the colonies had a "bachelor tax" as a further incentive to enter the married state. In Connecticut, Hartford taxed unmarried men twenty shillings a week, and New Haven enacted a law requiring unmarried persons of either sex to live with "licensed" families. Single men and women not living with relatives or in service as apprentices "are forbidden to diet or lodge alone," said the law. The city officials declared that such a law fulfilled the intent of the biblical commandment to obey parents by providing substitute parents for bachelors and spinsters (who were evidently suspected of acting in a wayward manner if they lacked the supervision and restraints of a family). The heads of the specially selected licensed families that took single persons under their care were ordered "to observe the course, carriage, and behavior of every such single person, whether he or she walk diligently in a constant lawful employment, attending both family duties and the public worship of God, and keeping good order day and night or otherwise" (vol. 1, 1919:67–68).

Bachelors were especially under continual surveillance in the New England colonies, being watched by the constable, the watchman, and the tithingman. Whereas today a person might choose singlehood in order to be free, it was marriage that freed a man in Puritan society. Only upon taking a wife could he escape the restrictions just mentioned. Furthermore, many New England towns provided building lots when a man exchanged his bachelor existence for the role of husband. In a society that placed a high value on family life and which needed to grow in population, pressures and incentives toward marriage were in abundance.

The main incentives to encourage persons to marry were economic. The bachelor tax drained off part of the single man's income, and in addition he was without the benefits of a wife and children to care for household needs and help him with farm chores or in the shop. Benjamin Franklin's (1745) advice about marriage was that "a single man has not nearly the value he would have in that state of union. He is an incomplete animal. He resembles the odd half of a pair of scissors."

Women, too, were constantly reminded that marriage was expected of them. Almost no other way of securing financial support was open to them. Even so, an early Maryland law was designed to make sure they got the message. A woman, who had inherited land was required to marry within seven years. Otherwise, the land would be forfeited to the next of kin or else she would have to dispose of it. The reason for the law was clearly spelled out: "That it may be prevented that noe woman here vow chastity in the world." She was to realize that her land "is gonne unless she git a husband" (quoted in Calhoun, vol. 1, 1919:247). Despite certain laws and informal pressures, some women did choose to remain single. The Plymouth church records of 1667 list the death of Governor Bradford's ninety-one-year-old sister-in-law, describing her as "a godly old maid never married." Other records indicate that Taunton, Massachusetts, was founded by "an ancient maid of forty-eight" (Calhoun, vol. 1, 1919:69).

The old song about the married man who wished he were single so that his pockets would jingle gets to the root of an attitude held by many bachelors—especially in the eighteenth-century South. This was true despite the costs involved (Maryland's part in the French and Indian War was financed by taxes on light wines, billiard tables, and bachelors, for example), because many men felt the responsibility of providing for a wife and children would be an even higher price to pay. In addition, there were men who felt that a free-swinging sex life with a variety of women was to be preferred over the restraints of settled domesticity with one spouse and attention-demanding children (Calhoun, vol. 1, 1919:246; vol. 2, 1919:208).

Some men remained single not by choice but by circumstance. With the movement westward, there arose a situation in which the supply of women did not match the supply of men. Miners, traders, trappers, loggers, and cowboys often remained single even though many of them might have preferred marriage. Yet both the nature of their work and the scarcity of available women placed obstacles in the way. Newspapers in the 1830s suggested that "the excess of spinsters in our large cities" could be alleviated by transporting them to the new settlements. Such women came to be spoken of in terms of some commodity to be shipped. An 1837 newspaper, for example, reported that "a wagon load of girls for the western market lately past through Northhampton, Mass" (Calhoun, vol. 2, 1919:104).

Sociologist Jessie Bernard (1979:xiii) illustrates the intensity of the pressures urging young women to marry by citing an old parochial school rhyme:

St. Catherine, St. Catherine, oh lend me thine aid,
And grant that I never may die an old maid!
A husband, St. Catherine!
A good one, St. Catherine!
But anyone better than no one, St. Catherine!
A husband, St. Catherine!
Handsome, St. Catherine!
Rich, St. Catherine!
Young, St. Catherine!
Soon, St. Catherine!

SINGLENESS AS A LIFE-STYLE TODAY

In 1973 a new magazine was launched. Its title? Simply one word—*Single*. That a special-interest magazine would come on the scene devoted solely to the concerns of unattached persons would have seemed strange in earlier periods of United States history. But at the present time, the single life-style is being chosen by growing numbers of persons—in some cases temporarily (but for a longer period as we saw in Chapter 6 in our discussion of rises in age at marriage) and in other cases permanently. Persons seem to be more cautious about when (and even *if*) they eventually will enter a legal union—another indication of trends toward rationality in choices about marriage. In terms of exchange theory, we may say that as more persons begin to calculate the costs and benefits of marriage, the greater the likelihood that some of them will assess a pattern of ongoing singleness to be basically more rewarding than legal marriage.

At various times the single person may or may not share an apartment with someone of the same or opposite sex, live in a commune, or have a trial marriage. But the significant point is that the traditional notion in our society that persons *must* marry for maximum happiness and well-being is increasingly being questioned.

How Many Stay Single? Most persons eventually marry. As Figure 9-1 shows, few persons over age thirty-five have never been married; and by the time they are in the age forty-five–fifty-four bracket, only 6 percent of men and 4 percent of women have been single all their lives (Rawlings, 1978).

However, this "all-time low rate of lifetime singlehood" must be understood in view of the fact that these middle-agers had been in their peak years for marrying at a time when both marriage and birthrates were high and people tended to marry early (Glick, 1979:2). The picture may very well be changing in view of the postponement of marriage among a considerable percentage of young persons today. "The longer the pattern of increasing postponement of marriage persists, the more likely the prospect becomes that the extent of lifetime singlehood among young adults of today will increase,"

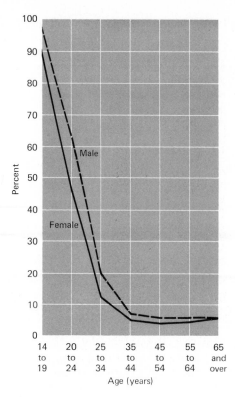

FIGURE 9-1 Never-married persons, by age: March 1977. (SOURCE: *Stephen Rawlings, "Perspectives on American Husbands and Wives,"* Current Population Reports: Special Studies, *Series P-23, No. 77, December 1978, p. 3.)*

reports demographer Paul Glick (1979:2), emphasizing the changes that are especially pronounced among women. In 1960, among women between ages twenty and twenty-four, only 28 percent had never been married. By 1977, the percentage had climbed to 45 for the same age bracket.

Education and Singleness   If trends toward increasing singleness and later age at marriage are showing up among women as a whole, we may expect such trends to expand most rapidly among those women who have access to socioeconomically rewarding alternatives to marriage. Highly educated women have most to gain from greater female autonomy and individualism since they are best prepared to enter occupations that offer the greatest benefits in terms of prestige and income.

Sociological studies in recent years have shown that higher levels of intelligence, education, and occupation are associated with singleness among women (Spreitzer and Riley, 1974:536). In the past, this association has sometimes been explained by the suggestion that women of high education and achievement are "marital rejects" or "pathetic misfits," persons who are "unfeminine" and "undesirable" to males and who therefore remain unchosen. However, the explanation may very well lie in the opposite direction. The active choosing may be on the part of the *women*. One sociologist, after a study of census data which showed a direct relation between female economic attainment and unmarried status, concluded that high-achieving women may

Studies in recent years have shown that higher levels of intelligence, education, and occupation are associated with singleness among women. (Randy Matusow)

consider marriage confining and therefore reject the institution—which is an altogether different matter than saying such women are unwanted by potential husbands (Havens, 1973:980). Such a tradition has not been uncommon in the academic world, for example. The pioneers of higher education for women often themselves provided positive role models of richly fulfilled and successful single women (Bernard, 1964, chap. 14).

Among whites, high education makes much less difference in the chances for male singleness. (See Table 9-A.) Highly educated men have not faced the dilemma faced by highly educated women. For well-educated women, the situation has generally been one of *either/or*—either major

TABLE 9–A *Percentage of single (never–married) persons in 1970 aged thirty–five to forty–four years with five or more years of college*

RACE	FEMALES	MALES
White	*20%*	*8%*
Black	*11%*	*11%*

SOURCE: U.S. Bureau of the Census, *1970 Census of Population*, PC (2) 4C, 1972, PP. 107–116.

attention to occupation and a life of singleness on the one hand, or marriage on the other (with occupational interests secondary or put aside). But for highly educated men, it has been a matter of *both/and*. No one would think of telling a man upon marriage that he should now seriously consider giving up his career. If anything, marriage may be considered as an aid to his career aspirations, since having a wife in the traditional sense is expected to relieve him of concerns about everyday household matters (laundry, meals, good order), increase his opportunities for entertaining important guests and clients, and in general to provide him with the emotional support and encouragement that can be so helpful in advancing his career. This is partly what sociologist Jessie Bernard (1972) has in mind in speaking of the contrast between the "his" marriage (marriage from the male's perspective) and the "her" marriage (marriage as traditionally defined for females).

It will be noticed in Table 9-A that the 1970 census showed no sex differences between the percentages of singleness among blacks. Eleven percent of thirty-five- to forty-four-year-old black males and black females with five years of college or more are single. Also of interest is the fact that singleness is much less common among highly trained black women (11 percent) than is the case among highly trained white women (20 percent).

For reasons noted earlier, blacks tend to be more responsive to individualistic rights for women than are whites. Thus, it may be that the educated black woman has faced less of a dilemma than her white counterpart. It has been less "either/or" and more "both/and." Apparently such black women have been able to negotiate marriage arrangements that they consider fair and just with black men who are probably willing to concede more autonomy than are white men. It thus becomes more "profitable" for highly trained black women to marry than is true of highly trained white women who may perceive greater costs to pay in marriage. Therefore, fewer of these black women remain single.

Incidentally, for both sexes of both races, it is the *least* educated (less than five years of any kind of schooling) who are least likely ever to marry (U.S. Bureau of the Census, 1972, PC(2)-4C). Demographers Hugh Carter and Paul Glick (1970:311) indicate that such persons may be "functionally illiterate" and "uneducable" and thus constitute a "hard core of unmarriageable" persons. In short, such persons simply possess few if any assets that would make other persons desire to enter into marriage bargains with them.

Persons who remain single not because they are "unmarriageable" but because they have voluntarily chosen this life-style do so because they perceive the costs of traditional marriage to be greater than its rewards.

Singleness over the Life Cycle   Thus far, we have been speaking of singleness only in the sense of never having been married. As we saw in Chapter 8, some persons live in paired relationships even though they are technically considered single (persons who cohabit and homosexual couples). Persons who are homosexual—whether in couple relationships or living as homosexual singles—make up a certain proportion of the never-married percentage cited earlier; but it's wrong to assume a simple equation between singleness and homosexuality per se; because as we saw, many homosexual persons are or have been married to a heterosexual partner. (We cannot say, in other words, that the estimate that 5 percent of the male population is homosexual corresponds to the fact that 6 percent of middle-aged men have never been married.)

Sociologist Peter Stein (1976), in studying the life-styles of single persons, broadened his definition to include those who may have been in either an actual marriage or a marriagelike situation at one point in life but live as singles at some other point. For the purpose of his study, Stein's working definition of "single" persons was "those men and women who are not currently married or involved in an exclusive heterosexual or homosexual relationship" (p. 11). Another author, Margaret Adams (1976) suggests that the "least ambiguous" definition of single persons is a legal definition that includes the never-married, the divorced, and the widowed. "These three groups share the common fate of not having a legal spouse and many similar practical issues of living," writes Adams (p. 18). For her own interviews, Adams concentrated on those within these groups that she felt had most in common in terms of a single life-style: the "authentically single" (never-married) and persons who were either widowed or divorced for five years and who had no children.

In 1947, the Census Bureau created a new classification called "primary individuals" to replace the older category of "one-person families" and limited the word *family* to mean "two or more persons related by blood, marriage, or adoption, living together" (Kobrin, 1976:233). According to the Census Bureau (*Current Population Reports*, P–20, no. 306, 1977:4), *primary individuals* are "persons who either live alone or with persons not related to them." This classification change has made it easier to observe patterns involving persons in nonfamily situations, since it allows for a broader spectrum of living arrangements than the "one-person family" category that "could only be studied in those tabulations which cross-classified families by size" (Kobrin, 1976:233).

Households containing primary individuals increased by about 40 percent during the period between 1970 and 1976 (U.S. Bureau of the Census, *Current Population Reports*, P–20, no. 306, 1977:4). Sociologist Frances Kobrin (1976) observes especially the increase in primary individual households at two stages of the life cycle: "the premarital independence stage" (most pronounced among young males) and the "postfamily independence stage" (most pronounced among older females who have been widowed and for whom the experience of living alone in their own household may be a first). "What was once the living style of a small proportion (3–4 percent) is now a significant alternative, claiming nearly 10 percent of Americans aged twenty to seventy-four, and much higher shares of some subgroups, such as widowed women," writes Kobrin (p. 238).

Choosing Singleness The concept of singleness embraced by Adams in her examination of this life-style is based on three basic criteria. "The primary criterion—or vital prerequisite—of being single is the capacity and opportunity to be economically self-supporting," writes Adams (1971). Also important in singleness as a life-style is social and psychological independence. Third, says Adams, there is "a clearly thought through intent to remain single by preference." In other words, one doesn't feel forced into singleness because an opportunity for marriage hasn't presented itself. One is single because of *choices* one has made— whether at the outset or later, or as a decision after an earlier marriage has ended.

"The possibility that some people might actually choose to be single because they want to be, because they feel it would contribute to their growth and well-being to remain so, is simply not believed possible," asserts Stein (1976:4), pointing to the intense societal pressures to marry and the tendency for social psychologists to refer to singles negatively as "those who fail to marry" or who cannot "make positive choices." To choose singleness means that a person perceives the rewards of that life-style to be greater than the rewards of marriage and that any costs perceived are less than the costs that would be required of one in marriage.

From his in-depth interviews with persons who had chosen to be single for the forseeable future, Stein worked out a chart of what he termed "pushes" and "pulls" that might move a person away from one situation (pushes) and toward another (pulls). This is, of course, another way of looking at relative rewards and costs. Loneliness and pressure from parents to marry, for example, are costs of singleness *pushing* toward marriage. And the desire for emotional attachment and for a family are perceived rewards of marriage *pulling* one toward that status. Conversely, a feeling of being trapped and suffocated in a marriage relationship is perceived as a cost to be avoided or eliminated and thus pushes a person toward singleness. Or one might be pulled toward singleness by such expected rewards as opportunities for more varied experiences and psychological and social autonomy. (See Table 9-B.)

Living as a Single Person   Stein points out that persons tend to think of singles in terms of two basic stereotypes: on the one hand, "*swingers*—the beautiful people who are constantly going to parties, who have uncommitted lives— and a lot of uncommitted sex"; and on the other hand, "the *lonely losers*," who are depressed much of the time and sometimes even suicidal (pp. 2–3). Actually, says Stein, the idea that "single men and women are either 'with it' or 'out of it' " is highly inaccurate. Single people, like married people, have a variety of experiences and moods. They have good days, bad days, and in between days. They have happy times, lonely times, exciting times, and dull times. "Yet, overall," reports Stein, "single men and women report many more positive experiences than negative ones" (p. 3).

While independence is the most valued part of being single, a fear of loneliness appears to be the biggest drawback; and singles soon become aware of the need for supportive friendship networks (Stein, p. 99). At the same time, many single persons are grateful for lives that permit solitude and privacy and don't consider loneliness as any special problem. Some reported to Adams (1976, chap. 5) that after a busy day in their occupations, they were

TABLE 9–B   *Pushes and pulls toward being married and being single*

TOWARD BEING MARRIED	
PUSHES (NEGATIVES IN PRESENT SITUATION)	PULLS (ATTRACTIONS IN POTENTIAL SITUATIONS)
Pressure from parents	Approval of parents
Need to leave home	Desire for family
Fear of independence	Example of peers
Loneliness	Romanticization of marriage
Cultural expectations, socialization	Physical attraction
	Emotional attachment and love
Guilt over singlehood	Security, social status, prestige
No sense of alternatives	Sexual availability

TOWARD BEING SINGLE	
PUSHES	PULLS
Restrictions within relationship:	Career opportunities
Suffocating one-to-one relationship, feeling trapped	Variety of experiences and plurality of roles
Obstacles to self-development	Self-suficiency
Boredom, unhappiness, and anger	Sexual availability
	Exciting life style
Role playing and conformity to expectations	Freedom to change and mobility
	Sustaining friendships
Poor communication with mate	Psychological and social autonomy
Sexual frustration	
Lack of friends, isolation, loneliness	
Limited mobility and availability of new experiences	

SOURCE: Peter J. Stein, *Single* (Englewood Cliffs, N.J.: Prentice–Hall, 1976), p.65.

glad to be able to go home to a quiet house or apartment to unwind without the distractions and demands of a family. This was true of both men and women. One woman told Adams that "in her opinion the type of loneliness with which single people have to reckon produces far less wear-and-tear on the psyche than the more pernicious emotional alienation that can develop between two people when the physical environment is shared but psychological and social exchange are at a minimum, or totally lacking" (p. 91).

Capitalizing on both the "swinging single" stereotype and the image of singles as lonely persons eager to find a mate, various businesses, services, and advertising practices have sprung up in recent years specifically aimed toward the singles market. At the same time, various religious groups are becoming more sensitive to the needs and concerns of single persons and are developing special programs on their behalf.

Jewish 'Singles' a New Problem after Years of Focus on Family

"We have no traditions by which to be guided," Rabbi Eugene Sack said, "We're really at the beginning of dealing with the problem."

The problem Rabbi Sack referred to was that of involving unmarried Jews in Jewish communal life.

At a conference on the subject at the Federation of Jewish Philanthropies last week, participants said the number of Jewish singles in the New York area had increased in recent years to at least 50,000—some estimated twice that number—as a result of such factors as increased divorce and extended education.

Synagogues and other institutions have had little experience in dealing with them, since Jewish tradition always has focused on the family.

"In the shtetl [Jewish village in Eastern Europe], being an 'old maid' was an unmitigated disaster and a single male roaming around was a dreadful danger to the family," Rabbi Sack said.

Or, as Leslie Gottlieb, another participant, put it: "In the Jewish Establishment you get born, bar mitzvahed or bas mitzvahed, hurry up and get married and have some Jewish babies. How are [singles] going to plug in? The sisterhood is not for us."

An underlying concern of the conference was that Jewish single people could be, as Rabbi Shlomo Balter put it, "lost to Judaism by default."

To confront the problem, and to provide an alternative to singles' bars, the Federation· in 1974 formed a Task Force on Jewish singles, headed by Rabbi Balter.

It published a newsletter, which now has a circulation of 2,000, and a manual, by Miss Gottlieb, describing coffee houses, sabbath dinners, discussion groups and other singles' programs that had been explored. It also organized the conference, held last Wednesday at the Federation's offices, 100 East 59th Street. The conference drew some 60 rabbis and lay directors of Young Men's and Women's Hebrew Associations and community centers in the New York area.

Rabbi Sack, spiritual leader of Congregation Beth Elohim in Brooklyn, said he had found that large mixers involved "ruthless competition" in which people came looking for "the one doll" or "the one guy." What is needed, he said, are smaller groups whose members meet regularly and "develop loyalties to each other."

Rabbi Sack said Jews who previously attended church singles programs were beginning to attend those at Beth Elohim, indicating a search for "a Jewish rootage."

One speaker described the success of havurot, informal communal groups that form to share some aspect of Jewish tradition. Others emphasized the needs of what one woman called "peripheral Jews who may only be interested in stepping inside a synagogue to meet someone."

SOURCE: The *New York Times*, May 2, 1976, p. 60.

SINGLE PARENTHOOD

The "First Baby of the Year" contest in Iowa City had always been a happy event. As in many other American cities and towns, a local newspaper sponsored the project and the business community joined in with enthusiasm, offering a variety of prizes to the new year's first arrival. But 1974's first baby was different. His mother wasn't married. The newspaper refused to award the prizes, giving them to the second child born instead. Baby number two had married parents (*National Observer*, January 19, 1974:4).

That same year, an elementary school teacher wrote to the Washington State Human Rights Commission for advice on a course of action she was considering. Divorced and the mother of a young son, she wanted to have another child but said she had not met anyone with whom she would be compatible in marriage. "I don't think I should marry for the sole purpose of reproduction," she wrote. Her plan? She wanted to remain unwed but to conceive a child by artificial insemination. Her question for the Commission centered around whether or not she could be fired from her job if she gave birth out of wedlock (*National Observer*, February 2, 1974:6).

And again in that same year, a national women's magazine featured a story of an unwed mother who told of why she kept her child rather than having an abortion or giving him up for adoption. She was not a young teenager, poorly educated, or from a deprived background. Rather she had a master's degree and was working on a doctorate at the time the conception occurred. The baby's father was a Ph.D. She had chosen the life-style of single parenthood as a better alternative than entering an unsatisfactory marriage (*Redbook*, February, 1974).

By the end of the 1970s, such stories were becoming accepted as one more evidence of alternative life-style choices. Fewer eyebrows were raised; fewer tongues prattled. American society's tolerance level had a much higher threshold than in the days when Hawthorne's fictional Hester Prynne was required to wear a scarlet letter indicating "A" for "Adultery"—a symbol of Puritan society's attitude toward the unwed mother and her illegitimate offspring. As the 1980s began, not only were there examples of women who advertised for a willing male to impregnate them so that they could have a child apart from marriage; there were also numerous court cases in which unwed fathers were attempting to gain custody of their children and to prevent the unwed mothers involved from giving the babies up for adoption. In addition, solo parenthood because of divorce or the death of a spouse is not at all uncommon (Orthner, Brown, and Ferguson, 1976). (This category of persons living a single parenthood life-style with children *from a former marriage* will be discussed in Chapter 18.)

ATTITUDES TOWARD MARRIAGE AND CHILDREN

Persons seem to fall into four categories when it comes to the matter of children. Traditionally, men and women have considered children as a major reward of marriage and thus have contemplated marriage with the "joys of parenthood" in mind. But in contrast to such couples, there are others who feel that the costs of children outnumber the rewards and thus remain voluntarily childless after marriage. A third category consists of single persons who have no desire for *either* marriage or children since they perceive the benefits of both to be outweighed by the disadvantages and costs.

However, there is a fourth group which we want to consider at this point—single persons who want children but who don't want marriage.

In recent years, many states have begun permitting unmarried persons to adopt children. This practice is upsetting to some unwed mothers who years ago were persuaded to give up their children for adoption because social workers advised them that children need to grow up in two-parent homes. However, data from available studies do not seem to provide support for the old fears about a child's being emotionally harmed by growing up in a one-parent situation (Kadushin, 1970). Unmarried persons of both sexes have proven to be excellent parents of adopted children. A Roman Catholic priest, for example, has adopted four over the years, bringing home each child during early infancy. A physician adopted two boys after she was well established in her practice and enough years had gone by to make her feel that marriage was unlikely. A bachelor in his thirties adopted a tiny boy who had been abandoned. A writer, whose engagement was broken when her fiancé found she couldn't have children, later adopted children as a single woman.

The other way to become an unmarried parent is, of course, through the normal processes of conception and birth. Some single women in recent years, including some active in the feminist movement, have chosen to continue out-of-marriage pregnancies, giving birth and rearing their children

Unmarried persons of both sexes have proven to be excellent parents of adopted children. (United Press International)

themselves rather than giving them up for adoption or having abortions. Historically, there have always been unmarried women who bore children. When these born-out-of-wedlock children were adopted by married couples, they did not have to grow up bearing the stigma "illegitimate." But if their mothers kept them, they were labeled "illegitimate" or "bastards." The baby was of course the same person in either case at the time of birth, but it was the situation into which he or she would be placed that would determine "legitimacy." This labeling would in turn have a profound effect on the child's entire life. But why has such categorization of children taken place? What does it mean?

PRINCIPLE OF LEGITIMACY

According to the anthropologist Bronislaw Malinowski (1930), there is a universal rule that "no child should be brought into the world without a man—and one man at that—assuming the role of sociological father, that is, guardian and protector, the male link between the child and the rest of the community." Malinowski calls this rule "the principle of legitimacy." He claims that throughout cultural variations, "there runs the rule that the father is indispensable for the full sociological status of the child as well as of its mother, that the group consisting of a woman and her offspring is sociologically incomplete and illegitimate. The father, in other words, is necessary for the full legal status of the family" (pp. 13–14 in Coser, 1964 reprint).

The principle of legitimacy stems from a functionalist view of marriage and parenthood. You'll recall that in the structural-functional framework the family is seen as an organism with interdependent parts, each having a particular function to perform, as in the human body. Under the principle of legitimacy, the focus is on the function of the economic provider, a role assigned to the father. Thus a child is said to require a social father in order that the child can receive the status and material benefits that are rightfully his or hers.

TRENDS RELATING TO THE LEGITIMACY ISSUE

Perhaps in some times and places it may have made sense to talk about the necessity of a social father to serve as a pipeline to the status and economic rewards of a particular society. But in modern times, such a requirement is not essential and inevitable for at least two reasons. One has to do with legal redefinitions of legitimacy, and the other relates to the changing roles and status of women.

Legal Redefinitions of Legitimacy   It is possible for societies simply to abolish the legal distinction between legitimate and nonlegitimate. Sweden, for instance, has done precisely that (Linner, 1967:36). A child born out of wedlock has full inheritance rights from its father as well as its mother. Thus, if a man sires two children in marriage and one outside the marriage, all three

The daughter of actress Liv Ullman and filmmaker Ingmar Bergman, Linn Ullman, though born out of wedlock, is considered to have full legitimacy status and inheritance rights from both parents according to Swedish law. (United Press International)

would share equally in their claims on his support, his status, and his estate. This assumes, of course, that paternity can be proven and that the father has any status and assets to transmit to the child. If either or both of these conditions cannot be met, the Swedish state is committed to provide for the child. According to government policy in Sweden, every child without a father is granted the same kinds of social and economic benefits enjoyed by other children.

Similarly, legislation that went into effect in the Union of Soviet Socialist Republics between 1968 and 1970 "has substantially changed the position of children born out of wedlock, and has given them the same status as legitimate children," reports one Soviet author who specializes in family law (Sedugin, 1973:73). In the USSR, an unmarried mother and her child are considered a family—a family just as valid as a nuclear family composed of two wedded parents and their children. If the child's father has not voluntarily acknowledged paternity and if the courts have not given a ruling establishing paternity in a particular case, an unmarried mother may receive state funds to aid in her child's upbringing; or she may send the child to a children's establishment run by the state where he or she is cared for entirely at the state's expense. On the other hand, if a male Soviet citizen "voluntarily acknowledges paternity by making a declaration to a registrar's office, his child enjoys the same rights and has the same obligations with regard to his parents and relatives as children born in wedlock" (Sedugin, p. 74). One of the rights the child enjoys is the right to be supported by both parents.

Supreme Court cases in recent years indicate that the United States may be moving in precisely the same direction as Sweden and the Soviet Union toward eventual abolishment of the legal distinctions between legitimate and nonlegitimate, especially in matters of support and inheritance (Krause, 1971). However, there is no indication as yet that the United States is prepared to undertake the kinds of programs necessary to equalize opportunities for children who have no male pipeline to the status system.

Legitimacy and Changing Female Roles The question arises: Why not a female pipeline to the status system? Why couldn't a woman provide for a child the resources that have traditionally come from a man? Increasingly, women are becoming better educated and are gaining access to jobs with levels of income and prestige formerly restricted to white men. Many such women are highly individualistic and extremely achievement-oriented. Among those who have never married, there may be some who choose to legally adopt a child. There may be others who conceive and bear a child out of wedlock and who choose to rear the child alone. Given their high level of resources, there is no reason to suspect that they could not be as adequate a pipeline for conveying society's benefits to a child as any man could be. They can provide adequate objective benefits, and they can socialize the child into achievement-type behaviors through their own example and guidance.

Thus, we see a second reason why a social father may not be requisite in modern society. From the studies of Blau and Duncan (1967), we already know that children who have lost their fathers through death or divorce achieve in later life as well as children from husband-wife households *from the same social class.* Apparently it is not the presence or absence of the father per se that affects the child's later attainments; rather, it is the benefits that the father provided while he was alive and in his estate, or else that he presently provides through child support. It therefore seems reasonable that a well-trained woman who opts for a life-style in which she raises a child alone can do at least as well as women who have been thrust into a status they did not choose nor necessarily want, namely that of provider and solo parent.

PRINCIPLE OF STATUS ADEQUACY

For the kinds of reasons just discussed, Malinowski's functionalist principle of legitimacy becomes dubious indeed. It needs to be changed and restated to fit the complexities of modern society. Perhaps instead of a "principle of legitimacy," we could think in terms of a *principle of status adequacy.* Very simply, a principle of status adequacy means that every child requires some sociological parent (father and/or mother) or the equivalent in a communal, kin, or political arrangement that can provide the child with adequate socialization and access to the opportunity system.

For some time, demographers have been collecting figures on the incidence of illegitimate births. Such data are available from thirty-nine states and the District of Columbia, which require the reporting of marital status (U.S. Department of Health and Human Services, *Monthly Vital Statistics Report*, vol. 29, no. 1, 1980:19).

In 1978 (latest statistics available), for every 1,000 unmarried women between fifteen and forty-four years of age, there were 26 live births. For every 1,000 unmarried black women, 83 out-of-wedlock births occurred; and for every 1,000 unmarried white women, 14 out-of-wedlock births occurred.

Another way to examine the extent of unmarried parenthood is to compare the number of births classified "illegitimate" with the total number of live births and to observe the rate per thousand. In 1978, out of every 1,000 live births, 163 were births in which the mothers were unmarried. Out of every 1,000 black babies born, 532 had unwed mothers. And out of every 1,000 white babies born, 87 were born out of wedlock (*Monthly Vital Statistics Report*, vol. 29, no. 1, 1980:19). Even more significant is the fact that the vast majority of both black and white births outside of marriage occur to women around or below the poverty line (Cutright, 1972b:382). The economic discrimination that has especially limited educational and occupational opportunities for black persons helps explain their higher percentages of births out of wedlock. (It might be useful to refer back to the discussion on pages 127–130.)

Unmarried women of lower social status tend to be more sexually active and to be poorly informed about effective contraception. Thus, out-of-wedlock conceptions are not unusual among this group; and carrying the baby to full term and delivering it while still remaining single is not unusual either. Not only do unwed mothers generally tend to come from lower status backgrounds; they also tend to be very young. According to the National

10-Year-Old Is Mother of Twins

INDIANAPOLIS (AP)—Twins born to a 10-year-old girl are healthy and gaining weight without use of an incubator, a doctor at Indiana University Hospital said Friday.

Dr. Robert Munsick, who is a professor of obstetrics and gynecology at the university's medical school, said the twin girls, born May 24, were "doing just fine," but will be kept in the hospital "a couple more weeks."

Each of the girls weighed 3 pounds, 6 ounces at birth, and were delivered six weeks premature. The names of the twins and their mother, who was released from the hospital Wednesday, have not been made public.

The twins were delivered normally after labor was induced on their mother.

Munsick said the youngest girl ever to give birth was a 6-year-old Peruvian, whose child was delivered by Caesarian section in the 1930s.

Ten-year-olds have given birth here in recent years, and "11-year-old mothers are almost common," Munsick said.

But a multiple birth for a 10-year-old mother is "extremely unusual," he added.

SOURCE: *Greensboro (NC) Daily News*, June 2, 1979.

Center for Health Statistics, of the 543,900 live births to unmarried women in 1978, close to half—about a quarter of a million—occurred to young women 19 years of age and younger. More than 9,000 occurred to women under age 15 (*Monthly Vital Statistics Report*, vol. 29, no. 1, 1980:19).

To disadvantaged young women with few alternative rewards, it may appear as if children—even "illegitimate" ones—provide one of their few sources of major life gratifications. Hence there may be little motivation to resist unmarried motherhood, perhaps even to the extent of experiencing several illegitimate births. And that is precisely where the principle of status adequacy has relevance. Households headed by poor women tend to be large. Consequently, the children are exceedingly disadvantaged and simply do not receive the kinds of benefits they need to adequately compete in modern society. It is a life-style very different from the one described previously in which the unmarried well-educated woman *chooses* both singleness and a child. Women with high levels of resources choose such a life-style from a variety of alternatives, are well-equipped to provide the child with substantial benefits, and are likely to limit the number of children they will rear to only one or two. In contrast, the unmarried woman who lacks educational and economic resources may find that single motherhood is something thrust on her rather than freely chosen. She becomes an unwed mother because few other viable options appear open to her. For her, the rewards of being a solo parent are few and costs high. If she is young, her schooling has probably been disrupted. She is poorly equipped to provide for her child and is quite likely to have more than one illegitimate offspring. In terms of the principle of status adequacy, her child requires an *outside* source to serve as the pipeline to the economic and opportunity system. Some support may come from both her family and from public assistance programs (Furstenberg and Crawford, 1978; Moore, 1978).

In sum, there seem to be trends in the direction of increased single parenthood, partly due to liberalized adoption procedures which permit unmarried persons to adopt children and partly due to a desire on the part of many unmarried mothers to retain their children rather than electing abortion or giving their children up for adoption.

Where parenthood is voluntarily chosen by a single person equipped to provide the child with necessary resources, the experience can be beneficial to both parent and child. But where parenthood is forced upon a young unmarried woman poorly equipped to handle the situation, the situation may be paradoxically entrapping (cutting her and her child off from educational and economic opportunities, for example) at the same time that it may seem somewhat rewarding (providing a certain sense of gratification in the midst of an impoverished life). The basic issue in such a case is not so much a matter of "illegitimacy" as it is of "status *inadequacy*."

UNWED FATHERS AND LEGITIMACY

State laws vary on specifics; but traditionally, men who fathered children out of wedlock have not been able to count on legal rights to custody or visitation.

Mike Johnson is an unmarried teenage father. He won custody of his daughter Jodi, whose fifteen-year-old mother wanted to give her up for adoption. (Dale Wittner/People Weekly © 1979 Time Inc.)

In that respect, it would seem that laws regarding unmarried parents and their offspring have favored the mother. However, the father has been the one who has had the power of "legitimating" a child—either by marrying the child's mother or else by taking the child into his own family, acknowledging the child publicly as his, and treating the child as legitimate. On the other hand, a woman who has given birth out of wedlock can block such efforts toward legitimation by the child's father, since she is the one who traditionally has had custody rights. The way she herself could secure the child's legitimation has been to give the child up for adoption. "Courts, asked to decide between the mother's desire to have the child adopted by strangers and the father's competing claim to custody, have gone both ways," report three law professors in summarizing trends in this area of family law (Davidson, Ginsburg, and Kay, 1974:315).

In 1979, the United States Supreme Court ruled unconstitutional a New York law that gave to unmarried mothers, but not to unmarried fathers, the sole right to make decisions on the adoption of their offspring. In the case before the Supreme Court, the unmarried father's attorney argued that his client, Abdiel Caban, was being denied due process and equal protection of the laws. The children's mother and her new husband wanted to legally adopt the girl and boy who had been born to Caban and her during a long-term cohabitation relationship. Had the adoption request not been stopped, Caban would have been denied even visitation rights and would have had no claim to his son and daughter even in the event of their mother's death.

In another situation, the strains of an unplanned pregnancy resulted in a broken engagement, and the young woman decided to give the baby up for adoption. However, the baby's father objected and sought legal custody of the boy. Upon being granted custody, he subsequently formed the New Orleans–based Foundation for Unwed Fathers to aid other men in similar circumstances.

A number of such stories have been in the news in recent years, and they serve to underscore a basic theme of this book—*change*. Such examples indicate changing definitions of what constitutes a family, just as the phenomenon of cohabitation has been forcing a new look at definitions of marriage. But even more, such examples illustrate changing ideas about sex roles.

As we've seen, the principle of legitimacy rested on the notion that it was the *father* who brought income and status to a family and on that account was essential to a child's legitimacy. The emphasis was on the "instrumental" function of fatherhood. We have challenged that assumption in view of the opportunities now open to women, making it possible for many mothers to bring the economic system's rewards to their children just as fathers have traditionally been expected to do. The principle of status adequacy therefore seems more appropriate to the situation in the United States today.

Another traditional idea has held that if a baby is born out of wedlock and not given up for adoption, the *mother* is the parent best qualified to be the "expressive" caretaker of the child. Now that idea too is being challenged by a number of unmarried fathers who see their role as encompassing much more than having sired a child. They love their children and want to be actively involved in their children's lives, either through visitation privileges or through actual custody. In other words, unmarried fathers are demanding *expressive* rights and duties at the same time that unmarried mothers want recognition of their own *instrumental* capabilities and contributions that should allow them to rear their children without the traditional stigma of illegitimacy.

Because of such changing attitudes and circumstances, some authorities in family law call into question the Proposed Uniform Legitimacy Act which would base legitimacy on the identification of paternity through a court order. Children of fathers who were not known or not available would continue to be regarded as illegitimate. Legal authority Kenneth Davidson and his colleagues (1974) summarize arguments of two outspoken opponents:

> The underlying premise of the Proposed Uniform Legitimacy Act has . . . been sharply attacked by Tenoso and Wallach [Book Review, U.C.L.A. *Law Review* 19:845 (1972)]. In their view, the law's primary goal should not be a search for the father whose identification by a court would then serve to legitimate the child.

Rather, the law should recognize that a woman and her children constitute a legitimate family unit and should support this "woman-centered and defined family" as a viable alternative to the existing nuclear family dominated by males. Toward that end, the authors propose a broad legislative program that would recognize all children as legitimate at birth regardless of whether the father can be identified; allow the mother to choose whether the father should be identified at all; require the payment of state support as a substitute for the father's duty rather than as welfare; and provide social welfare resources for all children regardless of the support received from either parent. (p. 324)

Such critics see the Proposed Uniform Legitimacy Act as nothing more than improving a faulty system; instead they wish to see the whole system radically changed.

COMMUNAL LIVING AND SUBSTITUTE KINSHIP

A wall plaque carries this message:

We need to have people
who mean something to us;
   People to whom
we can turn,
   Knowing that being with them is
coming home.

—R. Cooke

Traditionally, those people "who mean something," to whom one can turn in time of need, and who provide a sense of "coming home" have been the kin, those persons to whom one has become related either through blood or through marriage. At the same time, there may be other persons who serve as a kind of "substitute kin" even though they are unrelated to one another. In recent years, there has been much talk about building community. There have been experiments with communal living as well as efforts to create a kind of chosen family of friends with whom joys, sorrows, problems, anxieties, and dreams can be shared even though the friends don't share a common household—an arrangement one sociologist calls an "intimate family network."

In this section, we want to look at some of these "functional equivalents" of the extended family.

INTIMATE NETWORK AS A KIN SUBSTITUTE

An anonymous writer in *Ms.* magazine told of how sentimentality over "family solidarity" repeatedly drove her to plan elaborate holiday get-togethers with relatives only to be disappointed again and again. "Generally, the family for which I have sweated so generously ruins my evening," she wrote, adding that this didn't happen when she invited her friends. "My friends, I choose myself. They were not a gift from God." This woman eventually solved her problem by a formula of inviting "eight friends per biological family member" ("The Gift of Honesty," *Ms.*, vol. 2, December, 1973:46).

Some persons find kin relationships more costly than rewarding and seek other relationships to serve as substitutes. There are also persons who look for substitutes because they have no "effective kin" with whom significant contacts can be maintained on a regular basis. Relatives may live at great geographical distances, or they may no longer be living at all.

One behavioral scientist, Frederick Stoller (1970), has introduced in family workshops an idea he calls the "intimate family network." Such a plan could serve to alleviate any impoverishment some modern families may feel by being denied the richly varied experiences and emotional support traditionally associated with kin relationships. According to Stoller, "an intimate network of families could be described as a circle of three or four families who meet together regularly and frequently, share in reciprocal fashion any of their intimate secrets, offer one another a variety of services, and do not hesitate to influence one another in terms of values and attitudes."

Stoller suggests that the number of families should be more than two (to provide richness, varied role models for children, and more problem-solving resources) but usually not more than four, since too large a group would be hard to manage and might also cut down intimacy. Regular and frequent get-togethers would be important in order for the families to come to know one another deeply and develop the capacity to be honest and open with each other even in painful situations.

Reciprocal sharing would mean opening up to one another about how each family lives, its concerns, problems, and so on. Stoller is aware of the value the American family system places on privacy but points out that human life is enriched if *both* privacy and connectedness are experienced. The intimate-network idea would not force a surrender of the right to privacy but rather would provide an opportunity for a "voluntary movement back and forth between open sharing and self-contained areas of living."

The intimate network of families could also provide an exchange of services in the manner that the extended kin has traditionally done—not only through aid in times of crisis, but also in exchanges of advice, helping one another in special projects (such as painting a house), or providing such benefits as child care so that a husband and wife are free to take a trip together. Stoller also emphasizes the influence intimate-network families could have on one another's values and attitudes, helping one another to grow and develop in new directions.

Although the intimate-family-network concept emphasizes relationships between and among families, there is no reason why such networks could not be formed among any combination of unrelated individuals—single persons, widowed persons, divorced persons, couples with or without children, and so on. Many such informal networks already exist, particularly in urban areas where many persons live at great distances from kinfolk. A close network of friends (some of whom may be work colleagues) forms and meets together for dinners, picnics, trips, holiday celebrations, and so on. Thanksgiving, for example, may become not so much a matter of going "over the river and through the woods to Grandmother's house" as it is a situation of going across the streets and through the halls to someone's apartment opened up to friends.

COMMUNE AS A KIN SUBSTITUTE

Communes are intentional communities. Like intimate networks, they bring together biologically unrelated persons in order to build a kind of large *chosen* family. The purpose of this chosen family is to fulfill many of the functions traditionally fulfilled by the extended kin. Communes differ from intimate networks in several ways, most notable of which are the living arrangements (persons in communes maintain a common dwelling place) and economic sharing. The word *commune* itself is a wide umbrella, covering several different types of living patterns and philosophies. Yet, communes have much in common in their endeavors to serve as the functional equivalent of the kin. Let's examine some ways they do this.

Affection Traditionally, the extended kin have provided a main source of primary relationships. A person could derive a sense of belonging by saying,

A sense of togetherness is experienced by those in communal living arrangements. (The Book Publishing Co.)

"I'm a member of such-and-such family clan." A similar sense of togetherness is experienced by those in communal arrangements. They use family terminology, such as brotherhood and sisterhood, to express their deep feelings for one another and their commitment to the life they share. Common-unity or *community* based not on genealogy but on ideology (shared goals and values) holds them together in an affectionate bond.

Interdependence The sense of togetherness experienced promotes among group members the feeling that they need one another and need the group as a whole. Again, there is a resemblance to the "we can count on each other" feelings characterizing the extended kin. Commune members expect to give and receive mutual aid. Though the vows may be unspoken, there is a commitment to care for one another "for richer, for poorer, in sickness, and in health."

Rituals Group solidarity is reinforced by bringing group members together for regular participation in activities, ceremonies, and recurring events that symbolize commitment to the group as a whole. It might be so simple a matter as joining hands around a common table to recite a prayer or sing a song before eating. Or there might be a celebration in honor of a member's birthday or a couple's engagement or regular community songfests, holiday celebrations, and the like. Family rituals and traditions, whether they involve actual extended kin or the adopted chosen kin of a commune, can enhance what various writers call a sense of "communion . . . the mingling of self with the group," "we-feelings," and "we-consciousness" (Kanter, 1968:509–510).

Migration An additional way in which communal arrangements function like that of the kin relates to the bringing of new members into the commune. Sociologist Bert Adams (1968:3) points out the part played by the extended kin in residential migration. One unit of the kin (whether a nuclear family or an individual) may move to a new location and establish "an economic and residential 'foothold' in a community, to be followed there later by other kin." Similarly, individuals or families that join a commune may then invite other persons of their acquaintance from "back home" (such as single persons, lonely or troubled persons, individuals who have been widowed or divorced, and so on), suggesting that joining the commune might provide a solution to their problems and sense of aloneness. This may be compared to the Appalachian family which, after settling in Chicago, writes to relatives with the suggestion that they, too, should migrate.

Influence and Control Communal relationships also may resemble traditional kinship arrangements in the control they exercise over the lives of group members. Jay and Heather Ogilvy (1972:89), an academic couple who live in an urban commune, point out one aspect of this in their statement: "If a single person feels ill at ease bringing a prospective mate home to meet the parents, imagine the possibilities for tension bringing a prospective mate home to meet the commune." Their comment fits in with our discussion on mate selection where we saw that the degree of family control is associated with the degree of economic dependence.

ECONOMIC SIDE OF COMMUNE LIFE

Economic arrangements vary greatly in communal living. In some cases, two or three families might own a house jointly and share household tasks and meals but might otherwise be economically independent of one another. In another case, a large number of persons might give up all personal ownership and pool resources so that all possessions are held in common. This is true of certain urban communes where earnings from outside jobs are handed over to a committee in charge of finances, just as it is true of various rural communes which try to earn a living off the land as each member pitches in and works, or in arrangements in which commune members run their own industries—such as the Bruderhof, with colonies in New York, Pennsylvania, and Connecticut, supporting themselves through the manufacture of wooden toys, sold under the name "Community Playthings."

TYPES OF COMMUNES

Although there are no hard and fast rules when it comes to classifying communes, it is helpful to make some basic distinctions. Rosabeth Moss Kanter (1974), a sociologist who has written a number of books and articles based on her studies of communes, says that a simple way to describe communes is in terms of three underlying themes: the land, the spirit, and the home. Rural communes emphasize the land, getting back to nature; religious communes emphasize spiritual values and goals; and urban communes seem to place major stress on the shared home. Sometimes communes may be many things all at once—"a domestic unit (a large household), a production unit (a farm and/or a series of businesses), a political order (a village or town), and a religious order" (Kanter, 1973:xii).

Urban Communes and Rural Communes Sociologist Bennett Berger and his colleagues (1972) suggest that a fundamental distinction between communes has to do with whether they are located in the city or in the country. They point out that urban communes are easier to start ("all it takes is a rented house and a group of willing people") but that they are harder to sustain and have a more fluid membership. Rural communes, on the other hand, seem to call forth a more thorough commitment from their members; and this commitment is no doubt related to the profound consequences involved in choosing to work and live in the collective life of a communal farm. In a sense, one takes on a new identity by being isolated from one's former environment, having one's daily life structured in radically different ways than before, and engaging in unfamiliar tasks which present the constant challenge of developing new skills. In urban communes, persons usually continue with their occupations in the "outside world," but come together for meals, sharing household tasks and child care, recreation, meetings, and so on in their common dwelling, which is often enhanced with the "extras" made possible by their collective incomes (appliances, well-equipped music rooms, saunas, gym equipment, and the like) (Kanter, 1974).

INDIVIDUALISM VERSUS GROUP INTERESTS

A recurrent problem in the history of communes is the issue of community versus personal freedom. In communes that stress individualism, questions of preserving group solidarity and unity must be faced. On the other hand, in communes which give primary emphasis to group unity, there arise questions of where individual freedom fits in. Inevitably, communal movements must face the question: Can the *many* be *one* at the same time that the *one* can be *many*?

Zablocki (1971:250, 280–288) reports that for the Bruderhof the answer lies in how the word *freedom* is defined. "We must consider the possibility that the problem stems from confusing individualism with freedom," he writes. Bruderhof members firmly believe that they possess freedom—even though they possess nothing of their own, must ask for the simple necessities of life, must do the work chosen for them, and are required to attend communal functions and multiple meals at set times throughout the day, no matter how greatly personal schedules might seem interrupted. Emphatically, then, the members of the Bruderhof do not possess the freedom of individualism.

However, individualism has been the form in which Western peoples have looked for freedom, Zablocki points out, asking if this might not be why the issue of community then becomes difficult. "It seems undeniable," he writes "that community, which means bonds, obligations, and mutual interdependence, is fundamentally incompatible with individualism." Zablocki suggests that freedom can be discussed in two dimensions: "(1) the ability to decide to do something and then go ahead and do it; (2) the ability to change one's mind at any moment as to one's goal, and to act effectively to implement that change."

In the sense of the first dimension, the Bruderhof provides freedom for its members by giving them a structure for their lives, freeing them to get on with the life-goals they have chosen, and insulating them from the distractions of the outside world as well as from individual tendencies to swerve from the path they have chosen for themselves, much as a secretary might protect a busy executive from callers and unnecessary interruptions.

The second dimension of freedom mentioned by Zablocki is virtually unknown in the Bruderhof community. Psychically, economically, and socially, it is extremely difficult to change one's mind and leave the group once such a total commitment has been made; and those who do manage to break their ties are quick to admit that in their hearts they have never completely left. The way that the Bruderhof has dealt with the problem of freedom versus community is no doubt one of the most important reasons it has been such a long-lasting communal movement (it was founded in Germany in 1920 and later migrated to the United States and elsewhere), in contrast to the vast number of communes that fail after very short lives.

WHAT HOLDS COMMUNES TOGETHER AND MAKES THEM LAST?

The questions of *continuance* (why some communes last for a long period while others do not) and *cohesiveness* (what causes the feelings of sticking together in some communes while others rather quickly become "unglued") are intriguing ones. Rosabeth Moss Kanter's (1968) study of thirty nineteenth-century American communes (from among the nearly one hundred such utopian communities that sprang up between the Revolutionary and Civil wars), showed that nine could be rated successful (lasting thirty-three years of more), while twenty-one were unsuccessful (lasting less than sixteen years, with an average existence of four years). Included in her study were such well-known historical intentional communities as the Shakers (successful, 180 years), Harmony (successful, one-hundred years), the Oneida Community (successful, 33 years, with its name still familiar through the silverware industry it began), Brook Farm (in which Nathaniel Hawthorne participated, but unsuccessful as a commune, lasting only six years), New Harmony (unsuccessful, two years), and Yellow Springs (which lasted only six months).

Successful nineteenth-century communes, according to Kanter (1972: 313), built strong group commitment in at least four ways: (1) through the investments and sacrifices required of members, (2) through developing a strong in-group or family feeling which discouraged ties outside the group, (3) through identity-change processes so that the thinking and behavior of the individual was brought into conformity to the group, and (4) "through ideological systems and authority structures which gave meaning and direction to the community."

PROBLEMS COMMUNES FACE FROM WITHOUT AND WITHIN

Communal living is by no means a recent phenomenon. The practice stretches far back into history, long before the nineteenth century's utopian experiments. The discovery of the Dead Sea Scrolls in 1947 provided a new understanding of the Essenes, a Jewish sect which lived communally about two thousand years ago. And the Bible records the life of the early Christians who "were together and had all things in common; and they sold their possessions and goods and distributed them to all as any had need" (Acts 2:44-45).

Yet, communes have always faced difficulties from both without and within. How successful they are in meeting such difficulties has much to do with how lasting the commune will be.

Problems with the Outside World   One of the most basic practical considerations in forming an intentional community is finding a suitable place to live.

The zoning laws of many communities make it hard for a group of unrelated individuals to set up a household in a residential area. Even though the commune members consider themselves a family, their neighbors may think differently. In some communities, there is intense hostility toward the commune.

While the outside world may give evidence of hostility toward the commune, the commune may often just as strongly reject the outside world. In modern communes, just as in historical ones, the question of "we" versus "they" is still a very big issue. This comes to light first of all with regard to entrance procedures. Though often with some reluctance, many modern communes have begun to follow the nineteenth-century pattern of setting up selective procedures for membership. Others have a more open policy; to them, anyone who comes automatically belongs. But where member-nonmember distinctions are nonexistent, group cohesion is often weakened, and the group is demoralized as it tries to define itself.

Other difficulties of relating to the outside world may come up with regard to members who hold outside jobs and thus have contacts away from the commune all day long. Then there is the matter of friends and visitors. Strong communes are those which believe their way of life is superior. The old way of life is renounced, sometimes with great bitterness being felt toward it and the people in it (even parents in some cases). Relating to persons who still belong to that despised and "inferior" way of life may prove difficult, and the commune itself may want to ensure insulation by putting controls on such contacts.

Problems within the Commune   Communal experiments not only face problems from without but also from within the group itself. One of the biggest issues is the matter of authority. Kanter's study of nineteenth-century communes indicated that authority structures and strong leaders were characteristic of those communities that endured over a long period of time. Group members were willing to obey and submit to the persons in charge, believing that these leaders had a right to rule over them and that they did so with the members' best interests in mind.

Many communes today attempt to be democratic. However, a reluctance to make formal rules and a stress on minimal organization often mean that tasks go undone and that group solidarity is not built. Eventually such communes are apt to break up.

Problem of Sex Roles and Division of Labor   Often communes begin with high ideals about the equality of the sexes. Here is one place on earth, it is thought, where the "brothers" and "sisters" can relate to one another free of stereotypes and role assignments of the larger society. Yet, the ideals are often hard to implement. The group begins to find that men are speaking up more in the meetings and making the decisions, while the women are relatively silent. Work begins to be divided along traditional lines—women in the kitchen, men in the fields. We have already seen how this has occurred in the kibbutz where in recent years women have been allotted the more traditionally "feminine" tasks of the collective—cooking, laundry service, child care, nursing, teaching, and the like.

Sometimes male dominance in communal living is actually supported by an ideology of male supremacy and female subordination. A group of researchers who studied a rural commune of persons popularly called "Jesus people" found that the group had a clearly spelled-out "theology of sex roles" based on selected Bible verses, so that the women "knew their place." This meant a male-female hierarchy that prevented women from being included in the decision-making processes of the group. Even the one woman with the title of "deaconess" had authority only over other women, primarily with regard to their kitchen chores. All women were expected to bow to male authority (Harder, Richardson, and Simmonds, 1972).

Sometimes the explanation given for sex-role differentiation in communes is that such differentiation is "natural"—that women are simply better suited for some tasks and men for others. Interestingly, this type of explanation was even used among the Shakers, a group founded by a woman and which included an equal number of male elders and female eldresses in its governing bodies. In the early days of the movement, before the various profitable Shaker industries had begun, the elders maintained that "every commune . . . must be founded . . . on agriculture." In this agricultural stage, the men did the clearing and cultivation of the soil, planting, and harvesting. The women occupied their time with household tasks such as cooking, cleaning, spinning and weaving, doing the laundry tending the garden and dairy, and sewing. But in addition, notes one historian (slipping in a bit of personal opinion!), "Some feminine instinct was probably satisfied by the custom of assigning each brother to a sister who became responsible for the care of his clothes and his laundry and for general oversight of his habits and appearance" (Tyler, 1944:155).

In agricultural communes, the more physically demanding tasks tend to be considered the province of men, simply because of assumed greater male strength and the fact that males are unhindered by pregnancy, childbirth, and child-care responsibilities. (This latter fact does not, of course, apply to the celibate Shakers.) In any social system, certain tasks come to be defined as being more crucial for the maintenance of that system. Thus, from a structural-functional perspective, the chores connected with *producing* the food came to be regarded as more significant than the chores associated with *cooking* the food. The food must be produced before it can be cooked.

Since men control the production of the food, it follows that they have more power. Furthermore, since assumed greater physical strength is involved, men have more options than women. It would be possible for a man to do *either* the more demanding task (food production) or the less demanding one (food preparation), whereas woman's only option is considered to be the less demanding one (kitchen duty).

Some groups are attempting to break this pattern, both in ideals and in practice. Kathleen Kinkade (1973:171), a commune member who tells of the "Walden Two experiment" at Twin Oaks Community (a rural commune in Virginia) writes: "We have no sex roles in our work. Both men and women cook and clean and wash dishes; both women and men drive trucks and tractors, repair fences, load hay, slaughter cattle. Managerial responsibility is divided almost exactly equally—this in spite of the fact that our women are on the average two or three years younger than our men."

There is also evidence that certain urban communes have been moving away from traditional sex-role differentiation toward a more equal sharing of both tasks and power (Polk, Stein, and Polk, 1973). By jointly sharing the breadwinner role with the men, rather than living as dependents or as household servants, urban commune women in general tend to be regarded as equals to a greater extent than has been true of rural communes.

Other Problems Faced by Communes In addition to the various kinds of problems already discussed, commune members face the multitudinous daily problems involved in living together and trying to become molded into a family. This means there may be "family fights," conflicts of interest, personality clashes, and other difficulties of interpersonal relationships. There may be problems with members who shirk their duties and refuse to share in the work of keeping the community going. There is the issue of sheer economic survival which can place considerable pressure on the group. There are decisions to be made about household chores and other practical matters. In one study of urban communes, "disagreement over housekeeping responsibilities" and "personality clashes" were at the top of the list of problems (Hershberger, 1973).

Examples of Everyday Irritations in Communal Living

---

1. Betty believed that one should show beautifying behaviors in a house—for example, one should open or close the window curtains in the living room, straighten up furniture as needed, and so forth. Sally did not show these behaviors.

2. Communally prepared meals seemed to take a long time to prepare, eat, and clean up after—often several hours. I often wished that I could just eat quickly and run, as I had been accustomed to doing at my apartment or at a restaurant.

3. Jim and Elaine, poorer than the others, wanted to spend little on food; Randy, Alice, and I didn't mind spending a little more to get variety and quality. Jim and Elaine were vegetarians; the rest of us all enjoyed meat.

4. Jim sometimes irritated others by his sloppy manner of dress and his way of dishing out food.

5. In Rutland Square House, Jim and Randy were learning to play the saxophone, sometimes practicing late into the evening. I did not enjoy having to hear this, but had no choice.

6. Betty, brought up in Holland, liked the temperature in the house to be about 68. I preferred 71 or 72. Betty and I sometimes played little games with the thermostat.

7. Alice and Randy liked simple, uncluttered surroundings. Jim was one of the biggest collectors of junk imaginable.

8. Jim felt that since we were living communally, we should all be willing to share *each other's property. One day Jim borrowed my new car, gave it to a third party to drive (without my permission), and the third party (not a member of the house) got into an accident causing $700 damage. Jim never said he was sorry about the incident.*

9. Different persons had different ideas about how Evelyn (the 3-year-old) should be raised.

10. Some persons became irritated at having to answer telephone calls frequently for others. Sometimes Sally seemed to aggravate me deliberately, by talking too long on the telephone when she knew that I was waiting.

11. Betty became irritated at the large number of times the house was used for community-building social functions, such as potluck suppers. In particular, Betty found it very distasteful to discover dirty leftover dishes in the sink the next morning, or to find that dishes had been stored in the wrong place.

SOURCE: Excerpted from Matthew L. Israel, "Two Communal Houses and Why (I Think) They Failed," *Journal of Behavior Technology*, 1 (Summer, 1971) pp. 13–15 (as reprinted in Kanter, 1973:397–398).

Then there is the issue of sex. How will the group handle it? Will there be experimentation with free love or group marriages? Or will monogamy and the nuclear family unit be the ideal family form so that the commune will be one "big family" made up of many little families? Will parents have chief responsibility for the children, or will the children be considered to belong to the entire group? Who will be responsible for their socialization and how will this be carried out?

Although some married couples may find communal living beneficial to their relationship, many find that living in a group household places unique strains on their relationship (Brown and Brown, 1973:417; Jaffe and Kanter, 1979). A husband and wife may find themselves either separating from the group or from each other—although of course neither eventuality is inevitable. Sociologists Dennis Jaffe and Rosabeth Kanter (1979) explain:

> The operation of a joint household over which the couple does not have complete sovereignty, plus the presence of others in the immediate intimate realm, presents the couple with the necessity for making choices and intentional decisions about matters that could easily be taken for granted or derived from tradition in a single-family household—e.g., when to be alone together, when and how to include or exclude others, how to divide chores, what territory to carve out as the couple's own domain. (pp. 114–115)

These are only a few of the questions that arise in connection with communal arrangements. It becomes clear that, as an alternative to the family, the commune finds itself heir to many of the same issues that confront the traditional family—plus many more besides.

MODIFIED COMMUNAL LIVING ARRANGEMENTS

Some joint households may not consider themselves "communes" in a strict sense. A group of persons may decide to live together simply as a matter of convenience and to share rent costs. In this way, persons may be able to afford living in parts of a city not possible otherwise and can enjoy valued aspects of city life as well as being close to their employment. Some groups get together through word of mouth or advertisements and rent old mansions in deteriorating neighborhoods. Such groups have been described as being either hotel-like or familylike (Mooney, 1979). Hotel-like situations are those where housemates hardly know each other and go their separate ways, except for living under the same roof. Familylike households value and encourage togetherness.

One single woman who lives in such a household in Washington, D.C. says, "Family houses are typified in an ad I saw in a vegetarian restaurant: 'We give each other a lot of support, so don't answer this ad if you hate to be hugged.' " She describes what living with several other persons has meant to her:

> Sharing a house means you can come down to the living room Sunday morning in your bathrobe, have someone to read something funny to, have someone to go with you afterward to the art gallery.
> I came from the suburbs. This is warmer, wider, more real, better. (Quoted in Mooney, 1979)

Others have also reported that *companionship* ranks at the top of the list of benefits of communal living (Hershberger, 1973). This may be especially true for many single persons who have found that shared living arrangements are "an effective way of dealing with previously felt isolation and loneliness" (Stein, 1976:96–97).

GROUP MARRIAGE

One sometimes-mentioned alternative to conventional marriage is group marriage. Its current incidence is unknown, although from available evidence it appears to be practiced by only a very small minority (Ellis, 1970; Constantine and Constantine, 1971, 1973a). Anthropological research indicates that it has also been extremely rare in other cultures (Murdock, 1949). A group marriage differs from a commune, although the two are often confused. However, most intentional communities (communes) have as their goal the formation of a family of *brotherlike* and *sisterlike* relationships. Group marriages, on the other hand, emphasize *spouse* relationships between members. The sparse information presently available seems to show that group marriages are rare among communes, and efforts to press for such arrangements have even caused the disruption of some intentional communities (Constantine and Constantine, 1973a:68–69; Ellis, 1970).

GROUP MARRIAGE IS NOT POLYGAMY

Most persons in our society think of marriage in terms of *monogamy*—a marital relationship between one husband and one wife. Another form of marriage

Grouped by sex, Shakers danced in a ritual designed to shake out sin through the fingertips.
(Library of Congress)

practiced in many cultures throughout the world has been *polygamy* (one person with two or more spouses). Polygamy may occur either in the form of *polygyny* (one husband with two or more wives) or *polyandry* (one wife with two or more husbands). The terms are easily remembered by thinking of their Greek roots; for example, the *gyn* in polygyny is the same root found in the familiar term *gynecologist. Poly* plus *gyny* means "many females." *Poly* plus *andry* means "many males."

According to anthropological evidence, monogamy is the prevailing marital form in all societies. However, some permit polygamy in some form as well. A study of 238 societies by the anthropologist George Murdock (1949) showed that in 81 percent a male was allowed to marry more than one female (polygyny) but in only 1 percent of the societies could a wife have more than one husband (polyandry). Societies that recognize polygamous unions consider them to be nothing less than *marriages,* even though more than two persons are involved. This means that such arrangements entail all the responsibilities of marriage, including publicly declared commitment to the relationship and economic and sexual interdependence.

While often it is assumed that co-wives in a polygynous union regard themselves as unfortunate, one study of women in western Nigeria showed that many such wives are not necessarily unhappy with the arrangement. "In some cases," writes sociologist Helen Ware (1979:194), "wives in polygynous marriages may have greater autonomy because they have less invested in the

Societies that recognize polygamous unions consider them to be nothing less than marriages, even though more than two persons are involved. (Susan Berkowitz)

marriage and because, in losing part of their husbands' economic and moral support, they also gain independence." She added that many of the women in her study indicated they placed little value on husbands, while great value was attached to children; and she observed that "polygyny promotes competition in childbearing between co-wives" (p. 192).

When asked if polygyny provided any advantages for wives, the majority of women in Ware's study (some of whom were already in polygynous unions, while others knew their husbands might take additional wives some time in the future) cited the benefits of having help with household chores. "The most commonly cited second advantage was that wives could plan together to advance the welfare of the household as a whole through trade or other economic ventures," says Ware, pointing out this advantage applies only "to the traditional culture of farmers, traders, and artisans, in which the extended family is the unit of production and consumption and women can make a major contribution to the economic welfare of the family" (pp. 189–190). It would have little application where employment opportunities for women are limited.

A much smaller proportion of women in Ware's sample saw polygyny as advantageous for "sharing the burden of the husband's sexual demands," a finding that may seem understandable in view of the custom in that culture of child spacing through a wife's sexual abstinence for around two years after giving birth. Few wives were actually enthused over the idea of polygyny; but

Multiple Wives and Female Autonomy

There are two ways of viewing the differences in autonomy between wives in monogamous and polygynous unions. One is to argue that monogamous marriages (or rather marriages in which the husband is monogamous from choice rather than from lack of opportunity) represent a more modern, "Westernized" form in which spouses are more equal and, therefore, wives have greater opportunities for participating in decision-making.

The other view argues that wives in polygynous unions have greater freedom precisely because they are not in a one-to-one relationship with their spouses and must, to a certain extent, live lives of their own. Traditionally [in that society], wives knelt in respect to serve food or drink to their husbands, yet, at the same time, their money and possessions could not be used by their husbands without their consent (in marked contrast to nineteenth century Britain). In a "modern" marriage, pooled resources may actually represent a loss of autonomy for the wife.

SOURCE: Helen Ware, "Polygyny: Women's Views in a Transitional Society, Nigeria, 1975," *Journal of Marriage and Family* 41 (February 1979), p. 191.

given a choice, they said they would rather their husbands took on extra wives than have ongoing affairs with mistresses. Why? Ware's respondents reported that "men spend less money on their wives than on their mistresses" (which would mean less money leaving the household) and that "the position of a wife is defined rather than fluid and uncontrollable" (p. 189). Wives with some amount of formal "Western-style" education were found to view polygyny more negatively than was true of more traditional and uneducated wives.

WHAT IS GROUP MARRIAGE?

Group marriage is not the same as polygyny and polyandry but has been traditionally defined as consisting of two or more males married to two or more females (Nimkoff, 1965). Two writers who have given much attention to group marriage, Larry and Joan Constantine (1971), raise the objection that the traditional definition leaves no allowance for a three-person group situation in which all partners are equal in rank (in contrast to traditional polygamous situations). They suggest the term *multilateral* (or many-sided) marriage, which they define as an arrangement "in which all participants are married to at least two other participants; usually all participants are married to all others." James Ramey (1972a, 1972b) of the Center for the Study of Innovative Life Styles prefers to retain the familiar term *group marriage* while utilizing the Constantines' definition, substituting the word *pair-bonded* for the word *married* (since persons may be pair-bonded without being legally married). Ramey makes the following distinctions: The commitment in a dyadic (two-person) marriage is to the individual. The commitment in a commune is to the group as a whole. The commitment in a group marriage is to both the group as a whole and to each individual. His conclusion is that "group marriage, which combines commitment to the group with multiple pair-bonding among the members of the group, is the most complex form of marriage."

WHO ENTERS GROUP MARRIAGES AND WHY?

Finding persons in group marriages who are willing to be interviewed about their life-style is not easy. The Constantines (1973a) were able to identify only 101 groups in the United States which could be confirmed as multilateral marriages, 66 of which had already dissolved by the time they came to the interviewers' attention. Twenty-six groups were willing to become informants or respondents for the Constantines' survey. Less than half of the groups were still together at the end of one year, while 17 percent of the groups were still intact at the end of a three-year period.

It is commonly believed that only the very young are interested in multiperson marriages, but the limited information available suggests otherwise. In the Constantine project, the median age for female participants in group marriages was found to be twenty-eight, for males thirty-one. James Ramey's report on persons interested in alternate forms of marriage showed that couples who had participated in group marriages or in communes (with nearly three-quarters of the latter reporting they had been sexually involved with other couples at some time) had a median age of thirty (females) and thirty-five (males). Thus, while it is true that those wishing to try group arrangements are often young, frequently they are over thirty and sometimes considerably older. In fact, some behavioral scientists have discussed *polygyny* as a possible solution to the loneliness of old age (where widows outnumber widowers) and as a means of alleviating some of the problems of household care and financial needs among the elderly (see Duberman, 1977:13, Kassel, 1970).

Ramey's (1972a) information was gleaned from eighty couples who were either interested in group marriages or communes or else had already participated in such arrangements. Of these, over 90 percent of husbands and wives, if employed, held academic, managerial, or professional positions. Nine out of ten men and four out of every ten women had a college education or more.

In the group marriages examined by the Constantines, a wide variety of occupations were represented, including college professors, students, salespersons, farmers, carpenters, mechanics, engineers, psychologists, social workers, nurses, a physician, a minister, and a theologian. The reasons they gave for forming group marriages related to love, personal fulfillment and growth, the desire for community and for a richer family life for children, intellectual stimulation, and interest in sexual variety. According to the Constantines, "Most of them are *not* rebelling, seeking escape, acting on religious principles, or improving what they consider to be unsatisfactory marriages." In many respects, the reasons cited for forming group marriages appear to be similar to reasons persons might give for forming intimate family networks or joining communes, with the added desire (in group marriages) for freedom to experience sexual intimacy as part of emotional closeness to more than one person (Constantine and Constantine, 1973a:73, 109; Ramey, 1972a:651).

SEX IN GROUP MARRIAGE

Although it is popularly believed that sex is the central focus in group marriages, participants in such arrangements disagree and tend to emphasize the overall relationships of caring and sharing. Sexual intercourse usually occurs in what psychiatrist Albert Ellis (1970) calls a "round-robin" fashion, with different persons pairing off day by day (or every few days) so that each man and each woman in the marriage regularly copulate together. Some group marriages have a fixed rotation pattern which is planned and structured by group consensus.

The term *group marriage* is not synonymous with *group sex*, which may be defined as sexual activity engaged in by three or more persons simultaneously. Usually group-married persons pair off privately as couples, although on rare occasions several or all of the partners may climb into bed together (Constantine and Constantine, 1973a, chap. 15, also 1973b).

Larry and Joan Constantine (1973a:166–168) found that, with few exceptions, sexual activity between persons of the same sex occurred only in such group sexual encounters. The persons involved made a distinction between ambisexuality ("the capacity to relate sexually to either sex as appropriate to the circumstances") and homosexuality, pointing out that they considered "the interaction *among* several partners (hence in part between members of the same sex) as different from sex *between* two members of the same sex." Although the co-wives are considered to be "marriage partners" in the sense of commitment to each other, and the co-husbands similarly, all were much more certain about warm physical demonstrations of affection between same-sex partners than about actual sexual relationships. While every observed group made provision for heterosexual pairs to sleep together, no group provided sleeping arrangements for same-sex pairs.

PROBLEMS IN GROUP MARRIAGES

As in most marriages and communes, difficulties may arise as persons endeavor to relate to one another deeply. In a group marriage, the problems are especially complex because of the number of persons involved. Thus, such marriages tend to last from only a few months to a few years. The problems only rarely relate to sex (jealousy, for example). Usually, the breakups occur for other reasons—incombatibility of personalities, inability to communicate and work out problems of decision-making about the multitudinous details of everyday living together, conflicts about childrearing, and so on. Some couples perceive the costs to exceed the rewards and choose to end the arrangements. Although there is no formal document, a couple or a single person may in a sense "divorce" another couple.

Forming a group marriage in the first place can be problematic. In entering conventional two-partner marriages, we have seen that the selection of one person by another involves a great deal of evaluating costs and rewards. However, the process of mate selection becomes extremely complex in forming a group marriage because it means two people must find a compatible third partner who can relate satisfactorily to each of them or else another couple who can be co-spouses. The Constantines (1973a, chap. 8) report that many people are surprised to learn that couples often carry on a courtship with other couples in much the same way that individuals do before forming traditional dyadic marriages. There may be love letters, frequent phone calls, dinner dates, and the like. In some cases, the couples begin cross-couple sexual intimacies only after deciding upon a commitment to each other, a kind of engagement to be group-married.

One of the biggest problems facing group marriages is the fact that they are not recognized as legal marriages in any state at present. The group arrangement is characterized by ongoing sexual and economic interdependence, which fits with the sociological definition of marriage provided earlier, but there is often a reluctance to disclose the arrangement publicly because of the costs involved.

Although the Constantines (1973a:13, 235) are of the opinion that "group marriage has the signal and unique advantage of providing for sexual variety for *both* men and women *within* a stable marital configuration," they predict that it will be practiced by only a minority of families because of the complexities involved.

CHAPTER HIGHLIGHTS

Statistics indicate that most persons eventually marry. However, as more and more young persons postpone marriage, the likelihood of lifetime singleness for many will increase. Over the course of a lifetime, a person may experience singleness (in the sense of not being in a paired relationship) at one or more points—as a never-married person or as a divorced or widowed person. Prerequisites listed by Adams for a *single life-style* are economic independence, social and psychological independence, and "a clearly thought through intent to remain single by preference." Persons are likely to choose singleness if they perceive the rewards of singleness to outweigh the costs of singleness—and the costs of marriage to outweigh the rewards of marriage. Some never-married persons are parents, either through adopting children or through keeping and rearing their own children born out of wedlock. In modern times, the universality of Malinowski's notion that a social father is necessary as a pipeline to a society's status and economic rewards may be challenged on two grounds: (1) changing legal definitions of legitimacy, and (2) changing gender roles which make it possible for the child's mother to be the pipeline to the opportunity system.

Communes may serve as the functional equivalent of the extended kin in terms of affection, interdependence, shared rituals, influence on migration patterns, and general influence and control over members. Communes differ from *intimate family networks* (close friendship networks that seem like "family") in the communal living arrangement (a shared residence) and in the common practice or total or partial economic sharing in communes. A major concern of communes centers around achieving a balance of individualism versus group interests. Research indicates that some persons form *group marriages* for the same reasons that other people form communes or intimate family networks, but with the additional goal of having freedom to experience sexual intimacy as part of emotional closeness to more than one person.

PART FIVE

STRUCTURE AND PROCESS IN MARRIAGE

CHAPTER 10

(Erika Stone/Peter Arnold, Inc.)

THE STRUCTURE OF TRADITIONAL MARRIAGE PATTERNS

Entering the state of marriage could be compared to entering a building. However, not all buildings are structured alike, and neither are all marriages. The following cases illustrate four basic blueprints or models. This doesn't mean that every marriage must fall neatly and totally into one or another of the patterns described (there are frameworks in between the categories, blurring into one another), but the case descriptions help us see some basic structural distinctions.

CASE ONE

During the first half of the nineteenth century, when physical punishment was sometimes used to enforce husband supremacy, a writer recalled a man in her neighborhood. This respected church and community leader regularly beat his wife with a horsewhip, claiming that such behavior was necessary "in order to keep her in subjection" and to stop her from scolding. Emily Collins commented on her neighbors: "Now this wife, surrounded by six or seven little children . . . was obliged to spin and weave cloth for all the garments of the family . . . to milk . . . to make butter and cheese, and do all the cooking, washing, making, and mending . . . and, with the pains of maternity forced upon her every eighteen months, was whipped by her pious husband, 'because she scolded' " (Calhoun, vol. 2, 1919:92–93).

CASE TWO

Cindy and Tom have been married for seven years. They have a five-year-old son and a daughter, age two. They consider their marriage and family life ideal and say they can't understand what all the shouting about women's "liberation" means. "What is there to be liberated from?" asks Tom. "Women never had it better. Look how nice Cindy has it—just being able to stay at home, be her own boss, have her own hours, while I go out and earn the living! She wouldn't have it any other way, and neither would I. We both like knowing that she's here when the kids need her, and I enjoy coming home to a neat, orderly house and a delicious dinner. Oh don't get me wrong! She isn't my slave or anything. We work together on a lot of household projects on weekends, and I'm always glad to pitch in and help her when she needs me—like helping out with the dishes some evenings when I don't have meetings to attend, or helping put the children to bed."

Cindy agrees that she enjoys her role as full-time homemaker. "I like to sew, and I like to have time to chat with friends on the phone or down at the park while the kids play in the playground. I don't feel at all trapped. Tom gives me an allowance every week in addition to the household money, so I always have spending money that I don't have to account to him for. Really, I like my life and feel I'm fulfilling woman's true role—to love, encourage, and serve my family. And I feel I can help Tom advance in his career best by being just what I am, a loving, devoted wife who supports and backs him up, believes in him, and tries to make life smooth at home. They say that behind every great man is a woman; I want to be that woman in Tom's life."

CASE THREE

Marilyn is an elementary school teacher. Her husband, Al, is the manager of a local department store which is part of a large national chain. Married eighteen years, they have three children, ranging in age from nine to fifteen. When her youngest child reached school age, Marilyn returned to teaching after not having taught for several years, except for serving occasionally as a substitute teacher.

Now back at full-time teaching, Marilyn still does not consider it her primary career. "If Al and I feel the children are being harmed in any way and that they need me at home, I'll not hesitate a moment to give up teaching," she says. "I enjoy my work and it's nice having my income for extra things, but it's not absolutely essential. Al and I believe that the husband should be the main breadwinner. He's the captain and I'm second mate. That means his work takes precedence over mine. For example, if the company asks him to move (and that's happened many times already during our marriage), my teaching position is no reason to insist we stay here. I'm sure I could always find a similar position at our new location; and if not, I'll just stay home and be a good wife and mother. Or I can always put my name on a list for substitute teaching."

CASE FOUR

Janet and Roger both have demanding careers to which they are highly committed. Arriving at a suitable life-style for them and their four-year-old daughter has not been easy, but they have determined to work out an equalitarian marriage in the fullest sense of that term. This means that each takes seriously the responsibility of being a parent and giving time and loving attention to Gretchen. They have not assumed that the task of arranging for child care is Janet's task, nor have the necessary funds come from Janet's salary—as though she were the parent holding major responsibility for their child. Rather, both Roger and Janet feel they must share *the responsibility for Gretchen's needs as well as share the responsibility for household chores.*

Janet and Roger also feel that they should have equal power in family decision-making and that neither one's career is more important than that of the other. Thus, if Janet (a psychology professor) decides to accept an offer from a university in another state, her lawyer husband is willing to leave his lucrative law practice and set up a new practice in the new location (following his wife, in contrast to the traditional custom of a wife following her husband). At the same time, if Roger wanted to pursue some new opportunity (in politics, for example), Janet is willing to seek employment at some school in the area where Roger's new plans would take him.

UNDERSTANDING THE STRUCTURE OF MARRIAGE

The story of the nineteenth-century authoritarian husband and the modern hypothetical case studies serve to illustrate clearly that people may structure their marriages quite differently.

In defining marriage earlier, we saw that there are two sides to marriage, two main parts of the structure—the practical or instrumental side (earning family income, performing household tasks) and the personal or expressive side (love, sex, empathy, companionship). What goes on in these two areas of marriage is affected by the positions and roles of men and women. The opening four stories showed that marriage may be structured as a relationship between an owner and his property (the nineteenth-century husband who beat his wife to keep her in subjection), or between a head and its complement (Tom and Cindy), or between a senior partner and junior partner (Al and Marilyn), or between two equal partners (Janet and Roger). The first two cases illustrate two traditional marriage patterns and will be discussed in this chapter. In Chapter 11, we'll look at two emerging marriage patterns, as represented by the third and fourth cases.

OWNER-PROPERTY MARRIAGE PATTERN

The story cited in case 1 was not unusual in the nineteenth century. The husband who used a horsewhip on his wife to keep her in subjection was held by the New York courts to be within his rights. If what was termed "a reasonable instrument" was used, wife beating was legal in almost all states as late as 1850. As social historian Alice Felt Tyler (1944:426) points out,

"Women were legally considered perpetual minors; if unmarried, the wards of male relatives; if married, a part of their husband's chattels. . . . In legal status servile and incompetent, by social canon revered and closely guarded, in cold fact a vitally necessary part of a dynamic economic and social system." A married woman and all she possessed (including any earnings she might make) were legally considered to belong to her husband. Her very being was considered to be merged into his; the two were one, and the one was the husband.

Writer Eva Figes (1970) speaks of such a concept of marriage as "basically the purchase of sexual favour in return for board and lodging." The limited alternatives for women meant that the bargain was harshly one-sided. From a Marxist perspective, it could be said that men historically have been the ruling or dominant group, the bourgeoisie; women have been the ruled or subordinate group, the proletariat. Helen Campbell, the writer of an 1893 publication on women wage earners, began with "a look backward," to show how "physical facts worked with man's will . . . and early rendered women subordinate physically and dependent economically." She quotes other writers of the period to the effect that "woman at once became property. . . . Marriage . . . became the symbol of transfer of ownership," just as a formal deed signifies a purchaser's right to possess his land. It is *economic dependence* on the oppressor, argues Campbell, that is the basis of all oppression (Campbell, 1893:26–27).

POSITIONS AND ROLES

In the picture of marriage just described, the position of the man is that of owner, and the position of the woman is that of property. This position or status indicates how the two persons stand in relationship to one another. But within this status, each has a distinct part to play—a role.

Under the owner-property arrangement, the woman's major role was that of wife-mother. It was a hyphenated role in more than word only. A woman who was a wife was expected to be a mother as well; there was no notion that wife and mother could be two separate roles. For a married man, the role of husband-father was likewise not separated. If a man were a husband, he was supposed to be a father as well. That his wife should provide him with children was considered furthermore to be one of his basic marital *rights*.

The marriage contract implies both rights and duties for both partners. The rights of one partner may involve having certain duties performed on the part of the other partner. And the duties a spouse carries out may be done in order to assure that the rights of the other spouse are met. For example, in a traditional marriage, a husband might arrive home from work (his *duty* to provide for his family) and expect to find dinner ready (his *right* to have household needs cared for by his wife). His wife has prepared the meal (her *duty* to cook and do other household tasks for her family) because her husband has put in a hard day's work (fulfilling her *right* to be financially supported).

WIFE'S DUTIES AND HUSBAND'S RIGHTS

Under the owner-property arrangement of marriage, the role of wife-mother carried with it certain duties in both the practical and personal sides of marriage. Looking first at her duties within the instrumental or task-oriented dimension (the practical side), we find the following *norms* or expectations of how she was to behave:

1 Her chief task in life was to please her husband and care for his needs and those of the household.
2 She was to obey her husband in all things.
3 She was to bear children that could carry on her husband's name.
4 She was to train the children so that they would reflect credit on her husband.

From the husband's standpoint, the fulfillment of these norms by his wife was a matter of rights—*his* rights. He considered himself to possess the right to have his wife please him, obey him, care for his household needs, bear him children, and so on. Such rights were inherent in the position of owner.

Two points stand out and summarize the role duties of the wife-mother within the position of property. One, the woman has no existence independent from that of her husband; legally she is considered a nonperson. By definition, she is merely an extension of him—of his interests, desires, needs, wants, ambitions, goals, and so on. Two, the power question is settled and beyond dispute. The husband is boss and the wife must be subject to him. Whenever there is a disagreement or clash of wills, the wife as his property merely submits to her husband's will. By this means, order and stability are maintained. Embedding the authority question in a fixed way within the normative structure of the wife's role duties is considerably different from what we shall observe in other marriage arrangements.

Did Women Feel Oppressed?   Campbell's classic economic history of women details the scope of household tasks performed by the woman of the preindustrial era. Not only did she have all the childrearing and household maintenance tasks that women have usually done and many still do, she also "had to spin, weave, and bleach; to make all the linen and clothes, to boil soap, to make candles and brew beer. . . . She frequently had to work in the field or garden and to attend to the poultry or cattle." (Campbell, 1893:50).

The question naturally arises: Did women feel oppressed? Most Marxists would probably admit that they did not but would label this as "false consciousness"; that is women *believed* they were as content as they could reasonably expect to be, but this was a false or inaccurate picture. Further, the Marxist might say that had wives realized just how bad their condition actually was, they simply would have revolted en masse and sought liberation from husband oppression long ago.

It is difficult to know how most wives felt historically in the position of property. A few put their feelings into writing so that we know there was discontent on the part of some. However, not many alternative roles were open to women besides that of wife-mother. Likewise, it is hard to think of alternative images other than the wife-mother role that little girls could observe as they grew up, given the rigid sex-role socialization that occurred during that era. It seems likely that most men and women believed in the appropriateness of the marital arrangement as they knew it—the owner-property model with its respective rights and duties for husbands and wives.

Campbell's study goes to the heart of the matter as she describes the situation in which even wage-earning women found themselves at first. "For ages, [the woman's] identity had been merged in that of the man by whose side she worked with no thought of recompense," wrote Campbell. All the traits that were considered "feminine" were expected to be cultivated (submissiveness, clinging affection, humility), while stronger traits such as assertiveness were suppressed. These combined factors stood in the way of any resistance to injustice and mistreatment. Campbell (1893:51–52) makes her point forcefully: "The mass of women had neither power nor wish to protest; and thus the few traces we find of their earliest connection with labor show us that they accepted bare subsistence as all to which they were entitled, and were grateful if they escaped the beating which the lower order of Englishman still regards as his right to give."

Some concerned feminists not only saw the inequities but called attention to the need for *consciousness-raising* if women were ever going to experience the removal of unjust laws and customs. At the 1848 Seneca Falls (New York) Convention, the first women's rights conference held in the United States, one of the resolutions adopted was "that the women of this country ought to be enlightened in regard to the laws under which they live, that they may no longer publish their degradation by declaring themselves satisfied with their present position, nor their ignorance, by asserting that they have all the rights they want" (reprinted in Rossi (ed.), 1973, p. 419 in 1974 Bantam edition). Injustices in owner-property marriage laws and customs were singled out for special attention.

HUSBAND'S DUTIES AND WIFE'S RIGHTS

Having seen the wife's duties (which are also the husband's rights), we might wonder about the husband's duties (and correspondingly, the wife's rights). It is at this point that we discover the most important reason that the owner-property arrangement could be maintained. The husband's chief duty was to provide economic resources for the family's survival and well-being. Because the wife depended on her husband for these essential resources, he had considerable power over her. In other words, her deference was exchanged for his benefits. His power was therefore *doubly* reinforced since it rested both on the norms which prescribed wifely obedience and on the needed benefits with which he supplied his wife.

In the owner-property arrangement, societal norms sanctioned wife-beating, and there was little women could do about it. (Feminist Art Journal)

In exchange, for performing her duties, the wife received her rewards and the fulfillment of her marital rights by being provided for. She also shared in whatever prestige her husband was able to attain. She received acclaim from kin and peers based on her husband's achievements and social status. In addition, she received esteem, support, and approval from others (including her husband) because she performed her own apportioned duties so well. ("What an excellent wife and mother she is!" "She certainly keeps a neat house, and she can bake the tastiest pies in the world!" "She makes sure her children are well-behaved and mannerly, too.")

These exchanges of husband-wife rights and duties constituted an ongoing cycle. The husband's duty to provide fulfilled the wife's right to be provided for. This provision in turn motivated her to continue performing her wife-mother duties, which meant that the husband's rights were thereby fulfilled. Because of this, he continued to feel motivated to keep on providing for her, with the result that there was an uninterrupted fulfillment of role duties in the prescribed fashion. The basis for these role exchanges lay with the husband as owner and the wife as property, with the man's having exclusive access to economic resources and possessing power that men and women believed to be legitimate and right.

EXPRESSIVE DIMENSION

All that has been said thus far has concerned the instrumental dimension of marriage with its emphasis on economic provision and task performance. What about the person-oriented side of marriage? Again, thinking in terms of rights and duties, the wife's chief duty in the expressive dimension apparently was to provide sexual gratification for her husband. And it was his right to receive that benefit or resource from her. In exchange, it was likewise his duty to provide sexual benefits to his wife. However, although provision of sex was incumbent on both partners, the quality of sexual performance was probably far less crucial. The husband was not obligated to sexually gratify his wife at a very high level. And the wife was not expected to be particularly sensuous toward her husband; all that mattered was that she be available and "not refuse him his pleasure." Moreover, it is not clear that the spouses were expected to provide one another with a very high degree of other expressive rewards such as companionship and empathy.

Finally, the husband's ultimate power meant that if there were any disagreements over sexual or other expressive matters, the wife simply had to give in to his will and judgment. If she wanted to visit relatives or neighbors and he wanted her to spend the evening at home with him, she did as he said. If he wanted to have sexual intercourse when she was not so inclined, she submitted to his will. Her own expressive satisfaction wasn't considered important. The double standard was widely practiced by men; they could get whatever kinds and degrees of sexual satisfactions they desired through prostitutes. Mary Wollstonecraft complained about this as early as 1792 when she published her *Vindication of the Rights of Woman*. She wrote: "Their husbands acknowledge that they are good managers, and chaste wives; but leave home to seek for more agreeable . . . society; and the patient drudge, who fulfills her task, like a blind horse in a mill, is defrauded of her just reward; for the wages due to her are the caresses of her husband" (p. 113). Undoubtedly many wives under the owner-property arrangement felt such deprivation, but there was little they could do except suffer in silence.

Between husbands and wives, "emotional isolation was accomplished through the strict demarcation of work assignments and sex roles," writes historian Edward Shorter (1977:55). Why? Because societal norms dictated that the traditional family be based upon considerations of lineage and property rather than on affection. What mattered were certain definitions of social order. Contrasting past and present attitudes, Shorter writes:

> Whereas the modern couple would brim over with expressive behavior, hand-holding, and eye-gazing as they embarked upon the interior search, the traditional husband and wife were severely limited: "I'll fulfill my roles, you fulfill yours, we'll both live up to the expectations the community sets, and *voilà*, our lives will unfold without disorder." It would never have occurred to them to ask if they were happy. (p. 55)

HEAD-COMPLEMENT MARRIAGE PATTERN

The positions of husband-as-owner and wife-as-property gradually evolved into those of husband-as-head and wife-as-complement. The kind of marriage Tom and Cindy have in case 2 is a head-complement arrangement. Here both the wife's rights and the husband's duties increase. No longer is it a one-sided system in which the wife has little more than survival rights (food, shelter, clothing), while the husband reaps benefits from her services. In marriages where wives are viewed as complements or counterparts to husbands, the husband is expected to meet his wife's love and affection needs, her desires for sexual pleasure, her yearnings for warm emotional support, campanionship, understanding, and open communication. Take Cindy and Tom, for example. Cindy's responsibilities may at first seem similar to those of wives in the "property" arrangement, but an altogether different marital compact is in effect. Tom is *not* considered Cindy's owner or master. In the head-complement bargain, two persons who have chosen to join their lives together decide to organize their living arrangements in a particular, convenient way. The husband fulfills his end of the bargain by going out into the world to earn the family income; the wife fulfills her end by remaining home to care for the house and children.

Freed from the necessity of earning a living, Cindy can give her time and attention to her role as family coordinator, keeper of the hearth, and emotional hub. At the same time, she is often able to arrange time for voluntary activities, thus representing the family in the community through participation in charitable work, religious service, political activities, scouting, and parent-teacher organizations.

Tom, on the other hand, is freed from many responsibilities and encumbrances related to the ordinary demands of daily life (such as meal planning, shopping, cooking, cleaning, washing clothes, sewing on buttons, answering social invitations, writing letters and birthday cards to relatives, and the myriad of other tasks that usually fall to wives). Thus, Tom is enabled to devote more time, attention, and energy to his occupation. He has a helpful, supportive, encouraging wife behind him, making it possible for him to achieve much more than if he had to be on his own. He has someone who fills up something that would be missing from his life otherwise, someone who completes him, rounds out his life—in other words a *complement*. He may fondly speak of Cindy as his "other half."

This marital arrangement fits with the structural-functional approach to marriage described in Chapter 1. It suggests a biological analogy, with an emphasis on the specialized function of each body part. The husband in this pattern is expected to function as the family's "head," while the wife is expected to function as the family's "heart."

RIGHTS AND DUTIES IN THE HEAD-COMPLEMENT ARRANGEMENT

As in the owner-property marriage arrangement, couples who follow the head-complement pattern are expected to fulfill both rights and duties with respect to one another. These rights and duties are associated with the husband-father role and the wife-mother role, and again the *duties* of each spouse serve the *rights* of the other spouse. The norms associated with the spouse roles spell out what the respective duties of the husband and wife are.

Instrumental Side of Marriage Looking first at the practical or instrumental side of marriage, we find that most of the norms associated with the wife-mother role under the earlier owner-property marriage arrangement have not changed much. The woman's chief task is still to please her husband and care for the needs of the household. She is still expected to bear and rear children who will carry on the husband's name and be a source of pride and gratification. And she is still expected to find her meaning by living through her husband and children rather than seeking a life of her own. Likewise, she is to make sure that she orders her life so that credit is reflected on her husband. Good complements are expected to bring good compliments!

Yet change has occurred in one of the expected areas of behavior—the issue of obedience. No longer is power rigidly fixed within the established norms as it was under the owner-property arrangement ("Wives must obey their husbands"). Now it becomes somewhat more problematic. The marital power issue is less settled. Gone are the days when the wife was expected to submit to the husband without question.

Instead, as her husband's counterpart, the wife is expected to give final deference. That is, she yields to her husband's will in the end and gives in to his wishes, but before that time she is free to discuss her own opinions on the particular issue. Under the owner-property arrangement, the husband could say, "Do this!" and the wife did it. Now he says, "Let's do this." The wife may reply, "Why?" or "No, I don't think so." The husband in turn asks why his wife feels as she does and then he decides, "We'll do this anyway!" or else, "You're right; maybe we shouldn't."

The final decision is still the husband's. But it differs from his rulership as exercised under the owner-property arrangement because, as head, the husband now takes into consideration the wishes of the wife as complement. To borrow from computer language, we may say that the husband permits the

"They have this arrangement. He earns the money and she takes care of the house." (Drawing by Weber; © 1977 The New Yorker Magazine, Inc.)

wife to make "inputs" into the husband's decision-making. Of course, she may or may not counsel in a particular matter, and he may or may not consult on certain issues. In some cases, the husband may "allow" his wife to make the decisions. In certain other cases, the two may decide on a course of action jointly. But always the final options are in the husband's hands; he is like a supreme court beyond which no further appeals are possible.

These shifts are subtle but meaningful in that they represent some increase in the wife's participation in power. At the same time, there are corresponding shifts in the husband's *rights*. He has now lost the right to be the absolute ruler. In terms of exchange theory, with its emphasis on costs, rewards, profit, and loss, we may say that the loss of absolute rulership rights has been a cost to the husband. Although he still retains final authority and control, his role is now that of a president in a democracy rather than that of a totalitarian dictator. This loss by no means deprives him of all profit in the marital exchange. He still receives ample rewards from his wife within the instrumental dimension of marriage and retains the rights to receive from her the fulfillment of her duties associated with the wife-mother role as described earlier.

But what about the husband's duties in the instrumental realm? Here again nothing much has changed insofar as his unique obligation to provide for his wife and children is concerned. This access to economic resources continues to be the basis for his still possessing considerable marital power. The wife's rights and rewards associated with her husband's provision for her also remain much the same as before—except for one important shift. In the head-complement pattern, the wife has the right to work—whether or not she exercises that option. With her husband's consent, she may become a wage earner under certain conditions (usually serious economic needs within the family). The existence of the work option elevates her power potential, as we shall see.

Expressive Side of Marriage Moving to the expressive or person-oriented dimension of marriage, we see once more the effects of the wife's improved negotiating position. Under the owner-property arrangement, sex was exchanged between the spouses on a duties-rights basis; but the degree of satisfaction was not terribly significant, nor were other aspects of expressiveness, such as companionship and empathy. However, throughout the nineteenth and into the twentieth century, there gradually arose the notion of companionship marriage, with emphasis on the centrality of the "affectionate function." Little by little, it was becoming normative for husbands and wives to be friends and lovers. They were expected to be much more to one another than merely sources of income, status, housekeeping, sexual exchanges, and children. They were expected to enjoy one another as persons, to find pleasure in one another's company, to take one another into confidence and share problems and triumphs, to go places together and to do things together.

Couples also came to expect something beyond the old just-go-through-the-motions kind of sex. They wanted sexual intercourse to be gratifying in a new way—an experience more special and delightful than it once was. Husbands and wives were expected to provide for each other's sexual rights in a reciprocal-duty fashion. If the wife did her best to make sure that the sexual expression of love was pleasurable to her husband (thereby performing her duty and fulfilling his right), she expected in turn that her husband would do his best to provide her with sexual pleasure as well (thereby performing his duty and fulfilling her right).

The same was true in serving as sounding boards for one another's problems, or in being open to each other's needs for self-disclosure regarding inmost thoughts and feelings, or in being companions to one another during leisure time. Each had rights and duties in all these areas. All of this was quite different from the former arrangement of owner-property where the emphasis was more on the wife's duties and the husband's rights with regard to sex, with little importance at all attached to companionship, empathy, and being a "best friend" to one's spouse.

One reason that these alterations occurred stemmed from women's sense of expressive inequities. (Recall Mary Wollstonecraft's complaint about wives who felt cheated when deprived of their husbands' caresses. And this was as early as the eighteenth century.) With improved negotiating power derived from economic opportunities and the option to become wage earners, women began pressing for greater rights within the expressive or personal side of marriage, desiring to make the rights-duties exchange more fair and reciprocal. Warm expressive exchanges surely must have been much more difficult to carry out between an "owner" and his "property" under the old system. The status and power differences were just too wide for the spouses to be deep friends very often or very long. But as power differences began to decline with wives in a better bargaining position, changes were gradually brought about in the personal side of marriage, making it more rewarding for both wives and husbands. In exchange terms, the cost (husband's loss of some power) was offset by gains in the expressive dimension.

What brought about the evolution of the owner-property status so that it has changed into the head-complement arrangement? To answer that question, we must look at the increasing economic opportunities afforded women beginning as early as the colonial period.

WOMEN IN THE LABOR FORCE UP TO 1900

As women gained independent access to economic resources, they inevitably improved their bargaining within marriage. Though changes were slight and gradual, women began to realize the inherent contradiction in being able to gain resources on their own while still being considered property of their husbands. In 1848, the first Woman's Rights Convention called attention to numerous grievances, pointing out wrongs perpetrated by men and reinforced by laws men had drawn up. Among the complaints were these: "[Man] has made [the woman], if married, in the eye of the law, civilly dead. He has taken from her all right in property, even to the wages she earns" (quoted in Rossi, 1973). There were many injustices under such a system. Some husbands even hired out their wives and then appropriated their wages. Such unfair practices gave rise to agitation for new legislation on property rights for married women, and various states began to enact laws that were more equitable.

Even prior to the modern era, some women did have certain limited occupational opportunities. Often such women were single or widowed, and they were involved in the guild system. During the Middle Ages, women worked as cobblers, belt and sweater makers, leather dressers, purse makers, furriers, bakers, saddlers, tanners, goldsmiths, lace makers, and embroiderers of such items as church vestments, hangings for religious display, and coats of arms. In some areas of Europe, guild records indicate that over 200 occupations were open to women (Campbell, 1893:46–49; Lasch, 1973; Oakley, 1974, chaps. 2–3). But when the guild system ended, women lost the few opportunities they had begun to possess.

During the colonial period in America (from 1620 to 1776), there were almost no female wage earners, except for those employed in domestic service. A few women did engage in homebased spinning and weaving and other types of work associated with textiles and clothing production. A woman named Betsy Metcalf discovered that meadow grass could be bleached and braided into straw goods, and this process led to a large and lucrative industry. And the American Revolution, like all wars, saw wives step into positions of heading family businesses and farms temporarily vacated by their husbands.

It should be kept in mind that this historical description refers chiefly to white women. The great majority of black women were laboring as slaves on Southern plantations. And just as it was cotton that kept black women in slavery past the 1790s, so it was cotton that at that time altered economic opportunities for white women. According to Campbell (1893:68–72), "It is with the birth of the cotton industry that the work and wages of women begin to take coherent shape." For the first time in history, large and ever-increasing numbers of women began to get out from under their own domestic roofs to work under commercial roofs (spinning mills), earning sums of money hitherto unknown. In this version of the factory system, women from the beginning took a larger part than men. For example, in the first federal count of spinning-industry employees in 1816, there were 66,000 women and female children. There were 24,000 boys under seventeen years of age, and 10,000 males seventeen years and older.

The women who worked in those New England factories throughout the first half of the nineteenth century were mostly young, single, and poorly educated. Their wages were about half or a third of those paid to men. Nevertheless, the numbers of women engaged in a variety of occupations continued to increase throughout the nineteenth century. The mechanization necessary to carry on the Civil War created a whole new series of trade-type occupations, and the reduced numbers of available men made it possible for many women to enter these newly emerging trades.

Exactly how many women were working is hard to answer accurately because the Census Bureau had difficulty getting families to admit that they contained employed females. This hesitancy was due to fear of disapproval, since many persons considered female employment undesirable and frowned on women who dared to deviate from tradition. The 1870 census recorded the number of women workers as 1,836,288. But it seems evident that there were additional women workers who were not enumerated. By 1880, the figure had risen to 2,647,157; but again there was concern about underreporting. The 1890 census showed a 10 percent increase in women wage earners over the 1880 figure. By 1900, 21 percent of all women over fourteen years of age were employed, although only 6 percent of all married women were working (Cain, 1966:2).

That 6-percent figure for married working women is probably higher than anything that occurred in the prior century, and the record in this century has been one of dramatic change upward in the actual numbers and proportion of working wives. By 1940, the proportion had doubled to 14 percent and by 1960 doubled again to 31 percent. That the trend for married women to work outside the home has continued may be seen in 1976 census figures, which showed that 48 percent of all white married women and 55 percent of all black married women had earned income that year (U.S. Bureau of the Census, *Current Population Reports*, P–23, no. 80, 1979:198).

WORK OPPORTUNITIES AND THEIR IMPACT ON MARRIED WOMEN

This steady increase in access to and control of economic resources by *married* women is perhaps the most significant point about the 200-year upward trend in female employment. The availability of work opportunities and the chance to gain resources on their own caused wives to question the existing marital-role structure. They began demanding more rights, more of a voice in decision-making, more control over their own property, and so on. During the nineteenth and twentieth centuries, numerous legal changes gradually took place which played a large part in removing the wife from the position of property and recognizing her as more of a person in her own right (Calhoun, vol. 2, 1919:126–129; Brownlee and Brownlee, 1976:265–266). When women were permitted to inherit, earn, control, and dispose of their own property to a greater measure than before, the traditional marriage arrangement was profoundly affected. The changes brought about in marital-role structures (increased rights and power for women) in turn would affect still further labor-force participation by women (with more women feeling they had the right to work outside the home); and again in feedback fashion, this would affect marriages still further (with increased power for wives because of their increased economic resources).

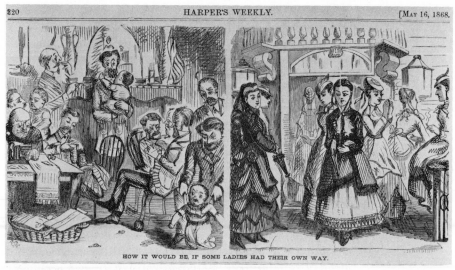

HOW IT WOULD BE, IF SOME LADIES HAD THEIR OWN WAY.

Various economic and legal changes meant a gradual recognition of women as persons in their own right, causing profound changes in the marital balance of power. (Library of Congress)

What we see at work here is the principle of alternative rewards described in Chapter 7. A person's power over another person depends on the resources he or she holds out to that person, how dependent that second person is on these resources, and whether or not that second person can find alternate sources for such benefits elsewhere. At the beginning of the nineteenth century, a woman had few options open to her besides marriage. If she wanted to be provided for, she needed a husband. This gave men a tremendous amount of power over women. Utterly dependent upon a man for economic resources, a woman became his property through marriage. However, as employment opportunities increased for women, a woman could provide for her own needs. Why sit idly by waiting to get married when one could engage in the numerous occupational pursuits opening up to women? As the nineteenth century ended, almost half (46 percent) of all single women were employed.

Although it was true that only 6 percent of married women worked outside the home and their rates of employment increased more slowly than those of single women, the *availability* of employment had a considerable impact on even those wives who didn't choose to enter the labor force. As the nineteenth century progressed, there opened up the possibility of choosing another set of rewards than those held out by husbands, and the existence of that option weakened the power of husbands—whether or not their wives actually worked. The *possibility* of a wife's becoming a wage earner gradually became part of the role rights of the wife-mother, thereby putting married women in a position where they had the capability of bargaining instead of merely yielding to their husbands' wishes. Women were no longer bound to unquestioning obedience out of a sense of helpless dependence on male economic support. Instead, wives could offer suggestions, disagree, counsel and advise, even try to insist on a particular course of action.

In moving from her status as property, the married woman could go in one of two directions. (See Figure 10-1.) The existence of the option to earn income meant either that she could stay at home to look after the household but would now be her husband's counterpart or *complement*, or she could work outside the home and thereby take on what we shall call the *junior-partner* status in marriage. In either case, the fact that the employment option was always there meant that her negotiating power in marriage was increased.

QUESTIONS RAISED BY SCHOLARS

Some scholars disagree over whether the status of women in Western culture has been raised or lowered through industrialization. Similar questions arose in Chapter 3 where we looked at "developing" societies—those currently experiencing movement from agriculture-based economies toward urbanization and industrialization. There we saw that modern technology and the factory system may eliminate many occupations in which women traditional-

FIGURE 10-1 *The movement away from the wife's position as property.*

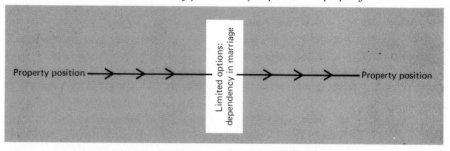

Where no alternatives existed for women, the property status continued in an ongoing line, as though a ray of light were passing through a plain sheet of glass, remaining unchanged.

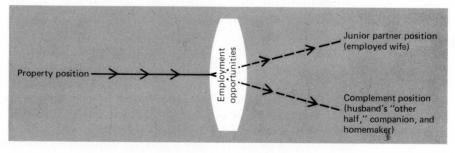

When alternatives for women opened up through employment opportunities and options, the property position "line" was bent like a ray of light passing through a special lens, bending it in two directions.

Scholars disagree over whether the status of women in Western culture has been raised or lowered through industrialization. (Hugh Rogers/Monkmeyer)

ly engaged, thereby hurting many women; but at the same time, industrialization has opened new opportunities for many women and has given them access to economic, status, and educational benefits previously denied them.

Sociologist Ann Oakley (1974) sees industrialization as devaluing women's work and status. Contrasting pre-industrial Great Britain with the situation afterward, she writes of the esteem that had been given to women's productive labors in agriculture, trade, and home-based industries and speaks of ways industrialization stripped women of their former status. The culmination was a removal of productive work *from* the home at the same time that women were expected to remain centered *in* the home. According to Oakley, the result was "the modern differentiation of gender roles and the modern division between domestic and productive work."

On the other hand, historian Edward Shorter (1977) is convinced that an examination of the "real lives of women in eighteenth-century farm-and-craft families" of the Western world reveals a status of considerable inferiority. He takes issue with those who argue that industrialization was "bad for women." "Over the long haul," writes Shorter, "the participation of women in the *paid* labor force was enormously increased rather than diminished—a fact that initiated the dismantling of the staggering patriarchy of the peasantry" (p. xviii).

In the early days of the New England settlement, it is true that women's productive work was recognized and valued, but at the same time "women were considered adjunct and secondary to men in economic life," writes social historian Nancy F. Cott (1977:20), pointing out that "divorce records of the eighteenth century clearly differentiated the two spouses' economic roles." The husband was expected "to supply or provide"; the wife was expected "to use goods frugally and to obey." Cott suggests that the meaning of women's economic status was "diluted" and less obvious during the period when all family members worked together as a "self-contained productive unit," but that the law made clear that the earnings and property of women belonged to their husbands. And when women did work outside the home, "wage rates reflected the expectation that they would rely on men as providers." Furthermore, women lacked opportunities to train for professions, since higher education was closed off to them (Cott, 1977:21–22).

While undeniably the transition to an industrialized society involves many complex factors, including the impact on women's status, it would seem inaccurate to say that women in the United States gradually came to be less valued as productive workers and more dependent upon men as providers. Ideologically at least, husbands were regarded as heads of households and primary breadwinners even in *pre*-industrial early settlements where husbands and wives labored side by side in cottage industries and on farms.

The picture may have been different in England, and it is that country on which Oakley (1974) focuses when she writes that "for men [industrialization] enlarged the world outside the home, chiefly by expanding the range of occupations available to them." For women, on the other hand, it came to mean a contraction of the world into the cramped space of the home, doing away with family labor and the family wage and creating the role of the dependent housewife who looks out on the world through the window above the dish-filled kitchen sink (Oakley, chap. 3). Industrialization took place earlier in Great Britain than in the United States; and further, the rigidly structured British class system separating the nobility and the commoners may have entered into the greater equality of female and male co-workers in crafts and farm work during pre-industrial days. Oakley writes that although the common law embodied the notion "that women ought to be subject to men," ordinary people ignored it in their everyday lives. She explains:

> "Common law" was the law of the nobles. Farming people and artisans depended in their dealings with one another on customs that decreed the independence of women and their equality with men. These customs dated back to the beginnings of English society, to the Anglo-Saxon era, when not only was there equality between the sexes in practice, but also, effectively, in law. (chap. 2; p. 28 in Vintage edition)

What we need to keep in mind is that, as Shorter reminds us, *over the long haul*—regardless of all that has been problematic along the way—women seem to have benefited by industrialization because of the increased options open to them. Oakley's comment about industrialization's role in enlarging the world outside the home for *men*, "chiefly by expanding the range of occupations available to them," could gradually over the years seem just as applicable to women. And it is this opening up of options beyond the four walls of the home that has, as we have seen, made its impact felt on how husbands and wives perceive the structure of marriage.

VESTIGES OF TRADITIONAL NOTIONS OF MARRIAGE IN THE LAW

Changes in laws often take place much more slowly than the changes in people's lives. In spite of increased economic opportunities for women and the fact that close to half of the wives in the United States are in the labor force, the traditional marriage contract and the laws that surround it assume husband dominance and wife dependency. This awareness prompts sociologist Lenore Weitzman (1974; Weitzman et al., 1978) to wonder how many persons would consent to the marriage contract if they knew its terms! "The marriage contract is unlike most contracts," says Weitzman (1974:1170). "Its provisions are unwritten, its penalties are unspecified, and the terms of contract are typically unknown to the 'contracting' parties."

What are the terms of contract? Weitzman lists three: the husband is regarded as head of the family; the husband is assigned the duty of support; and the wife is obligated to take care of the house and children. Joan Krauskopf, (1977), a professor of family law, adds a fourth characteristic of marriage in the eyes of the law—the separation of assets. This is a good-news, bad-news kind of situation. The good news is that married women today have the right to ownership and control over their own property, including income earned through outside employment—a right women did not have before the second half of the last century. The bad news is that the homemaker, busy in doing the domestic and childrearing tasks assigned her by the legal marriage contract, may one day find herself in a situation where the courts decide she doesn't *own* anything because she hasn't *earned* anything and her husband has listed all assets in his own name only. Her contributions as a homemaker are not considered to have monetary value.

Both Weitzman and Krauskopf are speaking of the forty-two states which follow the common law system based upon English common law and the idea that at marriage a wife's legal identity is merged into that of her husband. Blackstone's eighteenth-century *Commentaries on the Laws of England* sum up the notion that the wife ceases to exist as a person in her own right:

> By marriage, the husband and wife are one person in law; that is, the very being or legal existence of the woman is suspended during the marriage, or at least is incorporated and consolidated into that of the husband: under whose wing,

Wives and Property Rights

Because the law gives the homemaker no property rights during the marriage, she is totally dependent upon the husband's charity. In over half the families with small children, the husband earns all the funds; if he titles the family home and auto and bank accounts in his name, they are his alone. The common law courts presume that all household goods which do not have documentary title are the husband's (DiFlorida v. DiFlorida, 1975; State ex rel George v. Mitchell, 1950). In a recent Illinois case (Norris v. Norris, 1974) a farming couple who started out their marriage with nothing acquired considerable net worth in 20 years, but at the termination of the marriage the wife received only her personal belongings and clothing. The court noted that the ordinary services of a wife cannot be taken into account in deciding whether she has any property rights in the assets acquired during the marriage. Those "ordinary" services included the hard work of a farm wife, including preparing five or six meals a day for farmhands. When a Missouri farm wife tried to prevent her husband from disposing of their personal property, livestock, and canned goods (which she had probably grown and canned), she was told by the court that she had no property rights to them (State ex rel George v. Mitchell, 1950).

Even the wife who does earn money outside the home may find herself with no claim at all on the family assets. She may use her earnings for family expenses and thereby enable the husband to save more of his earnings. If the husband invests his savings in assets titled in his name, he may be allowed to retain them all for himself (Fisher v. Wirth, 1971; Popper v. Popper, 1975).

Only at termination of the marriage by death does a wife in common law jurisdictions receive a right to any share of her husband's property. At termination by divorce many courts have been given the power to award property to her. Although numerous writers are calling for recognition of "marital property" rights for the spouses during an ongoing marriage, none have been created in the common law jurisdictions. The current legal doctrine of separation of assets means that a husband may retain for himself all property or income over that needed for family support even though the wife's legal obligation to perform household services may prevent her from acquiring assets of her own.

SOURCE: Joan M. Krauskopf, "Partnership Marriage: Legal Reforms Needed," in Jane Roberts Chapman and Margaret Gates (eds.), *Women into Wives: The Legal and Economic Impact of Marriage* (Beverly Hills, CA: Sage Publications, 1977), pp. 96–97. (References deleted.)

protection, and *cover*, she performs everything. (Blackstone, as quoted in Stannard, 1977:9)

On the other hand, eight states—Arizona, California, New Mexico, Texas, Nevada, Idaho, Washington, and Louisiana—have marriage laws based not upon English common law but rather on law developed in Spain (Krauskopf, 1977:93). Called a "community property system," the law in these eight states assumes that wives and husbands legally own half of one another's property and are entitled to their share both during the marriage and in the event of termination by divorce (Weitzman et al., 1978:309–310).

However, even in community property states, there is held the common-law notion that primary responsibility for family support rests on the husband's shoulders (Weitzman, 1974:1180). "One effect of placing the primary support obligation on men is to further reinforce the husband's position as head of the household," write Weitzman and her colleagues (1978), "and, more specifically, his authority over family finances." They go on:

> The obligation is a mixed blessing for both the husband and wife. The husband is given power at the price of the pressures and responsibility of carrying a potentially crippling burden. The wife is given support at the price of limiting her economic capacity (and self-image), for the law assumes that she will always be economically dependent on a man. (p. 308)

Even though the husband is responsible for providing his family with life's necessities, it is up to him to determine what those necessities are. Courts are reluctant to interfere in private household matters when a marriage is intact. Thus, a wife cannot press for her right to be supported by her husband *as long as she is living with him*. If she leaves him and sets up a separate household, or if he leaves her, she can then go to court and demand the support to which she is entitled. "In other words, the husband may stay at home and starve his wife, but he may not desert her and starve her," quips Krauskopf (1977:100).

In one notorious 1953 case (*McGuire v. McGuire*), a husband with assets valued over $100,000 insisted that his family live in a house with no bathroom, no kitchen sink, a furnace that was inadequate for the house, and little furniture. He refused to give his wife any money for clothing, household necessities, or church donations; and to make sure he kept control of expenditures, he paid for groceries by check. When she took her complaints to court, the wife found how empty the right to be supported by her husband was. She was told that, although the husband's attitude left "little to be said on his behalf," it was not the court's business to determine a family's living standard. In her case, "as long as the home is maintained and the parties are living as husband and wife it may be said that the husband is legally supporting his wife and the purpose of the marriage relation is being carried out" (quoted in Weitzman, 1974:1184; see also Krauskopf, 1977:98).

In the story of Cindy and Tom at the beginning of this chapter, Cindy delighted in the fact that Tom gave her an allowance in addition to money for household expenditures. However, in terms of legal requirements as set forth by the courts, he could withdraw that allowance and cut down money for household expenditures at any time; and Cindy would have no legal recourse. At the same time, Cindy could not demand payment for her household services because those services are already considered to belong to Tom as part of his marital rights and one can't be expected to pay for something one already owns. (See boxed insert.) "The law's assumption that a wife 'owes' her domestic services to her husband thereby undermines the economic value of the wife's work in the home," assert Weitzman and her coauthors (1978:308–309). "It also allows the law to disregard the importance of the wife's labor in building the family wealth and property." Cindy spoke of being the support behind Tom, making life smooth for him and doing all she could to help him advance in his career. And Tom appreciates her contribution; he knows he wouldn't be where he is without her. Yet another man might devalue his wife's economic contribution and boast of being a self-made man—even though his wife carefully managed the budget, worked without compensation in the family business, and provided nonmonetary benefits in the form of service such as making the family's clothing, cutting her husband's and children's hair, cultivating a garden to keep food bills down, baking bread, and so on.

WHAT'S IN A NAME?

One other way in which the wife's merger into the husband is seen in symbolic terms is in the wife's taking her husband's surname. She is no longer who she was and may even be called "the former Mary Smith." Her identity is especially obliterated in the "Mrs. John Doe" form. Many couples today are electing to use a hyphenated form so that both the wife's and the husband's name are retained. Others choose various other ways of symbolizing their egalitarian ideals, including the option of the wife's keeping her birth name just as her husband keeps his. In a fascinating history of names used by wives, Una Stannard (1977) shows that at the beginning of the custom of taking the husband's name at marriage, women (already used to

Household Work: A Wife's Obligation?

Because a wife is obligated to provide domestic services for her husband, the courts have refused to enforce contracts under which she was to receive compensation for her labor. The courts have reasoned that if a wife already owes these services to her husband, a contract in which she is to be paid for them is void for lack of consideration. The courts thus have refused to honor contracts in which the husband agreed to pay his wife for housekeeping, entertaining, child care, or other "wifely tasks." Even when the husband and wife have agreed that the services the wife would perform were "extras" like working in the husband's business or doing farm labor, courts have voided the contract which obligated the husband to pay her for them.

SOURCE: Lenore J. Weitzman, "Legal Regulation of Marriage: Tradition and Change," *California Law Review* 62 (July–September 1974), p. 1189.

being known as "the wife of") actually viewed permission to use the husband's surname as a privilege—as symbolizing status through identification with a man! Rather than giving up something, it meant gaining something—the prestige available to women only through the accomplishments of a male rather than through their own achievements. Now that other options are open to women, women in increasing numbers want to be known through their own achievements. For many women, that may also mean a desire to be known by their own name continuously throughout life.

At the same time, other women who see their status as tied to that of their husbands are usually the most reluctant to use "Ms." instead of "Mrs.," and they guard jealously their right to carry their husbands' names even after a husband's death. Cindy is proud to be called "Mrs. Thomas Wilson." Another woman has refused to pay bills if they are addressed to her in her own first name prefixed by "Ms." Rather than viewing this as a recognition of her own individuality, she sees this form of address as robbing her of her highly esteemed status won through vicarious achievement.

Such examples provide further proof of the way both custom and law have combined to emphasize various elements of the owner-property and head-complement models of marriage. Certain assumptions are made about the roles of husbands and wives—assumptions based upon the economic side of marriage.

David and Janice—A Marriage of Champions

A week before Janice Champion and David Camesi of Manhattan Beach, California, planned to be married, David decided to change his name to hers.

Why? "I liked her name," says David, an associate professor of music at California State University at Dominguez Hills. "In fact, I loved it."

Janice, an air traffic controller, comments: "My mother thought David must be a very sensitive man to do such a thing. Now Mom, who has been divorced and remarried, is thinking about changing back to Champion, and that wasn't even her family name."

David found the court-petition method in a book, How To Change Your Name, *by David V. Loeb (Nolo Press). He registered copies of the correct forms with the clerk of the superior court in Torrance, California, published a notice of intent in the Torrance paper, and made a short court appearance.*

The court must allow you to change your name unless you're taking a well-known name or using your new name for a fraudulent reason such as to get out of bad debts. One hundred dollars was the cost of the two-month-long legal procedure.

David says that changing his name "made a lot of people realize that many of us are stuck with names we have never liked. I think others will see they can be freer with their names if they desire."

SOURCE: Joyce McWilliams, *Ms.,* vol. 7, no. 12 (June, 1979), p. 26.

Women's Unpaid Economic Contributions

(Charles Gatewood)

Our short-sightedness about women's economics also reflects the way statistics are compiled. Numerical measures universally fail to count women's unpaid contributions to the economic well-being of the nation, in their roles as homemakers and mothers, and as participants and volunteers contributing to the economic growth of civic and community life.

John Kenneth Galbraith gives us some insight into homemakers' unmeasured economic roles. As he states in his Economics and the Public Purpose:

"The value of the services of housewives has been calculated at roughly one-fourth of the total Gross National Product. However, the labor of women to facilitate consumption is not valued in the national income or product. This is of some importance for its disguise: what is not counted is not noticed *[italics added]. For this reason, it becomes possible for women to study economics without becoming aware of their precise role in the economy."*

(Along these lines, I find it interesting that the work of a maid or housekeeper is counted in the Gross National Product, but if the maid or housekeeper marries her employer, she is no longer counted.)

SOURCE: Dee Dee Ahern with Betsy Bliss, *The Economics of Being a Woman* (New York: Macmillan, 1976), p. 3.

Under the owner-property model of marriage, a wife had no existence independent of her husband. She was dependent upon him for financial support, was required to obey and submit to him, and was expected to fulfill her wife-mother duties according to his wishes. The husband, for his part, was expected to be a *responsible* "owner" and take care of the material needs of his wife and children. His power was doubly reinforced because it rested on (1) wifely obedience as a societal norm and (2) his role as the sole income earner. As women gained independent access to economic resources, they improved their bargaining position within the marriage relationship. The owner-property model of marriage began to give way to the head-complement model in which a husband and wife were expected to be more to each other than sources of income, status, housekeeping, sexual exchanges, and children; they were now expected to be friends and lovers as well.

While there has been some debate over whether the impact of industrialization on women's status has been positive or negative, it appears that over the long haul, women have benefited through the increased income-earning options opened up to them through industrialization. At the same time, even though close to half of the married women in the United States are in the labor force, the traditional legal marriage contract continues to be based upon notions of husband-dominance and wife-dependency. In the traditional marriage contract, the husband is considered the head of the family and is assigned the duty of support. The wife is obligated to care for the house and children.

In *common-law* states, each spouse is considered to own his or her own earnings and any property or accounts listed in the person's own name. In the eight *community property* states, wives and husbands legally own half of one another's property and are entitled to their share both during the marriage and after termination by divorce.

CHAPTER 11

(© Bruce Roberts/Photo Researchers, Inc.)

THE STRUCTURE OF EMERGING MARRIAGE PATTERNS

In Chapter 10, we examined traditional marriage patterns. Here we look at two emerging patterns: the senior partner–junior partner arrangement and the equal partner-equal partner arrangement. Both depend upon the wife's direct involvement in the economic-opportunity system.

SENIOR PARTNER AND JUNIOR PARTNER

When the husband is defined as the chief provider but the wife takes an income-producing job, her position as "complement" to the "head" is changed to that of junior partner. Correspondingly, her husband's position as head is changed to that of senior partner in the relationship. This shift results from the economic inputs the wife now brings to the marriage. Her income means that she is no longer totally dependent on her husband for survival; and furthermore, at least part of the family's living standard is attributable to her resources.

She also is likely to have more power in marital decision-making because, as various studies have shown, working wives tend to use their resources as a way of obtaining more bargaining leverage (Scanzoni, 1970; Blood and Wolfe, 1960). For some employed wives, this leverage may not be used often or at all; but the potential is always there. The wife is bringing money into the home just as the husband is, and she can always use that fact to gain what she feels is right in a particular decision.

Since she has helped earn the money, she wants to have a voice in how it is used. She may point out the unfairness of her husband's insistence on making huge expenditures without consulting her, particularly when she knows such expenditures would be impossible without her contributions to the family income. Or on the other hand, she might object to her husband's nagging about the price of something she purchased—even though it was purchased out of her own earnings rather than out of some "allowance" from him as in the days when she was a "complement." She might suggest ways they can negotiate about financial arrangements, perhaps coming to the conclusion that they should have separate bank accounts. Or they may decide on a plan in which each puts so much into family support and household needs and keeps another amount set aside for personal use, and so on.

The point to be stressed is that the actual or potential power stemming from a wife's employment removes her from the position of being an adjunct to a benevolent head whose ultimate jurisdiction is undisputed. As a junior partner, the wife has a greater share in the power and the husband a lesser share than in the other marital arrangements discussed. In the terminology of economics that lies behind exchange theory, we might say that the wife's *gain* in power (stepping up into partnership) becomes the husband's *loss* in power (stepping down from headship). This does not mean of course that there are

The actual or potential power stemming from a wife's employment removes her from the position of being an adjunct to a benevolent head whose ultimate jurisdiction is undisputed. (© Michael Hayman/Photo Researchers, Inc.)

not gains for him also—such as in the greater monetary resources now available to the family.

It must be kept in mind that power, in economics terminology, is a "scarce good." It is something that is limited in supply. How this commodity is divided up depends upon the respective resources of the bargainers. With the wife's greater access to the opportunity system, her resources for bargaining are increased, and so is her power. However, the husband still commands more power than his wife; because, although he is a partner rather than a head, he is the *senior* partner in the relationship. He continues to be viewed as the family's chief provider and is the one through whom the family derives its social status. But now the distance between the positions held by him and his wife is narrowed, and his power is not quite so final and definitive as in the head-complement arrangement.

Al and Marilyn, the department-store manager and schoolteacher in case 3 at the beginning of the preceding chapter, illustrate the senior partner–junior partner arrangement. Their marriage displays several characteristics that are common in this structural form. First, there is Marilyn's moving in and out of the labor force. She worked in the early years of marriage, then dropped out until the youngest entered school, then returned to work again.

Second, there is a lack of commitment to her career. If she feels she is needed at home, Marilyn says she won't hesitate to give up teaching. If her husband's company wants to transfer him, she is ready to move and take her chances at finding another teaching position in the new location. If she can't find a suitable job, she is willing simply to be a homemaker.

Third, the priority of the husband's career is emphasized. "Al and I believe that the husband should be the main breadwinner," Marilyn says. "That means his work takes precedence over mine." Al earns considerably more than Marilyn does, and with this higher income comes a higher degree of power in family decision-making. "He's the captain and I'm second mate," reports Marilyn. Furthermore, the family's social status derives primarily from Al and his position in the company rather than from Marilyn's schoolteaching.

The rights-duties exchange in a marriage where the spouses follow the senior partner–junior partner pattern is quite similar to that of the head-complement pattern. The main difference is in the wife's increased power and the husband's lessened power in marital decision-making. Her working and bringing in income means greater influence in both instrumental and expressive matters. However, it is still considered her duty to fulfill her wife-mother role in caring for the children and looking after household matters—although the husband might (when it is convenient) be more willing to help with such tasks than is the case under the head-complement arrangement where the wife is considered a full-time homemaker. But it is still considered the husband's right to have these domestic duties performed by his wife.

Likewise, the *primary* responsibility for providing for the family is still assigned to the husband. It is still the wife's right to have the husband support her (even though she might contribute to that support), and it is the husband's duty to be the main breadwinner (thereby freeing his junior partner to go in and out of the job market in a way that he cannot). In the expressive or person-oriented side of marriage, the rights-duties exchange is identical to that of the head-complement arrangement (except again for increased power on the part of the wife). Each partner has the right to receive and the duty to give marital rewards in the form of sex, empathy, and companionship.

MOVEMENT BETWEEN POSITIONS

The example of Al and Marilyn shows clearly that there is not some kind of chronological progression between the positions of head-complement and those of senior partner–junior partner. Rather, many wives (such as Marilyn) move back and forth between the junior partner and complement statuses, with their husbands correspondingly moving from senior partner to head and vice versa. Young wives often work at the beginning of marriage and are thus classified as junior partners. Many of them subsequently drop out of the labor force (usually to have their first child) and are thus reclassified as complements. After a period of time, they may return to work in order to help meet expenses, particularly the increased expense of rearing a child, and once again these women are junior partners. But they may go back to the complement status a year or two later—often because they wish to give personal care to the child or else because of the birth of a second child.

This type of shifting in and out of the labor force continues to occur among women past their twenties. And since most American women have by age thirty borne all the children they will ever bear (Glick, 1977:7), it appears that such shifting is not due chiefly to childbearing, though of course this is an important factor. However, the off-and-on labor-force participation by junior-partner wives beyond the childbearing age may simply indicate that these women do not share the same kind of work commitment that is true of their husbands. Except under certain circumstances (injuries, illnesses, work layoffs, and so forth), men do not start and stop repeatedly their participation in the labor force. Yet, when a national sample of married women aged thirty to forty-four was surveyed twice in the period from 1967 to 1969, it was found that among white women, 37 percent worked consistently, 40 percent did not work at all, and 23 percent fluctuated. In other words, out of 60 percent of white women who were in the labor force sometime during the three-year period, more than one-third of them participated in the labor force in an off-and-on manner. Among black married women in the sample, more than half were employed consistently during that time (51 percent), only 22 percent did not work at all, and 27 percent worked off and on (U.S. Department of Labor, *Dual Careers*, vol. 2, 1973:14). Since more black married women than white women work (more than three-quarters of the black married women in this sample, including the group that fluctuated during the three years), it means that at any given time we may expect to find more junior partners among married blacks than among married whites.

Even so, a substantial proportion of women within both racial groups are not employed, still another proportion get a job, quit, get another job, quit again, and so on. The lesser commitment to work on the part of many women as compared to men is due to many factors. Social pressures and sex-role stereotypes have meant that females have not been socialized to be committed to careers. Since men still have the major responsibility to be family breadwinners, there is not the same compulsion for women to work. By the same token, males are not given the option of *not* working. Their work commitment is reinforced by necessity and is not only a matter of choice.

Furthermore, since the major responsibility for child care and domestic chores has traditionally fallen on wives, some women may begin to wonder if the physical and psychological drain of two jobs (homemaking and employment) is worth it. Thus, they quit for a while until restlessness or a desire to earn some extra money drives them temporarily back into the labor force once again. Discrimination in hiring practices and advancement opportunities, plus unequal pay scales, have also undoubtedly lessened incentives toward career commitment on the part of many women—especially before rather recent legislation made possible legal redress for such grievances.

As we have seen, moving in and out of the labor force means marital statuses shift back and forth as well. It is quite likely that the negotiating advantages of junior partnership increase the longer and more consistently the wife works. The wife who has worked steadily for five years may be expected to have greater marital power than the wife who has been in and out of several jobs during that same period. Why? Because between jobs the latter wife repeatedly shifted into the complement position and thereby moved her husband into the position of head, while the wife with a steady employment pattern remained in the junior-partner position.

FACTORS ASSOCIATED WITH WIVES' EMPLOYMENT

Viewing a subject from the standpoint of demography (the study of population characteristics) helps us get an overall picture. By examining national census data, we can discover some of the factors associated with the employment of married women. Race, for example, is one such demographic factor.

Race Black wives are more likely to work than are white wives (Nye, 1974a; Kreps, 1971; Sobol, 1974; U.S. Bureau of the Census, *Current Population Reports*, P-23, no. 80, 1979). This reflects the combined effects of historical and current patterns discussed earlier—the long-standing economic discrimination against black males which forced black females into the labor force and the resultant norms which grew up among blacks so that female employment came to be accepted and respected. At the same time, the economic discrimination that black women themselves feel—both as blacks and as women—stands out in Table 11-A.

Many black wives work because they have to rather than because they necessarily want to. Sociologist Ivan Nye has pointed out that "for minority

TABLE 11–A   *Median personal incomes by sex and race, 1977*

	BLACK	WHITE
Males		
Any income during year	$6,290	$10,600
Year-round full-time work	$10,600	$15,380
Females		
Any income during year	$3,460	$4,000
Year-round full-time work	$8,290	$8,870

SOURCE: Figures are from the U.S. Bureau of the Census, "The Social and Economic Status of the Black Population in the United States: An Historical View, 1790–1978," *Current Population Reports*, P-23, no. 80 (June 1979), p. 187.

families, those without an employed wife are moderately deprived with respect to other minority families and extremely deprived compared to whites" (Nye, 1974a:28). In 1977, the median income for all black families headed by a husband and wife was $13,716. If the wife was not in the paid labor force, the median income was $9,697. But in families where the wife was employed, the median income jumped to $17,008—a figure that approaches the 1977 median income of white families headed by both husband and wife, and exceeds the median income of white families taken all together that year. (See Table 11-B.) Clearly, the wife's income makes a significant difference among those groups who otherwise would be granted fewer rewards from the economic-opportunity system.

On the other hand many black wives work not only because they *have* to but because in many cases they *want* to. Since among blacks it is normative for women to work, black females grow up expecting to work (Scanzoni, 1977:228–232). A study undertaken by the U.S. Department of Labor indicated that black women more than white women were committed to the idea of paid employment even if their financial situation made it unnecessary. In an attempt to measure attitudes toward work, women in the age range of thirty to forty-four years were asked: "If by some chance you (and your husband) were to get enough money to live comfortably without working, do you think you would work anyway?" In such a hypothetical situation, black women at all socioeconomic levels were interested in continuing to work to a greater extent than was true of white women, with the exception of those white women in higher-level occupations, who also indicated high work commitment. (See Table 11-C.)

The commitment to work that is generally found among highly educated women regardless of race is especially pronounced among blacks. Black women with four years or more of college are represented in the labor force

TABLE 11–B *Selected measures of family income, by type of family and labor–force status of wife: 1977*

	MEDIAN INCOME	
TYPE OF FAMILY	BLACK	WHITE
All families	$9,563	$16,740
*Male head**	13,443	17,848
Married, wife present	13,716	17,916
Wife in paid labor force	17,008	20,518
Wife not in paid labor force	9,697	15,389
Female head, no husband present	5,598	8,799

*Includes heads with wife present or without wife present.
SOURCE: U.S. Bureau of the Census, "The Social and Economic Status of the Black Population in the United States: An Historical View, 1790–1978," *Current Population Reports*, P-23, no. 80 (June 1979), p. 190.

TABLE 11–C   *Proportion of employed respondents who would work if they received enough money to live on without working, by occupation and race (percent)*

OCCUPATION	WHITE	BLACK
Professional and managerial	74	76
Clerical and sales	60	62
Blue collar	45	59
Domestic service	40	66
Nondomestic	56	74
Farm	57	84
Total or average	59	67

SOURCE: U.S. Department of Labor, *Dual Careers*, vol. 1, no. 21, 1970, p. 174.

"in the highest proportions of any female group," reports Nye (1974a:19; see also U.S. Bureau of the Census, *Current Population Reports*, P-23, no. 46, 1973:45).

Work, Women, and Children   In analyzing census data on the participation of women in the labor force, demographer Malcolm S. Cohen (1969) concluded that of all demographic factors associated with a married woman's working, it is the number of children she has and how young they are that most influence her employment behavior.

One fact that emerges from census data is that employed women tend to have fewer children than women who are not employed. This finding could be explained by either assuming that women who want to work choose to limit their family size so that employment is possible or easier, or one could argue that women who have larger numbers of children are not in the labor force (even if they would like to be) because child-care responsibilities at home act as barriers to employment. In other words, does having children keep women from employment, or does employment keep women from having as many children? These questions will be discussed more fully in a later chapter on reproduction.

Of course, many women with children *do* work—even women whose children are quite young. In 1950, some 12 percent of mothers with children under six years of age were working. By 1960, the figure had jumped to 19 percent; and by the end of that decade, it had increased another third to 30 percent and continued upward through the 1970s. (See Figure 11-1.)

Notice that over half of those mothers with children between the ages of six and seventeen are employed—an even higher percentage than among those with no children under eighteen years of age and where home responsibilities would be less. One explanation might be that women who have no children or whose children are grown may find their husbands'

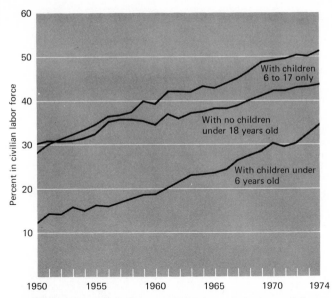

FIGURE 11-1 *Labor-force participation rates of married women by presence and age of children, 1950–1974. Married women with or without children under age eighteen have entered the labor force in increasing proportions over the past quarter century; the pace of the increase for women with preschool age children has accelerated in the past few years.* (SOURCE: *U.S. Department of Labor, Bureau of Labor Statistics,* U.S. Working Women: A Chartbook, *Bureau of Labor Statistics Bulletin 1880 [Washington, D.C.: U.S. Government Printing Office, 1975]. As reprinted in Jane Roberts Chapman and Margaret Gates (eds.),* Women into Wives: The Legal and Economic Impact of Marriage *[Beverly Hills, Calif.: Sage, 1977, p. 311.])*

income adequate for the standard of living they wish to maintain. But for others, the presence of children brings economic burdens. To attain a desired standard of living, the family may find that two incomes will be necessary; so the wife goes to work full- or part-time to buy that new freezer or color television or to help with house or car payments. There are also the direct costs of childrearing—providing for food, clothing, medical and dental needs, savings for college, and so on. Families with preschoolers face childrearing expenses too, of course; but in these cases the woman considering employment is hindered by the problem of finding someone to care for the children while she is gone. Mothers of *school-age* children simply find it much easier to enter the labor force.

The presence of preschoolers in the family does not affect the work status of black women as much as is true of white women (U.S. Bureau of the Census, *Current Population Reports*, P-23, no. 48, 1974:95). Again, this finding relates to economic need and the higher proportion of family income that is provided by these wives. It is also related to the tradition and norms supporting female employment among blacks.

One of the most fascinating ways of observing trends and changes is to

Staying home to care for young children is not an option for migrant farm workers. (Marcia Keegan/Peter Arnold, Inc.)

study the same group or panel of persons over a period of time. Sociologists call such studies *panel studies* or *longitudinal studies* (since the study takes place for some years and is in that sense a "lengthwise" study in contrast to "crosswise" surveys where a sample is drawn and information is obtained from a one-time interview only). In one longitudinal study, a large national sample of both black and white thirty- to forty-four-year-old women were interviewed over the three-year period between 1967 and 1969 in an effort to learn how labor-market participation is influenced by changes in marital status, age composition of children, and so on. In 1969, the researchers found significant increases in employment among women who in 1967 had reported having children under six years of age at home but who did not have children in this age range by 1969. In other words, when the children went to school, the mothers went to work. On the other hand, there was a decrease in employment among those wives who had reported no children under six in 1967 but who had preschoolers in the home by 1969 (U.S. Department of Labor, *Dual Careers*, vol. 2, 1973:22–24).

Maternal Employment and Effects on Children A question often arises at this point: How are children likely to be affected by their mother's employment? Until rather recently, the belief was widely held that children of working mothers would suffer emotional damage and be hindered in their development because of the long, daily physical separation from their mothers. However, in the 1960s, behavioral-science research brought to light findings that go a long way toward dispelling such beliefs. In various studies, as children of working and nonworking mothers were tested and compared, no important differences showed up. The evidence did not suggest that a mother's employment in itself has detrimental effects on her children. Psychological testing was used in order to compare the anxiety scores and personality-adjustment scores of children whose mothers were in the labor force and of children whose mothers were full-time housewives. In addition, social scientists compared children's school grades, observed their social and emotional development, and so on. Some studies focused on preschoolers and others on school-age children. But all in all, the findings did not support the old notion that a woman's working will somehow harm her children (see Ferriss, 1971:106 for a brief summary of these studies; also Hoffman, 1974).

But what about adolescents? Sociologist Ivan Nye, after a questionnaire survey of 2,350 high school students in the state of Washington, concluded from the evidence that if the familiar "concept of the neglected, maladjusted child of the employed mother has any validity, the effects involved are small." He concluded: "School performance, psychosomatic symptoms, and affec-

"School performance, psychosomatic symptoms, and affectional relationship to the mother appear unrelated to employment status of the mother." (Ginger Chih/ Peter Arnold, Inc.)

tional relationship to the mother appear unrelated to employment status of the mother. A small association appears to be present between employment status and delinquent behavior" (in Nye and Hoffman, 1963:140). The one negative finding in this sample, somewhat higher delinquency among teenage children of employed mothers, involved such things as truancy, ungovernability, petty theft, vandalism, driving without a license, and offenses involving sex and alcohol. Although there was more delinquent behavior among children of employed mothers than among children of unemployed mothers, the differences were not large. In rural areas, the delinquent behavior of adolescents whose mothers were employed was higher than in urban areas.

In a separate analysis of children from broken homes only, Nye found no significant differences between those whose mothers were employed and those whose mothers were not employed with respect to school grades, psychosomatic symptoms, delinquent behavior, and affectional relationship to the mother. In this sample, it will be noted, "no association was found between delinquent behavior and employment status of the mother" (Nye and Hoffman, 1963:139–140).

Nye's findings were reported in a 1963 book coauthored with Lois Wladis Hoffman. Entitled *The Employed Mother in America*, it attempted to gather together all available relevant research on the subject of maternal employment conducted between 1957 and 1962. Ten years after the book was published, Hoffman (1973:212) wrote: "The working mother had been considered quite a devil, and a great deal of the research reported in the book had originally been undertaken in the hope of documenting the ill effects of maternal employment. But the data simply would not cooperate."

She points out that it really shouldn't have been surprising that "examined as a general phenomenon, the standard study with adequate controls yielded no significant differences between the children of working and nonworking women," because maternal employment in itself is too wide a variable to study. All kinds of women work at all kinds of different jobs, under various conditions, with children of different ages, and so on. Such things as these would have to be considered. Hoffman points out that we may expect differences in effects of a mother's working according to whether the woman is a member of the working class or the middle class, whether she works out of necessity or out of choice, whether her children are younger or older, boys or girls. Other important considerations are the hours the woman works, the plans she makes for her household, child-care arrangements, her attitudes about her role, and so on. "But even those studies which introduced such breakdowns found few negative effects and several positive ones," Hoffman reports.

She does however, refer to one study that "suggested a bit of caution." In a study she conducted of working mothers of elementary school children, she found that children whose mothers feel *guilty* about working may be negatively affected. It is not the mother's employment in itself that seems to cause the problem, but rather the mother's attitude toward it and how she responds.

Hoffman found that some women who enjoyed working felt guilty about this and evidently tried to compensate by overindulging their children. For example, children of these mothers helped less around the house than children of nonworking mothers and were indulged in other ways as well. The results of this showed up in their interactions with other children and in their school performances. The children of mothers who worked and felt guilty about it "played more with younger children than with their age mates; they were less likely to initiate interaction with their classmates; their academic performance was not up to par." It is important to note that "the women who liked their work were more typically—though not exclusively—the middle class, and better educated." Thus, Hoffman's conclusions are significant: "These are almost the only negative effects of maternal employment found in the middle class to date, and they appear to result not from employment *per se* but from guilt about employment" (Hoffman, 1973:212–213; Nye and Hoffman, 1963:95–105).

On the other hand, writes Hoffman, there is considerable support for the idea that maternal employment can have a positive effect, particularly on girls. The daughters of high-achieving women are also likely to be high-achieving and to have less restrictive self-concepts because of the role models

Some Comments of Children from Two-Earner Families

Melinda, 13: There was never a time when both my parents didn't work. My parents are away a lot all through the week because besides having regular nine-to-five hours, my father sometimes works through the night and then he'll come home in the morning to change. Both my parents have a lot of meetings.

It seems special when they are home. We take more advantage of it. But it definitely makes me more independent, because they're not around to do everything for me and make all my decisions. If my mother were at home all day, she would do more cleaning and would always have everything ready for me. It's like babying me all my life, so I definitely think it's better that she work, because I am becoming much more independent. I feel free that I make my own decisions, because I've proven that I can by doing it. . . .

Jed, 12:. . . My mother hired a babysitter on a daily basis, so they don't need to be home most of the time. We've had this babysitter for about three years now and she's almost like a part of the family. So even if my parents aren't home, there's always somebody I can talk to.

A friend of mine told me he would like not having his parents home a lot, so that he could learn how to be independent when he grows up, but I think that's silly, because when you're a kid, that's your chance to have someone to depend on. Why not use that time to have somebody to depend on, and then when you grow older you can learn to depend on yourself?

SOURCE: Excerpted from Dorriet Kavanaugh, "Four Bright Children Speak Out on Having *Both* Parents Work," *New Woman*, (vol. 9, no. 2 (March–April 1979), pp. 28, 32. As reprinted from original source, Dorriet Kavanaugh, *Listen to Us* (New York: Workman Publishing Co., Inc., 1978).

The daughters of high-achieving women are also likely to be high-achieving and to have less restrictive self-concepts because of the role models their mothers provide. (© Joel Gordon, 1978)

their mothers provide. Such girls are less apt to limit their career horizons because of gender-role sterotypes (Hoffman, 1973:213; also see Hoffman and Nye, 1974).

With regard to the effects of a mother's working on sons, there is little data available except for a few very limited studies. Hoffman refers, for example, to a study of a small sample of gifted boys. The low achievers in the group had more employed mothers, but the high achievers had more mothers who were *professionally* employed—that is, they were women who did not merely hold a job but were committed to a career in a profession (Hoffman, 1973:214n; also see Hoffman, 1974).

Limited research on day-care centers thus far indicates that attendance at centers of high quality neither benefits nor harms children's intellectual development nor does it weaken their emotional ties with their mothers. In terms of *social* development, "the existing data indicate that day-care-reared children, when compared with age-mates reared at home, interact more with peers in both positive and negative ways" (Belsky and Steinberg, 1978:944).

These Employees Take Kids to Work with Them

Working mothers like the idea; sociologists like it; employers say they do, too, but it just isn't feasible or cost-efficient.

But Photo Corporation of America International (PCA), employing 1,400 people in their Matthews, N.C., office, has operated a successful company day-care center for seven years.

It is not only possible, but cost-efficient as well, Joan Narron, director of PCA's day-care center, is eager to talk about why.

"The No. 1 reason this company day-care center is cost-efficient is good public relations and good human relations within the company," she said.

"Our employees are more comfortable about the care their children receive while they work, and our supervisors can be more sure their employees are going to stay with us for a while."

"Our reduced turnover rate of parents due to child-care related problems is worth $40,000 a year to us—that figure is in my budget, in black and white," she said.

"Then there's the figure for public relations—that's worth $30,000 a year to us. And because some parents want us to use their children as models, we save $7,000 on model fees."

(PCA is the world's largest maker of color portraits and employs 2,700 people worldwide.)

"Furthermore, this program aids recruitment of new employees— that's worth $10,000 a year," said Ms. Narron.

"The annual unemployment rate in this area is only 2 to 3 percent, but last year we had 3,500 walk-in applicants. Many came because they had heard about child care on the premises," she said.

The center, housing 180 children, is large, cheerful and staffed by certified teachers and aides. A child can enter at six weeks and stay all the way through a fully accredited kindergarten.

Depending upon a parent's shift, she can leave her child at the center any time between 7 a.m. and 12:30 a.m., and will pay a maximum of $23 a week fee which decreases with each child.

Even nursing mothers are welcome to leave their babies. They are called when their babies are ready to be fed.

"Their infant attendant calls, says the baby is ready, and the mother literally drops everything and feeds her baby," said Narron.

"No, her boss won't mind and here's an example of why: We have an employee here, who designs the prototypes for our new equipment.

"Now, Mabel Donahue has a right to have a family—we know that. We also know we can't advertise and find another Mabel Donahue if she chooses to stay home with her family. We can't find anyone with equal ability and experience. So we don't mind her taking time to nurse her baby, because we need her," said Narron.

"She, meanwhile, isn't going to be worrying all day about her baby. Her baby is right here, and she can look in on him, nurse him and hold him from time to time throughout the day. It's fair to say Mabel is going to be more loyal to this company because of that and we benefit as much as she does.

"Company day care is certainly working, and it is definitely cost-efficient. We have 180 children now—including the grandson of our founder and the grandson of one of our maintenance workers and we'll have 200 by next year," she said.

"It's a warm, happy place for children to be; we don't believe they should sit in straight little chairs and walk in neat little rows. We make learning fun for them and while our discipline is consistent, its never angry or physical.

"We know this center is cost-efficient, and it's good human relations. But we know more than that. We know we're providing a sound basis for a child's future school success. For that, there is no dollar figure—because it's priceless."

Most working mothers have to work; they have no choice. For them, loving, professional child care which is down the hall not across town is priceless, too.

SOURCE: Niki Scott, "These Employees Take Kids to Work with Them," *Greensboro* (NC) *Daily News*, December 5, 1979.

However, most young children whose mothers are employed are not in day-care centers. According to government figures, nearly two-thirds of children ages three to thirteen whose mothers are in the labor force are usually cared for by the mother or father. Among families where the mother is employed full-time and the children are aged three to six years, 41 percent are cared for by one of the parents. This may be accomplished by juggling work schedules carefully, by taking advantage of "flexi-time" arrangements in some businesses which allow employees to choose their own hours rather than insisting that everyone work the same eight-to-five period, and by working at an income-earning profession or job in the home (see Bird, 1979). If neither parent can be home with preschool children, the children are most likely to be cared for by some other relative or a nonrelative either in the children's own home or in someone else's home. Only about 4 percent of three- to six-year-old children whose mothers are employed attend an organized day-care center (U.S. Bureau of the Census, *Current Population Reports*, P-20, no. 298, 1976:1–6). Figure 11-2 provides an overview of child-care arrangements among mothers who are in the labor force and those who are not.

Employed Wives and Education   Education is another important demographic variable associated with female employment. The higher a woman's education, the more likely she is to be in the labor force (U.S. Bureau of the Census, *Current Population Reports*, P-23, no. 46, 1973:45).

At first, it might seem surprising to note that better-educated wives are employed in higher percentages than are those with lower education, where family financial needs may seem greater. Again, it is a matter of rewards and costs. The more years of schooling a woman has, the more her market value is increased and the greater the earnings available to her. Furthermore, the better educated she is, the more likely she is to find employment in jobs that are professional-technical or managerial—jobs that economists William Bowen and T. Aldrich Finegan (1969:114–132) refer to as "more desirable" in

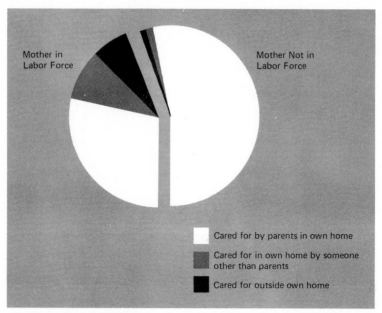

FIGURE 11-2 *Arrangements made for the daytime care of all children three to thirteen years old by labor-force status of the mother.* (SOURCE: *U.S. Bureau of the Census, "Population Characteristics: Daytime Care of Children: October 1974 and February 1975,"* Current Population Reports, *Series P-20, No. 298 [October 1976], cover page.)*

that they "offer more psychic income" than do other kinds of jobs. In other words, highly trained women are attracted to the labor force because of both the tangible and intangible rewards it offers them.

In contrast, the opportunity system doesn't offer lower-educated women the prized rewards it offers the highly educated. In the first place, jobs for those with little schooling are scarce, and even when they can be found, they are low paying. Furthermore, jobs open to women without skills and training do not offer "psychic income" in the form of prestige, power, enhanced self-esteem, opportunities for creative expression, and the enjoyment of interesting work. To such women, the costs of working may seem to outweigh the limited rewards— particularly the costs involved in leaving their children. Among whites especially, gender-role socialization in blue-collar and under-class homes prepares females to think of motherhood and homemaking as being the major sources of gratification in a woman's life. Being a junior partner may seem less rewarding to these women than being a complement. Hence the kind of statement sometimes made by women with fewer years of education who cannot understand some of the goals of feminism: "I can't for the life of me see why those women want to get out and get a job when they have husbands who can support them! I've *had* to work for many years and believe me, I'd give anything just to be able to stay home with my kids all day." Their jobs often seem dull and dead-end, and they would like to be free of them.

Employed Wives and Husbands' Income For some decades, government studies have shown a clear relationship between a married woman's employment behaviors and her husband's income. The more income a husband has had, the less has been the likelihood that his wife would be employed (U.S. Bureau of the Census, *Current Population Reports,* P-60, no. 64, 1969:2). However, the trend is changing. Many working wives are not in marriages where the husband is financially less advantaged. Rather, they are in marriages where the husband may be relatively well-off. In recent years, the greatest gains in wife employment have been among higher-income families (U.S. Bureau of the Census, *Current Population Reports,* P-60, no. 75, 1970:3).

How much difference do a wife's earnings make in family income? According to the U.S. Bureau of the Census, "The 1977 median income of all husband-wife families was $17,620" (*Current Population Reports,* P-60, no. 118, 1979:6). If only the husband was in the paid labor force, the median income was $15,060. But among families where the *wife* was employed as well as the husband, the median income was $20,270—a difference of over five thousand dollars. In speaking of *median income,* we mean the dividing point—the point at which half of the families in the particular category are above that income and half are below.

When it comes to actual dollars earned, it's important to remember that some of the wives at higher status levels earn much higher incomes because of their educational background and skills, whereas other wives at this same status level earn comparatively little because they work only part-time or are in and out of the labor force since they don't have to work out of necessity. On the other hand, lower status women who lack educational advantages may work full-time out of necessity and may find themselves bringing home earnings similar to those of more advantaged women who are not employed steadily. The overall earnings of women, whether married or single, however, continue to be substantially lower than those of men. Women working full-time the year round during 1977 had a median income of $8,620, whereas men who worked full-time year the year round earned a median income of $14,630 (U.S. Bureau of the Census, *Current Population Reports,* P-60, no. 118, 1979:2).

Nevertheless, the earnings of wives account for a sizable proportion of family income. As Figure 11-3 shows, about one out of four employed wives contributes 40 percent or more of the family income; and more than one-third of such wives contribute between 20 and 40 percent.

HUSBANDS' ATTITUDES TOWARD WIVES' EMPLOYMENT

Whether or not a married woman is employed is strongly related to how her husband feels about the matter. This was one of the findings of the longitudinal study of thirty- to forty-four-year-old women referred to earlier

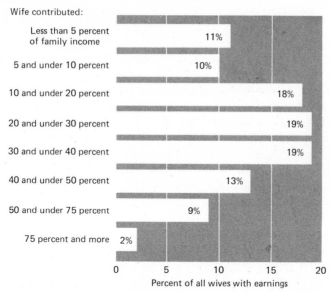

FIGURE 11-3   *Wives with earnings by percent of 1973 family income. In families where the wife was an earner, she most commonly contributed between 20 percent and 40 percent of the family income.* (SOURCE: *U.S. Department of Labor, Bureau of Labor Statistics,* U.S. Working Women: A Chartbook, *Bureau of Labor Statistics Bulletin 1880 [Washington, D.C.: U.S. Government Printing Office, 1975]. As reprinted in Jane Roberts Chapman and Margaret Gates (eds.),* Women into Wives: The Legal and Economic Impact of Marriage *[Beverly Hills, Calif.: Sage, 1977, p. 314.])*

(U.S. Department of Labor, vol. 2, 1973:43). At the time of the first interview during the three-year study, wives who thought their husbands were positive or at least neutral toward the idea of wives' employment were more likely to be in the labor force than were wives who felt their husbands were opposed to working wives. In the third year of the study, there were substantial increases in the percentage of employed wives among those women who at the first interview had indicated their husbands approved of a wife's being in the labor force. Evidently the knowledge that their husbands wouldn't object to their job seeking encouraged these wives to do just that. In contrast, among those wives who at the first interview reported their husbands' disapproving of a married woman's paid employment, there was a drop in the percentage of labor-force participation by the time of the third interview.

Another study found that among households where wives worked, the greater the husband's education the more likely he was to feel positively about the wife's working, and the more likely the wife was to *think* that her husband felt positively (Scanzoni, 1975b). Less-educated men are more likely to hold negative views about wife employment, probably because they feel that a wife's holding a job could be interpreted as a failure on the husband's part.

Since the income of less-educated men is lower than that of men with more education, their wives' income makes up a higher proportion of total family income. These earnings and the wife's participation in the labor force may be viewed as threatening to the husband's self-esteem. Such men may believe that wife employment casts aspersions on their attainments as men. "After all," they may reason, "what kind of man is it who can't support his own family? A real man should be able to make ends meet without having to send his wife out to work!" If a man has negative feelings toward employment for married women (no matter what his own education level happens to be), he is likely to voice his displeasure and try to influence his wife not to work.

Why Some Husbands Disapprove of Wives' Employment   But why should we expect some husbands to feel threatened and resentful about wife employment? Why can't they be glad for the added income or take pride in a wife's accomplishments or rejoice in the newfound satisfaction she is experiencing in her job? Recall that in terms of conflict theory men may be viewed as a dominant group and women as a subordinate group. A dominant group that feels it is losing power may seek to put a stop to such erosion. Thus, the issue of a married woman's working comes to be viewed as a challenge to male dominance. A negative reaction sets in because many men are reluctant to give up the power and privilege that have been associated with the traditional male role of sole provider.

Psychologist Daniel Yankelovich (1974:44–45) suggests that "for the approximately one out of five men who say that their work fills their psychological as well as their economic need (primarily in the professional and managerial categories), a working wife is no threat, especially when her economic contribution is not needed." However, for the noncollege majority, claims Yankelovich, a wage-earning wife could appear threatening by making the husband's work seem less valuable. For a man whose "job is just a job," providing few psychological rewards, daily labor is made worthwhile through priding himself on all the hard work and personal sacrifices entailed in taking care of his family's material needs. "Accepting these hardships reaffirms his role as the family provider and hence as a true man." For such a man, a wife's working deprives him of the unique breadwinning function that is so bound up in his concept of masculinity.

In research among low-income Puerto Rican families in New York City, social scientist Oscar Lewis (1968) found that notions of *machismo* or manliness characteristic of Latin cultures make it especially difficult for husbands to accept the idea of a wife's employment even though such income may be sorely needed. "The new-found independence of the working wife was probably the greatest source of domestic conflict among the sample families in New York," reports Lewis, adding that the conflict often was so intense that violence erupted and wife beating was quite common. The Puerto Rican husbands in the study were accustomed to being in control of both the family in general and the family finances in particular. Wives who worked no longer found it necessary to rely on their husbands for household and personal expenses. In addition, these wives had a new freedom to do as they wished and go where they pleased. Husbands resented such independence for wives, while wives for their part demanded more equal rights in the household. "The strains on family relationships were often severe," Lewis writes, "and almost every informant commented upon this problem." A psychologist who has given attention to Mexican-American families also refers to strains in family relationships that are occurring in male-dominant Chicano society as more and more women are unwilling to accept the traditional roles assigned them (Murillo, 1971).

Sex-Role Norms and Husbands' Attitudes toward Wives' Employment Our own research indicates that husbands who hold more egalitarian sex-role norms are more favorable to wives' employment than are husbands who hold more traditional ideas about gender roles (Scanzoni, 1975b). Traditionalism and egalitarianism were measured according to how much respondents agreed or disagreed with various statements about a wife's role. The more strongly that husbands believe a married woman's most important task in life is caring for her husband and children, that her greatest satisfaction should be through her family, and that if a wife does work she should not try to achieve as a man does nor expect to be paid as much as a man who must support his family, the less likely they are to favor wives' working.

On the other hand, husbands who favor wives' working do not accept beliefs such as those just mentioned which restrict a woman's options and emphasize a home-centered role. Men with more egalitarian gender-role norms disagreed with the notion that wives shouldn't have equal decision-making power with husbands, nor did they agree with the idea that women are somehow mentally and emotionally unsuited to certain tasks. More modern or egalitarian gender-role norms were also related to disagreement with such statements as these: "A wife should give up her job whenever it inconveniences her husband and children." And, "If a mother of young children works, it should be only while the family needs the money."

Husbands who are better educated tend to be more egalitarian in sex-role norms, believing that males and females should have equal opportunities to do whatever their abilities and training have suited them to do, without being restricted by roles based on gender. Such men are also less likely to feel threatened by wife employment. To wrap it up by a summary statement, we may say that where education is greater and sex-role norms are more egalitarian, husbands are less negative toward wives' working and are less likely to discourage or prevent wives' participation in the labor force.

WIVES' ATTITUDES TOWARD EMPLOYMENT

The longitudinal study of thirty- to forty-four-year-old women mentioned earlier included a question on how the women felt about work outside the home, under certain conditions, for mothers of children between six and twelve years of age. Women who favored the idea of mothers' working were classified by the researchers as "permissive" and those who were not in favor of such employment were classified as "opposed." In between was a group who expressed uncertainty about the desirability of a mother's working, and this group was labeled "ambivalent." The researchers found that the more permissive toward work a wife was, the more likely she was to be in the labor force (U.S. Department of Labor, vol. 2, 1973:39–40).

The study also showed that the women's personal beliefs about working affected their *future* behavior as well. By interviewing the same married women in 1969, the researchers were able to conclude that norms held by these women when interviewed in 1967 were predictive of what they had actually done about employment by the final interview. Working wives whose feelings were opposed or ambivalent toward working at the time of the first interview were less likely than the other working wives to still be employed by 1969. Similarly, wives who were not employed when interviewed in 1967 were more likely to be working by 1969 if their earlier attitudes had indicated approval of employment.

As we have seen, a variety of demographic and sociological factors are involved in a wife's working and thereby taking on the status of junior partner in the marriage. The age of a woman's children, her education, her race, her husband's income, the attitude of her husband toward wife employment, a woman's own attitudes toward working mothers—all of these issues enter into a woman's decision about taking a job. However, the question still arises: *Why* do some women choose to work?

Work Motivation   It is significant that questions are raised about why wives work and not about why husbands work. But the reason is simple. Up until this point in time at least, men haven't had the option *not* to work. Women, on the other hand, haven't had the option to work—except to a limited degree. Now that the option to work is open to them, women are increasingly exercising it; and many of them are expecting much more from their jobs than the income provided. As mentioned earlier in this chapter, the greatest increases in wife employment are among those who are already relatively well-off. In exchange-theory terms, the explanation lies in comparative levels of rewards. Bowen and Finegan (1969:22) make the point that "women with considerable formal education are likely to attach a high value to the social interactions and sense of professional accomplishment which market work can offer, as compared with the psychic rewards of staying at home."

If we ask working women if they work mainly because their family needs the money or because they enjoy working, about half say "money" and half say "enjoyment" (Scanzoni, 1975b). Those figures come from research conducted in 1971, whereas in a 1960 study only 30 percent of wives who had worked said that they worked because they "liked to" (Whelpton, Campbell, and Patterson, 1966:109). The remaining 70 percent worked for "other reasons"—mostly money. Thus, over a decade, the proportion of wives who say they work to supplement the family income seems to have decreased; and the proportion who work because they *enjoy* working has increased.

Now that the option to work is open to them, women are increasingly exercising it; and many of them are expecting much more from their jobs than income alone. (© Ginger Chih 1978)

Our research also produced the finding that the more education wives had and the more egalitarian the gender-role norms they held, the more likely they were to work for enjoyment. Similarly, the more egalitarian were husbands' gender-role norms, the more likely were husbands to report that their wives worked for enjoyment (Scanzoni, 1975b).

Meaning of Work   A wife's *reason* for working is an important consideration in examining the status of junior partner. For example, a woman who doesn't enjoy working and who never feels that her family needs her earnings is not likely to join the labor force and become a junior partner. But another woman may enjoy working regardless of family financial need, thereby becoming a junior partner by choice. A third woman may not want to work, yet becomes a junior partner out of necessity.

When a woman works for enjoyment, she is going after personal benefits. Her taking a job indicates a move toward autonomy. The woman who works to supplement family income, on the other hand, bases her employment behavior on group needs and interests— those of her husband and children. *Reaching for rewards* motivates the woman who works for enjoyment. In contrast, *avoiding costs* motivates the woman who works from necessity—the costs of having insufficient resources. Such a wife works out of coercion— because she has to, not because she wants to.

However, the evidence indicates that increasingly women are interested in working out of choice. Thus, their employment behaviors are becoming more and more like those of men. Although it is true that the option not to work has been closed to men, studies show that few men would care to exercise such an option even if it were available. This is true of both white-collar and blue-collar workers. From his studies in the sociology of occupations, Walter Slocum (1966:14) concludes that "no substantial group of able-bodied males between the ages of 25 and 65 in America is willingly without work." And, as we shall see later, one of the most traumatic consequences of retirement for older males is being forced to give up their jobs and the sense of meaning those jobs provided for them.

There are numerous reasons why work is so central, not only in America but in every industrialized society. Besides the obvious function of work in providing subsistence (and evidence continues to show that wages *do* matter), work is the means to individualistic achievement, the way of attaining highly valued rewards—a sense of self-worth, prestige, social status, fulfillment, enriching life experiences, satisfaction in service to others, power and influence, and so on. Women and men alike value these prizes offered by an industrial society, and thus we may expect work to have an attraction for both sexes.

Wives who move into the position of junior partner in the marriage relationship are often seeking occupational rewards similar to those of their husbands. However, in the senior partner–junior partner arrangement, the husband continues to be defined as the *chief* family provider, and his occupation is regarded as more important than his wife's. Although this marriage pattern means more power for the wife than is true of the owner-property and head-complement arrangements, there is not total equality. Senior-partner husbands are expected to be more committed to their occupations than are junior-partner wives. The norms attached to the provider role do not permit husbands to move in and out of the labor force.

Related to the significance attached to the husband's occupation are certain norms which help structure the roles of husband-father and wife-mother. In all three marital arrangements looked at so far, there is a basic assumption of parenthood. To enter marriage automatically assumes that an attempt will be made at some point to form a family. However, when the family is formed, the norms prescribe that the mother is ultimately responsible for child care, just as the father is ultimately responsible for economic provision.

The fact that the wife as junior partner is expected to have children and to be responsible for them tends to reinforce the subordinate nature of any occupation she might pursue. Household cares and family needs must predominate over her work goals, and therefore she is prevented from pursuing the direct-line, orderly sequence of occupational and achievement endeavors which characterizes her husband's life.

The vast majority of marriages in America and in other industrial societies are represented by the head-complement and senior partner–junior partner modes. Probably few of us can think of many contemporary examples comparable to the nineteenth-century illustration of the husband who insisted on his wife's subordination and whipped her to ensure the owner-property arrangement. Yet, most of us could name many couples who remind us of Tom and Cindy (head-complement) or Al and Marilyn (senior partner–junior partner) as described in the hypothetical case studies at the beginning of Chapter 10.

However, there is a fourth way that marriage may be structured, and an increasing minority of marriages may fit this pattern. We are speaking of an equal-partner arrangement. In other words, if we compare Figure 10-1 with Figure 11-4, we'll see that the option to work which removes a wife from the status of property not only opens up the possibility that she may become a complement or a junior partner; there is also a step beyond the junior-partner status—a wife may be an equal partner.

In an equal-partner marriage, both spouses are equally committed to their respective careers, and each one's occupation is considered as important as that of the other. Furthermore, there is role interchangeability with respect to the breadwinner and domestic roles. Either spouse may fill either role; both may share in both roles. Another characteristic of an equal-partner marriage is the equal power shared by husband and wife in decision-making. Lastly, this marriage form differs from the other forms in that there is no longer the automatic assumption of the hyphenated wife-mother and husband-father roles. The basic marital roles are simply wife and husband, and marriage is

FIGURE 11-4   *Three possibilities in the movement away from a wife's position as property.*

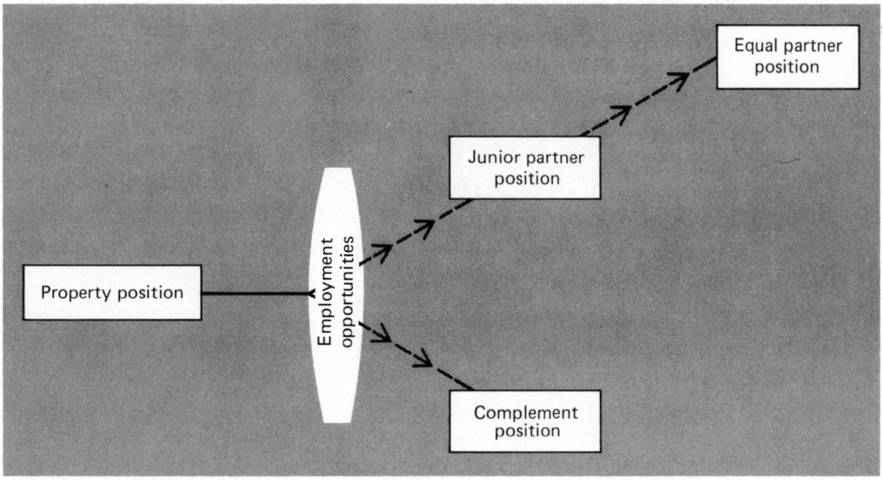

not considered automatically to require parenthood. In our opening case studies, the equal-partner marriage is represented by Janet, the psychology professor, and her lawyer husband, Roger.

EQUAL CAREER COMMITMENT

Based on research in England, a team of social scientists state that the "crucial element in distinguishing the dual-career family from other forms of family structure is the high commitment of both husband and wife to work on an egalitarian basis and a life-plan which involves a relatively full participation and advancement in work." Importantly, the term *dual-job family* is not used; these researchers use the word *career* deliberately. A career involves continuity and commitment. And in the dual-career setting, both the husband and the wife have high aspirations to achieve in the world of work, desiring to exercise to the full their individual competencies in their respective occupations, with both spouses performing tasks that are highly productive or that carry great responsibility (Fogarty, Rapoport, and Rapoport, 1971:334–335; see also Scanzoni, 1980).

A major feature, therefore, that marks off the equal-partner position from such positions as head, complement, senior partner, or junior partner are the *norms* endorsing the dual-achiever pattern. Speaking in terms of the rights of marriage, both partners have the *right* to careers (not merely jobs), and one career is not necessarily more significant than the other. That, of course, represents a radical departure from the other three ways in which marriages have been structured. In fact, some sociologists (arguing from the functionalist viewpoint) have suggested that such a marriage arrangement can't work.

Talcott Parsons (1955), for example, argues that sex-role segregation and specialization are necessary to the equilibrium or stability of a marriage. If the husband is chief breadwinner and the wife centers her life in home and family, a sense of competition is not likely to develop between the spouses as might be the case if both were achievers in the occupational realm. The development of such rivalries, according to Parsons, tends to disrupt the marriage. At the same time, even he has admitted that "it is, of course, possible for the adult woman to follow the masculine pattern and seek a career in fields of occupational achievement in direct competition with men of her own class." However, such departure from the traditional domestic pattern was rather rare at the time he was writing, leading him to conclude that "its generalization would only be possible with profound alterations in the structure of the family" (Parsons, 1942).

The equal-partner marriage *is* an attempt to alter the structure of the family. The goal of such an arrangement is not to destroy marriage but rather to change marriage so that the partners can fulfill individual aspirations unhindered by gender-role stereotypes and traditional ideas about the division of labor. Although, at the present time, the dual-career marriage has been called "a statistically minor variant" (Fogarty, Rapoport, and Rapoport,

1971:337), it is an emerging form—a life-style that may very well represent the wave of the future. In other words, out of all the new varieties of marital arrangements (trial marriage, group marriage, gay marriage, communal living, and so on), this is the one most likely some day to replace traditional marriage as we have known it.

Travel and Living Arrangements   Occupations are major factors in determining where persons live and where they travel. Traditionally, a married couple has lived together in one household, with the location of that household being determined by the husband's place of employment. If the husband's job meant settling in Michigan, the couple moved to Michigan—even if the wife's preferences might be to remain in Oregon.

Furthermore, if extensive travel was required in the husband's work, few questions were raised about his right to make such business trips or about the wife's duty to stay home and attend to the household while he was gone. In some cases, the husband's occupation might even mean long periods of actually living apart from his wife—such as in the case of a merchant seaman or fisherman, or if a man was in politics, the military, or fields of science which require extensive fieldwork. Such travel and living arrangements have been optional for men but rarely for women.

However, in the equal-partner arrangement, the wife gains these options as well. Her career may require her to travel a great deal, especially if she is in the professions, or in sports, journalism, the performing arts, business, and so on. In a very small sample of dual-career marriages in which the wives held positions in universities, research laboratories, hospitals, and business, sociologist Lynda Lytle Holmstrom (1972) explored attitudes and behaviors related to the issue of the wife's travel. She found in her sample that "most husbands in the professional couples were very supportive of their wives traveling without them and felt they should have this opportunity." Some couples "accepted very easily both the idea of being apart from each other and the fact that during the wife's absence additional domestic responsibilities would fall on the husband." Other couples emphasized the difficulties, particularly in cases where the wife was gone for a long time (such as a month) and there were children left under the husband's care; but even so, the wife's travel was viewed as a necessary part of her career. In one interview, after the husband had mentioned the hardships of having the full responsibility of the household fall to him while his wife was away, he was asked if he would prefer that his wife would not take such trips. His reply was, "No, no. It's just hard." He laughed and added, "I mean, if I feel that she shouldn't go away, then I feel that I shouldn't go away. . . . It's just part of the game."

"Commuter Marriages"   Not only do dual-career couples face the issue of the wife's traveling in connection with her career just as the husband travels in his work; there is also the possibility that the spouses' separate occupations

"I was shot out here to the New York office, my wife's company whisked her off to Denver, and Lord only knows what happened to the children." (Drawing by Martins; © 1977 The New Yorker Magazine, Inc.)

may require them to work in different geographical locations. The wife's career may require her working in Buffalo, New York, while the husband's career may require him to work in Chicago. Then what happens? Some couples may decide to spend their weekdays at their place of work and their weekends together in alternate locations or at some spot in between.

One of the most famous examples of such long-distance commuting over many years was the pattern worked out by Martha and Hicks Griffiths of Michigan. The couple met as college students, married, and went to law school together. Later they were partners in a Detroit law firm. When Martha Griffiths was elected to the state legislature, it became necessary for her to spend much of her time in Lansing, while her husband remained in Detroit. Later, when she won a seat in the House of Representatives, the couple no longer had the distance between Lansing and Detroit to consider but rather the much greater distance between Washington, D.C., and Detroit. The Griffiths solved the problem by living and working apart all week when Congress was in session, while making sure they were together from Friday through Sunday. Sometimes Martha Griffiths commuted to Detroit; other times Hicks Griffiths traveled to Washington. Apart from the high expenditure on air fares, they were said to be pleased with the arrangement since it made possible their giving attention both to their demanding jobs and to each other (Lamson, 1968).

Charlotte Curtis Is Asked about Her Commuter Marriage

You have a rather unique marriage arrangement from what I gather. You live together only on weekends.

Yes, I commute between Columbus, Ohio and New York.

Did you discuss this long-distance arrangement before you got married?

Yes. We knew it was the only way we could manage a marriage. My husband is a neurosurgeon. He has to be in the operating room by 8:00 A.M. and he's rarely home before 8:30 at night. If I lived in Columbus all the time, I wouldn't see him much more than I do now. He is a man who works. I am a woman who works. It never occurred to me to pull him away from the job he loves any more than he wanted me to quit the New York Times.

SOURCE: From an interview with the editor of the *New York Times* Op Ed page, Charlotte Curtis, by Patricia Bosworth. In *Working Woman*, vol. 2, no. 6 (June 1977), p. 36.

"People in two-location marriages are attempting to construct an alternative lifestyle which has few structural or cultural supports," write sociologists Betty Frankle Kirschner and Laurel Richardson Walum (1978:525). Most people's definition of marriage includes the idea that a husband and wife live under the same roof, and it isn't easy for relatives and friends to understand a couple's decision to live apart because of career demands. Acquaintances often wonder if the marriage is in trouble. One woman told Kirschner and Walum that only after months of patient explanation to her colleagues in her new location did they stop referring to her "ex" husband.

These researchers report that wives find it easier than husbands to find support systems, largely because of the Women's Movement and its encouragement of women's career aspirations. In traditional *male*-centered moves, such as leaving wives because of military service or immigrating into a new country before arranging for families to come, males had strong support systems. However, say Kirschner and Walum, "the woman-determined two-location family . . . leaves the male either as a new or renewed single. In either case, friendship and support systems may be difficult to establish or maintain because of lack of understanding and discomfort on the part of others" (p. 522). Friends of the couple may drop whichever of the spouses stays behind. But in addition, both the husband's male friends and the extended family may "denigrate his manliness" and wonder what kind of man he is to "allow" his wife to go off on her own or stay behind in her own career when he moves elsewhere. And some male friends may even feel envy, assuming he is now free to live as a swinging single.

To counteract such lack of support and the other stresses of living apart, couples develop various strategies for cultivating intimacy even though the geographical distance between them may be great. In spite of their high commitment to their respective careers, two-location couples who are making commuter marriage work make sure that they set aside time for interaction with each other in various ways. Kirschner and Walum explain:

> For example, the telephone for many couples becomes a daily or near-daily way of reaffirming coupledness. Some establish a regular time for their "phone date." One couple with limited financial resources would phone and after one ring hang up; the single ring was a symbolic hello, "I'm thinking of you." One woman reported that the knowledge that her husband would phone her at 11:00 P.M. each night sustained her through the day. Others write daily. The members of one couple agreed to write each other at the same time each day so they could sense a shared activity. One couple exchanged diaries. And couples plan occasions such as weekends, vacations, and holidays in which they will be together face-to-face. (p. 519)

For commuter couples, say these sociologists, time becomes extremely focused. "Time together is not 'wasted' on dutiful social obligations or meaningless socializing with uninterested others." It is spent with the realization that the hours together are short, and soon the wife and husband will have to return to their separate houses or apartments and their separate careers. Or they will have to put down the phone or end the letter.

At the same time, Kirschner and Walum report that the time apart also takes on an intensity of its own and shows up in heightened efforts to *achieve* in the spouses' respective careers. Career success may help them "justify to themselves their unorthodox living arrangements." But in addition, such couples "also report that it is easier to get work done since they have greater freedom to follow their own work rhythms without having to accommodate the needs of their spouse" (Kirschner and Walum, 1978:520). Nevertheless, such couples tend to think of their living arrangment as temporary and look forward to living together again when new career opportunities make such a move possible.

Kirschner and Walum (1978:523—524) report that those couples who are likely to have the least stressful two-location life-style are those who have high career commitment on the part of both parties; recognition by the husband of the importance of the wife's career; financial resources to meet the added expenses of maintaining two dwelling units, phone calls, travel to see

A Three-State Commuter Family

A year ago I left Roger and the baby in our big old house in Iowa. Roger was busy getting ready for the semester's teaching; I was off to my new job as assistant professor of psychology at a Pennsylvania state college. Teenagers Mary Ellen and Mark, 15 and 14, earned boarding school scholarships and headed north to Minnesota. We're a tristate nuclear family, and it's a peculiar life.

I was raised in a world where married women stayed home. In all my growing-up years I remember my mother spending a night away from her children twice: when she and my father took their first vacation in 10 years and when she went to her father's funeral.

For at least some families, the world has changed since then. Still, my new life seems to make people uneasy; they don't know what sexual label to pin on me. I can't be "married," or I'd be in my husband's house where I belong. I'm not "divorced and available," but am I planning to be? After all, I am "separated." I don't think their interest has much to do with me personally; it's just that a woman's sexual availability is crucial to evaluating her as a person.

But for us, there is little ambiguity: we are still a family. The seeds of our separation were in our marriage contract:

We value the importance and integrity of our separate careers and believe that insofar as our careers contribute to our individual self-fulfillment they will strengthen our relationship. We do not consider one partner's career to be more important than the other's. . . .

Still, there are problems. Roger and I have a feast-or-famine sex life—once a month I fly home to Iowa for three days. The distortions in our relationship are both funny and stressful. If we quarrel, we must explode-sulk-and-apologize in minutes. We haven't time for the luxury of fully developed bad moods. If we climb into bed weary, wanting just to sleep together spoon-fashion, we feel faintly guilty. This isn't what we've been fantasizing for the last month.

And then there's my relationship with Ben. . . .

I realize that I am the "second parent" now, less intimately involved and less knowledgeable than Roger. Of all the changes in our lives, it is the hardest to accept. I learn to watch while Roger eases Ben through his two-year-old's struggle for autonomy. . . .

There is some fundamental conflict here about deserving *to work. And I dare say it to myself at last:* I am entitled to do work that I care about. Its value to me is at least as important as its value to the world.

I meet many people who need to believe our experiment in living won't work. "You'll be divorced within a year" is a prediction I hear often, accompanied by a story of a couple who tried some bizarre long-distance relationship that ended in failure for the marriage. One person prophesies that Roger won't find another job within our two-year limit; the crunch will come if I refuse to give up mine. At first I'm wounded by my friends' cynicism. Don't they realize we care about each other and our marriage? I gradually see that their pessimism is too quick and too pervasive to be based on a realistic appraisal of the situation. It reflects their own needs for predictability and stability. Our experiment forces them to confront their own conflicts about risk-taking.

Our experiment is *risky. We are beginning to stabilize; we can live this way a while longer and still be a family. But we do not do it lightly. We do it only because we need so much to have both halves of the human experience—love and work.*

Roger has since found a teaching position at a nearby eastern college. Mary, Roger and Ben recently moved into an old Pennsylvania farmhouse and the family has one home base again.

SOURCE: Excerpted from Mary Crawford, "Two Careers, Three Kids, and Her 2,000-Mile Commute," *Ms.*, vol. 8, no. 2 (August 1979), pp. 76–78.

one another, and so on; shorter rather than greater geographical distances between the spouses' respective locations to allow for getting together more often; and long-established patterns of interaction. Couples who have been married for some time are better able than newlyweds to adjust to a commuter-marriage life-style.

Commuting Isn't Always the Solution   Some couples reject the idea of long-distance commuting, although they say they might be open to the possibility if no other solution were available. In some marriages, career-related moves may be decided on a husband's turn–wife's turn basis. If a husband has an occupational opportunity open to him that would require moving to another location, the wife may follow and seek to pursue her career in the new location also—even though it might mean sacrifices on her part. But then the next move will be determined by the wife's career. If better opportunities open to her elsewhere, it will be her husband's turn to follow.

Other couples might negotiate in other ways. In some cases, *neither* will accept a position elsewhere unless something really worthwhile is open to *both*; and no moves will be undertaken until such an arrangement is found. The point to be stressed here is that the traditional norm of a married couple's moving and living in conjunction with the husband's career interests is for dual-career couples no longer automatically assumed. In equal-partner marriages, the issues of residence and travel are likely to become increasingly problematic.

ROLE INTERCHANGEABILITY

The role of the wife in an equal-partner marriage is a radical departure from her role in the other positions discussed. The norms now prescribe that she has the duty to provide for her husband. At the same time, norms attached to the husband role also maintain that it is a husband's duty to provide for his wife—just as has always been the case. Since both the husband role and the wife role involve breadwinning, we have a case of *role interchangeability*. This is in contrast to the rigid *role specialization* that occurs under other marital positions. In situations of owner-property, head-complement, and senior partner–junior partner, each partner has a particular sphere according to his or her sex—for the male the occupational, for the female primarily the domestic.

Since there is role interchangeability in the equal-partner marital pattern and both sexes can fulfill breadwinner behaviors, there not only exists the norm that the wife as well as the husband has the right to a career; there also exists the norm that the husband as well as the wife has the right to be provided for. In other patterns of structuring marriage, it has been the husband's duty to provide and the wife's right to be provided for. But in the equal-partner situation, each spouse has both the duty to provide and the right to be provided for.

While it may be mind-boggling to some persons over thirty to conceive of the wife's having to provide, it may be even more unsettling to comprehend the healthy husband's having the right to be supported by his wife. The traditional work ethic, which assumed that one proved his self-worth and masculinity through occupational achievements, centered around a man's obligations to provide economic benefits, status, and prestige to his wife. But with the roles of both partners defined as interchangeable achievers, the husband can expect to share in the wife's status and bask in the prestige resulting from her accomplishments just as she has always done and will continue to do in his.

Option Not to Work   Although the provider-achiever role is interchangeable in an equal-partner marriage, such an arrangement does not necessarily require that both partners work full-time all the time. Either partner has the option not to work as well as the right to a career and the duty to provide. It may seem contradictory simultaneously to hold norms in which the husband or wife has the option not to work and yet at the same time has the duty to provide. However, while all the marriage structures we have examined are in constant process, the equal-partner pattern is especially in motion. It is continually being negotiated and renegotiated so that at one point a partner may be exercising his or her achievement rights, while at another time for various reasons the option *not* to work (the right to be provided for) is being exercised.

Will Men Become Househusbands?   The question raised earlier now becomes very real: will males, who have traditionally been work-oriented, be likely to exercise their option not to work? Occasionally, one hears reports of couples who trade off "house-spouse" and provider roles; that is, one year the husband stays home to look after the household and children while the wife works and supports the family, and the next year the pattern is reversed. However, at the present time few occupations allow for such flexibility. Even more than that, because of the way society's reward system is related to occupational achievement, it is not likely that many men for very long would find it rewarding not to work.

There might, however, be exceptions in certain types of work. A writer who works full-time for a newspaper, for example, might find it very rewarding to absent himself from his employment for several months to write a novel to which only evenings and weekends could be devoted were it not for his wife's financial support. A similar situation could arise in other creative arts as well—music, painting, sculpturing, and the like.

Note that in exercising the option not to work at a regular income-producing occupation, such men are not actually giving up work. They are changing the kind of work they do and are finding freedom for some pursuit that requires much time but is not always immediately income-producing. However, because of the reward system in an industrial society, they are seldom likely to be full-time "househusbands" in the tradition of the housewife role, although there are occasional exceptions. One man in

The happy "Hemmaman." (Enrico Sarsini/Life Magazine; © 1969 Time Inc.)

Sweden, for example, wrote a regular feature for a magazine in which he described his life as a *hemmaman* or househusband. His wife worked as an art director, while he stayed home to cook, clean, make beds, do the laundry, and care for their six-year-old child. He had previously worked in advertising but found his job boring, whereas he said he enjoyed child care, didn't mind housework, and thought a reversal of the traditional roles made sense in order to make it easier for his wife to pursue her career, since she made more money than he anyway ("The Happy 'Hemmaman,'" *Life* 67, August 15, 1969:46). Such a situation, it could be argued, is more like the head-complement form than the equal-partner pattern for marriage—only this time the wife is the unique provider and is likely to hold the greater power because of the resources she brings to the household, while the husband is the complement.

Division of Labor   In traditional marriage arrangements, the husband has had the duty to provide for his wife and the right to have his wife take care of household tasks. In the equal-partner pattern, role interchangeability means that both the husband and wife have the reciprocal duty to be breadwinners and the reciprocal right to be supported. But what about household tasks?

Does the wife as coprovider have the *right* to have these tasks performed by the husband? And does the husband, having the right to be provided for, have the *duty* to perform such household tasks? The answer is yes, if the exchange is to be fair. How this will be carried out will likely vary with the individual couple, but the mutual responsibility is there. Sharing household duties is a part of the equal-partner marriage pattern just as is the sharing of occupational duties.

That this is not simply "theory" with no relation to everyday life may be seen in some of our own research findings (Scanzoni, 1980; also 1978). Among a regional household probability sample of married white women aged twenty-two to thirty-three years, we found that nearly a quarter of the women (23 percent) reported that they shared the provider duty equally with their husbands. These equal partners also indicated that their husbands shared with them the tasks of child care, cooking, dishwashing, clothes washing, and food shopping to a greater degree than was true in the senior partner–junior partner and head-complement marriages in the sample. For their part, *wives* in equal-partner marriages were more likely to share with their husbands household repair tasks than was true of junior partner and complement wives.

EQUAL POWER IN DECISION-MAKING

As Figure 11-5 shows, the increasing power of the wife is perhaps the most prominent feature to be observed in moving through the four basic ways marriages may be structured. In the equal-partner position, it becomes standard or normative for both husband and wife to acknowledge that the balance of power is equal; neither spouse has more power than the other. The husband relinquishes any vestige of traditional ideas of masculine superiority, dominance, and the right to have the wife defer to her husband.

The basis for this normative egalitarianism lies in the equal career commitments of the husband and wife. A century ago, philosopher-economist John Stuart Mill (1869) argued that if two persons invest equally in a business, both partners will want equal power in order to protect their own and their mutual interests. Likewise, two spouses with equal investments in their marriage (because of the tangible and intangible resources contributed through their respective career commitments) will want equal marital power. Without this equal power, the career interests of one or the other could be threatened.

OPTION OF PARENTHOOD

In marriages structured around the positions of owner-property, head-complement, and senior partner–junior partner, major rewards were defined as coming from children—especially for wives. There were also certain costs involved—again especially for wives since they were mainly responsible for child care. Because of this responsibility, women tended to forgo serious

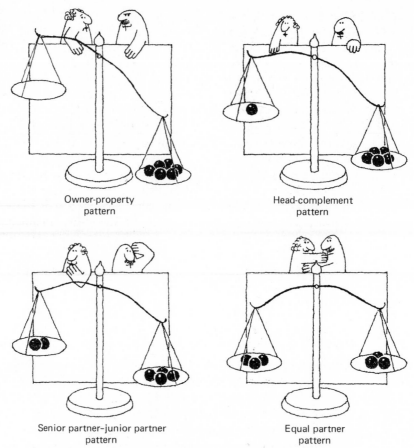

Owner-property
pattern

Head-complement
pattern

Senior partner–junior partner
pattern

Equal partner
pattern

The wife's power has more weight as her position moves from property to
complement to junior partner, until in the equal partner pattern the balance
of power between husband and wife is equal.

FIGURE 11-5   *How the balance of power changes according to the four marriage patterns.*

career commitment and its rewards. In fact, women who did choose to pursue
a career over children were generally considered selfish or neurotic.

In recent years increasing numbers of young women have rejected the
notion that it is selfish to want a life of their own. They refuse to subordinate
individualistic interests and rewards to the interests of husbands and
children. Indeed, the argument can be turned around to say that husbands
may be selfish to insist that wives have a certain number of children (or any at
all) and then be responsible for them. Some persons are raising the question:
If individualistic occupational rewards are so valuable, why should only
white men have access to them? And if children are so important, why
shouldn't husbands be responsible for taking care of them as much as wives
are?

Therefore, in equal-partner marriages, the roles of husband and wife are

If the choice is made to have children, both partners are equally responsible for their care. (Erika Stone/Peter Arnold, Inc.)

not attached to father and mother roles as they are in the other marriage patterns. The norms for both the husband role and the wife role make having or not having children a matter of choice. And if the choice is made to have children, both parents are equally responsible for their care.

Interestingly, our research has shown that equal partners (more than junior partners and much more than complements), control the spacing and the number of children they will have in such a way as to maximize the wife's career interests (Scanzoni, 1980).

MARITAL PATTERNS IN MOVEMENT

It should be clear by now that the positions of owner-property, head-complement, senior partner–junior partner, and equal partner–equal partner are not rigid, distinct categories in the sense that each marriage fits *exactly* into one of these "boxes." In the first place there may be movement between the categories. A wife may be a complement, take a job and become a junior partner, quit six months later and become a complement once again, and so on.

Second, few marriages would fit exactly and indisputably on *all* dimensions into any one of the categories. There is room for indefiniteness, a blurring and blending rather than clear-cut lines separating the statuses. It might be helpful to think of a continuum, a thermometer-like arrangement in which marriages attain degrees of equal-partner status, degrees of senior partner–junior partner status, degrees of head-complement status, perhaps even (though much less likely today) degrees of the owner-property status. In other words, couples may be more or less in or near one of the statuses.

It should also be kept in mind that while certain marriages may be found at particular points on the continuum today, they may be at a different point than they were two years ago; and they may be at another point two years from now. For example, a couple might be described as having a head-complement arrangement in their marriage. When the wife decides to take on a part-time job selling cosmetics door to door, pursuing it very casually as somewhat of a hobby in her spare time, she may move up to being slightly more than complement. As she begins devoting more time to her occupational interest, earning more money although still only on a part-time basis, she might become almost but not quite a full junior partner. A year later, she might move to a full-time job and take on wholly the junior-partner position in her marriage. If she were to save up money for special training and then were to embark on some career with equal commitment to that of her husband, she might take on an equal-partner status at some point.

WIFE AS SENIOR PARTNER OR SOLO PARENT BY DEFAULT

There are some situations where American wives are thrust into the position of senior partner—not necessarily because they seek it, but because they have no choice. It falls to them by default. They assume responsibility for the family simply because the husband has been unable or unwilling to fulfill his obligations.

MATRIFOCAL SITUATIONS

Anthropologist Helen Safa (1971:36–38) has written of a common pattern in cultures of poverty: the family becomes *matrifocal* or "mother-centered." The strong mother-child bond takes precedence over the husband-wife bond; the role of the husband (if he is present) is peripheral, almost as though the man is "excess baggage" in the family, without an important part to play.

Safa points out that this form of family life has arisen among lower-income families as a way of coping under conditions of poverty. The primary function of the family is viewed as childrearing, and "marriage is not expected to provide the intense emotional intimacy sought in the middle-class nuclear family." Both husband and wife have strong ties outside the family, either with kin or same-sex friends, and they tend to rely on these relationships rather than on each other for emotional support and assistance. "Lower-class women cannot invest the conjugal [marital or husband-wife] relationship with the heavy responsibilities it carries in the middle class," writes Safa. Why? Because such wives "cannot be sure that men will be adequate providers, or will not have to leave to find work elsewhere, or may not abandon them for another woman."

Another researcher who has studied lower-class family life-styles is sociologist Lee Rainwater (1966b:190–191). He points out that the matrifocal family is common among lower-class families in general and not only among blacks, as is sometimes thought. According to Rainwater, lower-class families "are matrifocal in the sense that the wife makes most of the decisions that keep the family going and has the greatest sense of responsibility to the family." Women in these families get advice from female relatives and tend to consider their husbands to be unconcerned about day-to-day problems of family life. Rainwater adds that since these tendencies are intensified among lower-class black families "matrifocality is much clearer than in white lower-class families."

Safa (1971:39, 46) makes the point that socioeconomic forces "have systematically robbed the man of any basis of authority in the black ghetto family; they have curtailed his role as economic provider, as leader in his own community, and as spokesman for his family in dealing with the outside world. As a result, the woman has been forced to take over many traditionally male roles." Safa argues that wife dominance is further reinforced by welfare programs: "Because men are temporarily or permanently absent from many black homes, or cannot be reached during working hours, social workers and other government officials dealing with these families often direct most of their attention to the women. In effect, they treat her as head of the household, whether she has a husband or not."

HOUSEHOLDS HEADED BY FEMALES ALONE

Safa (1971:36) and others who study the culture of poverty refer not only to matrifocal families but also to *female-based* families, a more restrictive term "referring only to those families actually headed by females alone." A lower-class woman might not only find herself in the position of senior partner in a marriage; she might also at some point find herself without a husband and in the position of solo parent. In Chapter 9, we looked at singleness as a life-style and also spoke of voluntarily chosen single parenthood—usually through adoption and most often among the well educated. Here we are thinking of situations where women are poor, have large numbers of children, and hold no particular commitment to the idea of solo parenthood. Yet, they find themselves forced into this role by circumstances. The circumstances may be the death of a spouse, desertion, divorce, or separation; or perhaps pregnancy out of wedlock.

In 1976, 11 percent of all white families and 36 percent of all black families were families maintained by a female householder with no spouse present (U.S. Bureau of the Census, *Current Population Reports*, P-20, no. 307, 1977). About half of the more than five million poor families in 1977 (those with incomes of less than $6,191—the "poverty threshold" set by the government for a nonfarm family of four) were families headed by women alone. Among black families below the poverty line, 71 percent were families maintained by a woman without a husband present (U.S. Bureau of the Census, *Current Population Reports*, P-60, no. 119, 1979).

At this point, perhaps a word of caution is in order. Statistics such as those just cited may lend themselves to the impression that such statistics describe the majority of black families. But this isn't true at all. Actually, less than a third of all black persons live below the poverty line, as do almost one-tenth of white persons (U.S. Bureau of the Census, *Current Population Reports*, P-60, no. 119, 1979). And 61 percent of all black families are headed by a husband and wife together (U.S. Bureau of the Census, *Current Population Reports*, P-23, no. 80, 1979:100).

BLACK FAMILIES MAINTAINED BY FEMALES ALONE

Throughout this book, while we have contrasted information on blacks and whites, the underlying premise has been that their family patterns are basically similar. Any differences do not spring from something innate or consciously planned but rather stem from the way society has been structured. Those blacks who have been most vocal about family life-styles have not made an effort to set up a unique and distinct family form (for example, a black matriarchy) but rather have moved toward the dominant form of the larger society in which the male has traditionally held the unique or chief provider role. The Black Muslims and other groups seeking to enhance black identity have placed great emphasis on male authority and female subordination, with the goal for marriage being the head-complement pattern (Malcolm X, 1964, chap. 13.).

This emphasis is apparently in reaction to decades of economic discrimination practiced against black males by the white society. Black women who were forced to work in order to survive came to possess economic resources that resulted in their gaining power in the family. Black males, deprived of access to economic rewards, were also deprived of power within the household. It was this situation which gave rise to considerable folklore about the so-called black matriarchy. The most unfounded assertion in this regard is the notion that there is something within black cultural values, traceable to plantation days or even to Africa, that predisposes blacks to favor female-dominant households.

All available evidence is to the contrary. Even among blacks who may not expouse the Muslim emphasis on female subordination, it is clear that the overwhelming majority do not prefer female-headed households but rather want the husband-wife form of family life-style (Rainwater, 1966b; Liebow, 1967; Schulz, 1969; Scanzoni, 1977). At the same time, although it's not preferred, the female-headed household is often accepted as an unavoidable means of economic survival.

But don't forget that more than two-thirds of black society live above the

Although it is a myth that blacks are predisposed to favor a matriarchal family form, female-headed households are—in some circumstances—accepted as an unavoidable means of economic survival. (Bob Adelman/Magnum)

poverty line and consist mostly of husband-wife units where sex-role equality is a pertinent issue. Here we are concerned *only with that one-third of black society which is a genuine American lower class or underclass.* These persons are different from poor whites and poor Spanish-speaking people in that they encounter much more severe economic discrimination due to their race. Paths to mobility out of the lower class are exceedingly limited; poverty is cyclical, generation after generation. Black males in this situation have been held back from fulfilling the provider role and have been forced into other kinds of behaviors in relation to women and to economic survival.

From his studies of black ghetto life, sociologist David Schulz (1969:82–85) describes several categories of such male behaviors. Some lower-class black men play the role of *pimp,* not only in the usual sense of living off the labors of several prostitutes but also in situations where they live off women who earn their income legitimately in domestic service or as clerks or welfare recipients. Often these are younger men who demand that their women provide them with a high standard of living (by ghetto standards), including the means to "dress like a dandy," while they reward the women with their capacity as lovers.

Another category listed by Schulz is the *supportive companion* who meets a woman regularly on weekends and gives her spending money and a good time but wishes to avoid the responsibilities of marriage and parenthood. Then there is the category of the *supportive biological father* who senses some responsibility for children he has fathered, even though he may be married to someone else. To the children's mother, he plays only the role of boyfriend but at the same time does not run away from certain economic duties.

One step beyond this category is that of the *indiscreet free man* who has a legitimate family plus one or more illegitimate families and who spends much of his time, income, and energies on the "other woman" and any children he has fathered by her. He does not hide his behavior from his legal wife and often compares her to his girl friend, causing much family conflict. The legal wife often feels trapped in the situation because she has numerous children and needs his support. With no alternative sources of rewards, she is forced to "make do" with the limited rewards her husband offers. In contrast, a fifth category, the *discreet free man*, keeps his extramarital activities covert or else has an understanding with his wife. He too showers large outlays of money and attention on his "illegitimate" family but doesn't flaunt these outside interests in such a way as to antagonize his legal family.

Schulz (1969:128) points out that the sixth category, *the traditional monogamous type of father*, is (although rare) considered the most desirable among underclass blacks. Such men are faithful to their wives and children and consider their homes and families to be their major concerns. "Typically such a father will have good relationships with his children and high status in the family regardless of his ability to earn a living."

The first five of these six patterns cast some light on why there are so many female-headed households in lower-class black society. Black women have had to interact with men who have largely been excluded from economic opportunity. These men have simply not been able to provide the kinds of socioeconomic rewards that members of modern societies (both black and white) have expected males to supply. Consequently, alternative strategies have evolved in which lower-class black men and women attempt to exchange economic and expressive benefits in ways that differ from the dominant societal pattern.

At the same time, black women are aware of exploitation by men who act out roles ranging from pimp to discreet free man. If actually married to such men, the sense of exploitation may lead some women to deep resentment. Thus, the high rates of black lower-class separation and divorce are more readily understood. The sense of exploitation may also explain why many black women are willing to remain *unmarried* female heads as well. Schulz (1969:136) explains that some black women "are very much afraid of marriage because no matter how good a man might seem before marriage, after he has papers' on you he might well change."

In short, many lower-class black women find themselves thrust into roles they did not seek, nor do they necessarily prefer, but which have been forced upon them as a result of economic discrimination against black men. When these women remain married, they often find themselves having considerably more power than their husbands who have difficulty functioning as providers. On the other hand, lower-class black women who live apart from their husbands may find themselves in situations made punishing through a combination of meager resources and numerous children.

FEMALE DOMINANCE NOT THE GOAL

Female leadership by default is something quite different from female dominance intentionally sought as a step beyond equality. Most feminists have not expressed a desire to be dominant over men, which would just be the old system in reverse. Rather they are interested in principles of egalitarianism.

Given the way work achievement, and its rewards are valued in industrial societies, it is unlikely that many males will be interested in a complete reversal of traditional sex roles so that the wife becomes the sole breadwinner and leader and the husband enjoys being supported and led. There are exceptions to this, of course. A common example is the situation in which a married male college student is financially supported by his wife.

There are other instances where personality factors play a part; in a particular husband-wife unit the wife may be stronger, more forceful, and seem to exercise greater decision-making power than her husband. The husband's psychological makeup may be such that he prefers his wife to be dominant and finds security in her strength. However, such cases are the exception. Because of the occupational-opportunity system, most marriages at present are structured in the ways that have been described, with husbands as heads and wives as complements, or husbands as senior partners and wives as junior partners, although there is movement in the direction of increasing numbers of equal-partner marriages. In the equal-partner arrangement, either spouse may take the leader-achiever-provider role, thereby allowing greater role flexibility for both. This pattern seems far more likely to be the wave of the future than a pattern that would totally reverse roles, placing women at the top and men at the bottom.

CHAPTER HIGHLIGHTS

When the husband is defined as the main provider but the wife takes a job that contributes to the overall family income, her position as "complement" to the "head" changes. She becomes the *junior partner*, and her husband is the *senior partner*. His occupation still has primacy, because the wife in this pattern of marriage is less committed to continuous labor force participation than is her husband. Wives in the junior-partner position are expected to put family and household needs before work goals, preventing such wives from pursuing the direct, orderly sequence of occupational and achievement endeavors that has traditionally characterized men's lives.

In an *equal-partner* marriage, both spouses are equally committed to their respective careers, and each one's occupation is considered as important as the other's. Both partners share equally the duty to provide and the right to be provided for, and both are equally responsible for household tasks. Both wife and husband have equal power in decision-making, including decisions about whether and when to have children. Parenthood is not automatically assumed in this pattern for marriage but is considered optional. The goal of the equal-partner arrangement is not to "destroy" marriage but to *change* it so that both partners can fulfill individual aspirations unhindered by gender-role stereotypes and traditional ideas about the division of labor.

CHAPTER 12

(© Joel Gordon, 1979)

PROCESS IN MARRIAGE: EXPRESSIVENESS

An incident a few years ago caused a publisher considerable embarrassment. The company had issued some full-color posters to illustrate a series of religious-education materials. But through some oversight, two picture captions were reversed and not noticed before the orders were shipped. A picture designed to illustrate marriage was labeled "John the Baptist in Chains." And the picture of the fettered prophet was entitled "Marriage."

No doubt the mix-up seems fitting to many people. Men have been known to speak of marriage as a kind of bondage, with freedom traded for the "chains of wedlock" (emphasis on the word *lock*). In recent years, large numbers of women have complained—perhaps even more than men—that marriage is a trap, shackling them into confining roles which prevent full development as persons and as achievers.

Such ideas about marriage come from traditional notions of wedded life as something rigidly fixed and static. Small wonder that the question has been raised: "Is there life after marriage?" (Bernard, 1972, chap. 10). The word *life* suggests energy, vitality, process. Actually, to picture marriage as a state of inaction fits neither with the realities of the husband-wife relationship nor with the cost/reward emphasis of this book. In the preceding two chapters, we examined marriage as a *structure*; now we want to see marriage as a *process*. The word *process* implies something dynamic, on the move; it derives from the Latin *procedere*, "to go forward." A process suggests continuous action taking place in a systematic fashion. Being in process means that ongoing changes and exchanges are occurring all the time. In this sense, the answer to the question, "Is there life after marriage?" is yes.

WHAT HOLDS MARRIAGE TOGETHER?

If marriage is constantly in process, what keeps the moving parts from spinning off in separate directions? In other words, what is the "glue" that holds a marriage together?

The question is similar to one posed in connection with communal living. Cohesiveness—sticking together—involves an effort to resolve the recurrent problem of group solidarity versus individual freedom. As marriage has been understood traditionally, a man and woman are said to become "one flesh." According to the biblical phrase used in many wedding ceremonies, they are "no longer two but one." In the minds of some persons, this merger into a new social unit must erase all traces of the two individuals as separate entities, somewhat in the manner of the juncture of the Allegheny and Monongahela rivers which lose their distinct identities at Pittsburgh, Pennsylvania, when they unite to become the Ohio River.

Yet many persons today reject the idea of a total submersion of individuality for the sake of group solidarity. To rephrase a question from our section on communes, they are asking, "Why can't the one be two at the same time that the two are one?" In one way of thinking, autonomy is considered to dissolve the glue that holds marriage together. But in another way of thinking, autonomy can be one of the basic ingredients cementing the relationship.

MARITAL-ADJUSTMENT SCHOOL OF THOUGHT

One of the earliest attempts to explore the glue of marriage was made by proponents of the "adjustment to marriage" school. The marital-adjustment idea fitted nicely with the notions of functionalism and its emphasis on an organism's need for smooth-working parts working together to preserve the structure.

According to the marital-adjustment school of thought, the glue of marriage is manufactured by submerging individual interests for the greater good of group solidarity. The major emphasis is on harmony and stability, the sustaining of "the commitment of husband and wife to their marriage" (Dizard, 1968:4). The goal, in other words, is group preservation rather than individual development. Sociologist Harvey Locke (1968:45) spoke of marital adjustment as "the process of adaptation of the husband and the wife in such a way as to avoid or resolve conflicts sufficiently so that the mates feel satisfied with the marriage and with each other." Similarly, sociologist Ernest Burgess and his colleagues (1963:294) wrote: "A well-adjusted marriage may be defined as a union in which the husband and wife are in agreement on the chief issues of marriage, such as handling finances and dealing with in-laws; in which they have come to an adjustment on interests, objectives, and values; in which they are in harmony on demonstrations of affection and sharing confidences; and in which they have few or no complaints about their marriage." The emphasis was always on "adjustment," "adapting," "harmonious relations," "agreement," and avoiding or minimizing conflict.

In describing how group standards may be designed to prevent disruptions based on individualistic interests, social psychologist Philip Brickman (1974:269) makes a comment that fits well with the basic premise of the marital-adjustment school: "In normative relationships [relationships with behavioral expectations clearly spelled out in advance], although conflicts of interest may exist, individuals are not supposed to be engaged in maximizing their own self interests. Instead they are supposed to be doing what is right or moral or normative, even if this is not in their self interest." In other words, persons are supposed to know what a "good" marriage is and requires. And then they try to fit into that mold, whether or not it "feels right" to them and even though it may mean a submerging of their "true selves"—that is, their own personal desires and aspirations. Often a great deal of pretense and game playing occurs to keep up the image of adjustment and harmony.

CRITICISMS OF THE MARITAL-ADJUSTMENT APPROACH

In recent years, there has been a reaction to the marital-adjustment school of thinking. Robert Seidenberg (1970:304–305), a psychiatrist, writes: "No marriage should ever be held of more importance than one of its participants. Persons, not marriages, are worth saving." In a similar vein, anthropologists George O'Neill and Nena O'Neill (1972) have given wide dissemination to the idea of "open marriage." What proponents of the marital-adjustment school call "successful marriage" corresponds to the O'Neills' definition of "closed marriage." In the closed-marriage contract, there is said to be a sense of belonging to the mate, denying one's self, maintaining a couple-front, behaving according to rigid gender-role sterotyping, and emphasizing total exclusivity. According to the O'Neills, the closed-marriage contract makes a couple slaves of their marriage because the expectations that surround such a marital pattern stifle individual wishes and potentials.

One reason for such critical reactions to the marital-adjustment school lies in a basic fact that champions of adjustment largely ignored, namely, that wives were doing more of the submerging of individual interests than was true of husbands (Bernard, 1972). The model of marriage that marriage-adjustment proponents worked with (and the pattern to which spouses were supposed to adjust) was what we have called the head-complement structure. At the same time, basic male-female inequalities were glossed over by mere *assertions* that modern marriage was now egalitarian. Such assertions may have been based on wishful thinking, but more likely they derived from observations that marriage was no longer an owner-property arrangement. It was assumed that if a wife wasn't "owned" by her husband, she must then automatically be his equal.

In its most sophisticated form, the argument that spouses are equal because they are *declared* to be such goes like this: Husbands and wives are specialists—the husband in his occupation, the wife in her household. Therefore, they complement one another; and because they complement one another, they are equal. They have differences in tasks, but no difference in rank (Miller and Swanson, 1958). One assumption made in this argument is that the rewards for doing household tasks are somehow comparable to rewards obtained for performing tasks in the occupational realm. Another assumption is that husbands are as dependent on wives as wives are on husbands. We have seen that neither assumption is valid. Women have been assigned the tasks that bring fewer rewards, lower rank, and greater dependence. It is difficult to see how this can be called "equality."

COSTS AND REWARDS: DYNAMICS OF MARRIAGE

Another way of thinking of the glue that holds a marriage together is to think of the exchanges the two persons make and the way they evaluate the costs and rewards of the relationship. When two persons choose one another and remain together sharing their lives, they are viewing their situation as one that is rewarding. It's profitable; they gain something from it. The benefits of the relationship outweigh any costs.

If the relationship should cease to be rewarding to one or the other spouse, efforts can be directed toward altering whatever situation seems

In marriage each partner pays certain costs and reaps certain rewards, both tangible and intangible. (© Ellen Pines/ Woodfin Camp & Assoc.)

to be costly and punishing. If no solution can be found, perhaps the relationship will be dissolved—although in some cases, the anticipated costs of dissolution may seem greater than the costs of remaining in an unsatisfactory situation.

In other words, the process of marriage involves getting and giving. Each person wants his or her "money's worth" out of the relationship—not necessarily in some crassly calculating way involving dollars and cents, but in terms of all sorts of rewards, both tangible and intangible. Gaining rewards involves costs and investments, which means there is going on in marriage a constant assessment of the reward/cost ratio to make sure that the individual and the marital unit are experiencing profit.

In thinking of the reward/cost ratio as being the glue of marriage, the emphasis may seem to be on the individual rather than on group unity. However, self-interest and group interest are not necessarily incompatible. What is best for the individual may also be best for the marital unit and vice versa. Most social scientists concur with a point made by Sidney Siegel and Lawrence Fouraker (1960) in their research on economic bargaining, namely that "the two parties, if they behave rationally and in their respective self-interests, will be forced inexorably to [an exchange] which maximizes their joint benefit." In other words, the most solid and cohesive social system is one in which all parties concerned experience what has been labeled *maximum joint profit* or MJP (Kelley and Schenitzki, 1972:307). There is no reason to think that this should hold less for a marriage than for a business partnership.

According to marital-adjustment notions, marital stability is thought to be achieved through long-suffering endurance and making the best of one's fate, with efforts being directed toward adapting to the marriage no matter how unsatisfactory it is. In contrast, the social-exchange or cost/reward model focuses on bargaining, change, and the rewards the spouses offer each other. Rather than being a process of adjustment, marriage becomes a *continual process of negotiation and profit seeking.* To some persons, this way of thinking may at first seem selfish and crass. Wouldn't it be simpler to say that *love* is the glue that holds marriage together?

LOVE AND RECIPROCITY

A song in the country-music tradition bears the title "The Cost of Real Love is 'No Charge.'" The lyrics tell of a child who compiles a list of all the things he does around the house and then demands payment from his mother. His mother in turn speaks of all she has done for her son, beginning with the nine months she carried him in her womb, the days of child care, the nights of sitting up while he was ill, the money put aside for his college education, and so on. However, in contrast to the child's list with specific monetary value attached to each task, the mother's list carries no price tags. After each item is a statement saying that the cost to the child is "no charge."

There is a prevailing sentiment that love—especially family love—should be freely given with no expectation of return, "no charge." However, the song itself describes reciprocity. The child wants payment, but the mother tells him he has already been paid and will continue to benefit from all that his parents do for him. At the same time, although she claims there is "no charge," the mother expects something from the child— affection, gratitude, respect, and the fulfilling of responsibilities assigned to him as a member of the family.

INTERDEPENDENCIES OF MARRIAGE

What is true of the parent-child relationship is also true of the husband-wife relationship. While popular sentiment would have us believe that this, too, is a situation of "no charge," the dynamics of married living suggest otherwise. In Chapters 10 and 11, we examined the exchange of rights and duties in the practical (instrumental) side of marriage. Now we want to see how such exchanges also take place in the personal (expressive) side of marriage as well. We'll also see that such exchanges take place *between* as well as *within* these two realms of marriage.

Perhaps it might be useful to think in terms of a two-story house. One story is the instrumental realm of marriage, and various changes go on between husband and wife on this level. The other floor of the house, the expressive realm is also the site of husband-wife exchanges. But there is in

Upper story: The *instrumental*
dimension of marriage (economic,
task-oriented, practical side
of marriage)

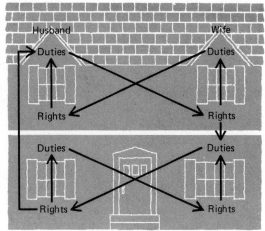

Lower story: The *expressive*
dimension of marriage (empathy,
companionship, physical affection;
the personal side of marriage)

FIGURE 12-1   *Dimensions of traditional marriage as a "two-story house."*

addition a considerable amount of running up and down the stairs between the two stories, with exchanges of rights and duties going on between the instrumental and expressive realms.

Figure 12-1 illustrates the way in which marriage, as explained by exchange theory, means continual reciprocity. There is an ongoing chain of obligations and repayments based upon a system of roles. Each role carries with it both rights and duties.

Marriage by definition means both instrumental and expressive interdependencies. We begin in Figure 12-1 with the husband's provider role, built around his duties to supply his wife (and any children) with economic and status rewards. As the husband fulfills these duties, the wife is having her rights to be provided for met. On one level, this motivates her to perform her instrumental role as homemaker, caring for the children and attending to domestic tasks. The husband, having his rights to a smooth-running household met by his wife's performance of her duties, is then further motivated to perform his own instrumental duties in the economic realm.

However, on another level, since the wife's rights to be rewarded by her husband in terms of economic and status benefits are met, she is also motivated to perform her expressive duties. Thus in Figure 12-1, the arrow moves down to the ground floor of the house. The wife's supportive, nurturant, affectionate behaviors (not only sexually, but including that) fulfill the husband's expressive rights. This in turn motivates him out of rectitude and gratitude to perform his expressive duties, thereby fulfilling his wife's expressive rights. It also motivates him further to perform his instrumental (breadwinning) duties.

It should be kept in mind that this entire process may not be at all conscious. Also, the marriage described is in *traditional* terms—the pattern for marriage that has been most familiar until now. Later, we'll examine how exchanges take place in an *equal-partner* marriage. But first, we want to focus on one particular dimension of process in marriage—expressiveness.

THE EXPRESSIVE DIMENSION IN TRADITIONAL MARRIAGE PATTERNS

What sociologists speak of as the "expressive" dimension of marriage is often that which first comes to mind when people think of the husband-wife relationship. Expressiveness includes three basic elements: *companionship* (someone to be with and do things with), *empathy* (someone who listens, understands, and cares), and *physical affection* (someone with whom love can be expressed through touch, caresses, and sexual intercourse).

At first it may seem strange to think of companionship, empathy, and physical affection as being somehow tied in with the instrumental side of marriage; but research has shown there are very real interconnections. These interconnections—particularly with respect to the economic system—are fascinating to explore.

HUSBAND'S OCCUPATION AND EXPRESSIVE SATISFACTIONS

Sociologists have found a relationship between social status and the degree to which couples are satisfied with the expressive dimension of their marriages. Couples with higher status (traditionally measured by the husband's occupation, education, and income) are more likely than lower-status couples to feel that their marital companionship, empathy, and physical affection are satisfactory.

In order to understand what are indeed complex relationships, it helps to think of the family and the economic-opportunity structure as two separate systems, each very much involved with the other. Figure 12-2 provides some idea of how the relationship of these two social structures affects what goes on in a traditional marriage in which the husband is the primary breadwinner.

The economic-opportunity structure may be thought of as a network of ways and means through which success and achievement may be attained in American society. It may also be thought of as a reward system, offering both tangible and intangible benefits. These benefits not only include money, prestige, and status; there are other significant rewards which may not seem so obvious without further reflection. For example, the degree to which a family is incorporated into the economic system is associated with such things as mental and physical health, educational, job, and cultural opportunities, and so on.

Families on the fringes of the economic-opportunity system have more problems with physical health, have more mental illness, have higher death rates and a lower life expectancy, and face problems of overcrowding, poor nutrition, excessive drinking, violence, lack of privacy, burdensome debts,

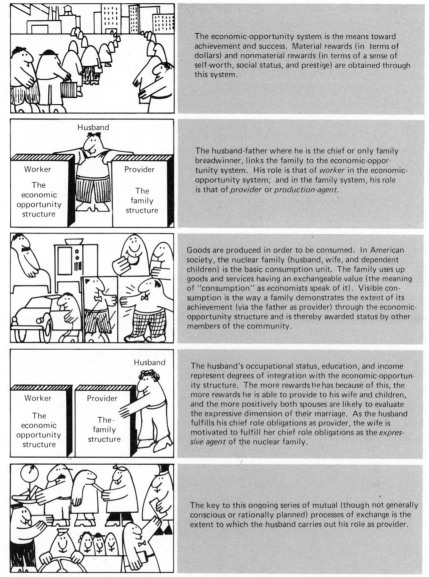

The economic-opportunity system is the means toward achievement and success. Material rewards (in terms of dollars) and nonmaterial rewards (in terms of a sense of self-worth, social status, and prestige) are obtained through this system.

The husband-father where he is the chief or only family breadwinner, links the family to the economic-opportunity system. His role is that of *worker* in the economic-opportunity system; and in the family system, his role is that of *provider* or *production-agent.*

Goods are produced in order to be consumed. In American society, the nuclear family (husband, wife, and dependent children) is the basic consumption unit. The family uses up goods and services having an exchangeable value (the meaning of "consumption" as economists speak of it). Visible consumption is the way a family demonstrates the extent of its achievement (via the father as provider) through the economic-opportunity structure and is thereby awarded status by other members of the community.

The husband's occupational status, education, and income represent degrees of integration with the economic-opportunity structure. The more rewards he has because of this, the more rewards he is able to provide to his wife and children, and the more positively both spouses are likely to evaluate the expressive dimension of their marriage. As the husband fulfills his chief role obligations as provider, the wife is motivated to fulfill her chief role obligations as the *expressive agent* of the nuclear family.

The key to this ongoing series of mutual (though not generally conscious or rationally planned) processes of exchange is the extent to which the husband carries out his role as provider.

FIGURE 12-2 *The Family (in the Traditional Pattern for Marriage) in Relation to the Economic-Opportunity System. Source: Partially adapted from Scanzoni, 1977, pp. 199–200.*

and low educational and verbal skills—to mention only a few handicaps associated with poverty (Herzog, 1967). The rewards associated with fitting into the economic-opportunity system come to the poor in only meager packages, and the dissatisfaction felt in receiving such scanty benefits carries over into marital dissatisfaction.

We have seen that marriage involves reward seeking. But the level of rewards that may be obtained depends upon the couple's socioeconomic status. In traditional marriages (where the husband is considered the unique or chief provider, whether it is a head-complement arrangement or in the senior partner–junior partner pattern) this socioeconomic status depends upon the husband's standing in relation to the economic-opportunity structure. This standing may be looked at both in objective terms (the actual *fact* of the husband's income) and in subjective terms (how the spouses *feel* about the level of rewards the husband is able to obtain from the opportunity system).

Research has shown that for both blacks and whites, there are positive relationships between economic factors and satisfactions within the marriage (Blood and Wolfe, 1960). Furthermore, economic satisfactions are strongly related to the family's actual economic position (Scanzoni, 1977). The flow of causes seems to go like this: The husband's education influences his job status, which in turn influences his income. The income in turn influences his wife's economic satisfaction, which in turn influences the expressive satisfaction of both partners (Scanzoni, 1975a).

Actual Income: The Objective Factor   A word of caution may be in order at this point. It is an oversimplification to try to formulate a neat, unqualified equation: more money equals more marital satisfaction. We would be telling only half the story if we were to say that the objective fact of income (the actual number of dollars the husband earns) is in itself the determining factor of expressive satisfactions. Such a simple summary of the situation applies mainly to those near or below the poverty line, where the strains of barely making ends meet do take their toll on the marital relationship and there is little doubt that expressive satisfactions would increase if income increased. One respondent from a black ghetto put it this way: "The men don't have jobs. The woman, she starts nagging. He don't have the money so he leaves. She ADC's it. If he had a job the family unit could come back together" (Rainwater, 1970:169).

A wife in such a situation feels an emotional estrangement from her husband because of his poor provision. Because of him, the family is not integrated into the economic-opportunity system with all its promises of success, money, and esteem. Since the objective rewards furnished by the husband are so few, both husband and wife feel a sense of alienation not only from the opportunity structure but also from each other.

This point becomes clear in sociologist Mirra Komarovsky's study of blue-collar marriages. She found that when husbands are inadequate providers wives tend to be overly sensitive to various faults in their husbands and may blame their failure on these factors. In reaction to such faultfinding, a husband may become more anxious about economic inadequacy and may take out his frustrations in drinking, angry outbursts, violence, or emotional

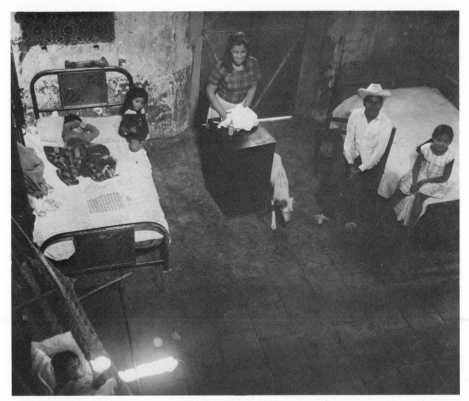

Money evidently takes on much greater importance to those couples who have the least. (© Joanne Leonard/Woodfin Camp & Assoc.)

withdrawal. The couple tends to avoid topics that matter most (bills, fears about illness, the uncertain future) because they are painful, with the result that a certain remoteness develops between the spouses (Komarovsky, 1962:291–292).

In another study, sociologists found that in nine cases out of ten, wives who ranked the economic aspect as "the most valuable aspect of marriage" were women married to men whose income was less than the median or men who were downwardly mobile (defined as having "failed to achieve the occupational level of their fathers"). Money evidently takes on much greater importance to those couples who have the least (Blood and Wolfe, 1960:81).

Feelings about Income: The Subjective Factor However, a standard of living that is considered satisfying to one person might not seem so at all to someone else. Economic satisfaction is, after all, a subjective matter. For example, suppose that Ann Jones and Barbara Smith both have husbands who earn $15,000. Ann is content with her family's standard of living. She and her husband work together on careful budgeting, own their own home, drive an economy car, and feel they are doing well. Their economic satisfaction extends over into satisfaction with the expressive aspects of marriage as well.

In contrast, Barbara is dissatisfied with the standard of living a $15,000 annual income forces her to maintain. "How can any family get along decently on that paltry amount in these days of rising prices?" she complains. She nags her husband to look for a better job or even to "moonlight" in order to bring in more money. Barbara would like a better home in a more prestigious neighborhood, more expensive furniture, nicer clothing, more luxury items, travel opportunities, more money to spend on the children, and so on. Her lack of economic satisfaction (despite the objective fact of her husband's income, which is exactly the same as that of Ann's husband) causes Barbara to be less satisfied with the expressive elements in her marriage also. She finds it hard to show empathy and affection to a husband who is not rewarding her as she feels she deserves to be rewarded.

The contrast between the hypothetical Ann and Barbara demonstrates the point of Figure 12-3. Marital satisfactions are related to both objective and subjective economic factors. For couples considerably below the national median income, the line between the objective factor (actual dollars) is likely to be direct. But as husbands' earnings increase toward the median income level and then beyond, the line becomes more and more indirect as subjective factors (*feelings* about economic rewards) increasingly influence expressive satisfactions.

The interrelationships between economic satisfaction and the expressive dimension of marriage showed up clearly in our study of more than three thousand married persons (Scanzoni, 1975a). The aspect of expressiveness found to be especially important was *empathy*, because according to the research findings it is empathy that affects the other areas of expressiveness—companionship and physical affection.

EMPATHY

Empathy means sharing another's thoughts, feelings, and experiences. We are empathizing with other persons when mentally and emotionally we enter into their sufferings, worries, triumphs, or joys. Empathy from others can banish feelings of aloneness and can bring a sense of affirmation, support, and encouragement. Psychotherapists of the transactional analysis school (made popular through such books as *I'm OK—You're OK* and *Games People Play*) have emphasized that there is a need for "stroking" in human relationships. People desire to be listened to, taken seriously, given recognition and approval. Psychiatrist Thomas Harris (1967) refers to this need as "the psychological version of the early physical stroking" which is so crucial during infancy (also Berne, 1964).

When people enter marriage, empathy is a sought-after reward. Spouses

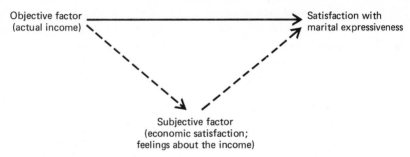

FIGURE 12-3 *The influence of economic factors on marital satisfactions.*

are expected to be able to confide in each other, talk things over, and find understanding and reinforcement. When such empathy isn't forthcoming from one's spouse, persons may seek alternate sources of rewards. A woman may phone her mother or a friend and pour out her heartaches. Or a man may proposition a female acquaintance with the familiar line, "My wife just doesn't understand me."

Sociological studies have attempted to measure the degree to which persons are satisfied with the empathy they receive in their marriages. Empathy can be looked upon as having two major components—communication and understanding. In three separate large-scale studies, satisfaction with *communication* was measured by asking each respondent how he or she felt about the way he or she could confide in the spouse and discuss anything that comes up. Was such communication perceived to be very good, OK, or not so good? The degree of satisfaction with *understanding* was measured by asking: "How do you feel about the way your wife (husband)

"You're always telling me you know exactly how I feel. Well, this time I'm calling your bluff. Exactly how do I feel?" (Drawing by Frascino; © 1977 The New Yorker Magazine, Inc.)

understands your problems and feelings? Do you feel her (his) understanding is: Very Good, OK, Not so good?" In general, our findings from all these studies combined may be summed up in the form of five generalizations, each of which will be examined in turn (Scanzoni, 1970, 1975a, 1977; also see Blood and Wolfe, 1960).

For Wives, Economic Satisfaction and Empathy Satisfaction Are Related First, our studies have shown that in general, *among both black and white women, the main positive influence on satisfaction with marital empathy is economic satisfaction.* More than any other variable measured, *economic satisfaction* most influences, explains, or predicts how wives feel about the communication and understanding they receive in their relationships with their husbands.

However, as we have seen, feeling materially rewarded is a subjective matter. How then can a sociologist assume to predict that wives who are economically satisfied will also be satisfied with the expressiveness in their marriages? Might not the degree of satisfaction in either realm simply reflect personality differences?

It is important to keep in mind that explanations and predictions in sociology are based upon research showing what is true of *most* people in a given situation. But this is not to deny that there may be exceptions. In this case, for example, while it is true that most wives' economic satisfaction relates to their husbands' actual income, there are some wives who are satisfied with a lower income and more simple life-style. One illustration might be that of a married couple who choose to carry out humanitarian or religious ideals by identifying with the poor in an urban ghetto or a rural depressed area. Perhaps the husband is a doctor or minister. The wife knows he could be earning a much larger income elsewhere, but she shares his vision and is content with a much lower standard of living than his education and profession would normally imply. However, we must keep in mind that such exceptional cases spring from free choice and are quite different from those cases where persons from birth onward are trapped in a cycle of poverty and forced to endure a life-style deprived of the rewards they yearn for. Such people are *not* economically satisfied.

Sociological research looks at random samples which are representative of a total population and draws conclusions based on *probability* or likelihood. It cannot tell us what will be true of each individual case, but it can show us what is likely. We may expect and predict therefore that the empathy a lawyer's wife receives will seem more satisfactory to her than does the empathy a janitor's wife receives. Such conclusions are based on statistics showing what is true of the vast majority, but any one case might not fit the overall picture. The lawyer and his wife might be on the verge of divorce, for example, while the janitor and his wife might have a warm, loving relationship that has spanned nearly half a century.

It is interesting at this point to notice a slight difference between black wives and white wives with regard to what accounts for economic satisfaction. Among white wives, the biggest indicator is clearly the objective fact of the husband's actual income. Among men, both black and white, feelings of economic satisfaction or dissatisfaction are also linked to the actual amount of money they earn. But among black wives, although their husbands' income and education are important, the research shows these items to be secondary to something else in importance. That "something else" is the wives' own "task-capability ranking." Black wives who rated themselves positively on such matters as intellectual ability, ability to organize things, ability to handle a number of responsibilites, knowledge and experience necessary to hold a job now or later, and abilities in such areas as budgeting, home management, cooking, and child care were also wives who were more apt to be content economically—in spite of the fact that their husbands earned less than the husbands of comparable white women (Scanzoni, 1975a).

Women who view themselves as more capable in skills and tasks may feel that they can therefore stretch limited income further. Economic deprivation has forced them to develop abilities that serve them well in coping with such deprivation. Apparently, the greater this coping ability, the less painful the deprivation is perceived to be; and this in turn means greater economic satisfaction.

The only exception to this pattern is among black wives whose husbands have high education. Then the pattern shifts so that it resembles that of whites; the husband's income becomes the strongest influence on economic satisfaction. It seems that where actual resources are greater (higher income is linked with higher education), there is less need to rely on a coping mechanism in order to feel a sense of economic satisfaction. Instead economic satisfaction is more directly related to one's actual economic situation (Scanzoni, 1975a).

For Husbands, Empathy Satisfaction Relates to Wives' Capabilities A second generalization from our research is this: *among both black and white men, satisfaction with empathy received in marriage is related to satisfaction with wives' capabilities in performing tasks.* There is no denying that economic satisfaction plays an important part in how satisfied a person feels about the communication and understanding received in marriage. This is true for men no less than for women. However, the research findings indicated that white husbands ranked economic satisfaction only in second place as an influence on satisfaction with empathy. And black husbands ranked economic satisfaction third, just after "expressive self-concept" (the degree to which the men considered themselves to be nurturant, supportive, and person-oriented). Placed at the top of the list as the major positive influence on satisfaction with marital empathy for both races was satisfaction with their wives' abilities and skills. Husbands who considered their wives to be doing a good job of carrying out mental, social, and practical tasks were likely to be husbands who reported they were satisfied with their wives' communication skills and understanding as well (Scanzoni, 1975a).

One explanation for this finding may be that women who are competent in general are also women who are competent in handling the demanding processes of talking things over and working things through in a marriage relationship. Such wives may have mastered empathy skills just as they have mastered other kinds of skills.

Another explanation, particularly applicable to traditional marriages, relates to exchange theory. Just as wives feel gratitude toward their husbands because of the status and material benefits the husbands provide, husbands may feel gratitude toward their wives because of the wives' competencies and the various benefits that spring from these abilities. Although it is not necessarily conscious, a sense of obligation may be felt by both spouses so that they respond to one another with open communication and warm understanding—in other words, with empathy. The wife responds because of her husband's role as breadwinner, his role outside the home. The husband's response to his wife, according to our research, is based on her competencies both inside the home (cooking, household management, child care, entertaining) and outside the home (knowledge and appreciation of literature, music, and art; intellectual ability, ability to organize things; knowledge and experience necessary to hold a job, and so on).

To try to pinpoint one exact explanation of the relationship between the husband's empathy satisfaction and the wife's task-capability rating is difficult because no doubt more than one explanation is involved. Again we must think in terms of process, perhaps in terms of a computer system with many feedback loops intertwined and affecting one another. If the wife is empathic toward the husband, he is likely to respond with empathy toward her. At the same time, his income enters in, as does her task-performance ability.

However, one finding did emerge which again gets us back to the matter of social status. There is no way of escaping its influence on marital satisfactions. The research data indicated that better-educated wives are the ones likely to be ranked as more competent and skillful. Better-educated wives are also likely to be married to better-educated husbands, and better-educated husbands are those most likely to confer the benefits of higher social status and income. These wives are therefore more likely to be economically satisfied and hence more responsive toward their husbands with empathy for this reason in addition to their possession of skills in communication and understanding. Again it becomes clear that many different interrelated factors feed into the marital exchange process.

Are Wives or Husbands More Satisfied with Empathy Received?   A third finding that emerged through our research centers on husband-wife differences. *Husbands are more likely than wives to be satisfied with the empathy received in marriage.* An "empathy gap" showed up in all three major studies—in the 1967 sample of over 900 white Indianapolis husbands and wives, again in the 1968 sample of 400 black Indianapolis husbands and wives, and once again in our 1971 five-state probability sample of 3,100 black and white respondents from metropolitan areas of Illinois, Ohio, Indiana, Michigan, and Wisconsin (Scanzoni, 1970, 1975a, 1977).

The finding that husbands are more satisfied than wives with marital empathy could mean either that wives actually receive *less* empathy than husbands do, or else that wives desire *more* empathy than husbands do and therefore cannot be satisfied so easily as husbands.

Perhaps at first glance, the explanation for the empathy gap may appear to lie in the alleged loneliness and isolation of wives in the traditional housewife role. While their husbands are gone all day interacting with colleagues who understand them and discuss subjects of mutual interest, wives have only fragmentary conversations with the postal carrier, supermarket cashier, and children's pediatrician, and must answer endless questions and settle the squabbles of preschoolers. While the husband may feel content with empathy received both on the job and at home, the wife may look to her husband alone for empathy. Yet not only is he not there to give it all day long, but he may also tend to expect *her* to give *him* empathy when he does arrive home and be unwilling to listen to the wife's problems. "I've had a hard day at work, honey. I want to relax and forget troubles for a while." He expects her to reward his economic efforts by soothing and bolstering his spirits.

One problem with the "isolated housewife" explanation for wives' lesser satisfaction with marital empathy shows up in the statistics which indicate that the level of satisfaction is directly associated with level of social status. Higher satisfaction with marital empathy is more likely to be found among wives of higher social status; yet these are the very wives who are more likely to fit the popular picture of the isolated suburban housewife.

Conversely, blue-collar wives are not nearly so isolated. They have relationships that provide intimacy and empathy. Studies have shown that many blue-collar wives have female confidants who serve as the "functional equivalents" of their husbands' workmates. Being less geographically mobile, such wives stay in neighborhoods longer and have time to develop and maintain close friendships. Furthermore, blue-collar wives are more likely to have kin living nearby (Komarovsky, 1962). Yet, they are discontent with the level of empathy found in their marriages. It is not that such wives lack communication and understanding per se; it is rather a case of not receiving empathy from their *husbands*.

Perhaps rather than looking for an explanation in terms of supposed isolation, we might better turn our attention to the matter of socialization. There are two sides to this: Females more than males are socialized to expect a high level of empathic gratifications from marriage. Males, on the other hand, not only may be satisfied with a lower level of empathy, but they are also not socialized to be able to give empathy to the extent that is expected of females (Fasteau, 1974; Balswick and Peek, 1971; Pleck and Sawyer, 1974).

Families, schools, churches, the media, and other influences join in getting across the message that girls are to think of marriage as their absorbing life interest. From the cradle onward, females hear nursery tales about the poor girl or princess who is awakened to life's meaning by the kiss of Prince Charming and whisked off to Blissful Castle to live out her days basking in the warmth of an adoring husband who devotes his life to catering to her every wish. To prepare for that day, little girls learn that females are to develop traits of kindness, tenderness, nurturance, understanding, and emotional expression. They enter marriage expecting to take on (and being granted) the role of "socioemotional hub" or "expressive leader" in the family (Seeley, Sim, and Loosley, 1956:178). And they likewise expect expressive gratifications in return. If they receive less empathy than anticipated, they feel cheated.

Males, on the other hand, are socialized to think of the world of work as their central life-interest. Marriage is viewed as an important part of life, but not the be-all-end-all of life as many women see it. Thus men tend not to be so totally absorbed in family affairs as are their wives. Being less absorbed, they are satisfied with what they feel are "reasonable" amounts of communication and understanding from their wives.

In the very same marriage, the husband and wife may view the situation quite differently from one another. Sociologists speak of this as the "definition of the situation," referring to how something *appears* to a person or is defined subjectively by him or her. One person may define the situation as favorable while the other may define the same situation as unfavorable. A husband might feel that the communication and understanding that takes place in a marriage is very good, but the wife might feel this area of marriage is very weak. Persons act and react according to their personal definition of the situation.

Another possible explanation for the differences in empathy satisfaction as perceived by husbands and wives also relates to gender-role socialization. Whereas girls are socialized to *give* empathy (and take for granted that they will receive it as well), boys are socialized to *receive* empathy far more than to give it. As children, they watch Mother kissing their bumps and bruises, relieving both physical and psychological hurts, and reassuring them in their fears and discouragements. And they see her do the same for Father. When they grow up, they expect to have wives who will perform the same function, because that's what women are "supposed" to do. Men may be satisfied with marital empathy to a greater degree than wives simply because husbands are *getting from* their wives more empathy than they are *giving to* their wives.

A familiar theme of cartoons and television situation comedies is that of the wife who tries to get her husband to listen and talk with her, only to be met by a series of grunts, "Yes, dears," or requests for a can of beer or a cup of coffee so that he can go on reading the newspaper or watching television in peace. Such scenes are far more likely to occur in lower-status homes than in higher-status families. Boys are taught to be tough, strong, nonintrospective, and to appear "manly" by keeping their feelings to themselves. The only kinds of emotions that may be expressed are those that fit with the masculine image—particularly anger and jealousy. Emotions of tenderness, compassion, and sorrow (especially when tears are involved) are considered to be the domain of the female sex; such behavior in males is looked upon with disdain as being "sissy."

Komarovsky (1962:156) speaks of the extreme difficulty which many lower-status men have when it comes to engaging in reciprocal exchanges of communication and understanding with their wives. The more disadvantaged a husband is (in terms of education, income, and occupational status), the harder he finds it to share feelings with his wife—even if he would like very much to do so.

However, our research showed that wives were less satisfied than husbands with empathy received in marriage *not only* at lower status levels but at higher status levels as well. Could it be that the gender-role socialization that emphasizes less expressiveness in males is also somewhat operative among higher-status husbands? Sociologists Jack Balswick and Charles Peek (1971) suggest that such may be the case. They point out that "American society is ironically shortchanging males" in terms of their ability to fulfill marital role expectations. "Society inconsistently teaches the male that to be masculine is to be inexpressive, while at the same time expectations in the marital role are defined in terms of sharing affection and companionship which involves the ability to communicate and express feelings."

Balswick and Peek describe the socialization process in which parents brag about a child's being "all boy." "All boy" is used in reference to behavior that is aggressive or "getting into mischief, getting dirty, etc., but never . . . to denote behavior which is an expression of affection, tenderness, or emotion." As a result of this socialization process, two basic types may emerge: the emotionally reserved "cowboy" who tries to convey a tough, he-man image and who does not express his feelings toward women even though he has such feelings, and the "playboy" who doesn't even have

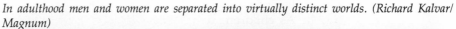

In adulthood men and women are separated into virtually distinct worlds. (Richard Kalvar/ Magnum)

When husbands' interests are so different from wives' interests, communication and understanding may be difficult. (Michael Hayman/Black Star)

emotional feelings toward women but views women as expendable commodities to be manipulated and used.

Sex-role stereotypes may cause problems not only with respect to sex-role socialization in childhood but also in the way they separate men and women into virtually two distinct worlds during adulthood. At the middle-class cocktail party the men gather in assorted groups to talk business, politics, or sports, while the women gather in other assorted groups to talk about children, recipes, schools, and problems of finding household help. In blue-collar settings, the men meet together at the corner bar or enjoy spending evenings "out with the boys" playing poker or bowling, while the women gather with female relatives and friends to share their problems and advice on babies, cooking, sewing, house care, and husbands. Husbands and wives whose interests are so different from one another may find open communication and understanding extremely difficult.

Comments of a Working-Class Husband

"They say married people live longer," he said one day, "but I think it just seems longer."

I once asked him why he got married when he views marriage with such lack of enthusiasm.

"What the hell you going to do?" he replied. "You just can't go on shacking up with girls all your life—I did plenty of that when I was single."

He paused to order another beer. "A man, sooner or later, likes to have a home of his own, and some kids, and to have that you have to get married. There's no way out of it—they got you hooked." . . .

. . . It seems clear that this man is not really complaining about his wife—he is unhappy with marriage. He also prefers men as a species to women; except for sexual purposes, he finds women dull and uninteresting. This is not the sort of man who would consider divorce. He is smart enough to know that he would find another wife just as restraining as this one. He also knows that he does not want to go through life as a bachelor.

Comments of a Working-Class Wife

"When I was a young girl I couldn't wait to get married—I thought it was the most wonderful thing in the world. Now I have my doubts."

The speaker is a woman who has been married for about thirty years. She has two grown children but no grandchildren as yet.

"The men go to work while the wife stays home with the kids—it's a long day with no other adult to talk to. That's what drives mothers to the soap operas—stupid as they are.

"Then the husband stops at some tavern to have a few with his buddies from the job—not having seen them since they left to drive home ten minutes ago. The poor guy is lonely and thirsty and needs to relax before the rigors of another evening before the television set."

She paused to sip her beer.

"Meanwhile," she continued, "the little woman has supper ready and is trying to hold the kids off 'until Daddy gets home so we can all eat together.' After a while she gives up this little dream and eats with the kids while the food is still eatable.

"About seven o'clock Daddy rolls in, feeling no pain, eats a few bites of the over-cooked food, sits down in front of the TV set, and falls asleep."

She ordered another beer. Then she said: "This little drama is repeated several thousand times until they have their twenty-fifth wedding anniversary and then everybody tells them how happy they have been.

"And you know what?" she added. "By now they are both so damn punch drunk neither one of them knows whether their marriage has been a success or not."

After a pause to light a cigarette, she said: "I think it's very funny—but I'm not laughing very hard."

I asked her why women seemed so anxious to marry in view of the gloomy state of marriage in our society.

"I don't really know," she said, "'but I think it is their desire for children. My children have meant a great deal to me and that is the part of marriage that women like most, in my opinion."

SOURCE: E. E. LeMasters, *Blue-Collar Aristocrats* (Madison: University of Wisconsin Press, 1975), pp. 37, 41–42.

Wives, having been socialized to be nurturant, might be able to give empathy to their husbands in spite of the "different worlds" they live in; but for men it may seem much harder. Not only have they grown up with the idea that inexpressiveness is associated with masculinity, they have also learned to consider women's interests trivial. Yet empathy involves entering into the emotions of another and seeing and feeling something as that person sees it. If a husband has difficulty entering into his wife's experiences because he feels a certain disdain for "woman's world" and at the same time is convinced that his wife wouldn't be able to understand and share in the most vital concerns of "man's world," it is not surprising that his wife will not be satisfied with the empathy her marriage offers.

Perhaps empathy would increase if sex roles were less rigid and husbands and wives had more in common. This point was made in a special television drama of recent years. A middle-aged, working-class wife, feeling bored and unfulfilled now that the children were grown and having had her "consciousness raised" through a women's group, tried to describe her deepest feelings to her cabdriver husband. But he refused to empathize and reacted to her communication efforts by falling asleep, turning away to watch television football broadcasts, or postponing discussion.

He *did* hear her and respond when she asked if she could get a job. The answer was clearly no. The idea threatened his masculine image. However, the wife went looking for a job anyway, and the husband had no idea where she was or if she'd ever come back. That night she phoned and asked him to meet her at a restaurant. Suddenly he didn't care about her job idea. He listened with genuine empathy as she told of waiting in employment offices, and then he said that he knew what that was like, for he too had often pounded the pavement looking for a job and had stood in lines of job applicants. A bond of comradeship and shared experience seemed to grow between the husband and the wife, and suddenly the strong, tough husband began to cry. His wife was moved. Reaching for his hand across the restaurant table, she said she had never felt closer to him. She was receiving the empathy she had longed for.

One reason that empathy satisfaction is greater at higher status levels may be that such couples live in less rigidly distinct male and female spheres and therefore have more in common. Another research finding indicates that husbands at higher levels are more likely to share information and news about their occupations with their wives, thereby giving wives a greater sense of participation in the totality of their husbands' lives than is true at lower levels. Husbands at lower income levels may feel less successful and prefer not to have their employment performances come under their wives' scrutiny any more than necessary (Scanzoni, 1970; Komarovsky, 1962:152ff).

Empathy Satisfaction Differences between Blacks and Whites   Another of our research findings is this: *whites are more likely than blacks to be satisfied with the empathy they receive in marriage.* This fourth generalization has nothing to do with inherent racial characteristics of either blacks or whites but rather may be explained by the relationship of each racial grouping to the economic-opportunity system (Scanzoni, 1977:204–210; 1975a).

Because of the limited opportunities afforded blacks in a white-dominated society, the blacks in our sample as a whole were found to have significantly less education and income and lower job status as compared to whites. Even when education levels are held constant, black men earn less money than white men. According to figures from the 1970 census, the earnings of black male workers employed the year round continued to be lower than those of the comparable age groupings for whites, although there were some signs of change, most notable among college-educated younger men. Furthermore, black men generally received lower earnings than white men, even when they held the same jobs. Black carpenters and construction workers, for example, had an income that was slightly less than two-thirds that of comparable whites. Black farmers earned slightly over one-third the amount white farmers earned. Black physicians and dentists earned between 82 and 85 percent of what comparable whites in these professions earned (U.S. Bureau of the Census, *Current Population Reports*, 1973:P-23, no. 46, 2, 52).

By 1977, "Blacks continued to lag behind Whites in the proportion holding high-paying, high-status jobs," reports the U.S. Bureau of the Census (*Current Population Reports*, P-23, no. 80, 1979:188, 218). That statement is illustrated by the fact that the majority of black men (58 percent) were employed in blue-collar jobs as compared to 45 percent of white men. Among white men, 42 percent held white-collar occupations (professional and technical, managerial, sales, and clerical); whereas among black men, only 23 percent held such occupations.

These inequities have an effect on black marriages. In discussing the exchanges that go on between a husband and wife we saw how important economic satisfaction is for exchanges of empathy. However, economic satisfaction among blacks is lower than among whites for the simple reason that the economic situation among blacks is less favorable. It is a matter of *relative deprivation*. Relative to whites, blacks earn less and have lower status.

The sociological concept of *reference group* sheds some light on the situation. A reference group is the group to which individuals or other groups compare themselves; it becomes a kind of measurement standard for assessing how well one is doing. While blacks have made considerable gains in social position as compared to the past, these gains have been accompanied by "psychological losses," according to social psychologist Thomas Pettigrew (1964:187), because many blacks have shifted their frame of reference in recent decades. Whereas formerly blacks tended to judge how well off they were by comparing present conditions with their previous situation, Pettigrew points out, "the rising expectations of the present are increasingly framed in terms of the wider white society."

Pettigrew and others claim that blacks at all status levels feel an intense strain resulting from relative deprivation. In fact, there is some evidence that the higher the status of blacks, the greater are the feelings of relative deprivation (Blau and Duncan, 1967). This may explain our finding that blacks with higher occupational status were no more satisfied with expressiveness in marriage than are blacks of less status—a finding that is not true of whites, where marital expressive satisfaction increases with higher social status.

Although these feelings of relative deprivation influence empathy satisfaction and processes of social exchange within the marriage relationship, they are not deliberate, conscious, and rational. Rather, they result from what sociologists speak of as a *socially structured* situation. Social forces rather than personal preferences and individual characteristics are influencing behavior in such cases. As white society denies equal benefits to blacks who have achieved the same educational and occupational position as whites, a sense of relative deprivation becomes very real to blacks. Since higher-status white wives take other white wives as their reference group, they can feel relatively satisfied with the objective rewards of money, prestige, and social status provided by their husbands. But black wives also take white wives as a reference group, and the comparision means relative dissatisfaction or deprivation (Scanzoni, 1977:208).

It is not that black wives respond with less empathy toward their husbands because they "blame" the husbands for not providing the material and immaterial rewards that white wives receive. Black wives know that their deprivation stems from the white-controlled economic-opportunity system. Yet, in traditional marriages where the husband is the link between the economic structure and the family, the wives are apt to react toward the husband simply because they can't react directly toward the reward-denying system itself. The process is subtle and usually not conscious. And even at higher status levels, since the husband represents the economic system, he meets with a response on the wife's part that because of *relative* deprivation is no more positive than that of black wives of lesser status who experience fewer *absolute* rewards.

Empathy Satisfaction Influences Other Satisfactions How couples feel about the empathy in marriage is not only important for its own sake but also for its effect on other aspects of the marital relationship. *Satisfaction with empathy in marriage influences satisfaction with the other expressive elements: companionship and physical affection.* This fifth generalization from our research is true of both blacks and whites. Empathy is in itself a coveted reward in marriage. But in addition to its own intrinsic benefits to the spouses, empathy evidently serves as a mechanism affecting other aspects of the couple's relationship as well. The more effectively husbands and wives can empathize or communicate and understand one another, the more likely they are to be able to handle satisfactorily decisions and disagreements about spending time together, leisure pursuits, sex relations, contraception, and so on. Thus they are likely to evaluate companionship and physical affection positively (Scanzoni, 1975a).

"Of course I'm happy, dear, if you call vaguely discontented happy." (Drawing by Weber; © 1976 The New York Magazine, Inc.)

COMPANIONSHIP

Several years ago, a women's magazine published a letter from a widow urging wives to take care of their husbands. She wrote: "There is, truly, no relationship like marriage. Someone chose you . . . gave you the gift of status . . . and the only attempt at understanding that will again come your way. Half a man's life on a platter. A built-in best friend. Someone to play with, walk in the first snow, wrap Christmas presents. *With.* Someone who remembers the same people and places and times . . . and your own young selves" (*Ladies Home Journal,* circa late 1950s).

This woman's letter sums up marriage in the way Americans idealize it, particularly from the standpoint of the role of the wife in a traditional marriage where the husband is the unique or chief provider. There is an awareness of the economic-achievement aspect ("gave you the gift of status") and an appreciation of the importance of empathy ("the only attempt at understanding"). But there is also much value placed upon a third expected characteristic of marriage— *companionship* ("A built-in best friend." "Someone to [do things] with.").

In other times and places, companionship in marriage has not been emphasized or expected. Ancient Greek men kept their wives secluded to assure the legitimacy of offspring but found companionship with highly cultured mistresses called *hetairai* (Seltman, 1956). And in the early days of the Israeli kibbutz, the husband and wife who were often seen in one another's company were scorned by the community because such spouse companionship was viewed as disloyalty to the larger collective life (Talmon, 1972:12).

Only recently has husband-wife companionship come to be a sought-after reward among some young married couples in Japan. Traditionally, social life has not been couple-centered but sex-segregated, with husbands finding companionship with work colleagues and "bar girls," while wives interact with relatives, children, and female friends. During research on Japanese life between 1958 and 1960, sociologist Ezra Vogel (1963) found that

Japanese wives were both curious and envious of American husbands and wives who went out together. Vogel writes: "One wife, upon hearing about a husband and wife going on a trip for a few days responded, 'how nice,' but after a moment's reflection added, 'but what would they talk about for so long?'"

In the United States, however, the companionship ideal of marriage is held up as a major goal toward which every couple is expected to aim. Husbands and wives are expected to accompany each other to most social occasions, to devote their leisure to mutual activities, and to enjoy simply being together as best friends. But how do American couples feel about the companionship they receive in marriage? Our research uncovered some findings that are similar to the findings related to empathy satisfaction.

Social Status and Satisfaction with Marital Companionship First of all, we found that *the higher the level of rewards provided by the husband (especially in terms of education and prestige), the more positively both spouses evaluate companionship* (Scanzoni, 1970:78). Several factors appear to be at work here. First, there is the familiar pattern of the exchange model in which the husband as the chief provider fulfills his instrumental role (financial support) which motivates the wife to fulfill her expressive role (emotional support). The better he fulfills his role, the more she reciprocates with greater expressiveness, calling forth more expressiveness on his part in turn. Companionship, as an important aspect of expressiveness, is thus rated as more satisfactory for higher-status couples.

Also not to be overlooked is that chain of events in which economic satisfaction (subjective), often stemming from economic success (objective), influences satisfaction with marital empathy. If a spouse evaluates positively the *empathy* received in marriage, he or she is likely to consider the marital partner to be a good *companion* as well. Someone with whom one can talk things over and find understanding is probably someone whose company is enjoyable in leisure pursuits, too.

Life-style factors may also enter in. Lower-status couples are accustomed to greater gender-role differentiation and sex-segregated leisure activities. Higher-status couples, on the other hand, are more likely to emphasize husband-wife togetherness in leisure pursuits. As a result, they rank the companionship aspect of marriage as more satisfactory than is true of lower-status couples.

The simple fact of money itself no doubt plays some part, too, in accounting for the relationship between higher social status and a positive evaluation of marital companionship. Leisure activities can require a considerable financial outlay. Camping and sporting equipment, travel, vacation cottages, theater tickets, dining out, entertaining friends, to name but a few of the leisure activities to which many contemporary Americans aspire, all cost money. Higher-status couples possess greater resources and thus have greater access to these means of fostering marital companionship.

Husband-Wife Differences in Satisfaction with Companionship We also found that *husbands are more satisfied than wives with the companionship received in marriage.* This second research finding is again similar to the finding with regard to empathy satisfaction. Husbands were more likely than wives to evaluate the companionship they received in marriage as "very good." Wives were more likely than husbands to evaluate marital companionship as either "OK" or "not so good." Why the difference? It appears that in both black and white marriages, husbands may feel they spend enough time in leisure activities with their wives, whereas wives may expect and desire more. Again, the explanation probably lies in the different socialization of males and females so that wives tend to invest the companionship element in marriage with greater meaning and importance than husbands do.

White-Black Differences in Satisfaction with Companionship A third research finding was this: *whites are more likely than blacks to be satisfied with the companionship received in marriage.* Even though as we have seen there are similarities in evaluations of companionship regardless of race, there are also differences clearly associated with race. When black couples and white couples are compared, the satisfaction with marital companionship is found to be less among blacks than among whites. Again, as we saw in the evaluation of empathy, the principle of relative deprivation appears to be operative.

PHYSICAL AFFECTION

Along with empathy and companionship, physical affection completes the trio called "expressiveness in marriage." Physical affection may include a wide range of behaviors—the squeeze of a hand, a kiss, a hug, resting one's head on the spouse's shoulder, stroking the spouse's hair, a tender caress on the back of the neck, a playful pat on the behind, snuggling up together on a couch, sitting on the partner's lap, petting, sexual intercourse.

In popular thinking, sex is considered the most important aspect of marriage; and when a divorce occurs, people often whisper that the couple must have had a sex problem. However, the causes of divorce are much too complex to pin all the blame on sexual dissatisfaction. In fact, marriage counselors can tell of cases where couples were quite happy with the sexual side of their relationship and continued to have intercourse up until the day of the divorce and even afterwards. "Good sex" doesn't necessarily result in overall marital satisfaction. On the other hand, satisfaction with other areas of marriage (economic satisfaction, empathy, companionship) is likely to show up in satisfaction with physical affection as well.

Sex and Sociological Inquiry Aware that sexuality is usually considered a personal and private matter, sociologist James Henslin (1971:1–3) has endeavored to answer the question, "What does sociology have to do with sex?" He writes: "The sociological point of view . . . is that while it is individuals who engage in any given sexual behavior, it is their group membership that shapes, directs, and influences the forms or patterns that their sexual behaviors take. . . . Although sexual behaviors have a biological base, it is membership in groups which shapes or gives direction to the expression of this sexual drive."

Psychotherapist Wardell Pomeroy (1972:469), formerly an associate of Alfred Kinsey at the Institute for Sex Research at Indiana University, has illustrated how a person's group classification is related to that person's sexual attitudes and behavior. Pomeroy put forth the rather dramatic suggestion that one could be able to tell which of two adolescent boys would be the more likely to attend college simply by looking at their respective sex histories. How? By comparing the boys' sex histories with the Kinsey findings on different categories of people (based upon racial-cultural grouping, educational level, occupation, parents' occupation, rural-urban background, religious group, and so on).

The sex history of one boy, for example, might indicate that he has had intercourse with a number of girls, doesn't take his clothes off for sex relations, cares more about the act than about emotional involvement with the girl, disapproves of mouth-genital contact, masturbates less than he did in his earlier teens, and has infrequent "wet dreams." The sex history of the other boy may indicate that he masturbates actively but has little or no sexual intercourse, reacts strongly to erotic stimuli, engages in petting a great deal and may try oral-genital contact, and considers sex more enjoyable in the nude. The first boy, says Pomeroy, is displaying a sexual pattern that stamps him as being from a lower social-status background, and few boys in this category would be likely to go on to college. It is the second boy who is likely to further his education past high school, because his pattern of sexual behavior shows that in all probability he is from a higher social-status background.

Pomeroy's way of drawing attention to the association between sex and status-level differences may seem a bit sensational but it helps make the point. His picture of the two hypothetical unmarried young men is based upon actual findings that emerged in the Kinsey studies of the 1940s and 1950s. Just as clearly, the data showed that social status affects the sexual behavior of married couples. For example, it was found that wives with higher educational backgrounds were more likely to reach orgasm during marital coitus and to achieve orgasm more frequently than wives with lower levels of education. Couples of higher educational background were also found to spend longer time in sexual foreplay before intercourse (Kinsey et al., 1953, chap. 9).

Marital Sex at Lower Status Levels   Couples with lower levels of education and socioeconomic status differ from higher-level couples in both sexual attitudes and practices. At the same time, researchers into sex behavior have found evidence that lower-level couples have much in common *with each other* in the same culture, in other cultures, and in other periods of history (Pomeroy, 1972:470).

Rainwater (1964), in comparing his own studies of American lower-status marriages with similar marriages in Mexico, Puerto Rico, and England, found several common characteristics. In all four "cultures of poverty," there was a central norm that "sex is a man's pleasure and a woman's duty." Second, a double standard was practiced both with regard to childhood sex education and later sexual behavior. Girls were shielded from sex information and expected to be sexually innocent until marriage; boys were left to their own devices and expected to experiment.

A third characteristic sexual pattern among these poverty groups in all four countries was the tendency for males to separate women into categories of "good women" and "bad or loose women." "Bad women" were defined as those who were sexually active and enjoyed sex—for example, prostitutes. Wives were expected to be "good women" who were disinterested in sex. In studies of a Mexican village, anthropologist Oscar Lewis (1951:326) found that men generally felt that sexual play was for the seduction of other women and deliberately refrained from arousing their own wives sexually because they didn't want their wives to "get to like it too much." The fear is sometimes expressed that female sexual enjoyment may lead to affairs with men other than their husbands.

What do marriages at lower status levels have in common that accounts for these attitudes toward sexuality? As Rainwater (1964) pondered that question, he came up with the hypothesis that *rigidly segregated gender roles* may be the key. Couples whose roles are widely separated are unlikely to have close sexual relations, and wives especially are unlikely to find marital sex gratifying.

Several years before Rainwater suggested his hypothesis, the British social anthropologist Elizabeth Bott (1957) had come to a similar conclusion in research on urban families in England. As representative of couples with segregated sex roles, Bott referred to a semiskilled factory worker and his wife who placed little importance on shared interests and joint activities, preferring instead a "harmonious division of labor." The wife's comments indicated that "she felt physical sexuality was an intrusion on a peaceful domestic relationship rather than an expression of such a relationship." In contrast, couples in Bott's study who stressed joint activities and male-female equality were couples in which the husbands held professional, semiprofessional, and clerical occupations. For these couples, a mutual enjoyment of sex was considered an important part of shared interests in general.

Change and Resistance According to sociologist Lillian Rubin (1976), some of the Kinsey researchers' findings about working-class sexual attitudes and practices no longer fit. In her nonrandom sample of fifty blue-collar families (with wives under age forty), whom she compared with a smaller sample of twenty-five professional families from the middle class, Rubin saw signs of change, which she summed up as follows:

> Among the people I spoke with, working-class and middle-class couples engage in essentially the same kinds of sexual behaviors in roughly the same proportions. But working-class wives express considerably more discomfort about what they do in the marriage bed than their middle-class sisters. (pp. 137–38)

Rubin illustrates by speaking of the conflicts that arise in working-class marriages as husbands become interested in spending more time in foreplay and experimentation with different sexual techniques, yet meet with resistance on the part of their wives. Some wives, for example, reluctantly go along with their husbands' desires for oral-genital sex because they feel it is their duty to please their husbands, or because they fear they will cause their husbands to fulfill sexual desires elsewhere if they refuse. Sometimes they give into their husbands' wishes out of genuine caring, even though they

Sex in Working-Class Marriages

. . . it is the men who now more often speak of their wish for sex to be freer and with more mutual enjoyment:

"I think sex should be that you enjoy each other's bodies. Judy doesn't care for touching and feeling each other though."

. . . who push their wives to be sexually experimental, to try new things and different ways:

"She thinks there's just one right position and one right way—in the dark with her eyes closed tight. Anything that varies from that makes her upset."

. . . who sometimes are more concerned than their wives for her orgasm:
"It's just not enjoyable if she doesn't have a climax, too. She says she doesn't mind, but I do."

For the women, these attitudes of their men—their newly expressed wish for sexual innovation, their concern for their wives' gratification—are not an unmixed blessing. In any situation, there is a gap between the ideal statements of a culture and the reality in which people live out their lives— a time lag between the emergence of new cultural forms and their internalization by the individuals who must act upon them. In sexual matters, that gap is felt most keenly by women. Socialized from infancy to experience their sexuality as a negative force to be inhibited and repressed, women can't just switch "on" as the changing culture or their husbands dictate. Nice girls don't! Men use bad girls but marry good girls! Submit, but don't enjoy—at least not obviously so! These are the injunctions that are laid aside with difficulty, if at all.

SOURCE:Lillian Breslow Rubin, *Worlds of Pain: Life in the Working-Class Family* (New York: Basic Books, 1976), p. 136.

personally feel uncomfortable. And sometimes their willingness "is offered as a bribe or payment for good behavior—not surprising in a culture that teaches a woman that her body is a negotiable instrument" (p. 140).

Whereas the middle-class women in Rubin's sample tended to be relaxed about the topic, recognizing that oral sex "is a widely practiced and acceptable behavior," working-class wives tended to be filled with guilt. One woman summed up the feelings of most of the others in the sample when she said:

> I always feel like it's not quite right, no matter what Pete says. I guess it's not the way I was brought up, and it's hard to get over that. He keeps telling me it's okay if it's between us, that anything we do is okay. But I'm not sure about that. How do I know in the end he won't think I'm cheap? (p. 141)

Rubin shows that the guilts and anxieties spring not only from past socialization but also from the mixed messages given by many blue-collar husbands who continue to think in terms of "cheap tramps," "those kind" of women, and so on. The men themselves, in spite of certain liberalized sexual attitudes, don't seem to shake off "good girl/bad girl" distinctions easily. Some wives are confused, knowing that on the one hand their husbands boast of wives' "innocence" and limited knowledge in sexual matters; but on the other hand, the husbands are suddenly expecting wives to engage in what might strike the women as strange and exotic behaviors that don't fit their image of themselves as good wives and mothers. Ambivalence on the part of husbands is also seen in their complaints about wives' not being more assertive and initiating sexual relations, while at the same time accusing wives of being too "aggressive" and "unfeminine" when they *do* try to take the initiative.

Even their husbands' new concern about wives' orgasms is not always welcomed by blue-collar wives. "For some," writes Rubin, "it has indeed opened the possibility for pleasures long denied. For others, however, it is experienced as another demand in a life already too full of demands." To illustrate, she quotes a mother of six children, who not only is employed part-time but also cares for an elderly, sick father in addition to all the housekeeping responsibilities:

> It feels like somebody's always wanting something from me. Either one of the kids is hanging on to me or pulling at me, or my father needs something. And if it's not them, then Tom's always coming after me with that gleam in his eye. Then, it's not enough if I just let him have it, because if I don't have a climax, he's not happy. I get so tired of everybody wanting something from me all the time. I sometimes think I hate sex. (p. 151)

Sexual Satisfaction and Social Status   Rainwater's (1965:63) studies of American marriages at different class levels are applicable here. In researching degrees of sexual interest, enjoyment, and commitment he found "a continuum from

TABLE 12-A   *Wife's gratification in sexual relations (percent)*

SOCIAL STATUS	VERY POSITIVE	POSITIVE	SLIGHTLY NEGATIVE	REJECTING
Middle class*	50%	36%	11%	3%
Working class†	53	16	27	4
Lower class‡	20	26	34	20

*Includes upper middle class (professionals, executives, and certain business proprietors) and lower middle class (accountants, engineers, supervisors of clerical workers, certain skilled workers and supervisors who have similar education and life-style in this category).
†Semiskilled and medium-skilled workers in manual jobs and certain service occupations such as police officers, fire fighters, bus and cab drivers, and so forth. (Rainwater speaks of this group as the upper lower class but the term *working class* seems more appropriate for our purposes.)
‡Rainwater refers to this as the lower lower class. It includes persons who consider themselves at the "bottom of the heap." Many work only intermittently or are chronically unemployed. When they do work, it is at unskilled jobs. Education is low, with few persons in this category having finished high school and many have no more than a grade school education. Their life-style is one of poverty, with substandard housing, usually in slum neighborhoods. Some sociologists call this the "underclass."
SOURCE: Adapted from Rainwater, 1965., Table 3-1 on p. 64 with category explanations from pp. 21-24.

strong positive involvement with marital sexuality to strong rejection'' (see also Bell, 1974). Social status plays an important part in one's position on the continuum, as Table 12-A shows. Among middle-class wives, 86 percent indicated very positive or positive feelings about marital sex, as did 69 percent of working-class wives. But among working-class wives there was an increase in the percentage reporting negative and rejecting attitudes—more than double that of middle-class wives who reported such feelings. Moving to lower-class wives, less than half reported positive or very positive evaluations of sex in marriage, and 54 percent expressed negative feelings to some degree.

Similarities between the middle class and working class in husband-wife enjoyment of sex are seen also in Table 12-B. It is the lower class that is most set off from the rest; here is seen the greatest degree of difference between how husbands and wives feel about sex. Both the more rigid gender-role segregation and the fewer economic rewards at this level are no doubt operating in the wife's lower satisfaction.

TABLE 12-B   *Comparative enjoyment of sex by husband and wife (percent)*

SOCIAL STATUS	HUSBAND ENJOYS SEX MORE	EQUAL ENJOYMENT	WIFE ENJOYS SEX MORE
Middle class	33%	59%	8%
Working class	47	51	2
Lower class	67	26	7

NOTE: More than half the couples in middle-class and working-class marriages report equal enjoyment of sex by husband and wife. This is only true of a quarter of those couples in lower-class marriages.
SOURCE: Adapted from Rainwater, 1965, p. 68, Table 3-5.

Blood and Wolfe's (1960:224–229) study of Detroit marriages also indicated that wives' satisfaction with marital expressiveness decreased as social status decreased. Our own findings concur with those of Blood and Wolfe and Rainwater. While it can't be denied that personality factors enter into physical expressiveness in marriage, social factors also play a significant part. In an achievement-oriented society, a sense of self-worth comes to be linked with success in the economic-opportunity system. It hurts to realize that one is only on the fringes of that system. This feeling of disappointment and dissatisfaction affects husband-wife empathy and carries over into feelings about physical affection as well (Scanzoni, 1970:79–107; 1975a).

Komarovsky (1962:93) observed this phenomenon in her study of blue-collar marriages. One twenty-nine-year-old woman said that sex was "wearing off" after ten years of marriage and five children. The wife indicated dissatisfaction with her economic situation and remarked that she might have more interest in sex if her husband were "getting along better." In Rainwater's interviews, a blue-collar wife complained of her husband's irresponsibility in money matters and his failure to be mobile into the middle class and indicated that these negative feelings about her husband negatively affected her feelings about their sexual relationship. And in another case, the couple was lower class, and the husband was unemployed. Because he had no interest in finding work and the rent was past due, the wife commented that

Sexual satisfaction in marriage is often related to social factors, such as a couple's economic situation and satisfaction with husband-wife empathy, as well as personality factors. (© Joel Gordon, 1979)

she had lost all desire for sexual intercourse, saying that now she just tolerated it (Rainwater, 1965:90–97).

Seeking Sexual Satisfaction Outside Marriage If persons feel their spouses aren't meeting their sexual needs, are they justified in seeking sexual satisfaction with other persons outside the marriage? Among the working-class men in a five-year participant observation study by sociologist E. E. LeMasters (1975), there persisted a belief that men had greater sexual needs than women and thus had the right to engage in extramarital sex when their needs weren't being adequately met within marriage. Except in highly unusual situations, however, no such rights were granted women; women were assumed to have less need for regular sex. "In other words," says LeMasters summing up the attitude of the blue-collar men in his sample, "a woman who seeks extramarital sexual partners is a 'slut,' whereas a man who engages in the same behavior is 'starved' for sexual relief by his wife" (p. 96).

Some observers suggest that, as such double-standard thinking disappears (as has been happening within the middle class especially), and as new and more open concepts of marriage are introduced, some couples may establish new ground rules for marriage that *allow* for sex with other persons besides one's spouse (Libby, 1977b). One idea is that a disappearance of the double standard would mean that women would have options for sexual permissiveness previously taken for granted by men only—an idea similar to the reasoning applied to premarital sex as seen in Chapters 4 and 5 of this book. Indeed some researchers have suggested a connection between greater permissiveness in *pre*marital sex and the expectation that *extra*marital sex will take place later on. In one study of unmarried college students, those students who were already engaging in sexual intercourse were more likely than other students to report that they expected to have outside sexual involvements after they were married (Bukstel et al., 1978).

However, sexual exclusivity and sexual possessiveness have been ideals bound up in the notion of marriage as we know it in our society; the two spouses are considered to belong to one another and to have unique rights of sexual access to one another. *Adultery* is the legal term for having sexual intercourse with someone other than one's own spouse, and it is negatively sanctioned by public opinion, the law (it is grounds for divorce), and Jewish and Christian religious teachings ("Thou shalt not commit adultery" is one of the Ten Commandments).

According to the 1974 National Opinion Research Center's national survey, 73 percent of adults consider extramarital sex to be "always wrong," as compared to 32 percent who answered that they consider premarital sex to be "always wrong." And throughout the 1970s, other national surveys continued to show that the general public is far more willing to tolerate premarital sexual permissiveness than it is to tolerate extramarital sex (Glenn, 1979). Sociologist Robert Bell (1971:63) suggests two reasons for the stronger societal disapproval of extramarital sex than of premarital sex: First, since a married person already has a socially approved partner to meet his or her sexual needs, it is assumed that there is no good reason to pursue outside sexual experience. Second, it is believed that sexual involvement outside of marriage will threaten the individual's marriage relationship. Thus, the condemnation of adultery is part of societal concern for the institution of the family.

Commuting Couples and Extramarital Sex   Sociologist Naomi Gerstel (1979) has questioned two assertions commonly made about extramarital sex: one, that whether or not spouses engage in sex outside of marriage depends in large measure on their opportunities to do so; and two, that changes in the *structure* of marriage (for example, movement to the egalitarian form) are linked almost inevitably with changes in basic *norms* that have governed marriage as an institution (for example, sexual exclusivity).

Gerstel shows that neither assertion can be indisputably supported. Using commuter marriage as a test case, Gerstel pointed out that here was certainly an example of structural change (equal-partner marriage in which the spouses' careers kept them in separate residences most of the week) and an example of "increased opportunity" for extramarital sex because the spouses were out of one another's sight so much of the time. Yet, among her seventy-four respondents, only 8 percent who hadn't had affairs prior to commuting became involved in extramarital sex after the commuting began. Sixty percent of the commuters had never had an extramarital sex involvement either before or during commuting, and 11 percent who had engaged in extramarital sex *before* commuting did *not* do so after the commuting pattern had begun. Another 21 percent had had affairs before commuting and continued to have them afterward.

Gerstel is making the point that over 80 percent of the persons in her sample behaved after commuting just as they had behaved before. Those who had previously incorporated extramarital sex into their life-style continued to do so. And those who were sexually exclusive both before and after commuting showed that *internal* constraints (norms and ideals held about marriage and/or a personal commitment to the spouse) were more influential in their behavior than the "reduction in *external* social constraints" (that is, "lowered observability and responsibility toward the spouse").

Among her respondents who had changed in some way after commuting, the 11 percent who stopped having extramarital involvements may have felt "that they must compensate for their separation with greater sexual fidelity," says Gerstel. "Alternative relationships might be more threatening, as there is a chance for them to develop into real substitutes" in the commuting situation. She continues by summing up the underlying reasoning that may lie behind many commuting spouses' decisions:

> Commuters have already tampered with the marital bond by living in separate residences. To tamper to an even greater extent by having affairs would reduce the marital ties to a near minimum. (p. 168)

But what about those who began having extramarital sexual affairs only after the commuting pattern began? From her in-depth interviews, Gerstel concludes that "in most cases, attitudes (that exist before separation) rather than opportunity seem to be the primary determinant of actual extramarital liaisons" (p. 157).

Extent of Extramarital Sex Leaving commuter couples, it's common knowledge that among married persons in general, a certain proportion do have sexual intercourse with persons other than their spouses. The exact incidence of extramarital sex today is not known, although in the Kinsey studies of the 1940s it was found that by age forty, half of the married men and slightly over a quarter of the married women in their sample had experienced extramarital sex. In studies since that time, certain sampling problems have made the results questionable—although some sociologists are persuaded that the percentage of persons engaging in extramarital sex has increased since the time of Kinsey's work (Libby, 1977b).

Kinsey and his associates referred to problems of jealousy encountered by many persons who reported extramarital coitus, with divorce as an outcome in a number of cases. The researchers concluded: "These data once again emphasize the fact that the reconciliation of the married individual's desire for coitus with a variety of sexual partners, and the maintenance of a stable marriage, presents a problem which has not been satisfactorily resolved in our culture" (Kinsey et al., 1953, chap. 10).

Mate Swapping ("Swinging") "Swing your partner!" is no longer just a square-dance call. The phenomenon of "swinging" (sometimes called "consensual adultery" or "spouse swapping") is being incorporated into the life-style of some married couples today who see it as a way to solve the dilemma posed by Kinsey— a have-your-cake-and-eat-it solution in which a person can enjoy sexual variety, a number of partners, and a stable marriage all at the same time. Some researchers have found that couples involved in swinging claim they have never participated in extramarital sex. To such couples, the term *extra* connotes the idea of something external to the marriage, whereas swinging is defined as a part of the marriage—a mutually agreed upon sexual experience. Two researchers on the subject, James Smith and Lynn Smith (1970, 1973) suggest that *co-marital sex* is a more accurate term for situations of consensual adultery in which both spouses participate. In another form of consensual adultery, either or both may have sexual intercourse outside the marriage but with the spouse's knowledge and consent, even though they do not participate at the same time or place as in swinging. Both forms of consensual adultery are in contrast to what the Smiths call "conventional adultery" which is characterized by concealment and deception (see also Libby, 1977b).

Sociologist Mary Lindenstein Walshok (1971) emphasizes that co-marital sex involves two distinctive qualities: (1) an agreement between a husband and wife that they will have sexual relationships with others, "but in contexts in which they *both* engage in such behavior at the same time and usually in the same place'' (perhaps in different rooms but under the same roof) and (2) that these sexual experiences will take place in an organized framework rather than permitting such experiences to occur spontaneously. Another team of sociologists refers to swinging as an *institutionalized* form of extramarital sex (Denfeld and Gordon, 1970). In other words, swinging is taking on the characteristics of an established, structured form of behavior. Swingers have their own subculture, including rules and norms. (Although there are regional differences, participants are expected to learn and conform to certain behaviors— a kind of swingers' ''etiquette,'' which may include such matters as waiting for the host to give the signal at a party by disrobing first (Symonds, 1971:95). The subculture of swinging also has its ideologies, its taboos (against gossip, and usually against emotional involvement and against male homosexuality—although female homosexual practices are encouraged), its communication networks, and its jargon (including code words for various sexual techniques and preferences). A number of swingers' organizations and magazines exist, and their classified ads provide one way interested couples find out about each other. Underground newspapers, clubs, personal referrals, and parties in homes are also ways persons interested in swinging may get together (Bell, 1975).

At present no valid data are available on the actual incidence of co-marital sex. Crude estimates arrived at by projecting from limited studies, subscriptions to swingers' magazines, and so on, have ranged from half a million couples upward (Bartell, 1971:20; Smith and Smith, 1974:78, 85, 263). Most studies have agreed that the types of people who participate in swinging are usually white-collar—and some skilled blue-collar—persons from a variety of occupations. (Physicians, lawyers, dentists, professors, high school teachers, airline pilots, salespeople, owners of small businesses, electricians, plumbers, housewives, and truck drivers have been represented in some studies.) For the most part, researchers have reported the level of education among swingers to be high, and the couples are generally considered to be

Classified ads in certain publications provide a way for swingers to find out about each other.

conventional, somewhat conservative, and "very straight" in areas of life other than their swinging. Ages of swingers have ranged from the late teens to seventy (Smith and Smith, 1974; Bartell, 1971; Denfeld and Gordon, 1970; Walshok, 1971).

According to O'Neill and O'Neill (1970), married couples decide to participate in co-marital sex for a number of reasons: Some spouses feel "they need more sex than their spouse provides." Others may be happy with their marriage relationship but yet feel that marital exclusivity is confining; the structured context of co-marital sex is viewed as a way to explore sex outside of marriage. Others are simply bored with sex with only one person over time and consider swinging as a "stimulant" or "sexual turn-on." And there are some who try group sex in a desperate effort to patch up a failing marital relationship. Sociologist Carolyn Symonds (1971:86) found that swinging sometimes has appeal to persons who feel vague dissatisfaction in marriage or who "have come to a point in their marriage where they feel a desire to expand or experiment."

Most studies have found that swinging was first suggested by husbands and also that men more than women initiate the sexual encounters at swinging parties—though women at swinging parties may covertly express preferences for certain men and provide clues to let them know of their interest and availability (Henshel, 1973; Symonds, 1971; Varni, 1973). Some researchers point out that many wives are hesitant about swinging at first and participate only to please their husbands, but that eventually they may come to enjoy it as much or more than their husbands (Varni, 1973; Smith and Smith, 1970). On the other hand, a study of drop-out swingers who later visited marriage counselors revealed that wives are usually the ones who want to discontinue participation in co-marital sex (Denfeld, 1974).

Sociologists Duane Denfeld and Michael Gordon (1970) suggest that the change in attitudes toward female sexuality, along with improved contraception, "is likely to have greatly increased the incentive for women to seek—as men have always done—sexual variety outside marriage"; and out of all available ways for both spouses to have such variety, "mate swapping is the least threatening and the one most compatible with monogamy." Swinging for recreation is viewed by the spouses as something that is only physical and unlike their marital sex which they view in terms of love and emotional involvement. Swinging involves rules (such as not getting together with sex partners outside designated swinging sessions) so that emotional attachments are discouraged and jealousy kept to a minimum. According to Denfeld and Gordon, swinging is not considered an alternative to monogamous marriage nor intended to disrupt the husband-wife relationship. Rather it may be viewed as "a strategy to revitalize marriage, to bolster a sagging partnership." Hence, the belief among swingers that "the family that swings together clings together." Smith and Smith (1973) make a similar point, viewing swinging as an evolutionary development that in the long run could be supportive of marriage by redefining the boundaries of marriage through the incorporation of extramarital sex into the relationship.

Other researchers call for caution. One study indicated that while some couples could incorporate swinging into their life-styles without apparent difficulty, other couples might find their marriage relationship deteriorating as a result (Gilmartin, 1974; see also Gilmartin and Kusisto, 1973). Denfeld's (1974) study of reports from marriage counselors on reasons couples drop out of swinging found that in nearly a quarter of the cases, jealousy was the main reason. Some of the other reasons were guilt, threatening the marriage relationship, becoming emotionally involved with other sexual partners, boredom and disappointment when swinging didn't live up to expectations and fantasies, and fear of discovery by the community and by the couple's children. Denfeld emphasizes that until a probability sample of past, present, and future swingers is used as the basis of a study, there will be many gaps in our knowledge of co-marital sex and its effects on the husband-wife relationship.

Different Views of Sexuality   In the seventeenth century, an English clergyman, Jeremy Taylor (1650, chap. 2, sec. 3–2), suggested these reasons for marital sex relations: "a desire for children, or to avoid fornication, or to lighten and ease the cares and sadnesses of household affairs, or to endear each other." Taylor's list suggests that persons may think of sexual intercourse in terms of various functions. Some persons may consider the main purpose of sex to be procreation, while others may emphasize recreation or mention the function of sex as communication. Or perhaps they think of it in terms of sheer physical release.

Lower-educated couples tend to have more children and to find birth control more problematic than is true of couples at higher status levels. Hence, sex-as-procreation no doubt looms high in the thinking of couples at lower levels, along with views of sex-as-release. Lower-status wives in Rainwater's studies made remarks like these: "It's just getting the sexual urge out of him." "He needs it like a starving man needs food." A husband reported that "a guy gets heated up and after he has it he feels good," adding that his wife felt better and slept better after intercourse, too (1965:113; 1960:135).

As education increases, couples may emphasize other kinds of gratifications associated with sexual intercourse (see Rainwater 1965:111, Table 3–15). Sex-as-communication ("endearing each other," to use Taylor's quaint seventeenth-century expression) is considered an important part of the overall communication and empathy in general that characterizes higher-status marriages. In addition, such husbands and wives appear to give more attention to sex-as-recreation. Sexual intercourse may be considered part of the companionship side of marriage, a pleasant leisure activity or fun time in which the spouses can delight together. Kinsey (1953, chap. 9) reported that couples who spent a half hour or an hour in sexual foreplay were likely to be couples from the better-educated groups in his sample. And Gebhard's (1966) data correlating marital satisfaction and wives' orgasmic experience showed that a couple's *spending time* in sexual activity was the key factor in enabling the wife to experience orgasm. As we have seen, the Kinsey studies showed that higher female orgasm rates occurred among higher-educated couples; and such couples were also found to be more willing to experiment with different sexual techniques (Gebhard, 1971:209). It may be that with higher education comes a greater acceptance and appreciation of the human body and all that sexuality has to offer in human experience. Also, higher-status couples have a greater sense of mastery with regard to birth control, and they may tend to have less fear that recreational sex will accidentally turn into procreational sex!

Frequency of Sexual Intercourse One area of marital sexuality where there seems to be little difference by social status is the matter of how often a husband and wife have sexual intercourse. Studies have shown weekly frequency to depend more on age and on the number of years married than upon social status. In Kinsey's sample, women who married in their late teens reported an average of nearly three times a week during the early years of marriage. By age thirty, the average was slightly more than twice a week. By age forty, the average had dropped to one and a half times weekly; and by age fifty, it was once a week. For sixty-year-old women, coitus was reported to take place about once every twelve days (Kinsey et al., 1953, chap. 9).

In the 1965 National Fertility Study, it was also found that social status was associated with little variation in coital frequency. Similarly, race was found to make almost no difference. White husbands and wives engaged in sexual intercourse an average of 6.8 times a month, while for nonwhites the average was 6.5. As far as religion is concerned, non-Catholics had a slightly higher average monthly frequency (7.1) than did Catholics (6.3). Couples as a whole who were married less than a year had sexual relations an average of ten or eleven times a month, whereas for couples married twenty-five years the average was about five times monthly (Ryder and Westoff, 1971:174; Westoff and Westoff, 1971:23–24).

When demographers began comparing data from the 1965 and 1970 National Fertility Studies, an interesting finding emerged. The evidence suggested that a real increase in frequency of sexual intercourse had taken place among married couples during the five-year interval. (See Table 12-C.)

The first explanation for increased coital frequency that might suggest itself is that contraceptive technology has improved and better methods are now available. Therefore, couples can have intercourse more often without worrying about the risk of pregnancy. This explanation seems plausible and may have some validity; the highest (age-standardized) frequencies of intercourse take place among couples where the contraceptive method employed is the pill, IUD, or vasectomy. However, the increase in frequency has also occurred among couples using all the other contraceptive methods as well—and even among couples not using contraception at all. (See Table 12-D.)

Demographer Charles F. Westoff (1974a) has suggested several possible reasons for these findings. Anxieties about unwanted pregnancies may have

TABLE 12-C   *Mean coital frequency in four weeks prior to interview, by age, 1965 and 1970, National Fertility Studies*

AGE	MEAN		NUMBER OF WOMEN	
	1965	1970	1965	1970
All women	6.8	8.2	4,603	5,432
20	10.7	11.0	203	223
20–24	8.4	10.1	835	1,127
25–29	7.4	9.0	828	1,223
30–34	6.8	8.0	913	1,017
35–39	5.9	6.8	878	947
40–44	5.1	5.9	946	895

SOURCE: Westoff, 1974a, p. 137.

been reduced not only by modern contraceptive technology but also through the availability of legal abortion. And an increasingly open climate regarding sexual matters also took place during the second half of the 1960s, with sex coming to be viewed more and more as something natural rather than as something taboo. "More fundamentally," reports Westoff, "there has been a developing emphasis on a woman's right to personal fulfillment. . . . Part of this growing ideology is that woman's traditional passive sexual role may be giving way to more assertive sexual behavior." The data showed that the more education a wife had, the more frequently the couple had intercourse. Furthermore, the more modern or egalitarian were her attitudes on gender roles, the higher was coital frequency. The researchers also found that wives who worked for reasons other than money had sexual intercourse more often than wives who were not employed or who worked chiefly for financial reasons. And wives who were seriously engaged in *careers* had sexual intercourse more frequently than all other wives. This brings us to our next topic.

THE EXPRESSIVE DIMENSION IN EMERGING MARRIAGE PATTERNS

Although some of what we have discussed so far in this chapter applies to marriages in general, and some even to emerging marriage patterns (such as the study of commuter marriages), the main thrust of the chapter has centered upon traditional marriage patterns. We have been focusing on the importance of the husband's position in the economic-opportunity structure, specifically in the case of head-complement marriages in which the husband is the unique family breadwinner. Now we want to move on to ask what happens to the expressive dimension of marriage in those emerging marriage patterns where the wife is also in the labor force—particularly in those cases where women have not merely jobs, but *careers*.

TABLE 12-D *Observed and age-standardized mean coital frequency in four weeks prior to interview, by type of exposure to the risk of conception, 1965 and 1970, National Fertility Studies*

TYPE OF EXPOSURE	MEAN OBSERVED		MEAN AGE-STANDARDIZED[a]		NUMBER OF WOMEN	
	1965	1970	1965	1970	1965	1970
All women	6.8	8.2	7.0	8.2	4,603	5,432
Noncontraceptive total	**5.9**	**7.2**	**6.0**	**7.2**	**1,681**	**1,907**
Pregnant	6.0	6.4	4.9	5.4	367	380
Postpartum	0.1	0.9	0.0	1.0	70	65
Trying to get pregnant	8.0	10.2	7.3	9.2	239	356
Sterile[b]	5.5	6.5	6.1	8.0	436	433
Subfecund[c]	6.0	7.3	7.0	8.4	201	265
Other nonuse	6.1	7.0	6.2	7.2	368	408
Contraceptive total	**7.3**	**8.8**	**7.5**	**8.8**	**2,922**	**3,525**
Wife sterilized[d]	6.5	7.0	7.1	7.6	234	322
Husband sterilized[d]	7.8	8.8	8.2	9.6	127	264
Pill[e]	9.2	10.0	8.4	9.2	690	1,211
IUD[f]	9.9	9.4	9.6	8.9	41	267
Diaphragm[g]	7.2	8.2	7.9	8.8	271	189
Condom[h]	6.6	8.1	6.9	8.5	629	490
Withdrawal	5.8	8.5	7.5	8.6	112	74
Foam	7.8	9.2	6.2	8.5	108	216
Rhythm	5.6	7.1	5.9	7.6	285	206
Douche	7.0	7.1	7.1	7.6	196	126
Other[i]	6.5	7.3	6.8	7.5	229	160

[a]The 1970 age distribution of the total sample has been used as the standard distribution throughout, thereby simultaneously eliminating both the effects of different age distributions associated with different exposure categories and the changes in age distribution from 1965 to 1970.
[b]Includes women who have had sterilizing operations for noncontraceptive reasons or who report that conception is impossible because of menopause or that they or their doctor are certain they cannot have another child.
[c]Includes women who believe they cannot have another child, but who are less certain than women classified as "sterile."
[d]Surgical procedures undertaken at least partly for contraceptive reasons.
[e]Includes combination with any other method.
[f]Includes combination with any method except pill.
[g]Includes combination with any method except pill or IUD.
[h]Includes combination with any method except pill, IUD, or diaphragm.
[i]Includes other multiple as well as single methods and a small percentage of unreported methods.
SOURCE: Westoff, 1974a, p. 138.

WIFE'S OCCUPATION AND PERSONAL AND FAMILY SOCIAL STATUS

Until recently, few questions were raised about the measurement of a woman's social status in terms of her relationship to a male. A 1966 book on college students, for example, asserted that "a woman's socially defined success is typically dependent not on her own occupational and job mobility but on her husband's," and that a female has but "one departure and arrival in her life cycle: her exchange of a father-determined social status for a husband-determined one" (quoted in Haug, 1973). Sociologist Joan Acker (1973:938) calls into question such assumptions. If women have such status-determining resources as education, occupation, and income, why don't these resources count as they do for men? Furthermore, asks Acker, why do we assume that such resources "are inoperative if the woman is married?"

Another sociologist, Marie R. Haug (1973:88), says that the practice of measuring a family's social status in terms of the husband-father alone might have seemed justified half a century ago when social scientists were beginning to introduce social-stratification measures. The proportion of employed married women was low at that time. "But there is no rational basis for persisting in outmoded practices in the face of changed realities in the work world," writes Haug.

Haug's criticisms of traditional measurement practices spring from an awareness that increasing numbers of women have occupational roles, that a woman's income added to her husband's can make a significant impact on a family's life-style (making possible a move to the suburbs or the sending of the children to college, for example), and that furthermore there are cases in which the wife's education and occupational status may be higher than her husband's (for example, where the husband has only a high school education and works as a door-to-door salesperson while his wife has a college degree and teaches school). Why should the family's social status be assigned according to his job rather than hers? Could their occupational rankings somehow both be taken into account? Or should social status be based upon the occupation or income of the one who would be given the higher ranking on the usual scales? These are questions to which some sociologists are giving attention.

Interestingly, a sensitivity to issues related to this matter was evident in the decision of the Census Bureau to move away from the traditional designation of the husband as "head of household" in the 1980 census. Instead, a "householder" ("the first adult household member listed on the census questionnaire") is considered to be the central "reference person." The reason? "Recent social changes have resulted in a trend toward more nearly equal status for adult members of a household and, therefore, have made the term 'head' increasingly inappropriate." (U.S. Bureau of the Census, *Current Population Reports*, P-60, no. 118, 1979:9).

However, most studies in existence have used one or all of the occupation-income-education factors in relation to the *husband* as the basis of determining a family's social position in the class structure. The explanation lies in the fact that most families up till now have followed the traditional pattern in which the husband is considered the chief provider. If his wife works (as in the senior partner–junior partner arrangement), his work is considered the more important. His commitment to his work is greater than hers, and his job rather than hers determines where the family moves. For all these reasons, the husband has been viewed as being more closely interwoven into the economic-opportunity system than the wife.

But this may change in the future as more and more women show a commitment to careers equal to that of men. A woman may be able to claim social status in her own right based on her own educational and occupational accomplishments. We may speculate that women with higher status will be able to bestow the benefits of that status on their husbands just as husbands presently reward wives with the fruits of the opportunity system. The roles and rewards will be equal and interchangeable. But what will this do to the husband-wife relationship? In what way, if any, does a wife's employment affect marital expressiveness?

EXPRESSIVE INTERACTION AND WIVES WITH CAREERS

If we think in terms of equal commitment to careers by husband and wife (an equal-partner arrangement rather than a senior partner–junior partner marriage), it is possible to theorize in terms of the model in Figure 12-4 and to suggest that expressiveness could be enhanced and strengthened rather than weakened by a wife's full participation in the economic-opportunity system. In the exchange model depicting traditional marriages in Figure 12-1, the movement of the arrows showed that the husband's fulfillment of his instrumental duties (breadwinning) called forth his wife's response in the expressive realm so that she fulfilled her duties of nurturance and affection. In Figure 12-4, we have *two* persons doing each of these things. Thus there is a reinforcement or doubling of the processes involved in the expressive side of marriage.

FIGURE 12-4   *The equal-partner marriage as a "two-story house" (to be compared with Figure 12-1). Source: Partially adapted from Scanzoni, 1972, p. 141.*

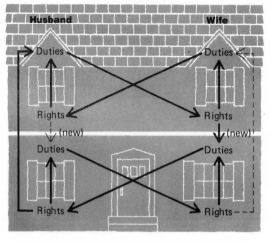

Upper story: The *instrumental* dimension of marriage (economic, task-oriented, practical side of marriage)

Lower story: The *expressive* dimension of marriage (empathy, companionship, physical affection, the personal side of marriage)

The model works like this: Where both partners are equally committed to careers and involved *directly* in the economic-opportunity system (rather than the wife's indirect involvement through her husband as in traditional marriage arrangements), the situation becomes one of husband-wife role reciprocity based upon equal-partner status and provider-role interchangeability. The process of fulfilling rights and duties changes from the process we examined in the traditional marriage model. No longer do the wife's instrumental duties include chief responsibility for household tasks; they are shared equally with the husband, for they are now included as part of his instrumental duties. But the wife's duties now also include equal responsibility with the husband for supplying the couple with economic and status rewards from the opportunity system. The rights of both husband and wife are met by these exchanges which in turn motivate them further to perform these instrumental duties (upper story of the house) as well as expressive duties (ground floor of the diagram). Their respective expressive rights are thereby fulfilled, further motivating each spouse in both expressive duties and instrumental duties.

As Figure 12-4 shows, what is new here is that now as the husband perceives that his economic and status rights are being met through his wife's provision, he has an *added* incentive for performing his expressive duties toward her (enhanced empathy, companionship, and physical affection). Another new feature is the way the husband's performance of expressive duties meets the wife's *rights* in the expressive realm in such a way that she is motivated to maintain ongoing occupational achievement. The husband-wife reciprocities that take place in equal-partner marriages are exactly the same for each spouse—which contrasts with the description of traditional marriages in Figure 12-1.

But isn't it rather crass to speak in terms of such reciprocities—the exchange of material benefits for expressiveness and vice versa? Actually, the idea isn't new in a *one*-sided way. Most persons have heard or read the laments of rejected suitors who complain, "She said she wouldn't marry me because I have nothing to offer her." It's the *two*-sidedness of what we're saying that may seem somewhat startling. The point being made isn't that love is something one buys. Nor do couples necessarily consciously think in terms of *rights* and *duties* in thinking of expressiveness in marriage. But what the model shows is that a process does occur in which the couple's relationship with the economic-opportunity structure has an impact on the spouses' relationship with each other as well; and that furthermore, their expressive interactions provide added motivation for achievement in the opportunity system so that they are able to provide one another with that system's rewards.

At present, there is not much actual data on how a wife's working affects the relationship between her and her husband. Much more research needs to be done as increasing numbers of women are taking seriously their option to seek employment outside the home, including strong commitment to demanding careers. However, let's examine what research is available at present and build upon that in order to speculate what future marital interaction might be like in the expressive realm, considering once again the three areas of empathy, companionship, and physical affection.

EMPATHY

In the past, the large-scale studies which have given attention to working wives and marital satisfaction have concentrated for the most part on marriages of the senior partner–junior partner variety. Equal-partner marriages have constituted such a small percentage of marriages until now that they have largely been ignored. Therefore, in trying to ascertain the effects of wife employment on marital expressiveness, we must keep in mind that we are speaking chiefly of marriages where the wife is in the junior-partner role; she has a job, but is not committed to a career with the same seriousness that characterizes her husband.

Even limiting our focus to junior-partner wives, we still do not come up with easy, clear-cut answers by examining the sociological literature on the subject. Occasionally, researchers even reach opposite conclusions. For example, after the Blood and Wolfe (1960:101–102) study of Detroit households, Blood (1963:304) concluded that a wife's employment was likely to lead to a more positive evaluation of the marriage if the couple were lower status than if they were higher status, presumably because of the tangible rewards provided by the wife in a situation where money is most needed. The findings of other sociologists suggest just the opposite. Marital dissatisfaction appears to be associated with the wife's employment at lower status levels much more than is likely in marriages where education, income, and job prestige are higher (Nye, 1963; 1974b).

Two researchers who studied a sample of 1,325 poverty-level families found employed wives indicating less general marital satisfaction than nonemployed wives. Employed wives also felt their husbands were less satisfied as well. The working wives perceived their husbands to be less satisfied with the time the couple spent together, the meals served, and just the fact of the wife's working. Actually, the wife's work was one of the two main areas in which conflict among lower-status couples with employed wives was greater than among comparable couples where the wives were not working. The other conflict area was sex (Feldman and Feldman, 1973).

These findings fit with Goode's observation that lower-status husbands tend to view their wives' working as a usurping of the husband's provider role. From his study of divorced women, Goode (1956) concluded that if a husband feels threatened in his traditional male role, it can negatively affect expressiveness in the marriage. Harold Sheppard and Neal Herrick (1972:27–28), who specialize in employment research, also found that blue-collar worker dissatisfaction was higher among those men whose wives worked. The researchers reported that these findings were "completely unexpected," because they had assumed that the higher family income would mean *less* discontentment. They surmised that perhaps at the blue-collar level "mach-ismo" might be a factor. "It may be that such men don't feel that they've really succeeded if, *all by themselves,* they can't provide their families with the necessary income to pay for the level of living to which they aspire."

In some of our earlier research, we found that although empathy satisfaction was higher in general among higher-status couples than among lower-status couples, a wife's employment did make a difference *within* these respective categories. A higher-status husband whose wife was employed was less likely to be satisfied with marital empathy than a comparable husband whose wife was not employed. In contrast, an employed wife in a higher-status marriage was likely to be more satisfied with marital empathy than was true of a nonemployed wife. It may be that the higher the status of the husband, the more he may have defined his wife's employment activities as a drain on time and energy that could have been better invested in empathy and attention to their life together. On the other hand, the wife in such a marriage may have felt satisfied that her rights were being granted her by being able to carry out her option to work; therefore in exchange she responded to her husband with what she considered to be a satisfactory level of empathy and defined his empathic responses as positive as well. Again, this may be a case of spouses' "reading" an identical situation quite differently (Scanzoni, 1970:129).

Such a husband-wife difference in the definition of the situation also characterized lower-status couples. But what happened was just the reverse of the husband-wife perceptions at higher status levels, and illustrates even further that the relationship between a wife's employment and satisfaction with various areas of expressiveness is not clear-cut. We found in the 1967 study (Scanzoni, 1970) that lower-status husbands were more satisfied with marital empathy if their wives worked, while employed wives at lower-status levels were less satisfied with empathy than nonemployed wives. It is possible that husbands placed such positive value on the money supplied by working wives that they were also able to empathize with them as persons who shared the burden of breadwinning. However, lower-status working wives, aware of the societal norms about the husband's primary role of provider, may have projected onto their husbands their fears that the men might feel threatened and "emasculated" by the wives' earnings. These fears and projections in turn might have caused wives to feel that processes of communication and understanding were less satisfactory than would have been the case in marriages where wives were not working.

In a study of employed wives and marital happiness, sociologists Susan Orden and Norman Bradburn (1969) found that *free choice* about working is highly important. They found that "marriages at all levels of the social structure are affected adversely when the woman is in the labor market only out of necessity," while on the other hand, a woman's working out of free choice has a positive effect on marital happiness. At only one point did these researchers find that the marriage relationship was strained by a wife's working out of free choice, and that was when there were preschoolers at home. "At other stages in the life cycle," report Orden and Bradburn, "the choice between the labor market and the home market makes little difference in an individual's assessment of his own marriage happiness" (pp. 405, 392).

Evidence from a later large-scale study of our own also seems to indicate that a wife's working may not be as important in evaluating marital expressive satisfaction as has been assumed in the past. Satisfaction with empathy, companionship, and physical affection was shown to be no different for either husbands or wives regardless of whether or not wives were employed (Scanzoni, 1975b). And after a study of Swedish working wives, Murray Gendell (1963:132–133) reported similarly: "On the basis of these data . . . we must conclude that working wives are neither more or less satisfied with their marriages than housewives." Fogarty and his associates (1971:475) came to a similar conclusion with regard to husbands after studying marriages with employed wives in England. "Taking all families together," they wrote, "it cannot be said that in the social group investigated 'wife working' has any clear-cut effect, whether positive or negative, on husband's estimate of happiness of the marriage."

Perhaps all we can say then with regard to marital-empathy satisfaction as it relates to wives' occupational achievement is simply that more research needs to be done—particularly with respect to equal-partner marriages. On the basis of very small samples and limited case studies, we might propose that empathy could conceivably be strengthened and increased in the dual-career marriage. Each spouse is rewarding the other with both economic-status benefits and expressive benefits. Since each is involved in a career, each can understand and empathize with the other's career concerns. There is a very real sense of putting oneself in the other's position and entering into that person's feelings and experiences because they are much like one's own and thus can be understood. Reciprocal advice and counsel can be exchanged between the husband and wife, since there is likely to be a feeling of colleagueship and equality that calls forth empathy. Such couples do not live in the separate worlds labeled "his" and "hers" which traditional sex roles have fostered (Fogarty, et al., 1971:477–478).

Colleagueship in Equal-Partner Marriages   In traditional marriages, a husband's colleagues are usually his work associates and not the members of his conjugal family. But in Holmstrom's (1972) study contrasting more traditional marriages with those that follow the dual-career pattern, she found that "when both marital partners have careers, the possibility exists that they will also be colleagues. If so, it adds a new dimension to the marriage" (p. 121). Holstrom found that a sense of professional colleagueship between married partners may take the form of working together jointly on the same projects (where their fields of specialty are similar or complementary) or in exchanging advice, making suggestions, and in general discussing one another's work. Sometimes, their influence on one another's careers takes more subtle forms, often in processes they may be unaware of at the time—such as in the books and magazines they bring into the home, the professional contacts each makes, the people to whom they may introduce one another, and so on.

In contrast, Holmstrom found that women who had given up their careers to devote full time to their marriages responded quite differently when asked about their influence on their husbands' work. They often replied "as a wife" rather than "as a colleague." They tended to see their roles as buffers between the husband and the pressures and demands of his work or as promoting the husband's career by playing various subordinate helping roles "rather than by collaborating or commenting as a colleague might."

Examples from dual-career marriages suggest a sharply contrasting pattern. An academic couple refers to the intellectual stimulation each provides the other with regard to their respective university careers: "Our collaboration now takes the form of long talkathons in which we discuss the subject, develop new points, downgrade old ones, and sharpen our wits on each other's thought" (Bernard, 1964:234). Joanne Simpson (1973), a meteorologist, provides another example as she tells of meeting her husband in a professional association and developing even before marriage into "a terrific research team with complementary skills." Where one was weak the other was strong, so that the two of them were able to create more than double the sum of their individual efforts. Even when federal Civil Service nepotism rules prevented their continuing to work together so that their work interests were brought into conflict, the sense of colleagueship continued. Simpson reports, "The conflict is compensated for in part by the common language, the associates, and the intellectual interests which we share."

The empathy that can spring from colleagueship in an equal-partner marriage does not necessarily require that the husband and wife be doing the same work. The mere fact of their both being active in the economic-opportunity system can result in the kind of sharing mentioned above—common intellectual interests, associates, and so on, plus the exchange of counsel, advice, criticism, and suggestions in the empathic spirit that can occur between persons equally involved in career achievement goals.

COMPANIONSHIP

Because of the sheer demands of time and energy required by an occupation, we might expect to find that husband-wife companionship suffers when the wife takes on outside employment. We did not find this to be true in recent research (Scanzoni, 1975b), although there was some indication of a negative effect of wife employment on companionship in the 1967 study of Indianapolis marriages (Scanzoni, 1970:38–41). In that particular sample at that particular time, there were indications that companionship satisfaction was greater if the wife was not working. But if the wife *was* working, once again there were variations by social status. In households where the wife held a higher-status job, both husbands and wives were much more satisfied with

In an equal-partner marriage, greater empathy satisfaction may derive from a sense of colleagueship. (Temple University)

marital companionship than was the case in households where the wife held a lower-status job. Women with higher-status jobs are usually married to men with higher education and higher-status jobs as well, men who have achieved and who are secure enough in their provider role not to feel threatened by their wives' working.

Earlier, Blood and Wolfe (1960) had found that wives most satisfied with marital companionship were those who concentrated on entertaining their husbands' business associates and clients, and who devoted themselves to understanding their husbands' business problems and helping their husbands get ahead rather than concentrating on careers for themselves. Those next most satisfied were wives who worked as collaborators with their husbands in joint enterprises. Employed wives were the least satisfied with companionship out of these three categories (because "her work partly separates her from her husband"), but such wives were more satisfied than were the traditional stay-at-home housewives. In the words of Blood and Wolfe, "Lowest of all [in companionship satisfaction] is the wife who 'sticks to her knitting' while the husband is absorbed in his own business. This traditional-type marriage involves relatively little companionship" (p. 167).

One of the findings that surprised Orden and Bradburn (1969) in their study of wife employment and marital happiness was that husbands whose wives worked part-time ranked companionship satisfaction higher than did all other husbands—including those whose wives were employed full-time and those whose wives were not employed at all. It was also found in this same study that the wives who freely chose part-time work were more happy than women who had freely chosen either to work full-time or to be full-time homemakers.

Gendell's (1963:133) study of Swedish working wives likewise led him to conclude that part-time workers were slightly more satisfied in their marriages than either full-time housewives or full-time employed wives—though the differences were really too small to be considered significant. And Fogarty and his associates (1971:478) also found some indication of greater satisfaction with part-time wife employment in England.

Companionship in career-oriented, equal-partner marriages requires planning and effort. On the one hand, companionship in such marriages could be enhanced by the spirit of colleagueship and the common interests that are discussed and mutually engaged in (such as travel together relating to one or the other's career where possible, or reading the same books and journals). On the other hand, companionship by definition means doing things together in leisure time; and where both husband and wife are fully committed to career interests, leisure time is likely to be at a premium and may at times seem nonexistent.

Part of the problem stems from what Fogarty and his associates call "overload"—the double job that is usually faced by an employed wife because of the traditional assumption that the management of the home is her responsibility in addition to her outside work. Trying to do two jobs might easily tax her energies and time so greatly that companionship is considerably reduced—something that her husband might resent. Perhaps this is why some of the studies indicated that there was greater satisfaction on the part of both husbands and wives if the wife chose part-time employment. Yet, this way of dealing with the problem is not satisfactory for many highly educated women. For one thing, suitable part-time employment is not easy to find; and for another, part-time employment does not bring with it the economic and prestige rewards that full-time work commitment does. Furthermore, many women simply prefer a continuous, highly committed work pattern. They are more apt to feel the solution to the time and energy problem lies in persuading husbands to share more of the overload, perhaps even finding companionship through jointly performing household tasks while also making more time available for leisure-time activities.

Dual-career families also need to make adjustments more than other families in ordering their social life. Fogarty and his colleagues (1971:477) concluded from their studies that dual-career families have special difficulties "in finding time for contacts with relatives and neighbours." And Bernard (1964:240) quotes an academic wife who said, "I must confess that entertaining for me is more of a chore than a pleasure because I keep thinking of all the time that its preparation takes away from my own work." Holmstrom

(1972:98) tells of one two-career couple who solved the problem through the husband's suggestion that they entertain friends by using some of their increased income to take them out to restaurants rather than serving a meal at home.

In marriages where husbands and wives can agree on priorities, the quality of their time together can make up for the lack of quantity. An art professor who says "there's a lot to be said for companionship in marriage" has remarked that her career could not have progressed as it has if she had been married to "a nine-to-five man with weekends off who expected attention" during his leisure time. The man she did marry is a highly respected photographer, photojournalist, and teacher who shares his wife's creative interests and who says, "The nice thing is we talk to each other. We always seem to have something to talk about" (Moore, 1974:15). In such marriages, the empathy of colleagueship seems to result in companionship that is considered highly satisfactory despite busy schedules necessitated by the spouses' equal involvement in the economic-opportunity structure (see Garland, 1972:213–214).

PHYSICAL AFFECTION

Persons who think in stereotyped sex roles often express worries that a couple's sexual relationship will be harmed if the wife shares the breadwinner role. Fogarty and his associates (1971:356) described these fears: "The assumption here is that women who want to enter the male world of competition would be highly motivated by competitiveness with men and, as a consequence, would tend to emasculate their husbands. The assumption follows that these couples' sex lives would be characterized by impotence and frigidity." However, while acknowledging that such a pattern might occur in certain cases, these researchers did not find evidence from their data that working wives are characterized by desires to lord it over men. Rather, the women in their sample indicated that they worked for reasons of financial security, the need to be creative, and "the desire to be effective as an individual person." As far as the sex lives of the couples in the Fogarty study were concerned, "the impression is one of a 'normal' range of sexual experience."

In our 1967 Indianapolis study, we found that husbands whose wives did not work were more satisfied with the love and physical affection received in their marriages than were husbands whose wives worked. This was true at all status levels. By the same token, wives who were employed were more satisfied with the love and physical affection in their marriages than were wives who did not work. Again, this was found at all status levels.

These husband-wife differences might relate to sex-role stereotypes and traditional notions of masculinity as it is tied into both the sexual realm and the provider role (especially at lower status levels) and a sense of resentment that the time and energy wives devote to their jobs may seem to be "stolen" from loving attention and affection that could have been given to husbands instead (particularly at higher status levels where wives are likely to have more education and higher-level jobs which make greater demands). For the wives' part, the sense of self-worth experienced through direct access to the economic-opportunity system and the sense of contributing financially to the family, plus the belief that their working meant their husbands had granted them something wives increasingly define as not only an option but a right—freedom to work—may have meant that the wives experienced a sense of contentment which carried over to their perception of the physical affection in marriage as well (Scanzoni, 1970).

Much more research needs to be done to determine the impact that wives' employment actually makes on the physical expression of love in marriage. Our more recent study indicated that a woman's working outside the home made no significant difference at all in husbands and wives' evaluation of satisfaction in this dimension of marriage (Scanzoni, 1975b). Indeed, some social scientists have suggested that, rather than hurting a couple's sex life, a wife's working might enhance it. The husband and wife can relate as two separate individuals who have developed their personal identities in the occupational world; thus each has more to bring to the other in the overall marital relationship, including the sexual aspects of that relationship (Fogarty et al., 1971:356).

Sociologist Alice Rossi (1964:139) has argued this point in countering charges made by defenders of traditional sex roles who claim that equality of the sexes would upset the male-female sexual relationship. While acknowledging that full sex equality would no doubt be the death knell of the traditional arrangement in which "the sex act presupposes a dominant male actor and a passive female subject," Rossi suggests that husbands and wives who participate equally in parental, occupational, and social roles "will complement each other sexually in the same way, as essentially equal partners, and not as an ascendant male and a submissive female." Rather than detract from the sexual experience, equality can enhance it since the "enlarged base of shared experience" in other realms can heighten satisfaction with the sexual experience as well.

Rossi's argument fits with an exchange-theory approach to the equal-partner marriage. If there are equal exchanges of rights and duties occurring in both the instrumental and expressive dimensions of marriage in general, might we not expect equal exchanges to go on in the sexual relationship as well?

Likewise, role interchangeability in the equal-partner marriage might be expected to extend to the realm of physical affection. Psychologist A. H. Maslow (1970) has alluded to such role interchangeability in sexual relations. Maslow devoted his attention to studying characteristics of persons with a strong sense of self-esteem and self-realization, persons "who have developed or are developing to the full stature of which they are capable." He termed such persons "self-actualizing" and found that one of their characteristics was that "they made no really sharp differentiation between the roles and personalities of the two sexes." Maslow explains:

That is, they did not assume that the female was passive and the male active, whether in sex or love or anything else. These people were all so certain of their maleness or femaleness that they did not mind taking on some of the cultural aspects of the opposite sex role. It was especially noteworthy that they could be both active and passive lovers and this was the clearest in the sexual act and in physical love-making. Kissing and being kissed, being above or below in the sexual act, taking the initiative, being quiet and receiving love, teasing and being teased—these were all found in both sexes. The reports indicated that both were enjoyed at different times. It was considered to be a shortcoming to be limited to just active love-making or passive love-making. Both have their particular pleasures for self-actualizing people. (p. 189)

As opportunities for women to exercise their full potentialities in the economic-opportunity system present themselves, the number of "self-actualizing" wives may be expected to increase. Thus the likelihood of growing numbers of couples in equal-partner marriages fitting the pattern Maslow describes may also increase.

Changes over Time In studying human sexuality, sociologists look for patterns, trends, and indications of what is happening among groups of people, rather than focusing on individual cases. We have already seen how social status can make a difference in the sexual attitudes and behavior of people. Similarly, a changing social climate over a period of time can also mean alterations in how people view sexual matters. Kinsey and his associates for example took into account changes in sexual practices which occurred over a period of forty years. Their sample of women was divided into categories according to decade of birth, beginning with women born before 1900, then those whose birth dates fell during the periods 1900–1909, 1910–1919, and 1920–1929. There were certain areas of sexual behavior where the decade of a woman's birth made much more difference than did her social class in how she had behaved sexually over the years.

Practices such as engaging in sexual intercourse in the nude or utilizing certain petting techniques in marital foreplay (for example, manipulating the husband's genitals or participating in oral-genital sex) were much less common among the older generation in Kinsey's sample than among the younger generation. Kinsey also found that a jump in the percentages of married women who had experienced orgasm had occurred over the four decades. He attributed these changes to a freer climate and more frankness about sexual matters, along with increased scientific understanding. "There were wives and husbands in the older generation who did not even know that orgasm was possible for a female," wrote the Kinsey researchers (1953, chap. 9), adding that even if persons did think female orgasm was possible, they couldn't conceive of it as being either pleasurable or proper.

In recent years, one of the biggest changes in attitudes toward marital sex has been with regard to the sexual needs, desires and behavior of women. The laboratory research of Masters and Johnson (1966) has clearly demonstrated the high capacity women have for sexual enjoyment, including the capability of experiencing multiple orgasms within a short space of time. Such findings would no doubt have shocked the sex lecturer who wrote in the early part of this century: "The best mothers [and] wives . . . know little or nothing of the sexual pleasure. Love of home, children, and domestic duties are the only passions they feel. As a rule, the modest woman submits to her husband, but only to please him (Shannon, 1917:162). Such lecturers and writers failed to realize that the lack of sexual interest in many married women was not a sign of the "natural order of things" or the "innate goodness of the female sex," but rather stemmed from the way females were socialized in a society that emphasized both sexual repression and the double standard. Such books helped perpetuate further the view that women were sexually disinterested and unresponsive.

Marriage Manuals and Changing Attitudes One way to get some idea of changing sexual attitudes over time is to examine marriage manuals from different historical periods. In an examination of American marital-education literature from the period of 1830 to 1940, sociologist Michael Gordon (1971) found a profound change in conceptions of the role of sex in marriage, a change he sums up in the title of his article on the subject, "From an Unfortunate Necessity to a Cult of Mutual Orgasm."

Many of the nineteenth-century books made it clear that sex should be viewed as a means to an end (procreation) rather than as an end in itself (pleasure). Warnings were sounded on the supposed dangers of excessive sex in marriage, and couples were alerted to the physical exhaustion and damage that might be incurred through overindulgence in sexual intercourse. Some books took pains to spell out exactly what "overindulgence" was, with the advice varying from calls for sexual abstinence except when a child was desired to suggestions that intercourse be limited to certain time periods. "Few should exceed the limit of once a week; while many cannot safely indulge oftener than once a month," instructed one sex manual written in 1866.

The emphasis on rationality, self-control, and moderation in marital sex was nothing new, but could be seen in writings from 200 years before. For example, the context of the comments of Jeremy Taylor, the seventeenth-century English divine quoted earlier, make it clear that he was just as concerned about misuses of sex in marriage as about its "proper" exercise. Avoiding fornication, seeking to have children, and desiring to find comfort from cares and to express endearment—these were legitimate ends; but "he is an ill husband that uses his wife as a man treats a harlot, having no other end but pleasure. The pleasure should always be joined to one or another of these ends . . . but never with a purpose, either in act or desire, to separate the sensuality from these ends which hallow it. Married people must never force themselves into high and violent lusts with arts and misbecoming devices, but be restrained and temperate in the use of their lawful pleasures." This statement was still being quoted as advice to couples in a 1917 sex-education manual (Shannon, 1917:162).

The typical Victorian wife and mother was expected to channel her passions in the direction of home, children, and domestic duties rather than to interest in or knowledge about sex. (The Bettmann Archive)

Toward the end of the nineteenth century and in the early decades of the twentieth, the winds of change began to blow—first a slight breeze and then a full-force gale. Sex took on a more important role in the marriage relationship, and pleasure for both partners began to be emphasized. Writers talked about "satisfactory sexual adjustment" and by the 1930s were giving instructions on how to achieve such adjustment. Learning and practicing such techniques was seen as an art, the goal of which was to be perfectly timed, simultaneous orgasm for husband and wife.

In almost paradoxical fashion, sex came to be viewed as *work* at the same time it came to be viewed as play. The growing societal approach to marital sexuality moved from the nineteenth-century emphasis on procreation to the twentieth-century emphasis on recreation, but as Gordon (1971:73) points out, it was recreation "at which one must work hard." "Work at sex because it's fun!" became the prevalent idea.

One of the first sociologists to point this out was Nelson Foote (1954), who responded to the 1953 publication of the Kinsey findings on female sexual behavior by writing an article called "Sex as Play." Referring to insights from the social psychology of play, Foote wrote that "'play—any kind of play—generates its own morality and values. And the enforcement of the rules of play becomes the concern of every player, because without their observance, the play cannot continue."

An examination of fifteen currently popular marriage manuals illustrates his point. Sociologists Lionel Lewis and Dennis Brissett (1967) found in these manuals an abundance of rules, duties, and do's and don'ts that husbands and wives are instructed to follow rigorously in their sexual relationship. Sex was presented almost as a chore, involving technical competence, skill development, a quest for mastery, a drive for success, and a fear of failure (defined mainly in terms of having or not having an orgasm). Deferred gratifications, self-denial, scheduling the various parts of the sexual act carefully, striving, performance, deliberation, management—these were the matters with which husbands and wives were to be concerned as they enjoyed themselves in recreational sex. Lewis and Brissett offered the thesis that "the American must justify his play . . . he has done this by transforming his play into work . . . work is felt to carry with it a certain inherent dignity." Lewis and Brissett speak of sex counselors and writers as "avocational counselors" in the same sense as teachers of other avocational interests (such as how to play tennis better, how to dance, ski, and so forth).

Sex researchers William Masters and Virginia Johnson (1973) also have written of "the influence of the work ethic on sexual attitudes in contemporary society" which convinces couples that "work is productive and he who works is virtuous, whereas play is wasteful and he who plays is sinful." Such a view, they emphasize, becomes goal-oriented and concerned with instant gratification rather than a mutual expression of affection between the partners in a context of overall communication and enjoyment of one another.

In Gordon's study of marriage manuals from 1830 to 1940, he noticed other patterns besides the swing from sex-as-procreation to sex-as-recreation to sex-as-work. For one thing, there occurred a change in attitudes toward birth control. Early writers were very negative about limiting family size, but some signs of change began to occur in the 1920s. In the 1930s (partially due to some legal changes), contraception came to be seen in a much more favorable light. Earlier, even writers who emphasized sex for pleasure tended to be reluctant to endorse birth-control practices—except periods of sexual abstinence.

The other most noticeable trend observed by Gordon in his study was the growing emphasis on female sexuality. Early books gave the impression that a woman could be expected to show little interest in coital relations with her husband. Later books still emphasized a woman's alleged lesser desire, but it was now suggested that a dormant sensuality lay within her, waiting to be awakened and called forth by her husband's skillful techniques of love. Full participation in *marital* sexual relations came to be viewed as a woman's right, and the husband's responsibility was to make sure she could exercise this right. As part of the trend toward recreational sex, some books began telling wives to seek to make sex pleasurable for their husbands as well.

What does any of this have to do with the subject at hand, namely the effect of a wife's working on the physical aspects of marital expressiveness? Gordon (1971:77) suggests, in view of trends he observed in his study of marriage manuals, that research is needed to find out "to what extent was the acceptance of female sexuality linked to the increasing number of women in the work force." As we have seen, the common owner-property arrangement of marriage began to change as the option to work opened to women. The wife's rights were increasing, as were her husband's duties toward her in the marital exchange— particularly with regard to fulfilling the wife's expressive rights. It is not surprising then that sexual satisfaction for wives began to receive increasing attention along with the rise in head-complement and senior partner–junior partner marriage patterns.

Yet, later research on female sexuality in more recent marriage manuals has caused Gordon and his coauthor Penelope Shankweiler (1971:465) to wonder if women have come as far as is sometimes thought. "Women in this century have been granted the right to experience sexual desire and have this desire satisfied," they write, "but always with the man calling the tune." They suggest that this is "a manifestation of the minority group status of women," since "if women have been encouraged to take more initiative it is in order that they might give more pleasure to their husbands rather than achieve more autonomy in the sexual realm." Gordon and Shankweiler refer to James Coleman's (1966) remark that female enjoyment of sexuality for its own sake can only come about "when a woman's status and ultimate position do not depend greatly on her husband."

Although the need continues for more research, evidence from the 1970 National Fertility Study cited earlier may indicate that many wives are already experiencing a greater degree of sexual autonomy and at least partially for the reason Coleman suggests. It could be argued that the increased frequency of sexual intercourse on the part of wives holding egalitarian gender-role norms, higher education, and career aspirations would seem to indicate more of a desire for sexual pleasure for its own sake than a desire to please husbands who "call the tune" on sexual matters because wives are economically dependent upon them.

But a wife's sexual autonomy need not rule out her desire to give sexual pleasure to her husband as well. In fact, in terms of exchange theory as illustrated in Figure 12-4, the wife in an equal-partner marriage has added reasons to provide such rewards to her partner just as he provides them to her. Some husbands may find that they are experiencing increased sexual enjoyment as egalitarian gender-role norms bring freedom from assuming the major responsibility for marital sex, and they may also find it rewarding to be released from pressures to perform and to view sex as a conquest. They may find that they like being able to receive as well as achieve. One man reported, after his wife became a feminist: "Our sex life has undergone a tremendous change, because I was no longer prepared for her to just lie back and look at the ceiling. . . . I deserve a little bit of looking at the ceiling too" (quoted in Fasteau, 1974:34).

The equal-partner marriage emphasizes role interchangeability. In such an arrangement, the responsibilities double in both the instrumental and expressive dimensions of marriage. But the rewards double as well. Thus, it is possible to postulate that as more and more marriages are built on the equal-partner pattern, marital expressiveness will be enhanced because of the broader base of joint interests and the increased and strengthened circuits of the marital exchange process.

CHAPTER HIGHLIGHTS

In the marital-adjustment school of thought, the emphasis is on avoiding conflicts and retaining harmony by adapting—even though such adjustment may mean submerging personal aspirations and interests. A major criticism of the marital-adjustment approach has centered on a realization that wives have been expected to adapt more than husbands. In contrast to the marital-adjustment school is an approach which stresses that marriage is a continual process of negotiation and benefit seeking. If the relationship ceases to be rewarding to one of the spouses, efforts can be directed toward *changing* the costly and punishing aspects of the situation instead of simply adjusting.

The *expressive* dimension of marriage includes three basic elements: *companionship* (someone to be with), *empathy* (someone who listens, understands, and cares), and *physical affection* (someone with whom love can be expressed through touch, caresses, and sexual intercourse). Research indicates that economic factors play an important part in the satisfactions husbands and wives perceive in the expressive dimension of marriage.

CHAPTER 13

(© Ginger Chih, 1978/Peter Arnold, Inc.)

PROCESS IN MARRIAGE: POWER AND NEGOTIATION

An experienced secretary and bookkeeper saw no reason that she shouldn't go back to work now that her children were in school. Her husband said no. Explaining the problem to a newspaper advice columnist, the woman wrote: "My husband said if I want to work outside the home I should work for him. (He owns a small retail business.) I don't want to work for him because he refuses to pay me. He says: 'You don't need any money of your own. If you want something, ask me and I'll give you the money for it.' (In the past when I've asked for money he has had to know where every dime is going.) He enjoys having me ask him for money. It makes him feel important" (*Bloomington-Bedford (Ind.) Sunday Herald Times*, "Dear Abby," June 9, 1974).

Persons who assert that marriage can stand on love alone are suggesting an imbalanced, precarious posture. Marriage requires two legs—love and justice. Aristotle in "The Nicomachean Ethics," defined justice as simply "the good of others." And Robert Seidenberg (1970:304), a psychiatrist, points out: "Love without justice is a yoke, which more often than not, not only enslaves but strangulates the human spirit." The wife in the letter quoted feels that she is being treated unfairly by her husband; she defines her situation as one of injustice, no matter what her husband may say about feelings of love for her.

However, if this wife presses for her rights and insists on furthering her own interests even though they are in opposition to her husband's interests, she is aware that a situation of conflict will develop. Negotiation will be necessary so that a satisfactory settlement can be reached and the relationship continued.

The issue of *power* also comes into play. The wife's power is limited by her dependence on her husband for resources. Aware of this, the husband refuses to allow her any discretionary income of her own even if she were to earn it in his place of business ("he refuses to pay me"). Instead he wants her to ask for any small amount as she needs it, thus keeping both himself and his wife alert to her dependence upon him and his power over her ("He enjoys having me ask him for money. It makes him feel important."). Further evidence of his power is the husband's demand for an accounting of how each dime is spent when he does give his wife money; there is a very real tie between his total control of the resources and his power in the marriage in general.

The wife senses that as long as she is utterly dependent upon her husband for material resources, his power over her will be great and she will find it necessary to go along with his wishes while submerging her own interests. Yet she seems to realize that if she can obtain resources of her own (the principle of alternate rewards as discussed in Chapter 7), her power will be increased and her husband's decreased.

Many persons have the mistaken notion that issues such as justice, negotiation, conflict, and power have no place in discussions of marriage. Such issues are thought to be appropriate when it comes to discussing political affairs or labor-management disputes but not when it comes to discussing the husband-wife relationship. Yet, since marriage is a social system, it involves social processes no less than do relationships between two parties negotiating business interests or two nations trying to work out a trade agreement.

WHAT IS POWER?

The word *power* derives from the Latin *potere,* which means "to be able." Power includes the ideas of ability and control. In this sense, "I can" is the essence of power. I can do something rather than being at the mercy of other forces. I can produce an effect on something or someone else. Thus, we speak of how science has increased the ability of humans to control the environment, to have power over nature, and so on.

As psychologist David Winter (1973) points out, the behavioral scientist is concerned specifically with *social* power. Winter's definition sums up the usual meaning of power as it is spoken of by psychologists, sociologists, and political scientists: "Social power is the ability or capacity of [one person or group] to produce (consciously or unconsciously) intended effects on the behavior or emotions of another person [or group]" (p. 5).

To put the whole matter very simply: power is the capability of having one's way and achieving one's goals—even though others may resist.

HOW SOCIOLOGISTS MEASURE MARITAL POWER

The concept of *marital* power has posed problems for sociologists, both in terms of defining it and measuring it. In fact, a great deal of controversy has raged over this subject in recent years as various sociologists who study the family have disagreed among themselves (Cromwell and Olson, 1975; Scanzoni, 1979b). The problem in defining marital power has occurred because some sociologists use the term synonymously with other terms, such as authority, decision-making, or influence, while other sociologists make distinctions between the various terms.

Sociologist Constantina Safilios-Rothschild (1970) makes the criticism that too many studies have examined only husband-wife *decision-making* in measuring marital power while failing to pay enough attention to what goes on behind the scenes, such as "the patterns of tension and conflict management, or the type of prevailing division of labor." She suggests that the total configuration of these behavioral patterns must be examined and not one aspect alone if power is to be understood. In Safilios-Rothschild's thinking, family power structure should be thought of in terms of three components: *authority* (who is considered to have the legitimate right to have the most say, according to prevailing cultural and social norms), *decision-making* (who makes the decisions, how often, and so on), and *influence* (less obvious maneuvering; the degree to which a spouse is able to impose his or her point of view through various subtle or not-so-subtle pressures even though the other spouse initially opposed that point of view.)

Another problem pointed out by some sociologists is that there may be various levels to familial power structure. Which level is being explored? Are we concerned with who makes particular decisions, or who decides that this person may make those decisions? Or even beyond that, who determines who will decide which spouse will make the decision? (Ryder, 1970; Komarovsky, 1962; Safilios-Rothschild, 1969, 1970). The picture begins to look like the proverbial "house that Jack built"!

In other words, suppose a husband and wife reach an impasse on a certain decision. Finally, just to get the matter settled so that the couple can go on with other things, one of them says to the other, "*You* decide. Since we can't make up our minds, I'll turn the matter over to you and I'll abide by your decision." The spouse who gets to make the decision may seem at first glance to be the one with the greater power; after all it is his or her wishes that will be carried out. However, as Safilios-Rothschild (1970:540) points out, "the one

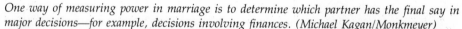

One way of measuring power in marriage is to determine which partner has the final say in major decisions—for example, decisions involving finances. (Michael Kagan/Monkmeyer)

spouse may relegate one or more decisions to the other spouse because he finds these decisions relatively unimportant and very time-consuming." The "relegating" spouse in such cases has considerably more power than the one who might appear to make the decisions, because the relegating spouse "can orchestrate the power structure in the family according to his preferences and wishes."

Survey Method of Studying Power   Sociologists study power in marriage by using two basic methods: *asking* or *watching and listening.* The "asking" method is sometimes called the survey method or the reputational method. A sample of husbands or wives (or both) is drawn, and questions are asked about the balance of power in their marriage. Sometimes a sample of children is drawn to find out which parent the children think has the greater power in the family. Variables such as social status, stage of the life cycle, and other factors are also introduced in an effort to find patterns that may aid in understanding marital power better. Questions used in the survey method may have to do with decision-making or with handling conflicts. Or a key question might be as direct as this: "Who is the real boss in your marriage?" A question used in several studies including our own research is this one: "When you disagree about [particular items the respondent has listed as areas of disagreement in his or her marriage], who usually gets his way, you or your spouse?" The spouse with the higher score of "winning out" in disagreements is considered to have the greater power.

One frequently used method of measuring marital power has been to ask respondents who makes the final decisions in each of a number of areas. The list might include matters like the choice of work for either spouse, vacation decisions, what kind of car to buy, and so on. Blood and Wolfe (1960) utilized this method in their pioneering Detroit study of husband-wife relationships. Yet, their approach to the issue of power has been criticized because each of the eight items they listed was given equal weight. In other words, when they tabulated the final results to find out a person's power score, decisions about the weekly food budget were treated as being just as important as the choice of the husband's job or the purchase of a house.

The problem of measuring power is further complicated by a lack of consistency in the kinds of questions asked even when marital power is thought of only in terms of decision-making. Blood and Wolfe (1960) singled out eight areas of household decision-making; and while some studies have duplicated these, other studies have utilized lists containing other items. Thus, it is difficult to compare studies (Safilios-Rothschild, 1970).

Another problem in connection with the survey approach relates to the respondents who are being queried. Some studies have focused on wives only, whereas other studies have sought to find out husbands' perception of decision-making power. There are also studies in which *both* husbands and wives are asked their perceptions of power within their marriages, and in addition there are studies in which children are asked to tell whom they perceive to have the greater power in their respective families. Comparison of various studies again becomes a problem, because it has been amply demonstrated that different members of the family may perceive the power structure differently (see Turk and Bell, 1972; Scanzoni, 1965; Safilios-Roths-child, 1969; Brown and Rutter, 1966; Hess and Torney, 1962).

In addition to the problems clustering around the kinds of questions that are asked and the persons who are asked them, there remains the more basic problem of limiting measurements of power to the matter of decision-making alone. Some sociologists suggest that rather than focusing on the *outcome* of decision-making, it might prove more fruitful to concentrate on the *process* by which decisions are arrived at (Olson and Rabunsky, 1972; Scanzoni, 1979b). But how can sociologists study the processes of decision-making that go on within family units? This brings us to the second commonly used method for investigating marital power.

Observational-Experimental Method of Studying Power Whereas the survey method is built around asking, the observational-experimental method is built around watching and listening. Laboratory situations are set up so that couples may be observed while they settle disagreements and make decisions. The sessions are usually tape-recorded and later evaluated by a panel of judges who code the observed behavior according to a specified rating scale. (For example, they might keep a record of who made the most interruptions in a family discussion, who made the greater number of suggestions in a husband-wife dialogue about some disagreement, and so on.)

Game techniques may also be utilized so that a couple is faced with decision-making in simulated situations (Greenblat, Stein, and Washburne, 1974). Sometimes a series of short stories are used as stimuli so that the husband and wife must come to an agreement about hypothetical problem situations and find ways to resolve conflicts. Their interactions are observed in an effort to see who exercises the greater power, who is most persuasive, or who gets his or her way (see summaries in Turk and Bell, 1972; Liu, Hutchinson, and Hong, 1973).

There are, of course, problems with the observational-experimental method just as there are with the survey method. Some critics point out that couples or families who know they are being watched may not act naturally and may present a picture somewhat different than they would in actual decision-making situations in their day-to-day living, thus creating an "onstage" effect. But other researchers have answered such criticisms with evidence that much accurate information about family interaction has been gained from observational methods. Two sociologists attempted to compare the two methods by using both on the same random sample of 211 families in metropolitan Toronto. One interesting finding was that "the questionnaire measures showed husband dominance to prevail, while the observational measures showed a balance between the spouses" (Turk and Bell, 1972:220).

Sociologist David Heer (1963) draws attention to a crucial problem common to both methods of researching marital power, namely, the fact that a person who has the greater power in one area of marital decision-making may have a much smaller degree of power in another area. It is not easy to find ways to ascertain and measure power since "power is not unidimensional." Heer's statement is but one more indication of the difficulties surrounding research on power in marriage. Sociologists speak of these as *methodological* problems, since they relate to methods of conceptualizing, gathering necessary data, and measuring findings. But an awareness of these problems should not mean that we despair of any understanding at all of marital power. While there are many things that sociologists do not know about this concept, there are many other things they do know. And it is on the basis of information we already have that we can proceed to build theory and seek explanations about the part power plays in the marital process.

HOW POWER IS OBTAINED AND MAINTAINED

A basic principle in sociology links power with resources. That is, the more resources a person, group, or nation possesses, the greater is the power held with relation to others who desire such resources. For example, suppose a country we'll call "Plentyland" has resources which another country ("Scarceland") lacks and desperately needs (oil, wheat, certain raw materials necessary for manufacturing, or other goods). Plentyland will then have a considerable amount of power over Scarceland and can force Scarceland to act in certain ways, either through threats of withholding the needed materials or through promises to increase such goods, provide better economic deals, and so on. If Scarceland's resources offered in exchange are not so essential to Plentyland as Plentyland's resources are to Scarceland, it follows that Scarceland is much more dependent upon Plentyland than is Plentyland on Scarceland. Therefore, Plentyland has the greater power and may be expected to exercise considerable influence and control over Scarceland. The point is illustrated somewhat in the price demands and other power exercised by some of the oil-producing nations during the energy crisis of recent years.

RESOURCE THEORY AND POWER IN MARRIAGE

But can resource theory be applied to *marital* power? Once again a certain amount of controversy has raged among sociologists (Safilios-Rothschild, 1970; Rodman, 1967, 1972). Safilios-Rothschild questions limiting the concept of resources to assets that will almost without question be found in greater abundance among *husbands* in traditional marriages (for example, education, income, occupational status), while other kinds of resources are ignored. "Does not the wife have at her disposal other 'resources' tangible and intangible which she can (and does) contribute or withdraw at will and thus 'control' even the most occupationally successful husband?" asks Safilios-Rothschild (1970:548). As examples of such control of resources, she names food preparation (poorly prepared or the husband's favorite dish), sloppy versus neat housekeeping, sexual enthusiasm or frigidity, the control of the home atmosphere and hospitality (or lack of it) through pleasant or sour moods, and so on.

In spite of her criticisms of resource theory, Safilios-Rothschild is herself speaking in terms of rewards, costs, and punishments. She does not appear to deny the basic sociological principle linking power with the ability to grant or withhold valued resources. Rather, her hesitancy seems to be associated with a reluctance to limit the definition of resources to an *economic* base.

However, in modern industrial societies, it is productive work in the marketplace that counts in terms of social worth. The work of women in the home is not assigned the same value as the work of men which is converted into dollars. "In a society in which money determines value, women are a group who work outside the money economy," writes Margaret Benston (1969:3–4). She goes on to point out that household work when performed by a wife is not considered to be worth money, and since it isn't, society considers it valueless and not even real work at all. This in turn leads to the conclusion that "women themselves, who do this valueless work, can hardly be expected to be worth as much as men, who work for money."

In commenting upon Benston's statement, sociologist Dair Gillespie (1971:457) emphasizes a point we have made throughout this book: Power is linked with one's degree of involvement in the economic-opportunity system. She writes: "Thus it is clear that for a wife to gain even a modicum of power in the marital relationship, she must gain it from external sources, i.e., she must participate in the work force, her education must be superior to that of her husband, and her participation in organizations must excel his."

Blood and Wolfe (1960) utilized the personal-resource theory to explain

"You say you're only a house-wife, and I say, what do you mean, 'only'?" (Drawing by Weber; © 1963 The New Yorker Magazine, Inc.)

their findings on marital power in the Detroit study. After seeing that a husband's degree of decision-making power was related to his education, income, and occupational status, these researchers concluded that "the higher the husband's social status, the greater his power." In other words, as the husband brings increasing amounts of resources into the marriage, his wife is increasingly willing to defer to his wishes and consider him to have the right to have his way in decisions. There was also evidence that the wife who brings educational and occupational achievements to the marriage has a greater share in the marital balance of power because of these resources.

A number of sociologists have criticized the interpretations of Blood and Wolfe, pointing out that even the findings of the Detroit study did not consistently fit with resource theory, because low-blue-collar husbands had more power than high-blue-collar husbands—just the opposite of the relationship between resources and power at other status levels. Also, when different areas of decision-making were measured by other sociologists, the findings did not always fit so neatly with the Blood and Wolfe explanation (Safilios-Rothschild, 1969, 1970; Centers, Raven, and Rodrigues, 1971; Rodman 1967, 1972).

Three sociologists who conducted a large study among husbands and wives in Los Angeles found that some of their findings clearly supported the resource theory of marital power as set forth by Blood and Wolfe, but other of their findings did not. Nevertheless, Centers, Raven, and Rodrigues (1971) do not toss out the notion that control of valued resources plays an important part in husband-wife power relations. They feel it is but one factor among several others. They call attention to personality factors, cultural factors (especially the influence of norms in the couple's culture or subculture about how much power husband or wife should have), and "role patterning" (the way the domain of authority varies by prevailing societal sex roles; in both their study and the Detroit study, wives had more to say about the choice of food for example, and husbands had more power in choices about the husband's job).

They also agree with Heer's suggestion that the *relative competence* and *relative involvement* of the spouses in specific decision-making areas must also be taken into account in examining family power. Certain decisions might require skills which one spouse possesses to a greater degree than the other. For example, in a particular marriage, one partner might decide on the color to paint the living room and the furnishings to buy because of that person's abilities in interior decorating; the other partner might make the decision about when to purchase new tires for the car based upon greater knowledge of auto maintenance. Also, the spouse who is more involved in or concerned with a specific matter might be expected to be the one to make the final decision on that matter.

Modifications of Resource Theory Several sociologists who see merit in resource theory as an explanation of marital power and yet are aware of certain weaknesses have suggested revisions or modifications. Heer (1963) suggests a theory of exchange which takes into account *alternatives* to resources provided by one's spouse. In Blood and Wolfe's interpretation, the emphasis had been on a comparison of the respective resources brought by each spouse into the marriage; and the conclusion had been that the more resources either one has in comparison to those of the other, the greater will be his or her power. Heer adds another comparison: What is the value of the resources provided by the spouse in comparison to resources available to that person outside the marriage? In other words, would the man or woman be better off married to someone else or not married al all? For example, if a wife thought the alternatives were better elsewhere, she might be less willing to defer to a dominating husband, thereby diminishing his power. The wife in such a case may be willing to risk terminating the relationship because she considers the cost of losing the husband less punishing than submitting to his control.

Heer's modification of resource theory fits with a point we have made repeatedly: a person's power over another diminishes as the second person finds that other sources of rewards are available. Sociologist Willard Waller's (1951:190–192) "principle of least interest" is also relevant. According to this principle, the person who is the less interested in keeping a relationship going has the greater power. The one to whom a relationship matters the most and who feels the greater need is more willing to defer to the other in order to preserve the relationship. When preservation of the relationship ceases to matter so much, the other party loses power.

In comparing cross-cultural studies, sociologist Hyman Rodman (1967, 1972) also found some difficulties in explaining marital power solely in resource terms and therefore suggested another modification. Rodman found that in France and in the United States it was true that the higher the husband's education, income, and occupational status, the greater his power in marriage; but just the opposite was found to be true in Greece and Yugoslavia. Husbands with the highest educational levels in these countries had the lowest marital-power scores. How can this be explained?

Rodman proposes a "theory of resources in cultural context" in which he sees the distribution of power in marriage as resulting from the interaction of two factors. One is the comparative resources of the husband and wife, and the other is the prevailing social norm about marital power in a particular culture or subculture. In other words, if a culture expects husbands to have the greater power in marriage, this norm can have a profound effect upon marital power in spite of the comparative resources of the husband and wife. On the other hand, if a culture favors a more equalitarian view of marriage, power is not automatically assumed and taken for granted as an inherent right of the male. Rather, any power one has must be earned, and this is where resources come in.

Rodman views the United States and France as being more flexible with regard to the distribution of power in marriage and more favorable to equalitarian ideology; therefore power is not something that is already "there" for males. Power comes instead from resources; it must be earned.

Thus the higher power of higher-status husbands in advanced, industrialized countries is not surprising. On the other hand, in developing nations with strong patriarchal traditions where social norms support the husband's right to dominate, the social classes more likely to embrace modern, egalitarian marriage ideals are those who have had opportunities for advanced education. Thus, in Greece and Yugoslavia, more highly educated, higher-status husbands have been more willing than lower-status husbands to grant wives more power, with a resulting decrease in power for themselves.

In looking at this cross-national data and Rodman's explanations, we are not by any means suggesting that higher-status Yugoslavian and Greek marriages within a strongly patriarchal society are somehow more equalitarian than higher-status marriages in the United States or other advanced, industrialized nations. Rather, the comparisons were concerned with degrees of authority *within* the respective countries under study in an effort to see how social status and power were linked in a particular cultural setting.

We have already seen how the option to work (expecially when it is exercised) increases a wife's marital power. And we may recall the example of West African tribes in which wives exercised high degrees of power because of their economic holdings. (See Kayberry, 1953, for more detail; also LaFree, 1974.)

All of this brings us back to resource theory once more. Elements of it are there even when we examine Yugoslavian and Greek data. In a 1966 study, two Yugoslavian sociologists found that in their country women who are employed gain in marital power (Buric and Zelevic, 1967). And Safilios-Rothschild (1967) also found this to be true in her study of wives in Athens. In spite of her misgivings about resource theory, she has written that there is some evidence for its holding true for Greek women more than Greek men. When a wife is employed and especially when her occupational accomplishments are higher than those of her husband, her power in the family tends to be increased, "because the possessed resources prove her abilities in such a way that even the traditional-minded males have to accept her competence."

A recognition of the part that beliefs and cultural norms play in marital power, as in Rodman's modification of resource theory, need not be seen as contradicting resource theory but rather as something that interacts with it and aids in an understanding of how power is distributed. Norms lend legitimacy to power; they do not create power.

It cannot be overstressed that power springs from resources. "Haves" possess more power than "have-nots" in a society. Norms are created to lend support to the possession of power and to show that it is "right" for those who hold power to do so. Thus, the norm that husbands should be more dominant in marriage than wives ultimately goes back to the fact that males have traditionally had greater access to the economic-opportunity system and therefore have had greater resources. Husbands *have* had greater power in marriage, and therefore behavioral expectations (or norms) have developed to support their right to this greater power. In turn, one's degree of acceptance of these norms can have an effect on marital power, along with one's resources as compared to those of the spouse. As women gain greater resources, and with these resources greater marital power, we may expect norms to develop sanctioning wives' rights to such power just as they have supported husbands' rights in the past.

POWER: LEGITIMATE AND NONLEGITIMATE

If the following two hypothetical statements by wives were heard, the observer would immediately be struck by both a similarity and a difference with respect to their comments on their husbands.

Joyce: My husband and I make most decisions together. We talk things over and then decide what to do. But he decides the really important things—particularly if we disagree. For example, he wanted to take a trip to Florida for our vacation and I wanted to visit relatives instead. Needless to say, he won! And I feel he had a right to. After all, he works hard all year to provide our family with a good standard of living. He deserves to decide how to use his time off work and what kind of vacation to take. I feel the same about major expenditures. He earns the money after all! Why shouldn't he be the one to decide how it's spent?

Martha: My husband bought this house trailer we're living in. He didn't even ask what I thought about it—just got it and moved us in. And now he can't even keep up the payments. He's never earned a decent living in all the years we've been married. You can tell that by just looking around our shabby place! But he sure acts like a king around here. "Get me a beer, Martha!" "I need clean socks. You'd better make sure you get to the Laundromat more often. What kind of a wife are you?" Yet he won't buy me a washing machine, and he takes the car every day so that I have to try to find neighbors who'll drive me to the Laundromat. And Pete is always telling me what I can't do, always bossing me around. Like the other night, my friend Judy called and wanted me to go to one of those parties in someone's house where they sell kitchen things, but Pete said, "No, you're not going! I don't want you to." And that was that. But it doesn't seem fair.

In comparing the two statements, we notice first of all that both wives indicate that their husbands hold greater power in marriage than they themselves do. But second, we notice that one wife feels this is right and fair while the other does not. The key factor here is involvement in the economic-opportunity system.

Joyce's husband has rewarded his family with status and material benefits; thus she feels he has the right to the greater power in the marriage. Martha's husband, on the other hand, has not provided such resources and therefore she resents the way he seizes power in the marriage and tries to control her life. Unconsciously, she is acknowledging that he hasn't earned the right to have authority over her. He has failed in what sociologist George Homans (1961:287) has called "the most important single factor in making a man a leader," namely, "the ability to provide rare and valued rewards for his followers."

Joyce feels that her husband's power in their marriage is legitimate. Martha feels that the power her husband exercises is not legitimate. This distinction is an important one which turned up in our Indianapolis study of marriages, and it throws light on many of the problems that have emerged in studies of marital power.

Some sociologist have sought to clarify the two kinds of influence and control over others by distinguishing between the terms *authority* and *power*. Authority is viewed as legitimate, power as nonlegitimate. Sociologist Walter Buckley (1967), for example, defines *authority* as "the direction or control of the behavior of others for the promotion of collective goals, based on some ascertainable form of their knowledgeable consent. Authority thus implies informed, voluntary compliance." *Informed consent* and *collective goals* are key points. In contrast, *power* according to Buckley, is "control or influence over the actions of others to promote one's goals without their consent, against their 'will,' or without their knowledge or understanding" (p. 186).

But since in normal, everyday usage, the word *authority* includes the notion of power, it may seem awkward to perch "power" and "authority" on two ends of a pole as opposites. The concepts involved, however, are valid. Control or influence over others that is deemed legitimate and involves knowledgeable consent certainly differs from control or influence that is *not* considered legitimate and which is exercised apart from the consent of the governed. But both cases involve power as defined at the beginning of this chapter. Thus, we suggest Figure 13-1 as an attempt to clarify the distinction. "Power is power," but it's possible to cross over the line into *nonlegitimate* power.

Nonlegitimate power is neither earned nor consented to. If it moves far enough, it becomes *domination*. Domination includes the idea of lording it over others against their will (the word derives from the Latin *dominus* meaning "master, lord, owner, despot"). In contrast, legitimate power is earned and consented to. As a process involving bargaining and negotiation, legitimate power moves toward *authority*—an institutionalized state. That is, we recognize that a person or group in a position of authority has the *right* to be in charge.

From the standpoint of cost/reward theory, nonlegitimate power is viewed by those under it as being undeserved, taken without having been earned, and as not providing sufficient rewards for the leader's followers. It is thus seen in terms of net loss (giving up one's own desires against one's will

FIGURE 13-1   *A continuum of power.*

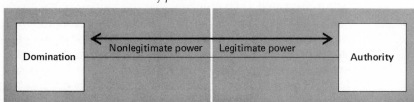

and giving in to the desires of another). In contrast, legitimate power is viewed by those who submit to it as having been earned and deserved by the one who holds the power. Therefore it is seen in terms of net profit (the rewards provided outweigh the costs of submitting to the will of another).

Nonlegitimate power tends to rely on coercion, threats, and punishment; whereas legitimate power relies on "friendly persuasion" and the provision of benefits. We might compare the distinction to the old problem of motivating the peddler's horse. The peddler might get his wagon moving again by either applying a stick to the animal from behind or by holding a carrot on a string out front to lure the animal onward. Legitimate power tends to emphasize the "carrot approach," while nonlegitimate power puts the emphasis upon the stick.

In the Indianapolis study (Scanzoni, 1970), we found that it is an oversimplification merely to state without qualification that with greater status comes greater husband power—unless we take into account the *kind* of power. Actually, the study showed that lower-status husbands tended to exercise more power in their marriages than did higher-status husbands. Men with less education, income, and occupational prestige tended to resolve conflicts unilaterally, carrying out their own wishes rather than paying attention to their wives' desires. Furthermore, they were less interested in working with their wives in making decisions about matters of spouse disagreement. In the processes of conflict resolution, wives were permitted little participation as compared to the situation in upper-status homes.

We saw earlier that Blood and Wolfe (1960:30–33) had also found that husbands in the lowest status group had more power than husbands in the next category (high-blue-collar) which broke the consistency of the pattern that had otherwise shown that husband power rises with social status. Their only attempt at an explanation was to comment that the group of lowest-status men with high power scores were presumably older men who were carrying on a pre–World War I patriarchal ideology which held that a husband should be the boss.

Komarovsky (1962:225–229), too, found in her sample of fifty-eight blue-collar marriages that the lower-blue-collar husbands had greater marital power than the higher-blue-collar husbands (skilled workers). She suggests that educational differences might account for this finding. The less-educated couples tended to have more patriarchal attitudes, with masculine dominance viewed as the norm. The better-educated couples (high school graduates) tended to have more equalitarian ideals. Furthermore, the wives in these marriages expected and demanded more of their marriages. Often they were better educated than their husbands, since the relatively high earnings of skilled workers make it possible for such blue-collar men to "marry upward." In some cases, men had even learned their skilled trades as a result of having married high school graduates who had encouraged them to enlarge their achievement aspirations. However, as Komarovsky notes, upper-blue-collar husbands, by marrying better-educated women, "lose the degree of power enjoyed by the semi-skilled over their less-educated wives."

Education is a resource wives may bring into a marriage, and again it is evident that resources bring greater power. The wife's educational resources and the husband's economic resources in skilled-worker marriages bring about more of a balance of power than in lower-blue-collar marriages. In upper-blue-collar families, decisions are more likely to be talked over and resolved jointly. This contrasts with the husband's unilateral decision-making and conflict resolution in lower-blue-collar families.

Beliefs and Practices Related to Power   In our own study, we measured both what respondents said they *believed* and what they said they *did* with regard to marital power. We found that beliefs do make a difference and that there was no support for Blood and Wolfe's contention that patriarchal traditions are no longer operative. Respondents were assigned a "male authority ideology" score based upon their replies to two questions read separately at different stages of the interview. The items were these: (1) "The wife should have equal authority with the husband in making decisions." (2) "The husband should be the head of the home." Structured responses (which made coding and assigning a score possible) were "strongly agree, agree, disagree, strongly disagree" (Scanzoni, 1970:151).

Among wives, it was found that the higher the social status (based on husband's education, occupation, and income), the more patriarchal were wives' beliefs. With increasing levels of social status, there appeared to be an increasing acceptance of traditional views regarding a husband's right to leadership within the marriage. Conversely, our research showed that the lower the level of social status, the less likely were wives to accept patriarchal beliefs. Lower-status wives rejected traditional notions of masculine authority and leaned toward modern equalitarian ideals. Husbands, for their part, were found at all status levels to believe that the husband should be the dominant person in the marital relationship.

The concepts of legitimate and nonlegitimate power fit nicely here. Husbands evidently feel they have the right to greater power in marriage. Lower-status husbands lean heavily on traditional norms which have given the male the final say as "head of the house." Higher-status husbands have both the traditional norms and economic achievement to support their claim to power. Wives seem to view matters somewhat differently. If husband power appears to be earned (by economic achievement and resources brought to the marriage), wives are willing to grant the right to power *ideologically* as well (by expressing a belief in traditional patriarchal ideals). Thus, with rising status, there comes a willingness on the part of wives to view husband power as *right*, legitimate, earned on the basis of rewards provided. Joyce, in our earlier illustration, is a wife who looks at the matter in this way.

However, lower-status wives are less willing to grant power to husbands ideologically, since the husbands have not earned such power economically, even though the husbands tend to feel that the patriarchal belief system in itself should be enough to assure their greater power in the marriage. The hypothetical Martha in our illustration demonstrated such a marital situation.

The husband feels the wife should defer to him simply because he is a man; the wife feels he doesn't deserve such deference since he has been so unsuccessful in the economic-opportunity system. Any power he takes is considered by her to be nonlegitimate and therefore *domination*. The higher-status wife, in contrast, sees her husband's greater power as legitimate and thus *authority*.

The same distinction between domination and authority emerged in our research as we focused on actual practice as well as on beliefs. The method of measurement used was based upon conflict resolution rather than routinized household decision-making (which, as we have seen, poses many problems in drawing conclusions from the data). We reasoned that a more realistic picture of marital power emerges if we examine matters considered important by a couple and over which there is disagreement, and then endeavor to find out which spouse has the final say in resolving the conflict.

In a nutshell, our findings were these: The lower the social status of the husband, the more frequent is his settling of issues unilaterally ("We will do what I say! And that's that!"), and the less he tends to share decisions with his wife ("Let's talk it over and try to find an answer that suits us both"). Conversely, the higher the status of the husband, the less unilateral is his power, and the more he is likely to share decisions with his wife. Rather than saying, "I have the last word by virtue of tradition and economic success," the higher-status husband is more likely to display an attitude that says, "Maybe we can come to a compromise," or "I don't want to make the final decision by myself; let's work on it together."

Thus, although as social status increases both husbands and wives believe the husband should have the greater power in marriage, in actual conflict resolution there is greater participation by both spouses than in lower-status marriages. Less frustrated in the occupational realm and more secure in the power they hold (because it is earned and thus considered legitimate in the eyes of their wives), higher-status husbands are willing to act in a way that is more or less equalitarian, even when contested issues are being discussed. Lower-status husbands, on the other hand, may hang on tightly to every shred of marital power that tradition has granted them since they have no power elsewhere, not having achieved in the economic system and thus lacking the resources that bring power. They therefore *take* power even though in their wives' eyes they have not earned it. In such marriages, in spite of the equalitarian ideals of the wives, husbands tend to make unilateral decisions in areas of disagreement. They are less apt to permit or encourage the participation of their wives in making such decisions, and this lack of shared power is resented by the wives.

In both cases (higher status and lower status), husbands hold the power. But how wives see that power is different. Higher-status wives tend to see it as right and proper; lower-status wives do not. Higher-status wives get to share in husbands' power; lower-status wives do not. In a certain sense, we might see here a distinction in types of power that has been made in psychoanalytic theory. Freud, Adler, and Horney all took pains to show a difference in *positive power* which originates in strength and *negative power* which originates in weakness (see summary in Winter, 1973:157). As viewed by lower-status wives, the domination of their husbands is negative power.

It must be kept in mind that we have been speaking here of marriages in the *traditional* sense in which the husband is the chief provider or only provider. Research on equal-partner marriages in which each spouse is equally committed to a career and equally a provider of economic resources might be expected to show a considerable change in the marital power picture. Hints of this were found in the Indianapolis data with regard to wife employment. We found, as have other researchers, that a wife's employment is associated with greater power in her marriage—both in terms of her beliefs (more favorable to equality than to patriarchy) and her actual behavior (she tends to make more decisions alone rather than sharing them jointly with her husband) (Scanzoni, 1970:159–162; Heer, 1958; Blood and Wolfe, 1960; see also Scanzoni, 1978, 1979b).

NEGOTIATION

In marriage, as in any relationship between intimates (friends, lovers, parents and children, siblings), there is an ongoing give-and-take (Davis, 1973; Lederer and Jackson, 1968). The power structure plays an important part in this exchange, but simply knowing who has the greater influence does not totally explain the exchange itself. Who gives what, and why? Who takes what, and why? Who gains? Who loses? What kinds of processes occur in making decisions, solving problems, resolving disagreements, working out compromises, developing plans, and so on?

Probably the best word to describe these kinds of social exchanges is *negotiation*. Negotiation may be defined as arranging the terms of a contract, transaction, or agreement through talking matters over and working things out. The word has its roots in the Latin *negotior* which refers to doing business or trading. The husband-wife relationship involves negotiation in that there generally is mutual discussion and an arrangement of terms of agreement concerning areas of married life. How will the spouses divide up household chores? How will they make decisions about whether or not to have children? How will they decide on leisure, friends, visits to relatives, and other aspects of social life? What kind of house or car should they buy? How can they arrange their sex life so that it will be satisfactory to both of them?

In arriving at terms of agreement, the husband and wife do not necessarily settle a particular issue once and for all. As circumstances change or as desires of one or the other change, various matters may need to be renegotiated. Again, the idea of process enters the picture. Marriage involves an *ongoing* series of exchanges—in other words, continuous negotiation and renegotiation. Even a relationship that over the years seems to have settled into very routinized ways of doing things often is caught unawares by new circumstances and faces the issue of renegotiation. Time brings changes. The

Marriage involves ongoing social exchanges and negotiations. (Sybil Shelton/Peter Arnold, Inc.)

children grow into different stages and require new kinds of guidance or have different needs than earlier. One spouse's health may fail, necessitating a renegotiation on how the household will be run or how the income will be produced. The retirement period of life may jolt a couple into seeing areas of their marriage needing re-examination and calling for efforts toward change.

The Latin origin of the term *negotiation* fits well with what goes on in such husband-wife interchanges. In a very real sense, it is a matter of "doing business" through a series of trade-offs. "I did that for him so he should do that for me." "If I gave up a big chunk of my day off to help her out, I don't see why she can't give up some time to bake pies for the guys coming over to play cards tonight—even if she doesn't like my friends!" "Of course, I'm going to hear my wife's speech at the PTA tonight. She always cheers me on when I do things like that; why shouldn't I encourage her, too?" "George got a big raise! Now we can take that trip we've been dreaming about! I'm going to do something special tonight. I asked my mother to take the children overnight, and George and I can have a special evening together making plans—and making love. I'll cook his favorite meal and maybe we'll even eat by candlelight!" "Well, it seems to me that if a wife works at a job all day, she shouldn't have to come home and do all the housework, too. That's why I try to help Sue with the dishes and cleaning and stuff."

Statements such as these illustrate how rewards and costs shape everyday marital life. The husband who gave up much of his day off to help his wife (costs) expects her to likewise give up time for him (costs again) in order to reward him as he rewarded her. The husband who has been rewarded with his wife's encouragement and approval is willing to take the time (costs, the extent of which depends on how else he might have used that particular block of time) in order to provide her likewise with encouragement and approval by listening to her speech. The wife who is delighted by the increased rewards of her husband's raise tries to find a way to reward him in turn; she chooses to go the "expressive" route by planning a romantic evening. The husband who is rewarded by his wife's monetary earnings accepts the costs of added participation in household chores to reward his wife with more free time.

CASE STUDY: BOB AND JULIE

A hypothetical couple named Bob and Julie illustrate how marital negotiation works. Their case seems particularly apt because it combines elements of both traditional marriage (in that Bob is the chief provider) and modern, equalitarian ideals (in that Julie has a job which gives her a greater degree of power than would be likely otherwise). In terms of the four main kinds of marital structures, we would say that Bob and Julie come closest to the senior partner–junior partner arrangement.

Let's assume that Bob and Julie have been married about six months. Without necessarily thinking in terms of bargaining, the two have negotiated with one another as to how their marriage should be structured in terms of rights, duties, and options. Bob was already established as a real estate agent at the time of their marriage, and they have mutually agreed that Julie will teach elementary school for two or three years before they think about having children. Household chores are divided between them. Bob straightens up the apartment and does the laundry. Julie takes care of the meal planning, shopping, and cooking. Additional arrangements have been worked out for other areas of marriage, both in the expressive and instrumental realms. Birth-control methods, use of leisure time, budgeting, visiting relatives, personal habits—these and more have all been subjects of negotiation.

Implicit in such a set of marital negotiations is the question of legitimate power or authority. Bob and Julie have agreed to pattern their marriage so that Bob is the chief provider, which means that he has certain fixed, fully structured rights and duties which are inherent in the breadwinner role. Julie shares in breadwinning, but her commitment to work is less than Bob's. It is understood and agreed upon by both husband and wife that the main support of the family will be Bob's responsibility. He is the senior partner.

Bob's position gives him the stronger leverage in decision-making processes and conflict resolution within the marriage. Thus, when Julie suggested Bob's doing the cooking several evenings a week, since her own schedule seemed pressured with commuting and extracurricular school activities, Bob rejected the suggestion. "Sure, my hours are more flexible than yours," he said, "but still my work requires me to be on call constantly. If a prospective customer wants to look at a house, I've got to be free at *their* convenience, not mine. I can't be tied down with cooking! But I'll tell you what I will do. I can help you out by doing the shopping, and that will give you some extra free time. You'll still have to plan the meals and make out the list so I'll know what to buy; but I'm willing to save you the time and energy that you'd have to spend on picking up the stuff. How's that for a compromise?"

As we have seen, the person in an exchange relationship who has the greater resources to offer tends to have more legitimate authority. Therefore, that person tends to shape or influence decision-making in his or her favor. If, for example, Julie were the full-time support of her husband while he completed college, she might have considerably more authority than in her present situation. Or if she were not employed at all, she would have less.

As matters now stand, however, Bob has more legitimate power than Julie does. This is true not only because of his greater financial resources, but also because of the chief provider role he fills. His job is looked upon by both him and his wife as being more important than hers. He can always argue that whatever might interfere with his career, will be punishing or costly to both of them. Sociologist William Goode (1963:21–22) has pointed out that upper-status men obtain many rights and have a high degree of power because they can always claim that family demands must not interfere with their work. Such a man, writes Goode, "takes precedence as *professional, not* as family head or as a male; nevertheless, the precedence is his. By contrast, lower-class men demand deference as *men*, as heads of families" (italics in the original, p. 22).

So long as Julie accepts the senior partner–junior partner structural arrangement and values the rewards Bob supplies her, she will tend to recognize as legitimate Bob's authority. "After all," she says, "*someone* has to have the final say if we can't agree on something. Somebody has to be the last court of appeals. We feel it's only right that it should be Bob. Even though we like to think of each other as equals, and we certainly talk everything over, there's still a sense in which Bob is sort of 'in charge' of the marriage. He has the main responsibility to provide for us. My income comes in handy, but it's his that we always depend on. Mine might stop someday because we'll probably have children and I'll quit work. But Bob can't do that. He has to shoulder the greater load, so I guess he deserves to have the greater power."

Maximum Joint Profit Bob and Julie are maintaining a relationship in which each considers the exchange to be profitable. They are providing benefits to one another (at cost to each individually), but in return they are receiving certain rewards. They are maintaining an ongoing situation of *maximum joint profit,* to use a term from economics. The situation is comparable to that in which a single buyer of a certain commodity and a single seller of that commodity enter into bargaining. Maximum profit for each is the goal.

Psychologist Sidney Siegel and economist Lawrence Fouraker (1960:1, 9) have pointed out that such a situation "appeals to the mutual interests of the participants, and would seem to call for harmonious cooperation between them." But at the same time, "the interests of the participants are exactly in opposition, and acrimonious competition would seem to be the behavior norm." If these two opposing factors (cooperation and competition) can be made to work together in the decision-making process, it becomes possible for the two parties in the negotiations to be forced into a contract which is in their *mutual* interest. Each individual and the relationship as a whole benefit. Both buyer and seller are satisfied that profit has been maximum for each. At the same time, the transaction sets up a bond between the bargainers and a climate conducive to doing further business together.

In the ongoing exchanges of Bob and Julie, the greater authority of Bob as senior partner and chief provider has been acceptable to Julie. The "costs" of her deferring to him in certain decisions and stalemates are considered to be fewer than the rewards she receives from him; therefore she is satisfied with her margin of profit in the relationship. Bob too feels that his rewards from the marriage are high. The offers and counteroffers of their various negotiations have resulted in a situation of maximum joint profit.

Distributing Rewards and Costs Justly However, at any point in these exchanges, one or the other partner may come to define the distribution of rewards and costs as being unfair. Homans (1961:74) calls such a perception of inequity "the problem of *distributive justice*." In other words, has the distribution of rewards and costs between the persons been just and equitable? Rewards should be comparable to investments for person A relative to person B if the bargain they have struck is to be considered fair by each.

To illustrate, let's assume that there comes a time when Bob's sales have fallen off and his commissions are down. Julie's salary has remained constant and her income is now higher than Bob's. Yet, she is continuing to do the cooking and finds it a real hardship in view of her tight schedule—expecially now that she is helping the fifth graders put out a school newspaper and is staying an extra hour after school. Bob, in contrast, has more free time on his hands than ever and is almost always back at their apartment long before she arrives home. Julie has begun to resent his unwillingness to prepare the evening meal. She feels that she is providing many rewards to him at the same time that she is incurring costs which she considers unacceptable (the necessity of rushing home to cook after an exhausting day of teaching), while in her opinion, Bob isn't bearing sufficient costs. She feels he "has it a lot easier" than she. Her schedule is fixed while his is flexible, he is home more hours than she is, he is providing less income now than she does. In view of all this, his refusal to cook seems unjust. Julie begins to negotiate, making clear her feelings about the matter. Since there has been a shift in the relative resources of this husband and wife over time, the gap in their relative authority is much less.

Being able to listen to, understand, share with, and enter into the feelings of another person is particularly important in the daily interactions of a husband and wife. (© Sylvia Johnson/ Woodfin Camp & Assoc.)

In order for the situation to change and the problem to be resolved, Julie and Bob will have to have some honest discussions. Earlier, we saw the important role that empathy plays in marriage. Being able to listen to, understand, share with, and enter into the feelings of the other person is important in any close relationship—and particularly so in the daily interaction of a husband and wife. Thus, social psychologist Philip Brickman (1974:27, 228) makes the important point that in the process of bargaining over a particular issue so that a situation will be changed, "a prerequisite . . . is the ability of the parties in the situation to communicate with one another about their various alternatives and intentions." At the same time, he stresses that problems of communication should not be considered the *cause* of the need for renegotiation or the cause of conflict. The prime cause of a bargainer's desire to change situational profits is a sense of inequity rather than a lack of communication. But communication is essential if renegotiation is to take place. An inability to communicate could only worsen the difficulties and delay the solution.

Going back to Bob and Julie, we find that as soon as the sense of unfairness crystallizes in her own mind, Julie brings up the matter again to Bob. She makes a suggestion to alleviate the unfairness (Bob should cook), and in view of their changed circumstances and her better bargaining situation, Bob is more open to her proposal than previously. Julie has not let her resentment smolder but has acted immediately. After time spent in negotiation, the couple arrive at a new exchange in which Bob agrees to do the cooking—with certain qualifications. He will cook for a three-month trial period to find out how costly it will be to him and also to find out how things go with his job situation. But for the time being at least, Julie has persuaded him that it is only fair for him to take on this household duty. Bob accepts the legitimacy of Julie's request, and both persons begin to maintain their new, renegotiated sets of costs and rewards. Both have established what has been variously called "balance" or "equilibrium" (Alexander and Simpson, 1971), and there is a sense of "distributive justice." Once again, both parties feel that current exchanges are operating for maximum joint profit and mutual gain.

The process of negotiating and renegotiating exchanges in marriage is illustrated as a series of steps in Figure 13-2. Bob and Julie's story focuses on just one area of renegotiation, but such renegotiations may take place in many other areas as well—often concurrently. For example, in the area of sex relations, one spouse might suggest having intercourse more frequently or trying new positions and techniques, and this matter could be renegotiated. For another couple, leisure time and companionship might be issues requiring renegotiation as one spouse complains of the other's absorption in occupational interests.

Written Contracts   All of the ongoing exchanges between a husband and wife are interconnected. And altering one exchange is bound to have certain effects on other exchanges as well. These complex webs need to be kept in mind in cases where couples decide to write their own marriage contracts.

Circumstances change, and people change. To sit down at the beginning of a marriage and spell out in advance *all* the possibilities and contingencies that might emerge, all the negotiations and renegotiations that would have to take place, would require writing something as intricate, detailed, and meticulous as the most complex legal document. Even then, as new situations would arise, there would have to be constant amendments (and negotiations about making the amendments!). A couple might find such an exhaustive contract cumbersome to follow and burdensome to change.

A major theorist in sociology, Emile Durkheim (1893), noted that much of the force even of legal contracts lies with the noncontractual rules that surround them. It simply isn't possible to write everything into a contract. In social exchange, trust is essential—just as "good faith" is highly important in ongoing exchanges between buyers and sellers in the business world (Blau, 1964, Fox, 1974, Kelley and Schenitzki, 1972, Siegel and Fouraker, 1960).

Persons must *believe* that others will fulfill their obligations—that they will do what is fair and just by them. And in a dyad (two-person relationship) such as marriage, many behaviors must be left relatively unspecified with the understanding—implicit or explicit—that each person is seeking the best interests of both (maximum joint profit).

Apart from such confidence that others will reciprocate, it is exceedingly difficult for stable, ongoing social relations to exist (Blau, 1964:99). However, trust cannot be written into a contract. It develops because two parties

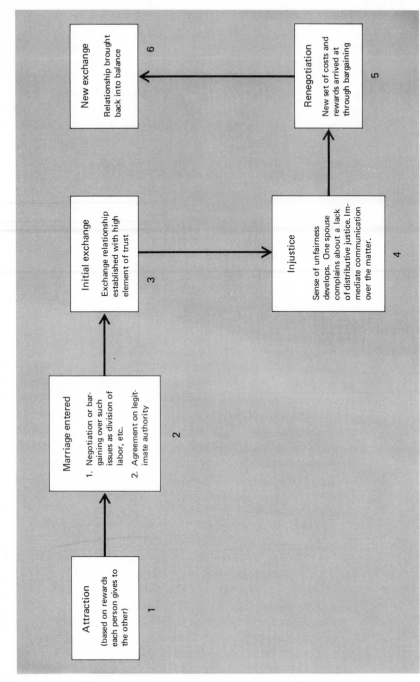

FIGURE 13-2 Marital negotiation and renegotiation.

Example of Couple Negotiation in a Homosexual Partnership

Those couples reporting that their income disparity had a negative effect on their relationship may have had an experience similar to Kathy and Toni's, where the disparity was so great it was bound to cause some problem. Kathy, a stockbroker, earned in excess of $40,000 a year. Toni, a freelance writer, averaged only about $8,000. Recalled Kathy, "When we started our relationship I did not want to make Toni feel like she was dependent on me. So we sat down and made out a budget for household necessities and we each contributed half. This soon became a major problem. Because of the fact that she didn't earn nearly as much as I, I had to lower my standard of living to accommodate a budget that she could afford. This didn't work out at all and continually caused us problems."

Added Toni, "When we started out, I didn't want her to get off on a trip of her feeling like she 'had to support' me. No one has supported me since I was sixteen."

Eventually, the couple negotiated a settlement that seemed to satisfy both. Explained Kathy, "We finally looked at money and its relative importance in our lives. Money didn't actually mean that much. What was important was our time and we felt that our time was equally valuable. What we got paid for our time was something that had very little to do with anything about or within ourselves—what we got paid for our time was all based on decisions we had little input into and seemed fairly irrational anyway.

"So we finally agreed to contribute to household expenses according to our income. If I earned four times as much as she, then I contributed four times as much to the household account. This gave us a lot more freedom and we began to live in a lifestyle that I was more comfortable with. Naturally, if our income relationship changes, then the percent contribution will also change. After all, she could strike it rich one of these days, or the stock market might fold tomorrow."

SOURCE: Sasha Gregory Lewis, *Sunday's Women: A Report on Lesbian Life Today* (Boston: Beacon Press, 1979), p. 142.

strongly value the rewards that each supplies to the other. Neither person wants to risk losing them, and therefore, each puts forth an effort to act toward the other in good faith.

At the same time, the idea of personally tailored marriage contracts should by no means be dismissed as having little value. Even though trust cannot be written into the contract, and even though changing circumstances cannot be foreseen, a couple's decision to work out a verbal or written agreement of what they expect of one another and the marriage *is nothing more nor less than negotiation.* Couples who work out such a set of ground rules for their relationship at the very outset may not only find the end product—the contract they come up with—useful for their situation. They may also find that the exercise of developing their own set of expectations has served as a training ground for future negotiations as well. (For suggestions on what might be included in a personal marriage contract, see Weitzman, 1974:1249–1255.)

To Love, Honor, and Negotiate

In 1973, Ms. magazine published the detailed personal marriage contract of Harriett Mary Cody and Harvey Joseph Sadis. The couple had drafted the contract "in order to define a marriage relationship . . . which preserves and promotes their individual identities as a man and a woman contracting to live together for mutual benefit and growth." The contract spelled out their agreements (and the reasons behind them) on such matters as keeping separate names, their relationships with others, religion, children, careers, where they would live (including how they would decide whether or not to move if an opportunity arose in either's occupation), how they would share their living space and allocate household tasks, and financial matters. The couple also included an agreement to periodically evaluate their partnership and a section on basic agreements that would be honored if they ever mutually decided to terminate the contract.

In Article X, "Decision-Making," the couple worded their contract as follows:

Harriett and Harvey share a commitment to a process of negotiations and compromise which will strengthen their equality in the partnership. Decisions will be made with respect for individual needs. THE PARTIES HOPE to maintain such mutual decision-making so that the daily decisions affecting their lives will not become a struggle between the parties for power, authority, and dominance. THE PARTIES AGREE that such a process, while sometimes time-consuming and fatiguing, is a good investment in the future of their relationship and their continued esteem for each other.

Four years later, Ms. published a follow-up article in which the couple spoke enthusiastically of the positive value the contract (including amendments) had demonstrated in their relationship. Harvey reported, "the marriage has been a lot of work. . . . I love Harriett very much, but without the contract I would have been finished long ago."

SOURCE: Based upon material from "To Love, Honor, and . . . Share: Marriage Contract of Harriett Mary Cody and Harvey Joseph Sadis," *Ms.*, vol I, no. 12 (June, 1973), pp. 62–64, 102–103; and "Marriage Contract Renewed," *Ms.*, vol. VI, no 1 (July, 1977), p. 21.

CHAPTER HIGHLIGHTS

Power may be defined as the capability of having one's way, achieving one's goals, and having intended effects on others' behaviors and emotions. A basic principle in sociology links power with resources. Because males have traditionally had greater access to the economic-opportunity system and have thus had greater resources, husbands have held greater power in marriage. Therefore, behavioral expectations (or *norms*) have developed to support husbands' rights to this greater power. But as women gain greater resources, we may expect norms to develop supporting *wives'* rights to greater marital power. Power may be exercised in a way that is *legitimate* (by being earned by the one who exercises it and consented to by those over whom it is exercised) or in a way that is *nonlegitimate* (by being seized by someone who has not earned it and who doesn't have the consent of those over whom it is exercised). Legitimate power relies on "friendly persuasion" and the provision of benefits to those under it. Nonlegitimate power, in contrast, tends to rely on coercion, threats, and punishment.

Negotiation may be defined as arranging the terms of a contract, transaction, or agreement through talking matters over and working things out. Marriage involves an ongoing series of negotiations and renegotiations as couples work out agreements about the many areas of married life. This continuous openness to negotiation is another example of marriage as *process* rather than as something static. Written contracts must take this into account. Where persons each gain rewards from one another and seek to act in the best interests of both, they are maintaining a situation which aims for *maximum joint profit*, that is, highest possible gains and benefits for *both* persons as individuals and a desire for what is best for the *relationship*.

CHAPTER 14

(Joel Gordon)

PROCESS IN MARRIAGE: CONFLICT AND ITS MANAGEMENT

Remember Bob and Julie, the couple we met in the preceding chapter? Let's observe them again as something new happens in their ongoing exchanges. Their situation isn't one of negotiation this time, but rather one of *conflict*.

It started when Bob decided they should buy a new car. Julie insisted they couldn't afford it and there was no use even thinking about it. Bob now feels a sense of "distributive injustice." He feels that his investment in the relationship is not producing desired payoffs.

Bob seeks to renegotiate the matter, and communication is established quickly; but in the bargaining that follows, it becomes clear that Bob's authority in this particular matter is less than his wife's. Real estate sales have continued to be low and Bob's earnings have remained less than Julie's for several months. There is no assurance that matters will change in the near future. If the couple were to buy a new car, Julie's larger income would be the main resource to make the monthly payments. At a certain point in the negotiations between Bob and Julie, *conflict* emerges.

WHAT IS CONFLICT?

Social conflict may be defined as *a struggle over limited resources and/or incompatible goals so that it appears that the more one party gets, the less the other party can have* (this definition is based on a combination of Coser, 1956:8; Kriesberg, 1973:17).

The struggle concerns *limited* resources, because if the resources were infinite there would not be the problem of dividing them up so that all parties would feel they had enough. Farmers in an area with abundant rainfall are unlikely to engage in conflict over water supplies. But in an area where water is scarce, two farmers are likely to engage in conflict when one finds the other has dammed the creek to hoard the scanty water supply for his own farm needs. Two children who race for the one remaining swing in the playground are also likely to engage in conflict because the resources are limited ("I got here first!" "No, I did! It's mine!"); but on another day when all the swings are empty, they will each take one and play together amiably.

Similarly, *incompatible goals* may be the basis of conflict. If one person wants to go one way and the other person wants to go in the opposite direction, they cannot walk together and simultaneously reach both goals. One can yield to the other so that they pursue one of the goals, or they might take a third goal as a compromise. Or they might go their separate ways with each pursuing his or her own goal. In a marriage, for example, one spouse might desire a large family while the other desires maximum freedom from anything that would tie them down. One person sees marriage in terms of child-centeredness and wants at least four children; the other person sees marriage in terms of couple-centeredness and wants no children. Their goals are clearly incompatible. Another illustration might be that of a spouse who is deeply involved in social issues and wants a simple life-style with much of their income given to humanitarian causes, but the other spouse wishes to live lavishly. Again, the two goals are incompatible, and conflict is likely to emerge.

STRUGGLE AND RESISTANCE

Struggle and *resistance* are key words in defining conflict (Kriesberg, 1973:4). Struggle occurs when counteroffers are refused outright or no modifications are suggested. The negotiations have reached a seeming dead end. Yet, one or both parties continue to press their claims, and one or both keep *resisting* because they believe that it is *not* in their best interests to accept the claims of the other. Each perceives that it would be too costly to do so. In the case of Bob and Julie, Julie feels the financial cost. Because their material resources are limited at this particular time, she wants to put as much money as possible into regular savings rather than spending it. Bob's goal, on the other hand, is to have a new car. He not only feels that the reward of the car is being denied him but that his status and authority are being undercut as well—a loss that is costly to him.

During the process of conflict, communication may continue in the sense that both parties press their claims and each completely understands and accurately perceives what the other wants. Clear communication in itself, however, is no guarantee that conflict will cease. In other words, it's not enough to talk things over and clear up possible *misunderstandings* (although that's important). Rather, the two parties have to work at *changing the situation* so that grievances and inequities are removed in a way that is satisfactory to both sides.

COMMUNICATION PROBLEMS AND CONFLICT

At the same time, it would be foolish to say that communication plays no part in situations of conflict. Conflict often tends to be associated with garbled communication or with a breakdown of communication. Data from laboratory studies and from investigations of wars show that misperceptions, miscalculations, and misinterpretations can seriously affect conflict (Kelley and Stahelski, 1970; White, 1966). Many Americans became deeply concerned about the seriousness of the cold war between the United States and the Soviet Union some years ago when Premier Khrushchev made the statement: "We will bury you." They interpreted it to mean that the Soviets planned to destroy the United States. However, Khrushchev was simply using a Russian phrase that means, "We will outlive you" (Klineberg, 1964:153 as quoted in Brickman, 1974:153). In other words, the thought was something like, "Our nation will outlast yours. We'll be around long after you."

Misperceptions especially can affect the resolution of conflict. In the case

"I never said I was going to put you in the movies. I said I was going to take you to the movies." (Drawing by Weber; © 1976 The New Yorker Magazine, Inc.)

of Bob and Julie, Bob might be saying that he wants *any* new car, whereas Julie may be understanding him to insist on a luxury car—since this is what he has always spoken of in the past. Bob might be understanding Julie to say she wouldn't even consider *any* new car under *any* circumstances, whereas Julie's resistance has mainly been buttressed against the idea of an expensive, luxury car that she is persuaded lies beyond their means. Somehow these two persons have failed to convey their own feelings and to hear what the other is saying. By attributing to one another motives and intentions that are not there at all, they have hindered effective communication.

Sometimes communication is simply broken off at some point during the conflict process. The parties concerned may decide they have nothing more to say to one another, and attempts to negotiate are given up. However, silence itself may become a form of communication. Social scientists T. C. Shelling and M. H. Halperin (1961:8) note that "failure to deny rumors, refusal to answer questions, attempts to take emphasis away from certain issues, all tend to communicate something" (as quoted in Brickman, 1974:153).

Whether or not verbal communication exists, and whether or not it is garbled, one or both parties may move toward trying to settle the conflict. In the case of our hypothetical couple, Julie seeks to resolve it by fiat—by giving an order or issuing a directive. Her pronouncement is, "No, we're not going to get a new car for you at this particular time." By using her authority based on their relative incomes, she attempts to end the conflict by simply refusing Bob's wishes outright.

NONLEGITIMATE POWER IN CONFLICT SITUATIONS

However, at any point in the conflict process, legitimate authority can be transformed into nonlegitimate power. When one person or group makes demands that seem excessive, the party on whom the demands are being made tends to feel exploited (Blau, 1964:22). Demands become "excessive" when they are not justified by sufficient levels of rewards. In our illustration, the wife makes a demand ("Forget about the car"), but the husband considers it excessive. Bob doesn't feel that Julie is offering any reward that would justify her demand or that would somehow "make up" for the sacrifice that would be required on his part by giving up his wishes for the new car. Second, Bob still thinks of himself as chief provider deserving to exercise the greater power in the marriage. He considers his current financial setbacks to be merely temporary, and he doesn't feel that his wife has the right to be as arbitrary as he feels she is.

When demands become excessive in the eyes of persons who are nevertheless forced to comply with them, such persons feel they are being coerced into situations they would not choose for themselves. These situations are regarded as painful, punishing, and costly. The power being exercised over them is no longer viewed as right or legitimate authority; rather it is seen as raw, nonlegitimate power. An example of such a conflict situation occurred in the 1974 feud between members of the National Football League Players Association (NFLPA) and the team owners. Players demanded numerous changes in the way summer training camps and exhibition schedules were being conducted. Life in the training camps was austere and uncomfortable. Rigid restrictions governed virtually every aspect of the men's lives. Curfews kept the players confined to the camp after a certain hour. Lights-out rules and bed checks demanded that they be in bed when they were ordered to be, and guards made regular rounds to make sure everyone was asleep. There were rules against using alcohol, wearing mod clothes, and dating local women (with heavy fines for those who failed to comply). Not surprisingly, the football players began to call such regulations "leash laws" and insisted that they be eliminated. Some men, resentful of being told how to run their lives and of being penned up in what they regarded as a kind of detention camp, were willing to give up football. Others engaged in all-out conflict in the form of a strike. They felt the power of the owners was nonlegitimate because of demands the players considered excessive. "It's the owners' way of showing their power and maintaining their monopoly of all decision making," the NFLPA executive director was quoted as saying. He went on to say that whereas that kind of control had worked in the past, it would not work any longer. On the other side, the team owners felt that their power was legitimate, and that since they paid the bills they had every right to tell the players what they may or may not do (Stump, 1974).

BREAKDOWN OF TRUST

One consequence of nonlegitimate power is that the trust we spoke of earlier can become corroded. Parties who feel exploited begin to doubt that the other party really cares about their best interests. Instead, the other person appears to be unduly selfish and more concerned with profit for *himself* or *herself* than with maximum joint profit. This became a common gripe among the football players. They felt underpaid and complained that the owners had worked out a system in which the men were working almost for nothing during the preseason months of practice and exhibition games. The owners appeared to care only about lining their own pockets. Similarly, this breakdown of trust was beginning to occur between Bob and Julie. Bob resented her telling him they could not purchase the car, and he began to wonder if she was hoarding her earnings selfishly toward her own goals rather than caring about him.

REGULATED CONFLICT IS NOT RESOLVED CONFLICT

By trying to settle the conflict through simply giving an order, Julie was seeking to reestablish the kind of exchange relationship that existed prior to the conflict. She wanted the conflict to "be over with." Thus, she took advantage of her present position of power based on control of the resources. But to Bob, that power seemed nonlegitimate. He is unwilling to let the conflict end in such a manner. He wants the conflict to be *resolved*, not merely *regulated*.

Any relationship based on nonlegitimate power is potentially unstable and can easily become unbalanced or even unglued. Persons who feel exploited want to change the status quo and thus are apt to resist and struggle in the face of what they consider unfair demands and insufficient rewards. Therefore, Bob simply refuses to accept his wife's decision and persuades her to reopen communication. "The conflict is *not* settled," Bob declares, convincing Julie that they should engage in renegotiation. This time he is able to strike a bargain with her. While it is true that originally he had set his heart on a particular luxury model, he had begun thinking matters over and became increasingly willing to settle for a less expensive car—even a subcompact. Julie concedes that with careful budgeting they can try to afford a car of this kind. They decide to visit various automobile showrooms and will choose a car together.

The conflict has been resolved satisfactorily in the sense that the original injustice has been removed along with the sense that nonlegitimate power is being exercised. Feelings of exploitation are also gone, and the sense of trust is restored. The struggle over authority and allocation of material resources is ended in that each party feels not only that his (her) own aims have been achieved, but also perceives that the other feels the same way. The renegotiation has led to a new exchange relationship in which the relative authority of each party is deemed legitimate, and the costs and rewards experienced by each are considered fair. In other words, a new balance of genuine mutual profit has been accomplished. (See Figure 14-1.)

Something else has likely been taking place in the relationship of Bob and Julie—though not necessarily consciously. Persons or groups in any social situation are continually making "comparison levels for alternatives" (Thibaut and Kelley, 1959:21–23). Comparisons are made between the current profit level (rewards minus costs) and what profit levels might exist in other potentially available situations. Persons are more likely to remain in their

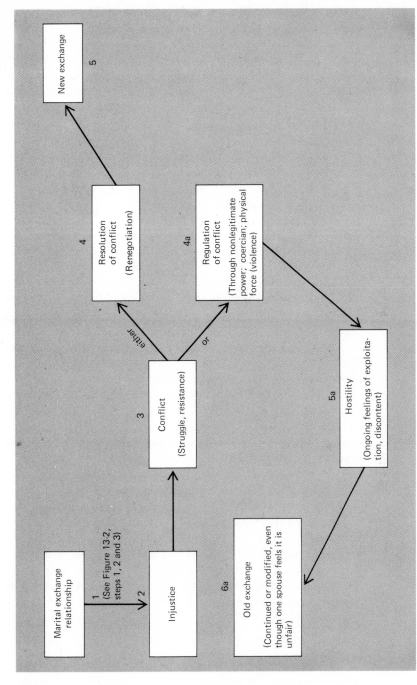

FIGURE 14-1 *Directions in which marital conflict may move: resolution or regulation.*

present situation if they define the rewards offered there as being greater than those elsewhere. In the case of Bob and Julie, their renegotiation and conflict resolution have reinforced their sense of overall profit so that the situation in which they find themselves seems more desirable than any alternative one. They have no desire to end the relationship.

TYPES OF CONFLICT

In order to more fully understand conflict, it helps to look at some ways it may be categorized by type.

ZERO-SUM AND MIXED-MOTIVE CONFLICT

In a bullfighting contest, either the matador or the bull will win—not both. The goal of the game is to conquer the opponent. Social conflict may also be of this type and is sometimes called *zero-sum;* the contesting parties expect to have either all or nothing.

However, another type of conflict has different objectives. Rather than a "winner take all" approach, there occurs a "mixed-motive situation." This kind of conflict is far more frequent in social interaction than is the zero-sum type. In *mixed-motive* conflict, the contesting parties also want to gain benefits at the other's expense, but they do not wish to totally crush the other. It is in the interests of both, their maximum joint profit, to continue the relationship if at all possible. The term *mixed motive* is used, writes social psychologist Philip Brickman (1974:5), "since each party may be partly motivated by a desire to cooperate around the common interests in the relationship and partly motivated by a desire to compete for the more favorable share of those resources which must be divided up."

In our story of Bob and Julie's negotiations over the new car, the conflict was mixed-motive. Each wanted to gain at the expense of the other, but neither wanted to wipe the other out in zero-sum fashion. Each saw value in maintaining their relationship and wanted to cooperate on the basis of all they held in common, even though their competing interests were pulling in different directions. Bob was not ready to insist on a new car to the point of breaking up the marriage, nor was Julie ready to resist to this point. Thus, they had to deal with mixed motives: competition on the one hand and cooperation on the other.

PERSONALITY-BASED AND SITUATIONAL CONFLICT

Another hypothetical couple, the Wilsons, sought a counselor's help because of severe conflicts in their marriage. Ted Wilson complained that his wife neglected household chores to read or watch television. "And she's always nagging me to give her time off from taking care of the kids. What kind of woman is she if she can't stand taking care of her own children and can't keep

"First of all, is this new anger or merely some old anger you're just getting around to expressing?" (Drawing by Frascino; © 1977 The New Yorker Magazine, Inc.)

the house decently clean? Something's wrong with her!" At this point, Betty Wilson broke in: "He's always saying something's wrong with me! Why doesn't he ever look at himself? The first thing he says when he comes in the door each evening is, 'What's for dinner?' or 'Don't you have anything cooked *yet*?' He's only affectionate if he wants sex. He only cares about himself. He won't even baby-sit so that I can take some evening-school courses."

Viewing the Wilsons' problem solely as a *personality-based* conflict, the counselor told Betty she should accept her wife-mother role and "adjust to her womanhood" rather than fight against it. She should stop rebelling against her responsibilities as a homemaker and should leave her husband free to pursue his occupational interests. Her interests should be secondary to those of Ted and the children. Ted, for his part, must learn to be more understanding. "Show Betty more affection and consideration," the counselor advised.

The Wilsons went home, tried out the counselor's advice, and found it didn't work. After a few more months of conflict, they visited a different counselor.

To the second counselor, the Wilsons' case was one of *situational* conflict. Resolution of such conflict lies in changing the situation rather than trying to change the people to fit the situation. The Wilsons were helped first to see what lay at the root of their problem. Betty felt frustrated in her homemaker role not out of malice or laziness but because she felt blocked from finishing college. She watched programs on public television and read books constantly to keep stretching her mind beyond what she felt housekeeping would allow. The counselor helped the couple see that trying to force Betty to "adjust" or "adapt" wasn't the answer. What they needed to do was to negotiate and find ways to make it possible for her to continue her education.

The Wilsons worked out a plan for sharing household chores and child care, and both the negotiation process and the sharing has strengthened their relationship. Watching his wife's accomplishments and happiness, Ted has a new respect for her and finds himself being much more affectionate now that the old hostilities are gone. Betty is so grateful for Ted's willingness to finance her education as well as his sharing child care and home responsibilities that she feels a new love for him. And even housework isn't the same old drudgery that it was in the days of her sulking and resentment. The Wilsons are finding that the changed situation is removing their old complaints about each other.

While conflicts may have either a situational or personality base, perhaps far more than is generally realized, marital conflicts stem from factors relating to situations which spouses could seek to remedy, instead of simply complaining about one or the other's "unpleasant personality" or how hard it is to get along with him or her. Resolving social conflict over incompatible goals or limited resources is not a matter of "adapting" or "adjustment"; rather it calls for *change*.

BASIC AND NONBASIC CONFLICT

It is one thing to engage in conflict within agreed-upon rules of a game; it is quite another to have a conflict about the rules. The first kind of conflict is *nonbasic*. When the rules themselves are called into question and contested, the conflict is clearly *basic*.

When Congress passes a bill and the President vetoes it, Congress may or may not override the veto. But the whole sequence of events is a struggle within the rules set down by the Constitution. That sort of conflict is routine nonbasic conflict. However, what happens when Congress overrides a President's veto and instructs the executive branch to spend money for sewers and roads, only to have the President impound the funds? When that actually happened during the Nixon administration, the conflicts were resolved by court decisions ordering Nixon to use the funds. Again, the rules provided by the Constitution were able to resolve the resistance and struggle.

But at another point in the Nixon administration, journalists were talking about a "constitutional crisis" in which the President was ordered by the courts to release certain papers and tapes which he claimed were covered by "executive privilege." A "crisis" could occur if Nixon did not back down. Would the court use physical coercion to enforce its will? Yet, how could it proceed against the head of the Armed Forces and of the Justice Department? As it turned out, Nixon complied with the basic rule of political conflict that the courts have ultimate legitimate authority in such matters and thus the last word. Had he acted in any other way, it would have been seen as a gross use of raw nonlegitimate power.

Principles involved in conflict-resolution processes at the macro level also may be applied at the micro level. In other words, the same principles that apply to struggles between executive, courts, and Congress apply as well to marital conflict. To illustrate, let's return once again to our story of Bob and Julie. We saw how they resolved their conflict over a new car by renegotiating within the existing rules or role norms which characterize their kind of marriage arrangement. However, at another point, Bob is offered a job in another locale—a position he considers much more challenging and financially rewarding than his current job. But an exciting opportunity has also come up for Julie in their present location. She has been invited to develop and direct a special-education program in the local schools, while at the same time pursuing a master's degree at a nearby university. The stage is set for conflict over their different goals.

Under the rules or norms of a senior partner–junior partner marriage, Bob would expect Julie to forgo her opportunities in special education and move with him, since his role has been defined as chief provider. As such, his occupational demands necessarily take precedence over most other family demands. Another norm characterizing traditional marriage arrangements has been the expectation that marriage will mean children. It is virtually taken for granted that the union of a husband and wife should produce children at some point in order that the gratifications of the father and mother roles may be experienced.

To complicate Bob and Julie's situation further, Bob has started to talk about having a child soon. He feels that his new position will make it possible to manage the economic costs of a baby and suggests that it's time to have one. Julie need not continue working, Bob says, since he will be able to support a family totally if he takes the new job. Thus, still acting under the "rules of the game" for the kind of marriage Bob and Julie have been maintaining, Bob begins to negotiate a new exchange with his wife. He believes that the rules furnish him with legitimate authority to ask her to move with him and to undertake motherhood soon after.

Julie, however, has other ideas. Having always leaned toward modern, equalitarian sex-role norms, she is now beginning to ask questions about the senior partner–junior partner arrangement. The opportunity of a career in developing and administering special-education programs seems challenging. Bob's requests therefore strike her as unjust. She feels that her costs will rise and her rewards drop substantially if she goes along with her husband. She begins to struggle and resist. Conflict has emerged.

Julie bargains, saying she is willing for Bob to move and for them to commute alternately on weekends. Through her conflict and in her specific negotiating process, she is in effect beginning to challenge the norms that govern the senior partner–junior partner arrangement. Open communication was established as negotiations began, but as the conflict progresses certain deep issues begin to move to the fore. Should Julie have children or should she remain voluntarily childless? Should their marriage continue to be based on role specialization, or should they shift patterns to one based on role interchangeability so that Julie would be considered an equal partner in a dual-career arrangement?

These conflicts are clearly basic in that they involve contention over what the rules of the game should be. The game (marriage) will be very different if fundamental rules are changed. Rules governing American football are very different from those governing European football (soccer). In politics, the rules in the United States say that the President shall not use force to resist the courts or Congress. But in many countries today generals and presidents openly use military force to get their way when parliaments or courts cross them. These are two very different political games.

The earlier conflict of Bob and Julie over the purchase of a new automobile was nonbasic. We saw that even nonbasic conflict is likely to bring about situational changes. This is doubly so for basic conflict. But in addition, for any social system, basic conflict can mean instability or even total collapse. For instance, if an American President could persuade a general to mobilize troops to resist a congressional order to remove him from office, there would occur the most serious and devastating disruption of American democracy in two centuries. Or if two companies were to experience basic conflict over the rules of their buyer-seller relationship, they might simply terminate the association. Such a breaking off of the relationship would not be so likely to occur over nonbasic conflict, which is more easily negotiable.

Issues Involved in Basic Conflict Both in personal (expressive) and practical (instrumental) realms of marriage, basic conflict may occur. We have defined marriage as a relationship involving sexual and economic interdependence between the partners. The norms surrounding the relationship include the expectation that the husband and wife will have sexual intercourse with one another and that they will share their material wealth. If one partner arbitrarily decides to change those rules, we have a classic illustration of basic conflict.

For example, a distressed middle-aged woman wrote to a newspaper advice columnist with the following story: She and her husband were both in their second marriages, and for six years they had found together what she described as a happiness neither had dreamed possible. Almost nightly, they had sexual relations which both enjoyed immensely. Then the husband joined a religious cult and changed his attitudes entirely. The wife wrote: "He said he could no longer kiss me, or touch me, or sleep in the same bed with me because if he did he could not enter the kingdom of heaven because he would be committing adultery since we had both been married before!" After eight months of living this way, the wife was seeking help because the conflict was of the most basic sort (Bloomington (Ind.) *Herald-Telephone* "Dear Abby," March 16, 1973).

How basic conflict may occur over economic sharing is illustrated in the later life of novelist Leo Tolstoy and his wife, the Countess Tolstoy. Tolstoy had become obsessed with a concern for nonmaterialistic values and a desire to share his royalties and other wealth with those who were poor. His wife considered him selfish and neglectful of his own family. Why should he give away *their* money to strangers? Didn't she deserve some reward for all her years of hard work in caring for their home and rearing the children? For Tolstoy to give away his royalties appeared to his wife as a breaking of the fundamental rules of the game as they applied to economic provision and sharing. The *consumption* of resources for survival and for status is a basic issue in marriage just as is economic *production*.

As we have seen, each of the four ways marriage may be structured also has rules about which partner is the unique or chief provider. The issue of whether or not to have children is also basic—particularly where marriage has been viewed in traditional terms.

At the same time, there may occur *nonbasic* conflicts within the same general areas that have been discussed (sex, the provider role, the consumption of resources, and the issue of children). Such secondary conflicts may center around the hours the husband or wife is working, how to discipline the children, how often and with what techniques should sex relations take place, or how to keep expenditures within the budget. But underlying each of these secondary conflicts is an assumption that there is agreement as to the four basic core issues (that is, that there will be sexual intercourse, that the provider role has been acknowledged to be the primary responsibility of one or both partners, that parenthood will be undertaken or avoided voluntarily, and that consumption and life-style will be of a certain kind). To the degree that such basic consensus exists, struggles which are less central can more satisfactorily be resolved.

In the case of Bob and Julie, Julie's objective is to resolve their basic conflict in such a way that she will become an equal partner with her husband, with her career and interests considered just as important as his. She is also increasingly open to the possibility of remaining childless and avoiding the mother role entirely. This is a very different "game" or arrangement than the couple had before when Julie seemed content to be a junior partner and planned to work only a few years before settling down to have a family. Yet it is precisely those former rules and that earlier game which Bob wants. Since each spouse wants to play a different game with a different set of rules, how can they resolve their mutual struggles and resistances? How can they hold their relationship together and avoid separation or divorce?

Some persons might argue that if the husband could somehow retain final authority, as was traditionally the case, then basic conflicts such as these could be resolved. The husband could simply declare, "This is what we will do," and the issue would be settled. However, that argument overlooks the twin questions of justice and accountability. Husbands have generally tended to resolve conflicts in ways they thought best, with "best" meaning ways that seemed favorable to themselves simply because they were considered to have the final authority. Again it seems appropriate to echo John Stuart Mill's argument of a century ago that there is no inherent structural reason for one partner in a voluntary association to be the final authority. It would be unjust in a business partnership, and it is unjust in a marriage.

Moreover, traditionally husbands had authority but *no accountability*, much as did preparliamentary monarchs. But today even a president who says the "buck stops here" is accountable for the exercise of nonlegitimate power. He is accountable to Congress who can impeach him, the courts who can reverse him, or to voters who can turn him out of office. Thus, in marriage, an appeal to some ultimate authority based on gender whose decisions cannot be disputed, modified, or rejected, or who could not be removed from his position of authority is simply not considered fair or wise in modern society. What Lord Acton said about political power applies as well to the notion of the male (or female) as absolute final arbiter in marriage. "Power tends to corrupt, but absolute power corrupts absolutely."

There are several alternative modes of conflict resolution that Bob and Julie can pursue. Assuming reasonable communication and willingness to negotiate, Bob can agree to a bargain in which the rules are indeed changed. Julie would then become an equal partner. As for the matter of starting a family, neither having nor not having children is essential to the equal-partner marriage pattern. The matter is optional. Thus, Bob may try to negotiate with Julie about having a child. If they do decide to have one, issues such as timing and child care become additional matters for negotiation. How extensively should they rely on nursery and day-care facilities? How responsible will Bob be for child care?

Besides bargaining for a child, Bob may also aim negotiation toward persuading Julie to move with him. Let us assume she can find educational and career opportunities in the new locale comparable to those in the old. When Julie agrees to pursue these opportunities rather than her original plans, a new exchange is established in which both spouses experience maximum joint profit. Julie has a new game; she is now an equal partner. At the same time, she has conceded to relocate and also to have a child—both however under conditions that she does not consider excessively costly or punishing. Bob, for his part, has gained the benefits he wanted (the move and the child), but he agrees to a new game based on role interchangeability in which he is now merely a coprovider and in which Julie possesses as much authority and autonomy as he does.

However, the story could have a different ending. Upon facing their basic conflict, Bob and Julie may simply decide on another mode of resolution—ending the marriage. The key is whether or not Bob is willing for the basic changes in the rules for which Julie is pressing. In other words, is he willing for a new game? If he is not, it is difficult to see what meaningful concessions Julie can make, given her objectives. They are resisting each other over very basic issues; and since both perceive that so much is at stake, no significant negotiations or bargaining can take place. The couple may therefore decide that it is in the best interests of both of them simply to separate and file for divorce. (See Figure 14-2.) Each compares the level of alternatives (rewards and costs) within the marriage with alternatives outside it. Each concludes that the latter alternatives are more desirable or "profitable" (fewer costs, greater rewards) than those in their present situation. And so they leave it.

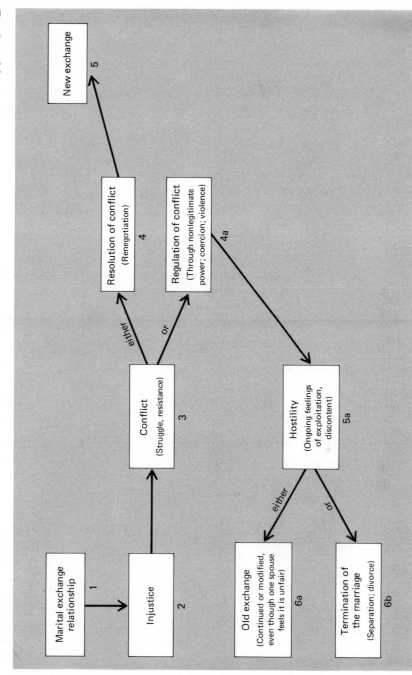

FIGURE 14-2   Three possible outcomes of marital conflict: resolution, regulation, or termination of the marriage (to be compared with Figure 14-1).

The overwhelming evidence suggests that conflict is an inevitable part of any ongoing social relationship—including marriage. (Kenneth Karp)

INEVITABILITY OF CONFLICT

Up until recently, sociologists tended to view social conflict as "bad." In terms of the structural-functional approach, conflict was thought to disrupt and tear apart social systems. Conflict within the institution of marriage was thought to have only negative consequences and was to be avoided at all costs.

Currently, the overwhelming weight of evidence suggests that conflict is an inevitable part of any ongoing social relationship—including marriage. Given the processes of social exchange and given the likelihood that all parties involved are seeking to maximize rewards and minimize costs, a certain amount of conflict on occasion is to be expected. There are bound to be occasions of struggling over incompatible goals or resisting the profit seeking of others because of the costs to oneself.

BENEFICIAL CONFLICT

Given its inevitability, the issue becomes not how to avoid conflict but how to resolve it. Increasingly, social scientists agree that conflict may often strengthen the bonds of a social relationship and make it more rewarding (Blau, 1964; Coser, 1956). Conflict, when satisfactorily resolved, removes injustice and punishments. The end result of conflict can be such that maximum joint profit is greater than it was before. "Opposition," says sociologist Peter Blau (1964:301), "is a regenerative force that introjects new vitality into a social structure." The new bargains that grow out of the conflict mean that numerous aspects of the total relationship can be revised, altered, and made more rewarding than if resistance and struggle had not occurred.

This "regenerative" process can be viewed not only from the micro perspective, such as the husband-wife unit; it can also be viewed on the macro level, where nations contend with one another or groups within society dispute with one another (for example, labor and management). Historically, the feminist movement has meant social conflict between women and men. Females have sought to increase their share of scarce resources (material rewards, education, prestige, power) inevitably at the expense of male dominance and control. The struggle of blacks against whites has been of the same type. When a minority group presses for a greater share of rewards disproportionately enjoyed by a majority group, there is conflict. During the conflict, there is likely to be suffering (costs) on both sides; but when the conflict is resolved satisfactorily, both sides are likely to benefit and experience maximum joint profit.

Looking back over the past two centuries, virtually all social scientists would conclude that the conflicts between blacks and whites and between males and females have indeed been "regenerative" or "healthy" for Western societies. American society is probably stronger and more stable than it would have been had not resistances occurred. And it is not only that these minority groups are becoming better off. It may be assumed that men and whites in general are also better off as a result of gains made by women and blacks. Although it has been costly to males and whites in terms of traditional rewards (privileged position, unchallenged economic advantages, greater power, and so on), new rewards have been emerging as compensation. For

"Let's face it, Ron. The only time we meet each other's needs is when we fight." (Drawing by Joe Mirachi; © 1977 The New Yorker Magazine, Inc.)

example, society benefits through a greater utilization of talents when certain persons aren't blocked from achievement because of race or sex. Freedom from racial or sex-role stereotypes may enable persons to be themselves and relate as human beings with much in common to unite them rather than stressing differences that separate. Husbands might find that they are emancipated from many pressures as wives come to share the economic load. And wives may prove to be more interesting companions as well.

DESTRUCTIVE CONFLICT

However, Coser (1956:73) raises the question: "If conflict unites, what tears apart?" In saying that conflict has the potential of being cohesive (holding social groups together and bringing benefits), we are not denying that conflict also has the potential of being divisive (tearing groups apart, breaking up relationships). Conflicts can bring about the dissolution of business partnerships, entertainment teams, alliances between nations, friendships, and marriages. If a husband and wife, for example, try to resolve conflicts by continually resorting to nonlegitimate power, feelings of exploitation, discontent, and distrust may be generated. The partner who feels exploited might eventually leave the relationship. As we saw earlier, there is some indication that working-class husbands try to resolve conflicts through exercising power that their wives do not recognize as legitimate, since the husbands have fewer resources and give their wives fewer economic-status benefits than is true of middle-class husbands. This may be one reason why divorce rates are higher among working-class marriages than among middle-class marriages. Conflicts tend not to be resolved in ways that are regenerative but rather in ways that are disruptive.

AREAS OF CONFLICT IN MARRIAGE

What kinds of issues are involved in conflicts between husbands and wives? In our study of Indianapolis marriages, we asked each respondent to name in rank order the four things the respondent and spouse disagreed about most often. The question was open ended; that is, no prepared list of areas of potential conflict was read. Thirty-eight percent of the respondents said that the major area of contention in their marriages was money (producing it and spending it); 19 percent cited issues connected with children, 10 percent indicated problems over friends, and 3 percent said problems over kin. Twenty-one percent were placed in a category called "miscellaneous" since they indicated problems common only to a few families, problems too individualized to warrant a special category for each one; and 9 percent of the respondents reported nothing (Scanzoni, 1970:157–158).

Among areas of disagreement placed in the miscellaneous category were issues sometimes called "tremendous trifles" (matters pertaining to personal habits, preferences, and manners of conducting day-to-day living). Slightly more than one-fifth of our respondents cited some such issue as the major area of disagreement. Examples were decisions about colors to paint the home interior, concerns about punctuality, disagreements over the thermostat setting, and so on. Such matters can become highly significant in a husband-wife conflict, particularly when one feels the other is exercising nonlegitimate power and taking unfair advantage.

Although many people think that sexual problems are the major cause of husband-wife disagreements, the number of respondents who mentioned sex as their number one contention area was too few to warrant listing sex as a separate category. The seven-tenths of 1 percent who did name sex were included under "miscellaneous." Blood and Wolfe (1960:243–244), in their Detroit study, also found that only a very small percentage of their respondents (less than one-half of 1 percent) specified sexual conflict as their major trouble area. Perhaps folklore, movies, the popular press, and reports of case studies by marriage counselors and sex counselors have combined to present an exaggerated picture of the part sexual disagreements play in marital conflict and dissolution.

On the other hand, Blood and Wolfe may have a point in saying that there may be an *underreporting* of sex problems as the major area of disagreement. These researchers suggest that persons might be shy and hesitant to name this area of marriage, since sex is generally considered to be a personal and private matter. Yet, the social climate regarding sexual matters has become increasingly open. Considerable time has passed since the Blood and Wolfe findings; and while it is possible that the shyness-privacy explanation may have been a factor in the low reporting of sexual conflict in their study, it would seem to be less valid as an explanation of the low percentage in more recent research. For example one large-scale study indicates that only 1.4 percent of husbands and wives consider sex to be their major area of disagreement (Scanzoni, 1975b). While there is no denying serious conflicts over sex do occur in some marriages, it appears that among marriages in general, other disagreement areas are of far more concern. Money and children continue to be the main issues over which there is husband-wife conflict.

Table 14-A compares the findings of Blood and Wolfe with those of our Indianapolis study and also with our more recent study in which 3,096 husbands and wives in ten major northern metropolitan areas were interviewed (Scanzoni, 1975b). In this latter study, nearly one-third of the respondents reported money matters as the major area of marital disagreement, and close to one-fifth percent specified child-related matters. Each remaining category shows a lower percentage then either of these.

ECONOMIC MATTERS

Given the interrelationship of the family with the economic-opportunity system, it is not surprising that issues relating to money and jobs are so important to husband and wives. Self-worth is intricately bound up with

TABLE 14-A   *Major conflict areas in marriage (percent of respondents reporting each area)*

CHIEF DISAGREEMENT	BLOOD AND WOLFE, 1960	SCANZONI, 1970	SCANZONI, 1975
Money-related matters (producing and spending)	24%	38%	33%
Child-related matters (e.g., discipline and number)	16	19	19
Friend-related matters		10	1
Kin-related matters	6	3	3
Companionship, leisure, recreation (kind, quality, and quantity)	16		8
Activities disapproved by spouse (problem drinking, gambling, extramarital affairs, etc.)	14		3
Roles, household division of labor	4		3
Miscellaneous (all else, including religion, politics, sex, communication in marriage, "tremendous trifles," etc.)	3	21	13
"Nothing" reported, "Nothing specific," not ascertained	17	9	17
Total	*100%*	*100%*	*100%*
Number	*(731)*	*(916)*	*(3,096)*

SOURCE: Adapted from Blood and Wolfe, 1960, p. 241; Scanzoni, 1970, p. 157; Scanzoni, unpublished data from the study described in 1975b.

achievement and acquisitiveness in a modern industrial society, and husbands and wives are apt to have great concern about whether or not they are living up to personal and societal expectations. Their concern might sometimes take the form of disagreements over occupational matters (the *production* aspect of the economic side of marriage) or over matters of expenditure (the *consumption* aspect). The couple might disagree about the wife's career aspirations or about the husband's working overtime or moonlighting on a second job, or about changing jobs. They might have conflicts about how much they should pay for new furniture, about how far to go into debt, about a spouse's extravagance (or conversely, a spouse's miserliness and hoarding), about having a joint checking account, about savings, investments, credit cards, and a myriad of other matters.

DISAGREEMENTS OVER CHILDREN

Since children require a considerable investment on the part of parents, they constitute another area of great importance and potential husband-wife disagreement. Emotionally and financially, as well as in terms of time and energy, parents are spending a great deal on children. In spite of these costs, parents also may view children as sources of rewards. Husbands and wives may disagree about the best way to ensure that the rewards of children will exceed the costs. To one spouse, the very idea of having children in the first place might appear to be too costly; while to the other spouse, "starting a family" may be a cherished goal. Similarly, there may be conflict about the spacing of children or the number desired. In one situation, a father continued to pressure his wife to "try one more time for a boy" after they had eight daughters. The wife balked at the suggestion.

Child-related marital conflicts are not only centered around having children (if, when and how many) but also about how to rear them. One spouse might be strict, while the other is lenient; the result is often severe disagreement about matters of nurture and discipline. Clashes about techniques of securing obedience from small children, or about how much allowance to give the elementary schoolchild, or about how much freedom to grant adolescents are not uncommon as husbands and wives share the task of parenting.

OTHER CONFLICT MATTERS

In a follow-up study of *wives only* from the earlier (Scanzoni, 1975b) study of marriages in ten major northern metropolitan areas, we tapped areas of conflict in a different way by first asking respondents to name the one most important thing they wished their husbands would either do or stop doing, and then asking whether or not they felt their husbands' behavior in this matter was fair to the wives (Scanzoni, 1978).

Fourteen percent were unable to name any such area that was a problem at the time of the interview. But among the remaining wives, socioeconomic issues again topped the list. Slightly less than a quarter wished their husbands would either work harder and earn more or else *not* work so hard and be away from the family so much; or they wished their husbands would stop spending so much money, or start spending more on certain items, and so on. Issues related to children concerned 15 percent and comprised the third largest set of conflicts.

However, in contrast to the other studies, a new set of conflicts was in second place—matters related to peer/kin relations. Nearly 23 percent of the wives wanted their husbands to stop spending so much time with the husbands' relatives or the husbands' friends, or to "stop wanting other women." Or they wanted their husbands to let them visit their own relatives more or let them entertain more often.

Other areas of conflict involved husbands' failures to perform household tasks (12 percent); socioemotional issues—such as wanting more attention, affection, and empathy from husbands and either more or less sexual interest (8 percent); issues centering around the wives' desire for autonomy and their husbands' resistance or lack of support in that desire for independence (4 percent); and various miscellaneous issues (16 percent).

Conflicts in marriage, whether about money or children or anything else, may be settled amiably through negotiation, or they may lead to a breakup of the marital relationship. Sometimes, however, they explode into actual violence—a possibility that until recently has often been overlooked by researchers, perhaps because of the "touchiness" and unpleasantness of the subject and the common belief that violence only occurs on occasion in "abnormal" families (O'Brien, 1971).

VIOLENCE IN MARRIAGE

One June day in 1974, an Indiana minister and his wife went for a drive. The trip ended tragically. When their bodies were found one week apart floating in the Wabash River, law officers theorized that an assailant must have slain the couple and stolen their car. Later, however, the automobile was found submerged at the point where it had been driven 200 feet into a stream. After an extensive investigation, a coroner's jury concluded that the plunge into the water had been deliberate and that the minister planned to kill his wife and possibly himself. The charge of homicide was considered definite, although there was some doubt about the suicide attempt in view of evidence that the minister had tried to escape but had been trapped when his shoe caught on something in the car. In its study, the jury learned that the couple, both in their mid-thirties and married only six months, had been having severe marital difficulties.

This case may seem as bizarre as it is tragic. Yet, according to the National Commission on the Causes and Prevention of Violence, what appear to be automobile "accidents" have not infrequently been found to have been intentional acts of murder and suicide (Mulvihill, Tumin, and Curtis, 1969). Not only is the family car sometimes the murder weapon itself; it also serves as the setting for many murders in which other weapons are used—such as in the case of a woman depressed over her forty-fifth birthday who asked her husband to go for a drive with her and then, as he slid behind the steering wheel, shot him and then herself.

Other common settings for family murders are the kitchen (a central location for interaction between family members and often the site of arguments) and the bedroom (where husband and wife are closed off in privacy with one another at the end of the day, providing an occasion where built-up tensions and hostilities may suddenly erupt) (Steinmetz and Straus, 1974:39, 93). Sometimes both settings are involved, as in a 1979 North Carolina case in which a husband became upset with the cold breakfast his wife had served. They continued their argument in the bedroom, where the husband allegedly reached for a gun and shot his wife in the head, then killed himself. And in a bedroom of a California rest home that same year, an eighty-one-year-old woman was charged in the murder of her eighty-five-year-old husband after she allegedly beat him severely during a quarrel.

"People are more likely to be hit, beat up, physically injured, or even killed in their own homes by another family member than anywhere else, and by anyone else, in our society," writes sociologist Richard Gelles (1979:11). But the problem isn't limited to our society. Gelles goes on: "Nearly one out of every four murder victims in the United States is killed by a member of one's own family, and this is the case in Africa, Great Britain, and Denmark." Family homicide is a gruesome reality in which husbands kill wives, wives kill husbands, parents kill children, children kill parents, brothers and sisters kill one another, people kill in-laws and grandparents, and so on. Viewed this way, the family looks more like a bloodstained battlefield than a peaceful haven of love and tenderness.

Most families, of course, are not broken up by the murder of one family member by another family member. Yet, many other kinds of violence may be far more common than is generally realized. Until recently, sociologists have given little attention to family violence, and research has been scanty. We simply do not know the actual incidence of physical force or the threat of physical force between spouses. Similarly, even though the problem of the "battered child syndrome" has been more publicized, there are no statistics on the actual number of children who are physically abused by their parents—although over the course of a year suspected cases of child abuse reported run around 300,000 (Steinmetz, 1977). We'll be examining the child-abuse aspect of family violence in our discussion of childrearing in Chapter 16. Here we want to focus primarily on the use of violence in conflicts between wives and husbands, as well as introducing the topic of family violence in general.

WHY NOT MORE RESEARCH INTO FAMILY VIOLENCE?

Since in the minds of most people, the family is considered to be a place of warmth, love, affection, tenderness, and caring, it seems hard to accept the idea that so much violence can occur within family settings. When it does occur, people tend to want to look the other way—as though not seeing something means it isn't there; or they may dismiss it as a rare exception involving some kind of personal pathology. Members of families where violence occurs don't want to admit that their families are not living up to what families are "supposed" to be and feel ashamed that they are somehow different from other families. Thus they may not seek help until the situation is extremely desperate.

Sociologist Suzanne Steinmetz (1977) speaks of how this "myth of family nonviolence" is perpetuated and reinforced:

> Evidence suggests that lawmakers, historians, and social scientists, as well as the general population, tend to deny the existence of family violence or to assume violence only occurs in sick families, families living in inner-city ghettos, or families characterized by some other pathology such as drugs, alcohol, gambling, or mental aberrations. By this means it is possible to resolve the dissidence between the socially desirable view of the family and the unpleasantness of reality. (p. 5)

However, in recent years the fact of family violence has been acknowledged, and research on the topic (though still limited and with many shortcomings) has been conducted (Steinmetz, 1978). Steinmetz (1977:xxi) points out that attention to child abuse became evident during the 1950s and 1960s. Studies of spouse abuse—especially wife abuse—began appearing increasingly in the 1970s. She predicts that the decade of the 1980s will be a period of increasing concern over abuses of the elderly and attention to the problem of battered elderly parents.

HOW WIDESPREAD IS VIOLENCE IN MARRIAGE?

Husband-wife violence is not a subject persons talk about with ease; and as we have seen, research has been scanty until recently, making it impossible to say with absolute certainty the *exact* amount of such violence that takes place. But we can gain some idea by looking at studies available thus far.

Some of the earliest pioneering researchers on the topic of marital violence endeavored to find some answers through interviews with applicants for divorce. In one such study, 17 percent of those interviewed spontaneously mentioned physical abuse as a reason for the deterioration of their marriage and a major factor in initiating divorce action (O'Brien, 1971).

In another study, George Levinger (1966) examined records of 600 applicants for divorce in the greater Cleveland area, where, by order of the court, divorce applicants with children under fourteen years of age were required to meet with experienced marriage counselors. In analyzing the counselors' interview records, Levinger found that physical abuse was a complaint in more than one-third of the cases, with wives complaining far more than husbands of being physically hurt by the spouse. Nearly 37 percent of the women applying for divorce voiced such a complaint, compared to 3.3 percent of husbands. Social-class differences were also found. Among middle-class couples in Levinger's sample, 22.8 percent of wives and 2.9 percent of husbands complained of being physically abused by the marital partner. Among working-class and lower-class couples, 40.1 percent of wives reported that their husbands hurt them physically, and 3.5 percent of husbands complained of physical abuse by their wives. While such figures may provide some rough idea of the extent of physical violence in marriages that end in divorce, they do not furnish us with data on marriages in general. Thus, generalizations from these figures should be avoided.

Since violence has often been regarded as almost exclusively a phenomenon of the lower socioeconomic strata of society, the extent to which it occurs in middle-class marriages may strike many as surprising. While it is true that more violence occurs in lower-class marriages than occurs at higher levels, there is nevertheless evidence that a considerable amount of physical abuse does occur among middle-class couples. Slightly more than one out of five middle-class wives in Levinger's study of divorce applicants reported violence, as compared to two out of five working-class and lower-class wives.

Murray Straus is a sociologist who has devoted much attention and exploratory study to the issue of violence in marriage. In one study, 385 university students filled out questionnaires indicating whether or not their parents were known to have used or threatened physical force during the last year in which the student lived at home. Sixteen percent of the students indicated that one or the other parent had *threatened* to hit or throw something at the spouse, or had actually done so, or had pushed, grabbed, or shoved the other during a disagreement. However, as Straus (1974) cautions, "An obvious limitation of this data is that it describes only unbroken families with a child in college, which is far from representative of the population as a whole. . . . Consequently, a description of the amount of violence between family members based on this data is likely to be an underestimate." Also, the information tells us only about a single year of a couple's married life, and it may be incomplete inasmuch as parents might be hesitant to engage in violence in the presence of their children—even though they might resort to it in private.

Another sociologist, Richard Gelles (1973a), in a series of depth interviews with eighty couples, found that in more than half of these marriages at least one instance of husband-wife physical force had occurred at some time.

Several years later, Gelles, Straus, and Steinmetz joined together in a large-scale research effort designed to study family violence in a national sample of over two thousand families. These researchers found that "one out of six couples in the United States engage in at least one incident of violence each year" (Gelles, 1979:92; Straus, Gelles, and Steinmetz, 1980). Furthermore, writes Gelles (1979:92), "over the course of a marriage the chances are greater than one in four (28%) that a couple will come to blows."

However, as Murray Straus and his colleague Suzanne Steinmetz (1973) write, "The fact that almost all family violence, including everyday beating, slapping, kicking and throwing things, is carried out by normal everyday Americans rather than deranged persons should not lead us to think of violence as being desirable or even acceptable." Rather, they suggest asking *why* so many families resort to violence. Gelles (1973b) emphasizes that psychological explanations in which "mental illness" is viewed as the major reason for physical abuse are inadequate in themselves. There needs also to be an examination of social situational factors such as childhood socialization patterns, socioeconomic status, community or subcultural values regarding violence, structural stress (unemployment, excess children, and so on), and an awareness of immediate precipitating situations that bring on acts of violence in some families.

WHY VIOLENCE OCCURS

To understand violence, we may want to recall our definition of conflict as a struggle over limited resources and/or incompatible goals in which it appears that one person or group will have its way at the expense of the other party or group. Conflict need not and often does not result in violence. However, in some situations persons may resort to violence because it may seem there is no other way out. Sociologist William Goode (1971) points out that when persons begin to feel a continuing imbalance between investments and payoffs in the daily exchanges of family life they may engage in conflict over this imbalance. For various reasons, they may feel they cannot take one of the other roads usually open in such a situation—escape, submission, or righting the balance. As a result, the conflict "can escalate to the point of violence because no simpler or easier resolution emerges."

In some marriage and family situations, one of the other routes may be chosen. Some persons decide that escape is the answer; thus, the child runs away from home or a spouse deserts the family or files for divorce. In other cases, submission (though given grudgingly and with resentment) might appear to be the only way to "keep the peace." Yielding to the demands of a domineering spouse, for example, may seem easier to the other spouse than bringing injustices out into the open and engaging in conflict. Goode's third alternative, righting the balance, would seem the most desirable way to handle what one or the other spouse feels are imbalances in the husband-wife exchange. This is the renegotiation process we spoke of earlier as exemplified in the way Bob and Julie handled their conflict over the new car.

Articles and books have been written to help couples approach the problem of conflict in this way and to fight "creatively," "fairly," and "properly"—in other words, to fight constructively rather than destructively (for example, Bach and Wyden, 1968). As sociologist Jetse Sprey (1971) has written, "The successful management of conflict requires the ability to negotiate, bargain, and cooperate: a range of behavioral skills." However, some persons fail to develop such behavioral skills and seek a solution to dissension by either escaping or submitting to the wishes and demands of the other person even if they seem unfair. Or out of desperation, either party in a conflict may resort to the fourth alternative mentioned by Goode—actual violence.

It should not be assumed that the *absence* of conflict means everything is fine in a husband-wife relationship. Seething resentments and hostilities may underlie an outwardly calm marital life. In the example of our hypothetical couple, suppose that neither had expressed feelings of injustice. Julie might have kept to herself (or shared with some relatives or women friends) her feelings that Bob was acting unfairly by not doing the cooking. Resentments could have piled up, but to avoid conflict she would not have voiced her complaints to Bob. Instead, she might have acted increasingly distant and cool toward him. As it was, she was able to bring up the matter and work with Bob toward a constructive solution through negotiation—even before an actual conflict emerged in which each would have struggled for his or her own way. The couple did engage in actual conflict over the car Bob wanted, but again they were able to resolve it since they didn't try to bury the problem but instead were willing to renegotiate after Bob pressed for what he felt was fairness.

WHY THE FAMILY MAY BE A SETTING FOR VIOLENCE

Suppression of perceived injustice in order "not to rock the boat" or to be "selfless" or "altruistic" can generate strong feelings which could explode at some unexpected time. Several observations of sociologist Lewis Coser (1956:62) are worth noting in this regard. He points out that "there is more occasion for the rise of hostile feelings in primary than in secondary groups." Primary groups are composed of persons having a close relationship to one another in which, as much as possible, the total range of roles and the complete personality of each is known to the other. The family is probably the most obvious example of such a group. Secondary relationships, on the other hand, involve persons who know and relate to one another segmentally; they share only certain aspects of their lives and see one another only in specific roles. A patient may know a doctor only in the role of physician and know nothing of the physician's role as spouse, parent, church or club member, friend, and so on. The patient and physician are involved in one another's lives only on a secondary level; the physician's relationship with his or her spouse, children, and closest friends, however, is on a primary level. Areas of one's personality and interests which are not disclosed in a secondary relationship are revealed and out in the open in a primary one, such as the family. "If you could see him at home, you'd know what he's really like," is a common bit of folk wisdom.

Coser emphasizes that since primary relations tend to involve the total personality, feelings of intimacy are strengthened. Sharing all aspects of life makes people feel close to each other. Paradoxically, however, such intimacy has the potential of breeding hate as well as love. This happens because persons in close contact are bound to "rub one another the wrong way" on occasion. But since conflict is usually considered "bad" and disruptive for primary relationships, deliberate efforts are made to avoid it. The desire to engage in conflict is suppressed out of concern for affectionate sentiments, peace, and group cohesiveness. However, suppression of conflicts often means that an accumulation of hostilities is occurring, and any eruption of these feelings is likely to have great intensity both because persons in primary relations are so totally involved in one another's lives and also because the hostile feelings have grown to huge proportions by not having been allowed expression earlier (Coser, 1956:62–63, 79).

An outburst in which spouses furiously unleash their gathering storms of hostilities is not likely to solve problems or help their situation. Hostilities and conflict are not one and the same. In the words of Coser (1956:40), "Whereas conflict necessarily changes the previous terms of the relationship of the participants, mere hostility has no such necessary effects and may leave the terms of the relationship unchanged." To renegotiate, bargain, or engage in actual conflict is like the safety valve on a boiler. "Letting off steam" keeps the entire mechanism from exploding (Blau, 1964:304).

When husbands and wives keep hostilities and resentments to them-selves, sudden convulsions might occur at any time in the form of devastating, heated verbal exchanges or actual physical violence. Often *both* verbal aggression and physical violence take place. Straus (1974) conducted a study to test the hypothesis that verbal aggression is a substitute for physical aggression. The results showed just the opposite: "The more verbal expression of aggression, the more physical aggression." In using the term *verbal aggression*, Straus is not referring to settling an argument through rational discussion, negotiating, and talking over and working through disagreements. Rather, he focused on such aggressive tactics as yelling and insulting the spouse, calling the spouse derogative names, sulking and refusing to talk (the "silent treatment" can be very aggressive), and angrily stomping out of the room.

TYPES OF VIOLENCE

John O'Brien (1971), a social researcher who has given attention to violence in divorce-prone families, defines violence as "any behavior which threatens or causes physical damage to an object or person." Examples of family violence in the divorce records he examined included wife beating, child beating, threats with a gun, extreme sadomasochism in sex relations, and the starving of the spouse's pet cats. Some sociologists suggest that a distinction should be made between two types of violence. Steinmetz and Straus (1974:4), for example, speak of violence in which physical force is used to cause pain or injury as an end in itself in contrast to violence in which "pain or injury or physical restraint" is used "as a punishment to induce the other person to carry out some act."

Perhaps we could think of the distinction in terms of what we might call "explosive" violence and "coercive" violence. The child who throws a temper tantrum, the wife who suddenly begins pounding her husband's chest when he tries to smoothe over a disagreement by making sexual overtures when she wants to talk, the husband who kicks over a chair in a fit of rage all may be expressing *explosive* violence. They feel angry and frustrated and feel some need to "get it out of their system" through striking out. *Coercive* violence, in contrast, is goal-oriented and is directed toward accomplishing a task, namely to persuade someone to do or not to do something, or to punish the person, or in some other way to exercise control through physical force. The parent who shakes the child in order to extract the truth when lying is suspected is an example of coercive physical force. "You'd better tell me the truth or I'm just going to shake it out of you!" The husband who reacts to finding his wife in bed with another man by beating them both black and blue is another example of coercive violence (though no doubt combining "explosive" elements as well). "There, that'll show you both! That'll teach you never to do anything like that again, you no-good whore!"

Coercion may of course be verbal and involve threats of rewards withheld or certain nonphysical punishments; but as a stressful situation escalates, actual physical aggression may be resorted to as one person tries to control the other. The husband blocks the door and snatches away the car keys, yelling at his wife, "I said I don't want you to go!" Conversely, the person who is attempting to resist the coercion may resort to violence. The wife kicks her husband, scratches his arm with her fingernails in an attempt to get back the car keys, and tries to push him away from the doorway as she shouts, "Let me go, you bully!"

SOCIOECONOMIC STATUS AND VIOLENCE

We have already seen that husbands who are blocked from success in the economic-opportunity system are likely to attempt to resolve disagreements through exercising power that their wives consider nonlegitimate. There is also some evidence that violence is one of the ways this nonlegitimate power may be exercised in marriage (Allen and Straus, 1980).

A husband might turn to brute force as a means of dominating his wife if it seems the only way he can persuade her to comply with his wishes. As one blue-collar wife told Komarovsky (1962:227), "Women got to figure men out, on account of men are stronger and when they sock you, they could hurt you." Another wife told of a time her husband pulled off a banister and ripped up three steps in a fit of anger toward her—which caused her to stop and think of what might happen if that physical strength were applied *directly* toward her. Thus, according to Komarovsky, "the threat of violence is another ground of masculine power," particularly at lower socioeconomic levels. In her sample of blue-collar marriages, Komarovsky found that 27 percent of husbands with less than twelve years of education and 33 percent of wives with less than twelve years of education reported that conflicts were handled through violent quarreling, with occasional beating and breaking things. Among the high school graduates in her sample, 17 percent of the husbands and 4 percent of the wives reported such violence in marital quarreling (p. 363). In another study, Steinmetz (1977:126) found that the higher a husband's and wife's education and the higher their socioeconomic status (measured in her study by husband's education and occupation), the less likely they were to use physical force to settle marital conflicts and the more likely they were to use discussion (see also Gelles, 1979:141).

O'Brien (1971) likewise reports evidence of a connection between violence and a family's relationship to the economic-opportunity structure. O'Brien's sample of 150 divorce applicants included 24 percent upper middle class, 29 percent lower middle class, and 47 percent working class. In one out of six families, violence had occurred to such an extent that it was considered a major reason for initiating divorce.

O'Brien separated the 25 cases of families spontaneously reporting violence from the 125 cases where violence had not been reported as a reason for divorce. He found evidence that physical force on the part of the husband-father was commonly linked with underachievement in the bread-winner role. (See Table 14-B.) Since his sample did not include families with husbands chronically unemployed, the lower class was not represented. Otherwise even more evidence of violence would likely have shown up. The

TABLE 14-B *Comparison of achievement status of husbands in violence and nonviolence subgroups of unstable families*

ACHIEVEMENT STATUS OF HUSBAND	PREVALENCE IN:	
	VIOLENCE SUBGROUP (NUMBER = 25)	NONVIOLENCE SUBGROUP (NUMBER = 125)
Husband was seriously dissatisfied with his job	44%	27%
Husband started but failed to complete either high school or college	44	18
Husband's income was the source of serious and constant conflict	84	24
Husband's educational achievement was less than his wife's	56	14
Husband's occupational status was lower than that of his father-in-law (wife's marital mobility downward)	37	28

SOURCE: O'Brien, 1971, p. 695.

greater incidence of violence characterizing underclass families in ghetto areas says O'Brien, "reflects, not a subcultural disposition toward violence, but rather a greater incidence of men in the father/husband role who fail to have the achievement capacities normally associated with this role" (p. 697).

But why should men become violent with their wives and children because they as husbands and fathers haven't been achievers in the economic-opportunity system? Some men may react aggressively out of a sense of frustration at being blocked from the rewards which achievement in that system would have brought them. Unable to attack the system directly or the forces which they feel hold them back from its benefits, such men turn their attacks upon their families. Their reaction is what we have described as explosive violence.

On the other hand, it is quite possible that coercive violence takes place as well as explosive violence in homes where the husband has not achieved at a high level. Lacking legitimate authority earned by his accomplishments in the realm of work, such a husband may nonetheless feel that he has the right to domineer over his wife. He accepts an ideology of male supremacy, even if his wife views his power as nonlegitimate and does not submit to it unquestioningly or happily. If there is no other means of getting his way, such a husband may try physical force. One behavioral scientist says that the husband's perception of a failure to be in control underlies his violent outbursts (Whitehurst, 1974b:76). In the thinking of such a husband, not to be "in control" of his wife and children is not to be fully a man.

Goode (1971:624) points out that social systems contain four major elements by which persons may move others to carry out their wishes: (1) money or other material resources, (2) prestige or respect (such as commanded by a person in a position to which others look up), (3) winsomeness (likeability, attractiveness, friendship, love), and (4) force or the threat of force. In other words, we are back to the "carrot and stick" analogy. Persons may get their way either through rewards or punishments meted out to those whom they wish to control. Husbands who lack positive resources with which to reward their wives are likely to find it more difficult to extract submission or compliance from them. Thus, they turn to the one resource that appears to remain to them—physical force.

O'Brien has taken ideas from conflict theory as it applies to the larger society and has shown how these same ideas may be applied to the family. He points out that those in a superior position in a social system may hold such a position because of an *ascribed* status—a status they have not earned but have been granted by virtue of their membership in some social category (whites in a white-dominant society, males over females, feudal lords over peasants, and so on). In such a social system, those in an inferior position may accept and support the arrangement, believing that the group in the superior position has the right to rule because of its advantaged skills and resources. However, says O'Brien (1971:695), "One of the most common situations leading to a rejection of the legitimacy of those in high status is when their achieved status fails to measure up to their ascribed status." If the superior group is not able to back up its privileged position with a display of adequate resources, or if it fails to distribute such resources fairly to those over whom it holds power, a conflict situation emerges which may erupt in violence (Grimshaw, 1970). Perceiving a threat to the legitimacy of its superior position, the dominant group may resort to coercive action (violence) against the subordinate group that has dared to challenge its supremacy. Applying these ideas to the family, O'Brien concludes that "one should find that violence is most common in those families where the classically 'dominant' member (male-adult-husband) fails to possess the superior skills, talents or resources on which his preferred superior status is supposed to be legitimately based" (p. 693).

Another researcher emphasizes the importance of the *wife's* resources or lack of them. Wives who are not employed and who have little education are those most likely to remain in situations where their husbands beat them and are least likely to seek outside intervention. Such wives may feel trapped in an undesirable situation but are persuaded they have few if any alternatives. In contrast, those with jobs are less dependent upon their husbands and are more likely to seek help from social service agencies or the police and are also more likely to leave the marriage (Gelles, 1979:103–104).

An additional reason for more violence at lower socioeconomic levels may relate to childhood gender-role socialization in which boys are encouraged to develop what Jackson Toby (1966) has termed "*compulsive* masculinity," with an exaggerated emphasis on roughness and toughness as a sign of manhood. Toby suggests that boys at such levels, having grown up with little opportunity to understand, appreciate, and wield *symbolic* power (such as the power of a physician or business executive), may look on violence as "the most appropriate way to protect one's honor, to show courage, or to conceal fear, especially fear of revealing weakness" (see also Straus and Hotaling, 1980).

SEX ROLES, BATTERED WIVES, AND BATTERED HUSBANDS

The whole issue of the part sex roles play in marital violence is one to which researchers have been giving increasing attention.

"The cultural norms and values permitting and sometimes encouraging husband-to-wife violence reflect the hierarchical and male-dominant type of society which characterizes the Western world," writes sociologist Murray Straus (1977:68). He points out that the development of "compulsive masculinity," beliefs in male superiority which give men rights over their families, beliefs about wives as being "childlike" and "property" over whom husbands may exercise control, and the sex-based division of labor which gives women primary responsibility for child care and makes them financially dependent on husbands (thus often locking the wives into emotionally and physically injurious marriage situations)—all of these notions have a part to play in the battering that goes on in families. "Wife-beating is not just a personal abnormality," stresses Straus, "but rather has its roots in the very structure of society and the family; that is, in the cultural norms and in the sexist organization of the society and the family" (p. 61).

While wives may use violence on husbands just as husbands may be violent toward wives, wives are far more likely to resort to violence only to protect or defend themselves from sexual abuse and physical attacks by their husbands (Gelles, 1979). Thus, although there are battered husbands—and even murdered husbands, "the real issue is the social, political, and legal context of the violence," writes Gelles. "This becomes a question of victimization. When men hit women and women hit men, the real victims are almost certainly going to be the women" (p. 141). Sociologist Susan Steinmetz (1977) explains why:

> When the wife slaps her husband, her lack of physical strength, plus his ability to restrain her, reduces the physical damage to a minimum. When the husband slaps his wife, however, his strength, plus her inability to restrain him, results in considerably more damage. (p. 90)

On the other hand, Steinmetz is quick to add that women are equally capable of performing violent acts toward their husbands when conditions are equalized—such as through the use of a weapon or where a husband is much physically weaker. Steinmetz reports a case in which an elderly husband was scarred and bruised from assaults by his wife who was thirty-one years younger than he and considerably stronger. She had severely bitten his ear on one occasion, blackened his eyes on another, and another time inflicted such a serious injury that physicians feared he might lose the vision in one eye! If we look at homicide statistics for *spouse murders only*, we find that about half the victims are husbands murdered by wives and half are wives murdered by husbands (Straus, 1977:60, Steinmetz, 1978:3; Gelles, 1979:139).

Rideout Innocent of Raping Wife

SALEM, Ore.—A jury of eight women and four men found John Rideout innocent Wednesday of a charge of first-degree rape brought by his wife, Greta.

The verdict was unanimous.

The trial was the first of its kind in Oregon since the state revised its rape law in 1977 to eliminate immunity of husbands to such charges. Rideout also is believed to be the first man in the nation to stand trial on a charge of raping his wife while they were living together.

Tuesday, Mrs. Rideout, 23, and Rideout gave their conflicting accounts of what happened on Oct. 10, the date of the incident that led to the rape charge.

Mrs. Rideout testified her husband beat her into "submission" and raped her on Oct. 10. Rideout admitted that he had slapped his wife on that date, but he said that the sexual activity afterward "was voluntary."

The district attorney, Gary Gortmaker, and the defense attorney, Charles Burt, made their summations to the jury and after the judge's charge, the jury began deliberations around 2:30 P.M. Wednesday. Those deliberations lasted three hours.

The courtroom and halls in the Marion County courthouse here were packed with feminists, lawyers, journalists and curious local residents.

Lawyers observing the trial said that they believe conviction of Rideout and any subsequent appeals would have tested the constitutionality of a state's right to legislate on matters involving marital privacy.

Feminists here said they hope the trial will cause other states to follow Oregon's lead and revise their rape laws to exclude immunity for husbands.

In addition to Oregon, Iowa and Delaware have also revoked the common law doctrine of immunity for husbands, and New Jersey has revised its rape law to revoke this doctrine, effective Jan. 1. 1979.

SOURCE: New York Times News Service, *Greensboro (N.C.) Daily News*, December 28, 1978.

Gelles (1979) calls attention to two violence situations where wives are particularly the persons at risk: *marital rape* and *beatings during pregnancy*. Since sexual intercourse is considered a right of marriage, only a handful of states have legislation that recognizes forced intercourse by a husband as being no different than forced sexual acts by someone else—in other words, rape. Some men, particularly those lacking resources that could act positively in the power balance in marriage, may consider an act of marital rape as a way to exercise nonlegitimate power. They see it as a way to coerce or humiliate or dominate their wives (Gelles, 1979:127).

Similarly, when wives are pregnant they may be victims of beatings by their husbands (Gelles, 1972:145). Gelles (1979:113) suggests several possible reasons. Some couples are poorly informed and may think that sexual intercourse must cease during pregnancy; thus some husbands may take out their sexual frustrations by beating their wives. In other cases, the transition to parenthood and the changes associated with expecting and having a baby may bring stress which, when coupled with economic stress, erupts in violence. Gelles also speaks of some husbands' reactions to wives' mood changes, complaints, and irritability brought about by biochemical changes during pregnancy. In still other cases, husbands may be responding angrily to the prospect of an unwanted child and may show their rage by battering their pregnant wives. The act may be in part a kind of "prenatal child abuse," Gelles (1979:116) suggests, or it may be an effort to prevent a live birth from taking place, since "for many families violence which brings about a miscarriage is a more acceptable way of terminating an unwanted pregnancy than is abortion." Several wives in one of Gelles's own studies reported having experienced miscarriages after beatings by their husbands, and one wife who had been beaten while pregnant told of giving birth to a handicapped child.

While Gelles (1979) underscores a number of factors—including economic problems—that contribute to what he terms a "deadly tradition of domestic violence," one point is particularly pertinent in view of a basic theme of this book. He writes:

> An underlying cause of family violence is the fact that the family is perhaps the only social group where jobs, tasks and responsibilities are assigned on the basis of gender and age, rather than interest or ability. An elimination of the concept of "women's work"; elimination of the taken-for-granted view that the husband is and must be the head of the family; and an elimination of sex-typed family roles are all prerequisites to the reduction of family violence. (pp. 18–19, references omitted)

Although, in the short run, some men may react violently to the idea of relinquishing the power and privilege inherent in the traditional male role; in the long run, movement toward equality for the sexes may be expected to decrease acts of violence between spouses (Straus, 1977). Research by Gelles (1979:141) already indicates that the lowest rates of marital violence are found in those families where decision-making is shared by husbands and wives.

CHAPTER HIGHLIGHTS

Social conflict may be defined as a struggle over limited resources and/or incompatible goals. *Struggle* and *resistance* are key words in understanding conflict. When one party *resists* the other's wishes or claims, they are engaged in conflict. *Struggle* occurs when counteroffers are refused outright or no modifications are suggested. Communication isn't enough to settle conflict; beyond talking about the conflict situation, the parties must work to change it.

In *zero-sum* conflict, each party seeks to have all or nothing. Only one can win. In *mixed-motive* conflict, the parties are motivated by a desire to compete with each other on the one hand, and to cooperate with each other on the other hand. *Personality-based* conflict has a psychological base and is rooted in problems within the person, whereas *situational* conflict is engendered by structural factors outside the person. Resolution of situational conflict lies in changing the situation rather than trying to change the people to fit (or adapt to) the situation. *Basic* conflict is conflict over the rules of the game and wanting to change the rules. *Nonbasic* conflict, on the other hand, is conflict within mutually agreed-upon rules without calling the rules themselves into question.

The overwhelming weight of evidence suggests that conflict is an inevitable part of an ongoing social relationship—including marriage. Conflict may strengthen a relationship because, when satisfactorily resolved, it removes injustice and can mean greater maximum joint profit. On the other hand, conflict can be divisive (tearing groups apart, breaking up relationships). Disruptive conflicts are likely to be those where nonlegitimate power is exercised, trust is destroyed, and the person who feels exploited and unfairly treated wants out of the relationship. Sometimes conflicts explode into violence. Although family violence occurs at all socioeconomic levels, there is greater likelihood for it to occur among husbands and wives of lower education and social status. "Compulsive masculinity" and other ideas associated with traditional sex-role norms appear to play a major part in family violence.

PART SIX

CONTINUING PROCESSES OF THE FAMILY EXPERIENCE

CHAPTER 15

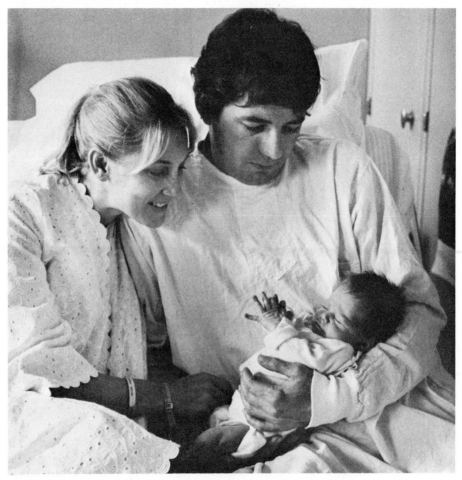

(© Ed Lettau/Photo Researchers, Inc.)

CHILDREN: TO HAVE OR NOT TO HAVE?

Ellen and Bill Peck decided not to have children. Soon the pressure was on! People reacted to their childless state with varying degrees of curiosity and hostility. Ellen points out that the question, "Are you going to have any children?" was never asked. Instead it was, "When are you going to have children?" (Katy, 1972; Peck, 1971).

According to a popular (but scientifically unsupported) folk belief, nature has programmed women so that their life's purpose is to have and rear children. Women are thought to possess some sort of mysterious quality deep within, a "maternal instinct" that produces yearnings for offspring. The folk belief is reinforced by a network of formal and informal societal pressures urging couples to become parents, and those who don't are stigmatized or pitied. These attitudes and societal pressures collectively are sometimes labeled *pronatalism* (from the Latin, "in favor of birth"). *Antinatalism* ("against birth") is the opposite term.

Attempting to counteract subtle and not-so-subtle pronatalist influences, Ellen Peck wrote a book entitled *The Baby Trap;* and in addition, she and her husband helped found an organization called the National Organization for Non-Parents (NON), which didn't hesitate to proclaim that "None is fun!" and emphasized advantages of remaining childless (or *child-free,* to use their preferred term). More recently, NON has changed its name to the National Alliance for Optional Parenthood, while retaining its original vision. "In order for people truly to have an option," states the organization's promotional materials, "we must continue to work to make nonparenthood a socially accepted and respected lifestyle."

But is it true, as some antinatalist groups claim, that couples have babies merely because of societal pressures (since societies cannot continue without replacement of their members)? Or is having babies simply a matter of nature's trickery—a kind of cosmic con game in which persons are carried away in the ecstasy of sexual pleasure only to be rudely awakened by a squirming, squealing, demanding infant who emerges to mock the lovers with an attitude of "Aha! You thought you were just having fun, but look what you got instead—me!" Or might it be that people have children because they want them or value them? No doubt all three explanations contain elements of truth.

REWARDS, COSTS, AND THE MOTIVATION TO HAVE CHILDREN

We have seen how the comparison of costs and rewards operates in the husband-wife relationship, beginning even before marriage in the mate-selection process and continuing through the negotiation and renegotiation process after the marriage takes place. Now we want to see how a theory of rewards and costs helps to explain how couples make decisions concerning reproduction. Assuming they are physically able to have children, will a particular husband and wife *want* to have them? If so, how many and when?

In ancient Hebrew society, no one would have thought to ask if married couples should have children. Had not the Creator commanded, "Be fruitful and multiply"? Children were considered God's gifts, "the fruit of the womb . . . his reward." The scriptures declared that a man needed a quiver full of children as an archer needed arrows. A barren woman was to be pitied. "Give me children or I die!" cried Rachel, the wife of the patriarch Jacob. Married couples desired children to help at home and in the fields and to support them in old age. Sons were needed to carry on the family name and inherit the land. Such an attitude toward children has been common throughout history in traditional, patriarchal, agricultural societies.

A sociological study of *why* people have children would have seemed out of place in biblical times. But such studies are of great interest in today's world. All too little research has been carried out in this area, and what has been done has often been faulty on methodological grounds. Increasingly, however, in dealing with questions of population growth (on the macro level), or "Why are John and Jane Doe going to have another baby?" (on the micro level), social scientists see the need to give attention to the matter of motivation. The birthrate at a given time in history cannot be explained simply and solely in terms of effective contraceptive technology or the lack of it. Although some persons are inclined to explain declines in the birthrate since the late 1950s by pointing to "the pill," it should be noted that there was also a low birthrate before and during the Great Depression in the United States several decades before the advent of the pill. And even in the early days of the Roman Empire, the emperor Augustus was concerned about low birthrates and therefore devised various incentives to encourage Roman citizens to have large families. By the time of the late Roman Empire, the problem had grown even more acute, because crushing tax burdens and unpaid forced public service made it difficult to support a family of any size (Boak, 1955).

Clearly, the perceived rewards and costs of having children play their part in family planning. In ancient Hebrew society, the *rewards* were uppermost in mind, and large families resulted. In Imperial Rome, the *costs* were of prime concern, and population replenishment was insufficient. But what about today? Why do some couples want children while others do not?

REWARDS OF PARENTHOOD

Psychologists Lois Wladis Hoffman and Martin L. Hoffman (1973) have examined research studies and theoretical literature focusing on reasons why children are valued. Drawing upon their findings, we might group incentives for having children into four main categories according to the rewards children may provide parents (see also Berelson, 1972).

REWARDS OF SELF-ENHANCEMENT

Embarking on parenthood brings a new social identity and a sense of arriving at adult status. "More than finishing school, going to work, or even getting married," Hoffman and Hoffman (1973:47) claim, "parenthood establishes a person as a truly mature, stable, and acceptable member of the community. . . . This is especially true for women, for whom motherhood is also defined as their major role in life." Since few alternative roles are available for uneducated, lower-status women in particular, having a baby is looked upon as perhaps the most important way of gaining identity at this class level.

Closely related to the new sense of self and adult status may be a sense of achievement through parenthood. It might be thought of as *personal* achievement either through having physically produced a child (or several children in social or religious circles where large families are highly esteemed), or through meeting creatively the challenges of rearing children and gaining a sense of pride in a job well done.

On the other hand, parents may experience *vicarious* achievement, a sense of sharing in their children's accomplishments as though these accomplishments were happening to the parents themselves. The mother who never had a chance to take music lessons basks in the reflected glory of her child's performance at a piano recital. The football-loving father swells with pride when his son is chosen high school player of the year. Later, as grown children do well in the occupational sphere, parents feel that their own prestige is enhanced as well. "My son, the doctor" is more than an old joke.

Hoffman and Hoffman (1973:56) also call attention to the reward of power and influence that parenthood brings people, along with a sense of making an impact on one's own life and the lives of others through bringing a child into the world. They suggest that particularly for persons who feel powerless in other areas of life, producing and molding a human being can provide a sense of having an effect on the world that is not otherwise possible. Studies have shown that persons who feel powerless are less likely to use contraceptives (Kar, 1971; Groat and Neal, 1967), and the Hoffman and Hoffman explanation may fit. On the other hand, of course, the overall sense of powerlessness might *contribute* to the nonuse of contraceptives because the couples involved may feel that contraceptives would do little good anyway—that getting along in life is a matter of fate and "breaks" rather than self-mastery and rational control.

Power and influence over others' lives can provide persons with feelings of importance. Contacts with social agencies and on the job usually put lower-status persons in positions where others have power over them, while they have little if any power over others. But at home they can experience a sense of power denied elsewhere. Social customs and laws allow parents to exercise tremendous control over children. Parents can issue commands; they can insist on having their wishes followed and can, within reasonable bounds, force children to comply. Parents can experience that power which stems from being the chief or only source of material and emotional benefits to others who need them (their children). Such "power benefits" in parenthood may play a part in explaining why lower-status couples tend to have larger families.

Socioeconomic Status and Fertility   Demographers have long noted the inverse relationship between social class and fertility. That is, fertility (the number of children born) goes *up* as socioeconomic status goes *down*. In the words of a 1920s song, "The rich get richer and the poor get children." These statements do not tell the whole story, because much more is involved than social status alone in explaining fertility rates, but in general we may say that lower-status families have more children on the average than do higher-status families.

This point becomes clear in government studies, based upon the 1970 United States census, which separated families (with wives aged thirty-five to forty-four years) into two groups: those with *lower status and early marriage* and those with *higher status and late marriage*. Lower-status families in this case were defined as those in which neither husband nor wife were high school graduates, the husband was a blue-collar or service worker, and the wife was between fourteen and twenty-one years of age at first marriage. The higher-status group contained couples who had one or more years of college

Why do lower-status couples have more children? (Paul Conklin/Monkmeyer)

TABLE 15-A   *Average number of children born to ever-married women thirty-five to forty-four years old, by socioeconomic status and age at marriage, United States, 1970*

| | WHITE WIVES | | BLACK WIVES | |
CATEGORY	NOT IN LABOR FORCE	IN LABOR FORCE	NOT IN LABOR FORCE	IN LABOR FORCE
Lower status and early marriage	3.9	3.3	5.6	5.0
Higher status and late marriage	2.9	2.4	2.5	2.0

SOURCE: Adapted from U.S. Bureau of the Census, *Current Population Reports*, P-23, no. 49, 1974, p. 38.

(both husband and wife), with the husband's occupation being white-collar and the wife's age at first marriage twenty-two or over. Among white families, the lower-status group had on the average one child more per family than did the upper-status group. Among black families, the lower-status group had on the average three more children per family than did the higher-status blacks. (See Table 15-A.)

The answer to the question "Why do lower-status couples have more children?" may be that often they want more. They are not so motivated as higher-status couples to prevent births. True, the costs of having children (particularly in the financial realm) are great for lower-status couples, but apparently many feel such costs are more than compensated for by the rewards. As we have seen, for women with few outlets or opportunities for achievement outside the home, the bearing and rearing of children can be extremely gratifying. And for lower-status men, large families can be a source of pride and an opportunity for exercising power not possible elsewhere. Various studies have shown that lower-status men tend to be more authoritarian in their families than are higher-status men (Sears, Maccoby, and Levin, 1957; Hoffman, 1963), underscoring a point made by Blau and Duncan (1967:428): "Whereas successful achievers have their status as adult men supported by their superior occupational roles and authority, the unsuccessful find a substitute in the authority they exercise in their role as fathers over a number of children." In addition, children may be looked upon as a form of wealth. In a report for the Population Council, Bernard Berelson (1972) has written that childbearing is one of the few ways the poor can compete with the rich. "Life cannot make the poor man prosperous in material goods and services but it can easily make him rich with children" (see also Blake, 1979).

At the same time, we need to realize that women at or below the poverty level are three times more likely than others to have one or more *unwanted* births during a lifetime (Alan Guttmacher Institute, 1979:20). The poor don't always have more children simply because they want more, but because of circumstances over which they feel they have no control. Their socioeconomic condition has restricted educational opportunities; and lower education, in turn, is associated with a higher likelihood of contraceptive failure. Poor persons often don't have access to reliable contraceptive methods nor understanding of effective usage. Similarly, access to safe abortions in cases of unwanted conceptions may be denied them because of governmental policies on funding. (On June 30, 1980, the U.S. Supreme Court upheld the constitutionality of the Hyde Amendment—the controversial 1976 congressional funding ban that stopped Medicaid payments for abortions unless a poor woman's life was in danger or in cases of promptly reported rape or incest.) According to the Alan Guttmacher Institute (1979), a corporation for research, education, and policy analysis:

> Many Medicaid-eligible women denied governmental help in paying for their abortions, and unwilling to face possible death or injury at the hands of illegal abortionists, are carrying their unwanted pregnancies to term. The consequences of such unwanted births for the young mothers, the young fathers, their children and society are deep and long-lasting. (p. 31)

REWARDS OF SELF-PRESERVATION

In "Hallowed Ground," the nineteenth-century poet, Thomas Campbell, wrote: "To live in hearts we leave behind/Is not to die." One way to make sure there are hearts left behind in which to "live on" is to have children. Offspring assure the continuation of the family line, the carrying on of the family name, uninterrupted control of a family business, perpetual ownership of family property, and other benefits associated with permanence.

It has long been common folk knowledge that persons desire children as a way of achieving a kind of immortality, and sociological studies provide verification. Men, more than women, tend to mention the survival of the family name as a reason for wanting offspring (Rainwater, 1965:147–148; Hoffman and Hoffman, 1973:48). In India, for example, demographic research showed that when men were asked to state the benefits of having a wife, a common response was "so our descent will continue." Such an evaluation of a wife's benefits was second only to the wife's value in looking after the husband's needs and performing services for him (Poffenberger, 1969).

Self-preservation benefits in having children not only relate to continuing the family line. In traditional societies, children have been valued for their economic utility. Particularly in agricultural societies, children have been considered assets because they provide families with a supply of workers. In the household, children can help with domestic chores; and older children can care for younger children, freeing mothers for other work (in the fields, for example). Children themselves can assist in agricultural tasks from a very early age.

In societies lacking adequate government plans for old age, children are expected to take responsibility for aging parents, often providing them with a home and nursing care as well as with financial support. Especially in underdeveloped and developing nations, a prime motivation for having large numbers of children is to assure that some will be living to provide for the parents in the parents' old age (Hoffman and Hoffman, 1973:57–58).

REWARDS OF PLEASURE, AFFECTION, AND BELONGING

Children may be desired because of widely held sentiments about the enrichment they bring to a couple's lives. Youngsters can mean fun, excitement, and laughter in the home. They are persons adults can relax with and play with, enjoying jokes, riddles, teasing, and roughhousing. Sparkle and zest are brought into adult lives. The novelty of a new baby ends the old, dull routine. Such an ideal picture is in the minds of many in anticipating children as pleasure sources for parents.

Furthermore, by having a baby, parents feel they have brought into being someone to love and be loved by. Children provide the promise of warm affection, a sense of belonging. A strong primary group is formed. Even if it seems that no one else in the whole world cares, having children is considered to mean that there is always someone who does care, thereby banishing feelings of aloneness. Parents expect that a loving relationship with their children will continue even if the husband-wife relationship itself comes to an end through death or divorce.

Men may find that children provide opportunities for them to be physically affectionate in a way that is discouraged elsewhere. (Nancy Hays/Monkmeyer)

There is some evidence that, especially in blue-collar homes, the companionship and affection provided by children compensates for a lack between the spouses in these expressive areas. Rainwater (1960:87) found in his studies of blue-collar homes that wives especially tended to form intense relationships with their children, because the children seemed to provide a sense of worthwhileness that they did not receive from their husbands. Rainwater reports: "The children (at least when young) seem easier to manage and arouse fewer conflicts than does the difficult task of relating to grown men whom they do not understand too well and of whom they are often a little afraid."

As far as the men themselves are concerned, they too may find that children provide opportunities for physically demonstrating affection in a way that is discouraged elsewhere. In Chapter 12, we discussed the effects of the socialization of men which may inhibit open expressions of affection toward their wives—particularly in blue-collar homes where greater sex-role differences are emphasized. However, with children, such men may feel more comfortable about giving open demonstrations of feelings. They can feel free to touch, cuddle, hug, kiss, tousle children's hair, hold them on their laps, and so on. "It is possible . . . that children provide for men one of the few relationships where they can express warmth and tenderness," write Hoffman and Hoffman (1973:53).

ALTRUISTIC AND RELIGIOUS SATISFACTIONS IN HAVING CHILDREN

In a study sponsored by the Planned Parenthood Federation of America, sociologist Lee Rainwater interviewed 409 husbands and wives at various socioeconomic levels in an effort to find out why couples want and have particular numbers of children. In examining his respondents' rationales for large and small families, Rainwater (1965:181–182) found that he could abstract one central norm, namely the belief that "one should not have more children than one can support, but one should have as many children as one can afford."

Altruistic Considerations Rainwater found a widespread belief that parents who didn't have as many children as they could afford were "selfish." Such an opinion was especially prevalent among men who wanted large families. It was less true of women who wanted large families for themselves but at the same time could understand that other couples might choose to limit family size in order to provide more benefits for children already born rather than for reasons of self-indulgence. Yet, the notion has persisted that persons who have large families are somehow more virtuous, self-sacrificing, altruistic, less materialistic, and less apt to spoil their children than are persons with small families. However, in recent years, concerns about a worldwide "population explosion" have challenged this way of thinking to a considerable extent, and the opinion is frequently voiced that the truly altruistic couple may be the one willing to forgo the pleasures of an additional child, whereas "selfish" people are those who insist on adding new persons to an already crowded planet.

A Black Leader Speaks Out on the Abortion Question

It had begun to seem to me that the question was not whether the law should allow abortions. Experience shows that pregnant women who feel they have compelling reasons for not having a baby, or another baby, will break the law and, even worse, risk injury and death if they must to get one. Abortions will not be stopped. . . . The question becomes simply that of what kind of abortions society wants women to have—clean, competent ones performed by licensed physicians or septic, dangerous ones done by incompetent practitioners.

So when NARAL [the National Association for the Repeal of Abortion Laws] asked me to lead its campaign, I gave it serious thought. For me to take the lead in abortion repeal would be an even more serious step than for a white politician to do so, because there is a deep and angry suspicion among many blacks that even birth control clinics are a plot by the white power structure to keep down the numbers of blacks, and this opinion is even more strongly held by some in regard to legalizing abortions. But I do not know any black or Puerto Rican women who feel that way. To label family planning and legal abortion programs "genocide" is male rhetoric, for male ears. It falls flat to female listeners, and to thoughtful male ones. Women know, and so do many men, that two or three children who are wanted, prepared for, reared amid love and stability, and educated to the limit of their ability will mean more for the future of the black and brown races from which they come than any number of neglected, hungry, ill-housed and ill-clothed youngsters. Pride in one's race, as well as simply humanity, supports this view.

SOURCE: From Shirley Chisholm, *Unbought and Unbossed* (Boston: Houghton Mifflin Co., 1970), excerpted from pp. 113–122, as reprinted in Lerner, 1972.

Hoffman and Hoffman call attention to another aspect of altruism, namely the concerns of various minority groups for an increase in their numbers and power. They refer to a study of black and Chicano college students in which there was support for the idea of having large families, with typical responses being, "We should double the actual number of Chicanos as soon as possible," and "Black people need more power and you can't have power without people; birth control for blacks is legalized genocide" (Buckhout et al., 1971; Hoffman and Hoffman, 1973:50–51). Among these politically conscious college students, having children is viewed as a service performed in the interests of bettering the conditions of an oppressed people.

Some black leaders disagree strongly. After describing the economic hardships large numbers of minority persons face in a society that has discriminated against them and the sense of entrapment an unwanted pregnancy can mean to poor families, U.S. Congresswoman Shirley Chisholm (1970) has made this comment:

Which is more like genocide, I have asked some of my black brothers—this, the way things are, or the conditions I am fighting for in which the full range of family planning services is freely available to women of all classes and colors, starting with effective contraception and extending to safe, legal termination of undesired pregnancies, at a price they can afford? (p. 122)

Religious Considerations Religious satisfactions in having children provide another kind of reward for parents. For some couples, having children is looked upon as a sacred duty. Parenthood provides these husbands and wives with a sense of fulfilling a divine command to "be fruitful and multiply," or brings an assurance that "God has blessed the union," or gives couples an opportunity for outwardly demonstrating compliance with church teachings against contraceptives.

A major difficulty in studying the relationship between religion and fertility springs from the successful efforts of various pressure groups in the late 1950s to eliminate a question on religious affiliation that was considered for inclusion in the United States census. However, enough other research exists to show that religion has been a factor in the number of children couples are likely to have. In the 1965 National Fertility Study, for example, married women under forty-five years of age who were Protestant had an average of 2.3 children and expected a total of 3.0. Catholic women had an average of 2.8 and expected a total of 3.9 children. Jewish women had 2.1 children and expected to have a total of 2.9 (Westoff and Westoff, 1971:164–161, 227; Ryder and Westoff, 1971:68).

Roman Catholicism Numerous studies have shown that Roman Catholics, as a result of their religious ideology, both *have* more children and *intend* to have more children than do couples of other religious groups. At the heart of Catholic teachings on marital sexuality has been an emphasis on a special mission assigned to husbands and wives "to collaborate with God in the generation and education of new lives." The point was reiterated in *Humanae Vitae* (1968), the Encyclical on Birth Control issued by Pope Paul VI: marriage is considered to be ordained toward begetting children. This teaching has traditionally influenced the actual number of children in Roman Catholic families and birth intentions for the future among both the general population of Catholics and those who are university students (Scanzoni, 1975b, 1975c; Coombs, 1978).

However, in recent years, signs of change have begun showing up—especially in contraceptive practices (see "Digest" section, *Family Planning Perspectives* 10 (July/August, 1978:240–241). Demographers Charles Westoff and Elise Jones (1977a) illustrate that change dramatically by pointing out that among women married between 1951 and 1955, eight out of ten Roman Catholic women conformed to their church's teaching on birth control during their first five years of marriage. That is, they had either used no method of contraception at all or else used only the rhythm method which is approved

Roman Catholics, as a result of their religious ideology, both have *more children and* intend *to* have *more children than do couples of other religious groups. (Ken Heyman)*

by the church. However, among women married during the 1971–75 period twenty years later, less than one out of ten conformed to church teaching during their first five years of marriage. Using data from the 1975 National Fertility Study, Westoff and Jones noted a "convergence of Catholic and non-Catholic contraceptive practice" in spite of official church teachings which remain unchanged among the Roman Catholic hierarchy. Table 15-B shows the similarities in contraceptive practice between Catholics and non-Catholics who intend no further births and also between Catholics and non-Catholics who want more children but who intend to plan when they will have them.

Judaism Studies have consistently shown the fertility of Jewish women to be the lowest of the three major religious groups (Ryder and Westoff, 1971:70). One reason may be that Jewish teachings have not emphasized procreation as a religious duty in the way that Catholicism has. Methods of birth control were known even in biblical times (Genesis 38:9), although large families were strongly encouraged. But with changing conditions over time—exile, movement to cities, dispersion, and so on—the older laws were modified. A man's duty in preserving the human race was considered fulfilled if he had fathered two children (Himes, 1936:69ff. in 1970 edition). The Talmud includes passages permitting contraception and even sterilization for women under

TABLE 15-B *Current contraceptive exposure of white, US non-Catholic (NC) and Catholic (C) married women younger than forty-five, by whether woman intends more births, 1975*

TYPE OF EXPOSURE	INTENDS NO MORE BIRTHS		INTENDS MORE BIRTHS	
	NC	C	NC	C
Total number	1,568	552	866	343
Percent total	100.0	100.0	100.0	100.0
Using contraception	86.2	83.2	67.7	64.1
Not using contraception	13.8	16.8	32.3	35.9
Pregnant, post-partum or trying to get pregnant	4.7	5.3	26.2	27.7
Sterile	6.8	8.3	0.0	0.0
Other nonuse	2.2	3.3	6.1	8.2
Number of users	1,352	459	586	220
Percent total users	100.0	100.0	100.0	100.0
Wife sterilized	24.0	18.5	0.0	0.0
Husband sterilized	21.6	18.3	0.0	0.0
Pill	24.4	23.7	61.9	60.0
IUD	7.8	7.0	11.4	8.6
Diaphragm	3.8	3.3	4.4	4.5
Condom	9.3	13.9	10.2	15.9
Withdrawal	1.8	2.6	1.7	2.3
Foam	3.6	2.6	4.8	2.3
Rhythm	1.3	6.3	2.6	5.0
Other	2.3	3.7	2.9	1.4

SOURCE: Charles F. Westoff and Elise F. Jones, "The Secularization of U.S. Catholic Birth Control Practices," *Family Planning Perspectives* 9 (Sept/October, 1977) p. 205.

certain circumstances (such as health problems or out of concern for her other children). These liberal views of birth control were challenged during the Middle Ages, however, when Jewish leaders began opposing contraception and urging couples to have as many children as possible to enlarge the Jewish population which had suffered great losses through persecution, massacre, disease, and malnutrition. But times have changed. Rabbi Robert Gordis (1967:36–41), a seminary professor, writes that today Judaism recognizes "that family planning is a necessity of modern life, in view of complex moral, hygienic, and economic factors."

Westoff (1974b:111–112) reports that fertility among Jews in Israel is considerably higher than that of the Jewish population of the United States and probably higher than the Jewish populations of other developed nations as well. Nevertheless, some concern has been expressed in Israel because the average number of births per Jewish woman is 3.2, while among Arabs in that nation it is 7.3. In the early 1950s, Jewish fertility reached a high of slightly more than 4.0 births per woman on the average, but since then the trend has been downward. Westoff refers to one "demographiç cynic" who calculates that "if current trends continue, the Jewish population will be a minority in Israel within three generations."

Protestantism   Only during this present century have Protestant churches moved away from a position on birth control that in many respects was like that of the Roman Catholic Church (Kennedy, 1970:153). Most major Protestant denominations today, however, would agree with this 1952 statement by a commission of the American Lutheran Church: "Married couples have the freedom so to plan and order their sexual relations that each child born to their union will be wanted both for itself and in relation to the time of its birth. How the couple uses this freedom can properly be judged not by man but only by God. The means which a married pair uses . . . are matters for them to decide with their own consciences" (quoted in Rehwinkel, 1959:41–42).

Some research has indicated that, among non-Catholic groups, members of certain fundamentalist sects and Mormons are likely to have more children than do other non-Catholics (Ryder and Westoff, 1971:70–71; Westoff and Potvin, 1967:130ff).

OTHER REASONS CHILDREN ARE VALUED

As part of a large international study of why children are valued and how fertility patterns are affected by the satisfactions children are considered to bring parents, researchers Lois Wladis Hoffman and Jean Denby Manis (1979) examined data for the United States according to whether the respondents were male or female, parents or nonparents, and according to racial or ethnic membership. Table 15-C provides an expanded list of reasons why children are valued. These reasons were given by respondents to the open-ended question: "What would you say are some of the advantages or good things about having children compared with not having children at all?" Both women and men attached great importance to the fun and stimulation children can bring, along with various aspects of love and companionship.

COSTS OF PARENTHOOD

In an effort to alert children to the problems of an overcrowded world, a book for elementary children contains this exercise in imagination: Youngsters are told to picture the life-styles of two different families. One family has two children, and these children have bikes and skates, nice clothes, music lessons, and a chance to go to summer camp. The parents take vacations, enjoy good food (including steaks), and occasionally take the whole family to restaurants. Plans are already being made for the children to go to college.

The other family in this exercise of the imagination has ten children. They have to share two bicycles among them. There isn't enough money for these children to take music lessons or go to summer camp. The younger children seldom wear anything but hand-me-downs. This family almost never has steak or goes to restaurants or even has very much meat or other nourishing foods—at least not in the way the two-child family does. The children in the large family therefore have colds more often. They also don't do as well in school and can't study quietly at home because of the lack of privacy. Their parents don't feel the family can afford to send the children to college (Frankel, 1970:48).

Readers of this children's book are being confronted with a traditionally unpopular and underrated fact: There are *costs* as well as rewards involved in having children.

MATERIAL COSTS IN HAVING CHILDREN

From prenatal care through delivery, from childrearing days through college, children are expensive. Economists point out that the financial costs of children are twofold: direct costs (money spent for children's needs) and indirect or "opportunity loss" costs (alternatives which have to be passed by or given up for the sake of the children).

Direct costs of having children are quite obvious: food, clothing, shelter, medical and dental care, toys and recreation, vacation trips, education, and much more. Exactly what such costs add up to varies according to social class, the ages of the children, the number of children (the more children in a family, the less spent per child, but the more spent altogether), and the family's life-style (for example, are they rural or urban?). One sociologist, Thomas J. Espenshade (1973), used data from the 1960–61 Consumer Expenditure Survey to calculate the monetary costs of rearing children to the age of eighteen. Although present-day costs have risen, Espenshade's estimates are illuminating. For example, he found that a lower-income family with one child will spend 40 percent of its income in childrearing over the eighteen-year period. An upper-income family, in contrast, spends only 26 percent of its income in rearing one child to age eighteen. Costs rise as the child grows older, and of course costs rise as more children are added to the family. However, the cost of the first child is approximately twice as much as the cost of a second child in a two-child family.

Indirect costs of having children may not appear so obvious. They include such losses as doing without that extra room planned for a den, because the new baby needs a bedroom. Or parents may have to forgo savings and investment plans because children make it necessary to spend most of the income immediately. The family's standard of living might be lower because caring for children's essential needs means less money left over for consumption items desired by parents (Mueller, 1972).

One indirect or "opportunity cost" of having children is the loss of potential family income which often results from a mother's being kept from labor-force participation. If a mother does work, some of the family's income will likely be used to pay for child care during the hours she is employed. Such consequences of having a child (or an additional child) are included when economists compute estimated material costs of parenthood.

At the same time, couples may be well aware of the sacrifices and

TABLE 15-C *The advantages of having children—specific responses*[a,b]

SPECIFIC ADVANTAGE	WOMEN					MEN		
	PARENTS			NONPARENTS		PARENTS		NON-PARENTS
	WHITE	BLACK	HISPANIC[c]	WHITE	BLACK	WHITE	BLACK	WHITE
Primary group ties and affection:								
Bring love and companionship	33.9	45.7	25.0	21.4	28.6	23.8	26.9	11.8
To have a complete family	16.3	12.0	21.9	19.3	21.4	21.9	19.2	21.5
To benefit the H/W relationship	13.4	7.6	15.6	19.7	7.1	12.2	11.5	12.9
To give love to the child	11.8	13.0	15.6	11.9	28.6	11.0	7.7	10.8
To give to child (not spec. love)	4.0	2.2	6.3	6.7	7.1	4.1	7.7	3.2
Love and companionship in old age	4.6	2.2	0.0	7.4	7.1	3.5	3.9	4.3
Stimulation and fun:								
Stimulation, fun, activity	52.3	45.7	50.0	35.8	21.4	46.7	65.4	23.7
Pleasure from watching them grow	16.6	12.0	12.5	10.5	14.3	16.3	26.9	12.9
Expansion of self:								
Purpose to life	14.0	7.6	18.8	7.4	7.1	10.3	19.3	4.3
Learning experience	11.3	6.5	12.5	7.7	0.0	6.9	3.9	3.2
Self-fulfillment	5.5	2.2	0.0	6.0	7.1	3.1	0.0	2.2
Part of experiencing life fully	4.2	1.1	3.1	3.9	7.1	3.1	0.0	2.2
To recreate myself; a child like me	4.0	1.1	3.1	2.8	0.0	6.6	7.7	4.3
Carry on the family name	1.4	2.2	0.0	6.0	0.0	3.1	15.4	7.5
Carry on the family line	0.6	1.1	3.1	2.1	0.0	1.9	3.9	5.4
Immortality	0.0	1.1	0.0	1.8	0.0	1.3	0.0	4.3
Adult status and social identity:								
Something useful to do	8.9	2.2	12.5	3.5	14.3	3.8	0.0	1.1
You feel adult; more mature, etc.	6.4	5.4	3.1	4.2	0.0	6.3	3.9	1.1
Socially expected and/or natural	6.6	3.3	3.1	4.6	14.3	6.3	3.9	2.2
Gives man an incentive for working	0.3	1.1	0.0	0.0	7.1	5.0	0.0	3.2

Achievement and creativity:								
To create a life, a human being	2.8	3.3	0.0	6.7	7.1	2.5	0.0	7.5
Satisfaction from doing a good job	5.3	5.4	3.1	7.0	7.1	4.4	3.9	11.8
Economic utility:								
Security in old age	1.2	5.4	0.0	4.6	0.0	1.9	3.9	2.2
Help in household chores	2.3	10.9	3.1	1.4	0.0	2.2	3.9	1.1
Morality:								
Makes you a better person	4.1	5.4	9.4	2.8	0.0	2.2	7.7	0.0
Miscellaneous:								
You can teach them	3.0	3.3	3.1	2.8	0.0	4.4	0.0	3.2
Vague positive attitude	2.2	2.2	6.3	4.2	0.0	1.9	0.0	1.1
There are no advantages	0.4	0.0	0.0	5.3	0.0	0.6	0.0	6.5
N	1125	92	33	288	14	321	27	95

[a]A maximum of four responses per person were coded.
[b]Racial categories with fewer than ten cases have been omitted.
[c]Includes Chicano or Mexican-American, Latin American, and Puerto Rican.
SOURCE: Lois Wladis Hoffman and Jean Denby Manis, "The Value of Children in the United States: A New Approach to the Study of Fertility," *Journal of Marriage and the Family* 41 (August, 1979), p. 586.

expenses involved in childrearing and still feel the experience of parenthood is worth it all. "Economic considerations appear to be important in setting an upper limit to the number of children desired," write Hoffman and Manis (1979:595), "but it also appears that, if the needs that children satisfy are important enough and, if there are no acceptable alternative ways of satisfying these needs, considerable costs will be endured in order to achieve the benefits" (see also Blake, 1979).

COSTS OF CHILDREN TO THE HUSBAND-WIFE RELATIONSHIP

According to popular folklore, having children is supposed to draw a husband and wife closer together. It doesn't always work that way. Social psychologist Jum C. Nunnally (1972) points out that for years psychologists have given attention to the effects of parents on children, but only in recent years has some attention been given to the other side of the coin, the effects of children on parents.

Nunnally became impressed with this aspect of parent-child relations while working with a colleague on studies of schizophrenic children. "Although it could not be firmly established from the research results," Nunnally writes, "I developed the definite impression that the disrupted home from which the schizophrenic child frequently came was more a product of the child's disrupting the rest of the family than the cause of the child's schizophrenia." He explains further: "The child was a constant source of strain for the other family members—causing embarrassment before neighbors and continual trouble in school, indifferent to affection, requiring many forms of expensive care, and a source of shame to parents and contention between them." Nunnally found that in a number of case studies there appeared to be a gradual deterioration of the families as time went on.

Traditionally, marriage has been viewed as a step in which "two become one." Parenthood means that two become three—or four or even more. And this can spell difficulties even in homes that do not face the kinds of problems Nunnally studied.

On the basis of research among a probability sample of more than five thousand adults, sociologist Karen Renne (1970) has reported that "people currently raising children were more likely to be dissatisfied with their marriages than people who had never had children, or whose children had left home, regardless of race, age or income level." She offers several explanations for this finding. First, there is the possibility that couples are less apt to file for divorce if there are children at home. Thus, couples with children may continue in unsatisfactory marriages while childless couples would feel more free to separate. Although she did not test this assumption, Renne suggests that "presumably the unhappiest marriages among childless couples and those whose children have grown up have already been dissolved."

A second possible explanation has to do with the demands parenthood makes on a woman and man, since it means an abrupt role transition—one for which many couples are not prepared (Rossi, 1968). It is one thing to be a wife or husband; it is quite another to be a mother or father as well. The relationship between the spouses may be altered drastically by the baby's arrival. Robert Ryder's (1973) research analysis of a study conducted by the National Institute of Mental Health indicates that having a child may result in a wife's feeling dissatisfied with the amount of attention her husband pays to her—either because husbands are less attentive after a baby arrives or else because wives simply desire more attention and assistance at this time.

Sociologist Harold Feldman's (1971) research among couples both before and after having their first baby likewise produced the finding that marital satisfaction declined with parenthood. Feldman also found that husbands and wives who had a close relationship with one another during pregnancy were not brought closer together by the child's birth but rather felt their marital satisfaction dropped. He postulates that to such closely knit couples, a baby may be an "interference factor," producing a decline in husband-wife companionship, with the husband in particular feeling cheated of his wife's attention. Where an *increase* in marital satisfaction occurred after becoming parents, the couples were less likely to have had a closely knit husband-wife relationship beforehand. It may be that such couples expect to be drawn closer together as they find in the baby a common interest, a conversation piece, and a reason to work together in joint tasks.

Feldman (1971) and other researchers have found evidence that the sexual relationship of a husband and wife may be negatively affected by parenthood (see also Christensen, 1968). Infants mean interruptions and require parents to be constantly "on duty." Time and energy demands required in parenting may mean less time and energy for the kind of sex life a couple had enjoyed previously. As children grow older, privacy increasingly becomes a problem. Spontaneous moments of romance at unusual times become difficult, and plans and strategies for uninterrupted lovemaking may have to be arranged.

In considering the overall impact of children on a marriage relationship, factors such as family income, race, and wife employment may enter in. Much more research needs to be done taking these and other variables into account. (See Houseknecht, 1979.) For example, Renne's research cited earlier showed that couples with children present were more likely to be dissatisfied than those couples with no children present at this particular point in their marriage—regardless of whether the family income in 1965 was more than $10,000 or less than that amount. However, among black couples, an interesting finding emerged. Forty-three percent of black husbands and wives reported dissatisfaction with their marriages when children were present and family income was less than $10,000. However, in black families where the family income was over $10,000, only 16 percent of husbands reported dissatisfaction in marriages where children were present. Evidently for black men, the *economic* pressures involved with parenthood are what determine feelings of dissatisfaction or satisfaction rather than parenthood itself.

For women, another factor may enter in. Black wives with children present did not show greater satisfaction with their marriages when 1965 family income was over $10,000. Forty-three percent continued to indicate marital dissatisfaction. However, less than half that percentage (20 percent) reported such dissatisfaction if there were no children present and income was over $10,000 (Renne, 1970). One possible explanation is that black wives are likely to be contributing to the family income, and the presence of children makes employment much more difficult.

Another way that having children may affect the husband-wife relationship is in the area of disagreements. In Chapter 14, we saw that husbands and wives tend to disagree over money and children more than over other concerns of marriage. One cost of having children is the necessity of spreading family income over a wider range of persons and needs. Disagreements over childrearing practices may also be costly to the husband-wife relationship, causing dissension that would have been avoided had the couple not had children.

COSTS OF CHILDREN IN TERMS OF FREEDOM

Even if husbands and wives agree on childrearing practices, the actual carrying out of all the day-to-day responsibilities involved may seem costly in terms of freedom. Parents are expected to be concerned about their children's mental, emotional, physical, spiritual, and social development. Such a task means an investment of enormous amounts of time and energy which the parents might otherwise have put into individualistic pursuits.

Children complicate life, not only in terms of the sheer physical work they occasion, but also in the way they can upset schedules, interfere with plans, and make exceedingly complex what were once simple procedures— things like going on a trip ("We'll have to take the playpen." "Did you get Cindy's diaper bag and baby food, honey?" "Where is Michael's medicine for car sickness?") or planning a night at the movies ("But, Darling, I've tried every baby-sitter I know of! It's not *my* fault Judy called us at the last minute to cancel out.") or even a trip to the grocery store ("Peter! Where are your boots? Oh, why must it always rain on shopping day?" "No, the baby gets to ride in the shopping cart; there isn't room for you." "Jennifer! Don't stand on the shelf like that—watch out for those jelly jars! Oh, no!" *CRASH*).

Other costs of children include being inconvenienced, making adjustments in living conditions (such as growing accustomed to noise, messes, less privacy, and crowding), emotional stress (worrying over a sick child, fearing the worst when a teenager is late getting home with the car), and feeling tied down and unable to carry out travel and recreation plans freely.

Hoffman (1972a) found in one study that some university students felt their own parents had been failures at childrearing and were afraid they might not be any more successful themselves in bringing up children. To these students, the difficulty of rearing a child and the fear of failure meant viewing childrearing as costly. But for those students who expected success in

Children complicate life, not only in terms of the sheer physical work they occasion, but also in the way they can upset schedules, interfere with plans, and make exceedingly complex what were once simple procedures. (Ken Heyman)

parenthood, childrearing and all its difficulties were thought of in terms of a challenge—a value, not a cost.

GENDER ROLES AND FERTILITY CONTROL

Bob and Julie, the hypothetical couple we followed in Chapters 13 and 14, found that attitudes toward sex roles and attitudes toward having children are closely linked. When their outlook on marriage was more traditional, they both considered Bob to occupy the chief provider role even though Julie worked too. During the early months of marriage, Julie was not committed to a career but fully expected to drift in and out of the labor market, depending on the needs of her family. Both she and Bob planned that she would quit work when they had a baby and would probably remain at home while the children were small.

Then things began to change. As Julie became interested in commitment to a career, her conception of her role moved from *traditional* (being a wife and mother is a woman's most important calling, and a woman must subordinate her interests to those of her family) to *egalitarian* or *modern* (a woman should strive to use all her talents and abilities to achieve in the economic-opportunity sphere, just as a man is expected to do). No longer was Julie so willing to give up her work in order to bear and rear children. She began wondering if she even wanted any children. A large part in the ongoing negotiations of this couple centered on decisions about children.

Increasingly, social scientists have begun giving attention to how fertility control relates to gender roles. Do choices to bear or not to bear children have anything to do with how men and women conceive of the "proper" or "desirable" roles for males and females? How does employment affect a woman's fertility? Working wives have fewer children than nonworking wives, but does this mean that they deliberately choose to have fewer children because they want or have to work? Or do they work because they have no or few children and therefore fill up their time with a job?

"To beget or not to beget; that is the question." One writer reports first hearing this play on Shakespeare's words in Moscow— "and in Russian!" he adds. Journalist George St. George (1973:155) points out that the birthrate in the Soviet Union has been declining, and the state needs children. Yet women are reluctant to give up their roles as productive workers in the economic sphere and don't want to exchange "the fruits of advanced civilization for the glory of motherhood." The rewards of working are viewed as being greater than the gratifications of large families. To encourage women to have more children, various authorities have suggested government policies such as cash subsidies for families having a second and third child, or even a practice of paying wages to women who are willing to quit working in order to stay home to bear and rear children. Many educated Soviet women consider such suggestions insulting, writes St. George, "a vicious attempt to push women back into nurseries and kitchen."

Valentina Tereshkova-Nikolaeva, the world's first and only woman cosmonaut, delivered an address at the World Women's Congress in Helsinki on June 15, 1969, in which she criticized attempts to curtail women's economic opportunities in order to allow them more time for child care and domestic concerns. She drew attention to three suggestions by social scientists, sharply disagreeing with each. First, to urge citizens to return to the old division of labor in which men worked and supported families while women stayed home with children was simply unrealistic. Second, to tell women to break up their lives into various parts, rearing children at one stage and concentrating on careers at another stage, would also be unrealistic since a professional woman would lose her qualifications by being out of her field for so long. The third suggestion, that women work part-time so that the rest of their time could be given to children, was also rejected by Tereshkova-Nikolaeva on the grounds that "such part-time workers cannot count on any solid professional careers, and would be used mostly as supplementary and

As alternative rewards such as educational and employment opportunities become available, women in developing countries may choose to have fewer children. (Barbara Kirk/Peter Arnold, Inc.)

temporary labor." Her own proposed solution lies in more child-care facilities, communal dining rooms and the like, with the adjustments being made not in a woman's professional life but in her home life, thereby giving her maximum release from tasks that would hinder economic productivity (St. George, 1973:172).

One way of securing such maximum release is to limit fertility—that is, to cut down on the number of children a woman has. And this is exactly what Russian women have been doing, along with women in many other industrialized countries. There are many studies, for example, which show that employed mothers in the United States have fewer children than nonworking mothers and also that unmarried females who plan to work desire smaller families (see summary in Hoffman and Hoffman, 1973:64; Hoffman and Manis, 1979:595).

On the other hand, this pattern of wife employment and lower fertility is not so clean cut in nonindustrialized societies. Sociologist Paula Hass (1972) has examined the proposition that the crucial variable in determining the relationship between wife employment and family size is the extent to which the mother role and the worker role are viewed as incompatible. In developing nations, women have often had a tradition of combining work and motherhood, and working has not meant a lowering of fertility. Women could easily be workers and mothers for at least two reasons. First, the home is the center of economic activity, with women often working in simple cottage industries (such as weaving or pottery making) or in agricultural tasks, with children close by. Second, child care is readily available in the form of the extended family, with a number of relatives usually willing to serve as substitute mothers.

However, the changes involved as societies move toward urbanization and industrialization make the worker and mother roles less compatible. Extended families are not so close by, and child-care arrangements become more difficult. Employment normally takes place away from the home in developed societies, geographically separating mothers and children. In such cases, it becomes exceedingly difficult for a woman to be employed and at the same time to be the mother of many children. We may expect her to have fewer children if she wants to continue working. But even more crucial, according to Hass, are the woman's attitudes. If she is highly educated and does not think in terms of traditional sex-role stereotypes, and if she is motivated to achieve occupationally and views the role of worker as an alternative to motherhood, she is likely to limit her family size to avoid role incompatibility as much as possible.

Hoffman and Hoffman (1973:65–67) make a distinction between viewing employment as an alternative to fertility and as a barrier to fertility. A woman who chooses the gratifications of occupational achievement as an *alternative* to the gratifications of children will have lower fertility not because employment prevents her having more children but because she wants fewer children in order to devote herself more fully to her occupation. In contrast, the woman who views employment as a *barrier* to higher fertility will have fewer children because working makes motherhood more difficult; she might prefer to have a larger family but knows that as long as she must work or wants to work, it would be hard to have additional children.

Hoffman and Hoffman suggest if employment operates as only a barrier and not as an alternative to motherhood, child-care facilities could have the effect of increasing rather than decreasing fertility by removing the obstacles that cause much of the mother-worker role incompatibility. Social policy planners sometimes overlook these distinctions between employment-as-barrier and employment-as-alternative by simply stating that providing job opportunities for women will bring about declines in birthrates. The attitudes, motivations, and gender-role norms held by women are more crucial than is the fact of employment in itself.

Our own large-scale study which investigated whether and how sex-role norms affect fertility provided data which clearly show that *the sex-role norms women hold affect both the number of children they intend to have and the number of children they actually do have* (Scanzoni, 1975b). Let's take four hypothetical case studies to see how this association between norms and fertility works.

HYPOTHETICAL CASE ONE

Dorothy is twenty-eight years old, black, and has a master's degree in social work. Her father is a high school teacher and her mother is a librarian. Dorothy's husband is a gynecologist. The couple have been married for three years and have no children at this time, although they would like to have children later. Dorothy has been employed as a social worker since before her marriage, and she plans to take off only a couple months when they have a baby and then return to work.

HYPOTHETICAL CASE TWO

Ginny is twenty-two years old. In answer to the question "Occupation?" she replies, "Housewife—or better yet, homemaker." Ginny is white, Catholic, and married her high school boyfriend at age eighteen, the same month they graduated. Ginny comes from a family that is religiously devout, participating in the Mass regularly; and she and her husband also devoutly practice their religious faith. During Ginny's growing-up years, her father was an auto mechanic and her mother was a full-time housewife. Ginny's husband presently sells appliances in a large department store. The couple have two children and are expecting a third in two months. "This one wasn't planned for," Ginny laughs, "but we'll be glad to welcome him to the family anyway—especially if it's a boy! Our first two are girls." She reports that they had their first daughter in the first year of marriage, and thus she has never held a job.

HYPOTHETICAL CASE THREE

Twenty-year-old Debra is black and the mother of three children. The first child was conceived before her marriage, and the last two were born ten months apart. "We tried to keep from having the babies so close together," she says. "But things just didn't work out. It's just too easy to get pregnant. We couldn't keep it from happening, and I expect it'll happen again." Debra's mother works as a cook in a school cafeteria, and her father is a service station attendant. Debra did not complete high school and works part-time as a housekeeper whenever her husband's mother can come over to take care of the children. Debra's husband is employed as a taxicab driver and is seldom home, a point of contention between them.

HYPOTHETICAL CASE FOUR

Linda—thirty-two years old, white, non-Catholic—is a lawyer with a busy practice. She and her husband (also an attorney) have been married seven years and have two children carefully spaced three years apart. Their son is four years old; their daughter is one. Both are cared for by a live-in housekeeper who loves them as though they were her own grandchildren.

If a sociologist were to interview these same women twenty years from now, which women would be likely to have the most children? Which would be likely to have the least?

Based upon data from our research project as well as from other studies, it is likely that Dorothy (case 1) and Linda (case 4) would have the fewest number of children. Both Ginny (case 2) and Debra (case 3) would be likely to have larger families than either of the other two women. Gender-role norms play a large part in explaining these differences. But remember these are hypothetical case studies used for purposes of illustration only. Sociologists are not concerned with predicting the behavior of particular *individuals* but rather give attention to patterns of behavior and trends among groups of persons who have certain characteristics in common. These hypothetical cases are presented in an effort to illuminate some of our findings from a large probability sample.

HOW GENDER-ROLE NORMS AFFECT DECISIONS ABOUT HAVING CHILDREN

Earlier in this chapter, we looked at United States census figures that showed higher-status black families to have an average of two children when the mother worked—a lower average than among either black or white higher-status families with nonemployed mothers and also lower than higher-status white families where the mother worked. Why do employed higher-status black women have fewer children than all other women? The answer appears to lie in the greater career commitment and more egalitarian sex-role norms held by higher-status black couples. We saw earlier that the tradition of labor-force participation for black wives has encouraged more egalitarian sex

Employed higher-status black women have fewer children than all other categories of women.
(Ken Heyman)

roles at all status levels than has been true of comparable whites (Scanzoni, 1977). But at higher status levels, additional factors enter in to reinforce this traditional bent toward greater egalitarianism. Take Dorothy's case, for example.

Dorothy's Case Dorothy comes from a family in which both parents had a college education and both held professional positions. Their higher socioeconomic status indicates that they were likely to socialize their children toward more egalitarian sex roles than is true in families of lower socioeconomic status. Furthermore, Dorothy herself is highly educated and committed to a career, and at age twenty-five married a man whose education, occupation, and income indicate high social status. All of these factors fit well with findings that were true of both black and white women in our research project (Scanzoni, 1975b).

The study showed that the higher the family background social status, the greater would be the egalitarianism that showed up in sex-role norms. Similarly, greater egalitarianism was also associated with higher levels of education. Higher education and greater egalitarianism in sex-role norms meant such women were likely to marry later than other women. Also, *married* women who were found to score high on egalitarian sex-role norms were more likely than other married women to be employed full-time. Finally, the data all fit together in such a way as to make this point: The greater the *egalitarianism* in sex-role norms and the fact of *full-time employment*, and the *greater the education* and the *later the age at marriage,* the lower the total number of births younger married women intended to have.

Ginny's Case   Moving on to the second hypothetical case study, we find that Ginny illustrates some other patterns that showed up in our research. Unlike Dorothy, Ginny grew up in a blue-collar home where the parents held traditional sex-role norms and socialized their children accordingly. Ginny herself holds traditional sex-role norms, which are reinforced by her religious faith, which she adheres to devoutly. She married young, did not go on for further education after high school, had children early in marriage, and has experienced one timing failure in child spacing. Some findings from our research clearly relate to Ginny's situation.

In research of this sort, certain factors fit with one another much like pieces of a jigsaw puzzle so that gradually the whole picture begins to be seen. For example, the lower the family social status background was and the lower the level of education a woman had reached, the more traditional were the sex-role norms she held. Similarly, the more traditional a woman's sex-role norms were, combined with lower education, the more likely she was to marry much earlier than other women. Also, the more traditional were the sex-role norms held by a married woman, the less likely she was to be employed full-time. And among Roman Catholic women, the more tradition-al were the sex-role norms they held, the greater their religious devoutness was found to be.

What does this have to do with how many children Ginny is likely to have? Traditionally, the greater the religious devoutness, the greater has been conformity to church teachings on birth control. Thus, religiously devout Catholics have been those least likely to have fertility-control patterns resembling those of white non-Catholics in comparable life situations. Recently, as we have seen however, the gap seems to be narrowing and Ginny's childbearing career may be less predictable on this count. Westoff and Jones (1978) found that if the current rate of reproduction among women married between 1971 and 1975 continued throughout their married lives, non-Catholics would have an average of 2.17 children each, "devout Catholics" (those who receive communion at least once monthly) would have 2.32 children each, and "less observant" Catholics would have 2.27. This contrasts markedly with the projected fertility of Catholic women married during the 1956–60 period, which was 4.83 children each for the devout and 3.99 each for the less devout.

Remember Ginny's comment about their third child's being unplanned? This could also be an indicator of more children later on. Our research showed that couples who report having children when unintended (timing failures) also tend to report having more children overall. At the same time, something interesting showed up among the Roman Catholic women in the study. Catholics who had experienced timing failures in the past were more likely to hold more egalitarian sex-role norms in the present (Scanzoni, 1975b). It is not clear whether this means that displeasure with contraceptive failures caused women to become more individualistic later on, or whether there had been individualistic tendencies which were put aside for the sake of family-centered interests during the earlier years of marriage and then reemerged.

Our study also showed that among nonemployed Catholic wives, there was a positive relationship between the husband's income and the number of children. More income meant more children—both in the present and intended in the future. Catholics have tended to accept more than non-Catholics the idea that "good persons would have as many children as they can afford." If the earnings of Ginny's husband increase, the couple is likely to have more children.

Shall We Try One More Time for a Girl? (Boy?)   There is another way in which gender may enter into the number of children Ginny will have. Recall her statement that the first two children were girls and they were now hoping for a boy. Several studies have indicated that couples like to have children of both sexes (Williamson, 1976). If a husband and wife have two or more girls and no boys or two or more boys and no girls, they are more likely to "try again" for another child than are couples who have a child of each sex. The Princeton Fertility Study, a longitudinal study in which the same couples were studied over a sixteen-year period, provided data which indicate that the sex composition of the family does affect family size. Couples who fail to achieve the desired sex composition within the number of children originally intended are likely to change their plans and have additional children in an effort to have the sex composition they want (Westoff, Potter, and Sagi, 1963:205–207). Couples are more likely to have a third, fourth, or even fifth child if all the preceding offspring were of the same sex; and this is especially true if the preceding offspring were girls. The final report of the Princeton Fertility Study, published in 1970, showed that "couples whose first two children are boys are 11 percent more likely to have another child than are couples whose first two children included a child of each sex." But "if the first two children were girls the probability of a third birth is 24 percent higher than if there was a child of each sex" (Bumpass and Westoff, 1970:93–94).

Other social scientists have pointed out a continued preference for boys, not only in traditionally patriarchal societies such as among Chinese families in Taiwan (Wu, 1972), but also in modern industrial societies. After an exhaustive survey of studies conducted in the United States and Europe between 1931 and 1975, social demographer Nancy Williamson (1976:63) reports "evidence of slight boy preference especially for firstborns, desire for one of each sex, and preference for a predominance of boys over a predominance of girls if a balanced number of each was not chosen." And while men have a *stronger* preference for sons than women do, women also lean toward boy-preference—though to a lesser degree.

One recent study based upon a large nationwide probability sample showed that just under one-half of fifteen- to forty-five-year-old married women in the United States have a preference for male children. Just under

Couples who fail to achieve the desired sex composition within the number of children they originally intended to have are likely to change their plans and have additional children in an effort to have the sex composition they want. (Sybil Shelton/Monkmeyer Press Photo Service)

one-third prefer female children, while slightly less than one-fifth express a preference for boys and girls equally (Coombs, 1977). Preferences were measured according to how respondents replied to the question: "If you were to have exactly three children, would you most like to have three girls, one boy and two girls, two boys and one girl, or three boys?" Unless the respondents indicated the strongest possible preference for one sex or the other (5 percent said they would like all boys, and 3 percent said they would like all girls), they were asked a series of questions about *alternate* choices and then scored according to the way their preferences leaned.

A 1954 study of men and women of marriageable age was duplicated nearly twenty years later among university students by different researchers. Similar findings emerged both times: when asked which sex these men and women would prefer their first child to be or when asked which sex they would like an only child to be, they overwhelmingly chose a boy ("Sexism on the Stork Market," *Human Behavior,* January, 1974:45–46 [comparison of Dinitz, Dynes, and Clark, 1954, with Peterson and Peterson, 1973]). There was, however, a slight increase in the percentage of persons to whom the sex of their firstborn didn't matter; and when it came to the sex of an only child, the percentage of men who wanted a boy decreased from 92 percent in 1954 to 81 percent in 1973. Among women there was little change as to preferred sex for an only child; about two-thirds indicated a preference for a boy in both surveys. Since the shift in attitudes occurred only among the men, psychologists Candida Peterson and James Peterson felt that the explanation lay in economics rather than the ideology of the feminist movement. Girls are no longer considered a financial liability as they were in the days when they were considered extra mouths to feed until the day they were married off. Now daughters grow up and support themselves just as sons traditionally did—which may in itself be more indicative of feminism (in the sense of changes toward egalitarian sex roles) than these researchers were ready to admit (Peterson and Peterson, 1973).

Sociologist Gerald E. Markle (1973, 1974) found that among university students one-third had no preference regarding the sex of their first child; but among those who did indicate a preference, the choice was 12 to 1 in favor of a boy. And in a general sample of persons living in Tallahassee, Florida, Markle found that the preference for a boy was 19 to 1. Markle's studies showed that respondents holding *traditional* sex-role ideologies were much more likely to state that they preferred their first child to be a boy than were respondents holding *egalitarian* sex-role ideologies. This research demonstrated what Markle had hypothesized from a survey of literature showing that in virtually all cultures around the world male babies are preferred; namely, that "an ideology of male superiority" affects first-child sex preference.

But what if there were a movement away from notions of male superiority and male privilege? An egalitarian ideology tends to abolish ideas about the unique character of boys, thus lowering their "market value" and reducing desires for them. As a result, the overall number of children desired by couples should be lowered, because the pressure to "keep trying for a boy" would be eliminated. But in our hypothetical case study of Ginny, the desire for a boy is strong and is reinforced by the traditional sex-role norms held by her and her husband. Chances are that they will have more children in an effort to make sure they have one or more sons.

Debra's Case Moving on to hypothetical case 3, we find that Debra's lower social status (both in terms of the present and her parental background), lower education, early age at marriage, premarital pregnancy, and past timing failures are all factors calling for predictions of high fertility over the course of her married life. A return visit by an interviewer twenty years after the first interview would likely turn up information that Debra had become the mother of a large family.

Why? In addition to the factors mentioned, plus some of those that applied to Ginny in case 2, three other findings from our research apply to Debra. First, a shorter interval between the time of marriage and the time of the first child's birth is a good indication that a higher number of children will be born in the marriage than if the interval had been longer. Second, the higher the number of children, the lower are the satisfactions that are felt to be experienced in both the economic and expressive dimensions of marriage. And third, the greater the traditionalism in sex-role norms (related to socialization in childhood, socioeconomic status, education, age at marriage, and so on), the less likely are wives to be currently using efficient and effective means of contraception, and the lower is their confidence that they will be able to prevent unintended births and "spacing and number failures."

Linda's Case   The remaining hypothetical case study focuses on Linda. The propositions that describe Dorothy in the first case study also apply to case 4. Linda's egalitarian sex-role norms, high education, high socioeconomic status, later age of marriage, full-time employment before her children were born, as well as full-time employment at present, all combine to indicate the likelihood that her family will remain small. In fact, her family may already be completed in that she has two children, a boy and a girl (although given her egalitarian sex-role views, this one-of-each-sex composition shouldn't matter), and she has confidence that unintended births will be prevented because she has had no timing failures in the past, having effectively used efficient methods of contraception. Two final propositions from our research fit Linda's case: First, among working wives, the greater the job status and income, the lower the number of children. And second, among white non-Catholic wives who are employed or who are well-educated, the greater the egalitarianism in sex-role norms, the less likelihood there is of past contraceptive timing failures. Thus the lower the fertility overall, since among all groupings (black, white, Catholic, and non-Catholic) timing failures and number of children are positively related. (In other words, the more "slipups" or accidental conceptions, the larger will be the family.)

The one reason that Linda might possibly choose to have an additional child relates to her having found satisfactory child-care arrangements with the result that her mother role and career role are not incompatible at this time. But given all the other information we have on Linda, it is unlikely that she will have further children.

Summary Statement on Gender-Role Norms and Fertility   In summarizing these hypothetical cases illustrating our research on how gender-role norms affect fertility, we may state the following: The greater the *individualism* (a woman's desire for personal and occupational achievement and for freedom to pursue her own interests), the less will be the *familism* (a woman's desire to center her life around husband and children). And the lower the familism, the lower will be the number of children intended and the number of children actually born. Similarly, we found that among unmarried university students, the more egalitarian were the sex-role norms held, the fewer were the number of children intended (Scanzoni, 1975c).

What about men? It appears that men who hold egalitarian views and are open to achievement aspirations in women are also willing to have fewer children. But men have a relatively lower sense of compulsion in the matter. In marital negotiations, we may expect that more egalitarian husbands will simply go along with their wives' limited birth intentions rather than actively taking a part or assuming a leadership role in formulating such plans. On the other hand, husbands who are more traditional might actively attempt to influence their wives' thinking, particularly if the husbands desire more children than do their wives. Or such husbands might simply be less cooperative with respect to contraception. ("Ah, come on, Joanie, don't be a spoilsport! Nothing's going to happen just this one time! And so what if it does? It might be kinda nice to have a new baby.") However, a great deal more research needs to be done on marital decision-making about having or not having more children.

CONTRACEPTION, STERILIZATION, AND ABORTION

A century ago, a federal statute known as the "Comstock Law" (named for a self-appointed vice hunter named Anthony Comstock) made it illegal to distribute birth-control information and materials through the mails. Druggists who sold contraceptive devices were arrested. Various states had their own legislation which made it a crime to distribute contraceptive literature, illegal for physicians to prescribe contraceptive devices, or even (as in Connecticut) against the law for couples—single or married—to use contraceptive devices.

Many of these anticontraceptive measures continued into this present century, some until recently. The clergy denounced birth control as sinful, and Theodore Roosevelt warned of "race suicide." Condoms were referred to as "rubber articles for immoral use." In the 1920s, when the birth-control-movement leader Margaret Sanger needed diaphragms to distribute to women who came to her birth-control clinic, she was unable to obtain such contraceptives in the United States and had to purchase them from abroad. American manufacturers were by then permitted to manufacture contraceptive devices but refused to make the reliable Mensinga diaphragm and instead made unsatisfactory cervical caps. However, it was illegal to import contraceptives. Margaret Sanger's clinic therefore obtained them through illegal channels, importing them from Germany by way of Canada from where they were smuggled across the border in oil drums (Kennedy, 1970:42, 183, 218).

Times have changed. Birth control is a fact of life in modern industrial societies, having gained widespread public acceptance and support. How successfully couples practice the limitation of their families depends on a combination of motivation and methods.

CONTRACEPTIVE PRACTICES

The 1970 National Fertility Study showed a large drop in the rate of unwanted births between two different time periods (1961 through 1965 and 1966 through 1970). Westoff (1972:9) attributes this decline to improvements in controlling unwanted births, improvements resulting from using contraceptives earlier and more extensively, more usage (or more consistent usage) of the more efficient methods, and greater motivation to avoid pregnancy.

However, even though there has been a drop in unwanted births, studies indicate that about one-third of all married couples who are attempting to prevent a pregnancy will nevertheless have an unwanted conception within five years. (N. Ryder, 1973; Jaffe, 1973; Tietze, 1979). Norman B. Ryder (1973:141–142), a sociologist who specializes in population research, illustrates in Figure 15-1 how both *methods* and *motivation* enter into the matter of contraceptive failure. The information again comes from the 1970 National Fertility Study.

Ryder defines contraceptive failure as "an unplanned pregnancy which occurs in an interval during which use of contraception is reported." Respondents who reported using contraception prior to a pregnancy and who replied that conception was accidental rather than intentional were asked whether they were attempting to *delay* the next pregnancy or to *prevent* it altogether. It was found that, regardless of the method used, more failures occurred when couples planned only to delay a pregnancy. Evidently, if there are plans to have another baby sometime anyway, more chances are taken, whereas efforts at contraception are more rigorous if the desire is to prevent an *unwanted* pregnancy. Motivation makes considerable difference.

Methods of Contraception Used   Dramatic changes in contraceptive methods occurred between 1965 and 1970 as more and more couples used the more reliable methods and an increasing percentage of couples chose to be surgically sterilized (Westoff, 1972). The move toward more effective contraception continued through the 1970s. Table 15-D shows what currently

FIGURE 15-1   *Percent of contraceptors who fail to delay a wanted pregnancy or to prevent an unwanted pregnancy in the first year of exposure to risk of unwanted conception, by selected contraceptive method. Source: N. Ryder, 1973, p. 141.*

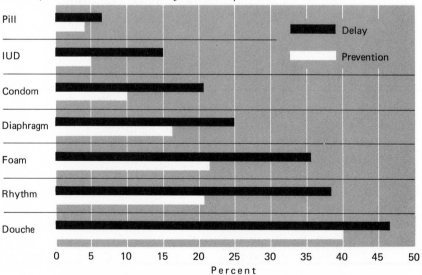

TABLE 15-D Number of currently married women aged fifteen to forty-four and percent distribution by contraceptive status, according to race and Hispanic origin: United States, 1973 and 1976

CONTRACEPTIVE STATUS	TOTAL		WHITE		BLACK		HISPANIC ORIGIN	
	1976	1973	1976	1973	1976	1973	1976	1973
	NUMBER IN THOUSANDS							
All women	27,185	26,646	24,518	24,249	2,144	2,081	1,673	1,676
	PERCENT DISTRIBUTION							
Total	100.0	100.0	100.0	100.0	100.0	100.0	100.0	100.0
Sterile couples								
All sterile couples	30.2	23.8	31.0	24.0	24.3	22.7	20.5	21.6
Nonsurgical	1.9	0.9	1.9	0.8	2.6	1.9	1.5	0.7
Surgical	28.3	22.9	29.1	23.1	21.7	20.8	19.0	20.9
Noncontraceptive	9.0	6.5	9.0	6.6	8.8	6.2	7.8	5.2
Female sterilized	8.2	6.3	8.2	6.3	8.7	6.1	7.0	5.2
Male sterilized	0.8	0.2	0.8	0.3	0.0	0.0	0.9	—
Contraceptive	19.3	16.4	20.1	16.5	12.9	14.6	11.2	15.7
Female sterilized	9.6	8.6	9.6	8.2	11.0	13.6	7.0	10.7
Male sterilized	9.7	7.8	10.5	8.4	1.9	1.0	4.2	5.0
Couples able to have children								
Noncontraceptors:								
Pregnant, postpartum, seeking pregnancy	13.4	14.2	12.8	14.2	16.6	14.0	20.8	18.9
Other nonusers	7.7	8.7	7.2	7.8	13.5	17.9	10.5	9.7
Contraceptors:								
All methods	48.6	53.2	49.0	54.0	45.4	45.3	48.1	49.8
Oral contraceptive pill	22.3	25.1	22.5	25.1	22.0	26.3	20.7	22.9
Intrauterine device	6.1	6.7	6.1	6.6	6.1	7.6	10.4	8.7
Diaphragm	2.9	2.4	3.0	2.5	1.8	1.2	2.4	1.8
Condom	7.2	9.4	7.4	9.9	4.5	3.2	6.1	7.0
Foam	3.0	3.5	2.9	3.5	3.8	3.0	3.5	1.8
Rhythm	3.4	2.8	3.5	2.9	1.4	0.7	3.1	2.1
Withdrawal	2.0	1.5	2.0	1.6	1.8	0.4	1.1	2.2
Douche	0.7	0.6	0.5	0.5	2.7	1.8	0.1	0.6
Other	0.9	1.3	0.9	1.3	1.2	1.0	0.5	2.7

SOURCE: Adapted from National Center for Health Statistics, U.S. Department of Health, Education, and Welfare, "Contraceptive Utilization in the United States: 1973 and 1976," *Advance Data from Vital and Health Statistics*, no. 36, August 18, 1978, p. 2.

married white, black, and Hispanic women were doing to prevent or postpone pregnancy in 1973 and 1976.

Pregnancy Risk and Gender-Role Norms It is possible to place current contraceptive behavior on a continuum of risk-taking (Figure 15-2). At the "extremely high risk" end of the continuum would be the couple who use no contraception whatsoever. If the wife were physically able to conceive, the probability of her becoming pregnant would be high indeed. But moving down and into the "high risk" section of the continuum, we would find couples who use such methods as husband withdrawal before ejaculation, or the wife's douching immediately after intercourse, or rhythm (having sexual relations only at the time of the month when the wife is considered to be infertile, the one method officially endorsed by the Roman Catholic Church).

At the "extremely low risk" end of the continuum would be husbands who have had vasectomies (the severing of the sperm-carrying tubes from the testicles) and wives who have undergone surgery in which the fallopian tubes were cut and tied so that the ovum could not be reached by sperm cells. This operation is called a tubal ligation. Women who have had hysterectomies (the removal of the uterus) or total oophorectomies (the removal of both ovaries) are also sterile—although such surgery is ordinarily performed for purposes other than contraception. The next lowest risk method of contraception is the pill, followed on the continuum by the IUD, condom, and diaphragm with contraceptive jelly or cream.

In analyzing our research on how fertility relates to gender-role norms, we found that women who sought individualistic rewards more than familistic rewards were low-risk takers when it came to contraceptive techniques (Scanzoni, 1975b). They tended to use the most efficient

FIGURE 15-2   *Continuum of risk-taking in contraceptive practice.*

Likelihood of Pregnancy	Method
Extremely high risk	No contraception at all
Very high risk	Postintercourse douching
High risk	Rhythm, foam, withdrawal, contraceptive jellies (without use of diaphragm), suppositories
Low risk	IUD, diaphragm with jelly or cream, condom
Very low risk	The pill
Extremely low or no risk	Sterilization (tubal ligation, vasectomy, hysterectomy)

methods—the pill or intrauterine devices (IUD), or else very diligent use of the diaphragm with jelly, or their husbands carefully used condoms. Women who ranked higher on familism than individualism, on the other hand, were using methods that placed them on the high-risk section (top half) of the continuum.

It became apparent that the risk-taking level in contraception indicates the degree to which women are indifferent to the *costs* of children or even actually desirous of the *rewards* of children. Women who hold more traditional sex-role norms may think of an unplanned pregnancy as a "surprise" perhaps, but they are not likely to think of such an event as a "disaster" as might be the case with women holding egalitarian sex-role norms and individualistic aspirations. Women who strongly believe in pursuing their own interests (such as career achievement) cannot afford to be indifferent to the costs of children. Any children to be born to them must be carefully planned both as to numbers and timing. Egalitarian wives are therefore more motivated than traditional wives to choose the most efficient birth-control methods and then to use those methods with great care to avoid failures.

This finding is one more piece of evidence that motivation plays a highly significant role in fertility control. Improved methods made possible by advances in research and technology are of great importance but are not in themselves enough. No matter how *theoretically* effective a particular contraceptive technique is, its *actual* effectiveness will in large measure depend upon the user. Women who forget to take their birth-control pills or couples who occasionally neglect to insert diaphragms or to use condoms can expect contraceptive failures, not because the perfect birth-control method is yet to be discovered, but rather because their motivation in using presently available methods is not strong enough.

One problem pointed out by some feminists is that while some of the most efficient contraceptives may carry low pregnancy risks, they carry other kinds of risks. And for the most part, these risks must be taken by women, not men. For example, certain dangers and serious side effects have been associated with use of the IUD or the pill by some women. Barbara Seaman (1972:219) writes: "If you doubt that there has been sex discrimination in the development of the pill, try to answer this question: Why *isn't* there a pill for men?" Male biomedical researchers counter with claims that the greater availability of female contraceptive methods is not part of a "male chauvinist plot," nor are scientists "proceeding to research and test contraceptives in order to provide more fun for men, while ignoring the health needs of women." Rather, they point to certain complexities in the male reproductive system that have limited the approaches that can be taken (Segal, 1972). However, research on male contraceptives continues, including investigations into the possible use of sex steroids that would inhibit the production of sperm, and possible techniques that could immunize a male against certain components of his own body so that antibodies might stop the production of sperm or cause sperm to be infertile (Bremner and de Kretser, 1975). Of course, the risk of side effects could be a possibility with a "male pill," too.

But for the present time at least, side effects of oral contraceptives for women have kept some individualistic, egalitarian wives from using or continuing to use them—even though the pill is generally considered to be the most reliable means (apart from sterilization) of cutting down the risks of unwanted conceptions. Data from our research indicate that while women with egalitarian sex-role norms do tend to gravitate toward pill usage, women who are equally committed to individualism and egalitarianism may avoid the pill because of concern about physiological effects, choosing instead other reliable, low-risk methods, and making them work because of strong motivation (Scanzoni, 1975b).

Among the general population, "the increase in the use of oral contraceptives observed from the 1960's through 1973 has come to a halt," writes demographer Kathleen Ford of the National Center for Health Statistics in the report cited in Table 15-D. "However," she continues, "for couples in which one partner was not sterile, no other method comes close to it in popularity" (p. 6).

STERILIZATION

Three out of every four married couples who used any contraception at all in 1975 were using the pill, the IUD, or had been surgically sterilized. Commenting on this finding from the 1975 National Fertility Study, two researchers point out that "a decade earlier, just a little more than one-third were using these highly effective methods" (Westoff and Jones, 1977b:153). Sterilization now rivals the pill, and in fact exceeds it in popularity among couples who don't want any more children. While 24.1 percent of couples who have had all the children they desire rely on the pill for contraception, 43.5 percent of such couples have elected to be sterilized (either the husband or the wife). Among couples who have been married from twenty to twenty-four years, 56 percent report that one or the other spouse has been sterilized (Westoff and Jones, 1977b:155).

Since sterilization is considered to be the lowest-risk method of contraception of all, the question may arise: do couples with egalitarian sex-role norms choose tubal ligations or vasectomies to a greater degree than do couples holding traditional sex-role norms? Much more research needs to be done to answer this question as well as other questions about why couples choose contraceptive surgery, how they feel about it afterward, and so on. In our own research (Scanzoni, 1975b), we were unable to find any meaningful pattern of variables (not even education) to account for the choice of this "radical" means of birth control by either younger or older couples in our sample.

As of 1979, women with limited education and lower socioeconomic status were more likely to have experienced a tubal ligation than were women with more schooling (Westoff and McCarthy, 1979; Westoff and Jones, 1979:6). Lower-educated women may have turned to contraceptive surgery in a desperate attempt to control fertility after several children and unsuccessful attempts to use other contraceptive techniques. Sometimes pressures for such surgery have come from outside, for example from social agencies. In 1974, the Department of Health, Education, and Welfare issued strict guidelines designed to protect poor and minority persons against *coerced* sterilizations— particularly in the case of minors and adults considered legally incompetent. The guidelines resulted from public protests after federal funds were reported to have been used for the sterilization of two black adolescent girls in Alabama. In another case, physicians were requiring that pregnant women on Medicaid who had two or more children must agree to a tubal ligation or else the physicians would not deliver their babies (Vaughan and Sparer, 1974).

Since lower-educated women have traditionally had more children than higher-educated women, it has been easier for them, if they wanted to be sterilized, to meet contraceptive surgery eligibility requirements set up by the medical profession. Restrictive policies of physicians, hospitals, and health insurance companies have in the past meant that more than free choice was involved if a couple chose sterilization. For example, up until 1969, the official manual of the American College of Obstetricians and Gynecologists (ACOG) recommended that contraceptive operations be performed on women *only* if they were at least twenty-five years old and had five living children. A thirty-year-old woman could not be sterilized unless she had four living children, and a woman thirty-five years old had to have at least three living children before she could have a tubal ligation. These suggestions were adopted by most hospitals, some of which had even more restrictive requirements for sterilization. However, many of these restrictions were dropped after 1969 when the ACOG manual discontinued mentioning the old recommendations. Although vasectomies have generally been performed in physicians' offices rather than in hospitals, they too have been subject to restrictions— often the doctors' own ideas about the desired age of a man and number of children he must have before being sterilized (Presser and Bumpass, 1972:20).

With the growing acceptability of sterilization, it is quite possible that more and more younger couples will elect to have such operations when they want either no additional children or no children at all. Already, sterilization has become "the single most popular method [of preventing conception] for couples married 10 years or more" (Westoff and Jones, 1979:6). Among white couples, the percentage of wives who are sterilized for contraceptive reasons is similar to the percentage of husbands. Among black couples, the person sterilized is far more likely to be the wife. (See Table 15-D.) Though the percentage difference is not so striking, sterilization among Hispanic couples is also more likely to have been performed on the wife. Female sterilization shows signs of becoming increasingly popular now that newer and simpler procedures can be used and hospital stays are shorter. In many cases the woman may be discharged the same day she has entered ("Digest," *Family Planning Perspectives* 11, July/August, 1979:254; Westoff and Jones, 1979:6).

ABORTION

Up until the historic Supreme Court decision in 1973 which swept aside antiabortion laws, abortion had been illegal in most states except in certain situations (such as rape, incest, or danger to the mother's life). Although illegal abortions occurred in great numbers, it was difficult to study who had them and why. After July, 1970, New York was one state that permitted abortion on request; and early studies of the impact of legalization indicated that from 70 to 80 percent of abortions performed in New York City would have been performed anyway—but illegally—had the law not been changed (Cutright and Cutright, 1973:8; Tietze, 1973, 1975; Sklar and Berkov, 1974).

In the years since 1973, it has been possible to study what the legal right to abortion has meant nationwide. As Table 15-E shows, most abortions are performed on very young women up to twenty-four years of age. In fact, about one-third of abortions involve teenagers. Three-fourths of women who have abortions are unmarried.

Researchers note that one result of the Supreme Court ruling "has been a steady trend toward performance of abortions earlier in gestation, when the procedure is safer. Ninety percent of all abortions in 1976 were performed at 12 or fewer weeks' gestation; nearly half were performed at eight or fewer weeks" (Forrest et al., 1978:274). The use of the safest abortion method, suction, has also increased as Table 15-E shows.

About one-third of abortions are performed on black women and those of other nonwhite races. That about two-thirds of abortions are performed on white women should not be surprising since there are more white women than those of other races in the general population. However, if we separate the racial groupings and look at abortion *rates* (number of abortions per 1,000 women aged fifteen to forty-four), a different picture emerges. Among white women, the abortion rate is 19; while among women of black and other races, the rate triples to 58. We have already seen in Chapter 9 that racial discrimination and the resultant economic hardship are major factors in explaining the higher rates of births out of wedlock among blacks. The higher rates of abortion presented here no doubt have similar explanations. Furthermore, very poor women—those eligible for Medicaid—were those regardless of race who had the highest rates of abortion in 1976 and who were thus most affected by the legislation of late 1976 which limited the circumstances under which federal funds could be used to pay for abortions.

If most abortions are taking place among the poor, the very young, and the unmarried, what about the general population of married persons? As we saw in Table 15-E, only one out of every four abortions is performed on a married woman. As Cutright and Cutright (1973) point out, it appears that "the bulk of the decline in marital fertility is coming from contraception—not legal abortion."

However, among married couples who feel that children would be costly and in conflict with individualistic interests, abortion may seem a viable

TABLE 15-E   *Estimated number and percentage distribution of legal abortions, by selected characteristics, United States, 1973–76*

CHARACTERISTIC	NUMBER				PERCENTAGE DISTRIBUTION			
	1973	1974	1975	1976	1973	1974	1975	1976
Total	744,610	898,570	1,034,170	1,179,300	100.0	100.0	100.0	100.0
Age								
<15	11,550	13,630	15,520	15,820	1.6	1.5	1.5	1.3
15–19	231,890	279,790	326,780	362,680	31.1	31.1	31.6	30.8
20–24	238,110	285,370	330,200	392,280	32.0	31.8	31.9	33.3
25–29	131,800	162,500	188,610	220,500	17.7	18.1	18.2	18.7
30–34	73,970	90,070	100,420	110,050	9.9	10.0	9.7	9.3
35–39	40,870	48,460	52,380	56,720	5.5	5.4	5.1	4.8
≥40	16,420	18,750	20,260	21,250	2.2	2.1	2.0	1.8
Race								
White	539,600	626,560	701,110	784,890	72.5	69.7	67.8	66.6
Black and other	205,010	272,010	333,060	394,410	27.5	30.3	32.2	33.4
Marital status								
Married	203,990	245,880	269,640	290,030	27.4	27.4	26.1	24.6
Unmarried*	540,620	652,690	764,530	889,270	72.6	72.6	73.9	75.4
No. of living children								
0	361,880	429,810	486,930	562,610	48.6	47.8	47.1	47.7
1	140,240	176,040	208,800	244,430	18.8	19.6	20.2	20.7
2	105,680	133,300	160,520	181,520	14.2	14.9	15.5	15.4
3	64,560	78,330	89,690	97,690	8.7	8.7	8.7	8.3
4	35,590	40,520	45,200	47,930	4.8	4.5	4.4	4.1
≥5	36,660	40,570	43,030	45,120	4.9	4.5	4.2	3.8
Weeks of gestation								
≤8	273,160	387,270	466,830	559,900	36.7	43.1	45.1	47.5
9–10	223,020	260,920	296,780	333,770	30.0	29.0	28.7	28.3
11–12	135,510	139,860	156,270	171,270	18.2	15.6	15.1	14.5
13–15	47,060	45,920	47,240	49,010	6.3	5.1	4.6	4.2
16–20	54,340	54,240	57,170	55,120	7.3	6.0	5.5	4.7
≥21	11,520	10,360	9,880	10,230	1.5	1.2	1.0	0.9
Method								
Suction curettage	574,000	711,480	869,360	990,660	77.1	79.2	84.1	84.0
Surgical curettage	91,710	101,800	79,170	110,760	12.3	11.3	7.7	9.4
Saline infusion	70,530	64,620	58,960	56,230	9.5	7.2	5.7	4.8
Hysterotomy/ hysterectomy	4,550	5,010	3,640	2,680	0.6	0.6	0.4	0.2
Other†	3,820	15,660	23,040	18,970	0.5	1.7	2.2	1.6

*Never-married, widowed, divorced, separated.
†Includes prostaglandin.
SOURCE: Jacqueline Darroch Forrest, Christopher Tietze, and Ellen Sullivan, "Abortion in the United States, 1976–1977," *Family Planning Perspectives* 10 (September/October, 1978), p. 275.

Number of Abortions Growing

WASHINGTON (AP)—A survey by an international population study group indicates that one in four pregnancies worldwide ends in abortion, according to a report released Sunday.

The report by the Population Crisis Committee estimated that at least 40 million and perhaps as many as 55 million legal and illegal abortions were performed or induced last year and said the number appears to be growing."

"In most parts of the world, the incidence of abortion is expected to grow as a result of wider preference for smaller families, lack of alternative family planning services and an increase in the number of women of childbearing age," the committee said.

The committee, a privately funded organization, reported a year ago that sterilization had become the principal method of birth control in the world.

Cynthia Green, one of the staff members who prepared the latest report, said there were 122 million live births last year and an unknown but relatively small number of spontaneous abortions, or miscarriages, which weren't counted in the panel's calculations.

The Soviet Union, Japan and Austria have among the highest abortion rates in the world, the report said. More than half of all pregnancies in those countries end in abortion, compared to about one in four in the United States, India, China, Sweden and Denmark.

The committee explained the high rates in the Soviet Union and Japan by saying abortions there not only are legal but the two nations "share a heavy historical reliance on abortion as a method of family planning due to the lack of oral contraceptives, IUDs (intrauterine devices) and voluntary sterilization."

In most of Latin America and Africa, abortion is either strictly illegal or permitted only under very restricted circumstances, such as to save the life of the mother, the committee's survey showed.

But the report said such restrictions don't always hold down abortion rates. It said there is at least one abortion for every five live births in Belgium, Burma, Colombia, Indonesia, the Philippines, Portugal and Taiwan, all of which prohibit abortion under any circumstances.

The study found there has been a trend throughout the world in recent years to liberalize abortion laws. It predicted nations would continue to rely on the procedure as a form of birth control because no perfect contraceptives are available.

SOURCE: Associated Press report, *Greensboro (N.C.) Daily News*, April 30, 1979.

---

option in the event of an "accidental" conception. Sociologist J. E. Veevers (1973a:358), for example, found in a sample of fifty-two voluntarily childless couples that although most of the wives had never been pregnant, they reported that if pregnancy should occur they would seek an abortion. One-fifth of these women had already had at least one induced abortion. Demographers Charles Westoff and Norman Ryder (1977:170) also found a relationship between individualistic interests and a more permissive attitude toward abortion. Married women who were *least likely* to believe abortion was permissible were women who had never been employed. Married women *most likely* to believe that abortion was permissible were women who not only were employed but who worked for reasons other than financial considerations. Education was also found to be an important factor. Women with a college education have been found to be more approving of abortion than are women with a high school education or less (Westoff and Ryder, 1977:167–170).

VOLUNTARY CHILDLESSNESS

In the children's story "The Gingerbread Man," we are presented with the sad spectacle of a lonely old couple so desperate for a child that they set out to make one out of cookie dough. In Edward Albee's play *Who's Afraid of Virginia Woolf?* childless George and Martha, constantly at odds with one another, railing with insults and hostilities, nevertheless drew solace from a shared secret—the illusion of the imaginary son they had dreamed up together.

According to popular folk belief, married couples without children are to be pitied. Their lives are considered by outsiders to be incomplete. Surely, the reasoning goes, no couple would remain childless unless it couldn't be helped. Perhaps the husband or wife is infertile, physically unable to reproduce. But even then, adoption is always a possibility. That some couples would deliberately choose not to have offspring would strike many persons as absurd.

There is evidence that most people do want children, but there are others who do not. According to both United States and Canadian census data, about 5 percent of couples prefer voluntary childlessness (Veevers, 1972; Silka and Kiesler, 1977:24; Polonko, 1979). Several studies indicate that among student samples of young unmarried persons, the percentage of those saying they plan not to have any children over their lifetime is three or four times the 5 percent figure above—though, of course, many may be expected to change their minds later (see summary of such studies in Silka and Kiesler, 1977; Polonko, 1979).

If it is true that 1 out of 20 currently married women deliberately wants to avoid motherhood despite all the pronatalist pressures of relatives, friends, the media, and even the government (such as income-tax laws), the question becomes *Why?* The little research that has been done thus far on voluntarily childless couples indicates that the answer lies once again in perceived rewards and costs (Polonko, 1979). Veevers (1974) points out that some couples who choose not to have children think chiefly in terms of cost avoidance, but other couples look at the reverse side of the coin and emphasize the rewards of an adult-centered life-style.

It is possible to think of the rewards of *not* having children in much the same way that we earlier considered the rewards of having children. Couples who desire the child-free life-style might think in terms of the following:

REWARDS OF SELF-ENHANCEMENT AND SELF-PRESERVATION

Social identity and a sense of adult status can come through means other than parenthood—most notably through individual achievement in a career or public service. We have already seen that some couples may look upon having children as a way of gaining a sense of self and experiencing vicarious accomplishments (by "living through" their children), but other couples feel that children could hinder self-enhancement and block a husband and wife from being all that they could otherwise be. Such voluntarily childless couples feel that children would drain away time and energy that could otherwise be devoted to pursuing individualistic interests and making their own name for themselves. They want to be remembered for their own contributions to the world rather than the contributions of their children.

REWARDS OF AFFECTION, BELONGING, AND PLEASURE

Whereas couples who want children speak of the expressive rewards expected in parenthood, couples who don't want children may view children in a "three's a crowd" fashion and fear that commitment to parenthood would detract from commitment to the marriage itself. Veevers (1974) reports that some of her respondents made such comments as, "A child would come between us. I wouldn't be able to be as close to my husband if I had a child. . . ." or "If you have children, then not all of your emotional involvement would be with each other anymore and you would have lost something." Couples who opt for the child-free life-style are willing to "put all their emotional eggs into one basket" as one respondent told Veevers. Affection and belonging are important for such women and men, but they want to find such affection and belonging in the husband-wife relationship alone rather than seeking these rewards through children. As Veevers has expressed it: "A dominant component [of the child-free life-style] is commitment to the ideal that a married couple should be a self-sufficient unit, who look to each other for the satisfaction of most (and perhaps all) of their social and psychological needs. . . . They relate to each other not only as man and wife, but also as lover and mistress and as 'best friends.' The presence of children makes such dyadic withdrawal difficult if not impossible" (p. 397).

In another study, sociologist Karen Polonko (1979, chap. 4) compared voluntarily childless wives with wives who intend to have children and found that the majority of the voluntarily childless "believe that children will decrease their satisfaction with spouse closeness, companionship, romance, and the opportunity to experience new things with their spouse."

This theme of "experiencing new things" and freedom to pursue individualistic and couple interests and adventures also shows up in other studies of child-free couples. Veevers (1974) reports that a recurrent theme among her respondents was the search for novelty, the avoidance of routine, the quest for new experiences, new situations, new tasks, a desire to travel, the freedom to just "pick up and go" at a moment's notice. Childless couples also reported that they enjoyed being able to pursue adult activities and adult entertainments without having to be concerned about family recreational activities, child-centered play, and constant consideration of "what is good for the children." They liked, for example, being able to attend movies with adult themes rather than being limited to Disney-type films in the interest of family togetherness.

ALTRUISTIC AND RELIGIOUS SATISFACTIONS IN NOT HAVING CHILDREN

"People who don't want to have children are simply selfish! They think only of themselves and their own convenience." Such has been the familiar accusation hurled at couples who voluntarily choose to remain childless. But with growing concern about population pressures, food and energy shortages, crowding, and all the related problems of too many people on too small a planet, the accusation of selfishness has been aimed toward a different target. Couples who want the rewards of children in great abundance are the ones who are now likely to be labeled self-indulgent and unconcerned about the good of humanity. Couples who forgo the experience of parenthood may be considered by others to be altruistic.

And indeed altruistic motives may very well figure into the decisions of some couples to remain childless. In our own university student sample, although no question was asked about preferred childlessness per se, we did find that a prime motivation for limiting family size was a deep concern about population pressures (Scanzoni, 1975c). Two researchers, Susan Gustavus and James R. Henley, Jr. (1971), who studied seventy-two childless couples applying for sterilization, found that concern over population growth was one of several reasons these men and women gave for not wanting any children.

Veevers (1973a:363–364) reports that concern with population problems "does provide a supportive rationale indicating that one is not necessarily being socially irresponsible and neglectful of one's civic obligations if one does not reproduce," but that among her sample, such concern was not a motivating force for not having children but was "an *ex post facto* consideration." It was something a childless couple could latch onto after making their decision, but primarily "their satisfaction with being childless is related to concerns other than to their contribution to the population crisis."

Hoffman (1972a) makes a similar point. Referring to the report of a psychiatrist working with couples having marital difficulties, she states that a recurring theme that emerged during therapy was that of the husband who didn't want children but *pretended* to want them in order not to appear harsh and unloving. "With the socially negative view so prevalent," writes Hoffman, "it has probably been unacceptable to admit the desire for childlessness even to oneself." Such individuals may be the ones most open to concerns about not adding to the world's population since these concerns provide an altruistic rationale for their personal preferences. At the same time, there is no denying that among some socially conscious couples, consideration of population pressures may be a very real motivation in their initial decision not to have children rather than simply a rationale to justify their decision later.

When it comes to the question of *religious* satisfactions in not having children, the issue may seem harder to determine. To some persons, the very notion of religious satisfactions in childlessness would seem absurd, since religious beliefs have traditionally been bound up with notions that children are "blessings from heaven" and that parenthood is a sacred duty. Indeed, in both the Veevers and the Gustavus-Henley samples of childless couples there is an indication that rejection of such notions includes rejection of the religious beliefs and institutions from which they derive. Veevers (1973a:357) writes of her sample of fifty-two voluntarily childless wives: "Most individuals are either atheists or agnostics from Protestant backgrounds, and of the minority who do express some religious preference, almost all are inactive." Respondents in the study by Gustavus and Henley (1971) were also likely to report that they had no religion. And in Polonko's (1979) sample of 95 voluntarily child-free wives, participation in religious services averaged less than once a year. Nearly one-third reported no religious preference, "and most of these women further classify themselves as atheists or agnostics," reports Polonko (chap. 4). Although two-thirds stated a religious preference, one-fifth of them attended religious services less than once a year, and close to another fifth reported they never attended. Only one of the wives said she attended church more than once weekly. Only 12.6 percent of the voluntarily childless wives in Polonko's sample were Roman Catholic.

Traditionally, religious supports for voluntary childlessness have been nonexistent. However, at least one Protestant scholar sees in voluntary childlessness the possibility of a church-sanctioned commitment somewhat like that of celibacy for reasons of religious service. Just as a person might renounce marriage in order to devote himself or herself to serving God and others with a maximum of freedom, mobility, and time available for one's mission, so might a married couple choose not to have children in order to give full concentration to their ministry. So writes Mennonite theologian John Howard Yoder (1974) as he suggests that church mission and service agencies could benefit by encouraging voluntarily childless couples who embrace this life-style in order to dedicate themselves to religious ministries. Similar thinking is taking place among some Roman Catholics. An article in *U.S. Catholic,* for instance, proposes "a new alternative . . . made possible only in this time—that childless marriage be recognized as a religious ideal when it is undertaken in order that the couple might pursue a higher calling of service to God and humanity" (Everett and Everett, 1975:39).

CHOOSING THE CHILD-FREE LIFE-STYLE

J. E. Veevers has given much study and consideration to factors related to the decision of couples not to have children. Several of her findings are of special interest because of what they tell us about how and why the decision not to have children is made.

Many of Veevers' (1973b) respondents reported having come from unhappy homes in which their parents remained together rather than getting a divorce. The children learned not only that having children doesn't necessarily mean either personal or marital happiness, but also they learned that children can even be the cause of strife in marriage. Furthermore, parents who endure miserable situations "for the sake of the children" may be teaching children that parenthood is entrapping, preventing the option of divorce. Women in the sample who grew up in such homes had negative impressions of motherhood, which were made all the stronger by the fact that their mothers had been "basically dissatisfied with their housework and child-care roles."

Some voluntarily childless wives in Veevers' sample had been "only" children. Thus it may be that the absence of role models and the lack of opportunities to interact with siblings caused some of these women to feel incompetent for or uninterested in the mother role for themselves.

On the other hand, some of the wives in the sample came from large families in which they were the oldest of the children and had responsibility for all the younger brothers and sisters. Being cast in the "little mother" role, these women learned early that children limit one's activities. Often during girlhood, these women had to baby-sit when they would rather have pursued their own interests or attended school events. Taking care of real children provided an experience quite different from that known to little girls who play only with dolls. "The dolls never misbehave in unmanageable ways," writes Veevers, "they never preempt or preclude other activities, and when they become burdensome or boring they can be readily but temporarily abandoned." Not so with real babies. And girls who grow up in the oldest-daughter position in the family often learn that early. They may thus have little desire for taking on the mother role in adulthood.

Egalitarian gender roles and wife employment may also enter into the choice not to have children. Earlier we saw that these factors were related to limiting family size; but for some couples they are also related to avoiding parenthood altogether. Veevers (1974) writes: "Most of the childless wives interviewed report that their marriages are characterized by very egalitarian sex roles, with an orientation in which the husband and wife are considered to be of equal value to the relationship, with equal levels of authority and equal levels of competence." Furthermore, "egalitarian role relationships may be both a consequence and a cause of childlessness."

With one exception, all of the childless wives in Veevers' sample work and plan to work indefinitely. About half of the women reported a deep commitment to their work and derive a sense of identity from it, and many have high professional aspirations. "The remaining half work mainly for extrinsic rewards, such as money and the satisfactions of interacting with others in job situations," Veevers (1974) reports.

Polonko also found the voluntarily childless in her study to be "characterized by intensely egalitarian gender-role and pro-childless norms." Such women "perceive children to be very costly to their satisfaction with their spouse relationship, standard of living and career," writes Polonko (1979,

Many voluntarily childless women report a deep commitment to work and high achievement goals. (© Ginger Chih, 1978)

chap. 4), and all three of these areas are quite highly valued. The voluntarily childless women in her study had achieved higher income and occupational prestige than had the wives who had not voluntarily chosen childlessness. Polonko suggests that for voluntarily childless wives, career *success* is a key factor in decisions to remain child-free, along with perceptions that the wife's career and the care and attention required by children would be incompatible. Other studies have indicated that occupational success in high status jobs is associated with intentions to remain child-free (see Silka and Kiesler, 1977).

How the Choice Is Made   Veevers (1973a:359–360) found that nearly a third of childless couples decide before marriage that childlessness will be a part of an informal marriage "contract." From the very beginning there is no intention to have children. In most cases, these women in Veevers' sample had made the decision during adolescence and later sought future mates who agreed; although in some cases, the women had not considered a childless marriage until meeting their future husbands.

Among the other two-thirds, childlessness comes about as the result of continually postponing having children until a future time. But the "right time" never comes. For most couples, this postponement seems to come about through a series of four stages—first, a definite period of waiting; second (when the agreed-upon time is up), an indefinite period of postponement when the time to have a baby becomes increasingly vague; third, a critical state in which the possibility of permanent childlessness is openly

Adoption Is the Choice of Some

During the late 1950's and throughout the 1960's, adoptions increased in the United States, both in actual numbers and in relation to both births and women in the childbearing ages. Since 1970, there has been a decline in the number of adoptions and in the ratio of adoptions to currently married women in the childbearing ages. This decline since 1970 is observed for white adoptions, but not for other adoptions which have continued the upward trend of the fifties and sixties. The decline in white adoptions since 1970 appears to be a combination of more white mothers keeping their illegitimate babies rather than putting them up for adoption (a trend starting around 1960) and a depression of white illegitimate births in the early seventies.

About 4 percent of the women in the United States adopt a child, other than a stepchild, by the time they complete their childbearing years. Although few young women have adopted, over half say they would resort to adoption as a means of achieving their expected family size if they should be unable to bear the children they want. As age increases, the proportion who indicate the possibility of future adoption decreases, while the proportion who have adopted increases to 4 percent of women age 40–44 in 1973. The average age at adoption appears to be about 30 years old.

Women who have adopted children are found in all racial, educational, economic and religious groups. These characteristics of women show little relationship to the amount of adoption. However, labor force participation is related to adoption. Women working full time are least likely to adopt if they are white, but not if they are black. The most significant characteristics related to those who have adopted are the relative inability of the women to bear children in the future and their experience of childbearing in the past. Subfecund or sterile women and women who have no children born to them are much more likely to have adopted a child than are fecund* women or women who have had children born to them.

There has been a major change between 1955 and 1973 in who adopts children. Adoptions by 1955, at least among white wives 18–39, were much more likely among sterile and childless women than among women who could have or have had children. In 1973, it was not the sterile but those with some problems in having children that were most likely to have adopted, and although childless women were still more likely to have adopted than women with children, the difference between them had greatly diminished. Over half of the women who had adopted a child by 1973 had borne children of their own, with the majority of these women giving birth to children before adopting rather than after adopting.

*Fecundity is the ability of a woman to bear a child if she so desires.

SOURCE: Gordon Scott Bonham, "Who Adopts: The Relationship of Adoption and Social-Demographic Characteristics of Women," *Journal of Marriage and the Family* 39 (May, 1977), p. 303–305.

acknowledged for the first time; and fourth, an explicit decision (or the recognition of the implicit decision that has been gradually made) that they will never have children. Other researchers write of ongoing patterns of negotiation rather than a series of postponements (Cooper et al., 1978).

In another study focusing on the respective power in the husband-wife relationship when there is *disagreement* about whether or not to have children,

Some couples experience parenthood through the adoption of children. (Erika Stone/Peter Arnold, Inc.)

it was found that if the husband first suggested childlessness, the wife was likely to come around to agreement with him, often after years of negotiation. But if the wife wanted a child-free marriage and the husband did not, the husband was not likely to be persuaded by her wishes. Divorce in such cases tended to be the outcome (Marciano, 1978).

Interestingly, in Veevers' sample of wives who wished to be child-free, the door was not closed on possible adoption of children some day. Veevers (1973a:362–363) points out that the importance of the option of adoption lies in the twofold symbolic importance: "the reaffirmation of normalcy" [because of the societal view that "normal, well-adjusted" people will want and like children] and the avoidance of irreversible decisions."

MACRO VIEW OF REPRODUCTION

If the nursery-tale introduction to childlessness is "The Gingerbread Man," the equivalent introduction to a macro view of the world population situation could be the story of the old woman who lived in a shoe and had so many children she didn't know what to do.

What About Having One Child Only?

While most couples decide to have two children, a small but growing number remain childfree. About 10% choose the third alternative—to have one child. . . .

Parents of only children are quick to point out the advantages of the one-child family for themselves. "Being the parent of one child is having the best of two worlds" in the view of one parent. "I can experience the joys and frustrations of being a parent without getting so tied down by parenting responsibilities that I haven't time to pursue my own interests". . . .

The image presented by one-child parents of a close, democratic, affluent family-style is considerably different from the long-admired American portrait of the "Walton" family-style with its tangle of relationships and clear lines of authority. One mother in a one-child family observed that the end results are different. "Parents with several children often seem to view parenting as an all-consuming job. For my husband, daughter, and me, life is more like a three-way adventure."

SOURCE: Sharryl Hawke and David Knox, "The One-Child Family: A New Life-Style," *The Family Coordinator* 27 (July, 1978), excerpts from pp. 215–217.

Ansley J. Coale (1974), for many years director of the Office of Population Research at Princeton University, vividly describes what is taking place as world population increases at a rate more rapid than at any time in history. He points out that the *growth rate* (the number of persons added per year per 1,000 population, taking into account both births and deaths) was up until 10,000 years ago about .02, and it took at least 35,000 years for the population to double. Between A.D. 1 and 1750 (the year when the modern accelerated growth phenomenon began), the growth rate was .56 per 1,000, which meant the world population doubled every 1,200 years. However, according to United Nations studies, the growth rate is expected to be about 20 per 1,000 over the next several decades—which would mean a doubling of the world population this time in just under thirty-five years!

Coale illustrates the cumulative effect of even a small number of doublings by referring to an old legend in which a king offered his daughter in marriage to any man who could supply one grain of wheat for the first square on a chessboard, two grains for the second square, double that amount for the third square, and so on. "To comply with this request for all 64 squares," writes Coale, "would require a mountain of grain many times larger than today's worldwide wheat production."

In 1973, the world population was 3.9 billion. According to United Nations projections, there will be 6.4 billion people in the world by the year 2,000. Coale points out that if the present growth rate of 20 per 1,000 were to continue so that the population would double every thirty-five years, the earth would be in a similar situation to the legendary king's chessboard. "The consequences of sustained growth at this pace are clearly impossible," says Coale. He explains why. "In less than 700 years there would be one person for every square foot on the surface of the earth; in less than 1,200 years the human population would outweigh the earth; in less than 6,000 years the mass of humanity would form a sphere expanding at the speed of light."

BIRTHRATES IN THE UNITED STATES

Throughout most of the developed world, there appears to be a trend toward two children as the preferred family size (Westoff, 1974b:113). The United States is no exception; and as part of the trend toward smaller families, birthrates dropped to record lows between 1972 and 1976. (The *birthrate* is the number of births per 1,000 population.)

Then, according to the National Center for Health Statistics, the birthrate increased in 1977 for the first time in seven years (*Monthly Vital Statistics Report*, vol. 27, no. 11, 1979:1). Before jumping to the conclusion that this signals another "baby boom" as happened in the 1950s, it's important to notice where the biggest increases occurred. Figure 15-3 shows that the most rapid increases between 1976 and 1977 occurred among women in the twenty-five to twenty-nine-years-of-age bracket (a 5 percent increase) and in the thirty- to thirty-four-years-of-age bracket (a 5.5 percent increase). The largest increases among these groups occurred among women having their first babies. In that one-year period, there was an 11 percent increase in first births among women between thirty and thirty-four years of age, and during 1978, there was another 12 percent increase. In addition, there was a 10 percent increase in first births to women aged thirty-five to thirty-nine years. The explanation appears to be that these women are now having the children they had delayed having earlier—no doubt in many cases due to a desire to act upon individualistic interests, such as becoming launched in a career before embarking on parenthood. The overall birthrate, however, had declined slightly again by the end of 1978 (latest available figures) to 15.3 live births per 1,000 population (from 15.4 the year before). And the *fertility rate* (births per 1,000 women aged fifteen to forty-four years) was down from 67.8 in 1977 to 66.6 in 1978, second to the lowest rate ever recorded although there were indications of a slight rise in both the birthrate and fertility rate as 1979 statistics were being tabulated (*Monthly Vital Statistics Report,* vol. 29, no. 1, 1980:1–4, 10).

WHERE POPULATION GROWTH IS OCCURRING

It should be kept in mind that not all parts of the world are growing equally. In some nations, there is even governmental concern that not enough people are being born. In other nations, the annual population increase seems staggering and is associated with poverty, inadequate food supplies, extremely crowded living conditions, and other social problems. To understand this imbalance, it helps to think in terms of the United Nations' classifications for

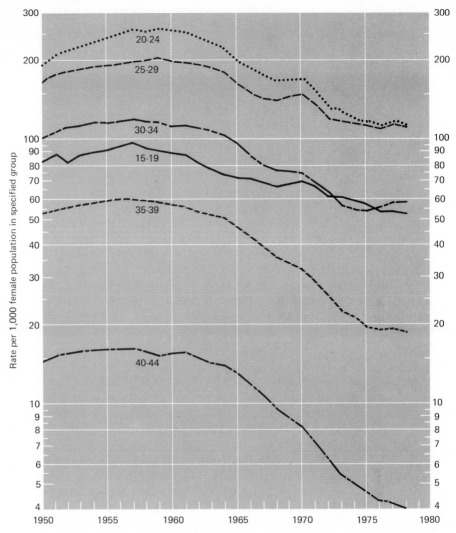

FIGURE 15-3   BIRTH RATES BY AGE OF MOTHER: UNITED STATES, 1950–78. Source: "Advance Report: Final Natality Statistics, 1978," Monthly Vital Statistics Report, vol. 29, no. 1, Supplement (April 28, 1980), p. 2. Published by the National Center for Health Statistics, U.S. Dept. of Health and Human Services.

areas of the world. "Less developed" societies are those which are "largely rural, agrarian, and at least partly illiterate." "More developed" societies are those "primarily urban, industrial, and literate" (Coale, 1974:48). Particular populations may be at various points along a continuum of change from being "less developed" to being "more developed."

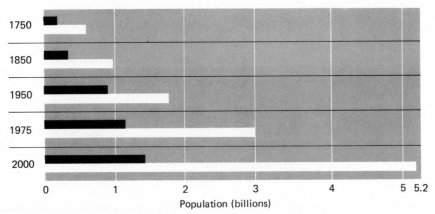

FIGURE 15-4   *World population increase since 1750 is charted for developed countries (dark bar) and underdeveloped countries (light bar). Classification as developed or underdeveloped is according to economic and demographic differences now prevailing. Data for the year 2000 are based on a United Nations projection that assumes slowly ebbing growth rates. Source: Demeny, 1974, p. 153.*

The less-developed nations are growing in population at a very high rate of increase at the same time that population growth in the rest of the world is more moderate or even low. (See Figure 15-4.) In fact, according to United Nations projections, 90 percent of the anticipated population increase by the year 2000 will have been contributed by the less-developed nations. However, we must be careful in interpreting what this projection means. Demographer Paul Demeny (1974:152) of the Population Council warns: "The frequent references to 'soaring' birth rates in popular interpretations of contemporary demographic changes in the underdeveloped world have little factual basis and in many instances no basis at all. Rapid population growth is mainly a result of falling death rates unaccompanied by adjustments in birth rates."

Demographers speak of this lag between death rates and birthrates as the "demographic transition." During the transition, as less-developed countries undergo changes through which they move toward urbanization and industrialization, death rates decline because of medical advances, improvements in sanitation, nutrition, and the like. At the same time, the birthrate in these countries continues as before for a considerable period of time. Population then grows because of this difference in birth and death rates. After the transition to urbanization and industrialization is completed, the birthrate also declines. The wide gap between numbers of deaths per 1,000 population and numbers of births per 1,000 becomes much smaller. (See Figure 15-5.)

At the same time that less-developed nations are growing so rapidly (with growth rates of 2.5 percent per year), the population growth rate in developed nations is now less than 1 percent and falling. In fact, observes sociologist Charles Westoff (1974b:109), in the twenty countries that have 80 percent of the world's "developed" population, fertility is "at, near or below

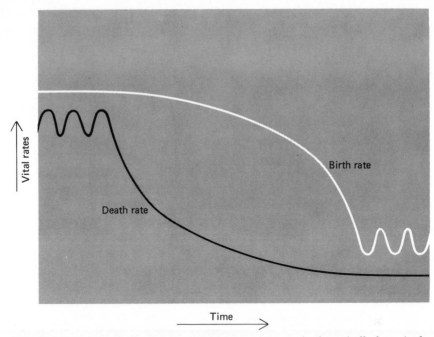

FIGURE 15-5 *The* demographic transition, *represented schematically here, is the central event in the recent history of the human population. It begins with a decline in the death rate, precipitated by advances in medicine (particularly in public health), nutrition, or both. Some years later the birth rate also declines, primarily because of changes in the perceived value of having children. Before the transition the birth rate is constant but the death rate varies; afterward the death rate is constant but the birth rate fluctuates. The demographic transition usually accompanies the modernization of nations; it began in Europe and the United States late in the eighteenth century and early in the nineteenth, but in the underdeveloped nations it began only much later, often in the twentieth century. In the developed countries the transition is now substantially complete, but in much of the rest of the world only mortality has been reduced; the fertility rate remains high. In the interim between the drop in mortality and fertility population has increased rapidly. Source: From Coale, 1974, p. 49.*

the replacement level." Replacement level means an average of 2.1 births per woman over a lifetime of childbearing. (Demographers speak of the likely average number of births per woman over an entire lifetime of childbearing as a nation's *total fertility rate.* It is based on births per woman at different age levels in a given year.)

TRENDS AND GOVERNMENT POLICIES

Governments are aware of the consequences of population growth or the lack of it, and they may utilize various measures to either cut down growth or encourage greater fertility. Where there is a concern about *too rapid growth* and the problems of crowding, housing, pollution, limited resources, burdens placed on community services, and similar matters related to the well-being of a country and its citizens, governments may seek to encourage birth control through varied programs. For example, in 1979, China's national leaders began a strict program of costs and rewards intended to keep couples from having more than one or two children. And government leaders in India have tried a variety of incentives—and even coercion at some points—to lower that country's rapid population growth (Landman, 1977; Potts et al., 1977). Reports from the World Fertility Survey are showing indications of a decline in the average number of children born to women in fourteen Latin American and Asian countries as a result of family planning efforts (Kendall, 1979). Even so, fertility levels in these developing countries remain considerably higher than those of developed countries. For example, in Bangladesh, only 10 percent of married women use contraceptives; there a woman now bears 6.3 children on the average over a lifetime, as compared to 7.1 earlier. But in Costa Rica, where 78 percent of wives use contraception, fertility has been reduced from 7.1 children per woman to 3.8.

On the other hand, if a government becomes alarmed that a decline in fertility may mean military, economic, and political disadvantages, and may cause such problems as a labor shortage in future years, policies and programs and changes in laws may be instituted in an effort to raise the fertility rate. For example, Romania's *total fertility rate* in 1955 was 3.1 births per woman, but by 1966 it had reached a low of 1.9. Disturbed by this decline, the government repealed its permissive abortion law. By the next year, fertility had doubled to 3.7. This large upsurge in births in 1967 later caused severe overcrowding in the Romanian school system. Westoff (1974b:112–115) predicts that by 1984 when this group of children enters the labor force, there will be very high unemployment or an outmigration of surplus labor. At the present time, Romanian fertility has again been lowered despite the restrictions on legal abortion, as couples rely on diligent usage of contraception and, when necessary, illegal abortion. Another government which became concerned over a low population growth rate was that of President Peron of Argentina. Before his death in 1973 he told the women of Argentina that they had maternal responsibilities to fulfill—and promptly made oral contraceptives illegal (Westoff, 1974b:118).

COSTS, REWARDS, AND POPULATION

It seems clear that on the macro level, no less than on the micro level, reproduction is a matter of costs and rewards. Too many people can be costly, but so can too few. Governments around the world are increasingly aware of population concerns and have set up various commissions to study demographic trends and to suggest policies (Berelson, 1973). Where there is concern about too much population growth, as is occurring in the less-developed nations, attention must be given to the rewards and costs of children on the micro level in order to affect trends at the macro level. Especially is there a need to present alternative rewards, for (in the words of Hoffman and Hoffman, 1973:69), "as long as children satisfy an important

China Will Reward Couples with No More than One Child

WUHAN, China—In a series of unusually strict directives, Chinese officials have announced new bonuses for couples with no more than one child and income cuts, housing and promotion restrictions for families that grow beyond two children.

The toughened birth sanctions apparently grew from a major Peking conference on population control in January. They reflect widespread official distress at the state of the economy and the difficulties of modernizing a country with 900 million mouths to feed.

A difficult reappraisal of China's economic needs, continuing in a series of high-level meetings, even has produced a startling official admission by Radio Peking that "the average amount of food grain distributed to each person in China is now even less than in 1957."

If each married woman had only two children, said a broadcast from Guangdong Province, ancestral home of most Chinese-Americans, the province's population would still increase by 10 percent in the next five years and "any improvement in the people's living standards can be forgotten."

Nationally, the numbers are even more staggering. The country's annual population growth has been estimated at 1.5 to 2 percent. Although that is below such countries as India, with more than 2 percent, or Mexico, with more than 3 percent, it represents an increase of 13 to 18 million Chinese a year. The higher estimate would mean China grows every year by about the population of the state of New York.

Birth control is nothing new in China. It is even mentioned in a new constitution approved last year. Shanghai was reported two years ago to have reduced its population growth rate to only 0.6 percent through a tough system that required every woman to report her contraception method to local authorities and then wait until she was told it was her turn before having a baby.

China's national leaders have never been as blunt about their population problems as they seem to be now, or as willing to impose sanctions on parents seeking a third or fourth child. As in other countries with population problems, such as India, resistance to population control has been particularly strong among peasant couples who depend on sons to help run farms, earn food for the family and support elderly parents.

SOURCE: L.A. Times–Washington Post News Service, *Greensboro* (N.C.) *Daily News,* May 1, 1979.

value for which there is no alternative, people will climb over a great many barriers and put up with a great many costs before they will diminish fertility. As long as children satisfy important values, even very trivial reasons for another child will seem valid."

CHAPTER HIGHLIGHTS

How couples perceive the costs and rewards of having children plays a major part in family planning. Incentives for having children tend to fall into four main categories: (1) self-enhancement, (2) self-preservation, (3) pleasure, affection, and belonging, and (4) altruistic and religious satisfactions. Persons at lower socioeconomic levels tend to have more children than those at higher levels. One reason is that children are a source of rewards for poor people when other rewards are denied them; another reason may relate to a sense of helplessness in controlling their lives, including a failure to prevent unwanted births in many cases. The material costs involved in having children are twofold: *direct costs* (money spent for children's needs) and indirect *opportunity costs* (opportunities passed by or given up for the children). Some studies have indicated that couples who are rearing children are less satisfied with their marriages than are childless couples or those whose children are grown.

Research shows that sex-role norms held by women affect both the number of children they intend to have and the number they actually do have. A summary statement of gender-role norms and fertility is this: The greater a woman's *individualism* (desire to pursue her own interests and fulfill her own achievement goals), the lower will be her *familism* (desire to center her life around her husband and children). And the lower the familism, the lower will be the number of children intended and the number actually born.

Three out of four couples are now using the pill, the IUD, or have been surgically sterilized. Sterilization of either the husband or wife is the most popular method of birth control for couples married ten or more years. Most abortions take place among the poor, the very young, and the unmarried; only one out of four abortions is performed on a married woman. About one out of twenty married women now chooses to have no children at all because she views children as more costly than rewarding and prefers an adult-centered life-style.

Governments may take action to decrease or increase population, depending upon how fertility trends appear to be helping or hindering national self-interest. Where the concern is over too much population growth, as in less-developed countries, attention must be given to the rewards and costs of children on the *micro* level (the "small picture" of individuals and couples) in order to affect trends at the *macro* level (the "large picture" of nations and the world as a whole).

CHAPTER 16

(Erika Stone/Peter Arnold, Inc.)

THE YEARS OF CHILDREARING

How would you like to take care of an egg for a week? That seemingly preposterous question was put to a high school class in Philadelphia a few years ago in an effort to show students what it's like to be responsible full-time for an infant.

The egg had to be raw, not hard-boiled, and thus susceptible to breakage. Careless students who broke their Humpty Dumpties over the week were subject to a trial for "egg abuse," and at the end of the experiment a mock trial was held for such offenders. Some of the instructions for the project went something like this: "If you want to go out, the egg goes with you or you have to hire an egg-sitter. WHAT IF YOU HAVE TWINS??!! Look at the bright side—eggs don't wake you up in the middle of the night" (National Alliance for Optional Parenthood, 1978).

BECOMING PARENTS: A CRISIS?

The egg experiment illustrates the life-style changes that occur when persons become parents. As a number of sociologists have pointed out, "if the family is conceived of as a small system of interrelated roles and statuses, then it follows that the addition or removal of a family member necessitates changes and reorganization which may produce stress" (Hobbs and Cole, 1976:723). During the late 1950s and throughout the 1960s, this concern with possible stress gave rise to a number of studies and reports that suggested that parenthood was nothing less than a *crisis* for many wives and husbands.

Some of the first "parenthood as crisis" studies indicated that the majority of couples in particular samples experienced an "extensive" or "severe" crisis when their first child was born (LeMasters, 1957; Dyer, 1963). It was suggested that couples had held an idealized image of what parenthood would be like and were not prepared for the reality of a demanding, helpless infant.

On the other hand, later studies presented a different picture. While a baby's entrance into a household obviously changed—even disrupted—the usual routine of husbands and wives, the majority of couples reported gratifications in parenthood. Most spoke of their marriages as being no different (and in some cases, even better) after the first child's birth and did not report a severe crisis experience. If a crisis was perceived, it tended to be measured as only "slight" or "moderate" (see Russell, 1974; Hobbs and Cole, 1976; Hobbs and Wimbish, 1977; Hill, 1978).

AN EXAMPLE OF TRUE CRISIS

The word *crisis* may at first call to mind a psychological definition which includes an "upset in a state of equilibrium caused by a hazardous event which creates a threat, a loss, or a challenge for the individual" (Bloom, 1963, as quoted in Klaus and Kennell, 1978:24). For example, two professors of pediatrics have summarized studies of the emotional crisis parents undergo upon the birth of a child with a birth defect. At the moment of impact when the news is first received, the parents go through a period of shock, then one of denial, followed by a period of sadness and anger. Gradually, equilibrium is restored as the parents learn to cope and adapt. The process has been compared to the grieving process that takes place when a child dies. In the case of a malformed infant, the parents are in a sense mourning the loss of their expected, perfectly formed child. But at the same time, something else is being required of them. They must become attached to the actual, living, malformed infant that *has* been born; and they must handle this concurrently with the "grief work" or mourning process. However, as such parents get to know their baby and learn to give him or her the required physical care, feelings of closeness to the child develop and the initial feelings of sadness begin to diminish in most cases (Klaus and Kennell, 1978:23–26). (For a summary of studies of families with handicapped children, see Rapoport et al., 1977:117–129.)

INADEQUACIES OF THE FAMILY CRISIS APPROACH TO STUDYING PARENTHOOD

While it isn't difficult to think of parenthood as a "crisis experience" in cases such as that just described, some scholars have suggested that the term is a bit too strong for the ordinary experience of parenthood. While some studies, as we've seen, did show that some couples perceived their experience with their first baby to be a "crisis" (according to sociologist Reuben Hill's (1949, 1978) definition of crisis as a sharp change in which old patterns are no longer adequate and new ones have to be developed), others suggested calling such an experience a "normal crisis" (Rapoport, 1963). Parenthood was thus viewed as a normal event in the lives of most couples, a developmental stage that could be looked forward to and prepared for in advance since it was an experience common to most people. Yet at the same time, the changes in status from nonparent to parent were such that the term *crisis* still seemed appropriate.

Sociologist Alice Rossi (1968), however, is among those who suggest that "the time is now ripe to drop the concept of 'normal crises' and to speak directly, instead, of the transition to and impact of parenthood." She feels that the words *normal* and *crisis* don't really fit together— for two reasons. If a couple successfully makes the transition to parenthood, the word *crisis* seems inappropriate. And second, the word *normal* appears to suggest only successful transitions to parenthood and would seem to rule out the possibility of unsuccessful transitions and negative parenthood experiences. Hobbs and Cole (1976:730) likewise conclude that "it is more accurate to think of beginning parenthood as a transition, accompanied by some difficulty, than a crisis of severe proportions."

BECOMING PARENTS: A TRANSITION

One may leave an unsatisfactory job or marriage, but there is no turning back once parenthood has been undertaken. "We can have ex-spouses and ex-jobs," writes Rossi (1968), "but not ex-children." The word *transition* derives from the Latin for "going across." With parenthood, a new way of life is beginning for the couple.

Several of the crisis studies have indicated that wives are more likely than husbands to report having found the transition to parenthood difficult (Hobbs and Wimbish, 1977:686)—not a surprising finding in light of the greater disruptions in wives' lives beginning with pregnancy and continuing through their traditionally greater involvement in child care. And in a study of black first-time parents, sociologists Daniel Hobbs and Jane Maynard Wimbish (1977) concluded that the transition to parenthood for these couples was slightly more difficult than was the case for the white couples in earlier studies in which Hobbs had been involved (Hobbs, 1965, 1968; Hobbs and Cole, 1976). However, they offer no explanation as to why this might be but call for further research. At the same time, they point out that the higher difficulty scores in the sample of black couples did not (any more than in the case of white couples) "warrant the label of crisis to describe their experience" (Hobbs and Wimbish, 1977:688).

The transition to parenthood is less difficult when a couple has been married for some time and the pregnancy is planned. (Erika Stone/Peter Arnold, Inc.)

What Black Parents Want

Black parents have all the problems other parents have, and more. They have to bring up their children to be comfortable with their blackness, to be secure, to be proud, to be able to love. . . . They have had to raise their children under the most horrendous of circumstances. In social, economic, and emotional deprivation. Educational deprivation, too. The quality of black life, while it is improving, has been unspeakable. And not because of anything blacks have done. Because of what has been done to blacks. . . . no other group has had the experience of being treated as less than human for generation after generation after generation. . . .

What do blacks want for their children?

Nothing more than every parent in every latitude and longitude wants for his [or her] child. And nothing less.

SOURCE: From Dr. Phyllis Harrison-Ross and Barbara Wyden, *The Black Child: A Parent's Guide to Raising Happy and Healthy Children* (New York: Peter H. Wyden, Inc., 1973), pp. 20–21 in the Berkley Medallion paperback edition.

What are the most bothersome elements in the new parenthood role? Some of the most common complaints relate to the baby's interruption of routine habits of sleep and freedom to go places, fatigue, money problems due to the increased expenses of an infant, interference from in-laws, the loss of the wife's figure and worry over personal appearance, additional work, decreased sexual responsiveness, and a decrease in contacts with friends (Hobbs and Wimbish, 1977; Russell, 1974).

FACTORS INVOLVED IN DIFFICULT TRANSITIONS TO PARENTHOOD

Sociologist Candyce Smith Russell (1974) did not discard the term *crisis* in her study of the degree of crisis experienced by first-time parents and what factors might be associated with difficult transitions to parenthood. But she used the word in a special sense. "It is important to make clear that crisis as used in this study is defined as change in self, spouse, or relationships with significant others which the respondent defines as 'bothersome,'" writes Russell (p. 295).

What were some factors associated with a perception of parenthood as a "crisis" (in Russell's sense) or a "bothersome," difficult transition? Premarital conception, a mother's poor health, and (for men) a low ranking of the role of fatherhood in their scale of values. On the other hand, parents indicated less difficulty in undertaking their new role if the pregnancy was planned and without complications and if the delivery was problem-free. The more months a woman had been married before having her first baby also was linked with a less stressful transition to parenthood.

In addition, the baby's temperament entered into how distressing the new experience of parenthood was perceived, with quieter babies associated with lower stress for the parents. Russell writes:

It is likely that there is a reinforcing interchange between a parent's ideal image of a baby and the infant's objective behavior. Quiet behavior may reinforce a parent's image of a cuddly baby and elicit a warm response from the parents, which in turn satisfies the infant's desires. Noisy, active behavior, on the other hand, may not fit parental expectations and may elicit non-soothing behavior which will further excite an already active baby. (p. 300)

DO REWARDS OUTWEIGH COSTS?

Russell not only looked at the problems parents experienced in having their first baby; she also measured *gratifications* associated with parenthood. And overall, her research showed that "respondents perceived their first year of parenthood as only moderately stressful and as well supplied with rewards" (p. 300).

This emphasis on the gratifications of parenthood must not be over-looked. Otherwise, we see only one side—and the negative side at that. As psychologist Lois Wladis Hoffman (1978:340) emphasizes, "This negative portrayal does not seem to jibe with the overall positive evaluation of new motherhood that many women indicated and with the reports of older women looking back." By "negative portrayal," she means the social science literature in which both theories and research have focused on a variety of problems associated with new parenthood—for example, evidence of greater traditionalism in sex roles as husbands and wives begin functioning as parents, certain anxieties and marital dissatisfactions during early stages of parenthood, theories about the loss of marital intimacy when the twosome becomes a threesome, and all the "bothersome" elements in first parenthood that have given rise to the "crisis" label already examined.

Hoffman is persuaded that we must take into account the *subjective* experience of motherhood in order to get the total picture. "To summarize the effects of the first child on the woman's role without asking the woman how she felt," writes Hoffman, "might lead to the conclusion that motherhood would soon be on its way out" (p. 366).

Thus, in her research based on a large national representative sample of white married women under age 40, Hoffman used two approaches. One, she asked the women themselves how they felt about motherhood. And two, she compared the women who had already had their first child with those who had not, looking for any differences between the two groups with respect to sex-role attitudes, employment, education, power in marital decision-making, how much husbands participated in household task performance, and friendship patterns.

She points out that if we paid no attention to women's feelings about their experience of motherhood but looked *only* at objective comparisons between the two groups (mothers and nonmothers), motherhood might be described in "severe" terms. In comparison to the nonmother, the woman who has had her first child

has more responsibilities and less freedom; she is more likely to leave employment, and sometimes to curtail education. Her husband helps less with household tasks, to some extent her power in decision-making is diminished, and she is more likely to develop a set of friends separate from her husband. (p. 366)

At first glance, we might expect from this that those women who had actually experienced such changes and restrictions in their lives would be the most likely to rate motherhood negatively, whereas nonmothers might hold in mind an idealistic image and rate motherhood more positively. But Hoffman's findings show just the opposite. "In all open-ended questions, mothers viewed motherhood more favorably than nonmothers," writes Hoffman, "and women with no more than a high school education saw it more positively than those with further education" (p. 364).

Hoffman found that new mothers often changed their sex-role ideology in the direction of more traditionalism in order to feel more comfortable psychologically with what indeed tended to happen when the first child was born: an "increased separation of husband-wife roles along the traditional, sex-typed lines" (p. 366). In spite of such separation along sex-role lines and more apartness between husbands and wives in general (such as an increase in having separate friendships), most respondents felt that having a baby brought them closer to their husbands because it involved the husband and wife in a common task and goal—the child's well-being. Hoffman concludes:

> Whether it is the human capacity to learn to live under the conditions that exist, whether it is a bill of goods that has been successfully sold, or whether motherhood is in fact a very gratifying experience, one effect of the first child is a more positive view of the experience, and even to some extent a change of attitudes to fit, and accept, the new situation. (pp. 366–367)

PARENTHOOD: THE INSTITUTION AND THE EXPERIENCE

Increasing numbers of women and men are questioning traditional sex roles, however, as we have seen throughout this book. And we may expect such questioning to show up in less willingness to fit into traditional assumptions about motherhood and fatherhood as well and to seek instead for new patterns. Yet, such questioning need not devalue parenthood; for many, it may enhance and enrich the experience.

To question the traditional assumptions about parenthood doesn't mean an undermining of the parent-child *relationship* but has more to do with the conventional way in which parenthood has been conceptualized and in which child-care responsibilities have been assigned. That's why it is important to distinguish between parenthood as a *relationship* or experience (which can indeed be gratifying as the Hoffman data showed) and parenthood as an *institution* (the form or patterned way of parenthood that has been set up with certain roles and behavioral expectations spelled out in advance for women and men to follow) (see Bernard, 1974; Rich, 1976).

Fatherhood: Four Myths versus Reality

Myth #1: Men do not have a natural inclination toward parenting or nurturing behavior. Reality: *Parenting skills, like most other skills, are basically learned behaviors, not biological endowments. Social customs have taught women and girls to care for the young: social customs could also teach, encourage, and reward men and boys for the same types of skills and behavior.*

Myth #2: Infants (both male and female) show no interest in their fathers. Reality: *Recent research by Lamb (1975) and others casts serious doubts on our earlier assumptions. When the father takes an active role during the first few months of the infant's life, a strong bond seems to develop between them, just as it does between infant and mother. An infant may be more concerned with basic needs of nourishment, comfort, sleep, and a predictable, positive environment than with the sex of the person who meets these needs.*

Myth #3: There is a single and universal description of a "successful father." He is financially secure, emotionally tough, and has a natural strength and inclination to control his environment through rational thought and behavior. Reality: *As women and men honestly raise questions about traditional sex-role definitions and expectations, both are acknowledging much broader characteristics and options for being a successful woman or a successful man. There is no single definition for masculinity or femininity; neither is there a single or universal definition for a good father or a good mother.*

Myth #4: Fathers do not want to be bothered with the daily routines of childrearing. Reality: *Although many fathers have accepted a narrow definition of their role and feel that their time should be spent on non-child-related tasks, many are eager to participate in direct interaction with their children at all levels. Many more fathers would feel this way if they were encouraged to realize their capabilities as parents.*

SOURCE: James C. Young and Muriel E. Hamilton, "Paternal Behavior: Implications for Childrearing Practice." Pages 135–145 in Joseph H. Stevens, Jr. and Marilyn Mathews (eds.), *Mother/Child, Father/Child Relationships* (Washington, D.C.: National Association for the Education of Young Children. 1978).

MOTHERHOOD

Keeping in mind the distinction between motherhood-as-institution and motherhood-as-relationship, we can see the point sociologist Jessie Bernard (1974:10) is driving at when she asserts that young mothers "are beginning to tell us, it's true: they find joy in their children, but they do not like motherhood." Bernard explains why:

> The way we institutionalize motherhood in our society—assigning sole responsibility for child care to the mother, cutting her off from the easy help of others in an isolated household, requiring round-the-clock tender, loving care, and making such care her exclusive activity—is not only new and unique, but not even a good way for either women or—if we accept as a criterion the amount of maternal warmth shown—for children. It may, in fact, be the worst. It is as though we had selected the worst features of all the ways motherhood is

structured around the world and combined them to produce our current design. (p. 9)

Bernard emphasizes that this view of motherhood is largely based upon a nineteenth-century Victorian idealization—a conception of motherhood that was "male and middle-class" and which ignored the reality of women's lives even of that period of history. The focus was on "mother as symbol."

FATHERHOOD

Some scholars and researchers have been calling attention to a myth that has grown up which assumes that parenting and mothering are one and the same (Rapoport et al., 1977:3; Young and Hamilton, 1978:137). Fathers have been given relatively little attention except for their traditional role as primary breadwinner. Author-poet Adrienne Rich (1976) points out that even the expression *to father* a child is generally taken to mean "to beget, to provide the sperm which fertilizes the ovum." In contrast, the expression *to mother* carries with it the idea of nurturing and caring for someone.

Many men are beginning to see such a narrow definition of fatherhood as

Role-sharing means both parents take equal responsibility for their children and consider this responsibility when they integrate occupational and family roles. (Charles Gatewood)

Rethinking Parenthood: Who Benefits?

"Everyone can benefit from the reinvention of family roles. Mother is being recognized as a person, and as a person who can think. Father must be recognized as a person, and as a person who can feel."

SOURCE: Maureen Green, *Fathering: A New Look at the Creative Art of Being a Father* (New York: McGraw-Hill, 1977).

having cheated men of the rewards of greater involvement with their children. Thus, unwed fathers are in some cases today demanding visitation rights and custody rights. Divorced fathers are also indicating a desire for more than a provider role but want total or joint custody in many instances. And many fathers in intact marriages now question the wisdom of pouring their energies so totally into occupational pursuits that involvement in family life is shoved aside. They are less likely to believe the simplistic equation: "good provider" equals "good father."

The rethinking of women's roles has had an impact on men's roles as well and is a major factor in the new attention to the responsibilities of fatherhood today. "Young women now entering the scene want more than merely supportive husbands," writes Bernard (1974:175). "They want fatherhood itself expanded. The sharing of the provider role by the mother is felt to call for a sharing of the parental role by the father in the child-care and socializing function." Bernard emphasizes that role sharing is not the same as role *reversal* (in which the mother is the family provider and the father is the caretaker of the children and house)—although of course some couples may choose the role reversal arrangement if it particularly suits them. But role *sharing* means both parents take equal responsibility for the children and take this responsibility into account as they integrate occupational and family roles.

STAGES OF PARENTHOOD

Rossi (1968) points out that the development of a social role has various phases and lists four basic stages of adult social roles: the anticipatory stage, the honeymoon stage, the plateau stage, and the disengagement-termination stage. For example, in the case of a person's role as spouse, the period of engagement is the *anticipatory* stage for that role; the *honeymoon* period is made up of the early days when the role is new and the spouses are enjoying a special closeness to one another and exploration of one another's uniqueness; the *plateau* stage is the "protracted middle period" that makes up the major part of married life; and the *disengagement-termination* stage occurs when the marriage ends in divorce or death.

Early Stages   Applying these four broad stages to parenthood, Rossi speaks of pregnancy as the anticipatory stage. (Making the preparations for adopting a child would be the equivalent for adoptive parents.) The "honeymoon stage" of parenthood, says Rossi, is "that postchildbirth period during which, through intimacy and prolonged contact, an attachment between parent and child is laid down." She emphasizes that there is a major difference between this "honeymoon" stage and that of marriage, however; because in the early stages of parenthood, parents are getting acquainted with the child for the first time, in contrast to marriage where the persons knew each other in advance to a considerable degree.

Interest in *sharing* the anticipatory and honeymoon stages of parenthood may be seen in the participation of young husbands and wives together in preparation-for-childbirth classes, the desire of many couples to have the husband present during childbirth (either in a hospital that cooperates with such a plan or, in some cases, by arranging an at-home birth, possibly with the assistance of a midwife rather than a physician where legal), and in the interest of many young fathers in sharing the care of babies and small children (see Rapoport et al., 1977:161–175, 352).

The honeymoon stage of parenthood seems especially important with the first baby because the parents are conscious of trying out various aspects of the parental role for the first time. Sociologist Sandra Titus (1976) calls attention to one illustration of this. By studying records of family life as shown in family photo albums, she found that not only do parents tend to take more pictures of the first baby than of subsequent children; they also take special kinds of pictures. First-time parents seem interested in preserving on film a record of their own learning of various tasks associated with their new role; thus, there are photos of the parents as they hold, feed, diaper, bathe, and otherwise care for the baby.

Later Stages   There is no precise point marking the transition from the honeymoon stage of parenthood to Rossi's "plateau" stage—the bulk of the years in which parents are preparing their children for life. It is during this plateau period that parents confront various child-developmental issues, such as sex-role socialization, moral development, the child's growth toward independence, discipline, and motivation for achievement (Rapoport et al., 1977:353).

The Committee On Public Education of the Group for the Advancement of Psychiatry (1973) has described what is taking place in parents' lives during those years:

> Parenting involves reliving one's own childhood experiences during each stage through which the child passes. Parents and children develop together and interact with each other. To be able to feel what the child feels enlarges the parents' capacity for empathy in other interpersonal relationships. (p. 16, as quoted in Rapoport et al., 1977:16.)

At the same time, the Committee emphasizes that parents need not feel guilty for recognizing their own needs as individuals and attending to them:

> Parents are not only vehicles for the care of their children. They were persons before the child arrived; are persons while they are parents; and will be after the children leave. . . . They were once told to listen to their parents. They are now told to listen to their children. Both directives are valuable. They must, in addition, listen to themselves. (Group for the Advancement of Psychiatry, 1973:131–132, as quoted in Rapoport et al., 1977:18.)

The final stage of parenthood, Rossi's "disengagement-termination stage," like the plateau stage, is not marked by some specific event signifying that parental authority, obligations, and responsibilities have ended. "Many parents, however, experience the marriage of the child as a psychological termination of the active parental role," says Rossi (1968). At the same time, as we have seen, Rossi has emphasized in that same article that a parent can never become an ex-parent in a strict sense. Even after their offspring reach legal age or marry or otherwise strike out on their own, parental interest and involvement usually to some degree will continue.

CHILDREARING IN AN ACHIEVEMENT-ORIENTED SOCIETY

Childrearing, like marriage, is a complex process involving actions, interactions, and reactions; and all parties concerned—father, mother, and each child—play a part in this process. In other words, we're back again to exchange theory.

EXCHANGE THEORY AND CHILDHOOD SOCIALIZATION

Sociologist Stephen Richer (1968) has developed a theoretical model of how social exchange may be expected to work in parent-child relationships. Building upon the premise that power is associated with resources, Richer attributes the high degree of power parents hold over very small children to the fact that in the earliest years children are totally dependent upon parents for both material rewards (food, clothing, shelter) and social rewards (comfort, love, affirmation, approval, and so on). Children have few if any alternative sources of such rewards, nor do they in themselves possess equivalent resources which would permit bargaining from an equal power base.

The relationship is one-sided until somewhere in the toddler stage when children discover a resource of their own—one highly valued by parents and which therefore gives children a measure of power in the bargaining process. That resource, according to Richer, is *compliance*—doing what others want them to do. Children perceive that their compliance means a great deal to parents and can make parents happy or unhappy. ("Melissa, please eat your

The child's growing awareness of the ability to produce effects on others is a crucial occurrence.
(Joel Gordon)

peas. Come on now, be a good girl. It makes Mommy sad when you won't obey." "Timmy! You know you're supposed to tell me when you have to go to the potty!" "Kim, say 'thank you' to Grandma. Kim! Come back here this minute! Say thank you for the present. Oh, that child makes me furious!")

Richer points out that the child's growing awareness of the ability to produce effects on others (the parents' pleasure or displeasure) is a crucial occurrence. "For, though still dependent for basic material and social rewards on his parents, the child begins to experience feelings of autonomy, a necessary prerequisite for later involvement in self-interested exchange (p. 463).

When the child starts school, compliance is found to be valued by other adults as well. Now the teacher's praise and approval can be obtained in exchange for the child's conformity to the teacher's wishes. Schoolmates also increasingly become sources of social rewards. No longer is the child quite so dependent upon parents, and with the availability of alternative rewards for the child comes a diminishing of parental power. The child may now place a higher price tag on compliance: hugs, smiles of approval, and expressions of pleasure may not always be enough any more. Thus the parent may suggest material rewards (a dollar for a good report card or a gift for cooperation in something the child doesn't want to do) or may bargain for the child's compliance in a spirit of quid pro quo: you do this for me and I'll do that for you. The early dependence stage has given way to a reciprocity stage.

During adolescence the child's power increases even more because the resources offered by the peer group take on such importance. One way parents may try to obtain and maintain compliance is through offering new kinds of rewards which will bring greater peer group approval for the adolescent (the keys to the car, opening the home for parties, and the like). However, if the young person has alternative material rewards (money from a part-time job) as well as alternative social rewards (peer approval), dependency on parents is all the more decreased—as is parental power.

Richer acknowledges that the picture just presented may seem a bit overdrawn, but it is intended simply to provide a basic illustration of how social exchange theory may be applied in parent-child relationships. Of special importance is the part socioeconomic status plays in the exchange. For example, parents may view a child's increasing realization that compliance can be granted or withheld as a situation calling for reasoning and reciprocity or as a situation posing a threat to order and therefore calling for coercion (the stick instead of the carrot). Social class has a great deal to do with which of the two approaches parents will take. Studies have shown that parents at lower socioeconomic levels are more likely to use coercion and parents at higher levels are more likely to employ reasoning and bargaining. "The middle-class home is thus more conducive to the development of an exchange system," says Richer, "whereas the cultural patterns at lower status levels inhibit such a system." And when a child reaches adolescence and physical force and coercion are more difficult to utilize, lower-status parents may find themselves relatively powerless because they have few rewards to offer in comparison to alternate sources of benefits now open to their offspring.

Sociologist Robert Winch (1962) has tested exchange theory in a study comparing the influence on college males of two social systems: the family and the fraternity. *Identification* was the term he used to denote the lasting influence of one person or social system on another person. (We have already, seen in Chapter 2 how important parents consider the reward of such identification on the part of a child who models his or her life after the parent's example and values.) Winch found that since upper-status families (fathers in particular) are better able than lower-status families to reward their sons with such resources as material goods, time, and expertise, sons from families at higher socioeconimic levels are more likely to identify with their fathers than with the fraternity peer group. But when a family lacks resources and expert power, the son looks to another social system for rewards; therefore, the fraternity's influence increases as socioeconomic status decreases (Winch, 1962; Winch and Gordon, 1974, chap. 3).

CLASS DIFFERENCES IN SOCIALIZING FOR ACHIEVEMENT

"Members of different social classes, by virtue of enjoying (or suffering) different conditions of life, come to see the world differently—to develop different conceptions of social reality, different aspirations and hopes and fears, different 'conceptions of the desirable,'" writes sociologist Melvin Kohn (1969:7). Another way of saying that persons hold differing "conceptions of the desirable" is to say they hold different values.

Kohn (1969:200) has done extensive research which shows that parental values differ by class, and consequently parents at different status levels socialize their children in dissimilar ways. "Parents tend to impart to their children lessons derived from the conditions of life of their own social class—and thus help prepare their children for a similar class position." For example, in a study of men and work, Kohn found that at higher socioeconomic levels more than at lower levels there was great value placed upon self-direction characteristics—curiosity about how and why things happen as they do, interest in making sound judgments, self-reliance, taking responsibility, facing facts squarely, being able to work under pressure, and so on. At higher status levels, the men tended to evaluate jobs in terms of *intrinsic* qualities (characteristics inherent in the occupation, such as how much freedom it offered, how interesting it was, the opportunities it afforded to use talents or help other people). But at lower status levels, the men tended to judge jobs according to *extrinsic* characteristics (externals such as pay, job security, fringe benefits, work hours, supervisors and co-workers, and so on) (p. 76).

Not only was the conception of the world of work found to differ by socioeconomic status, the conception of the social world was also found to differ. The lower the social status, the more likely were the men to emphasize a rigid conservatism which opposed questioning old, established ways. They were more likely to resist innovation and change and were unable to tolerate nonconformity to the dictates of authority. "The most important thing to teach children is absolute obedience to their parents," was the kind of statement which received much greater agreement among lower-status men. The lower the social position, the more likely were men to view personal morality in terms of conforming to the letter of the law (again emphasizing the external over the internal), and also the less trustful they were of other people.

These outlooks carry over to the socialization of children. Kohn found that the higher the socioeconomic position of fathers the more highly they valued self-direction in their children and the less likely they were to value conformity to standards imposed from the outside. The contrasting values of higher-status self-direction and lower-status conformity also showed up in a study of mothers. Although Kohn found that mothers at all status levels considered it important that their children be happy, considerate, honest, dependable, obedient, and respectful of others' rights, the higher the social status of mothers, the more likely they were to emphasize curiosity and self-control as desirable qualities for their children. And the lower the status, the more likely were mothers to select obedience, neatness, and cleanliness as desirable. Of particular interest is Kohn's finding that a mother's own educational and occupational attainments (rather than her ascribed status based on her husband's attainments) are related to the values she holds for her children. Kohn found also that those working-class mothers who held high aspirations and wanted their children to attend college tended to be women who themselves had had some educational advantages but who had married down. "One gets the impression," writes Kohn, "that for many of them, the child's upward mobility represents an opportunity to recoup the status that they, themselves, have lost" (p. 34).

Kohn's findings on different parental values largely held for both blacks and whites. Socioeconomic status, not race, was the key factor in determining whether parents emphasized in their children either self-determination or conformity to external controls. As a further test of his findings, we included in our 1968 Indianapolis study of black families some of Kohn's items for measuring parental values. Our results were similar: The lower the status of black parents, the more likely they were to respond that *obedience* was the most important thing a child should learn. The higher the status, the more likely they were to indicate that *autonomy* was the most desired value for their children. We also found, as Kohn did, that the greater the wife's own occupational status, the more likely she was to transmit autonomy values to her children (Scanzoni, 1977).

RESOURCES PROVIDED BY PARENTS

When Gertrude Hunter entered high school, she enrolled in the college-preparatory program without so much as a second thought. "What happened next," she says, "is, tragically even today, all too familiar to blacks." A faculty adviser called her in and handed her back the form that had contained her carefully worked-out class schedule. But all the college-prep courses had been crossed out! Home economics courses had been substituted. The dazed young woman took the paper home, whereupon her outraged mother promptly marched to school to confront the adviser. Gertrude Hunter describes the scene in her own words: "The adviser attempted to placate my mother. 'Mrs. Teixeira,' she pleaded, 'what is a colored girl going to do with college? If she learns cooking and sewing, she can always get a good job.' But when we left the office. I was enrolled in the college course."

Years later, as a pediatrician in a high administrative position with the United States Department of Health, Education and Welfare, Dr. Gertrude Hunter looked back with gratitude to her parents' influence on her life. Knowing they expected her to do well in school, she endeavored to fulfill those expectations. Her father and mother helped her see that who and what she was was good. "As a woman," she says, "I was told I would be able to do whatever I wanted. I was taught that my skin had a beautiful color. This constant, implicit reinforcement of positive self-image was my parents' most valuable gift to me" (Hunter, 1973).

Self-Esteem In the ongoing exchange between parents and children, the resources passed on by parents may be tangible (music lessons, summer camps, college or trade school tuition, and the like) or they may be intangible in the form of attitudes conveyed and aptitudes developed. The building of a child's self-esteem, as in the case of Gertrude Hunter, is one example of such an intangible resource.

Sociologist Alan Kerckhoff (1972:56) calls attention to the way children's

Intangible resources, such as self-esteem, are among the most valuable gifts parents can pass on to children. (Charles Gatewood)

interactions with their parents profoundly affect their definition of the world around them so that they come to view it as "friendly or threatening, as a source of opportunity or danger, as controllable or chaotic." In that interaction, a child's self-image begins to evolve; and the world and the self will seem quite different to someone who believes, "I can do anything I set out to do," and someone who believes, "People like me don't have much of a chance in life." Kerckhoff writes: "The self-image is thus a view of oneself in relation to one's environment. Part of that environment is the opportunity structure—how much access to rewards different kinds of people have."

Persons at lower socioeconomic levels tend to see the social stratification system in much the same way as higher-status persons; that is, they rank certain occupations as being more prestigious than others. They generally consider *themselves* to be in lower-status positions in addition to being defined by others in this way, which means, says Kerckhoff, that these attitudes will be conveyed to lower-status children who then follow their parents in developing a "sense of impotence in society." Since such parents have little faith that the American Dream will actualize for them or their children, they emphasize security and risk avoidance rather than looking for opportunities to seize. The child thus develops an attitude of passivity rather than a sense of mastery. In a home where there are low expectations for achievement and great pressures for compliance, a child is likely to develop low self-esteem.

However, where parents endeavor to build a strong self-image in children, encouraging them to be upwardly mobile, they provide them with a valuable resource for achievement. Some comments of respondents from our study of black families illustrate how parental encouragement and confidence serve as resources that benefit children. "He has given me the incentive to get ahead," said one male respondent of his father. And these comments were made about mothers: "She had a value system that was a middle-class standard, not like poor people." "She always taught me to save money—what little I could get hold of—and take advantage of every opportunity that would help me to get ahead" (Scanzoni, 1977:79).

Education and Work Attitudes   Since occupational achievement is so bound up with education, a family that values education provides children with a particularly valuable resource in that children will be encouraged and aided in obtaining as much schooling as possible. We found that considerable educational and occupational mobility had occurred among our sample of Indianapolis black families, and there is little doubt that parental attitudes aided in such upward mobility in a great many cases.

Numerous respondents made comments such as these: "She saw that I went to school." "Lots of times I didn't plan on going and he saw to it I got there." "He kept telling me I needed an education." "She wanted me to be very smart." "He helped me by financing the things I needed for school." Several spoke of parental sacrifices which made it possible to finish school instead of having to drop out to get a job. "He went without clothes so I could go to school," said one respondent. "She washed and ironed for white folks and helped out so I could go to school," said another. Others spoke of parents making it possible to attend college, art school, or trade school. Respondents reported emotional support, aid with homework, and other forms of help and encouragement parents had given as well.

Attitudes toward work were also conveyed to them by parents. "I used to jump from job to job," said one respondent. "He told me I couldn't get ahead like that—to stay on the job until I could get to know whether I liked it or not." Some told of fathers who had spoken of hardships they themselves had faced so that their children would know what to expect in the job market. Overall, although these parents were aware of the relative deprivation of blacks, they nevertheless endeavored to encourage their offspring to accept the dominant value system of American society with its emphasis on achievement.

However, not all parents had conveyed such positive attitudes. Some respondents spoke of being taught to expect disappointment and some were actually hindered from movement toward achievement. Some parents were indifferent, offering no advice about getting ahead and doing nothing to encourage educational attainments. One male respondent said of his father: "He hindered us because he wanted us to quit school and go to work; he did not allow us to participate in school activities." A woman said of her mother: "Because I had to do all the housework, she didn't care if I went to school or not" (Scanzoni, 1977, chap. 3).

Among both blacks and whites, a family's position in the economic-opportunity system has a great deal to do with attitudes conveyed to children. Kohn (1969, chap. 11) suggests that the values parents emphasize in their children are generated and maintained by the parents' own occupational experiences. Lower-status jobs are more constricting and seldom provide opportunities for self-direction, emphasizing instead conformity to authority; hence, the lower the status, the more likely does the conformity discussed earlier come to be regarded as a value in its own right on or off the job. In contrast, higher-status occupations permit self-direction and encourage flexibility, creativity, and making one's own analyses and decisions rather than simply obeying orders. Persons with opportunities for self-direction on the job place high value on self-direction in other areas of life as well and seek to convey such attitudes to their children. According to Kohn's studies, children at higher status levels are thus better equipped to get ahead in a society that stresses achievement. They are more likely to have learned to think for themselves, handle responsibility, meet new and problematic situations and to initiate change instead of merely reacting to it. Lower-status children are less prepared for achievement because their parents have placed primary emphasis on externals and consequences.

Other studies have shown that even the way parents talk in the home affects a child's thinking and speaking abilities and that language patterns vary according to socioeconomic class. As a result, children at higher status levels become better able to label, classify, analyze, conceptualize, and communicate than children at lower socioeconomic levels (see summary in Kerckhoff, 1972:48–52).

ACHIEVEMENT MOTIVATION AND GENDER ROLES

There is some evidence that high achievement motivation is associated with certain childrearing patterns, namely, early independence training, encouragement of self-reliance, fewer restrictions, and holding high aspirations (McClelland, 1961; also see Brown, 1965, chap. 9). Such patterns would seem to be the opposite of the value orientations of lower-status families (passivity and conformity) and suggest rather the mastery and autonomy more likely to be found at higher status levels.

However, not only are differences in achievement socialization related to class; they are also related to gender. Female socialization at all class levels seems to reflect value orientations generally associated with lower-status levels; that is, girls more than boys are pointed in the direction of passivity and conformity, and boys more than girls are encouraged toward mastery and autonomy. The actual *degree* of gender typing varies by class, but elements of it are there at all status levels.

Sociologist Alice Rossi (1965) has shown that the qualities that have been shown to be characteristic of great scientists are the very qualities that have traditionally been discouraged in the childhood socialization of females: high intellectual ability, intense channeling of energy in the pursuit of work tasks, extreme independence, and apartness from others. On a similar note, psychologist Lois Hoffman points out that socialization practices have usually encouraged females from earliest childhood to want to please others and to work for approval and love. Achievement in tasks is motivated by these learned *affiliative* needs, and "if achievement threatens affiliation, performance may be sacrificed or anxiety may result." Boys, on the other hand, learn to value achievement much more for its own sake and to become involved in work for the sheer joy of mastering a challenging task.

In view of studies which show that gifted girls are less likely than gifted boys to fulfill their intellectual potential in adulthood, Hoffman's (1972b) thesis is that females are not given adequate parental encouragement in early strivings toward independence. Parents tend to worry over and protect girls more than boys, fostering dependence and discouraging feelings of confidence and competence. If one is female, there is also less pressure to develop one's own self-identity. "Separation of the self is facilitated when the child is the opposite sex of the primary caretaker," writes Hoffman. Since the mother is usually the primary caretaker, both male and female children form their first attachment to her. However, a boy is encouraged to identify with his father, which prompts an earlier and more complete separation form the primary caretaker and fosters the building of a sense of selfhood. "The girl, on the other hand, is encouraged to maintain her identification with the mother," Hoffman explains: "therefore she is not as likely to establish an early and independent sense of self." She also points out that boys more than girls engage in conflict with their mothers, another way in which the formation of a separate self is facilitated.

But perhaps more than building a sense of selfhood through *separation from* the mother, it is the male child's *identification with* the achiever role of the father that encourages greater autonomy. Hoffman is not unaware of that possibility and refers to studies which show that high-achieving females have also identified with their fathers. Changing attitudes and more egalitarian gender-role norms might show that a female's identification with the mother doesn't in itself hinder self-direction. "The significant factor may be identifying with a mother who is herself passive and dependent," Hoffman states. "If the mother were a mathematician, would the daughter's close identification be dysfunctional to top achievement?" Research is needed to answer that question, but already there is some evidence that the answer is no. Rather, close identification with such a mother might be likely to encourage the daughter to follow the mother's example and become an achiever herself. Other conditions conducive to female achievement are also more likely to be found in those families where the mother is professionally employed, namely, early independence training and a close relationship with a father "who encourages the girl's independence and achievement while accepting her as a female" (Hoffman, 1974:162–163; 1973:213).

Childhood Experiences of Female Executives   For her doctoral dissertation in business administration at Harvard University, Margaret Hennig studied female presidents and vice-presidents of male-oriented nationally recognized medium-to-large business firms and compared them with a control group of women "who appeared overtly to match the top women executives in all factual data but who had never succeeded in rising beyond middle management." The difference between the two groups' achievements appears to lie in the family dynamics of their respective childhoods (summarized in Hennig, 1973; Hennig and Jardim, 1977).

Each high-achieving executive was either an only child or the firstborn in an all-girl family with no more than three siblings. Both parents highly valued in their daughter *both* femaleness and achievement; being a girl and being a success were not viewed as contradictory or mutually exclusive. Although all but one of the mothers represented the traditional feminine role model in homemaking, they actively encouraged their daughter to explore roles that were usually considered masculine. Both parents warmly supported their daughter and delighted in her accomplishments. In addition, they sought to help her internalize achievement values and satisfactions. They seemed to want her to learn early to set her own goals and standards of excellence and to experience the pleasure of rewarding herself through a job well done.

The executives also reported that their parents had had unusually strong relationships with each other and with them, respecting each person as a distinct individual. As one respondent expressed it: "I had the fortune to have two full and complete parents. That is, both my mother and my father were separate real people and I had a separate and real relationship with each. Most girls have such experience of sharing common interests with their mothers; few share common interests with their dads."

Overall, the father and mother in such homes created a supportive climate free from gender-role limitations so that over the years their daughter could try out a wide range of roles and behavioral styles. This "security base" prepared these future executives to overcome any obstacles they might encounter from having been born female. When gender-related conflicts came up, "it was the conflict itself, rather than the achievement, that was perceived as needing to be eliminated," writes Hennig. All during childhood, these women had developed high self-esteem—both from their parents who reinforced and encouraged them and from their own experiences of successful accomplishments. Hennig (1973:30) concludes: "During those early experiences, they accepted such a strong concept of themselves as people that even years of later conflict and pressure to split them into two segments—the feminine affective person and the masculine instrumental person—could not cause them to reduce their achievement drive.''

SOCIAL STATUS AND CHILD DISCIPLINE

The word *discipline* may be defined as training to act in accordance with certain standards, or it may be defined as chastisement or correction for failure to conform to such standards. Sociologist Leonard Pearlin (1972) refers to the second sense of the word in speaking of discipline as ''a systematic reaction to the behavior of children that parents judge to be either a direct threat to parental values and aspirations or an insufficient effort by children to attain these distant ideals'' (chap. 6).

Pearlin's use of the word *systematic* is deliberate: he is making the point that although parents differ in disciplinary practices, these differences are *patterned* and cannot be explained simply as the result of personality variations or as momentary reactions to situations in which parents give vent to certain feelings. Pearlin's study of families in Turin, Italy, produced findings that correspond to Kohn's findings in the United States. According to their evidence, disciplinary practices in the home are tied to parental values; and parental values, as we have seen, are linked with social status.

Both middle-class and working-class parents emphasize control in the lives of children; but for middle-class parents the emphasis is on control from within (self-direction), whereas working-class parents stress control from without (obedience to rules and authority). Both social status and the sex of the misbehaving child enter into the reaction of parents with regard to discipline.

Kohn (1969, chap. 6), for example, found that working-class mothers in his sample were more likely than middle-class mothers to employ physical punishment when children (particularly sons) engaged in wild play (boisterousness, aggressive behavior, belligerent and destructive actions) or when children fought with brothers and sisters. The focus was on ''the direct and immediate consequences of the disobedient acts'' rather than on perception of the child's motivations. From the mother's point of view, what has occurred in such a case is a violation of good order; such nonconformity to acceptable standards of behavior calls for punishment according to working-class values.

Middle-class mothers, on the other hand, were able to tolerate wild play even in its extreme forms. But they could *not* tolerate violent outbursts of temper. The overt behavior in the two instances might be exactly the same (''shouting, wrestling, slamming doors, stamping feet, running''), but what these mothers were concerned about was the child's intent rather than the situation itself. Children's rowdiness and excitement in play weren't viewed as alarming as long as their actions were perceived as ''letting off steam.'' However, if the same actions were viewed as violent outbursts—temper tantrums resulting from a child's feeling frustrated at not getting his or her own way—middle-class mothers tended to resort to physical punishment.

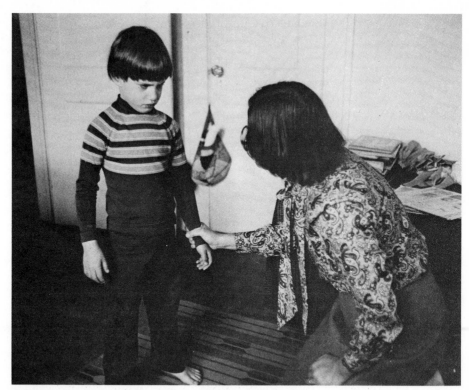

Disciplinary practices in the home are tied to parental values, and parental values are linked with social status. (Michael Kagan/Monkmeyer)

Why? Again, parental values seem to have been involved—in this case, the middle-class value of self-control. Parents refused to put up with behavior that indicated the loss of such control.

GENDER-BASED DIFFERENCES

Misbehavior in children may be thought of either in terms of their doing what they shouldn't do (as in the above illustrations) or in their *not* doing what they *should* do (refusing to carry out parents' requests). Kohn found that working-class mothers tended to punish sons for the first kind of misbehavior but not for the second kind. When boys defiantly refused to comply with their mothers' wishes, the mothers tended to refrain from any form of punishment and instead simply did nothing at all. But when daughters refused to do as they were told, they were swiftly punished. At this social status level, "more is expected of girls than of boys," writes Kohn. "Girls must not only refrain from unacceptable behavior; they must also fulfill positive expectations" (p. 101).

Working-class girls were more likely than boys at this level to be punished for such activities as smoking, swiping something, or fighting with friends. Once again we see the part class differences play in gender-role norms. Kohn points out that for working-class parents, "what may be taken as acceptable behavior (perhaps even as an assertion of manliness) in a preadolescent boy may be thought thoroughly unladylike in a young girl." Middle-class parents, in contrast, tend not to make such distinctions based on gender. Their main concern in matters of discipline is that children of either sex will act according to internalized principles (pp. 105–106).

TYPES OF DISCIPLINE

In 1958, social psychologist Urie Bronfenbrenner published a comprehensive review of socialization studies from the 1930s onward. Bronfenbrenner was especially interested in class differences in childrearing, and one of his conclusions was this: "In matters of discipline, working-class parents are consistently more likely to employ physical punishment, while middle-class families rely more on reasoning, isolation, appeals to guilt, and other methods involving the threat of loss of love (as quoted in Kerckhoff, 1972:42).

However, in recent years a number of studies have caused sociologists to raise questions about alleged class differences in the usage of physical punishment, and inconsistencies in earlier studies are being reexamined as well (Erlanger, 1974; also Straus, 1971). Pearlin (1972:103) wrote of his Italian study: "By itself, class bears only a modest relationship to physical punishment: Only 8 percent more middle- than working-class parents reported that they had not resorted to any physical punishment in the past six months."

Another sociologist, Murray Straus (1971), found that 52 percent of a sample of university students had experienced actual or threatened physical punishment from their parents during the last year of high school; but there was no relationship between physical punishment and socioeconomic status. Straus was surprised that such class differences didn't show up—especially since the study showed that the highest frequency of physical punishment took place among students who reported their parents emphasized obedience as the most important characteristic of children, and the lowest frequency took place where parents considered self-control and thinking for oneself to be the most desired traits in children. Straus suggested that the explanation for the lack of differences according to class may lie in the fact that working-class students in the sample were from homes where upward mobility was emphasized and where parents had identified with higher-status values and socialization practices. Thus the incidence of physical punishment was no greater among them than among middle-class students.

Kohn's (1969) research showed that mothers responded to children's misbehavior in numerous ways—ignoring it, scolding and admonishing, removing the child from the situation or diverting attention, restricting activities, isolating the child temporarily, or punishing the child physically ("everything from a slap to a spanking"). Both working-class and middle-class mothers reported that they generally ignored misbehavior or else admonished their children at this stage (Kohn's sample included only mothers of fifth-graders). Few reported using isolation or restriction, and even fewer punished physically under usual circumstances. Although there was a slight tendency for working-class mothers to be more likely than middle-class mothers to use physical punishment, coercion was not quickly resorted to in either class. Only *persistent* misbehavior was seen to call for punishment. "It would seem, then," says Kohn, "that the difference between middle- and working-class mothers' use of physical punishment is not in the frequency with which they use it, but in the conditions under which they use it" (pp. 93–95)—conditions which we have already examined.

DISCIPLINE AND ACHIEVEMENT VALUES

In the socialization process, parents seek to guide their children in the development of characteristics and behaviors which the parents consider to be important for the future—particularly as sons and daughters prepare to fit into the economic-opportunity system in some way. Evidence from the studies of Kohn and Pearlin suggests that the parents' values come from their own place in the economic structure, and these same values are then passed on so that children will find a place there that will quite often be similar to that of the parents. When children deviate from behavior consistent with the parents' values, discipline is employed. In this sense, discipline is an important part of socializing for achievement (Pearlin, 1972:99).

CHILD ABUSE

In recent years, increasing attention has been given to the problem of battered children. The subject of child *discipline*, just examined, is different from child *abuse*—although authorities may not always agree on the exact line of

(The Advertising Council)

demarcation. What starts out as discipline may sometimes become abuse, especially if a parent feels a child's behavior indicates the parent's loss of control over the situation. Sociologist Suzanne Steinmetz (1977:39) explains: "Just as normal discipline is an attempt to restore authority, abuse is a more desperate attempt to do so."

The Child Abuse Prevention and Treatment Act passed by Congress in 1974 provided this definition of child abuse:

> Child abuse and neglect means the physical or mental injury, sexual abuse, negligent treatment, or maltreatment of a child under the age of eighteen by a person who is responsible for the child's welfare under circumstances which indicate that the child's health or welfare is harmed or threatened thereby. (Quoted in Gelles, 1979:45.)

As we saw in an earlier chapter, about 300,000 cases of suspected child abuse are reported annually in the United States (Steinmetz, 1977:98). But the actual incidence may be much higher, with reliable estimates ranging from one-half million to one and one-half million (Steinmetz, 1978:4–5; Gelles, 1979:25, 44).

WHY DO PARENTS ABUSE THEIR CHILDREN?

While the idea has been prevalent that parents who abuse their children are thereby showing that they are "sick," "pathological," or "abnormal," sociologist Richard Gelles (1979) points to the research he and his colleagues have conducted, as well as other studies, and comes to a different conclusion. "It is now necessary to stop thinking of child abuse as having a single cause: the mental aberrations of the parents," he writes. "It is time to start thinking about the multiple social factors that influence child abuse" (p. 40).

What are some of these social factors? Economic factors, for one. *Unemployment* can be a factor in producing family stress that may show up in violence toward children (Gelles, 1979:35–37). *Social status* also enters in. Numerous studies have indicated that child abusers tend to have lower education, occupational status, and income (see summary in Gelles, 1979:33).

This is not to say that middle-class abusive parents don't exist. They do, but their numbers are fewer. Moreover, the differences in child abuse by social class can't simply be written off as differences in labeling and reporting—even though it's true that physicians and helping agencies are more likely to take a middle-class parent's word for it that a child's injuries resulted from an "accident"; whereas a poor or minority person is more apt to be "caught," reported to authorities, and given the label "child abuser." Also, an injured child brought into an emergency room or clinic is far more likely to be diagnosed as abused than is a similarly injured child brought to a private physician's office (Gelles, 1979:63–64). But even keeping these matters of labeling and reporting in mind, enough research evidence exists to indicate the greater incidence of child abuse at lower socioeconomic levels. The pressures of feeling cut off from the economic-opportunity system may build up to the point of explosion, with children bearing the consequences.

Gelles also reports that child abuse is likely to occur *if the parents themselves had been abused as children,* or if *the family is large* (four or more children), or if the child is the result of an *unwanted pregnancy* (pp. 36–37).

Other important patterns emerged in a study conducted jointly by the Human Resources Department of the state of Georgia and the Atlanta-based National Center for Disease Control, which focused on 2,000 cases of child abuse, including 26 cases in which the children died. Children born out of wedlock were found to be two and one-half times more likely to be abused than were children of married parents.

Of natural parents who abused their children, half were mothers. And half of these had given birth to their first child while still in their teens. Fifty-eight percent of all child abusers in the study were male, and many were not the natural fathers of the children they abused. The Georgia study showed that 90 percent of children who were *sexually* abused were girls. Types of abuse suffered by boys included burns, malnutrition, skull fractures, cuts, brain damage, and other multiple injuries (*Greensboro Daily News,* Associated Press report, January 28, 1979). Of course, girls may suffer such injuries, too.

In view of the stereotypical image of motherhood as synonymous with gentleness, it may come as a surprise to learn that large numbers of mothers abuse their children. Gelles (1979:34) writes: "The child who is perceived by the mother as impinging on her freedom and desires seems to be vulnerable to abuse from the frustrated mother." He also points out that the mother's greater contact with and responsibility for the child may in some cases cause her to feel so exasperated and frustrated by the child's demands that she gives way to a violent outburst and beats or otherwise inflicts pain on him or her.

THE MOST DANGEROUS AGE

"The most dangerous period for the child is from 3 months of age to 3 years," says Gelles. "The abused, battered, or murdered child is most vulnerable during those years when he is most defenseless and least capable of meaningful social interaction" (p. 34).

According to Gelles, three interrelated factors may account for this. First, a very small child is simply less physically durable than an older child and thus can't withstand as much physical punishment or force without severe damage or even death occurring.

Second, parents may become frustrated because infants and toddlers cannot be reasoned with as the parents try to persuade them to do something or stop doing something. Gelles refers to case studies in which parents who have abused their children speak of doing so in desperation when they couldn't get a baby to stop crying or to cooperate in toilet training efforts or otherwise obey some command.

Third, just by virtue of her or his birth, an infant can be distressing to parents. "The new-born child may create economic hardship for the family, or may interfere with professional, occupational, educational, or other plans of the parents," explains Gelles. "Thus, the new child may create structural stress for parents which is responded to by abuse" (p. 35).

WHAT CAN BE DONE?

The complexity of child abuse as a societal issue is summarized by Saad Nagi (1977), whose study was designed to aid human service agencies in developing programs and policies. Having commented on advancements in medical technology that have aided physicians, surgeons, and radiologists in diagnosing and treating abused children, Nagi goes on to say:

> Unfortunately, the complexity of the problem goes beyond the diagnosis and treatment of physical problems. It entails identifying and treating whatever emotional damage the children might have sustained, motivating parents and others to report cases of suspected abuse, changing the behavior of abusive parents and guardians in order to prevent repetition, deciding when children should and should not be left with their families, and collecting legally admissible evidence for protecting the rights of children. (p. 22)

Nagi points out that the two basic approaches that have been used in dealing with parents who have abused their children are *punitive* approaches (parents are punished for what they have done) or *therapeutic* approaches (parents are directed to counselors for help).

In addition to involvement in psychological and family counseling programs, some parents who are concerned about their violent actions toward their children join self-help groups such as Parents Anonymous (modeled after Alcoholics Anonymous) so that they can talk over their problem with other parents in a similar situation. In addition, service agencies and socially concerned organizations have set up shelters and "crisis nurseries" for victims of family violence (Gelles, 1979:17; Nagi, 1977:22–23).

Yet, Gelles argues that as commendable, useful, and necessary such programs and efforts are, they are not enough. They are like "an ambulance service at the bottom of the cliff," because they wait until after the child abuse has occurred before they step in to help. The need is to "fix the road on the cliff that causes the accidents," says Gelles (p. 41). And that means research and theory to aid in predicting child abuse and putting forth effort to deal with the various social factors that we have seen lie behind much of the maltreatment of children.

Sociologist Suzanne Steinmetz (1977:138) refers to examples of some persons who were able to survive brutality in childhood without the disastrous consequences that so often occur or who were able to overcome those that did occur, even though the abuse left its mark (as in the case of Thomas Edison whose hearing was damaged by the frequent severe beatings he received as a child). Nor is the pattern doomed to be repeated in some fatalistic way. Steinmetz provides a note of hope for former victims of child abuse by referring to a personal communication from an authority in child development who was herself a beaten child. The woman reported that she is requently asked, "Do all children who are abused grow up to be abusing mothers?" Her reply: "No, some of us grow up to study empathy."

CHAPTER HIGHLIGHTS

A first baby changes a couple's lives so that the "transition to parenthood" is sometimes difficult and has even been called a "crisis" in some sociological studies. The transition has been found to be more difficult for wives than for husbands because of traditional assumptions that mothers will have the greater responsibility for child care and will make the greater sacrifices of individualistic interests. Russell's research has turned up some factors that are associated with a greater or lesser degree of stress in the transition to parenthood.

Russell's research also focused on gratifications of parenthood. And Hoffman found that mothers view motherhood more positively than do nonmothers. However, mothers often feel compelled to change their sex-role ideology in a more traditional direction to fit with the segregation of husband-wife roles that tend to become more pronounced when the two become parents. On the other hand, many young mothers notice a discrepancy between motherhood set up as an *institution*, with specific patterns of expected behavior (which they view negatively) and motherhood as a *rich experience of relating to their children* (which they view positively). Many fathers today also want a larger part in their children's lives than has been traditionally expected, required, or even allowed (because of work demands and schedules).

Rossi has written of parenthood in terms of four stages: the anticipatory stage, the honeymoon stage, the plateau stage, and the disengagement-termination stage. Each stage has unique features and challenges.

Socioeconomic class differences have been found in how children are socialized for achievement and in ways children are disciplined. And while child *abuse* occurs at all class levels, it occurs with greater frequency where education, income, and occupational status are low and the stresses occasioned by economic deprivation (including actual unemployment) are great.

CHAPTER 17

(© Joel Gordon, 1979)

THE MIDDLE
AND
LATER YEARS
OF MARRIAGE

According to folk wisdom, as the years of marriage go on, the fires of love burn down. The theme is a familiar one in novels, plays, and films. "You just bite the nail and hang on," was the advice given by an elderly father to his middle-aged son in view of the son's marital discontent in Robert Anderson's drama *Double Solitaire*. A public-television presentation of 1975, the play took its title from the mother-in-law's counsel to the daughter-in-law. While the disenchanted husband heard his father's advice to "just remember, bite on the nail," the middle-aged wife was listening to the older woman's recipe for ongoing marital happiness: playing double solitaire. Most people of course play the card game alone, but, emphasized the mother-in-law, in marriage the spouses can play alone while together. A "double solitaire" marriage was exactly the kind of marriage the younger woman didn't want.

MARITAL SATISFACTION OVER TIME

Descriptive literature by writers, family counselors, and a certain number of studies by behavioral scientists have reinforced the belief that marriages deteriorate in the middle years. "By and large such observations are based on clinical experiences with persons who have so much difficulty in making the transition that they must seek outside help," writes researcher Irwin Deutscher (1962), whose own findings did not support commonly held notions about the "empty nest" period of life, for example, when children are grown and gone and parents allegedly have little to bind them together any longer.

While cautioning that definite conclusions cannot be drawn from the responses of such a small sample (forty-nine urban, middle-class, postparental couples, forty to sixty-five years of age), Deutscher (1962) wrote that the majority of wives and husbands viewed this stage of the family life cycle "as a time of new freedoms." In particular, his respondents spoke of the freedom from economic responsibility for the children, freedom to travel or move to another location, freedom from housework and other tasks, "and finally, freedom to be one's self for the first time since the children came along."

At the same time, while many early reports of diminished marital satisfaction over time were based on little more than impressions and clinical findings, some data from more rigorous studies lend support to such findings (see summary in Rollins and Feldman, 1970:21). For example, Blood and Wolfe's (1960:264) widely cited Detroit study produced the finding that wives became less satisfied as the length of marriage increased. And the Burgess/ Wallin longitudinal study, begun in 1937 with 1,000 engaged couples and followed up twenty years after their marriages, showed that among the 153 couples left from the original sample there was widespread disenchantment, less intimacy, and decreased "marital adjustment" (Pineo, 1971; Troll, 1971).

Our own studies have yielded inconsistent results, again showing the uncertainty and need for further research in this area. In our large-scale study of white Indianapolis husbands and wives, we found that, in general, satisfaction with empathy (communication and understanding) increases—although there are certain variations by socioeconomic status and sex that must be taken into account (Scanzoni, 1970). In a more recent study, however, we found that the age of a wife or husband (highly correlated with the stage of marriage in most cases) made virtually no difference at all in how satisfactory both black and white persons evaluated their marriages (Scanzoni, 1975a). Marital satisfaction or dissatisfaction was found to be tied to socioeconomic factors and perceptions of the wife's abilities rather than to the number of years the couple had lived together.

Some studies have shown a decline in marital satisfaction during the childbearing and childrearing stages, but an increase in satisfaction during the postparental years (Rollins and Feldman, 1970). Such findings have led to the widespread generalization that marital satisfaction follows a U-shaped curve, dropping when the first child is born, leveling out over the childrearing years, then moving back up again when the children have left home. Yet, although there *is* some empirical evidence for such a pattern, the decline in satisfaction is not so dramatic as it may at first appear. The "U" isn't very deep, and in fact is rather flat "inasmuch as only 4–8% of the variation in marital satisfaction is associated with stages of the family career," emphasize researchers Boyd Rollins and Richard Galligan (1978). These sociologists and others call for caution in view of the way some writers tend to *overstate* the U-shaped effect and thereby give couples entering marriage the impression they "should prepare for the storm" (p. 82; see also Spanier et al., 1975; Schram, 1979).

Some couples may feel that their marital satisfaction remains high or even increases over the years, while other couples experience a decline and may feel that the descriptive terms sometimes used for mid-marriage disappointment are on target. There may be "disenchantment" (a loss of enthusiasm for the partner and the relationship, a cooling of feelings), and there may be "disengagement" (lessened companionship and interaction between the spouses) (Blood, 1969:325–333). These are the marriages which sociologists John Cuber and Peggy Harroff (1965) have categorized as "devitalized" because of "the clear discrepancy between middle-aged reality and the earlier years." In such cases, the couples report that once they were closely identified with each other, shared many interests, spent a great deal of time together, and thoroughly enjoyed their sex life. Now things have changed, and they do things for and with each other out of duty more than out of the sense of love and delight in one another they once felt. According to Cuber and Harroff, although "the original zest is gone," those couples in their sample who fit into this category tended to "believe that the devitalized mode is the appropriate mode in which a man and a woman should be content to live in the middle years and later" (pp. 49–50).

In attempting to understand the complexities suggested by the various studies on changes in marital satisfaction over the years, perhaps we need to see even *more* complexities rather than trying to boil it all down to a simple truism, such as, "Marital satisfaction does (or doesn't) decline as time goes on." There are structural and situational factors—and not merely personality considerations—to keep in mind. If marital satisfaction is related to socioeconomic status, we need to consider changes in access to the economic-opportunity structure over the family life cycle. How does either spouse's loss of employment on the one hand, or a sizable promotion on the other, affect satisfaction within marriage? How will the marital relationship be affected by a husband's feelings at middle age that he has not reached the goals of which he had dreamed? What if a wife feels unfulfilled in her career goals? How will a wife's decision to seek employment after the children are grown and gone affect her relationship with her husband at this stage of life especially after a marriage built on traditional sex-role assumptions? Research is needed which takes such situations as these into account. Also, since some studies indicate that marital satisfaction decreases and levels out during the childrearing stages but increases again at the postparental stage, questions need to be raised about whether we are seeing the effect of children on a marriage or simply the effect of the passage of time. Comparative research on marital satisfaction among childless couples over the years would be fruitful in this regard.

"Two many other uncontrolled variables such as ages of husband and wife, number of years married, and stage in the occupational career of the husband (and wife) are highly correlated with child-referenced transitions over the family career," say Rollins and Galligan (1978) in commenting on the common assumption that the presence or absence of children or their stage of development accounts for the U-shaped curve of marital satisfaction. They go on to say that "the data are, however, congruent with the notion that the presence of dependent children in the home put a 'crunch' on the time, energy, and economic resources of parents and result in a decrease in the marital satisfaction of the parents" (p. 83). These sociologists call for further research and suggest that the lowered marital satisfaction during the childrearing years may be related to the increased accumulation of family roles over the years and the stress or strain experienced in trying to live up to the expectations and obligations of these multiple roles (see also Hoffman and Manis, 1978).

Another factor to keep in mind is the personal growth that one or both spouses may experience over time. People change, but not always at the same rate or in the same direction. New experiences, new interests, new contacts, new goals, even adopting a whole new philosophy of life may mean that one spouse ceases to be the person the other spouse thought he or she knew and married. Anthropologist Paul Bohannan (1970:36), an authority on divorce, suggests that an inability to tolerate change in the spouse often lies at the root of the growing estrangement associated with a marital breakup. As a person changes over the years, the rewards he or she offers to the spouse (and the costs to the spouse) are likely to change as well. This will require renegotiation such as that described in Chapter 13, if the couple is to reach new agreements of expectations so that each spouse experiences maximum joint profit.

Perhaps we might also speculate that a certain amount of disenchantment occurs because of unrealistic expectations stemming from romantic love. When the helplessness of "falling in love" and being swallowed up in a mystery beyond comprehension gives way to the daily routines of living together, a great deal of magic and passion may seem to disappear. In the words of psychoanalyst Erich Fromm (1956): "After the stranger has become an intimately known person there are no more barriers to be overcome, there is no more sudden closeness to be achieved." Thus the exhilaration of falling in love may be sought with someone else, and once again "the stranger is transformed into an 'intimate' person." The intensity again becomes less and ends in the desire for a new adventure in romantic love—"always with the illusion that the new love will be different from the earlier ones" (pp. 44–45 in paperback edition).

SUBJECTIVE EVALUATION OF MARITAL SATISFACTION

Marital satisfaction is really a subjective matter, depending upon how a marriage lives up to the expectations of the individuals concerned. One couple may consider their marriage deeply satisfying, whereas an outsider might see the marriage as dull and undesirable. Whether or not wives and husbands are satisfied with their marriage relationship in the middle years depends upon the rewards they expected to receive and felt they deserved and whether or not these rewards materialize. In exchange-theory terms, we can think of Thibaut and Kelley's (1959:21) *comparison level* or CL, an imaginary point on a scale by which persons evaluate costs and rewards in a relationship (just as a certain point on a thermometer serves as the dividing line between temperatures above and below freezing). If the marital rewards minus costs are at a level that meets the expectations of the particular husband or wife, he or she rates the marital relationship above the comparison point (CL)—though the rating is not necessarily conscious. On the other hand, if the outcomes of a particular relationship (the rewards as compared to costs) fall below an individual's personal CL, the relationship will be rated unsatisfactory.

It's possible that in some marriages the level of profit diminishes over the years so that the relationship ceases to be as rewarding as it once was. In other words, to one or both spouses, the marital relationship slides below the CL point. This may explain some cases of disenchantment in the middle years. In other cases, one or both spouses may *raise* their CL point and come to expect *more* from the marriage than they did earlier, with the result that the outcomes of the relationship may be evaluated quite differently than was once the case. A person may not be so easily satisfied as was true earlier in the marriage but may feel that he or she deserves a great deal more at this point in life.

Thibaut and Kelley also speak of another standard of comparison—the *comparison level for alternatives* or CL_{alt}. The CL_{alt} marks the lowest level of outcomes or profit a member of a relationship will accept in the light of available alternatives. Persons consider the reward/cost ratio of the best other situation available to them and weigh the anticipated profit there against their present situation. For example, a husband or wife might have reason to believe that the rewards minus costs in a relationship with a third party would yield greater profit than in the present relationship with the spouse. In some cases, this might mean divorce and remarriage; in other cases, an extramarital "affair" might result, even though the marriage continues. Or a spouse might come to the conclusion that a *single* life-style is a desirable alternative and would offer a more favorable reward/cost ratio than the present marriage. Chapter 18 will focus on the many facets of divorce and remarriage.

THE MIDDLE YEARS: EMPTYING OF THE NEST

Couples who remain married may expect to have a longer period of time together after the children have grown and gone than has ever been the case before. Demographer Paul C. Glick (1977:11) suggests that this extended empty nest period may be "the most dramatic change that has occurred in the

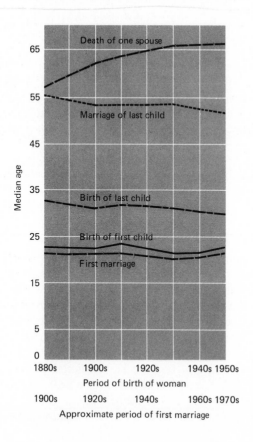

FIGURE 17-1 *Median age of mothers at the beginning of selected stages of the family life cycle. (Source: Paul C. Glick, "Updating the Life Cycle of the Family,"* Journal of Marriage and the Family 39 *February 1977: 7.)*

Contrary to the stereotype of the middle-age woman, depressed over the physical changes associated with menopause and experiencing a sense of uselessness upon the emptying of the family nest, many wives at midlife today are likely to be energetically attending to their own interests and thankful for the freedom to pursue them at last. (Mimi Forsyth/Monkmeyer Press Photo Service)

pattern of the typical life cycle.'' Increased survival rates, plus the fact that couples are likely to be relatively younger when their last child marries, mean that a husband and wife can look forward to an average of thirteen postchildren years together before one of the spouses dies. This contrasts with the two-year empty nest period which couples who married at the beginning of this century could expect, as is illustrated in Figure 17-1.

WIVES IN THE MIDDLE YEARS

Contrary to the stereotype of the middle-aged woman, depressed over the physical changes associated with menopause and experiencing a sense of

Midlife: A Stage Rather than an Age

Appearances notwithstanding, for women, at least, midlife is not a stage tied to chronological age. Rather, it belongs to that point in the life cycle of the family when the children are grown and gone, or nearly so—when, perhaps for the first time in her adult life, a woman can attend to her own needs, her own desires, her own development as a separate and autonomous being. Thus, the mid-thirties career woman, married two years and about to bear her first child is not concerned with midlife issues. She's worried about diapers and feedings, about hard days and sleepless nights, about how she'll continue her career, about whether she can manage motherhood and wifehood without sacrificing one to the other, or her own life to both. Compare her with a woman of the same age, married eighteen years, whose youngest child is fifteen. For good or ill, she has answered the questions that now face the recently married new mother. For good or ill, that part of life is done. Now, she must find a way to give meaning to the rest of her life—something to do, some way of being, that makes each day worth living.

SOURCE: Lillian B. Rubin, *Women of a Certain Age: The Midlife Search for Self* (New York: Harper & Row, 1979, pp. 7–8.

uselessness upon the emptying of the family nest, many wives at midlife today are likely to be energetically attending to their own interests and thankful for the freedom to pursue them at last. The stereotype no doubt arose from observing individual cases that seemed to support it, especially in clinical settings where troubled women sought out help. But it's a mistake to generalize from these instances and to assume that the periods of *launching* (when children are getting ready and beginning to leave home) and *empty nest* (when children have left) must necessarily be difficult and distressing for all mothers. When sociologist Norval Glenn (1975) analyzed data from six national surveys, he found that middle-aged wives whose children had left home reported greater general happiness and greater marital happiness than middle-aged wives with a child or children still at home. Although he cautions against the assumption that the results would be the same in the case of widows left entirely alone and acknowledges that there *are* cases of individuals who experience negative effects from the postparental stage, he says that in general he did not find evidence that "the 'empty nest' or postparental stage of the family life cycle is a traumatic and unhappy period for the typical woman." Other studies have yielded similar findings. Summarizing some of these, Joan Robertson (1978), a *gerontologist* (a specialist in the study of aging), writes:

> The childbearing years are over for most women in early midlife. Longitudinal data indicate that both men and women respond to the *empty nest period* with a

sigh of relief and freedom from responsibilities. Most women welcome the freedom to revive or intensify old and new interests. Most seek opportunities for self-definition, new careers, and inner souces of strength. Conversely, some (but fewer than has been traditionally assumed) remain the same by choice and others stagnate—remain the same without making a conscious choice. Some become acutely or chronically depressed and dependent on spouses, families, or others. (p. 378)

Who are the women most likely to experience difficulty as the nest empties? According to family studies specialist Dena Targ (1979:381), they are "women who define themselves primarily as mothers . . . women who have accepted the traditional feminine role, who have invested themselves in their children, who have not created alternative roles for themselves . . . women who have not anticipated and planned for the empty nest period." Wives who have been employed outside the home before the nest empties, or who have developed outside interests other than paid employment (such as voluntary work or further education), tend to adapt to this period most successfully (Schram, 1979:10; Rapoport et al., 1977:274–275).

HUSBANDS IN THE MIDDLE YEARS

Another family development specialist shows how males at midlife experience the negative effects of earlier traditional sex-role socialization. "The 'male mystique' requires men to be strong, aggressive, unemotional, and tough, all characteristics which may be called into question during the decades from forty to sixty when the male is confronted with the beginnings of bodily decline, career stagnation, and drastic changes within his family unit," writes Jessica Field Cohen (1979:469).

Cohen refers to a number of studies that indicate that the gender-role paths traveled by males and females may cross at middle age, with males becoming more sensitive and nurturant (expressive) at the same time that females are becoming more independent and assertive (instrumental). Since for many men, middle age is a time of taking stock of life and recognizing their own mortality, they may feel anxious and uncertain about what lies ahead and feel threatened by their wives' growing autonomy (Cohen, 1979:467; Brim, 1976). They may yearn for attention, support, and nurturance from their wives at the very time their wives are feeling that a new world is opening up to them as women—a time of life in which women at last can attend to their own interests after years of putting husbands and children first.

Sociologist Lillian Rubin (1979), in interviewing 160 women aged thirty-five to fifty-four, found repeated instances of husbands who missed the old comfortable routines of their marriages when wives' behavior had been predictable and traditional. Some husbands began complaining about their wives' lack of interest in spending money for clothes and other items, whereas earlier they had complained because they considered their wives extravagant! "I don't really want clothes any more," one respondent told Rubin, "I only bought them before because I didn't have anything else important to do with my life" (p. 182). One husband wondered why his wife didn't want to redecorate the house any longer—something she had wanted so much when it wasn't possible earlier (and something "that would have kept her happily in the house a few years ago"). But now she spoke of changed priorities. Commitments to new interests (including paid employment and further education) meant that often their husbands' once-wished-for offers of movies and dinners were now viewed as impositions in wives' busy schedules, with the result that husbands felt hurt, rejected, and confused. Rubin describes what the changes in a wife's life can mean for the marriage:

> That "different kind of commitment" means that, even when she still takes care of the physical needs of family and household, she may not be so readily available to manage their social and emotional needs as well. It means she can't entertain so often because she has work to do. . . . It means that she doesn't want to go to a movie because she's studying for an exam. . . . It means that she may be too preoccupied with a conference tomorrow to want to have sex today. (pp. 179–180)

Midlife Transition: His and Hers

Because he has spent his life in the work world, he knows its limitations. Even if he enjoys his work, he's beginning to slow down, to look for other interests, to experience the shallowness of his interpersonal relationships. In her life, it's just the other way around. She knows all about those things he misses. She has spent her life developing emotional closeness with others, honing her interpersonal skills to a fine edge. That's where she's most expert. For her, the time has come to test her competence in other ways. She goes to school or gets a job—fearful perhaps, but also filled with excitement, the promise of adventure filling her fantasies. For her, the world often seems shiny and new.

Every day I go to work is a thrill. I love walking into my office, closing the door, and getting at the things on my desk. I feel like a kid who has a new toy to play with every morning when she gets up. [Slightly abashed at what she's just said] I hope you won't think that's too silly.

In fact, her excitement about her life is anything but silly; it's a refreshing delight to see. But again, it often means new problems in the family. Sometimes they're felt immediately because he's ready to slow down at just the moment she's accelerating her investment in a new career.

SOURCE: Lillian Rubin, *Woman of a Certain Age* (New York: Harper & Row, 1979), p. 207.

One woman reported that after she had trimmed down from 300 pounds, her husband's initial delight gave way to brooding and comments about wishing she hadn't lost all that weight. He saw her advancement in her job and her new self-confidence and began worrying that she would no longer be the same person. She told Rubin:

> All I can say to him is, "I love you, but I can't go back to being what I was. I can't do that for anybody." I finally feel that I'm a person with something to offer the world. I'm not going back to what it was like before for anything—no matter what. (pp. 197–198)

Some husbands find such determination on the part of wives hard to accept.

Furthermore, for many husbands, the midlife transition not only brings changes to their marriages; it also means changes in their *job* outlooks. Social scientist Rhona Rapoport and her colleagues (1977) call attention to the rapid technological and organizational changes that often catapult men to the peak of their careers earlier than was once the case. Upon reaching this peak, they may move in any of several directions. They "may feel depressed at a sense of futility in life; they may embark on a second career, or change their life styles completely by opting out of the occupational ladder altogether, or they may recreate their current interests" (Rapoport et al., p. 274). According to these researchers:

> For men in occupations which require competitive effort to make their way up organizational ladders, this may be a period of choice—between moving upward into more taxing senior positions with greater rewards of pay, power and prestige (though feeling perhaps that one is not as fit or as driven for such things as previously) *vs* de-emphasizing work aspirations in favour of rewards in family life or other interests. (p. 274)

Rapoport and her colleagues go on to point out that men who choose to become more involved in their families not as top priority but because of a feeling that they have failed or are likely to fail in occupational advancement may show signs of dissatisfaction, irritability, and depression in response to what is actually second choice. In contrast, those men "who choose [family involvement] as a primary option, emphasizing 'humanistic' values rather than success, may have higher levels of satisfaction than their more 'successful' colleagues" (p. 274).

In addition to changes in their physical bodies, marriages, and occupational aspirations, men at midlife are facing another change—the same one experienced by wives and which has sometimes been considered unique to wives: the change associated with the emptying of the family nest.

Few studies have focused on how fathers react to their children's leaving home—a neglect that three social scientists label "both difficult to understand and unfortunate." Robert Lewis, Phillip Freneau, and Craig Roberts (1979) speculate that "because males are currently increasing their involvement in the home and some are becoming more nurturing and caring toward their children, it would seem that more fathers will be experiencing unhappiness at the time that their last child leaves home" (p. 515). In their random sample of 118 postparental fathers, these researchers found that 35 percent had neutral feelings about having all their children gone from home, 26 percent felt somewhat happy, 16 percent felt very happy, and the remaining nearly one-fourth reported feelings of unhappiness.

Focusing on the fathers who reported unhappiness over the empty nest, Lewis, Freneau, and Roberts found that men who felt most unhappy "were also apt to be those who felt most neglected by their wives, received the least amount of understanding from them, were most lonely, were least enthusiastic about their wives' companionship, and had the least empathic wives" (p. 517). As we have already seen, many wives at this stage of life are stepping outside the nest themselves—just at the time when many husbands are turning more inward toward their families after years of concentrating on occupational achievement. Yet it may seem that now that the men have come home, everyone else has gone!

Another finding of Lewis and his associates was that the fewer the children fathers had, the greater was the unhappiness felt when the children left home. And the fathers' age seems to be a factor, too. "The fathers who reported most unhappiness were also the oldest fathers," say these researchers, "and those who reported the greatest happiness were the youngest fathers" (p. 517). The data also suggested that fathers who perceived themselves to be most *nurturant* felt most unhappy when all their children had moved away from the family household. Lewis, Freneau, and Roberts say it all adds up to this: when the last child leaves home, the fathers who feel the most unhappiness tend to be those who have the "most to lose." They go on to describe this finding among the men in their sample:

That is, they had the fewest children and, therefore, had more to lose emotionally with each child's leaving. They tended to be older fathers and, therefore, may have perceived fewer years to share with this child whom they feared would probably never again be so close. They also tended to perceive themselves as more nurturing and caring men, who may have had more to lose with the diminution of the full-time father role and loss of accompanying identities as care-givers and nurturing persons. Finally, these were fathers who probably had the most to lose with their last child's leaving because they tended also to report less satisfactory marriages. (p. 518)

One problem, say these researchers, is that there are "few normative guidelines for fathers at this stage, since males traditionally have been expected to concern themselves primarily with instrumental tasks, such as earning the family's livelihood" (p. 519). Thus, they don't expect the postparental period to be problematic and are likely to reach this point in life without having prepared for what they have been led to believe was something that concerned only mothers.

Time for Launching: Breaking Away yet Sticking Together

It is only recently that there have been concerted efforts to analyse the interlocking *nature of parents' and adolescents' needs at this stage and to understand them in terms of normal psychodynamic development. . . . The efflorescence of sexuality in the adolescent has repercussions on parents who may be on the wane in this respect, and more or less uncomfortable about it. Similarly, the fluctuations between exaggerated independence and child-like dependence in the child may have particularly acute repercussions for parents who, at mid-life, may be seeking new patterns of independence or dependence for themselves in relation to their families. The adolescent's wish to 'fly', to find adventure and new experience may repercuss particularly poignantly on the psychic equilibrium of parents who feel trapped in the ruts of their social roles and responsibilities. . . . Parents may feel it particularly difficult to be self-confident in their encounters with their children who seem so mature, so competent, so sexually precocious and independent-minded, with values of their own which may be sharply at variance with them. . . .*

Parents who can open themselves to influence by their adolescent children in respect of some of their expectations may find the experience very rewarding. Those who do not find some of their adolescent's ideas compelling in themselves may still tolerate behaviour and attitudes from their children that conflict with parental expectations. This may be rationalized in terms of the child's individuality, or in terms of his or her identity formation. There are, however, many parents who find the expression of behaviour that conflicts with their expectations very distressing. It may be that they 'confuse the rebellion in manners for a rebellion in morals' (GAP, 1973, p. 43), or alternatively they may personalize their children's deprecation of parental standards and authority as attacks directed at them as individual parents and people.

A major element in parent-child relations in this phase is the requirement of parents to facilitate their adolescent children's launching. From the adolescent's point of view, it may be difficult to seek adequate guidance and direction without feeling it to indicate a lack of competence; to seek support and reassurance needed without feeling smothered; to seek one's own patterns, without feeling selfish.

SOURCE: Rhona Rapoport, Robert Rapoport, and Ziona Strelitz with Stephen Kew, *Fathers, Mothers and Society: Towards New Alliances* (New York: Basic Books, 1977), pp. 290–291.

THE SQUEEZE BETWEEN GENERATIONS

"I feel like a nut in a nutcracker," one middle-aged woman told us. "I'm caught between pressures from my aging parents on one side and my teenagers and their needs on the other."

She was describing a common situation at this stage of life (Rapoport et al., 1977:270). Health, emotional, and possibly financial needs of older parents may make heavy demands upon the middle generation at the very time they are launching their own children and looking forward to time for their own self-realization. A husband and wife at midlife may even find that, once they reach the empty nest stage, the nest will soon become refilled— either with an elderly parent or a grown son or daughter who has experienced a divorce, loss of job, or other circumstance (Hess and Waring, 1978:250). "Role allocation in our society is such that those now in middle adulthood easily fall victim to overcommitments," write social scientists Beth Hess and Joan Waring (p. 249). Too many needs, roles, and responsibilities are clamoring for attention at the same time. And there isn't enough time and emotional energy to go around.

MIDLIFE COUPLES AND THEIR GROWN CHILDREN

For one thing, parents don't cease being parents just because their children are approaching adulthood or have already reached it. Rapoport and her associates (1977:307–309) therefore prefer not to use the term *postparenthood* but speak of "parenting with adult children" instead. They point out that while it's true that "the *active* element of the parenting role recedes" and "the physical energy and time spent on daily parenting activities decreases and may stop altogether," parents continue to be concerned about their children and involved in their lives to some extent. Counsel, mutual aid, and a desire to spend time together often continues into and throughout the empty nest period. Yet regrettably, say these researchers, "the actual experience of parenting with adult children has received very little systematic study" (p. 308).

During the launching period, as parents head toward the time when their children reach legal age, marry, or otherwise strike out on their own as adults, the parents themselves may be going through a period of questioning and change—as we've already seen. Parents are likely to be experiencing "middlescence" while their children are experiencing adolescence (Robertson, 1978:377). And while parents may continue to influence their children, their children at this stage of life may influence considerably the values and behaviors of the parents in a kind of "reverse socialization" pattern (Bengtson and Troll, 1978:225). Witness the impact of young adults of the 1960s and 1970s on the political ideologies, clothing, and hairstyles adopted by the parent generation.

What is occurring is a "complex feedback system of transmission and differentiation involving generations of youth and their parents," report behavioral scientists Vern Bengtson and Lillian Troll (1978:234). Since parents have made such great investments in their children, they may feel they have a stake in assuring generational continuity by transmitting their values to them. But at the same time, their children are asserting their independence and may have a different perspective on the goals their parents consider most important (Bengtson and Troll, p. 218). There is give and take from both directions, and it may lead to deepening friendship on the one hand or alienation on the other.

At the time that their young adult children are asking, "What shall I do

Parents are likely to be experiencing "middlescence" while their children are experiencing adolescence. (Erika Stone/Peter Arnold, Inc.)

with my life?" the parents may be asking, "What have I done with my life? Have I made the best choices? What lies ahead in the years that are left?" Once again a weighing of costs and rewards is taking place. Rapoport and her colleagues (1977) talk about the "critical evaluation" typical of these midlife years. Have life investments been satisfying and worthwhile? "Are they paying off—psychologically, interpersonally, and in terms of how well the children seem to have developed?" (p. 271).

And while looking at the generation following after them intensifies the midlife couple's questions about personal identity, values, and achievements, looking at the generation ahead of them— their aging parents—may jolt them into a vivid realization of their own mortality.

MIDLIFE COUPLES AND THEIR AGING PARENTS

"In helping the aged parent, the offspring rehearse for their own future," write Hess and Waring (1978:252), "and conversely, the older person, having already lived through middle-age transitions, can serve as a role model and source of advice." But, they go on to say, the way is not always easy nor is the relationship between the generations necessarily without problems and strains.

Caring for Elderly Parents

The financial independence of the generations . . . enables them to maintain the separate residences that most prefer until such arrangements are no longer feasible or possible. Thus, when elderly parents need to call upon children for assistance, they are apt to be frail, greatly disabled, gravely ill, or mentally incompetent. Although ill health typically increases the number of contacts between parents and offspring, these frequently fail to engender feelings of closeness and satisfaction between the generations. Rather, family members are often reluctant and feel ill-prepared to take on such responsibility, regardless of a value commitment to the desirability of home-based health care. Some children define such care taking as a sacrifice.

Generally, institutionalization is not considered a desirable alternative by either parent or child. Not only is there a stigma attached to the perceived "dumping" of a parent—evidence of persisting obligation norms—but it also tends to limit intergenerational contacts. However, intergenerational stress may be alleviated through transfer to a nursing home when the condition of the parent becomes physically and emotionally difficult to manage. This advantage, however, is offset by the high cost of such care over a long period.

SOURCE: Beth B. Hess and Joan M. Waring, "Parent and Child in Later Years: Rethinking the Relationship," in Richard Lerner and Graham Spanier (eds.), *Child Influences on Marital and Family Interaction* (New York: Academic Press, 1978), p. 249.

Aging parents may require time, emotional energy, and financial aid just when middle-agers are already overcommitted and faced with pressing career demands, community responsibilities, and heavy involvement in the lives of their own growing or grown children (which may include paying for expensive college educations). If a parent is widowed or becomes severely ill, the pressures on the middle generation may be especially acute. "The expenses associated with a parent's protracted illness are a financial as well as an emotional drain," write Hess and Waring. "But demands for companionship can be even more trying" (p. 260). And such demands for attention and companionship may be present where older parents are in good health as well as in cases of sickness and disability.

Hess and Waring speak of some of the psychological barriers that often block close relationships between middle-aged persons and their parents, including leftover resentments and hostilities from the years when the middle-generation persons were growing up in the family household:

> Although years of separate residence and greater self-knowledge may erase some of the minor difficulties and blunt the edge of some of the major ones, struggles for control, patterns of blaming, and disappointments about achievement, etc., may linger to undermine the possibility of a comfortable relationship between parents and children in the later years. Or they may be transferred onto the in-law relationship, creating a different but no less difficult kind of strain. (p. 251)

The resulting "emotional distance" may mean that the prospect of caring for an aged parent will cause considerable anxiety for many persons. Hess and Waring emphasize that "the expressed reluctance to take on primary care of an ailing parent may not reflect 'hardheartedness' so much as a strong reality orientation—the situation may be more emotionally stressful than the offspring can cope with" (p. 251). In other words, it isn't only a case of overcommitment in which the offsprings' time and energy resources are so taxed that they are unable to give themselves fully to their parents' needs. It's often a fear that one's own marriage or emotional health will suffer if one (or one's spouse) takes on caretaking responsibilities for an aging parent. Yet, even that realization may arouse pangs of guilt. At the same time, the aging parent may feel just as reluctant to become dependent upon a son or daughter—especially if the relationship has been a difficult and strained one in the past.

Hess and Waring suggest that as health care and income needs of older persons increasingly come to be viewed as societal concerns (rather than personal concerns of the individual and her or his family), "resentment and hostility between the generations may be lessened." The middle generation isn't forced then to make painful choices between providing for their children's needs, their own retirement needs, and the needs of their elderly parents. And at the same time, "the aged parent is spared being placed in the position of petitioner for favors from those for whom they were once responsible" (p. 247).

Of course, the middle generation is still making possible the provision of funds through the social security system and other taxes (which have meant a heavy burden as the elderly segment of the population increases). But "the essential change has been that the adult child now provides for an aged parent in the *citizen* role rather than the familial one," say these researchers (p. 247). Does this mean that affectionate caring for aged parents is thereby diminished? Not necessarily. Hess and Waring suggest that what is occurring is a shift in intergenerational exchanges. Once the emphasis was on fulfilling *instrumental* needs directly (financial provision for parents in old age as a mark of duty and responsibility if not always of love and caring), but now the emphasis appears to be more and more on direct *expressive* exchanges— striving where possible to build friendship and intimacy between the generations. Other social scientists point out that not everyone sees the shift of responsibility for older persons from the family to the state as something positive. "The spectre of an increasing percentage of the population retired and 'living off' young workers is haunting members of American society," writes social gerontologist Sarah Matthews (1979:170). "Sharing income with spouses and children is one thing; helping to support retired persons, relatives, or nonrelatives, is quite another."

What Hess and Waring wish to emphasize, however, is this: valued relationships between middle-aged parents and their parents are most apt to be cultivated and continued where both the offspring and the parents regard and treat one another as *adult equals.* If the middle-generation person perceives that he or she is still treated as a dependent child and not as an adult friend, that person is less likely to want to keep up the relationship with parents on anything more than a "duty" basis. Conversely, if the aging parent takes on the characteristics of a dependent child or is treated as such in a reversal of roles, similar difficulties in relating may arise. (Of course, this situation sometimes cannot be avoided because of an aging parent's physical impairments; and many offspring may try to give the same loving care to a helpless parent—or in some way provide such care—as they themselves once received from that parent.)

"The best model for examining intergenerational relations in later life may not lie in the family system," say Hess and Waring, "but in friendship patterns—relationships based upon mutual respect, common interests, affection, and emotional support" (p. 244). Friendship is voluntary and based upon what these social scientists speak of as *homophily*—"the tendency for liking to be based on shared traits and attitudes." The greater the homophily between adult children and their parents, the greater is the likelihood that the relationship will be strong, enduring, and satisfying to both sides.

THE LATER YEARS

Esther and Fred Blake are both sixty-two years old. Although everyone tells Fred that he should be looking forward to his retirement, he rather dreads giving up the work that has meant so much to him for so long. Esther, who has devoted her life to homemaking, has mixed feelings. She looks forward to time for travel and hobbies together, but she also knows from the experience of friends that her own daily routines will be drastically changed with Fred around the house all day. In addition, both are concerned about Fred's eighty-two-year-old mother who lives alone in an apartment near their home. Her health is failing, and they wonder whether they should consider a nursing home for her or invite her to live with them—which would cut down their own freedom.

Neither Fred nor Esther feels "old." As they recently showed some friends their honeymoon pictures, Fred had said he would like to go back to hike over some of those rugged mountain trails again. "At *your* age?" his wife had teased. "What do you mean, 'At my age'?" countered Fred, "you're only as old as you *think* you are!"

THE OBJECTIVE MEANING OF AGING

Half-joking remarks like "At *your* age?" or "Act your age!" imply the existence of social norms associated with various stages of life. Since social norms generally guide us throughout life as to how we should or shouldn't act, older people sometimes feel confused and alienated because at this stage behavioral expectations are less clear.

Some sociologists suggest that decreasing social requirements for behavior could actually be viewed as bringing increased freedom for elderly persons

*"We haven't much time left, Jake. What do you say
we take a stab at la dolce vita?"*

(Drawing by Weber; © 1976 The New Yorker Magazine, Inc.)

(Bengtson, 1973:23–26). Irving Rosow (1973:36–37) points out that this freedom results from the fact that, as persons grow older, limitations are placed on their responsibilities and power; therefore their ability to affect others adversely is sharply reduced. "There is less social stake in their behavior," he writes, "and correspondingly little concern with the options that older people exercise and the choices they make." What they do in their private lives is up to them. "So long as they do not become a burden to others or indulge in virtually bizarre behavior, within their means they can do very largely as they want and live as they wish."

It is no doubt true that, for some persons, freedom from normative constraints is considered a reward—as illustrated in the remark of a woman who said, "You have a perfect alibi for everything when you're eighty," since people readily overlook spilled soup, forgotten appointments, "acting silly," and even insisting on one's own way (letter to "Dear Abby," *Bloomington* (Indiana) *Herald Telephone*, May 20, 1975). On the other hand, freedom from social expectations because of decreased power and responsibility to affect the lives of others can be experienced as a punishment or loss. "I'm no longer important to anyone; people don't care what I do anymore" could be the feeling.

Not knowing what is expected of oneself is especially hard in cases of what sociologist Leonard Cain (1964:289) calls "asynchronization": the timing of various events in a person's life in a way that doesn't synchronize with other events (quoted in Bengtson, 1973:17). According to social expectations, people marry, have children, advance in their occupations and enter retirement and widowhood at certain taken-for-granted times. Yet the timing of certain events in one area of life doesn't always correspond with what is taking place in another area. Sociologist Vern Bengtson tells of interviewing a fifty-five-year-old steelworker who, having just retired, was considered to have reached *old age* in the economic-occupational sphere of life. But in his family he was relatively *young* in that he was the father of a thirteen-year-old daughter. In a fraternal order, his activities and position caused him to be considered *middle-aged*. This man found it difficult to define himself or know what was expected of him. Friends from work kidded him about being an old man. He didn't know what to do with his time. And his wife was annoyed with his being underfoot all day long (Bengtson, 1973:17–18).

What is Old Age? There is no simple answer to the question, When does a person become old? Surveys in both Great Britain and the United States have shown that the older a person's chronological age, the later he or she tends to think old age begins (Riley, Foner, and associates, vol. 1, 1968:311). Concepts of old age also vary by social status, with lower-status persons tending to believe old age begins earlier (for example, in the fifties), while persons of higher status tend to think old age begins later (about age sixty-five). Bengtson (1973:21) points out that persons of lower status move through their family careers and their work careers more quickly than do higher-status persons. At lower levels, persons tend to marry earlier, have their children sooner, and become grandparents earlier. In addition, because of limited education they usually reach as high as they will ever go occupationally at an earlier age than is true of persons at higher status levels. Not surprisingly then, "old age" seems to arrive sooner.

The Census Bureau defines old age as beginning when a person has lived sixty-five years. By this definition, there were 23 million elderly persons in 1976, a figure that is expected to nearly double to 45 million elderly persons by the year 2020 (Siegel, 1979:7). Table 17-A shows what percentage of persons over sixty-five years are in various age categories. Advances in medical science have meant considerable increases in life expectancy with the result that persons born in 1977 may expect to live seventy-three years on the average as compared to forty-nine years for persons born at the beginning of the century. And persons who had already reached their sixty-fifth birthday by 1977 could expect to live sixteen more years. The *median* age at death in 1977 was 76.8 years, compared to 58 years at the beginning of the century (National Center for Health Statistics, 1980, *Vital Statistics of the United States, 1977*, vol. II, sec. 5, 1980:4).

The arbitrary setting of age sixty-five as the beginning of old age provides a *social* definition of old age, just as age eighteen or twenty-one socially and

TABLE 17-A *Percent distribution of the population sixty-five years old and over, by age: 1950 to 2020*

AGE	1950	1960	1970	1976	1980	PROJECTIONS 1990	2000	2010	2020
65 years and over	100.0	100.0	100.0	100.0	100.0	100.0	100.0	100.0	100.0
65 to 69 years	40.7	37.7	35.0	36.1	34.9	33.6	28.9	33.4	35.4
70 to74 years	27.8	28.6	27.2	25.8	27.3	26.1	25.9	23.4	26.9
75 to 79 years	17.4	18.5	19.2	17.7	17.3	18.4	20.1	17.0	16.8
80 to 84 years	9.3	9.6	11.5	11.9	11.3	12.2	13.3	13.1	10.2
85 years and over	4.8	5.6	7.1	8.6	9.2	9.7	11.8	13.1	10.6

SOURCE: Jacob S. Siegel, "Prospective Trends in the Size and Structure of the Elderly Population, Impact of Mortality Trends, and Some Implications," in U.S. Bureau of the Census, *Current Population Reports*, series P-23, no. 78, January, 1979, p. 10.

legally defines adulthood. However, there is a big difference. The change in classification from a minor to an adult is usually viewed as a gain; it means a highly regarded status with new social and legal privileges and responsibilities has been conferred upon a person. In contrast, moving from middle to "old" age (as it has been defined by social security regulations, for example) may be viewed as a loss. Many privileges and responsibilities are taken away. The status conferred—"elderly person," 'golden ager," "senior citizen"—is *not* a highly regarded one, because in an industrial society being old is not esteemed as in other societies where prestige is granted on the basis of accumulated wisdom from many years. In industrial societies, education and innovation rather than past experience are valued keys to the occupational system's rewards. Change is rapid, and new technological skills are required. Practical knowledge of old ways of doing things is considered of limited worth. Thus older persons are expected to move out to make room for the young.

Social scientist Sarah Matthews (1979) concludes from her research that old age in our society is nothing short of a *stigma*—something that "spoils" one's identity in the eyes of others and makes one seem somehow not fully "normal" as a human being and as an adult (Goffman, 1963). Matthews explains:

> Old people are assumed by virtue of their age to be physically, and, therefore, mentally incapacitated. The stigma theory that age and poor health are synonymous is used to justify a mandatory retirement age, but it also has an effect on everyday interaction. Old people because of their advanced age are more easily assumed to be incapable of performing adequately as adult members of society. (pp. 61–62)

THE SUBJECTIVE MEANING OF AGING

To lump together all persons who have passed a certain number of birthdays under the labels "the elderly" or "senior citizens" gives the impression that "the aged" make up a homogeneous category. The word *homogeneous* comes from the Greek and means "of the same kind." But persons at age sixty-five and beyond don't suddenly all become alike any more than all persons at twenty-five are alike. Increasingly, social scientists emphasize that much more than age itself must be taken into account. People vary in their outlooks, goals, self-concepts, and social resources. Social status is particularly important because, as sociologist George Maddox (1970) stresses, this variable summarizes previous life experience. He goes on to point out that what individuals bring to old age determines to a large extent what old age will mean to them. "Social competence, adaptive flexibility, and a sense of well-being displayed by persons in the middle years of life predict the probable display of these same characteristics in the later years," he writes, adding that in a sense the life-cycle is a process in which "success predicts success."

From our earlier discussions of social status, we know that persons with higher education are more likely than those of lower education to possess the social and personal skills mentioned by Maddox. Sociologist Zena Blau (1973) provides evidence from various studies showing that the lower the social status level, the more likely persons are to respond to old age with attitudes of *alienation*, "characterized by the feeling that 'there is just no point in living,' by feeling regret over the past, by the idea that 'things just keep getting worse and worse,' and by abandonment of all future plans." Such persons tend to feel they have been failures (having been poor in a society that stresses success) and consider their lives useless. "You know what they ought to do with old men like me?" asked one respondent. "Take us out and shoot us. We're no good for anything" (pp. 156–157).

Old age may also seem difficult for persons at higher status levels, especially when it is accompanied by the loss of significant roles such as that of worker or spouse; but rather than reacting with alienation, the major response is what Blau calls *conformity*—an attitude of adjustment. "Lots of times you don't like the new things," said one respondent referring to the changes brought by the transition to old age, "but there isn't anything you can do about them. You just have to accept them" (pp. 163–166). (However, Blau found another small category which she labeled *innovators*, those persons who—regardless of social status—were able to take old age in stride, enjoy life in the here and now, and continue to develop new interests and friendships. Persons of both sexes who were both socially active and employed were the most likely to be innovators.)

Research has shown that a person's attitude has a great deal to do with aging. "You're only as old as you think you are" has much truth in it. Blau refers to the writer E. B. White, who said at age seventy, "Old age is a special problem for me because I've never been able to shed the mental image I have of myself—a lad of nineteen." Although the years brought changes, he was able to maintain a sense of inner sameness, continuity, and knowing who he was. Such ongoing self-identity and "agelessness" was due in large measure to the fact that he was able to keep up in his craft in spite of the passage of years, a privilege denied most people today. Blau asserts that it is the loss of one's occupational role, "the mainstay of one's identity," that leads people to form a new concept of themselves (pp. 103–104). In an extensive review of research findings on aging, sociologists Matilda Riley, Anne Foner, and associates (1968:302) emphasize that, "in the main, identification of the self as old is most pronounced among the disadvantaged and those who have experienced sharp discontinuity with the past." Widowhood, retirement, and poor health are cited as examples of such sharp discontinuity. We tend to form a sense of who we are through what we do and through relationships with other people. To find it necessary to leave the most significant role associated with *doing* (occupation) because of ill health or compulsory retirement, or to leave what for the majority of persons is the most significant *relationship* role (spouse), is to leave what seems like a part of one's very self.

ROLE EXITING

As we've seen, being old is much more than having reached a certain chronological age or of having undergone certain physical changes; it has a social meaning, and it is this social meaning that is most crucial. Zena Blau (1973:xiii) uses the term *role exiting* to describe the social meaning of aging and to show why persons in our society tend to dread being labeled old: "For it is the sustained experience of being necessary to others that gives meaning and purpose to the life of all human beings. Opportunities to remain useful members of the society are severely undermined by the exits from adult social roles that are typical of old age." While role exits occur constantly before old age (one leaves the student role to become a wage earner, for example), the role exits most often associated with old age are different, because "retirement and widowhood terminate a person's participation in the principal institutional structures of society—the nuclear family and the occupational structure" (pp. 17–18). A person comes to be viewed as a dependent, not a producer—a person with diminished power in society (Dowd, 1975).

Retirement   Retirement is a relatively new social institution associated with industrial society and without past precedent (Loether, 1964:518). As sociologist Ethel Shanas (1972:222) emphasizes, giving up work at a set age in order to spend the remainder of one's life in retirement "emerges as a widespread practice only when the level of living within a society is such that persons can be supported by society without themselves being workers." In simpler societies, the productivity of the elderly is needed, since almost everyone is living near the subsistence level and enforced idleness would be out of the question. But in modern societies, automation, diminishing opportunities for self-employment, and pressures to make room for job-seeking younger workers all combine to make retirement the rule rather than the exception.

   The passage of the Social Security Act in 1935 institutionalized retirement and formally defined old age by establishing pension eligibility at age sixty-five. But what this means is that at a certain arbitrarily fixed point in time, a person is suddenly excluded from the occupational structure—the structure that in American society provides such highly valued rewards as prestige, income, and a sense of worth. Blau points out what this role exit means to a male's self-image in particular. Both the material and social rewards associated with the opportunity system are taken away. After having been socialized to consider occupational achievement as the chief aspect of adult identity, males in retirement find themselves not only without a job but without the identity that went with that job. Adding to the strain is the realization that "retirement is a *social* pattern that implies an invidious judgment about old people's lack of fitness to perform a culturally significant and coveted role." It is a form of social banishment and exclusion and is therefore the hardest kind of role exiting one is called upon to bear (Z. Blau, pp. 105, 211–215).

Matthews (1979) refers to recent legislation that raises to age seventy the earliest age at which mandatory retirement may be legally required for persons in most occupational groups and suggests that in time "there is a real possibility that specific retirement age will be eliminated altogether." One reason is that, in reaction to funding problems in the social security system, Congress has begun shifting away "from an emphasis on what the aged *cannot* do to what the aged *can* do," the goal being to reduce old age "dependency." Increasingly, retirement would be based on choice and ability, not age. Matthews believes that even with such changes, "most workers will probably choose to retire 'on schedule,' that is, between the ages of sixty and sixty-five." But those who want to work may continue to do so. And, says Matthews, "Elimination of chronological age as the legal criterion of the beginning of old age, while it may have minimal economic effects, may have far-reaching effects on the social definitions of the aged"—and on their self-image as well because of the knowledge that they would be regarded as persons capable of contributing to the economy (pp. 170–171).

A number of things happen in retirement. No longer can a husband bring home the monetary and status rewards which played such a part in marital power and in the instrumental and expressive exchanges of rights and duties discussed in Chapters 10, 11, and 12. Because of the traditional meaning of the breadwinner role, retirement is experienced as much more demoralizing to males than is the case with females who retire from the work force (Z. Blau, 1973:29). This might be changing, however, as more women are becoming committed to careers and taking on the equal co-provider role. But for wives who have been full-time homemakers, life goes on much the same as before the retirement period, except that their husbands are now around home all the time.

For men, the changes are many. The daily pattern is disrupted because the once-structured time built around the job is now empty. Social participation is curtailed, since male friendships are usually highly dependent upon their occupational involvement. After a man's retirement, his still-employed,

Retirement: Reward or Punishment?

Dear Dr. Donohue: My husband retired recently, and since has been nothing but a grouch, complaining of this or that ailment. I have heard, but never believed it till now, that these guys just retire to die. Why? It is distressing me terribly. Any comment on this "non-medical" question?—Mrs. R. T.

It may not be as "non-medical" a question as you think. This retirement syndrome is real for many men. Why this downhill slide occurs at a time when life should be most pleasant, without the worries of work, is a puzzle. Some studies have, in fact, shown some sort of a correlation between retirement and heart-related illnesses. Some men need and thrive on the anxieties of daily work. In a discussion of this recently, one physician remarked, "There are some individuals who feel retirement is a just reward for a lifetime of work and others who regard it as a punishment for growing old." We are not sure whether there are direct links between physical ailments and retirement, but we have suspicions that there may be several.

SOURCE: From "Dr. Donohue" syndicated column, *Greensboro* (N.C.) *Daily News*, March 20, 1980.

former work associates continue to talk, joke, and gripe about job-related topics, and both he and they begin to realize that he no longer fits in (Z. Blau, p. 89).

Although blue-collar workers tend to report lower job satisfaction than white-collar workers and are more likely to volunteer for retirement, they tend to have greater difficulty in making the transition from worker to retiree. Losing the occupational role means a reduction in feelings of self-worth since blue-collar men are less likely to have other roles to fall back on or tangible evidences of accomplishment that remain (such as college degrees). The occupational role has been their major means of identity. The occupational role has also been highly important to white-collar men, but because of greater resources and role flexibility they have been found to be better able to make the transition to the retired state (Loether, 1964, 1967).

Widowhood   As with retirement, there are differences by socioeconomic status and by sex with regard to the other major role exit associated with old age—widowhood. Of course, a person may lose a spouse before this period of life, but the subject is considered here since it affects such vast numbers at this stage (especially women). The 1970 census showed that more than half the women over age sixty-five had lost a spouse, in contrast to 17 percent of men in this age range (U. S. Bureau of the Census, *We the American Elderly*, 1973). There are more widows than widowers for a combined reason: women tend to marry men older than themselves and men tend to die earlier than women. Among persons over age sixty-five in 1976, there were 69 men for every 100 women; and among persons seventy-five years and over, there were 58 men for every 100 women (Siegel, 1979:10–11).

Since in traditional marriage, a woman's identity and status have stemmed from rewards provided by her husband, the husband's death means not only the loss of a companion with whom one's life was shared but also the loss of the wife role. A new way of looking at life—a reconstruction of reality—takes place during the transition from wife to widow to being one's own person (comparable in a sense to what also happens after divorce). At first, many women continue to think in terms of their former wife role and order their lives after their husband's wishes for a time ("Bill wouldn't want me to. . . ." "I think George would expect me to do it this way." "Carl never wanted me to learn to drive."), but many arrive at a point of reaching out and building a new life (Silverman, 1972).

Sociologist Helena Lopata (1973a) found that widows of lower socioeconomic status (measured by education level) tended to live more isolated lives than did widows at higher status levels. Women with lower education have usually been married to men with low incomes, and husband-wife activities were usually highly segregated by sex which, as we saw in Chapter 12, tends to be associated with lower expressive satisfaction. In one sense, widowhood may be less costly to such women in that they do not experience the loss of a companionship they never had. For such a woman, writes Lopata, "isolation is made easy by the fact that she was always marginal to the social system and that she was not socialized into any skills for expanded re-engagement into society" (p. 270; Z. Blau, 1973:84). On the other hand, widowhood may be extremely costly in terms of money as such a woman experiences even greater financial restriction than when her husband was alive.

Lopata's research led her to conclude that losing a husband is less disorganizing to the identities of lower-status women than is true of women with higher education because higher-status women have invested more time and energy into constructing a world view built around their husbands. In such homes, there is likely to have been more shared interests, greater communication, empathy and involvement in one another's lives, and less stress on sex-segregated activities. Nevertheless, because of the personal and social resources associated with her educational advantages and other benefits, the higher-status woman is equipped to build a new image of herself and the world if she so chooses. Though the change may be painful, as the process goes on she may come to feel "like a fuller human being, more independent and competent than in the past" (Lopata, 1973b:416).

A number of studies indicate that, in general, males have greater difficulty adjusting to widowhood than do females. The loss of a spouse in old age takes its toll on men in many ways: low morale, mental disorders, and high death and suicide rates (Bock and Weber, 1972). Like retirement, widowhood is (in Blau's terms) a role exit. But unlike retirement, widowhood isn't a socially imposed exit but results in most cases from forces beyond human control. Therefore, widowhood doesn't carry with it the sense of having been judged and banished by others as retirement does. But there is still the sense of loss—of being deprived of highly cherished rewards.

The marital rights-duties exchange depicted in the two-story house diagram in Chapter 12 showed that in traditional arrangements, the instrumental side of marriage is characterized by an exchange in which the husband provides the wife with financial and status benefits and the wife rewards the husband by performing the necessary tasks of daily living such as maintaining the home. When death ends the marriage, the surviving spouse is left without these instrumental rewards to a great degree: a wife's husband-based status is gone and often her financial situation is a problem as well, and a husband has lost his means of domestic care. For the first time in his life he may have to cope with laundry, cooking, cleaning, and the like. One result of the traditional gender-linked division of labor in marriage is that an older widow's life goes on much as usual (in terms of housekeeping) while a widower is forced to take on new and often unfamiliar responsibilities. Not only has he lost the role of worker through retirement but now he must take on a different role (homemaker), and so many changes all at once in the later years of life can be difficult (Berardo, 1970; Vinick, 1978).

In addition to the instrumental or practical side of marriage, the expressive or personal side is deeply affected as well. Again, males appear to fare worse in widowhood. Men are more likely than women to have depended entirely on their spouses to serve in the role of confidant, meeting needs for empathy, understanding, affection, communication, and companionship. But women are more likely to have other sources of personal affirmation outside the marriage, not only because they are more likely than husbands to have kept in touch with kin networks over the years, but also because they are more likely to have deep friendships in which they are accepted and appreciated as total persons (and not viewed primarily in terms of a role such as worker) and from which they can draw rich emotional support. Many older women have friends who are already widows and who can serve as role models, providing older women with an opportunity to mentally rehearse for widowhood in advance. When widowhood strikes, the network of widow friends can provide the new widow with companionship in various activities as well as empathy and aid. Zena Blau (1973:72–75), emphasizes the importance of having at least one intimate friend to bring continuity to life and emotional support in old age. But at the same time, she shows how much more difficult it seems to be for men than women to form such close, long-lasting friendships, since gender-role socialization has traditionally discouraged the development in males of those qualities that are necessary for building deep interpersonal relationships (see also Lowenthall and Haven, 1968; Powers and Bultena, 1976).

We may speculate that adjustments to widowhood may be less difficult and demoralization less common as emerging forms of marriage replace the traditional head-complement model. As women and men come to share equally in breadwinning and domestic roles, they may be better able to cope

When widowhood strikes, the network of widow friends can provide companionship in various activities as well as empathy and aid. (© Hanna Schreiber/Rapho/Photo Researchers, Inc.)

with losses in the instrumental side of marriage. It also seems likely that the diminished rewards in the expressive side of marriage brought by widowhood will seem less devastating as both sexes become more alike in terms of nurturance qualities and, through having developed the capacity for intimacy, can build and maintain other close relationships to bring meaning to life in old age.

THE MARRIAGE RELATIONSHIP IN THE LATER YEARS

Some couples have many years together before death separates them. Research on the marriage relationship in the later stages of the life-cycle is limited at this time, but some of the findings provide the following picture (U.S. Bureau of the Census, *We the American Elderly*, 1973; Riley, Foner, and associates, 1968; Smith, 1965; Palmore, 1968; Stinnett, Carter, and Montgomery, 1972; Parron and Troll, 1978).

Only 3 percent of elderly men and 5 percent of elderly women live in homes for the aged. A growing proportion of widows and widowers are maintaining independent households, and elderly married couples tend to live in separate households from their children as well. In cases of illness, the spouses tend to care for each other, preparing meals, and so on. Gender-role differentiation tends to become lessened, and shared activities tend to increase, since so much time is available for the husband and wife to spend together in the later years of marriage. Companionship may be enhanced both through greater sharing of household tasks after the husband retires and more joint leisure projects (such as vacations or decorating the home) after all the children have been gone for several years. High marital satisfaction in the later years is also associated with high morale, but the reverse is true as well (Lee, 1978).

In other words, although many changes occur over the years as a couple go through life together, some sorts of exchanges both in the instrumental and expressive realms of marriage continue so long as the marriage lasts. And those couples who have learned to understand and empathize with one another, to enjoy activities together, and to negotiate in times of conflict have the potential of experiencing high rewards and maximum joint profit to the very end (Parron and Troll, 1978).

AGING AND SEXUALITY

Contrary to many commonly held beliefs and stereotypes about being sexually "over the hill," sexual interest and activity continue among elderly couples. Advancing age usually means a decline in frequency of sexual intercourse, but that doesn't mean that sex will necessarily be eliminated from marital interaction. Findings from the Duke University Longitudinal Study of Aging showed that the majority of husbands and wives were sexually active until over age seventy-five. And close to 15 percent of the couples indicated a pattern in which both sexual activity and interest were increasing rather than decreasing. Among those couples who reported having stopped having sexual intercourse entirely, however, the median age at which intercourse ceased was age sixty-eight for men and age sixty for women. Wives and husbands agreed that husbands were the ones most responsible for stopping sexual intercourse, the main reasons being loss of potency, loss of interest, and illness (Palmore, 1970, chap. 8).

The Sex Information and Education Council of the United States reports that pervasive stereotypes about the alleged "sexless older years" can be destructive in many ways, negatively affecting the older person's sex life, self-image, and the marriages of older people in general. Such stereotypes also cause problems between aged parents and adult children when widowed or divorced parents consider remarriage, can make diagnosing various medical and psychological problems difficult, and may even lead to false accusations and faulty administration of justice in cases of elderly men accused of certain sex offenses. (For example, if elderly women show an interest in small children, they are considered warm and affectionate. But for an elderly man to show such interest brings the risk of being labeled a "dirty old man." It is assumed that his interest in children could only be sexual; and since it's also assumed that old people have no interest in sex, the man's attitudes are thought to indicate a perverted interest which must be watched with fear and suspicion [SIECUS, 1970, chap. 8; Felstein, 1970].) Many persons in the helping professions are urging efforts toward greater sensitivi-

Despite widespread notions about the "sexless older years," many elderly couples continue to enjoy the physical expression of love. (Bruce Davidson/Magnum)

ty to and understanding of the sexual needs of the elderly—including elderly persons in nursing homes whose right to privacy and desire for physical affection have not always been recognized or treated wisely (Carroll, 1978). At the same time, Hess and Waring (1978:257) call attention to the concerns of some specialists in aging that "with the discovery of gerosexuality, too much may now be expected of elderly lovers." (The prefix *gero* there comes from the Greek word for "old age" and is the word from which *gerontology*—the scientific study of aging— comes.)

REMARRIAGE IN THE LATER YEARS

While difficulty in accepting the possibility of aging parents' active sexuality may be one reason that offspring often are less than enthusiastic about a parent's remarrying late in life, other reasons also enter in—for example, fears that a lonely parent is being taken advantage of by the prospective mate, or anxieties that the offspring's share of an inheritance will be diminished because of the parent's new spouse (Hess and Waring, 1978:253).

Even so, over 35,000 marriages each year involve either a bride or groom

Sex after Seventy

Of those who mentioned sex in marriage, the important aspect was not the physical act but the warmth of another body, the holding, the intimacy. One 73-year-old man expressed himself fully on the subject of sex:

I don't know if I'm oversexed, but I'm a lover. I like to pet, kiss, hug. I have more fun out of loving somebody I love than the ultimate end. You know, some people—and this is the failure of sex, too—some people want sex and forget the rest of it—the hugging and the petting and I think that's wrong. People say, "What will happen to me when I get older?" Well, I'm still alive! There's no thrill like that today. People try dope, they try smoking, they try drinking. This is the one thing that's good for the body.

SOURCE: Barbara H. Vinick, "Remarriage in Old Age," *The Family Coordinator* 27 (October, 1978), p. 362.

who is over sixty-five years old (Vinick, 1978:359). And many offspring not only approve but are happy for their parents' newfound happiness and are relieved from worries about their parents' loneliness and need for companionship reports sociologist Barbara Vinick (1978) after in-depth interviews with twenty-four remarried elderly couples. Her respondents had received positive affirmation from their children in over half the cases but found a surprising amount of negative feedback among their own peers upon learning of the remarriage prospects. "People mentioned friends who felt deserted by the remarriage," writes Vinick, "or, not having the courage to remarry themselves, felt apprehensive in regard to a friend's chances for happiness" (p. 361). Over time, however, friends tended to become more approving of the marriage; although getting together with both friends and relatives tended to decrease as the new spouse became the major "source of intimacy and services" (p. 362).

Most of the remarried elderly persons in Vinick's small sample reported satisfaction. "We're like a couple of kids," one woman told her. "We enjoy life together. When you're with someone, you're happy." Those who reported unhappiness were those who felt that external circumstances had forced them into marriages they later regretted. Vinick provides an example:

One such woman, Mrs. R., was approaching the age of compulsory retirement when she met her husband. She did not know how she would get along financially, and had a feeling of desperation about her situation. Mr. R. owned a home, and was financially well off. After a short courtship, they married. Mrs. R. now describes her marriage as like "having stepped into a dark room." Her husband is arbitrary, autocratic and miserly. She is full of apprehension but is pinning her hopes on a move to Florida where she hopes they will be happier. (p. 362)

Widows, Widowers, and Remarriage

A lonely man who wants to remarry can relatively easily assuage his loneliness by remarriage. . . . A lonely woman who wants to remarry will often have difficulty finding a mate because of the lopsided ratio of one widower to every five widows in the population. Women, therefore, more often than men stated that they had "adjusted" to being alone. As 68-year-old Mrs. H. explained, "Teaching kept me very busy. The type of work I did kept me from being lonely. I had adjusted, you know. I had a very happy life by myself. I had some very good friends, with whom I enjoyed doing things. So, we always had something to look forward to. We were always planning."

Women, in general, were financially less secure than the men. Many of the women had returned to work because of financial necessity. But in spite of their more fortunate economic position, men appear to need *remarriage more than women. In fact, twice as many men as women said that they had hoped to remarry.*

SOURCE: Barbara H. Vinick, "Remarriage in Old Age," *The Family Coordinator* 27 (October, 1978), pp. 360–361.

But, Vinick adds, Mrs. R.'s situation was illustrative of only a minority of persons in the sample. Nineteen of the twenty-four women, and twenty-one of the twenty-four men described themselves as "satisfied" or "very satisfied" with their remarriages.

AGING AND ALTERNATIVE LIFE-STYLES

Little empirical data have thus far been gathered concerning aging and alternatives to traditional marriage and family such as those discussed in Chapters 8 and 9—although a certain amount of research has begun to be focused on, for example, elderly homosexual persons (Minnigerode and Adelman, 1978; Raphael and Robinson, 1980; Friend, 1980), elderly never-married persons (Scott, 1979), and various group living arrangements for older persons (Streib, 1978). As we saw earlier, cohabitation has sometimes been an alternative chosen by some elderly couples who have desired love and companionship but who haven't wanted to lose widow's pension benefits or (until recent legislation) social security benefits—or who haven't wanted to run counter to their children's wishes that they not marry again (Hess and Waring, 1978; Dressel and Avant, 1978).

Sociologist Gordon Streib (1978) points to a need for more research on various points along a *continuum* of possible living arrangements for elderly persons—possibilities ranging from independent households on one end to a total-care nursing home on the other, with a wide range of collective living arrangements in between (see also Streib and Hilker, 1980).

Love's Labour's Lost and Found

FORT LAUDERDALE, Fla. (AP)—Two years ago, Martha Munzer and Isaac Corkland were reunited by coincidence and resumed a courtship interrupted by war—World War I.

They've been living together almost ever since, and today they'll be married in a Pompano Beach synagogue. Then Corkland, 83, and Mrs. Munzer, 80, will take a monthlong honeymoon in Israel. They say part of the reason they're getting married is to make it easier to register in hotels.

The couple met on a blind date in the summer of 1918 and say they fell in love over the next 10 days.

"It was so romantic at 18 to have a young Army lieutenant who was my lieutenant, Mrs. Munzer said.

"I thought she would make a wonderful helpmate." Corkland recalled. "She had such a bright outlook on life."

He was shipped to Europe, and despite their best efforts to keep in touch, they drifted apart after the war. She married after graduation from the Massachusetts Institute of Technology and he became a Tennessee lawyer and married there. But they never forgot each other.

"After Corky became a widower in 1960, he came to New York looking for me, but he didn't find me," she said.

Corkland retired to Florida and took creative-writing classes at Nova University. In one class project, he described his wartime romance.

Soon after, a fellow student showed him portions of a book a friend was writing. The friend was Mrs. Munzer, who was living in Mamaroneck, N.Y., and a widow.

"We thought it was kind of a miracle. Our lives had been apart for 60 years," she said.

The couple says, "our life is only beginning," and Mrs. Munzer's latest book, her eighth, is titled "It Might as Well Be Spring."

"We're just having a ball," she said.

She giggled when asked why the two lived together for the past two years.

"We took a leaf from the younger generation. We decided to see first how we liked living together," she said.

SOURCE: *Greensboro (N.C.) Daily News/Record*, Sunday, March 30, 1980.

The child-free alternative life-style elected by many married couples today also needs to be considered with regard to aging—both the couples' own future aging (what will be their support system?) and the fact that their parents may be pressuring them to have children simply so that the older generation may experience grandparenthood! In a humorous essay in the *New York Times Magazine* (July 25, 1976), columnist Russell Baker spoke of a real concern of some persons—the fear of being "grandchildless." "What right, one may ask, do these aging Americans have to expect grandchildren?" asks Baker. "The answer is that American society has conditioned them to construct their lives on the assumption that grandparenthood is inevitable, and as a class they have done so." He continues:

> The politicians they have chosen to govern them have been the politicians who boasted that they would make the world a better place for their grandchildren. They have borne taxation, taken up arms, supported huge mortgages and spent vast sums on the improvement of their own children, and all in the cause of making America a better place for their grandchildren.
>
> What was the point of all this if it turns out that there are to be no grandchildren to enjoy this better world. . . .? (p. 4)

The Homosexual Community Caring for Its Older Members

Since older persons represent a diversity of ethnic groups, religious backgrounds, and socio-economic status, they also include lesbians and gay men. However, the special needs of older gay men and women have often been overlooked.

Senior Action in a Gay Environment, Inc. (SAGE) was created to help meet these needs. SAGE is a part of the gay and lesbian community caring for its elders. . . .

SAGE is a group of trained volunteers—including social workers, doctors, lawyers, psychologists, gerontologists, and other concerned members of the gay community—who joined together in June, 1978, to incorporate the country's first volunteer service organization addressing the needs of older lesbians and gay men. SAGE's services are uniquely designed to enhance the older person's connection with the gay community.

SAGE Offers the Following Services by Trained Volunteers

1. Friendly visiting: at home, in the hospital, or in an institution
2. Escort services: to medical centers, gay religious services, shopping, on errands
3. Telephone contact: daily or as needed
4. Social activities: to provide a congenial setting for meeting, sharing and caring; to reduce loneliness, rebuild relationships, establish supportive connections with the gay and lesbian community
5. Bereavement support: for those facing the serious illness or death of a friend or lover
6. Information and referral in areas of concern to older persons: legal matters (including wills and bequests), home care and long-term facilities. SAGE makes referrals to appropriate social service agencies as well as to gay-oriented professionals including lawyers, therapists, and physicians.
Services are free, and confidentiality is fully respected.

SOURCE: From a brochure distributed by Senior Action in A Gay Environment, Inc., 487-A Hudson St., New York, N.Y. 10014.

GRANDPARENTHOOD

In her study of over 1,000 Chicago area widows, sociologist Helena Znaniecka Lopata (1979) found that while grandchildren were reported to be persons the widows enjoyed being with, they were less likely than nieces and nephews to be listed as persons to whom the widows could turn in times of crisis or when they felt in need of comfort. "What is quite possible is that the relation provides intense enjoyment for only a brief time while the grandchildren are little, and that the generations drift apart when the grandchildren become strongly involved in their own lives," explains Lopata (p. 246). The average age of the widows in her sample was sixty-five which would indicate that some of the grandchildren were likely to be heavily involved in the concerns of adolescence and early adulthood, including their own educational, career, and family interests and responsibilities, thereby making them less available as intregal parts of their grandmothers' social support systems.

Other studies have indicated that, when it comes to the morale of elderly persons, friends make a greater contribution than grandchildren since friends have much more in common with them (Wood and Robertson, 1978; Z. Blau, 1973). In summarizing a number of studies on grandparenthood, two specialists in the study of aging point out that in the United States the grandparent role is by and large an inactive role that is hedged about by certain restrictions ("Grandparents are expected not to encroach upon the

The ties between grandparents and grandchildren can bring some of life's richest experiences. (Myron Wood/Photo Researchers, Inc.)

parental responsibilities of their young adult offspring or to interfere with their authority"), but yet is seen by older persons "as at least one socially acceptable avenue for involvement in their children's families" (Wood and Robertson, 1978:369–370). According to Wood and Robertson, who interviewed 257 grandparents:

> While grandparents verbally attributed a great deal of significance to grandparenthood, the behavior of most grandparents in the role was relatively limited. It was true that most grandparents babysat, took their grandchildren to the zoo, movies, and so on, read to and played with them, and gave grandchildren gifts and remembered their birthdays, but the frequency of these activities for most grandparents was only a few times a year. Fewer than half of the grandparents reported ever telling their grandchildren about family history and customs or teaching them a special skill such as sewing, cooking, fishing, or a craft. (p. 369)

While folklore has presented us with the image of elderly white-haired grandparents in rocking chairs or in cozy kitchens with gingham curtains and the spicy aroma of cookies baking for the grandchildren, many grandparents are middle-aged rather then elderly. It is common today for persons to become grandparents in their late forties or early fifties (Rapoport et al., 1977:335). And this can mean a difference in grandparenting style—particularly for grandmothers. Social scientist Joan Robertson (1977) found that younger grandmothers with more education, high involvement in activities outside the family, outside friendships, and paid employment tended to consider grandmothering "a joyous role" but at the same time made it clear "that they are more involved in their own lives and place less emphasis on grandparenting" (p. 173). In contrast, the older grandmothers in her sample had less education, tended to be widowed and unemployed, and had fewer outside friendship and community ties. These grandmothers "speak of grandmotherhood in highly laudable and personal or affective tones," writes Robertson. "Grandchildren are viewed as important to their daily lives because they help fill lonesome hours. This is evidenced in the fact that these women have the highest frequency of interaction behavior with grandchildren—an interesting finding in view of their age" (p. 173).

Little research has this far been done on the grandfather role. Rapoport and her colleagues (1977:335–337) suggest that much more attention be given to grandfathers. They suggest that at the same time that the younger grandmother may be busy with her own interests, glad to be relieved of the duties of active parenting, and uninterested in heavy involvement in a grandmother role (such as caring for grandchildren while her offspring and spouse are at work), the opposite may be true of the grand*father* in many cases. "Having been denied the pleasures of active parenting, he may yearn for a phase of active grandparenting," say these behavioral scientists, calling for research to explore this possibility. If their speculation is found to be true, it will be one more instance of the impact of changing gender roles—just as we saw in our discussion of the launching and empty nest period of the middle years.

Some studies have shown that marital satisfaction over time tends to follow a U-shaped curve. Satisfaction is high at the beginning of the marriage, drops during the childbearing and childrearing years, then rises again during the empty nest period. Increased survival rates and a couple's relatively younger age at the time their last child marries mean that a husband and wife who remain together can now look forward to an average of thirteen postchildren years together.

Contrary to the stereotype of the middle-aged woman, many wives at midlife today are enthusiastically pursuing their own interests and thankful for time and freedom to do so. Those who have most difficulty when the children leave home are those who have defined themselves chiefly as mothers, accepted traditional sex-role assumptions, and haven't planned ahead by developing outside interests. At the same time that many wives are turning their attention to interests outside the home such as employment and further education, many husbands are questioning their own lifelong absorption in occupational endeavors and would like to develop and emphasize the expressive side of life more fully. As a result, some fathers at midlife are finding it difficult to see their children leave home. Some are also finding it hard to accept their wives' new aspirations.

Just at the time when the middle generation is already overcommitted with the many demands of growing or grown children, careers, and community responsibilities, they may find that their aging parents are requiring increased attention and possibly financial aid. Valued relationships between middle-aged persons and their parents are most apt to be cultivated where both the offspring and the aging parents regard and treat one another as equals and friends. The same is true of the middle generation in relation to their own adult children.

The Census Bureau defines old age as beginning when a person has lived sixty-five years. This definition, based solely on chronological age, arbitrarily classifies persons in a social category that in our society is devalued and considered nonproductive and powerless. Leaving important social roles ("role exits") at this stage of life may bring a painful sense of loss—especially the leaving of one's role as *spouse* (through the experience of widowhood) and one's role as *worker* (through compulsory retirement).

For those couples whose marriage continues into the later years, high marital satisfaction is associated with high morale. Some widowed older persons remarry. Over 35,000 marriages each year involve either a bride or groom aged sixty-five or older. Changing gender-role expectations and the fact that many persons become grandparents while in their forties or fifties have combined to bring changes in grandparenting style, particularly in the case of grandmothers.

CHAPTER 18

(Joel Gordon)

DIVORCE AND REMARRIAGE

When Larry and Sue, a couple in their late twenties, announced their plans for divorce, their friends were shocked. They couldn't believe it. Not Larry and Sue! If *they* couldn't stay married, who could?

Psychiatrist Arthur Miller (1970) points out that such reactions are typical of the feelings friends may experience in such situations. An impending divorce may cause friends to seriously examine their own marriages, and they may feel anxious and threatened. Sometimes there has been an idealization of the marriage of the divorcing couple, and the model with which one identified suddenly seems to be crumbling, bringing a sense of disillusionment as well as emotional loss.

The shock is intensified when the news is completely unexpected. In his classic study of divorce and readjustment, sociologist Williard Waller (1930: xiv, 107) wrote of a couple's teamwork in maintaining "the polite fiction" that all is well in their marriage even though they are moving toward divorce. The societal norm that family matters are private matters usually means that husbands and wives are reluctant to air their grievances or quarrel in front of their mutual friends. During the process of alienation leading toward divorce, the couple may make deliberate attempts to "manage their impressions" on others—in a sense giving what sociologist Erving Goffman (1959) speaks of as "a performance," trying to control how others see their situation. They are likely to act as they think they *should* act because others expect married couples to act in certain ways—even though such actions may be contrary to the realities of their particular case.

DIVORCE AS A PROCESS

The reference to a "process of alienation" underscores an important point: just as marriage is a process, so is the dissolution of a marriage. Marriage, with its ongoing exchange of rights and duties, rewards and costs, requires negotiation again and again. But sometimes the bargaining breaks down. The old pact no longer seems satisfactory to one or both; yet the couple seem unable to strike a new deal on which they can agree. One may try to coerce the other, seeking to get the conflict regulated rather than resolving it. This approach tends only to increase hostility and bitterness, especially when the coercion is viewed by the other spouse as an exercise of nonlegitimate power. The trust element and concern for maximum joint profit is damaged. "If you really wanted what is best for me and for our marriage, you wouldn't be ordering me to do something against my will!" says one spouse. But the other counters: "If you wanted what's best for *me* and cared about what *I* feel is best for our marriage, you wouldn't be resisting me. You'd go along with what I want."

Such was Sue and Larry's situation. Larry loved the outdoors and wanted to get away from the city life that meant so much to Sue. Increasingly concerned about energy conservation and environmental issues, Larry longed to join with some friends of theirs in an organic farming venture in a rural area where the other couple had inherited some land. But Sue cringed at the notion of what she called a "primitive, back-to-nature life-style" and couldn't envision herself "chopping wood, tending chickens, and raising goats or something." Furthermore, she had no plans to give up her studies in architecture at the university and the job opportunity she had been promised after graduation. She was stunned that Larry would even suggest it.

Larry told his friends he wouldn't be able to join them in their farming experiment; so they found another couple. But Larry blamed Sue for shattering his dream and making him miss out on what he considered an extraordinary opportunity. Over the months, Larry and Sue grew increasingly distant from each other. Their interests and life-goals seemed to pull them apart, and they found it harder to talk together about things that really mattered. Certain subjects (careers, life-styles, gender roles) were particularly explosive, didn't lend themselves to discussion and negotiation, and eventually came to be avoided entirely. Where each had once felt reinforced by the other, both now felt that the other was almost like an altogether different person, no longer providing the rewards of emotional support that had meant so much to the other's self-esteem. Instead, there were now psychic punishments—nagging, criticism, smoldering resentment, searching for faults to complain about, and a tendency to tear down instead of build each other up as they had once done. These punishments, along with the diminishing rewards, made the relationship seem increasingly costly to maintain. Outside alternatives became more and more attractive (for Larry, the prospect of living and working among like-minded persons; for Sue, the prospect of freedom to pursue her career interests unhindered). The thought of divorce alarmed them at first—they had thought such a thing could never happen to them—but it seemed the only way.

BOHANNAN'S "SIX STATIONS OF DIVORCE"

The process Sue and Larry underwent corresponds to what anthropologist Paul Bohannan (1970, chap. 2) calls the *emotional divorce*. Divorce may seem perplexing because so many things are taking place at once. Bohannan has isolated six aspects or overlapping experiences involved in each divorce. The emotional divorce centers around the deteriorating marriage relationship. The husband and wife "may continue to work together as a social team, but their attraction and trust for one another have disappeared," writes Bohannan. "The emotional divorce is experienced as an unsavory choice between giving in and hating oneself and domineering and hating oneself. . . . Two people in emotional divorce grate on each other because each is disappointed."

While the emotional divorce is taking place, other aspects of divorce may also be occurring. There is the *legal divorce* (the obtaining of an actual decree), the *economic divorce* (the settlement of money matters and the division of

Divorced Persons and Married Persons: A Statistical Comparison

In March, 1977, there were an estimated 8.1 million men and women who were divorced and who had not remarried, compared to 48 million married couples; there were 84 divorced persons for every 1,000 persons in an intact marriage. . . . In 1977, women had higher divorce ratios (101 per 1,000) than men (66 per 1,000), and persons under 45 had higher ratios (91 per 1,000) than those 45 years and over (76 per 1,000). These latter two developments reflect the facts that (1) women have a longer average duration of divorce before remarriage and a lower incidence of remarriage than men; and (2) most of the recent increase in divorce has been among younger couples.

SOURCE: U.S. Bureau of the Census, "Marital Status and Living Arrangements: March, 1977," *Current Population Reports,* series P-20, no. 323, April, 1978, p. 3.

property), the *coparental divorce* (decisions about the custody of any children, visitation rights, each parent's responsibilities, and so on), the *community divorce* (changes in ways friends and others in the community react as the couple's divorce becomes known), and the *psychic divorce* (the sense of becoming uncoupled and regaining a sense of identity as an individual rather than one of a pair).

HOW WIDESPREAD IS DIVORCE?

Questions sometimes arise as to how widespread divorce is. One common way demographers measure marital dissolution is through the *crude divorce rate:* the number of divorces per 1,000 persons in the population. Figure 18-1 shows trends in marriage and divorce rates for over a century.

CRUDE DIVORCE RATES

In 1867, when divorce statistics first began to be collected, there were about 0.5 divorces per 1,000 population. For the next sixty years, the divorce rate increased consistently, rising about 75 percent every twenty years. Had this pattern continued, the divorce rate in 1947 would have been 2.8. Instead, a very steep rise occurred in the 1940s. Most observers attribute the sharp increase to the high number of "quickie marriages" that took place amidst the uncertainties and upheavals of that period. As World War II came to an end, so did many of the hastily entered marriages it had spawned. The divorce rate in 1946 shot up to an all-time high—4.3 divorces per 1,000 population.

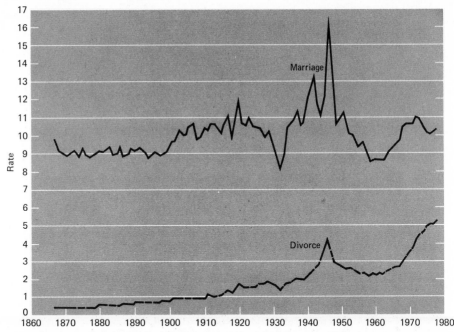

FIGURE 18-1   *Crude Rates: Marriages and Divorces per 1,000 population, United States,*
1867–1978. (Source: National Center for Health Statistics, 1973, series 21, no. 24, p. 10;
Monthly Vital Statistics Report, 1979, vol. 27, no. 13, p. 11.)

Then, just as suddenly, the rate fell again and leveled off during the
1950s, remaining at about 2.1 to 2.3 until 1963. That year the plateau ended
and another climb began. Within ten years the rate had nearly doubled, even
exceeding the 1946 figure. For every 1,000 persons in 1973, there were 4.4
divorces; and by 1975, the divorce rate was 4.9. However, in 1976 and 1977,
the divorce rate plateaued at 5.0. This was the first time in a decade that the
rate had not climbed from one year to the next, and it may signal a slowdown
of the spectacular rate increases that had been taking place previously. At the
same time, as Table 18-A shows, the rate rose slightly in 1978 to 5.2 divorces
per 1,000 population (National Center for Health Statistics, series 21, no. 24,
1973:9; *Monthly Vital Statistics Report*, vol. 22, no. 13, 1974; vol. 23, no. 12,
1975; vol. 27, no. 13, 1979).

REFINED DIVORCE RATES

Using *all* persons in the population as a base on which to calculate divorces
presents a problem since many persons aren't "at risk" when it comes to
divorce (children and unmarried adults). Demographers therefore sometimes
use another way of measuring divorces, taking only married women as the
base. The results are called *refined* rates. Refined rates are considered more

TABLE 18-A Marriages, divorces, and rates: United States, 1958–78
[Rates on an annual basis per 1,000 population. Data refer only to events occurring in the United States. Alaska included beginning with 1959 and Hawaii with 1960]

YEAR	MARRIAGE		DIVORCE	
	NUMBER	RATE[1]	NUMBER	RATE[1]
1978[2]	2,243,000	10.3	1,128,000	5.2
1977	2,178,367	10.1	1,091,000	5.0
1976	2,154,807	10.0	1,083,000	5.0
1975	2,152,662	10.1	1,036,000	4.9
1974	2,229,667	10.5	977,000	4.6
1973	2,284,108	10.9	915,000	4.4
1972	2,282,154	11.0	845,000	4.1
1971	2,190,481	10.6	773,000	3.7
1970	2,158,802	10.6	708,000	3.5
1969	2,145,000	10.6	639,000	3.2
1968	2,069,000	10.4	584,000	2.9
1967	1,927,000	9.7	523,000	2.6
1966	1,857,000	9.5	499,000	2.5
1965	1,800,000	9.3	479,000	2.5
1964	1,725,000	9.0	450,000	2.4
1963	1,654,000	8.8	428,000	2.3
1962	1,577,000	8.5	413,000	2.2
1961	1,548,000	8.5	414,000	2.3
1960	1,523,000	8.5	393,000	2.2
1959	1,494,000	8.5	395,000	2.2
1958	1,451,000	8.4	368,000	2.1

[1]Rates are based on population enumerated as of April 1 for 1960 and 1970 and estimated as of July 1 for all other years.
[2]Provisional.

SOURCE: U.S. Department of Health, Education, and Welfare, Monthly Vital Statistics Report, vol. 27, no. 13, 1979, p. 11.

precise because they focus on the logical group out of which a particular category comes. If you're interested in studying first-marriage rates, you take single persons as your base because they're the persons who enter first marriages. If you want to focus on divorce rates, you look at married persons—the category out of which divorces occur. If you want to study fertility rates, you look at women in the childbearing years. And so on.

For example, in Figure 18-2, Arthur Norton and Paul Glick (1979) are comparing the divorces per 1,000 *married* women aged fourteen to forty-four years with first marriages per 1,000 *single* women. And when they look at remarriage rates, their base is that group out of which remarriages take place—those women who have experienced widowhood or divorce.

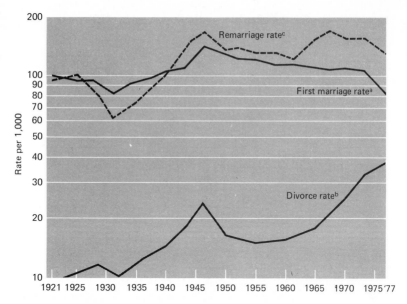

^a First marriages per 1,000 single women 14 to 44 years old.
^b Divorces per 1,000 married women 14 to 44 years old.
^c Remarriages per 1,000 widowed and divorced women 14 to 54 years old.

FIGURE 18-2   Rates of first marriage, divorce, and remarriage for women in the United States: 1921–1977. (Source: Arthur J. Norton and Paul C. Glick, "Marital Instability in America: Past, Present, and Future," in George Levinger and Oliver C. Moles (eds.), Divorce and Separation: Context, Causes, and Consequences. *New York: Basic Books, 1979, p. 8.)*

Using such refined rates for divorce, Norton and Glick (1979:7) have shown that during the three-year period between 1921 and 1923, the average annual rate was 10 divorces for every 1,000 married women. But in the period following World War II (1945–47), the annual average rose to 24 divorces per 1,000 married women. Then, like the crude rates (divorces per 1,000 general population), the refined rates (divorces per 1,000 married women) dropped. For the six-year period between 1954 through 1959, the average annual rate of divorce remained at 15 divorces per 1,000 married women. Then it began to climb again. By the 1975–77 period, there were—on the average— 37 divorces taking place annually for every 1,000 married women.

We must keep in mind, of course, that the word "every" shouldn't be taken too literally. By presenting global divorce rates, we are simply trying to bring the divorce picture into perspective in order to gain an overall view. But other factors enter in, making the likelihood of divorce greater within some populations than others. For example, if we were to look at a group of a thousand married women who had married very young, had little education, and whose family income was low, the number of divorces would be much higher than the number of divorces among another thousand women who had married later and who had more education and higher family incomes.

Speaking of "global" divorce rates, questions may arise about the term in the literal sense. What about divorce rates around the globe? How does the United States compare with other parts of the world in terms of divorce trends?

"The U.S. divorce rate has consistently far exceeded that of any other country," write Glick and Norton (1977:4), "but the gap has been narrowing." Some sociologists suggest that high divorce rates appear to be by-products of industrialization and urbanization. Modernization cuts across ideological, cultural, and national boundaries, making nations highly interdependent and structurally similar. Consequences of these interdependencies and similarities show up not only in such matters as energy distribution, inflation, and raw-material allocations, but also in marriage, family, and divorce patterns to a considerable extent. Especially noteworthy in this regard have been the demands of women throughout the world for greater autonomy, rights, privileges, and rewards (Goode, 1963).

Glick and Norton (1977:4) show how the 1976 rate of 5 divorces per 1,000 population in the United States compared with statistics for other countries considered to have "relatively high divorce rates" in that same year. The divorce rate for Australia was 4.3; and for the Union of Soviet Socialist Republics, the rate was 3.4. Sweden had a divorce rate of 2.7 (down from a peak of 3.3 two years earlier), and the divorce rate for Denmark was 2.5. Finland reported 2.1 divorces per 1,000 population, while Egypt reported 2.0.

Canada's divorce rate (2.4 in 1977) was slightly less than half the United States rate for that year (5.0). But as sociologist John Peters (1979:11) points out, "The divorce rate in Canada varies considerably from province to province." Whereas the rate for Ontario reflects the national average, the rate for British Columbia is much higher (3.3), for example. And the rate for Newfoundland is less than 1 per 1,000 (0.8).

AGE, DURATION OF MARRIAGE, AND DIVORCE

"Teenage marriages are twice as likely to end in divorce as marriages that occur in the twenties," write Glick and Norton (1977:15) of the U.S. Bureau of the Census.

Thus, reality is clouded somewhat by speaking of overall divorce rates without taking into account where the bulk of divorces occur—at lower age levels. The instability of teenage marriages, however, doesn't always show up in teenage divorce statistics because the persons involved may have left their teens by the time the marriage breaks up and the divorce decree is finalized.

Furthermore, the practice of "waiting until the children are grown and gone" may not be as common as is popularly assumed. There are such cases, to be sure; but statistically, such occurrences are not great. The older couples become, the less likely they are to divorce—especially after the early thirties when divorce rates drop sharply. Close to 65 percent of all women whose first marriage ended in divorce had, according to 1975 census figures, become

The older couples become, the less likely they are to divorce. (Catherine Ursillo/Photo Researchers, Inc.)

divorced between the ages of fourteen and twenty-nine. Another 24 percent divorced between the ages of thirty and thirty-nine years. Only 11 percent ended their first marriages in divorce after the age of forty (Glick and Norton, 1977:20).

RACE AND DIVORCE

"Although blacks and whites display generally similar patterns of divorce by social and economic characteristics," Norton and Glick (1979:15) point out, "the incidence of divorce is uniformly higher for blacks than for whites." In 1975, one-fourth of ever-married black men and black women in the thirty-five to forty-four-year age range had experienced a divorce; whereas among ever-married white men in this age bracket, less than one-fifth (19 percent) had experienced divorce, as had 21 percent of ever-married white women. Differences by race, age, and sex may be seen in another way in Table 18-B which shows the number of divorced persons for every 1,000 married persons.

But why should black marriages have higher rates of disruption than

TABLE 18-B   *Number of divorced persons per 1,000 married persons with spouse present by age, race, and sex: March 1977, 1970, 1965, and 1960*

SEX AND YEAR	TOTAL	RACE		AGE	
		WHITE	BLACK	UNDER 45 YEARS	45 YEARS AND OVER
BOTH SEXES					
1977	84	78	161	91	76
1970	47	44	83	44	51
1965	41	39	¹70	36	48
1960	35	33	62	30	42
MALE					
1977	66	63	106	73	59
1970	35	32	62	31	38
1965	34	32	¹56	28	40
1960	28	27	45	22	35
FEMALE					
1977	101	93	217	106	95
1970	60	56	104	55	67
1965	49	46	¹85	44	57
1960	42	38	78	37	51

¹*Black and other races.*

SOURCE: U.S. Bureau of the Census, "Marital Status and Living Arrangements: March, 1977," *Current Population Reports*, series P-20, no. 323, April, 1978, p. 4.

those of whites? A sentence from a census report provides a clue: "Black men . . . with incomes of $10,000 or more in 1969 were more likely than men with lower income—under $3,000—to have a wife living with them." Similarly, black men who had completed high school were more likely still to be married to their first wives than were blacks who had not completed high school. In other words, educational and economic opportunity have a great deal to do with marital stability. But because of discriminatory practices in a white-dominated society, blacks have not had equal access to such opportunities. While blacks in 1969 had greater chances of having intact marriages if their income reached or exceeded $10,000, their chances were cut by the very fact that only 27 percent of blacks had incomes at this level. But 53 percent of white families that year had incomes of $10,000 or above. And by the middle of the 1970s, the median income of black men was only 61 percent of that of white men (U.S. Bureau of the Census, *Current Population Reports*, P-23, no. 46, 1973:3; P-23, no. 42, 1972:31; P-23, no. 80, 1979:28).

SOCIOECONOMIC STATUS AND DIVORCE

Over the years, numerous reports from census data both in the United States and in other developed nations have shown that social status and marital stability are positively related: the greater the social status, the greater the marital stability (Goode, 1962; Cutright, 1971; Norton and Glick, 1979).

Reasons for the association between socioeconomic status and marital stability were already discussed in Chapters 10 through 13. There we saw the part played by an exchange of resources in terms of fulfilling marital rights and duties, and we saw how satisfaction with the instrumental and expressive sides of marriage is closely linked to socioeconomic factors. High marital satisfaction indicates that the partners view the relationship as providing rewards to a greater degree than it exacts costs. Why leave a situation where the profit margin is high? On the other hand, one or both partners may perceive the reward/cost ratio to be so low that the relationship doesn't seem worth maintaining—particularly if alternatives outside the marriage promise greater benefits (Scanzoni, 1979c; Levinger, 1979). Then the question ceases to be "Why leave?" and becomes instead "Why stay?"

Exchange theory also helps us see why particular social groups have higher rates of marital dissolution. For example, the heavy concentration of divorce among young persons cannot be adequately understood until we think in terms of economic factors. Persons with lower education tend to marry earlier. They also tend to hold more traditional gender-role norms and therefore prefer the head-complement form of marriage—or at most, a senior partner–junior partner arrangement. Such wives are socialized to want their husbands to provide for them; yet the lower education and resulting lower incomes of their husbands tend to result in less marital satisfaction and a greater likelihood of divorce. If the wife does go to work, the husband may feel threatened by her independent resources to a far greater extent than would a husband with a higher level of education. Likewise, the lower education of both partners quite likely means that they possess fewer negotiating skills and are less able to work through conflicts.

Or take the matter of higher divorce rates among blacks. Black men have been able to bring relatively fewer resources to their marriages than white men because of economic discrimination by whites and blocked educational and occupational opportunities. In traditional-type marriages, wives may be disappointed that their husbands are not providing them with a desired level of rewards, and the husbands themselves may feel frustrated by their limited access to the opportunity structure. Furthermore, black wives have often entered the work force out of necessity, providing them not only with alternative resources (money earned on their own rather than money provided by their husbands) but also giving them increased power in their marriages. The strong preferences many black women have developed for individualism and egalitarianism may result in their being more insistent on justice in terms of opportunities for self-determination and the pursuit of both extrinsic and intrinsic occupational rewards. Thus, the bargaining in black marriages may be "tougher." Black wives may be less willing than white wives to endure certain kinds of costs (or reduced net profit).

However, a similar situation may be arising in the case of white wives as well. We saw in Chapter 10 that employment rates among married women are increasing, and we have also seen that divorce rates are increasing as well. Historian William O'Neill (1967, chap. 1) sees a connection between the two, beginning in the last century. At the present, there is an additional element on the scene—the push toward equal partnership in marriage rather than simply the matter of "working wives" in the junior-partner sense. And this could mean a continuing rise in divorce rates. Educated women may be expected increasingly to desire marriages that are not only satisfying in terms of companionship and affection, but also marriages that provide opportunities to continue growing as a person, sharing the provider role and power in decision-making. To the degree that such opportunities are not forthcoming, many women may be willing to end their marriages.

We may see one indication of this in the fact that women who marry for the first time after the age of thirty (and thus who presumably have had a chance to demonstrate their self-sufficiency) are more likely to divorce than women who marry in their twenties. And among women with graduate school training, a higher percentage have been divorced than is true of women at any other educational level (Glick and Norton, 1977:16–17). Apparently, such women refuse to settle for unsatisfactory marriage bargains (Scanzoni, 1979c).

Income-Maintenance Programs: Do They Save Marriages? The question may arise: if marital well-being is associated with economic well-being, could the marriages of disadvantaged persons be helped by giving such families more money? Studies of the results of various financial aid plans have thus far provided conflicting answers (Moles, 1979; Galligan and Bahr, 1978; Hannan, Tuma, and Groeneveld, 1978). In some federally funded experimental programs, for example, families which received guaranteed incomes had higher rates of marital dissolution than families in a control group studied for comparison. It appeared that as wives were less dependent upon husbands for sustenance, the more likely they were to leave unsatisfactory marriages in which they had previously felt trapped because of a lack of alternatives. On the other hand, sociologists Richard Galligan and Stephen Bahr (1978:289) have examined data that "suggest that direct income supplements may have little effect on marital dissolution" and point out that other factors related to total family assets and consumership skills must be taken into account in examining the question.

Three other sociologists point out that income-maintenance programs have built into them two possible effects that are sometimes at cross-purposes with each other. The "income effect" could lower divorce rates by decreasing the tensions and conflicts generated by money worries. The "independence effect," on the other hand, works in an opposite direction "by reducing the economic dependence of the more dependent partner (usually the wife) on the marriage" (Hannan, Tuma, and Groeneveld, 1978:611). According to these sociologists, "the effect of an income-maintenance program on marital dissolution depends not only upon the magnitude of the payment a couple receives but also on their level of income before the program, the level of the wife's independence, and the magnitude of the change in the wife's independence." And while pointing out the inconclusiveness of currently available data and calling for further research, two other behavioral scientists observe that "whether or not public assistance payments encourage initial

separation, they do seem to retard the remarriage of the already separated"
(Levinger and Moles, 1979:136).

DIVORCE TRENDS

Since most divorces occur early in marriage, it appears that unsatisfactory
profit and unjust bargains become apparent to one or both spouses before
many years have passed. Many such couples are evidently unable to
negotiate situations of maximum joint profit, and therefore terminate the
marital relationship.

At the same time, Chapters 13 and 14 made clear that disagreements and
conflicts arise in virtually all marriages, and couples are continually faced
with the challenge of handling and resolving them. In some cases, situations
arise which sociologists term *institutionalized conflict*, particularly in matters of
personal habits and preferences. In one marriage, for example, the husband is
unhappy with his wife's obesity and has insisted for years that she lose
weight. At the same time, the wife has tried for years to persuade her
husband to give up smoking. Each resists the other's demands, but neither
one is willing to press the issues to the point of divorce. The conflict has been
incorporated into their marriage, and they accept it as part of their life
together. They avoid *overt* struggles about these matters as much as possible,
even though they feel strongly about them. As a taken-for-granted aspect of
their relationship, the conflict is thus "institutionalized."

The great majority of couples, black and white, seem able to negotiate in
such a way that their marital relationships are maintained. Marital stability is
enhanced if the husband has greater socioeconomic resources to contribute.
On the other hand, tangible resources contributed by wives may be either
beneficial or negative to marital stability. Much depends on how husbands
view wives' working. To some husbands, a wife's breadwinning activities are
viewed as a threat to the husband's provider role—a role he considers to be
uniquely his by virtue of being a male. But to other husbands, a wife's
working may be considered her right to fulfillment, bringing positive benefits
to the marriage as well. Still other husbands may fall somewhere in between
these two categories.

However, in the short run, many men may feel threatened by the
increasingly serious occupational commitment of women; and the ensuing
conflict over different notions of gender roles and marital rights and duties
may, for a time at least, keep the divorce rate at the present high levels. But no
one can say for sure (Scanzoni, 1979c).

WHAT ARE THE CHANCES THAT A MARRIAGE WILL END IN DIVORCE?

Statistics on divorce are often misused and sensationalized (see Scanzoni,
1972, chap. 1). For example, some writers like to compare the number of

marriages taking place with the number of divorces taking place that same year and then draw conclusions from the ratio. If there were, say, 2,000 marriages and 1,000 divorces in a certain locality, the popular media and various political and religious leaders might seize upon such information as evidence that the family is "breaking down," asserting that 1 out of every 2 marriages is ending in divorce and that young people entering marriage have only a 50-50 chance of making it last.

However, such a use of statistics is wrong. The same people getting married in that particular locality that particular year weren't the same people who were getting divorced (with a few possible exceptions, of course). The 1-out-of-2 statistic was based on a comparison of *two different groups!* On the one hand were the single and formerly married people who were taking out a marriage license that year; and on the other hand were persons already married (whether one year or fifty years) who had decided to end their marriages in divorce.

Because of such careless use of statistics, sociologists find it much more satisfactory to speak of crude rates (number of marriages, divorces, births, or whatever per 1,000 population) to have a constant and consistent base for comparison; or better yet, to speak of refined rates, as we saw earlier. These ways of reporting divorce statistics make them far less spectacular. To illustrate: if we take the average annual refined rate of 37 divorces per 1,000 married women during the 1975–77 period, we see that under 4 percent per year chose to end their marriages. In other words, in a given year during that period, over 96 percent of married women remained in their marriages.

However, this obviously doesn't mean that 96 percent of marriages will never be dissolved. Some of the women in the 96 percent "intact marriage" category in 1977 have by now moved into the "divorced" category. And that brings us to the question: what are the chances that a given marriage will end in divorce?

The answer appears to be somewhere in the neighborhood of 1 out of 3. By basing projections on divorce and death rates in a recent period, demographers have estimated that 27 percent of marriages formed in 1950 will end in divorce, as will close to 36 percent of those marriages that took place in 1964 (Preston and McDonald, 1979, as cited in Plateris, 1979:2). According to information from a June, 1975, current population survey by the U.S. Bureau of the Census which focused on persons born in the 1945–49 period, 34 percent of men and 38 percent of women are likely to have their first marriage end in divorce eventually (Glick and Norton, 1977:19).

Other statistics have been based upon a comparison of what percentage of persons end their marriages by a certain anniversary and how this has changed. Demographer Alexander Plateris (1979) has examined data from the National Vital Statistics System to see how the risk of divorce varies according to the year in which persons were married. To do this he studied "marriage cohorts." A *marriage cohort* may be defined as "a group consisting of all couples married during a given calendar year" (p. 1). Plateris emphasizes that "any change in the variety of conditions—social, economic, cultural, demographic—that may influence the overall risk of marital disruption at any given point in time, will affect the various groups of married couples differently, according to the respective stages in their married lives."

One example of change over time that Plateris observed in his cohort study was this: The 1950 marriage cohort reached the level of having one-quarter of the couples divorced by the time of the twenty-fifth wedding anniversary. But one-fourth of couples married in 1952 were already divorced by the time of their twentieth anniversary. For couples married six years later in 1958, one-fourth were divorced before they had a chance to celebrate their fifteenth anniversary. And among couples in the 1965 cohort, one-quarter of the marriages had ended in divorce by the time of the tenth anniversary (p. 2).

CHANGING ATTITUDES TOWARD DIVORCE

In the mid-1970s, a Chicago-area church introduced as part of Sunday worship services the announcement of marital separations. Members of the congregation are encouraged to go up to divorcing couples to express loving concern and acceptance. "We rejoice with Mary and Joe when they get married," the minister is quoted as saying, "but who anguishes with them when their marriage doesn't work?" (*Chicago Daily News*, April 19, 1975:10).

An article in a religious periodical suggested a step further—a ceremony of marital dissolution in which the officiant solemnizes the end of one period in a couple's lives and the beginning of another (Shideler, 1971). Some religious leaders caution against assuming that such ceremonies are promoting or condoning divorce; rather they signify a recognition of the *reality* of divorce and a concern to lend support to the persons affected (Powers, 1976). "A divorce ritual is no more against marriage than a funeral is against life," explains one denominational staff member (quoted in *Newsletter of the National Council on Family Relations Task Force on Divorce and Divorce Reform*, October, 1976:9).

Such support for divorced persons has not always been forthcoming from religious leaders. Around the turn of the century, a writer on Christianity and social issues called divorce the "worst anarchism." Simple anarchy could overthrow the state, Lyman Abbott declared, but the state could be reconstructed. Divorce, however, could destroy the family as an institution and bring about the downfall of civilization. Abbott, like many moral thinkers and writers of his time and since, considered the family (and more specifically, the traditional form of the family in which the husband-father has been the central figure) to be the very foundation of society. Good social order, according to this viewpoint, could not exist side by side with divorce (O'Neill, 1967, chap. 2).

Alarmist cries, religious controversies, and legal debates have surrounded the subject of divorce throughout much of history. Changing attitudes today (such as those reflected in the accounts of church-sanctioned divorce ceremonies) and suggestions for reforming divorce laws appear to be rooted in two basic ideals: (1) a concern for individual rights and best interests and (2) a demanding view of marriage, with high expectations for companionship, empathy, affection, and self-actualization.

INDIVIDUALISM VERSUS FAMILISM

The worth, dignity, and freedom of the individual are cherished ideals in our society. But at the same time, there is concern for that which is most beneficial for society as a whole, which sometimes necessitates putting aside individualistic interests. Again we see the old problem first observed in Chapter 9 in connection with communal living: autonomy (self-determination and self-interest) versus community (in which group interests are given primary emphasis, even if individualistic interests are submerged or sacrificed).

During the divorce controversies that accompanied the rising divorce rates from after the Civil War onward, much of the debate centered around opposing perspectives on marriage. There was the traditional view which held up *familistic* ideals, on the one hand, and an emerging view which emphasized *individualistic* ideals on the other. From the standpoint of *familism*, marriage meant subordinating personal prerogatives and interests for the sake of the family (and ultimately, for the sake of one's society, since the family was held to be the basic unit on which society rested). O'Neill (1967, chap. 3) writes of moral conservatives who demanded that persons in oppressive marriages remain in them no matter how great the pain. Good would come out of even a bad marriage because of spiritual growth resulting from the "purging, purifying influence of suffering." Providing a way out of an unsatisfactory relationship couldn't be reconciled with the ideals of familism. The availability of divorce was thought to discourage a couple's working at their relationship. Furthermore, according to an article in a religious periodical in 1903: "When people understand that they must live together they learn to soften, by mutual accommodation, that yoke which they know they cannot shake off. They become good husbands and good wives, for necessity is a powerful master in teaching the duties it imposes" (quoted in O'Neill, 1967, chap. 2).

From the familistic viewpoint, marriage was seen in terms of permanence, duty, and fidelity; but from the *individualistic* viewpoint, marriage was seen in terms of pragmatism or practical considerations. What would be best for the individuals involved? If a marriage didn't work out, why force persons to remain in it? Wouldn't it be better for the woman and man and for society in general if such marriages could simply end? These kinds of questions bring us to the second reason that attitudes toward divorce began to change.

HIGH EXPECTATIONS FOR MARRIAGE

O'Neill (1967, chap. 1) provides historical evidence that the form of family life idealized in the last century (the Victorian partriarchal family) was actually quite recent on the historical scene, having been gradually emerging since the sixteenth and seventeenth centuries. If we view the modern nuclear family as "an essentially new institution rather than as the last gasp of a dying one," it is easier to understand "why divorce became a necessary part of the family system." O'Neill points out that "when families are large and loose, arouse few expectations, and make few demands, there is no need for divorce. But when families become the center of social organization, their intimacy can become suffocating, their demands unbearable, and their expectations too high to be easily realizable." The system is made workable by the "safety valve" of divorce.

He goes on to emphasize that when divorce is viewed in this way, it can be seen as a necessary feature rather than a flaw in the marriage system. Divorce provides persons who are oppressed in their marrriages with a way of escape, "and those who fail at what is regarded as the most important human activity can gain a second chance."

RELIGION AND DIVORCE

As divorce rates were rising and attitudinal changes were taking place, churches were taking a new look at the divorce question. There was by no means a consensus of opinion. Those who argued according to traditional interpretations of the Bible called for strict opposition to divorce: Had not Jesus taught that man should not put asunder what God has joined together? But as early as the seventeenth century, writer-poet John Milton (1820 edition, pp. 126–128) had argued that this teaching itself legitimates divorce since some persons may not have been "joined by God" even though legally married. During the moral debates over divorce in the late nineteenth century, the same point was made by Carroll Wright, Commissioner of Labor and supervisor of the first United States government statistical report on marriage and divorce. Wright claimed that it was "blasphemous" to call the union of two ill-suited persons "a sacrament on the ground that God hath joined them together." Human beings, not God, were responsible for bad marriages, he argued, and persons who had made a mistake and "missed the divine purpose as well as the civil purpose of marriage" should be provided with a way out (quoted in O'Neill, 1967, chap. 7).

A modern Jewish position on divorce reflects a similar viewpoint: "Once it becomes clear that the marriage has failed irremediably, Judaism recognizes that the union has lost its sanction and its sanctity . . . the husband and wife are no longer joined together by God in any meaningful sense, and society stultifies itself by trying to ignore the truth" (Gordis, 1967:43).

Other arguments that have been used in attempting to reconcile divorce with religious teachings center around the ideals of love, mercy, and compassion, the recognition of human frailties, and the suggestion that "Christ saw marriage as an ideal state rather than an institution to be defended at all costs" (O'Neill, 1967, chap. 3). Even in the Roman Catholic

Church, which traditionally has firmly opposed divorce and remarriage, a great deal of rethinking on the subject is taking place today in spite of the official position.

LAW AND DIVORCE

Persons in the legal profession and legislators have also been forced to reexamine the divorce question in view of changing social conditions and attitudes. Will tougher laws preserve marriages? Will families break up at higher rates if divorces are easier to obtain? Some answers are provided by both history and cross-national comparisons.

Jilted Husband Wins Suit over Stolen Wife

PROVIDENCE, R.I. (AP)—A man who sued his best friend for stealing his wife and won an $80,000 court settlement said Tuesday the case will help protect the family structure in America.

"They said you couldn't win a case like this in 1979, but we did," said Gerald P. Zarella, the jilted husband.

Zarella, of West Warwick, was commenting on a Monday order by a jury that Sidney H. Robinson pay $80,000 of the $1 million requested in the suit.

"People are finally starting to wake up. Pope John Paul has pleaded for family unity, and President Carter has issued statements on it, too," said Zarella, 34. "We need to keep families as tight as possible, and this case may help avoid breakups."

A jury of four men and two women found that Robinson, 36, a building contractor in West Warwick, had had "criminal conversation" with Zarella's 33-year-old wife, Lila.

In his instructions to the jury, Judge Ronald Lagueux defined "criminal conversation" as violation of a spouse's right to "exclusive privileges of physical intercourse."

Robinson's lawyer, Joseph J. McGair, said he will ask for a new trial later this week and for a reduction in the jury's award.

Robinson and the former Mrs. Zarella, who is now his wife, could not be reached for comment.

Zarella said he and Robinson lived about three-quarters of a mile from each other.

He said he learned his wife was seeing Robinson about a year before she filed and received a divorce from him on March 29, 1976.

Zarella said he got into a fight with Robinson after learning of the affair and was arrested and jailed. He said Robinson agreed to drop charges if Zarella signed a release that prohibited him from suing for alienation of affection.

He signed the release and then started researching the laws on criminal conversation. He filed suit against Robinson on Jan. 11, 1977.

Zarella, who has custody of the two children, said he has filed a second suit against Robinson seeking $750,000 for his children. That suit is in the pre-trial stage.

SOURCE: Greensboro (N.C.) Daily News, October 24, 1979.

O'Neill (1967, chap. 1) points out that divorces were largely restricted to middle- and upper-class persons when it was both difficult and expensive to obtain a divorce. "But once the legal restraints on divorce were eased, divorce tended to become a lower-class phenomenon." However, this doesn't mean that less restrictive divorce laws *cause* the breakup of lower-status families. We saw earlier that the "glue" that holds a marriage together is not the law but rather the rewards it provides the partners. Spouses who perceive the costs to exceed the rewards may want to leave the relationship *without* divorce. Desertion and separation (sometimes called the "poor person's divorce") do not grant freedom to remarry as divorce does, but they do provide escape from an unsatisfactory marriage. However, when divorces may be obtained more easily, broken marriages among persons with limited opportunities in the economic system are able to take the divorce route rather than the desertion route.

Max Rheinstein (1972:406), a professor of law, has concluded after thorough research on divorce in the United States and across the world that "a strict statute law of divorce is not an effective means to prevent or even to reduce the incidence of marriage breakdown." Responding to those who blame divorce for "not only broken homes but broken lives," Rheinstein argues that what may harm homes and lives isn't divorce but rather the breakdown of the marriage that precedes divorce. Divorce is only a legal recognition that the marriage has already broken down; it restores the man and woman to freedom to enter new marital relationships. The freedom of remarriage can be good for society, says Rheinstein (chap. 5), because "it reopens the way for the creation of new homes for the ex-spouses and their children, a home . . . which at least holds the possibility of being more harmonious than that which has broken down."

In his opinion and that of many other concerned persons, society would be better served and marital stability better promoted by helping people to form and maintain satisfactory marriage relationships rather than tightening laws to keep persons locked in unsatisfactory relationships. Even the total banning of divorce wouldn't prevent marital breakups. A number of Latin American countries, for example, permit no divorce whatsoever, but evasive practices have been devised by which persons (especially those with means) do find ways out of unsatisfactory marriages (Rheinstein, 1972, chap. 16).

Therefore, there is a move today to make laws which will help alleviate some of the pain of divorce rather than adding to that pain through strict and severe legal requirements. One evidence of change is gradual movement away from the *adversary* approach, in which one partner sues the other for divorce (John Doe versus Mary Doe), toward divorce by mutual consent. The concept of "grounds for divorce" (adultery, cruelty, desertion, nonsupport, drunkenness, and so on) is giving way to the simple recognition of a *marital breakdown* and the partners' desire to separate. The National Conference of Commissioners on Uniform State Laws has proposed a model no-fault divorce law which would make marriage a totally voluntary relationship,

No Divorce, but Brazilians Find a Way

RIO DE JANEIRO—Lea Tavora, a 38-year-old Brazilian psychologist, has been separated from her husband for years and is living with Schmil Ochs, who is separated from his wife.

Each has a daughter by previous marriage. They have a son born out of wedlock.

For Mrs. Tavora and many thousands of Brazilians, Argentines and other Latin Americans whose countries refuse to recognize divorce and remarriage, the formation of new families has created few legal problems and little social stigma. . . .

"Desquites"—as legal separations are called in Brazil— and illegal second marriages have become an accepted part of life among the middle and upper class in this largest Roman Catholic country in the world. . . .

Although politicians have been struggling for 75 years to legalize divorce and have met steadfast resistance from the church and conservative sentiment, there are many legal protections for unlawful second marriages.

A separated woman who forms another family may be considered a concubine in the eyes of the law, but at the same time she has almost the same rights as a legal wife—including inheritance, accident insurance, the right to use her companion's name, and alimony should she separate again. Moreover, children born technically out of wedlock in illegal second marriages are considered legitimate.

"There is no stigma on my kids because of my situation," Mrs. Tavora asserted, recalling a recent incident at her 11-year-old daughter's school.

Mrs. Tavora was asked to attend a parent-teacher meeting. A problem had arisen because a majority of the students had parents who had entered a second marriage, and the children were teasing classmates whose parents were legally married.

The situation today is far different from that of just two decades ago, when a separated woman and her children were regarded as second-class citizens. Faced with disdain, suspicion and hostility, a separated woman encountered problems finding a job or remaining with her circle of friends and acquaintances.

The fact that the job market has opened up so considerably in recent years, particularly for professionals, has provided an important cushion for women.

SOURCE: Mery Galanternick, *The New York Times*, August 22, 1976, p. 60.

"lasting legally only so long as it meets the needs of both partners," emphasizes sociologist Jessie Bernard (1970). Over half of the states in the United States already have some no-fault provisions for divorce (Wright and Stetson, 1978). Bernard points out that sometimes state legislators hesitate to legitimize divorce by mutual consent because they fear that one partner might force or maneuver an unwilling partner to give consent. "But if one party is adamant in his or her insistence on divorce, the marriage has actually broken down," she writes. Forcing a couple to live together under legal duress wouldn't mean the marriage itself was somehow put together again. "The no-fault divorce recognizes this bitter reality."

At the same time, Bernard is convinced that divorce is not likely ever to become matter-of-fact. "It will probably always be an extremely painful experience for most people, as breaking ties always is, even outside of marriage," she emphasizes. But at the same time, "the idea of forcing people to remain together is repugnant to the present world view" (see also Wright and Stetson, 1978).

ALIMONY AND CHANGING IDEAS ABOUT MARRIAGE, DIVORCE, AND GENDER ROLES

One of the biggest differences between no-fault and traditional divorce law may be seen in the redefinition of alimony and its purpose. (The word comes from the Latin *alimonia* meaning "nourishment, sustenance.")

Sociologists Lenore Weitzman and Ruth Dixon (1976), in a careful and thorough analysis of changes in ideas about alimony, point out that traditional notions about its role and purpose were tied to traditional notions of gender roles in marriage. Alimony was designed to insure that wives were compensated for fulfilling their marital duties through devotion to homemaking, and it was also designed to reinforce the responsibility of husbands for supporting their wives—even if the marriage ended in divorce. The very existence of alimony reflected the legitimacy of the norms surrounding the exchanges of marital rights and duties as spelled out in the traditional marriage pattern. Furthermore, say these sociologists, in addition to compensating wives for past services and enforcing husbands' support obligations, alimony served as a way of punishing the person considered "at fault," while rewarding the innocent party. If a husband was considered at fault in the divorce, he could be penalized by being required to pay high alimony payments. If the wife was considered guilty (for example, in cases of adultery), she could be penalized by not being awarded alimony.

Under no-fault legislation, all such notions are challenged and changed. Weitzman and Dixon show that rather than being used to punish alleged wrongdoing and to reinforce traditional gender roles, the no-fault approach calls for a new concept of alimony based solely on the *needs* of the respective parties. Divorce is not thought of in terms of assigning blame to either person; thus the idea of alimony-as-punishment is discarded. So is the idea of alimony as compensation for a homemaker's services—which is the reason some feminists feel this aspect of newer divorce laws is unjust (see also Eisler, 1977).

According to provisions of the California Family Law Act of 1969 with its pioneering no-fault approach to divorce, judges are asked to set alimony by considering "the circumstances of the respective parties, including the duration of the marriage, and the ability of the supported spouse to engage in gainful employment without interfering with the interests of the children of the parties in the custody of each spouse" (Civil Code Section 4801, as quoted in Weitzman and Dixon, p. 11).

For the supported spouse (which is usually the wife), there exist three types of financial provision, two of which are considered temporary until the formerly supported spouse is capable of self-support. Weitzman and Dixon use the term *transitional support* for what is sometimes called "retraining support" or "support for displaced homemakers." The idea is that a woman who has devoted her life to homemaking may need to learn or update occupational skills to gain employment outside the home. Once she can support herself, she would no longer need or receive the transitional support payments from her former husband.

Another kind of support is *custodial support,* which Weitzman and Dixon are careful to distinguish from *child* support, which is support for the children's needs. Custodial support provides income for the parent who is caring for the children, freeing her or him to be a full-time caretaker, especially while children are very young. A third kind of financial provision sometimes granted under the "new alimony" system is what Weitzman and Dixon describe as *support insurance* and compare to a "disability pension." It is support awarded to older women who are divorced after a long marriage and are not able to be retrained for gainful employment.

When it comes down to the practical application of the new laws, however, Weitzman and Dixon found they make little difference. They call attention to the "alimony myth"—the belief that most divorced women receive alimony and that most divorced men pay it. Their data showed that under the new California law, only 15 percent of women receive alimony; and only 20 percent received it under the old law. Limited evidence from other states indicates similar percentages. These researchers conclude that "alimony can only be an instrument for justice in higher-income families where there is sufficient income to award support. But the vast majority of all divorcing women come from lower-income families—families in which a sufficient support award is impractical, if not impossible" (p. 31).

AFTER DIVORCE

Personal adjustment after divorce was a neglected area of study until Waller published his research and theoretical insights on the subject in 1930. A quarter of a century went by before another significant sociological work was published in an effort to understand how persons reorganize their lives after divorce—this time research on divorced women conducted in the Detroit metropolitan area by William Goode (1956). More recently, both behavioral scientists and family counselors have been increasingly focusing attention on postdivorce problems and challenges (Bohannan, 1970; Krantzler, 1973; Bloom et al., 1979; Weiss, 1975; Spanier and Casto, 1979).

Goode (1956, chap. 1) saw the process of readjustment in terms of changes in roles. A person leaves the role of husband or wife and must take on a new role. There are also changes and disruptions in existing social relationships when one is no longer part of a married pair. Postdivorce adjustment, according to Goode, involves incorporating such changes and disruptions into the individual's life in such a way that he or she moves beyond thinking of the prior divorce as the "primary point of reference." In other words, the person ceases to think in terms of "I am an ex-wife (or ex-husband)" but rather in terms of being an individual in one's own right.

Divorce involves a time of transition and grief, which isn't always easy since societal expectations are unclear (people wonder whether to extend sympathy or congratulations after a divorce), and support is often lacking both with regard to the mourning process itself and in terms of helping persons cope with building a new life. Divorce counselor Mel Krantzler (1973) speaks of divorce as "the death of a relationship" and suggests that a time of grief is essential for emotional healing just as when an actual person dies. In divorce, the individual is not necessarily mourning the fact that the ex-spouse is gone or wishing that he or she would return—the divorce itself signifies their disinclination to live together satisfactorily. What is happening is grief over the loss of the rewards no longer held out by the relationship, a realization that (in the words of a film title and song, popular in the 1970s) "the way we were" has ended. The enrichment found in the marital partnership has ceased to exist. The net profit is gone.

There is a sense of diminishment of one's very own self in the loss. Waller (1930, chap. 5) recognized this when he wrote:

> There is always an element of betrayal when we break with a friend, and our distress is made all the more poignant because we have betrayed not only the friend but the part of us that was in him. . . . The pathos of a marital break attaches . . . to the very essence of the process by which those who have been one flesh are made separate. Personalities that have been fused by participation in common enterprises and that are held together by their common memories can only be hewn apart at the expense of great psychic travail.

Persons who once learned to live together must now undergo learning to live apart. The interdependence, the daily routines, the regularized sex life, the companionship, the built-in habit systems that have developed over time as the two persons shared a life together—all are changed by divorce.

The adjustment is often difficult. The individual may begin longing for the ex-spouse and the rewards the relationship once held, even though he or she knows this chapter in life is closed and indeed may want it to remain closed. "The memory of a person [may be] dear after the person is dear no more," observed Waller (p. 135). He writes of a man who reported looking for the mail to arrive at all times of the day, even though he knew there couldn't possibly be any more for him. The man had ambivalent feelings, both longing for and dreading letters from his ex-wife (p. 54).

At the time of the breakup, the marriage partners may expect the divorce to bring feelings of relief and happiness and may be surprised at the sadness and moments of nostalgia that come up. Part of the reason may lie in what Bohannan (1970) sees as a *reversal* of the courtship process and the "rewarding sensation" of knowing one has been selected out of the whole world.

Divorce means being de-selected, and "it punishes almost as much as the engagement and the wedding are rewarding" (p. 33).

Yet for many couples an unsatisfactory marriage can be more punishing than divorce. Krantzler (1973, chap. 8) quotes poet-novelist Herman Hesse, himself twice divorced, to show that divorce may open the way for some persons to experience a new exchange of rewards and a creative, fulfilling life that would have been impossible otherwise. "Be ready bravely and without remorse," wrote Hesse, "to find new light that old ties cannot give."

CHILDREN AND DIVORCE

Even though life after divorce is a new life, ties with the old life may remain for some time. The after-divorce "continuities" may include such matters as occasionally helping a former spouse with some household chore, picking up mail at the old address, even going out to dinner or shopping together during the "uncoupling" process (Vaughan, 1979). The biggest continuity of all, as might be expected, is the ongoing tie that exists between the former spouses because of their shared interest in the children born or adopted during their marriage. They may no longer be wife and husband, but they are still Mom and Dad.

CHILDREN AS A LINK BETWEEN DIVORCED PARENTS

"Just as the relationship between married spouses is a critical determinant of family interaction," writes social scientist Constance Ahrons (1979:500–501), "so, too, is the relationship between divorced spouses critical to divorced family reorganization and interaction. One of the most stressful tasks facing divorced parents is the redefinition of their coparental relationship."

Prior to the divorce, the two persons each held the position of spouse-parent within the family. Now they must learn to continue their shared parental relationship to their children and also the shared relationship they have *with one another* on account of that parenting, but at the same time they are expected to learn to discard the spouse role that was formerly so intricately tied to the parent role. It's often a difficult task, because even the parental role is now different and has to be redefined as part of a new life-style in which the parents live separately. Ahrons suggests that a whole new family system comes into being:

> The reorganization of the nuclear family through divorce frequently results in the establishment of two households, maternal and paternal. These two interrelated households, or nuclei of the child's family of orientation, form one family system— *a binuclear family system*. The centrality of each of these households will vary among postdivorce families. Some families make very distinct divisions between the child's primary and secondary homes, whereas in other families these distinctions may be blurred and both homes have primary importance. (p. 500)

One example of such blurring observed among Ahrons' own sample of divorced parents was that of the divorced couple who owned and lived in the same duplex, with the mother occupying one half, the father in the other half, and the children moving freely between the two households. Child psychiatrist Richard Gardner (1977) refers to a similar situation in which former spouses lived in separate wings of a large house, with the children's rooms located in between. Such situations are, however, not usual.

Ahrons' sample consisted of forty-one divorced parents to whom the courts had awarded joint custody of their children and thus the term *binuclear family system* may be especially appropriate. In joint custody, both parents have "full custodial rights" and are given "an equal voice in the children's upbringing, education, and general welfare" (Cox and Cease, 1978:11–12). Since the parents are expected to consult with one another about important matters involving their children and in other ways share in their children's lives, a certain amount of postdivorce interaction between the two parents is necessary. The amount of such interaction and how the divorced parties may feel about it varies.

Ahrons (1979:505) found a continuum of "relational styles" among the divorced spouses in her sample, ranging from "my former spouse as best friend" to "my former spouse as bitter enemy," with most respondents falling somewhere in between as "neither friend nor foe."

The "best friend" former spouses were those who showed evidence of respect and caring for one another after the divorce, sometimes sharing news or seeking advice as *friends* as well as coparents. Some had business partnerships together. Such divorced parents chose to live near enough to have frequent get-togethers so that the children could share experiences with both parents at the same time in child-centered fun times, outings, and family conferences.

Divorced parents in Ahrons' second or "neither friend nor foe" category kept in-person contact to a minimum, discussing by phone most issues that concerned the children. When such parents did get together, the occasion was usually some special event in the child's life—perhaps a birthday or a performance in a school play or sports activity. "There was more unresolved anger in these former spousal relationships than in the first pattern," writes Ahrons, "and the joining together to share the child's experience was marked with some discomfort and formality. The parents had some disagreements about each other's child-rearing practices but most had decided to not interfere with the way the other parent related to the child" (p. 511).

Unlike parents in the "best friend" and "neither friend nor foe" categories, the third category observed by Ahrons— the "bitter enemies" category—chose not to get together at all. Even upon occasions in their children's lives that brought them to the same place, such as graduation ceremonies, these divorced parents did not sit together nor otherwise interact except for polite formalities. Ahrons points out that parents in this category tended to have custody arrangements that were closer to the traditional sole custody pattern, in that one parent had physical custody and a higher degree of control over the child's life than the other. "One illuminating finding of this study is that joint custody rights are not synonymous with equal parental responsibility," reports Ahrons (p. 508)—although, of course, that is the ideal that many strive for.

CHILD CUSTODY ARRANGEMENTS

Up until the middle of the nineteenth century, custody of children after a divorce was almost always given to the father. Some English judges had reasoned that God had appointed the father to be guardian of the child and that, furthermore, fathers could better prepare children for life since they (and not mothers) were involved in society and understood the workings of society. American judges tended to rule according to "best interests of the child" rather than the absolute or divine right of fathers, but the practical outcome of their decisions and the reasoning behind them echoed their English counterparts and English common law. Fathers were generally awarded custody because they were the financial supporters of the children, considered to be the natural protectors of both children and women, and better equipped to educate children for participation in society (Weiss, 1979:325–326).

Then something happened so that "preference for the mother was the dominant judicial outlook from the time of the Civil War through the 1960s," writes sociologist Robert Weiss (1979:326). What happened was a changed attitude toward the family; it came to be viewed as a haven *from* a cold, impersonal world rather than a school of preparation *for* that world. Under the older way of thinking about childrearing, the "best interests of the child" seemed to assign the custodial role to the father—the one who could train the child for society. Under the newer way of thinking, the child's best interests seemed to decree that the mother have the custodial role, since she was the one who could nurture and insulate the child from the hard knocks of life and patiently and soothingly help the child adjust to his or her environment. Ideas about a unique psychological bond between a mother and child and exaggerated claims about the child's needs for the special love only a mother was thought capable of giving led to "the doctrine of tender years"—the term used in law to indicate that the mother, if she is considered fit, should be granted custody of the children. More than half the states (twenty-seven) have statutes based on the tender years doctrine, and even in thirteen of the states with statutes giving both parents equal rights to custody, "the tender years doctrine still prevails" (Cox and Cease, 1978:12).

Yet, there are indications that another major shift is occurring. Just as attitudes in the 1860s changed from preference for the father in custody decisions, favoring the mother instead; in the 1960s, attitudes began showing signs of change from a preference for the mother to the notion that the sex of the custodial parent is irrelevant (Weiss, 1979:325–328). What arrangement serves the child's best interests according to the individual case is increasingly

Change Comes Slowly

With the social changes which have occurred in the last twenty years, particularly the blurring of traditional roles with an increase of employed mothers and increased involvement of fathers in household affairs, one might expect some erosion of the decided advantage realized by mothers in custody disputes; however, in this State, the impact of this revolution has yet to be felt to any substantial degree. Within the last two years, a Justice of the Georgia Supreme Court observed:

> *I believe that the Supreme Judge of the Universe had the first discretion, and it was he who ordained that the female of the species should replenish the earth, and built into her instincts and intuitions which aid a mother in protecting and raising her young. This love is not severed when the umbilical cord is cut. Yes, I believe the calf should follow the cow.*

SOURCE: Lucy S. McGough, *The Legal Status of Homemakers in Georgia* (Washington, D.C.: Homemakers' Committee of the National Commission on the Observance of International Women's Year, 1977), p. 17.

seen as what matters. Some states have changed their laws to reflect this. However, as Weiss notes, "Judges' courtroom practice may be changing more slowly than statute law" (p. 327). "If present practice continues, the custody of over 90 percent of these children will be entrusted to their mothers" (p. 324) (see also Weitzman and Dixon, 1979).

Sole custody is the name given to the custody arrangement in which one parent (whether the mother or the father) is given full responsibility for the child, who lives with that parent and is under that parent's control. The other parent (the noncustodial parent) is granted visitation rights but "has no legal right to make decisions regarding the rearing of the child" (Cox and Cease, 1978:10). However, even in this arrangement, the parents may discuss with one another certain major concerns and decisions with regard to their children.

Under *divided custody* or *alternating custody* arrangements, one parent has physical custody and legal authority for one designated period of time, and then the other parent has such responsibility for the child during another period of time. In other words, the parents take turns being solo parents with legal custody. "The most common divided custody arrangements provide for the children to spend alternating six-month periods with each parent, if the parents live in the same school district, or nine months with one parent and three months with the other if they live in different districts," explain two specialists in family law and counseling (Cox and Cease, 1978:10).

Split custody is another arrangement sometimes granted by courts. In split custody, the children are split up. One parent is given custody over some of the children, while the rest of the children will be under the other parent's custody.

Earlier, we referred to *joint custody* in which both parents are granted full custodial rights and are equally responsible for the child—not just during alternating periods but all the time. This arrangement, while apparently increasingly popular with many parents, is often discouraged by the courts which favor instead sole custody arrangements (Woolley, 1978; Cox and Cease, 1978). The reason for skepticism among some legal authorities usually relates to a belief that two people who can't get along in a marriage relationship aren't likely to agree on how to rear their children and also that

Societal Attitudes Have Presented Special Difficulties for Homosexual Parents Seeking Custody of Their Children

Sandy P. was abandoned by her husband while she was pregnant with her second child. At the hearing for divorce he denied paternity in an attempt to avoid an order for child support.

For seven years, Sandy raised her daughters alone. Although Sandy is a lesbian, at no time did her lover live in the house.

Sandy had neither psychological nor financial support from her ex-husband. His neglect was so complete that even the younger child's near fatal illness did not stir him to visit. When he sued for custody of both girls he was being pressed by the county to pay nearly $5,000 in back child support payments.

In court, the children's teachers and school principal testified that Sandy attended a community college, worked, was a girl scout leader, and showed herself to be an exemplary and devoted mother. Testimony introduced noted that her performance in Parent Effectiveness Training was such that she was invited to teach a course in the program.

During the seven-day hearing, a court-appointed psychiatrist, who had been recommended by the father's attorney, testified that the children were normal, well adjusted girls who had suffered no adverse effects from their mother's lesbianism. He also stated that the younger child, who barely knew her father, would be psychologically harmed by being moved out of the stable home her mother had provided all her young life.

The judicial decision acknowledged that Sandy was a warm and loving mother who adequately cared for her children. Nevertheless, custody was moved to the father solely on the basis of the lesbian relationship.

A LEGAL OVERVIEW

Sandy's case is typical; present case law both in family court and on appeal means odds on getting custody are greater than 90 percent against a woman who has had a lesbian relationship no matter how short its duration. The ten-year recorded history of these custody cases shows that not only the biological father, but also maternal and paternal grandparents, other relatives and the state fall into the plus 90 percent probability ratio.

SOURCE: Rosalie C. Davies, "Representing the Lesbian Mother," *Family Advocate* (A journal of the Family Law Section of the American Bar Association), vol. 1 (Winter, 1979), p. 21.

children's lives will lack stability without one place called "home" and one parent in charge. Yet, as Ahrons (1979) showed in the research we have already discussed, joint custody need not mean that a child is torn between two separate worlds but is rather incorporated into a binuclear *family system* that includes both parents, even though they are in two different households. The whole point of joint custody contrasts with the adversary idea of divorce in which the former spouses are considered bitter antagonists, with the children caught in between. "Joint custody decisions are based on the presumption that both adults are competent, responsible parents who want to continue to relate with their children, although they are choosing to terminate the spousal bond," emphasizes Ahrons (p. 513). Her research, as well as that of others (for example, Woolley, 1978), indicates a wide variety of innovative ways in which divorced parents work out the practical aspects of joint custody. One little girl in such an arrangement, far from feeling divided in her loyalties, explained, "My parents love me enough to let me love both of them" (Woolley, p. 33).

EFFECTS OF DIVORCE ON CHILDREN

Estimates based on government statistics suggest that nearly 1 out of 3 children presently growing up in the United States will see their parents' marriages end in divorce (Bane, 1979; Bumpass and Rindfuss, 1979). Or to look at it another way: according to the National Center for Health Statistics, 55 percent of divorces involved children in 1977 (latest available statistics). And during that same year, 17 children out of every 1,000 experienced parental divorce, as compared to about 10 per 1,000 ten years earlier, and 6 per 1,000 ten years before that (*Monthly Vital Statistics Report*, vol. 28, no. 2, 1979). (See Table 18-C.)

The question quite naturally arises: what does divorce do to these children numbering over a million annually? How does divorce affect their lives? No one simple answer can be given, because the questions themselves have so many dimensions and so many factors must be taken into account. Research up to this point has been limited and has yielded conflicting results. "Some studies argue that there is little measurable impact of divorce on the lives of children," write sociologists Larry Bumpass and Ronald Rindfuss (1979:50), "while others have attributed all manner of social ills to this experience."

Bumpass and Rindfuss refer to studies that show that children from disrupted families tend to have lower socioeconomic and educational attainments over the long-term and also higher rates of instability in their own marriages. Rather than settling the question of the consequences of divorce in the lives of children, however, such findings may be telling us less about divorce per se than about factors associated with divorce and the postdivorce period—especially the likelihood of economic hardship. Single-parent families—particularly those headed by mothers—are likely to find their living

TABLE 18-C   *Estimated number of children involved in divorces and annulments, average number of children per decree, and rate per 1,000 children under eighteen years of age: United States, 1954–77*
[Refers only to events occurring within the United States. For 1960–77 estimated from frequencies based on sample; for all other years estimated from total counts.]

YEAR	ESTIMATED NUMBER OF CHILDREN INVOLVED	AVERAGE NUMBER OF CHILDREN PER DECREE	RATE PER 1,000 CHILDREN UNDER 18 YEARS OF AGE
1977	1,095,000	1.00	17.0
1976	1,117,000	1.03	17.1
1975	1,123,000	1.08	16.9
1974	1,099,000	1.12	16.3
1973	1,079,000	1.17	15.8
1972	1,021,000	1.20	14.8
1971	946,000	1.22	13.6
1970	870,000	1.22	12.5
1969	840,000	1.31	11.9
1968	784,000	1.34	11.1
1967	701,000	1.34	9.9
1966	669,000	1.34	9.5
1965	630,000	1.32	8.9
1964	613,000	1.36	8.7
1963	562,000	1.31	8.2
1962	532,000	1.29	7.9
1961	516,000	1.25	7.8
1960	463,000	1.18	7.2
1959	468,000	1.18	7.5
1958	398,000	1.08	6.5
1957	379,000	0.99	6.4
1956	361,000	0.95	6.3
1955	347,000	0.92	6.3
1954	341,000	0.90	6.4

SOURCE: U.S. Department of Health, Education, and Welfare National Center for Health Statistics, "Final Divorce Statistics, 1977," *Monthly Vital Statistics Report*, vol. 28, no. 2, May 16, 1979, p. 5.

standard lower than before the divorce. The problem is especially acute at lower status levels. Mary Jo Bane (1979), a specialist in urban studies, in calling attention to the fact that lower-income families have higher rates of both divorce and death than higher-income families, concludes that "one would expect both men and women in disrupted marriages to be somewhat worse off than other families" because they are more likely to come from the ranks of the poor to begin with (p. 238). "These economic problems ought to be the main concern of policy-makers who worry about the children of marital disruption," asserts Bane (p. 286).

A similar point comes through in Bumpass and Rindfuss's (1979) analysis of a large national probability sample of mothers. They found, for example, that among white children whose mothers had not completed high school, 33 percent experienced a disrupted family before the children reached age fifteen, as compared to one-fifth of those children whose mothers had finished high school. "A mother's age at the birth of her child is correlated with education," say these researchers, "but the differences by mother's age are even more pronounced. Children born to mothers under the age of 20 are more than twice as likely to experience a disrupted family than children born to mothers aged 25 or older (39% vs. 15%); furthermore, they are, on the average, six years younger at the time of disruption (4.8 vs. 10.8 years of age)" (p. 60).

Among white children in the sample, about 1 out of 6 had experienced the disruption of the parents' marriage by age five. Among black children (for reasons we suggested earlier in this chapter), the rates were more than double those of whites, with more than 2 out of 5 black children experiencing marital disruption by age five, and 3 out of every 5 likely to experience the breakup of their parents' marriages before the children reached age sixteen. Bumpass and Rindfuss also point to "another significant aspect of children's experience with marital disruption that is missed by divorce statistics":

> Many children are born after the marital dissolution but before their mother remarries. Among twice-married women in 1970, more than one-fourth had given birth between separation and remarriage. (p. 52)

Such births complicate even further the economic hardship faced by many divorced mothers rearing children alone.

But of course, not all divorced mothers were married at an early age and lacked educational and economic opportunities; and regardless of a family's socioeconomic status, financial hardship isn't the only consideration to be taken into account in assessing the effects of divorce on children's lives. Children may undergo a great deal of personal pain when their parents' marriage ends (Gardner, 1977, chap. 4). Children sometimes blame themselves, feeling that they themselves somehow "caused" the divorce; or they may feel that the parent who left has rejected them rather than the marital partner. They may feel hurt, confused, angry, and insecure. They may display symptoms of grief that are similar to grief reaction in cases of death. They may entertain fantasies about their parents' reconciliation. After all, divorce is a crisis experience. But it need not be viewed as an absolute disaster with inevitably disastrous effects, damaging the child for life (Luepnitz, 1979).

In interviews with a small sample of twenty-four college students whose parents had divorced before the respondents were sixteen years old, psychologist Deborah Luepnitz (1979) found that exactly half the students reported that the initial conflict between their parents was what the students found most difficult and stress-producing. In other words, the predivorce period was harder for them as children than was the divorce itself. Another one-fourth found the postdivorce period the most difficult, and 8 percent found the transition period between the time of the announcement and the time their fathers moved out to be hardest. The remaining 16 percent reported no stress over their parents' divorce. Three of the four students reporting *no* divorce-linked stress attributed this to the lack of bitter antagonism between the parents during the divorce process, the supportiveness of parents, friends, and siblings, and the fact that they continued to have free access to both parents after the divorce. The other student reporting no stress over the divorce indicated relief that the family was now free of a father who had been violent and in constant trouble with the law.

Luepnitz suggests that perhaps "much of the literature on children of divorce ought to be retitled 'children of marital conflict' " because symptoms often thought to be reactions to divorce were reported in her subjects "in response to marital fighting *years* before they became 'children of divorce' " (p. 84). It may be far more distressing for a child to live in a conflict-ridden home than to come from a broken one. A number of Luepnitz's subjects reported that before age nine they experienced severe physical reactions to their parents' fighting—vomiting, losing or gaining weight, hair loss, even an ulcer.

Other research likewise indicates the detrimental effects of parental conflict. "It doesn't seem to matter if the conflict leads to separation or divorce," writes educator Cynthia Longfellow (1979) after a review of numerous studies. "The child who experiences his [or her] parents' marital discord is at greater psychiatric risk" (p. 305). Longfellow suggests that little is accomplished by looking for one broad-reaching answer to the question of divorce and its impact on children; rather we should be endeavoring to sort out those aspects of divorce that are troubling to children: for example, life-event changes (not only one parent's moving out, but possibly less income available, the necessity of moving to another location, and so on), parental depression, absence of adequate support networks for the single mother in many cases, the parental conflict surrounding the divorce, and how the divorce is understood and processed by the individual child.

SOLO PARENTING AFTER DIVORCE

An extensive review of the research literature, as well as a study they themselves conducted, also leads sociologists Helen Raschke and Vernon Raschke (1979) to conclude that it would be beneficial "to give more attention to conflict and its effects on children in all family forms, and less attention to ferreting out the 'ills' of the single-parent family" (p. 373).

Among the family forms examined by the Raschkes were those with both parents present (intact families), single-parent families, reconstituted families (new families brought into being through the remarriage of a divorced or widowed parent), and arrangements in which children lived with relatives or in foster homes. The particular *form* of a child's family was found to make no significant difference in the child's self-concept. (These researchers suggest that a child's self-concept "can be interpreted as a general measure of personal and social adjustment," [p. 369].) What *did* make a difference was whether or not children perceived an atmosphere of conflict in their families. Where there was greater conflict, the self-concept of the children was significantly lower. On the other hand, perceived parental happiness was positively correlated with children's self-concept—regardless of whether the family was intact, reconstituted, or a single-parent arrangement. The happier the child's parent or parents, the higher the self-concept of the child. Pointing out that their study of 289 third-, sixth-, and eighth-graders may not provide answers to all the questions surrounding the topic, Raschke and Raschke say one thing is sure: it doesn't provide any support for "the cliché that 'broken homes yield broken young lives'." Thus, the study "should play a role in helping to place the single-parent family in better perspective" (p. 373).

As Table 18-D shows, while 4 out of 5 children live with two parents (including families where one parent is a stepparent), the remaining children live, for the most part, in single-parent families. Table 18-D compares percentages of both black and white children living in each family arrangement in 1976, and Table 18-E shows the association between economic factors and likelihood of living in a solo-parent family. The likelihood goes up as income goes down.

Sixteen percent of children in the United States live with their mothers in a solo-parent situation, and only 1 percent of children live with their fathers in such an arrangement. However, this percentage may be expected to grow as no-fault divorce laws become more widespread and as custody decisions come to be based on factors other than the "tender years doctrine" with its assumption that mothers are automatically the better custodians. Two researchers who have given special attention to single-parent fatherhood refer to several dramatic changes in recent domestic litigation: (1) lawyers are increasingly willing to pursue cases of male custody, (2) more fathers are

TABLE 18-D   *Persons under eighteen years old,* by presence of parents and whether living with mother only, by marital status of mother: 1976*

LIVING ARRANGEMENT AND MARITAL STATUS OF MOTHER	PERCENTAGE IN EACH CATEGORY		
	TOTAL	WHITE	BLACK
Living with both parents	80.0	85.2	49.6
Living with mother only	15.8	11.8	40.1
Separated	4.9	3.1	16.0
Other married, husband absent	0.9	0.7	1.8
Widowed	2.1	1.6	5.1
Divorced	6.2	5.9	8.3
Single	1.7	0.5	8.8
Living with father only	1.2	1.2	1.5
Living with neither parent	3.0	1.9	8.8

*Excludes persons under 18 years old who were heads or wives of heads of families or subfamilies.
SOURCE: U.S. Bureau of Census, "Marital Status and Living Arrangements, March 1976," *Current Population Reports*, P-20, no. 306, January, 1977, p. 6.

TABLE 18-E   *Percent of own children living with both parents, by family income: 1960, 1970, and 1975*
(*Income in current dollars and refers to income received during 1959, 1969, and 1974*)

YEAR AND FAMILY INCOME	OWN BLACK CHILDREN		OWN WHITE CHILDREN	
	PERCENT LIVING WITH—		PERCENT LIVING WITH—	
	BOTH PARENTS	ONE PARENT	BOTH PARENTS	ONE PARENT
1960				
Total, own children	75	25	93	7
Under $4,000	64	36	77	23
$4,000 to $5,999	87	13	92	8
$6,000 to $7,999	92	8	96	4
$8,000 to $9,999	89	11	97	3
$10,000 and over	86	14	97	3
$10,000 to $14,999	87	13	97	3
$15,000 and over	81	19	97	3
1970				
Total, own children	65	35	91	9
Under $4,000	30	70	53	47
$4,000 to 5,999	63	37	79	21
$6,000 to $7,999	78	22	91	9
$8,000 to $9,999	90	10	95	5
$10,000 and over	91	9	97	3
$10,000 to $14,999	91	9	97	3
$15,000 and over	89	11	97	3
1975				
Total, own children	54	46	87	13
Under $4,000	17	83	37	63
$4,000 to $5,999	29	71	61	39
$6,000 to $7,999	51	49	73	27
$8,000 to $9,999	66	34	83	17
$10,000 and over	82	18	95	5
$10,000 to $14,999	79	21	92	8
$15,000 and over	86	14	96	4

NOTE: Universe is own unmarried children under eighteen years old living in families where at least one parent is present.
SOURCE: U.S. Bureau of the Census, "The Social and Economic Status of the Black Population in the United States: An Historical View, 1790–1978," *Current Population Reports*, P-23, no. 80, June, 1979, p. 108.

actually seeking custody—including custody of very young children, and (3) the success rate for fathers in contested custody cases is increasing (Orthner and Lewis, 1979:28). Furthermore, their research and that of others indicates that there is no reason to presume that fathers cannot successfully rear

There is no reason to presume that fathers cannot successfully rear children alone. (James H. Karales/ Peter Arnold, Inc.)

children alone. Many can—and do (Orthner, Brown, and Ferguson, 1976; Orthner and Lewis, 1979; Gersick, 1979).

Solo parents—whether mothers or fathers—face the challenges, joys, and problems that all parents face, but they face them without a partner. They have to balance the demands of home and career, find baby-sitters, provide guidance and discipline, actively support their child's school endeavors and other activities and interests, arrange appointments with physicians and dentists, shop for new shoes, bandage scraped knees, and allow plenty of time for fun, listening, telling stories, laughing, and hugging. And they have to do it all alone.

Supportive friendship networks, relatives who care, teachers who take a warm and personal interest, special community and religious activities designed with such families in mind, and groups such as Parents without Partners can make a tremendous difference in the emotional well-being of solo parents and their children at a time in their lives when encouragement is especially needed. Many of the divorce rituals mentioned earlier were designed to be symbolic of such support. "At precisely the time when individuals are most lonely and need to establish links of communication with others," writes Jeanne Audrey Powers (1976:80), a Methodist minister who has authored divorce ceremonies, "members of the Christian community know least how to respond, and the person is usually met with silence, embarrassment and whispered conversations that end abruptly when the person enters a room."

Her point is poignantly illustrated by an anecdote told to us by a woman who was first widowed and then saw her second marriage end in divorce. When the second marriage ended, one of her children asked, "Where are all the people, Mommy? Why aren't people bringing us casseroles this time and coming to visit like they did when Daddy died?" Apparently, persons in this woman's circle of acquaintances found themselves more willing to provide emotional support and practical assistance for someone whose spouse had died than for someone whose marriage had died.

While some divorced fathers rearing children alone also have reported negative reactions from others, the majority report they receive much support and a great deal of special attention (Orthner and Lewis, 1979:43). One researcher suggests a reason related to traditional gender-role expectations:

> Since, in our society, children of divorced parents usually live with their mothers, there is nothing especially commendable about a single female parent. When, on the other hand, the children live with their fathers, the men are frequently regarded as heroic, or at the very best, commendable for taking on the responsibilities they are not usually expected to do. In a sense, the single male parent may be viewed as a social widower, and as such receives much of the solicitations and direct help which is customarily offered to actual widowers. (Mendes, 1975, as quoted in Orthner and Lewis, 1979:44.)

Contrasting societal attitudes toward male solo parents with those toward female solo parents (who are seen to be simply "doing their job," even though the mothers are employed full-time), three other researchers point to the example of a divorced mother of a handicapped child who said:

> No one has felt any commitment to me as a result of my having to take care of Barbara alone—no one has offered any help. When she is with my husband, they get invited out all the time. When people come here, they take it for granted that I'll cook for them. But they'll take food all prepared out there [her husband's house]. (Kohen, Brown, and Feldberg, 1979:238)

Here, as in so many other areas, we see the impact of sex-role stereotypes.

REMARRIAGE

Remarriage after divorce is popular. "Evidently, divorced men strongly prefer being married, albeit with a different partner," write demographers Paul Glick and Arthur Norton (1977:6) after examining data showing that "divorced men are three times as likely to remarry as never-married men are to enter first marriage." Although divorced men have a slightly higher likeli-

FIGURE 18-3   *About one out of three brides and one out of three grooms in 1977 had been married before. (National Center for Health Statistics, "Final Marriage Statistics, 1977," Monthly Vital Statistics Report, vol. 28, no. 4, [July 20, 1979], pp. 2, 5.)*

hood than divorced women of remarrying, women, too, have a high probability of marrying again (U.S. Bureau of the Census, *Current Population Reports*, P-20, no. 297, 1976:3).

LIKELIHOOD OF REMARRIAGE

Of the 6 million divorced women between the ages of fifteen and forty-four in 1976, 21 percent had remarried within the first year after their divorce. And within five years after the divorce, 71 percent were remarried. According to the National Center for Health Statistics, during the first five years after divorce "the likelihood of remarriage was greater for white than for black women, greater for those who were divorced before age 25 than for those who were divorced later, and greater for those with less than a high school education than for those with one or more years of college" (National Center for Health Statistics, *Advance Data*, no. 58, February 14, 1980).

On the other hand, contrary to the impressions given by sensationalistic reports in the media, *most* married persons are in their first marriage. In 1975, among married individuals born between 1900 and 1959, 85 percent had been married only once, 13 percent had been married twice, and 2 percent had been married three or more times (U.S. Bureau of the Census, *Current Population Reports*, P-20, no. 297, 1976:2). In general, widowed persons are somewhat less likely to remarry than divorced persons; but one pattern is similar to that of divorced persons—men are more likely to remarry than women. The remarriage rate for widowers is four times the rate for widows (National Center for Health Statistics, *Monthly Vital Statistics Report*, vol. 28, no. 4, 1979).

In recent years, remarriage rates for both widowed and divorced persons have been dropping, which may indicate more caution and more deliberate weighing of costs and rewards before entering a new marriage—especially after having terminated the earlier marriage by choice as in the case with divorce. In Chapter 8, we saw that among younger divorced men especially,

Out of every five divorced persons . . . . .

Four may be expected to remarry eventually . . . . . .

And one may be expected to remain single.

FIGURE 18-4 *(Statistics from U.S. Bureau of the Census,* Current Population Reports, *Series P-20, No. 297, "Number, Timing, and Duration of Marriages and Divorces in the United States: June, 1975," October 1976, p. 3.)*

cohabitation has taken on increasing popularity in recent years, and we referred to speculations that this pattern may indicate an attempt to have many of the benefits of marriage while avoiding the risks of a second or third unsatisfactory marital union and the necessity of another divorce. Such cohabitation may be a substitute for marriage, or it may be a trial run to be "absolutely sure" next time.

DO REMARRIAGES WORK OUT?

Remarriages are somewhat more likely to end in divorce than are first marriages. On the basis of current divorce statistics, the U.S. Bureau of the Census has released estimates that among persons aged twenty-five to thirty-five years in 1975, one-third could expect their first marriages to end in divorce at some time; and 40 percent of those whose first marriages ended in divorce could expect to become redivorced eventually (*Current Population Reports,* P-20, no. 297, 1976:5–7).

However, these projections should not lead to the conclusion that divorce repeaters are simply "divorce-prone" and have personalities that hinder their remaining in a stable marriage situation. "The term 'divorce-prone' is pejorative and unnecessary," writes sociologist Lucile Duberman (1977), pointing out that situational factors rather than character flaws help explain the somewhat higher divorce rates among remarried persons as compared to first-married persons. "Remarried divorced people face unusual problems—self-doubt, communal skepticism, extra financial burdens, and extraordinary dyadic adjustment—yet most of them rate their marriages 'very happy,'" Duberman emphasizes, "and most of them stay married in spite of the fact that they fear divorce less than those who have never experienced it" (pp. 204–205).

How satisfactory are remarriages? "So far," say sociologists Norval Glenn and Charles Weaver (1977), "divorce and remarriage seem to have been rather effective mechanisms for replacing poor marriages with good ones and for keeping the mean level of marital happiness fairly high" (p. 336). After analyzing data on remarriage and reported happiness, they concluded that "remarriages of divorced persons which do not quickly end in divorce probably are, as a whole, almost as successful as intact first marriages" (p. 331). Of course, the concept "happiness" is subjective, can be difficult to measure, and can mean many things. Glenn and Weaver had scored marital happiness according to how respondents answered the question: "Taking all things together, how would you describe your marriage? Would you say your marriage is very happy, pretty happy, or not too happy?"

Another study (Albrecht, 1979) used a comparative approach: how did the remarriage compare in happiness with the first marriage, with the perceived happiness of acquaintances' marriages, and with the happiness the remarried persons had *expected* to find in the new marriages? Respondents tended to rate their remarriages better on all three counts.

In still another study, the researcher focused on "global happiness" rather than on *marital* happiness alone and found indications that, overall, "remarried women are *less* happy than women in first marriages," while "remarried men report themselves significantly *more* happy than men in intact first marriages" (White, 1979:869). Divorced women may feel forced into remarriage because of economic circumstances and the difficulties of rearing children alone. Such factors, among others, "suggest the hypothesis that divorced women wanting to remarry are not in a favorable marriage market, and, to continue the economic analogy, may have to settle for inferior goods," sociologist Lynn White points out. "Divorced men, however, are in a much more favorable market, such that remarriage should be a sign of desire rather than necessity, and of a wide rather than a narrow range of alternatives" (p. 871).

COSTS AND BENEFITS OF DIVORCE AND REMARRIAGE

Earlier, we looked at government data indicating that women with lower education are those most likely to remarry after divorce. Such women lack resources that could provide alternatives. Better-educated women, having other options open to them in the economic-opportunity system, may feel less constrained to remarry and less willing to run the risk on another unsatisfactory marriage. The costs are too great. Indeed, for some women at all class levels, divorce may be considered rewarding rather than costly. Some

Divorce—Not Always Negative

Divorce. It is a lonely, guilt-ridden, grief-filled experience for most men and women. But not for all.

When Penny was divorced, after eight years of marriage, she was left with two preschoolers, an inoperable car, piles of unpaid bills and an apartment she could no longer afford.

But she felt only a profound sense of relief.

"I had been working as a secretary, so employment wasn't a problem. I had been doing all the housework and parenting anyway, so that didn't change. And he'd spent every penny we earned, so being broke was nothing new," she said.

Now 46 years old, Penny is still single 18 years after that divorce. She's director of personnel for a company that is a household word, earns $43,000 a year, dates when she wants to and is still close to her now-grown daughters.

"I'm not saying divorce is necessarily a good thing. But I am saying that a lot of women are better off (not worse) after a divorce. Even with children. Even with low-paying jobs," Penny said smiling.

"It just isn't true that divorced mothers are miserable. . . .

"As for parenting, it was hard work but really easier without my husband. No arguments; no one saying I was spoiling them. They were good girls then and they still are.

"And they were relieved there was no more fighting, I'm sure. They knew—kids always do. . . .

"I would never say divorce is the best answer—but I know a lot of miserable women who are staying with men they can't stand just because the word 'divorce' is so frightening," she said.

"Well, I'll tell you what's a lot more frightening: Living with someone who gives you nothing emotionally. Bills can be paid; children will be fine as long as they know they're loved; and loneliness is a state of mind.

"But living with someone just because you're afraid not to? That's got to be the most frightening thing in the world."

SOURCE: Niki Scott, "Divorce May Be Relief for Some," *Greensboro* (N.C.) *Daily News*, October 1, 1978.

report that after divorce they experience autonomy for the first time in their lives, and it's a good feeling. They enjoy the control they can exercise over their own lives—how they use their time, how they keep the house, how they rear the children, how they use money, and so on. In citing evidence for this, Kohen, Brown, and Feldberg (1979) explain:

> If a couple divorces, the woman loses most of her right to the man's resources, but she also loses her personal dependence and obligations of service. She now stands in direct relationship to society as the head of her family. . . . Patriarchal authority is now outside the family, not inside, and the woman can choose to some extent the way in which she will relate to those authorities [employers,

welfare officials, lawyers and judges, and the like] and the use she will make of whatever formal and informal resources are available. (p. 229)

While not minimizing the very real financial hardships many women face after divorce, Kohen, Brown, and Feldberg report that some divorced women they interviewed tended to feel they had more money after divorce when in actuality they had less! Why? Because now they had control of the money (whether earned income or from AFDC or support payments); and such control made all the difference after having lived in marriages where husbands gambled, spent more than they earned, or withheld needed money from their wives and children. Thus, they felt "better off" in many ways, including financially. For such women, "divorce meant an end to the husband's power to impoverish the family" (p. 239). On the other hand, some women assessed the cost/benefit ratio differently. Women who had been married to high-income husbands especially tended to indicate that "problems from loss of income far outweighed the benefits of increased control" (p. 240).

IMPACT OF DIVORCE ON SEX ROLES

At the same time that divorce forces many women to become more autonomous and to develop skills along *instrumental* lines, divorce may be forcing some men to develop skills along *expressive* lines by involving them more fully in parenting—especially where fathers are awarded full or joint child custody.

Social scientists Kristine Rosenthal and Harry Keshet (1978) found that after-divorce parenting, whether part-time or full-time, can be an important resocialization experience for men. The experience makes necessary a rethinking of work commitments as over against commitments of time and energy to their children. Interaction with children may come to have higher priority than ever before. "Parenting which in a marriage was likely to come second to work obligations is now a legitimate function *on par* with the demands of work," say these researchers. "In fact, it acquires many of the characteristics of work, and fathers begin to develop competence, recognize cues for judging themselves as competent, and experience the familiar rewards of a job well done" (p. 471). Aware that this description gives the impression that men tend to make even expressive relations into something instrumental, Rosenthal and Keshet continue:

> The issue of competence and efficiency dominates the self-image of males. The cultural image of competence is cold and impersonal, but it also can be a way to think about feelings and to begin to learn how to function interpersonally. (p. 471)

In their study of 127 divorced and separated fathers, these researchers found that as men gained confidence in their parenting through caring for children's physical needs, such as giving the children baths, meals, and getting them to school, the fathers experienced good feelings between them and their children and gradually developed greater sensitivity to what was on their children's minds. "Once the feelings of competence begin to be introduced into the area of dealing with children's emotions, reinforced by the child's well being, the whole area of emotions becomes less threatening for men," say Rosenthal and Keshet. And "for men socialized to believe that feelings must be kept hidden and are a barrier to effective functioning, experiencing competency in this area can be a source of positive self-regard" (p. 472). These fathers' movement away from nontraditional sex roles and their greater skills in expressiveness might be expected to carry over into new relationships, including remarriage and what Rosenthal and Keshet call "refamilying."

BLENDED FAMILIES

After divorce in which there were children, remarriage involves not only two *persons* but means the blending of two *families*. "The child of divorced parents who both remarry will have two biological parents, two step-parents, biological siblings, step and half siblings, up to eight grandparents (even

"Will You Marry Us?"

I married a widower who had a 7-year-old boy and a 4-year-old girl. The three of them (father and children) proposed. My "son" said, "Will you marry us?" I willingly became wife and mother with one "I do."

Our first baby was born just before our first anniversary, but before she was born, I had already applied to adopt my husband's two children. This was my way of covering three issues. For one thing, this made all my children full brothers and sisters. In the second place, they would always be mine. I had a terrible fear that if something happened to my husband, someone would take my children away. Most importantly, I felt that in time to come my children would realize how much they meant to me by my making sure they were legally mine.

The greatest joy of my life may well have been the time my oldest daughter asked me if I could love an adopted grandchild. When I said that it wasn't fair to ask me because I have adopted children, she said, "Oh, Mommy, I forgot." Maybe that's the answer to Mrs. Maddox [referring to an earlier article on problems in stepparenting]. In our house we forgot.

SUE HERBACH
Delmar, N.Y.

SOURCE: "Letters" department, *The New York Times Magazine*, September 19, 1976, pp. 91–92.

After a divorce in which there were children, remarriage involves not only two persons but means the blending of two families. This husband and wife, who were just married, are seen here with fourteen of their sixteen children, seven his and nine hers, from previous marriages. (United Press International Photo)

more if any grandparents had divorced and remarried) and any number of additional extended relatives through the new spouses of the biological parents," Ahrons (1979:499–500) points out.

When divorced persons combine their families through remarriage, the resultant family form is variously called a "reconstituted" family (Duberman, 1975), a "blended" family, a "merged" family, or a "step" family (Roosevelt and Lofas, 1977). The term *step* comes from an old English word meaning "to bereave." A bereaved husband or wife who took a new spouse thereby gave the bereaved children a new parent. When reconstituted families were more likely to come about because of the death of a father or mother rather than the parents' divorce, the term *stepparent* made sense, argues Bohannan (1970:119); but it makes less sense now—at least in cases of divorce. In remarriage after divorce, the child still has both biological parents and thus "the stepparent is an addition, not a replacement." The remarriage of one or both parents leaves all parties concerned not only with inadequate kinship terms but also without helpful guidelines for behavior in these new relationships.

Of course, *either* husband or wife may be widowed or may be the parent who has custody of the children after divorce and thus may bring a new spouse into the home. But since traditionally mothers more than fathers have been awarded child custody, a common pattern in remarriage after divorce is the mother/children/ stepfather family form. At the same time, the children's biological father is likely to be involved in their lives to some degree— although in some cases he may feel pushed aside. Ruth Roosevelt and Jeannette Lofas (1977), authors of a book on remarriage and steprelationships, speak of this situation:

> When the ex remarries, the parent without custody is presented with the hard fact of a new person in his old place. This other person is his day-to-day replacement in the home with his children. And he didn't even choose the person. At the same time, he still continues to pay out child support.
>
> It hurts. A father hears his children calling another man Dad. Sometimes he hears them calling himself by his first name rather than Dad. One father wrote a letter to his former wife: "I have lost everything surrounding the relationship. At least let me keep my title and my name. Ask her to call me Dad, not Barry. Please."

Research on blended families has been limited and has yielded inconsistent findings. While admittedly complex factors are involved in the relation-

Challenges, Joys, and Problems of Steprelating

The stepfamily might be considered analogous, psychologically, to what happens physically in organ transplants. The most common cause of failure in transplants, as we know, is quite simple: the body responds protectively and rejects foreign tissue. Medical measures are taken to keep this from happening. Psychologically, the danger of similar pathology exists in the merged family situation. . . .

On the positive side, the stepfamily has in its favor the strength and effort inherent to all new ventures. The parents may also have a kind of second sight derived from prior experience.

In interviewing for this book we found an urgent poignancy in the point of view of each member of the stepfamily. Stepmothers poured out to us their feelings of being used and used and used. Stepfathers spoke of feelings of being strangers in their homes. Stepchildren described feelings of somehow never really belonging and at the same time being tugged in separate directions. Biological parents with children living with them in stepfamilies spoke of feeling split between children and mate. Absent parents communicated their sense of eroding loss and powerlessness over their children's development. . . .

In the merger of two companies, careful plans are laid for the realignment of possessions, offices, duties, responsibilities. In the newly merged family the setting in order of people and things must be just as carefully planned.

SOURCE: Ruth Roosevelt and Jeannette Lofas, *Living in Step: A Remarriage Manual for Parents and Children* (New York: McGraw-Hill, 1977), pp. 17, 24.

ships that make up such families, research has not supported the fairy-tale fiction that stepparents are cruel and unloving, nor the generalization that the remarriage of a custodial parent is somehow harmful to children. There can be satisfactory remarriages and unsatisfactory remarriages—just as is true of first marriages. And some remarriages may be beneficial to the children involved, while others may be detrimental in some way.

Therefore, one team of researchers take pains to point out that after carefully comparing children in stepfather families with those in natural-parent families, they found that the social-psychological and social characteristics of the two groups indicated no substantial differences associated with the particular family form in which the children lived (Wilson et al., 1975). "The child who is part of a stepfather family may have a predominantly positive, predominantly negative, or mixed experience in that family," say these social scientists in urging public policy makers and service agencies not to offer services "to stepfather families (indeed to all forms of reconstituted families) with a categorical assumption that such families are inevitably inferior to natural-parent families for the well-being of the child" (p. 535). Many persons who grow up in blended families report positive feelings about their experiences and feelings of affection toward their stepparents (Bernard, 1956). This is not to deny the special problems faced in reconstituted families with their multiple relationships, but it does mean that such problems need not be considered insurmountable (Roosevelt and Lofas, 1977).

CHAPTER HIGHLIGHTS

Divorce, like marriage, is a *process;* and it involves many aspects: emotional, legal, and economic. Statistics on divorce are often misused and sensationalized, and great care must be taken when assessing divorce trends and projecting the likelihood of eventual marital dissolution. Over the past century, changing attitudes toward divorce appear to be rooted in two basic ideals: (1) a concern for individual rights and best interests and (2) a demanding view of marriage with high expectations for companionship, empathy, affection, and self-actualization. These changing attitudes are reflected in laws, religious rethinking, and actual statistics (5.2 divorces per 1,000 population in 1978 as compared to 0.5 when divorce statistics were first collected in 1867).

After divorce, the ex-spouses may experience grief and a redefinition of themselves as they take on *new roles* and leave old ones (husband and wife). At the same time, to one degree or another, they must continue their roles as parents, including working out satisfactory child custody arrangements from a variety of possibilities. Studies of the effects of divorce on the children involved are inconclusive and inconsistent, but one finding has emerged repeatedly: it may be far more distressing for a child to continue living in a conflict-ridden home than to come from a broken one. Some behavioral scientists emphasize that no *one* answer can be given to the question of divorce and its impact on children and suggest research on the multiple issues surrounding the experience of divorce, examining what factors are most troubling to children and why.

After divorce, remarriage is popular—although in recent years remarriage rates for both divorced and widowed persons have been dropping. This may indicate more caution and more deliberate weighing of costs and rewards before entering a new marriage. Although remarriages are somewhat more likely to end in divorce than first marriages, those that remain intact are apt to be considered highly satisfactory to the persons involved. Sometimes remarriage involves uniting two families rather than two persons only, thus forming what is variously called the "blended" family, the "merged" family, the "reconstituted" family, or the "step" family.

EPILOGUE: WHAT'S AHEAD FOR MARRIAGE AND FAMILY?

As we went to press, new statistics from two different sources were released which underscore the central theme of this book: the roles and relationships of women and men no longer fit the old familiar patterns. Change isn't only a word in our title; it's the name of the game!

And yet, what is happening is not wild, unpredictable, chaotic change. Rather, it's a continuation of the trends we've seen in both editions of this text. Persons are asking a great deal more from relationships and are less willing to tolerate costly and punishing situations. And they're questioning basic assumptions about marriage, no longer content to let it be defined and scripted for them, no longer willing to follow sex-specific rules and roles, and no longer rushing into marriage without first allowing time to explore other alternatives.

A 1980 report of the United States Bureau of the Census indicates that the median age for a woman's first marriage (22.1 years) is now above the 1890 high of 22.0. That women no longer consider marriage the foremost or only option open to them is also seen in other statistics from this same report. In 1960, only 29 percent of twenty- to twenty-four-year-old women were still single; but as the decade of the seventies came to a close, *half* of all women in that age range had never married. And in the next older bracket, among women aged twenty-five to twenty-nine years in 1979, one out of every five remained unmarried. In contrast, only one out of every ten women in that age range in 1960 had remained single (*Current Population Reports*, 1980, Series P-20, No. 349, p. 1).

According to the Census Bureau, more than one out of every five households in 1979 consisted of a person living alone. And "the largest increases in one-person households during the 1970s occurred among divorced and never-married persons" (p. 3).

Persons in the "never-married" and "divorced" categories also accounted for the greater proportions of persons living in what the Census Bureau refers to as "unmarried-couple households." In 1979, about one-half of both women and men in such arrangements had never been married. Slightly more than one-fourth of the women in unmarried-couple households were divorced, as were just under one-third of the men. The remaining persons in unmarried-couple arrangements were widows (11 percent) and widowers (5 percent) and married persons who were separated or otherwise living apart from their spouses.

Over the decade of the 1970s, the number of unmarried-couple households more than doubled, reaching 1.3 million. Officials at the Census Bureau, however, caution against sensationalism in reporting this finding. They write:

> Despite the spectacular nature of the recent increase in this unmarried-couple living arrangement, the 2.7 million "partners" in these 1.3 million households represent a very small portion of all persons in "couple" situations. In 1979, there were an estimated 96.5 million men and women who were married and living with a spouse. Thus, the partners in unmarried couples represented only about 3 percent of all persons among couples living together in 1979. (p.3)

Table E-E shows that about three-fourths of unmarried-couple households

Table E-E   *Unmarried couples, by sex and age of householder and presence of children under fourteen years old: 1979.*

(NUMBERS IN THOUSANDS)

SUBJECT	NUMBER	PERCENT
All unmarried couples	1,346	100.0
Householder:		
Man	855	63.5
Woman	491	36.5
No children present	985	73.2
Householder:		
Man	644	47.8
Woman	341	25.3
Age of householder:		
Under 45 years	741	55.1
Under 25 years	274	20.4
25 to 34 years	370	27.5
35 to 44 years	97	7.2
45 years and over	244	18.1
45 to 54 years	53	3.9
55 to 64 years	78	5.8
65 years and over	113	8.4
Children present	360	26.7
Householder:		
Man	211	15.7
Woman	150	11.1

Source: U. S. Bureau of the Census, *Current Population Reports*, Series P-20, No. 349, "Marital Status and Living Arrangements: March 1979. " Washington, D. C.: U.S. Government Printing Office, 1980.

consisted only of two adults. The other one-fourth contained, in addition to two opposite-sex adults, one or more children under fourteen years of age. The table is also interesting in showing which age groups make up different proportions of unmarried couple households. The largest percentage of householders in such living arrangements are aged twenty-five to thirty-four years, followed by persons under age twenty-five, with persons sixty-five years of age and older making up the third highest percentage.

As the 1980s began, there were signs of an increasing acceptance of the unmarried-couple life-style—or if not acceptance, at least tolerance. In some circles, cohabitation evidently has come to be regarded as just one more marital status category. In a routine 1980 general reader survey questionnaire sent out by *Working Woman* magazine, respondents were asked in one question to check which of four categories described their situation: (1) single,

Lawyers: Repeal marriage tax penalty

Washington (AP)—The tax penalty on marriage resulted from stereotyped assumptions about the role of married women, a House committee was told Thursday.

Paul Mapes, an Arlington, Va., lawyer, said the authors of the 1969 tax legislation "were unconsciously proceeding under the assumption that married women did not work outside of the home."

Lynda Sands Moerschbaecher, an assistant general counsel at Yale University, said the tax law not only is discouraging marriage but is encouraging divorce and creating a reason for women to remain out of the labor force.

Both told the House Ways and Means Committee that steps are needed to rectify the situation, which Ms. Moerschbaecher said affects 38 million taxpayers.

The committee, which writes the nation's tax laws, is holding hearings on the provision, which causes two workers who are married to pay more in taxes than two workers who simply live together.

Mapes, who estimated his four years of marriage had cost him $7,000 in extra taxes, said "it is now clear that the marriage penalty substantially interferes with the free exercise of the right to marry."

"A significant number of couples have already divorced to avoid this tax and others have postponed their marriages or have been deterred from marrying at all," he said.

Ms. Moerschbaecher called the current law "unduly burdensome and harsh" and added "it is obvious that the tax burden on individuals changes arbitrarily with a wedding ceremony."

She suggested the simplest—and fairest—means of abolishing the marriage penalty would be to have everyone file individual returns and use only one income tax rate schedule.

"The couple is not a proper entity or tax unit; the individuals earning the income are proper tax units," she said.

The administration agrees the law should be changed, but says it has not decided which approach to take.

The Treasury Department says the United States is the only industrialized nation with an income tax that does not distinguish between one-income and two-income families.

SOURCE: *Greensboro (NC) Daily News*, April 4, 1980.

(2) living together (unmarried), (3) married, or (4) widowed, divorced, or separated.

And while many unmarried couples were no doubt living together for all the reasons discussed in Chapter 8, some spoke of another reason: inequity in income tax laws. Marriage was perceived as too costly in the most literal sense—money! The tax laws had been based on the husband-breadwinner assumption, and two-earner couples began finding they could save money by living together unwed or divorcing if they had been married. People began talking about a "marriage penalty" and demanding that Congress take a look at the problem.

Yet, most persons aren't ready to give up on marriage; they simply want to see changes made which take into account today's realities—especially the realities of changing sex-role definitions and expectations, the growing autonomy of women, and the increase in two-earner couples. As the accompanying boxed insert shows, the 1980 Virginia Slims American Women's Opinion Poll conducted by the Roper Organization indicates that, over the 1970s, attitudes on such issues changed dramatically among even the older and less educated segments of the population. Ideas that were once scoffed at or casually dismissed as "just a fad" are now widely accepted. Rigid definitions of "woman's place" and "woman's work" and "man's place" and "man's work" are increasingly seen as limiting to both sexes. *Sharing* the roles of provider, parent, and household caretaker, and working out a satisfactory personal marriage arrangement *by negotiation* seems more appealing to many couples than arbitrarily assigning privileges and responsibilities according to sex.

This worries certain social observers, however, who decry the death or decay of "the family" (Lasch, 1977). Their assumption is that "the family" is one particular model: a husband who supports his wife and children financially and a wife who devotes herself totally to caring for the house and children and standing by her husband as an emotional support. Any movement away from this pattern (which such writers consider the ideal) is assumed to mean some sort of "family breakdown."

Yet, families exist in many forms and show a great deal of variety. The senior-partner–junior-partner and equal-partner marriage patterns being chosen by increasing numbers of couples today are patterns that aren't likely to disappear. Why? Because more and more persons apparently view such alternatives to the traditional marriage pattern as something "better"—in other words, more rewarding in the long run for all family members. This is not to deny that there are also costs to pay as couples struggle to work out the logistics of daily living without the old rules and guidelines and with overcrowded schedules taking their toll on time and energy. Even so, signs do not point to a return to the head-complement traditional marriage pattern which, for many, would seem even more costly.

What then is happening to the family? Clearly, it's not dying. But it *is* changing. What we're seeing is not decay but "a metamorphosis into something different from what existed before, but equally viable" (Scanzoni, 1980:126-127). This is an exciting time to be studying marriage and family!

Survey finds major shifts in attitudes of women

Twice as many women hold full-time jobs today as did 10 years ago, and most women who were surveyed in a recent poll think it is likely that by the year 2000 almost all women who are able will be working.

This finding, which showed 35 percent of women hold full-time jobs today compared to 18 percent in 1970, was announced yesterday as part of the 1980 Virginia Slims American Women's Opinion Poll.

The poll was conducted last fall by the Roper Organization. It surveyed the attitudes of 3,000 women and 1,000 men, who were selected as representative samples of the female and male populations of the United States, age 18 and up.

Another of its findings was that a majority of women today (64 percent) approved of most of the efforts to strengthen and change the status of women in society, compared to a minority of women (40 percent) in 1970.

"But a single rather startling fact indicates even more dramatically how much women have changed in their attitudes during the 1970's," said Burns W. Roper, chairman of the Roper Organization, at a luncheon held to announce the poll's findings at the Pierre Hotel.

"Ten years ago, the group that was least in favor of changing women's status was older, less educated women," he said, "while the group that was most in favor of change was younger, more educated women." Today, he said, 55 percent of older, less educated women favor change, which is more than the 45 percent of younger, better educated women who favored change in 1970. . . .

Mr. Roper said that hour-long interviews were conducted in the homes of the respondents, who were asked 90 questions dealing with the status of women, women and work, sex roles, marriage, children, money, physical fitness, leisure time, social issues and the future.

This was the fourth poll of American women sponsored by Virginia Slims cigarettes, following similar studies in 1970, 1972 and 1974.

The study showed that money is the primary reason why women work—only 14 percent of working women surveyed said they work to have something interesting to do. And as they become more career-oriented, women are increasingly perceiving sex discrimination in jobs. A majority of women today (57 percent) believe that a woman who is aiming for an executive position in her company will meet with discrimination, compared to 50 percent who thought that in 1970.

According to the study, women today overwhelmingly (94 percent) continue to favor marriage as a way of life. But at the same time, a majority (52 percent) are redefining the traditional marital relationship of the male as breadwinner, female as housewife.

"Women are tending to perceive marriage as a responsibility to be shared between both partners in similar roles," Mr. Roper said, "with both husband and wife working to contribute earned income, and with both husband and wife sharing homemaking and child-rearing responsibilities."

The study also showed that more than four out of five women said that children are not an essential ingredient in a full and happy marriage.

"Today, therefore, motherhood, once an integral part of marriage, is no longer seen as an essential ingredient of marriage," Mr. Roper concluded.

He said that another finding he considered significant was the changing of "boy/girl" sexual sterotypes, to the point where it is "no longer thought feminine for boys to make beds and wash dishes, and no longer thought masculine for girls to mow lawns and take out the garbage". . . .

"This shift in attitudes may have far-reaching implications," he said. "When today's boys and girls become tomorrow's men and women, they may be less inclined than the men and women of today to define masculinity and femininity in terms of the kinds of jobs people do."

The study showed that in the case of an unsuccessful marriage, more women now favor divorce as an acceptable solution than did so 10 years ago—62 percent compared to 52 percent. And when it comes to child custody, the majority of women today (57 percent) said that both mother and father should be given equal consideration by the court.

SOURCE: Judy Klemesrud, *The New York Times*, March 13, 1980, pp. C1, C6.

REFERENCES

Abrahamson, Mark
1978 *Functionalism.* Englewood Cliffs, N.J.: Prentice-Hall.

Acker, Joan
1973 "Women and social stratification: A case of intellectual sexism." *American Journal of Sociology* 78:936–945.

Adams, Bert N.
1968 *Kinship in an Urban Setting.* Chicago: Markham.

Adams, Margaret
1971 "The single woman in today's society: A reappraisal." *The American Journal of Orthopsychiatry* 41:776–786. Reprinted in Arlene Skolnick and Jerome Skolnick (eds.), *Intimacy, Family, and Society,* Boston: Little, Brown, 1974.
1976 *Single Blessedness.* New York: Basic Books.

Ahrons, Constance
1979 "The binuclear family." *Alternative Lifestyles* 2 (Nov.): 499–515.

Aird, John S.
1972 "Population policy and demographic prospects in the People's Republic of China." Bethesda, Md.: Center for Population Research. National Institute for Child Health and Human Development.

The Alan Guttmacher Institute
1979 *Abortions and the Poor: Private Morality, Public Responsibility.* New York: The Alan Guttmacher Institute.

Albrecht, Stan L.
1979 "Correlates of marital happiness among the remarried." *Journal of Marriage and the Family* 41 (November): 857–867.

Aldous, Joan
1978 *Family Careers: Developmental Change in Families.* New York: John Wiley & Sons.

Aldridge, Delores P.
1973 "The changing nature of interracial marriage in Georgia: A research note." *Journal of Marriage and the Family* 35:641–642.

Alexander, C. Norman, Jr. and Richard Simpson
1971 "Balance theory and distributive justice." Pp. 69–80 in Herman Turk and Richard Simpson (eds.), *Institutions and Social Exchange.* Indianapolis: Bobbs-Merrill.

Allen, Craig M., and Murray A. Straus
1980 "Resources, power, and husband-wife violence." Pp. 188–208 in Straus and Hotaling.

Altman, Dennis
1971 *Homosexual Oppression and Liberation.* New York: Outerbridge and Lizard. Avon Books edition.

Alzate, Heli
1978 "Sexual behavior of Columbian female university students." *Archives of Sexual Behavior* 7 (January): 43–54.

Angrist, Shirley A.
1969 "The study of sex roles." *Journal of Social Issues* 25:215–233.

Arafat, Ibithaj, and Betty Yorburg
1973 "On living together without marriage." *Journal of Sex Research* 9: 97–106

Arizpe, Lourdes
1977 "Women in the informal labor sector: The case of Mexico City. *Signs* 3 (Autumn): 25–37.

Ashley, Paul P.
1978 *Oh Promise Me but Put It in Writing.* New York: McGraw-Hill.

Bach, G., and P. Wyden
1968 *The Intimate Enemy.* New York: Morrow.

Bahr, Howard M.
1976 "The kinship role." Pp. 61–79 in F. Ivan Nye (ed.), *Role Structure and Analysis of the Family.* Beverly Hills, Calif.: Sage Publications.

Baldwin, Wendy
1976 "Adolescent pregnancy and childbearing—Growing concerns for Americans." *Population Bulletin,* vol. 31, no. 2. (Washington, D.C.: Population Reference Bureau, Inc.).

Balswick, Jack O., and Charles W. Peek
1971 "The inexpressive male: A tragedy of American society." *The Family Coordinator* 20:363–368.

Bane, Mary Jo
1979 "Marital disruption and the lives of children." Pp. 276–286 in Levinger and Moles (eds.).

Barash, David P.
1977 *Sociobiology and Behavior.* New York: Elsevier.

Bardwick, Judith M.
1971 *Psychology of Women.* New York: Harper & Row.
1973 "Sex, maternity and self-esteem." Paper read at the National Institute for Child Health and Human Development and the Center for Population Research Conference on Family and Fertility. June 13–16, Belmont, Elkridge, Maryland. Mimeographed.

Barker-Benfield, Ben
1972 "The spermatic economy: A nineteenth century view of sexuality." *Feminist Studies* 1, (1). Reprinted in Michael Gordon (ed.), *The American Family in Social-Historical Perspective.* New York: St. Martin's. Pp. 336–372.

Barnhart, Elizabeth
1975 "Friends and lovers in a lesbian counter-culture community." Pp. 90–115 in Nona Glazer-Malbin (ed.), *Old Family/New Family.* New York: D. Van Nostrand Co.

Barron, Milton L.
1972 *The Blending American*. Chicago: Quadrangle.

Barry H. III, Margaret K. Bacon, and I. I. Child.
1957 "A cross-cultural survey of some sex differences in socialization." *Journal of Abnormal Social Psychology* 55:327–332.

Bartell, Gilbert
1971 *Group Sex*. New York: Wyden.

Batchelor, Edward, Jr. (ed.)
1980 *Homosexuality and Ethics*. New York: Pilgrim Press.

Becker, Gary S.
1973 "A theory of marriage." *Journal of Political Economy* 81:813–845.

Beit-Hallahmi, Benjamin, and Albert Rabin
1977 "The Kibbutz as a social experiment and as a child-rearing laboratory," *American Psychologist* vol. 32(July), as reprinted in *Family Factbook* (Chicago: Marquis Academic Media, 1978), pp. 272–281.

Bell, Alan, and Martin Weinberg
1978 *Homosexualities: A study of diversity among men and women*. New York: Simon and Schuster.

Bell, Robert R.
1966 *Premarital Sex in a changing Society*. Englewood Cliffs, N.J.: Prentice-Hall.
1971 *Social Deviance*. Homewood, Ill.: Dorsey.
1974 "Married sex: How uninhibited can a woman dare to be?" (with Norman Lobenz). *Redbook* 143 (September): 176.
1975 "Swinging: Separating the sexual from friendship." Pp. 150–168 in Nona Glazer-Malbin (ed.), *Old Family/New Family*. New York: D. Van Nostrand Co.

Bell, Robert R., and J. B. Chaskes
1970 "Premarital sexual experience among coeds, 1958–1968." *Journal of Marriage and the Family* 32:81–84.

Belsky, Jay, and Laurence D. Steinberg
1978 "The effects of day care: A critical review. *Child Development* 49:929–949.

Bem, Sandra Lipsitz
1975 "Sex-role adaptability: One consequence of psychological androgyny." *Journal of Personality and Social Psychology* 31:634–643.
1976 "Beyond androgyny: Some presumptuous prescriptions for a liberated sexual identity." In A. G. Kaplan and J. P. Beene (eds.), *Beyond Sex Role Stereotypes: Readings Toward a Psychology of Androgyny*. Boston: Little, Brown & Co.
1977 "Psychological androgyny," Pp. 319–324 in Alice G. Sargent, *Beyond Sex Roles*. St. Paul: West Publishing Co.

Bengtson, Vern
1973 *The Social Psychology of Aging*. Indianapolis: Bobbs-Merrill.

Bengtson, Vern L., and Lillian Troll
1978 "Youth and their parents: Feedback and intergenerational influence on socialization." Pp. 215–240 in Lerner and Spanier (eds.), *Child Influences on Marital and Family Interaction: A Life-Span Perspective*. New York: Academic Press.

Benston, Margaret
1969 "The political economy of women's liberation." *Monthly Rev.* (September): 3–4.

Berardo, Felix M.
1967 "Kinship interaction and communications among space-age migrants." *Journal of Marriage and Family* 29 (August):541–554.
1970 "Survivorship and social isolation: The case of the aged widower." *The Family Coordinator* 19:11–25.

Berelson, Bernard
1972 "The value of children: A toxonomical essay." *The Population Council Annual Report—1972*. New York: The Population Council.
1973 "Population growth policy in developed countries." Pp. 145–160 in C. Westoff et al., 1973.

Berger, Bennett, Bruce Hackett, and R. Mervyn Millar
1972 "The communal family." *The Family Coordinator* 21:419–427.

Berger, David, and Morton Wenger
1973 "The ideology of virginity." *Journal of Marriage and the Family* 35:666–676.

Berger, Miriam E.
1971 "Trial marriage: Harnessing the trend constructively." *The Family Coordinator* 20:38–43.

Bernard, Jessie
1956 *Remarriage. A Study of Marriage*. New York: Dryden Press.
1964 *Academic Women*. University Park, Pa.: Pennsylvania State University Press.
1966 "Note on educational homogamy in Negro-White and White-Negro marriages." *Journal of Marriage and the Family* 3:274.
1970 "No news, but new ideas." Pp. 3–25 in Paul Bohannan (ed.), *Divorce and After*. Garden City, N.Y.: Doubleday.
1972 *The Future of Marriage*. New York: World.
1974 *The Future of Motherhood*. New York: The Dial Press.
1979 "Foreword," pp. ix-xv in George Levinger and Oliver C. Moles (eds.), *Divorce and Separation: Context, Causes, and Consequences*. New York: Basic Books.

Berne, Eric
1964 *Games People Play*. New York: Grove.

Besanceney, Paul H.
1970 *Interfaith Marriages: Who and Why*. New Haven, Conn.: College and University Press.

Billingsley, Andrew
1968 *Black Families in White America*. Englewood Cliffs, N.J.: Prentice-Hall.

Bird, Caroline
1979 *The Two-Paycheck Marriage*. New York: Rawson, Wade Publishers, Inc.

Blake, Judith
1979 "Is zero preferred? American attitudes toward childlessness in the 1970s." *Journal of Marriage and the Family* 41(May):245–257.

Blau, Peter
1964 *Exchange and Power in Social Life*. New York: Wiley.

Blau, Peter, and Otis Dudley Duncan
1967 *The American Occupational Structure.* New York: Wiley.

Blau, Zena Smith
1973 *Old Age in a Changing Society.* New York: New Viewpoints.

Blood, Robert O., Jr.
1963 "The husband-wife relationship" Pp. 282–305 in Nye and Hoffman, 1963.
1967 *Love Match and Arranged Marriage.* New York: Free Press.
1969 *Marriage.* 2d ed. New York: Free Press.

Blood, Robert O., Jr., and Donald M. Wolfe
1960 *Husbands and Wives.* New York: Free Press.

Bloom, B.
1963 "Definitional concepts of the crisis concept." *Journal of Consulting Psychology* 27:42.

Bloom, Bernard, Stephen White, and Shirley Asher
1979 "Marital disruption as a stressful life event." Pp. 181–200 in Levinger and Moles (eds.), 1979.

Boak, Arthur
1955 *Manpower Shortage and the Fall of the Roman Empire in the West.* Ann Arbor: University of Michigan Press.

Bock, E. Wilbur, and Irving Webber
1972 "Suicide among the elderly: Isolating widowhood and mitigating alternatives." *Journal of Marriage and the Family* 34:24–31.

Bohannan, Paul (ed.)
1970 *Divorce and After.* Garden City, N.Y.: Doubleday.

Boserup, Ester
1977 Preface to special issue on "Women and national development." *Signs* 3 (Autumn): ix–xiv.

Bott, Elizabeth
1957 *Family and Social Network.* London: Tavistock.
1968 (Paperback edition)

Boulding, Elise
1976 "Familial constraints on women's work roles." *Signs* 1 (Spring): 95–117.

Bourne, Patricia, and Norma Wikler
1976 "Dual roles and double binds: Women in medical school," Paper presented at the 1976 annual meetings of the American Sociological Association in New York City.

Bowen, William, and T. Aldrich Finegan
1969 *The Economics of Labor Force Participation.* Princeton, N.J.: Princeton University Press.

Bower, Donald, and Victor Christopherson
1977 "University student cohabitation: A regional comparison of selected attitudes and behavior." *Journal of Marriage and the Family* 39 (August):447–453.

Brawley, Benjamin
1921 *A Social History of the American Negro.* New York: The Macmillan Company.

Bremner, William J., and David M. de Kretser
1975 "Contraceptives for males." *Signs* 1 (Winter):387–396.

Brickman, Phillip (ed.)
1974 *Social Conflict.* Lexington, Mass.: Heath.

Briggs, Kenneth
1976 "Jews said to ease view on marriage," *The New York Times* (May 16), p. 29.

Brim, O.
1976 "Theories of the male mid-life crisis." *Counseling Psychologist* 6:2–9.

Bronfenbrenner, Urie
1958 "Socialization and social class through time and space." Pp. 400–425 in E. E. Maccoby, T. M. Newcomb, and E. L. Hartley (eds.), *Readings in Social Psychology,* 3d ed. New York: Holt.

Brown, Howard
1976 *Familiar Faces, Hidden Lives.* New York: Harcourt Brace Jovanovich.

Brown, George, and Michael Rutter
1966 "The measurement of family activities and relationships." *Human Relations* 19:241–263.

Brown, L. Dave, and Judy C. Brown
1973 "Group process in the urban commune." Pp. 408–418 in Kanter, Rosabeth Moss, *Communes: Creating and Managing the Collective Life.* New York: Harper & Row.

Brown, Roger
1965 *Social Psychology.* New York: Free Press.

Brown, Sarah S., E. James Lieberman, and Warren B. Miller
1975 "Young adults as partners and planners." Paper presented at the Scientific Session of the 103rd Annual Meeting, American Public Health Association, Chicago, November.

Brownlee, W. Elliot, and Mary M. Brownlee
1976 *Women in the American Economy: A Documentary History, 1975–1929.* New Haven, Conn.: Yale University Press.

Buber, Martin
1958 *I and Thou.* New York: Scribner's.

Buckhout, R. et al.
1971 "The war on people: A scenario for population control?" Unpublished manuscript. California State College, Hayward.

Buckley, Walter
1967 *Sociology and Modern Systems Theory.* Englewood Cliffs, N.J.: Prentice-Hall.

Bukstel, Lee, Gregory Roeder, Peter Kilmann, James Laughlin, and Wayne Sotile.
1978 "Projected extramarital sexual involvement in unmarried college students." *Journal of Marriage and the Family* 40 (May):337–340.

Bumpass, Larry, and Ronald Rindfuss
1979 "Children's experience of marital disruption." *American Journal of Sociology* 85:49–65.

Bumpass, Larry L., and Charles F. Westoff
1970 *The Later Years of Childbearing.* Princeton, N.J.: Princeton University Press.

Burgess, E. W., and P. Wallin
1953 *Engagement and Marriage.* Philadelphia: Lippincott.

Burgess, Ernest W., Harvey Locke, and Mary Thomes
1963 *The Family: From Institution to Companionship.* 3d edition New York: American.

Buric, O., and A. Zelevic
1967 "Family authority, marital satisfaction and the social network in Yugoslavia." *Journal of Marriage and the Family* 29:325–336.

Buxembaum, Alva
1973 "Women's rights and the class struggle." *Political Affairs* LII:22.

Cain, Glen G.
1966 *Married Women in the Labor Force.* Chicago: University of Chicago Press.

Cain, Leonard, Jr.
1964 "Life course and social structure." In R. E. L. Faris (ed.), *Handbook of Modern Sociology.* Chicago: Rand McNally.

Calhoun, Arthur W.
1919 *A Social History of the American Family.* Reprint. New York: Barnes and Noble, 1960.

Campbell, Helen
1893 *Women Wage Earners.* Reprint. New York: Arno Press, 1972.

Carlier, Auguste
1867 *Marriage in the United States.* New York: Leypoldt and Holt. Reprint. New York: Arno Press, 1972.

Carns, Donald E.
1969 "Religiosity, premarital sexuality and the American college student." Unpublished doctoral dissertation, Indiana University, Bloomington.
1973 "Talking about sex: Notes on first coitus and the double sexual standard." *Journal of Marriage and the Family* 35:677–688.

Carroll, Kathy (ed.)
1978 *Sexuality and Aging.* Minneapolis: Ebenezer Center for Aging and Human Development.

Carter, Hugh, and Paul C. Glick
1970 *Marriage and Divorce: A Social and Economic Study.* Cambridge, Mass.: Harvard University Press.

Centers, R., B. Raven, and A. Rodrigues
1971 "Conjugal power structure: A reexamination." *American Sociological Review* 36:264–278.

Chafetz, Janet Saltzman
1978 *Masculine/Feminine or Human?* 2d edition. Itasca, Ill.: F. E. Peacock Publishers, Inc.

Chesser, E.
1957 *The Sexual, Marital and Family Relations of English Women.* New York: Ray.

Chinchilla, Norma S.
1977 "Industrialization, monopoly capitalism, and women's work in Guatemala." *Signs* 3 (Autumn):38–56.

Chisholm, Shirley
1970 *Unbought and Unbossed.* Boston: Houghton Mifflin.

Christensen, Harold T.
1968 "Children in the family: Relationship of number and spacing to marital success." *Journal of Marriage and the Family* 30:283–289.
1969 "The impact of culture and values." Pp. 155–159 in Carlfred Broderick and Jessie Bernard (eds.), *The Individual, Sex, and Society.* Baltimore: Johns Hopkins.

Christensen, Harold T., and Christina F. Gregg
1970 "Changing sex norms in America and Scandinavia." *Journal of Marriage and the Family* 32:616–627.

Clark, H.
1968 *The Law of Domestic Relations in the United States.* St. Paul: West.

Clatworthy, Nancy Moore
1975 "Living together." Pp. 67–89 in Nona Glazer-Malbin (ed.), *Old Family/New Family.* New York: D. Van Nostrand Co.

Clayton, Richard, and Harwin Voss
1977 "Shacking up: Cohabitation in the 1970's" *Journal of Marriage and the Family* 39 (May):273–283.

Coale, Ansley J.
1974 "The history of the human population." *Scientific American* 231 (September):41–51.

Cohen, Jessica Field
1979 "Male roles in mid-life." *The Family Coordinator* 28 (October):465–471.

Cohen, Malcolm S.
1969 "Married women in the labor force: An analysis of participation rates." *Monthly Labor Review* 92 (October):31–35.

Cole, Charles Lee
1977 "Cohabitation in social context." Pp. 62–79 in Roger W. Libby and Robert N. Whitehurst (eds.), *Marriage and Alternatives: Exploring Intimate Relationships.* Glenview, Ill.: Scott, Foresman and Company.

Coleman, James S.
1966 "Female status and premarital sexual codes." *American Journal of Sociology* 72:217.

Collins, Randall
1971 "A conflict theory of sexual stratification." *Social Problems* 19:3–21.

Constantine, Larry, and Joan Constantine
1971 "Group and multilateral marriage: Definitional notes, glossary, and annotated bibliography." *Family Process* 10:157–176.
1973a *Group Marriage.* New York: Macmillan
1973b "Sexual aspects of group marriage." Pp. 182–191 in R. W. Libby and R. N. Whitehurst (eds.), *Renovating Marriage.* Danville, Cal.: Consensus Publishers.

Coombs, Lolagene C.
1977 "Preferences for sex of children among U.S. couples." *Family Planning Perspectives* 9 (Nov./Dec.):259–265.

Cooper, Pamela, Barbara Cumber, and Robin Hartner.
1978 "Decision-making patterns and postdecision adjustment of childfree husbands and wives," *Alternative Lifestyles* 1 (Feb.): 71–94.

Coser, Lewis A.
1956 *The Functions of Social Conflict.* New York: Free Press.

Cott, Nancy F.
1977 *The Bonds of Womanhood: "Women's Sphere" in New England, 1780–1835.* New Haven, Conn.: Yale University Press.

Cottrell, Ann Baker
1973 "Cross-national marriage as an extension of an international life style: A study of Indian-Western couples." *Journal of Marriage and the Family* 35:739–741.

Cowing, Cedric
1968 "Sex and preaching in the Great Awakening." *American Quarterly* 20:624–644.

Cox, Mary Jane Truesdall, and Lory Cease
1978 "Joint custody." *Family Advocate* 1 (Summer): 10–13, 42–44.

Cromwell, R. E., and D. H. Olson (eds.)
1975 *Power in Families.* New York: Wiley.

Cuber, John, and Peggy Harroff
1965 *Sex and the Significant Americans.* Baltimore: Penguin.

Current Population Reports
(See U.S. Bureau of the Census.)

Cutright, Phillips
1971 "Income and family events: Marital stability." *Journal of Marriage and the Family* 33:291–306.
1972a "The teenage sexual revolution and the myth of an abstinent past." *Family Planning Perspectives* 4(1):24.
1972b "Illegitimacy in the United States: 1920–1968." Commission on Population Growth and the American Future, *Vol. 1: Demographic and Social Aspects of Population Growth.* Washington, D.C.: U.S. Government Printing Office.

Cutright, Phillips, and Karen B. Cutright
1973 "Abortion: The court decision and some consequences of a constitutional amendment." Mimeographed. Bloomington, Ind.: Department of Sociology, Indiana University.

D'Andrade, Roy G.
1966 "Sex differences and cultural institutions." Pp. 174–204 in Eleanor E. Maccoby (ed.), *The Development of Sex Differences,* Stanford, Calif.: Stanford University Press.

David, Deborah S., and Robert Brannon (eds.)
1976 *The Forty-Nine Percent Majority: The Male Sex Role.* Reading, Mass.: Addison Wesley Publishing Co.

Davidson, Kenneth M., Ruth Bader Ginsburg, and Herman Hill Kay
1974 *Sex-Based Discrimination: Text, Cases and Materials.* St. Paul, Minn., West Publishing Co.

Davis, Elizabeth Gould
1971 *The First Sex.* New York: G. P. Putnam's Sons.

Davis, Kingsley
1941 "Intermarriage in caste societies." *American Anthropologist* 43:376–395.

Davis, Murray S.
1973 *Intimate Relations.* New York: Free Press.

Delamater, John, and Patricia Maccorquodale.
1978 "Premarital contraceptive use: A test of two models." *Journal of Marriage and the Family* 40 (May):235–247.

Demeny, Paul
1974 "The populations of the underdeveloped countries." *Scientific American* 231 (September):148–159.

deMiranda, Glaura Vasques
1977 "Women's labor force participation in a developing society: The case of Brazil." *Signs* 3 (Autumn):261–274.

Demos, John
1972 "Demography and psychology in the historical study of family life: A personal report." Pp. 561–569 in Laslett, 1972.

Denfeld, Duane
1974 "Dropouts from swinging: The marriage counselor as informant." Pp. 260–267 in Smith and Smith, 1974.

Denfeld, Duane, and Michael Gordon
1970 "The sociology of mate swapping: Or the family that swings together clings together." *Journal of Sex Research* 6 (May):85–100.

De Rougemont, Denis
1940 *Love in the Western World.* New York: Harcourt, Brace.

Deutscher, Irwin
1962 "Socialization for postparental life." Pp. 508–523 in Arnold Rose (ed.), *Human Behavior and Social Processes.* Boston: Houghton Mifflin.

Dinitz, S., R. Dynes, and A. Clark
1954 "Preference for male or female children: Traditional or affectional." *Journal of Marriage and Family Living* 16:128–130.

Dizard, Jan
1968 *Social Change in the Family.* Chicago: Community and Family Study Center, University of Chicago.

Dowd, James J.
1975 "Aging as exchange: A preface to theory." *Journal of Gerontology* 30:584–594.

Drabek, Thomas, William Key, Patricia Erickson, Juanita Crowe
1975 "The Impact of Disaster on Kin Relationships." *Journal of Marriage and the Family* 37 (August): 481–494.

Dressel, Paula, and W. Ray Avant
1978 "Neogamy and older persons: An examination of alternatives for intimacy in the later years." *Alternative Life Styles* 1 (February):13–36.

Driver, Anne Barstow
1976 "Review essay: Religion." *Signs* 2 (Winter):434–442.

Duberman, Lucille
1974 *Marriage and Its Alternatives.* New York: Praeger.
1975 *The Reconstituted Family.* Chicago: Nelson-Hall.
1977 *Marriage and Other Alternatives.* 2d edition. New York: Praeger.

Duke, James T.
1976 *Conflict and Power in Social Life.* Provo, Utah: Brigham Young University Press.

Durkheim, Emile
1893 *The Division of Labor in Society.* Translated by George Simpson. New York: Free Press edition, 1933.

Duvall, Evelyn M.
1962 *Family Development.* 2d edition. Philadelphia: J. B. Lippincott Co.

Dyer, Everett
1963 "Parenthood as crisis: A re-study." *Marriage and Family Living* 25:196–201.

Eber, Irene
1976 "Images of women in recent Chinese fiction: Do women hold up half the sky?" *Signs* 2 (Autumn):24–34.

Ehrhardt, Anke
1977 "Gender development." Paper read at the Summer Program of the Institute for Sex Research, Indiana University, July 28, 1977.

Ehrhardt, A. A., R. Epstein, and J. Money
1968 "Fetal androgens and female gender identity in the early treated adrenogenital syndrome." *Johns Hopkins Medical Journal* 122:160, as cited in Ramey (1973).

Ehrlich, Annette
1976 "The adaptable primates." *Human Behavior* 5 (November):25–30.

Ehrmann, Winston
1957 "Some knowns and unknowns in research into human sex behavior." *Marriage and Family Living* 19:16–22.
1959 *Premarital Dating Behavior*. New York: Holt.

Eichler, Margrit
1977 "Sociology of feminist research in Canada." *Signs* 3 (Winter):409–422.

Einbinder, Michael P.
1973–74 "The legal family—A definitional analysis." *Journal of Family Law* 13:781–802.

Eisler, Riane Tennenhaus
1977 *Dissolution: No-Fault Divorce, Marriage, and the Future of Women*. New York: McGraw-Hill.

Elder, Glen H., Jr.
1975 "Age differentiation and the life course." Pp. 165–190 in *Annual Review of Sociology*, vol. 1. Palo Alto, Calif.: Annual Reviews, Inc.

Ellis, Albert
1970 "Group marriage: A possible alternative?" Pp. 85–97 in Herbert Otto (ed.), *The Family in Search of a Future*. New York: Appleton-Century-Crofts.

Emerson, Richard M.
1962 "Power-dependence relations." *American Sociological Review* 27:31–41.

Engels, Friedrich
1884 *The Origin of the Family, Private Property and the State*. Chicago: Charles H. Kerr, 1902 edition.

Erlanger, Howard S.
1974 "Social class differences in parents' use of physical punishment." Pp. 150–158 in Steinmetz, Suzanne, and Straus, Murray (eds.), *Violence in the Family*. New York: Dodd, Mead.

Espenshade, Thomas
1973 *The Cost of Children in Urban United States*. Population Monograph Series, No. 14. Berkeley: University of California Institute of International Studies.

Etzkowitz, Henry
1971 "The male sister: Sexual separation of labor in society." *Journal of Marriage and the Family* 33:431–434.

Euripides
Hippolytus. Translated by David Grene. Pp. 231–291 in David Grene and Richmond Lattimore (eds.), *Greek Tragedies*,

vol. 1. Chicago: University of Chicago Press.

Everett, William, and Julie Everett
1975 "Childless marriages: A new vocation?" *U.S. Catholic* 40(May):38–39.

Farber, Bernard
1964 *Family: Organization and Interaction*. San Francisco: Chandler.
1966 *Kinship and Family Organization* (ed.). New York: John Wiley.
1973 *Family and Kinship in Modern Society*. Glenview, Ill.: Scott, Foresman and Co.

Fasteau, Marc Feigen
1974 *The Male Machine*. New York–McGraw-Hill.

Fawcett, James T. (ed.)
1972 *The Satisfactions and Costs of Children: Theories, Concepts, Methods*. A summary report and proceedings of the Workshop on Assessment of the Satisfactions and Costs of Children, April 27-29. Honolulu: East-West Population Institute.

Feldman, Harold
1971 "The effects of children on the family." Pp. 107–125 in Andree Michel (ed.), *Family Issues of Employed Women in Europe and America*. Leiden, Netherlands: E. J. Brill.

Feldman, H., and M. Feldman
1973 "The relationship between the family and occupational functioning in a sample of rural women." Ithaca, N.Y. Department of Human Development and Family Studies, Cornell University.

Feldman, Harold, and Margaret Feldman
1975 "The family life cycle: Some suggestions for recycling." *Journal of Marriage and the Family* 37 (May):277–284.

Feldman, Saul, and Gerald Theilbar
1972 *Deviant Life Styles: Diversity in American Society*. Boston: Little, Brown.

Feline, Peter Gabriel
1975 *Him/Her/Self: Sex Roles in Modern America*. New York: Harcourt Brace Jovanovich and Mentor Books.

Ferriss, Abbott
1971 *Indicators of Trends in the Status of American Women*. New York: Russell Sage Foundation.

Felstein, Ivor
1970 *Sex in Later Life*. Baltimore: Penguin.

Field, Mark G., and Karin I. Flynn
1970 "Worker, mother, housewife: Soviet woman today." In Georgene H. Seward and Robert C. Williamson (eds.), *Sex Roles in Changing Society*. New York: Random House. Pp. 257–284.

Figes, Eva
1970 *Patriarchal Attitudes*. New York: Stein and Day.

Finkel, Madelon Lubin, and David J. Finkel
1975 "Sexual and contraceptive knowledge, attitudes, and behavior of male adolescents." *Family Planning Perspectives* 7 (Nov./Dec.):256–260.

Firestone, Shulamith
1970 *The Dialectic of Sex*. New York: Morrow.

Fitzpatrick, M. Louise
1977 "Review essay: Nursing." *Signs* 2 (Summer):818–834.

Fogarty, Michael P., Rhona Rapoport, and Robert N. Rapoport
1971 *Sex, Career and Family.* Beverly Hills, Calif.: Sage.

Foote, Nelson
1954 "Sex as play." *Social Problems* 1:159–164.

Forisha, Barbara Lusk
1978 *Sex Roles and Personal Awareness.* Morristown, N. J.: General Learning Press.

Forrest, Jacqueline Darroch, Christopher Tietze, and Ellen Sullivan
1978 "Abortion in the United States, 1976–1977." *Family Planning Perspectives* 10 (Sept./Oct.):271–279.

Fox, Alan
1974 *Beyond Contract: Work, Power and Trust Relations.* London: Faber and Faber.

Fox, Greer Litton
1974 "Powerlessness, pragmatics, and resentment; The female response to the male role in contraception." Paper presented at the Groves Conference on Marriage and the Family. Hot Springs, Ark. April. Mimeo.
1977a "'Nice girl': Social control of women through a value construct." *Signs* 2(Summer):805–817.
1977b "Sex-role attitudes as predictors of contraceptive use among unmarried university students." *Sex Roles* 3:265–283.

Frankel, Lillian B.
1970 *This Crowded World.* Washington, D.C.: Population Reference Bureau.

Franklin, Benjamin
1745 "Advice to a young man on choosing a mistress." In Leonard Labare and Whitfield Bell, Jr. (eds.), *The Papers of Benjamin Franklin*, Vol. 3. New Haven, Conn.: Yale University Press, 1961.

French Institute of Public Opinion
1961 *Patterns of Sex and Love.* New York: Crown.

Friedl, Ernestine
1975 *Women and Men: An Anthropologist's View.* New York: Holt, Rinehart and Winston.

Friedlander, Judith
1976 "Comment on Harriet Whitehead's Review of *Woman's Evolution.*" *Signs* 2 (Winter):501–503.

Friend, Richard A.
1980 "GAYging: Adjustment and the Older Gay Male." *Alternative Lifestyles* 3 (May):231–248.

Fromm, Erich
1956 *The Art of Loving.* New York: Harper & Row. Paperback edition, Bantam Books.

Furstenberg, Frank F., and Albert G. Crawford
1978 "Family support: Helping teenage mothers to cope." *Family Planning Perspectives* 10 (Nov./Dec.):322–333.

Gaer, Joseph, and Ben Siegel
1964 *The Puritan Heritage: America's Roots in the Bible.* New York: Mentor.

Gagnon, John H., and William Simon
1967a "Femininity in the Lesbian community." *Social Problems* 15:212–221.
1967b (eds.), *Sexual Deviance.* New York: Harper & Row.
1970 (eds.), *The Sexual Scene.* Chicago: Aldine.
1973 *Sexual Conduct.* Chicago: Aldine.

Galligan, Richard, and Stephen Bahr
1978 "Economic well-being and marital stability: Implications for income maintenance programs." *Journal of Marriage and the Family* 40 (May):283–290.

Gardner, Richard
1977 *The Parents' Book About Divorce.* New York: Doubleday.

Garland, T. Neal
1972 "The better half? The male in the dual profession family." Pp. 199–215 in Constantina Safilios-Rothschild (ed.), *Toward a Sociology of Women.* Lexington, Mass.: Xerox College Publishing.

Gebhard, Paul
1966 "Factors in marital orgasm." *Journal of Social Issues* 22:89–95.
1971 "Human sexual behavior: A summary statement." Pp. 206–217 in Donald Marshall and Robert Guggs (eds.), *Human Sexual Behavior.* New York: Basic Books.
1972 "Incidence of overt homosexuality in the United States and Western Europe." Pp. 22–29 in *Livingood,* 1972.
1973 "Sex differences in sexual response." *Archives of Sexual Behavior* 2:201–203.

Geiger, H. Kent
1968 *The Family in Soviet Russia.* Cambridge: Harvard University Press.

Gelles, Richard J.
1972 *The Violent Home.* Beverly Hills, Calif.: Sage.
1973a "An exploratory study of intra-family violence." Unpublished Ph.D. dissertation, University of New Hampshire, Durham, N.H.
1973b "Child abuse as psychopathology: A sociological critique and reformulation." *American Journal of Orthopsychiatry* 43:611–621. (Reprinted in Steinmetz and Straus, 1974.)
1979 *Family Violence.* Beverly Hills, Calif.: Sage.

Gendell, Murray
1963 *Swedish Working Wives.* Totowa, N.J.: Bedminster Press.

Genovese, Eugene
1974 *Roll, Jordon, Roll: The World The Slaves Made.* New York: Pantheon, 1974.

Gersick, Kelin
1979 "Fathers by choice: Divorced men who receive custody of their children." Pp. 307–323 in Levinger and Moles (eds.).

Gerstel, Naomi
1979 "Marital alternatives and the regulation of sex: Commuter couples as a test case." *Alternative Lifestyles* 2 (May):145–176.

Gillespie, Dair L.
1971 "Who has the power? The marital struggle." *Journal of Marriage and the Family* 33:445–458.

Gilmartin, Brian
1974 "Sexual deviance and social networks: A study of social, family, and marital interaction patterns among co-marital sex participants." Pp. 291–323 in Smith and Smith, 1974.

Gilmartin, Brian, and Dave V. Kusisto
1973 "Some personal and social characteristics of mate-sharing swingers." Pp. 146–165 in

Roger W. Libby and Robert N. Whitehurst (eds.), *Renovating Marriage*. Danville, Calif.: Consensus Publishers.

Glazer-Malbin, Nona
1976 "Housework." *Signs* 1 (Summer): 905–922.

Glenn, Norval D.
1975 "Psychological well-being in the post-parental stage: Some evidence from national surveys." *Journal of Marriage and the Family* 37:105–110.
1979 "Attitude toward premarital, extramarital, and homosexual relations in the United States in the 1970s." *Journal of Sex Research* (May).

Glenn, Norval D., and Charles Weaver
1977 "The marital happiness of remarried divorced persons." *Journal of Marriage and the Family* 39 (May):331–337.

Glick, Paul C.
1977 "Updating the life cycle of the family." *Journal of Marriage and the Family* 39 (February):5–13.
1979 *Current Population Reports Special Studies*, series P-23, no. 78, "The future of the American family." U.S. Bureau of the Census.

Glick, Paul C., and Arthur J. Norton
1977 "Marrying, divorcing, and living together in the U.S. today." *Population Bulletin*, vol. 32, no. 5 (Washington, D.C.: Population Reference Bureau).

Goffman, Erving
1959 *The Presentation of Self in Everyday Life*. New York: Anchor Books.
1963 *Stigma*. Englewood Cliffs, N.J.: Prentice-Hall.

Goldberg, Herb
1976 *The Hazards of Being Male*. Plainview, N.Y.: Nash Publishing.

Goldberg, Steven
1974 *The Inevitability of Patriarchy* (expanded edition). New York: William Morrow and Co.

Goode, William J.
1956 *After Divorce*. Reissued in 1965 as *Women in Divorce*. New York: Free Press.
1959 "The theoretical importance of love." *American Sociological Review* 24:38–47.
1962 "Marital satisfaction and instability: A cross-cultural class analysis of divorce rates." *International Social Science Journal* 14:507–526.
1963 *World Revolution and Family Patterns*. New York: Free Press.
1964 *The Family*. Englewood Cliffs, N.J.: Prentice-Hall.
1971 "Force and violence in the family." *Journal of Marriage and the Family* 33:624–636.

Goodman, Mary Ellen, and Alma Beman
1971 "Child's eve-views of life in an urban barrio." Pp. 109–122 in Nathaniel Wagner and Marsha Haug (eds.), *Chicanos: Social and Psychological Perspectives*. St. Louis: C. V. Mosby Co.

Gordis, Robert
1967 *Sex and the Family in the Jewish Tradition*. New York: The Burning Bush Press.

Gordon, Albert I.
1964 *Intermarriage: Interfaith, Interracial, Interethnic*. Boston: Beacon.

Gordon, Michael
1971 "From an unfortunate necessity to a cult of mutual orgasm." In James Henslin (ed.), *The Sociology of Sex*. New York: Appleton-Century-Crofts.
1978 *The American Family: Past, Present, and Future*. New York: Random House.

Gordon, Michael, and Penelope Shankweiler
1971 "Different equals less: Female sexuality in recent marriage manuals." *Journal of Marriage and the Family* 33:459–465.

Gould, Lois
1972 "X: A fabulous child's story." *Ms.* 1(December): 74–76, 105–106.
1978 *X: A Fabulous Child's Story*. Houston: Daughters Publishing Company.

Gouldner, Alvin
1960 "The norm of reciprocity: A preliminary statement." *American Sociological Review* 25 (April):161–178.

Graham-Murray, James
1966 *A History of Morals*. London: Library 33 Ltd.

Granovetter, Mark S.
1973 "The strength of weak ties." *American Journal of Sociology* 78 (May):1360–1380.

Green, Richard
1974 *Sexual Identity Conflict in Children and Adults*. New York: Basic Books.

Greenblat, Cathy, Peter Stein and Norman Washburne
1974 *The Marriage Game*. New York: Random House.

Greenwald, Harold
1970 "Marriage as a non-legal voluntary association." Pp. 51–56 in Herbert Otto (ed.), *The Family in Search of a Future*. New York: Appleton-Century-Crofts.

Grimshaw, Allen D.
1970 "Interpreting collective violence: An argument for the importance of social structure." *Annals* 391 (September)9–20.

Groat, H. T., and A. G. Neal
1967 "Social psychological correlates of urban fertility." *American Sociological Review* 32:945–959.

Gross, Harriet, Jessie Bernard, Alice Dan, Nona Glazer, Judith Lorber, Martha McClintock, Niles Newton, and Alice Rossi
1979 "Considering 'a biosocial perspective on parenting.'" *Signs* 4 (Summer):695–717.

Group for the Advancement of Psychiatry (GAP), Committee on Public Education.
1973 *Joys and Sorrows of Parenthood*. New York: Scribner.

Gustavus, Susan O., and James R. Henley, Jr.
1971 "Correlates of voluntary childlessness in a select population." *Social Biology* 18:277–284.

Gutman, Herbert
1976 *The Black Family in Slavery and Freedom*. New York: Pantheon.

Guttentag, Marcia, and Helen Bray
1977 "Teachers as mediators of sex-role stan-

dards." Pp. 395–411 in Alice G. Sargent (ed.), *Beyond Sex Roles*. St. Paul: West Publishing Company.

Hacker, Helen Mayer
1975 "Gender roles from a cross-cultural perspective." Pp. 185–215 in Lucile Duberman, *Gender and Sex in Society*. New York: Praeger Publishers.

Hallenbeck, Phyllis
1966 "An analysis of power dynamics in marriage." *Journal of Marriage and the Family* 28:200–203.

Haller, Archibald, and Irwin Miller
1971 *The Occupational Aspiration Scale*. Cambridge, Mass.: Schenkman.

Hammond, Boone, and Joyce Ladner
1969 "Socialization into sexual behavior in a Negro slum ghetto." Pp.41–51 in Carlfred Broderick and Jessie Bernard (eds.), *The Individual, Sex, and Society*. Baltimore: Johns Hopkins.

Hannan, Michael, Nancy Brandon Tuma, and Lyle Groeneveld
1978 "Income and independence effects on marital dissolution: Results from the Seattle and Denver income-maintenance experiments." *American Journal of Sociology* 84:611–633.

Harder, Mary White, James T. Richardson, and Robert B. Simmonds
1972 "Jesus people." *Psychology Today* 6 (December):45–50, 110–113.

Harris, Thomas
1967 *I'm OK—You're OK*. New York: Harper & Row. Avon edition, paperback.

Harrison, James
1978 "Men's roles and men's lives: Review essay." *Signs* 4 (Winter):324–336.

Hass, Paula H.
1972 "Maternal role incompatibility and fertility in Latin America." *Journal of Social Issues* 28(2):111–128.

Haug, Marie R.
1973 "Social class measurement and women's occupational roles." *Social Forces* 52 (September):86–98.

Havens, Elizabeth
1973 "Women, work, and wedlock: A note on female marital patterns in the United States." *American Journal of Sociology* 78:975–981.

Havighurst, Robert J.
1953 *Human Development and Education*. New York: Longmans, Green.

Heer, David
1958 "Dominance and the working wife." *Social Forces* 36:341–347.
1963 "The measurement and bases of family power: An overview." *Journal of Marriage and the Family* 25:133–139.
1974 "The prevalence of black-white marriage in the United States, 1960 and 1970." *Journal of Marriage and the Family* 36:246–258.

Hennig, Margaret
1973 "Family dynamics for developing positive achievement motivation in women: The successful woman executive." *Anals*

of the New York Academy of Sciences 208 (March):76–81.

Hennig, Margaret, and Anne Jardim
1977 *The Managerial Woman*. New York: Doubleday.

Henshel, Anne-Marie
1973 "Swinging: A study of decision making in marriage." *American Journal of Sociology* 78:885–891.

Henslin, James M. (ed.)
1971 *Studies in the Sociology of Sex*. New York: Appleton-Century-Crofts.

Henze, Lura F., and John W. Hudson
1974 "Personal and family characteristics of cohabiting and non-cohabiting college students." *Journal of Marriage and the Family* 36(November):722–727.

Hershberger, Ann
1973 "The transiency of urban communes." Pp. 485-491 in Kanter, 1973.

Herzog, Elizabeth
1967 *About the Poor: Some Facts and Some Fictions*. Children's Bureau Publication no. 451. Washington, D.C.: U.S. Department of Health, Education and Welfare.

Hess, Beth, and Joan Waring
1978 "Parent and child in later life: Rethinking the relationship." Pp. 241–273 in Lerner and Spanier (eds.).

Hess, Robert, and Judith Torney
1962 "Religion, age and sex in children's perceptions of family authority." *Child Development* 33:781–789.
1967 *The Development of Political Attitudes in Children*. Chicago: Aldine.

Hill, Reuben
1949 *Families Under Stress: Adjustment to the Crises of War, Separation and Reunion*. New York: Harper.
1964 "Methodological issues in family development research." *Family Process* 3:186–206.
1970 *Family Development in Three Generations*. Cambridge, Mass.: Schenkman Publishing Co., Inc.
1978 "Psychosocial consequences of the first birth: A discussion." Pp. 392–401 in Miller and Newman (eds.).

Hill, Reuben, and Roy H. Rodgers
1964 "The developmental approach." Pp. 171–211 in Harold T. Christensen (ed.), *Handbook of Marriage and the Family*. Chicago: Rand McNally.

Hill, Robert, and Lawrence Shackleford
1975 "The black extended family revisited." *The Urban League Review* 1(Fall):18–24. Reprinted in Staples (ed.), 1978.

Himes, Norman
1936 *Medical History of Contraception*. Reprint. New York: Schocken, 1970.

Hiner, N. Ray
1975 "Adolescence in eighteenth century America." *History of Childhood Quarterly* 3(Fall, 1975):253–280.

Hirsch, Barbara
1976 *Living Together: A Guide to the Law for Unmarried Couples*. Boston: Houghton Mifflin.

Hobbs, Daniel F., Jr.
1965 "Parenthood as crisis: A third study." *Journal of Marriage and the Family* 27(August):367–372.
1968 "Transition to parenthood: A replication and an extension." *Journal of Marriage and the Family* 30(August):413–417.

Hobbs, Daniel F., Jr., and Sue Peck Cole
1976 "Transition to parenthood: A decade replication." *Journal of Marriage and the Family* 38(November):723–731.

Hobbs, Daniel F., Jr., and Jane Maynard Wimbish
1977 "Transition to parenthood by black couples." *Journal of Marriage and the Family* 39(November):677–689.

Hoffman, Lois Wladis
1972a "A psychological perspective on the value of children to parents: Concepts and measures." In Fawcett, 1972.
1972b "Early childhood experiences and women's achievement motives." *Journal of Social Issues* 28(2):129–155.
1973 "The professional woman as mother." *Annals of the New York Academy of Sciences* 208(March):211–217.
1974 "Effects on child." Pp. 126–166 in Hoffman and Nye, 1974.
1978 "Effects of the first child on the woman's role." Pp. 340–367 in Miller and Newman.

Hoffman, Lois Wladis, and Martin L. Hoffman
1973 "The value of children to parents." Pp. 19–76 in James T. Fawcett (ed.), *Psychological Perspectives on Population.* New York: Basic Books.

Hoffman, Lois Wladis, and Jean Denby Manis
1978 "Influences of children on marital interaction and parental satisfaction and dissatisfaction." Pp. 165–213 in Lerner and Spanier (eds.).
1979 "The value of children in the United States: A new approach to the study of fertility." *Journal of Marriage and the Family* 41(August).

Hoffman, Lois Wladis, and F. Ivan Nye
1974 *Working Mothers.* San Francisco: Jossey-Bass.

Hoffman, Martin L.
1963 "Personality, family structure, and social class as antecedents of parental power assertion." *Child Development* 34:869–884.

Holmstrom, Lynda Lytle
1972 *The Two-Career Family.* Cambridge, Mass.: Schenkman.

Holter, Harriet
1970 *Sex Roles and Social Structure.* Oslo, Norway: Universitetsforlaget.

Homans, George C.
1961 *Social Behavior: Its Elementary Forms.* New York: Harcourt, Brace, and World.

Hong, Lawrence
1976 "The role of women in the People's Republic of China: Legacy and Change." *Social Problems* 23(June):545–557.

Hooker, Evelyn
1965 "The homosexual community." In *Perspectives in Psychopathology.* New York: Oxford. (Reprinted in Gagnon and Simon, 1967b).

Hoult, Thomas Ford, Lura Henze, and John Hudson
1978 *Courtship and Marriage in America.* Boston: Little, Brown & Co.

Houseknecht, Sharon K.
1979 "Childlessness and marital adjustment." *Journal of Marriage and the Family* 41(May):259–265.

Humanae Vitae: Pope Paul's Encyclical on Birth Control.
1968 St. Louis: Religious Information Bureau of the Knights of Columbus. Pamphlet No. 69.

Hunter, Gertrude
1973 "Pediatrician." In *Successful Women in the Sciences: An Analysis of Determinants.* Special issue of the *Annals of the New York Academy of Sciences* 208(March):37–40.

Ickes, William, Brian Shermer, and Jeff Steeno
1979 "Sex and sex-role influences in same-sex dyads." *Social Psychology Quarterly* 42(December):373–385.

Jaffe, Dennis T., and Rosabeth Kanter
1979 "Couple strains in communal households: A four-factor model of the separation process." Pp. 114–133 in George Levinger and Oliver C. Moles (eds.), *Divorce and Separation: Context, Causes, and Consequences.* New York: Basic Books.

Jaffe, Frederick S.
1973 "Commentary: Some policy and program implications of 'contraceptive failure in the United States.'" *Family Planning Perspectives* 5(Summer):143–144.

Jenkins, Jim
1978 "Wonder before you wander, mate: This is Carolina, not California." *The Greensboro (N.C.) Record,* July 5, 1978, p. A–6.

Jennings, Theodore
1977 "Homosexuality and the Christian Faith." *The Christian Century* 94(February 16).

Jensen, Mehri Samandari
1974 "Role differentiation in female homosexual quasi-marital unions." *Journal of Marriage and the Family* 36:360–367.

Jurich, Anthony P. and Julie A. Jurich
1974 "The effect of cognitive moral development upon the selection of premarital sexual standards." *Journal of Marriage and the Family* 36(November):736–741.

Kaberry, Phyllis M.
1953 *Women of the Grassfields.* London: Her Majesty's Stationery Office.

Kadushin, Alfred
1970 "Single parent adoptions: An overview and some relevant research." *Social Service Review* 44(3).

Kanowitz, Leo
1973 *Sex Roles in Law and Society.* Albuquerque: University of New Mexico Press.

Kanter, Rosabeth Moss
1968 "Commitment and social organization: A study of commitment mechanisms in utopian communities." *American Sociological Review* 33:499–517.
1972 "'Getting it all together': Communes past, present, future." Pp. 311–325 in Louise Kapp Howe (ed.), *The Future of the Family.* New York: Simon and Schuster.

1973 *Communes: Creating and Managing the Collective Life.* New York: Harper & Row.

1974 "Communes for all reasons." *Ms.* 3(August):62–67.

1977 *Work and Family in the United States.* New York: Russell Sage Foundation.

Kantner, John F., and Melvin Zelnik

1972 "Sexual experience of young unmarried women in the United States." *Family Planning Perspectives* 4(October):9–17.

1973 "Contraception and pregnancy: Experience of young unmarried women in the United States." *Family Planning Perspectives* 5(Winter):21–35.

Karr, S. B.

1971 "Individual aspirations as related to early and late acceptance of contraception." *The Journal of Social Psychology* 83:235–245.

Kassel, Victor

1970 "Polygyny after sixty." Pp. 137–143 in Herbert Otto (ed.), *The Family in Search of a Future.* New York: Appleton-Century-Crofts.

Katchadourian, Herant, and Donald T. Lunde

1975 *Fundaments of Human Sexuality,* 2d ed. New York: Holt, Rinehart and Winston.

Katy, Barbara J.

1972 "Cooling motherhood." *National Observer,* December 20.

Katzenstein, Alfred

1970 "Male and female in the German Democratic Republic." In Georgene H. Seward and Robert C. Williamson (eds.), *Sex Roles in Changing Society.* New York: Random House.

Kelley, Harold, and Anthony Stahelski

1970 "Social interaction basis of cooperators' and competitors' beliefs about others." *Journal of Personality and Social Psychology* 16:66–91.

Kelley, H. H., and D. P. Schenitzki

1972 "Bargaining." In C. G. McClintock (ed.), *Experimental Social Psychology.* New York: Holt.

Kendall, Maurice

1979 "The world fertility survey: The current situation and some findings." Paper presented at the Annual Meeting of the Population Association of America. Philadelphia, April 26–28. Summarized in "Digest," *Family Planning Perspectives* 11 (July/August):259–260.

Kennedy, David M.

1970 *Birth Control in America: The Career of Margaret Sanger.* New Haven, Conn.: Yale University Press.

Kephart, William

1964 "Legal and procedural aspects of marriage and divorce." Pp. 944–968 in Harold T. Christensen (ed.), *Handbook of Marriage and the Family.* Chicago: Rand McNally.

1977 *The Family, Society, and the Individual,* 4th ed. Boston: Houghton Mifflin.

Kerckhoff, Alan C.

1972 *Socialization and Social Class.* Englewood Cliffs, N.J.: Prentice-Hall.

Kim, Choong Soon

1974 "The *Yon' jul-hon* or Chain-String Form of marriage arrangement in Korea." *Journal of Marriage and the Family* 36(August):575–579.

King, Karl, Jack O. Balswick, and Ira E. Robinson

1977 "The continuing premarital sexual revolution among college females." *Journal of Marriage and the Family* 39(August):455–459.

Kinkade, Kathleen

1973 *A Walden Two Experiment.* New York: Morrow.

Kinsey, Alfred C., W. B. Pomeroy, and C. E. Martin

1948 *Sexual Behavior in the Human Male.* Philadelphia: Saunders.

Kinsey, A. C., W. B. Pomeroy, C. E. Martin, and P. H. Gebhard

1953 *Sexual Behavior in the Human Female.* Philadelphia: Saunders. New York: Pocket Books paperback edition.

Kirkendall, Lester

1958 "Understanding the problems of the male virgin." Pp. 123–129 in Isadore Rubin and Lester Kirkendall (eds.), *Sex in the Adolescent Years.* New York: Association.

Kirschner, Betty Frankle, and Laurel Richardson Walum

1978 "Two-location families: Married singles." *Alternative Life-Styles* 1(November):513–525.

Klatzky, Sheila R.

1972 *Patterns of Contact with Relatives.* Washington, D.C.: American Sociological Association.

Klaus, Marshall H., and John H. Kennell

1978 "Parent-to-infant attachment." Pp. 5–29 in Stevens and Matthews.

Klineberg, O.

1964 *The Human Dimension in International Relations.* New York: Holt.

Kobrin, Frances

1976 "The primary individual and the family: Changes in living arrangements in the United States since 1940." *Journal of Marriage and Family* 38(May):233–239.

Kohen, Janet, Carol A. Brown, and Roslyn Feldberg

1979 "Divorced mothers: The costs and benefits of female family control." Pp. 228–245 in Levinger and Moles (eds.).

Kohlberg, Lawrence

1966 "A cognitive developmental analysis of children's sex-role concepts and attitudes." In E. E. Maccoby (ed.), *The Development of Sex Differences.* Stanford, Calif.: Stanford University Press.

Kohn, Melvin L.

1969 *Class and Conformity: A Study in Values.* Homewood, Ill.: Dorsey.

Kolbenschlag, Michael

1976 "Dr. Estelle Ramey: Reclaiming the feminine legacy." *Human Behavior* 5(July):24–27.

Koller, Marvin

1974 *Families: A Multigenerational Approach.* New York: McGraw-Hill.

Komarovsky, Mirra

1962 *Blue-Collar Marriage.* New York: Random House.

Kraditor, Aileen S.
1968 *Up From the Pedestal.* Chicago: Quadrangle Books.

Krain, Mark, Drew Cannon, and Jeffery Bagford
1977 "Rating-dating or simply prestige homogamy? Data on dating in the Greek System on a midwestern campus." *Journal of Marriage and the Family* 39(November):663–674.

Krantzler, Mel
1973 *Creative Divorce.* New York: Evans. New American Library Signet paperpack edition.

Krause, Harry D.
1971 *Illegitimacy: Law and Social Policy.* Indianapolis: Bobbs-Merrill.

Krauskopf, Joan M.
1977 "Partnership marriage: Legal reforms needed." Pp. 93–121 in Jane Roberts Chapman and Margaret Gates (eds.), *Women into Wives: The Legal and Economic Impact of Marriage.* Beverly Hills, Calif.: Sage Publications.

Kreps, Juanita
1971 *Sex in the Market Place.* Baltimore: Johns Hopkins.

Kriesberg, Louis
1973 *The Sociology of Social Conflicts.* Englewood Cliffs, N.J.: Prentice-Hall.

Kristeva, Julia
1975 "On the women of China." *Signs* 1(Autumn):57–81.

Kutner, Nancy, and Donna Brogan
1974 "An investigation of sex-related slang vocabulary and sex-role orientation among male and female university students." *Journal of Marriage and the Family* 36:474–484.

Kutner, Nancy, and Richard Levinson
1976 "The toy salesperson: A potential gatekeeper for change in sex-role definitions." Paper presented at the Annual Meetings of the American Sociological Association, New York, August.

LaFree, Gary
1974 "Independence among the Igbo women of West Africa." Unpublished paper, Department of Sociology, Indiana University, Bloomington, Indiana.

Lamb, Michael E.
1975 "Fathers: Forgotten contributors to child development." *Human Development* 18:245–266.

Lamphere, Louise
1977 "Anthropology." *Signs* 2(Spring):612–627.

Lamson, Peggy
1968 *Few Are Chosen: American Women in Political Life Today.* Boston: Houghton Mifflin.

Landman, Lynn C.
1977 "Birth control in India: The carrot and the rod?" *Family Planning Perspectives* 9(May/June):101–110.

Lasch, Christopher
1973 "Marriage in the middle ages." *The Columbia Forum* 2(Fall).
1977 *Haven in a Heartless World: The Family Besieged.* New York: Basic Books.

Laslett, Peter (ed., with the assistance of Richard Wall)
1972 *Household and Family in Past Time.* London and New York: Cambridge University Press (second impression 1974).

Laws, Judith Long, and Pepper Schwartz
1977 *Sexual Scripts: The Social Construction of Female Sexuality.* Hinsdale, Ill.: The Dryden Press.

Leacock, Eleanor
1976 "Comment on Harriet Whitehead's review of *Woman's Evolution.*" *Signs* 2(Winter):504–507.
1977 "Review of *Toward an Anthropology of Women,* ed. by Rayna Reiter. In *Signs* 3(Winter):495–497.

Lederer, W. J., and D. D. Jackson
1968 *The Mirages of Marriage.* New York: Norton.

Lee, Gary
1977 *Family Structure and Interaction.* Philadelphia: Lippincott.
1978 "Marriage and morale in later life." *Journal of Marriage and the Family* 40(February):131–139.

LeMasters, E. E.
1957 "Parenthood as crisis." *Marriage and Family Living* 19:352–355.
1975 *Blue-Collar Aristocrats.* Madison: University of Wisconsin Press.

Lenski, Gerhard, and Jean Lenski
1978 *Human Societies,* Third Edition. New York: McGraw Hill.

Lerner, Gerda (ed.)
1972 *Black Women in White America.* New York: Random House.

Lerner, Richard, and Graham Spanier (eds.)
1978 *Child Influences on Marital and Family Interaction: A Life-Span Perspective.* New York: Academic Press.

Lever, Janet
1978 "Sex differences in the complexity of children's play." *American Sociological Review* 43(August):471–483.

Levine, Donald, Ellwood Carter, and Eleanor Miller Gorman
1976 "Simmel's influence on American sociology. Part I." *American Journal of Sociology* 81:813–845.

Levine, Robert A.
1970 "Sex roles and economic change in Africa." Pp. 174–180 in John Middleton (ed.), *Black Africa.* New York: Macmillan.

Levinger, George
1966 "Physical abuse among applicants for divorce," an excerpt from "Source of marital satisfaction among applicants for divorce." *American Journal of Orthopsychiatry* 36(October), as reprinted in Steinmetz and Straus, 1974, pp. 85–88.
1979 "A social psychological perspective on marital dissolution." Pp. 37–60 in Levinger and Moles (eds.).

Levinger, George, and Oliver C. Moles (eds.)
1979 *Divorce and Separation: Context, Causes, and Consequences.* New York: Basic Books.

Levi-Strauss, Claude
1949 "The principle of reciprocity." Chapter 5

of *Les Structures Elementaires de la Parente.* Presses Universitaires de France. Abridged and translated by Rose L. Coser and Grace Frazer. Pp. 74–84 in Lewis Coser and Bernard Rosenberg (eds.), *Sociological Theory,* 2d edition. New York: Macmillan.

1956 "The family." Pp. 261–285 in Harry L. Shapiro (ed.), *Man, Culture, and Society.* New York: Oxford.

Lewis, Diane K.

1975 "The black family: Socialization and sex roles." *Phylon* 36 (September):221–237.

1977 "A response to inequality: Black women, racism, and sexism." *Signs* 3(Winter):339–361.

1978 "Reply to Bernstein's comment." *Signs* 3(Spring):736–737.

Lewis, Lionel, and Dennis Brissett

1967 "Sex as work: A study of avocational counseling." *Social Problems* 15 (Summer):8–18.

Lewis, Oscar

1951 *Life in a Mexican Village: Tepoztlan Restudied.* Urbana: University of Illinois Press.

1968 *A Study of Slum Culture.* New York: Random House.

Lewis, Robert, Phillip Freneau, and Craig Roberts

1979 "Fathers and the postparental transition." *Family Coordinator* 28(October):514–520.

Lewis, Sasha Gregory

1979 *Sunday's Women: A Report on Lesbian Life Today.* Boston: Beacon Press.

Libby, Roger W.

1977a "Creative singlehood as a sexual lifestyle: Beyond marriage as a rite of passage." Pp. 37–61 in Robert W. Libby and Robert N. Whitehurst (eds.), *Marriage and Alternatives: Exploring Intimate Relationships.* Glenview, Ill.: Scott, Foresman.

1977b "Extramarital and comarital sex: A critique of the literature." Pp. 80–111 in Roger W. Libby and Robert N. Whitehurst (eds.), *Marriage and Alternatives: Exploring Intimate Relationships.* Glenview, Ill.: Scott, Foresman.

Libby, Roger W., and John E. Carlson

1973 "A theoretical framework for premarital sexual decisions in the dyad." *Archives of Sexual Behavior* 2:365–378.

Liebow, Elliot

1967 *Tally's Corner: A Study of Negro Street-Corner Men.* Boston: Little, Brown.

Liljestrom, Rita

1966 Knstroller i ungdomsbker och massmedia (Sex roles in literature for adolescents and in mass media). In *Kynne eller Kon? (Talent or Sex).* Stockholm.

Lindsey, Ben B.

1926 "The companionate marriage." *Redbook* (October).

1927 "The companionate marriage." *Redbook* (March).

Linner, Birgitta

1966 "Sexual morality and sexual reality—the Scandinavian approach." *American Journal of Orthopsychiatry* 36:686–693.

1967 *Sex and Society in Sweden.* New York: Pantheon.

Litwak, Eugene

1960 "Occupational mobility and extended family cohesion." *American Sociological Review* 25(February):9–21.

Liu, William T., I. W. Hutchinson, and L. K. Hong

1973 "Conjugal power and decision making: a methodological note on cross-culture study of the family." *American Journal of Sociology* 79:84–98.

Livingood, John M.

1972 *National Institute of Mental Health Task Force on Homosexuality: Final Report and Background Papers.* Rockville, Md.: National Institute of Mental Health.

Locke, Harvey J.

1968 *Predicting Adjustment in Marriage: A Comparison of a Divorced and a Happily Married Group.* New York: Greenwood.

Loether, Herman

1964 "The meaning of work and adjustment to retirement." Pp. 517–525 in A. B. Shostak and W. Gomberg (eds.), *Blue-Collar World.* Englewood Cliffs, N.J.: Prentice-Hall.

1967 *Problems of Aging.* Belmont, Calif.: Dickenson.

Longfellow, Cynthia

1979 "Divorce in context: Its impact on children." Pp. 287–306 in Levinger and Moles (eds.).

Lopata, Helena Znaniecki

1973a *Widowhood in an American City.* Cambridge, Mass.: Schenkman.

1973b "Self-identity in marriage and widowhood." *The Sociological Quarterly* 14 (Summer):407–418.

1979 *Women as Widows: Support Systems.* New York: Elsevier North Holland, Inc.

Lord, Edith

1970 "Emergent Africa." Pp. 44–66 in Seward and Williamson.

Lott, J., and B. E. Lott

1963 *Negro and White Youth.* New York: Holt.

Lowenthall, Marjorie Fiske, and Clayton Haven

1968 "Interaction and adaptation: Intimacy as a critical variable." *American Sociological Review* 33:20–30.

Luckey, Eleanore, and Gilbert Nass

1969 "A comparison of sexual attitudes and behavior in an international sample." *Journal of Marriage and the Family* 31:364–379.

Luepnitz, Deborah

1979 "Which aspects of divorce affect children?" *The Family Coordinator* 28(January):79–85.

Luker, Kristin

1975 *Taking Chances.* Berkeley: University of California Press.

Lyness, Judith, Milton Lipetz, and Keith Davis

1972 "Living together: An alternative to marriage." *Journal of Marriage and the Family* 34:305–311.

McAdoo, Harriette

1978 "The impact of extended family variables upon the upward mobility of black families." Summary report of research sponsored by the Office of Child Development. Department of Health, Education and Welfare, Grant No. 90-C-631(1). Washington, D.C.: Howard University.

McCall, Michal M.
1966 "Courtship as social exchange." Pp. 190–210 in Bernard Farber (ed.), *Kinship and Family Organization*. New York: John Wiley.

McClelland, David C.
1961 *The Achieving Society*. Princeton, N.J.: D. Van Nostrand.

McKinley, Donald Gilbert
1964 *Social Class and Family Life*. New York: The Free Press.

McNeill, John J.
1976 *The Church and the Homosexual*. Kansas City, Kansas: Sheed Andrews and McMeel, Inc.

Macciocchi, Maria
1972 *Daily Life in Revolutionary China*. New York: Monthly Review Press.

Maccoby, Eleanor Emmons, and Carol Nagy Jacklin
1974 *The Psychology of Sex Differences*. Stanford, Calif.: Stanford University Press.

Macklin, Eleanor
1972 "Heterosexual cohabitation among unmarried college students." *Non-traditional Family Forms in the 1970's*. (Reprint of a special issue of *The Family Coordinator*, October, 1972). Minneapolis: National Council on Family Relations, pp. 95–104.

Maddox, George
1970 "Themes and issues in sociological theories of human aging." *Human Development* 13:17–27.

Mainardi, Pat
1970 "The politics of housework." Pp. 447–454 in Robin Morgan (ed.), *Sisterhood Is Powerful*. New York: Vintage.

Malcolm X
1964 *The Autobiography of Malcolm X*. New York: Grove.

Malinowski, Bronislaw
1930 "Parenthood, the basis of social structure." In V. F. Calverton and S. D. Schmalhausen (eds.), *The New Generation*. New York: Macauley. Reprinted in Rose L. Coser (ed.), *The Family: Its Structures and Functions*, 2d edition. New York: St. Martin's, 1974.

Marciano, Teresa Donati
1978 "Male pressure in the decision to remain childfree." *Alternative Lifestyles* 1(February):95-112.

Markle, Gerald E.
1973 "Sexism and the sex ratio." Paper read at the annual meeting of the American Sociological Association, New York, August 1973.
1974 "Sex ratio at birth: Values, variance, and some determinants." *Demography* 11:131–142.

Martin, Del, and Phyllis Lyon
1972 *Lesbian/Woman*. New York: Bantam Books.

Martin, Del, and Paul Moriah
1972 "Homosexual love—woman to woman, man to man." Pp. 120–134 in Herbert Otto, *Love Today*. New York: Association.

Martin, Elmer, and Joanne Mitchell Martin
1978 *The Black Extended Family*. Chicago: University of Chicago Press.

Martin, Ralph G.
1969 *Jennie: The Life of Lady Randolph Churchill*. Englewood Cliffs, N.J.: Prentice-Hall.

Marx, Karl
1848 *The Communist Manifesto*. Chicago: Henry Regnery Co. Gateway Edition, 1969.

Maslow, A. H.
1970 *Motivation and Personality*. New York: Harper & Row.

Masters, William, and Virginia Johnson
1966 *Human Sexual Response*. Boston: Little, Brown.
1973 "Why 'working at' sex doesn't work." *Redbook* 140(April):87.
1979 *Homosexuality in Perspective*. Boston: Little, Brown.

Mattessich, Paul
1978 "The family life cycle and three forms of social participation." Unpublished manuscript, University of Minnesota. Mimeographed.

Matthews, Sarah
1979 *The Social World of Old Women: Management of Self-Identity*. Beverly Hills, Calif.: Sage.

Maraini, Dacia
1975 "Report from Italy." *Signs* 1(Winter):553–554.

Mead, Margaret
1935 *Sex and Temperament*. New York: Morrow.
1966 "Marriage in two steps." *Redbook* 127 (July):48–49.
1968 "A continuing dialogue on marriage." *Redbook* 130(April):44.

Melton, Willie, and Darwin L. Thomas
1976 "Instrumental and expressive values in mate selection of black and white college students." *Journal of Marriage and the Family* 38(August):509–517.

Meltzer, Bernard N.
1967 "Mead's social psychology." Pp. 5–24 in Jerome G. Manis and Bernard N. Meltzer (eds), *Symbolic Interaction: A Reader In Social Psychology*. Boston: Allyn and Bacon.

Meltzer, Bernard N., John W. Petras, Larry T. Reynolds
1975 *Symbolic Interactionism: Genesis, Varieties and Criticism*. Boston: Routledge and K. Paul (London and Boston).

Mendes, H.
1975 "Parental experiences of single fathers." Ph.D. dissertation, U.C.L.A.

Mernissi, Fatima
1975 *Beyond the Veil: Male-Female Dynamics in a Modern Muslim Society*. New York: Schenkman Publishing Co.

Merton, Robert K.
1974 "Intermarriage and the social structure: Fact and theory." *Psychiatry* 4:361–374.
1959 "Social structure and anomie: Revisions and extensions." In Ruth Nanda Anshen (ed.), *The Family: Its Function and Destiny*. New York: Harper & Row.

Meyer, J., and B. Sobieszek
1972 "Effect of a child's sex on adult interpretations of its behavior." *Developmental Psychology* 6:42–48.

Middleton, Russell
1962 "A deviant case: Brother-sister and father-daughter marriage in Ancient Egypt." *American Sociological Review* 27:603–611.

Mill, John Stuart
1869 "The subjection of women." Reprinted in John Stuart Mill and Harriet Taylor Mill, *Essays on Sex Equality*, edited by Alice Rossi. Chicago: University of Chicago Press, 1970, pp. 125–242.

Miller, Arthur A.
1970 "Reactions of friends to divorce." Pp. 56–77 in Paul Bohannan (ed.), *Divorce and After*. Garden City, N.Y.: Doubleday.

Miller, Brian
1978 "Adult sexual resocialization: Adjustments toward a stigmatized identity." *Alternative Lifestyles* 1(May):207–234.
1979 "Gay fathers and their children." *The Family Coordinator* 28(October):544–552.

Miller, Daniel, and Guy Swanson
1958 *The Changing American Parent: A Study in the Detroit Area*. New York: Wiley.

Miller, Howard L., and Paul S. Siegel
1972 *Loving: A Psychological Approach*. New York: Wiley.

Miller, Warren B.
1973 "Psychological vulnerability to unwanted pregnancy." *Family Planning Perspectives* 5(Fall):199–201.

Miller, Warren B., and Lucile F. Newman (eds.)
1978 *The First Child and Family Formation*. Chapel Hill, N.C.: Carolina Population Center, University of North Carolina.

Milton, John
1820 *The Doctrine and Discipline of Divorce*. London: Sherwood, Neely, and Jones.

Minnigerode, Fred, and Marcy Adelman
1978 "Elderly homosexual women and men: Report on a pilot study." *The Family Coordinator* 27(October):451–456.

Mirande, Alfredo
1977 "The Chicano family: A reanalysis of conflicting views." *Journal of Marriage and the Family* 39(November):747–756.

Mitchell, Juliet
1971 *Woman's Estate*. New York: Pantheon.

Moles, Oliver C.
1979 "Public welfare payments and marital dissolution: A review of recent studies." Pp. 167–180 in Levinger and Moles (eds.).

Monahan, Thomas P.
1973 "Marriage across racial lines in Indiana." *Journal of Marriage and the Family* 35:632–640.

Money, John, and Anke A. Ehrhardt
1972 *Man and Woman, Boy and Girl*. Baltimore: The Johns Hopkins University Press. (Mentor paperback edition used in citations.)

Money, John, and Patricia Tucker
1975 *Sexual Signatures: On Being a Man or a Woman*. Boston: Little, Brown.

Monthly Vital Statistics Reports (See U.S. Department of Health, Education and Welfare, or U.S. Department of Health and Human Services.)

Mooney, Elizabeth C.
1979 "I asked my daughter why she lives like she does." *Washington Post*, May 6, p. B8.

Moore, Kristin
1978 "Teenage childbirth and welfare dependency." *Family Planning Perspectives* 10(July/August):233–235.

Moore, Patricia
1974 "Interview with Art and Irene Siegle." *Chicago Daily News*, May 26, P. 15.

Morgan, Edmund S.
1966 *The Puritan Family*. New York: Harper & Row.

Mueller, Eva
1972 "Economic cost and value of children: Conceptualization and measurement." In Fawcett, 1972.

Mueller, Samuel A.
1971 "The new triple melting pot: Herberg revisited." *Review of Religious Research* 13:18–33.

Mulvihill, J. J., M. M. Tumin, and L. A. Curtis
1969 *Crimes of Violence*. Staff report to the National Commission on the Causes and Prevention of Violence. Washington, D.C.: U.S. Government Printing Office.

Murdock, George P.
1949 *Social Structure*. New York: Macmillan.

Murillo, Nathan
1971 "The Mexican American family." Pp. 97–108 in N. N. Wagner and M. J. Haug (eds.), *Chicanos: Social and Psychological Perspectives*. St. Louis: Mosby.

Murphy, Patrick E., and William A. Staples.
1979 "A modernized family life cycle." *Journal of Consumer Research* (June).

Nagi, Saad Z.
1977 *Child Maltreatment in the United States*. New York: Columbia University Press.

National Alliance for Optional Parenthood
1978 "Are you kidding yourself?" Pamphlet on teenage pregnancy.

National Center for Health Statistics
(See U.S. Department of Health, Education and Welfare, or U.S. Department of Health and Human Services.)

Nelson, James B.
1978 *Embodiment: An Approach to Sexuality and Christian Theology*. Minneapolis: Augsburg.

Nielsen, Joyce McCarl
1978 *Sex in Society: Perspectives on Stratification*. Belmont, Calif.: Wadsworth Publishing Co.

Nimkoff, M. F. (ed.)
1965 *Comparative Family Systems*. Boston: Houghton Mifflin.

Nisbet, Robert A.
1970 *The Social Bond*. New York: Knopf.

Noble, Jeanne L.
1966 "The American Negro woman." Pp. 522–547 in John P. Davis (ed.), *The American Negro Reference Book*. Englewood Cliffs, N.J.: Prentice-Hall.

Nock, Stephen L.
1979 "The family life cycle: Empirical or con-

ceptual tool?" *Journal of Marriage and the Family* 41(February):15–26.

Norton, Arthur, and Paul Glick
1979 "Marital instability in America: Past, present, and future." Pp. 6–19 in Levinger and Moles (eds.).

Nunnally, Jum C.
1972 "Major issues, measurement methods, and research strategies for investigating the effects of children on parents. In Fawcett, 1972.

Nye, F. Ivan, and Lois W. Hoffman
1963 *The Employed Mother in America.* Chicago: Rand McNally.

Nye, F. Ivan
1963 "Marital Interaction." Pp. 263–281 in Nye and Hoffman, 1963.
1974a "Sociocultural context." Pp. 1–31 in Hoffman and Nye, 1974.
1974b "Husband-wife relationship." Pp. 186–206 in Hoffman and Nye, 1974.

Oakley, Ann
1974 *Woman's Work: The Housewife, Past and Present.* New York: Pantheon. Vintage paperback edition.

O'Brien, John
1971 "Violence in divorce-prone families." *Journal of Marriage and the Family* 33:692–698.

Ogilvy, Jay, and Heather Ogilvy
1972 "Communes and the reconstruction of reality." Pp. 83–99 in Sallie Teselle (ed.), *The Family, Communes and Utopian Societies.* New York: Harper Torchbooks.

Olson, D., and C. Rabunsky
1972 "Validity of four measures of family power." *Journal of Marriage and the Family* 34:224–234.

O'Neill, Nena, and George O'Neill
1970 "Patterns in group sexual activity." *Journal of Sex Research* 6(2):101–112.
1972 *Open Marriage.* New York: Evans. Avon paperback edition.

O'Neill, William L.
1967 *Divorce in the Progressive Era.* New Haven, Conn.: Yale University Press.

Orden, Susan, and Norman Bradburn
1969 "Working wives and marriage happiness." *American Journal of Sociology* 74:392–407.

Orthner, Dennis, Terry Brown, and Dennis Ferguson
1976 "Single-parent fatherhood: An emerging lifestyle." *The Family Coordinator* 25(October):429–437.

Orthner, Dennis, and Ken Lewis
1979 "Evidence of single-father competence in childrearing." *Family Law Quarterly* XIII(Spring):27–47.

Ovid
Metamorphoses. Translated by Mary M. Innes. Baltimore: Penguin, 1955.

Pagelow, Mildred D.
1976 "Lesbian mothers." Paper presented at the annual meetings of the American Sociological Association, New York, August 31, 1976.

Pala, Achola O.
1977 "Definitions of women and development: An African perspective." *Signs* 3(Autumn):9–13.

Palmore, Erdman
1968 "The effects of aging on activities and attitudes." *The Gerontologist* 8(Winter): 259–263.
1970 (ed.) *Normal Aging: Reports from the Duke Longitudinal Study 1955-1969.* Durham, N.C.: Duke University Press.

Papanek, Hanna
1977 "Development planning for women." *Signs* 3(Autumn):14–21.

Parron, Eugenia, and Lillian E. Troll
1978 "Golden wedding couples: Effects of retirement on intimacy in long-standing marriages." *Alternative Lifestyles* 1(November):447–464.

Parsons, Talcott
1942 "Age and sex in the social structure." *American Sociological Review* 7:604–606.
1943 "The kinship system of the contemporary United States." *American Anthropologist* 45:22–38.
1951 *The Social System.* New York: Free Press.
1955 "The American family: Its relation to personality and to social structure." In T. Parsons and R. F. Bales (eds.), *Family Socialization and Interaction Process.* New York: Free Press.

Pearlin, Leonard
1972 *Class Context and Family Relations: A Cross-National Study.* Boston: Little, Brown.

Peck, Ellen
1971 *The Baby Trap.* New York: Bernard Geis.

Peterman, Dan, Carl Ridley, and Scott Anderson
1974 "A comparison of cohabiting and noncohabiting college students." *Journal of Marriage and the Family* 36(May):344–354.

Peters, John
1979 *Social Problems in Canada: Divorce.* Toronto: University of Toronto, Guidance Centre, Faculty of Education.

Peterson, Candida C., and James L. Peterson
1973 "Preference for sex of offspring as a measure of change in sex attitudes." *Psychology* 10(August):3–5.

Pettigrew, Thomas
1964 *A Profile of the Negro American.* Princeton, N.J.: D. Van Nostrand.

Piddington, Ralph
1965 "A study of French Canadian kinship." *International Journal of Comparative Sociology* 12(1). Reprinted in C. C. Harris (ed.), *Reading in Kinship in Urban Society.* New York: Pergamon, 1970, pp. 71–98.

Pineo, Peter C.
1961 "Disenchantment in the later years of marriage." *Marriage and Family Living* 23:3–11.

Plateris, Alexander A.
1979 "Divorces by marriage cohort." *Vital and Health Statistics,* series 21, no. 34 (August). Washington, D.C.: National Center for Health Statistics.

Pleck, Joseph and Jack Sawyer (eds.)
1974 *Men and Masculinity.* Englewood Cliffs, N.J.: Prentice-Hall.

Pleck, Joseph H.
1976 "The male sex role: Definitions, problems, and sources of change." *Journal of Social Issues* 32:155–164.

Poffenberger, T.
1969 "Husband-wife communication and motivational aspects of population control in an Indian village." Monograph Series no. 10 (December). New Delhi: Central Family Planning Institute.

Pogrebin, Bertrand B.
1972 "How does it feel to be the husband of . . .?" *Ms.* (Sept., 1972). Reprinted in *Scenes From Life*, Judy Blankenship (ed.), pp. 385–388. Boston: Little, Brown, 1976.

Polk, Barbara Bovee, Robert Stein, and Lon Polk
1973 "The potential of the urban commune for changing sex roles." Paper read at the annual meeting of the American Sociological Association, New York, August.

Polonko, Karen
1979 "Accounting for the conditions of voluntary childlessness." Ph.D. dissertation, Indiana University.

Pomeroy, Wardell B.
1972 *Dr. Kinsey and the Institute for Sex Research.* New York: Harper & Row.

Ponse, Barbara
1978 *Identities in the Lesbian World.* Westport, Conn.: Greenwood Press.

Potts, Malcolm, Peter Diggory, and John Peel.
1977 *Abortion.* Cambridge, England: Cambridge University Press.

Powers, Edward A., and Gordon L. Bultena
1976 "Sex differences in intimate friendships of old age." *Journal of Marriage and the Family* 38(November):739–747.

Powers, Jeanne Audrey
1976 "Rituals with the divorced." Pp. 73–96 in *Ritual in a New Day.* Nashville: Abingdon.

Presser, Harriet B., and Larry L. Bumpass
1972 "The acceptability of contraceptive sterilization among U.S. couples: 1970." *Family Planning Perspectives* 4(October):18–26.

Preston, S. H., and J. McDonald
1979 "The incidence of divorce within cohorts of American marriages contracted since the Civil War." *Demography* 16:1–23.

Pryor, Edward, Jr.
1972 "Rhode Island family structure: 1875 and 1960." In Laslett, 1972.

Queen, Stuart, and Robert Habenstein
1974 *The Family in Various Cultures*, 4th ed. Philadelphia: Lippincott.

Rabin, Albert I.
1970 "The sexes: Ideology and reality in the Israeli kibbutz." In Georgene H. Seward and Robert C. Williamson (eds.), *Sex Roles in a Changing Society.* New York: Random House, Pp. 285–307.

Rabkin, Leslie, and Melford Spiro
1970 "Postscript: The kibbutz in 1970." Chapter 9 in Melford Spiro, *Kibbutz: Venture in Utopia.* New York: Schocken.

Rains, Prudence
1971 *Becoming an Unwed Mother.* Chicago: Aldine.

Rainwater, Lee
1960 *And the Poor Get Children.* Chicago: Quadrangle.
1964 "Marital sexuality in four 'cultures of poverty.'" *Journal of Marriage and the Family* 26(November):457–466.
1965 "Family Design: Marital Sexuality, Family Size, and Contraception.* Chicago: Aldine.
1966a "Sex in the culture of poverty." *Journal of Social Issues* 22(April), as reprinted in a later version in Carlfred Broderick and Jessie Bernard, *The Individual, Sex, and Society.* Baltimore: Johns Hopkins, 1969. Pp. 129–140.
1966b "Crucible of identity: The Negro lower-class family." *Daedalus* 95(Winter):172–216.
1970 *Behind Ghetto Walls.* Chicago: Aldine.

Ramey, Estelle
1973 "Sex hormones and executive ability." *Annals of the New York Academy of Sciences* 208(March 15):237–245.

Ramey, James
1972a "Communes, group marriage, and the upper-middle class." *Journal of Marriage and the Family* 34:647–655.
1972b "Emerging patterns of innovative behavior in marriage." *Family Coordinator* (October). Reprinted in Smith and Smith, 1974.

Raphael, Sharon M., and Mina K. Robinson
1980 "The Older Lesbian," *Alternative Lifestyles* 3 (May): 207–229.

Rapoport, Rhona
1963 "Normal crises, family structures and mental health." *Family Process* 2(March):68–80.

Rapoport, Rhona, and Robert Rapoport and Ziona Strelitz, Stephen Kew
1977 *Fathers, Mothers and Society: Towards New Alliances.* New York: Basic Books.

Raschke, Helen, and Vernon Raschke
1979 "Family conflict and children's self-concepts: A comparison of intact and single-parent families." *Journal of Marriage and the Family* 41(May):367–374.

Rawlings, Stephen
1978 "Perspectives on American husbands and wives." *Current Population Reports: Special Studies*, Series P-23, No. 77. Washington, D.C.: U.S. Bureau of the Census, 1978.

Redford, Myron H., Gordon W. Duncan, and Denis J. Prager (eds.)
1974 *The Condom: Increasing Utilization in the United States.* San Francisco: San Francisco Press.

Reed, Evelyn
1975 *Woman's Evolution: From Matriarchal Clan to Patriarchal Family.* New York: Pathfinder Press.

Rehwinkel, Alfred M.
1959 *Planned Parenthood.* St. Louis: Concordia.

Reiss, Ira L.
1960a *Premarital Sexual Standards in America.* New York: Free Press.
1960b "Toward a sociology of the heterosexual relationship." *Journal of Marriage and Family Living* 22(May):139–155.

1967a "Some comments on premarital sexual permissiveness." *American Journal of Sociology* 72:558–559.

1967b *The Social Context of Premarital Sexual Permissiveness.* New York: Holt.

1972 "Premarital sexuality: Past, present, and future." Pp. 167–188 in Ira L. Reiss (ed.), *Readings on the Family System.* New York: Holt.

1973 "The role of sexuality in the study of family and fertility." Paper presented at the conference "Family and Fertility," sponsored by the Center for Population Research and the National Institute for Child Health and Human Development, June 13–16, Belmont, Elkridge, Maryland. Mimeographed.

Reiss, Ira L., Albert Banwart, and Harry Foreman

1975 "Premarital contraceptive usage: A study and some theoretical explorations." *Journal of Marriage and the Family* 37(August): 619–630.

Renne, Karen

1970 "Correlates of dissatisfaction in marriage. " *Journal of Marriage and the Family* 32:54–67.

Rheinstein, Max

1972 *Marriage Stability, Divorce, and the Law.* Chicago: University of Chicago Press.

Rich, Adrienne

1976 *Of Woman Born: Motherhood as Experience and Institution.* New York: Norton.

Richer, Stephen

1968 "The economics of child rearing." *Journal of Marriage and the Family* 30:462–466.

Richman, Judith

1977 "Bargaining for sex and status: The dating service and sex-role change." Pp. 158–165 in Peter J. Stein, Judith Richman, and Natalie Hannon (eds.), *The Family: Functions, Conflicts, and Symbols.* Reading, Mass.: Addison-Wesley.

Ridley, Carl, Dan Peterman, and Arthur Avery

1978 "Cohabitation: Does it make for a better marriage?" *The Family Coordinator* 27(April):129–136.

Riley, Matilda White and Anne Foner, in association with M. Moore, B. Hess, and B. Roth

1968 *Aging and Society,* vol. 1. New York: Russell Sage.

Roberts, Helene

1977 "The exquisite slave: The role of clothes in the making of the Victorian woman." *Signs* 2(Spring):554–569.

Robertson, Constance Noyes (ed.)

1970 *Oneida Community: An Autobiography, 1851–1876.* Syracuse, N.Y.: Syracuse University Press.

Robertson, Joan

1977 "Grandmotherhood: A study of role conceptions." *Journal of Marriage and the Family* 39(February):165–174.

1978 "Women in midlife crises, reverberations, and support networks." *The Family Coordinator* 27(October):375–382.

Robins, Lee, and Miroda Tomanec

1962 "Closeness to blood relatives outside the immediate family." *Marriage and Family Living* 24(November):340–346. Reprinted in Farber, 1966.

Rodgers, Roy H.

1964 "Toward a theory of family development." *Journal of Marriage and the Family* 26:262–270.

1973 *Family Interaction and Transaction: The Developmental Approach.* Englewood Cliffs, NJ: Prentice-Hall.

Rodman, Hyman

1967 "Marital power in France, Greece, Yugoslavia, and the United States: A cross-national discussion." *Journal of Marriage and the Family* 29:320–324.

1972 "Marital power and the theory of resources in cultural context." *Journal of Comparative Family Studies* 3:50–67.

Rohrlich-Leavitt, Ruby

1976 "Comment on Harriet Whitehead's review of *Woman's Evolution.*" *Signs* 2(Winter):498–500.

Rollins, Boyd, and Harold Feldman

1970 "Marital satisfaction over the family life cycle." *Journal of Marriage and the Family* 26:20–28.

Rollins, Boyd, and Richard Galligan

1978 "The developing child and marital satisfaction." Pp. 71–105 in Lerner and Spanier (eds.).

Roosevelt, Ruth, and Jeannette Lofas

1977 *Living in Step: A Remarriage Manual for Parents and Children.* New York: McGraw-Hill.

Rosaldo, Michelle Zimbalist

1974 "Woman, culture, and society: A theoretical overview." Pp. 17–42 in Michelle Zimbalist Rosaldo and Louise Lamphere (eds.), *Woman, Culture, and Society.* Stanford, Calif.: Stanford University Press.

Rosaldo, Michelle Zimbalist, and Louise Lamphere (eds.)

1974 *Woman, Culture, and Society.* Stanford Calif.: Stanford University Press.

Rose, H. J.

1958 *Gods and Heroes of the Greeks.* Cleveland: World Publishing.

Rosenberg, Bernard, and Joseph Bensman

1968 "Sexual patterns in three ethnic subcultures of an American underclass." *Annals of the American Academy of Political and Social Science* 376:61–75.

Rosenthal, Kristine, and Harry Keshet

1978 "The impact of childcare responsibilities on part-time or single fathers." *Alternative Lifestyles* 1(November):465–491.

Rosow, Irving

1973 *Socialization to Old Age.* Berkeley: University of California Press.

Rossi, Alice

1964 "Equality between the sexes: An immodest proposal." Pp. 98–143 in R. J. Lifton (ed.), *The Woman in America.* Boston: Beacon Press Daedalus Library.

1965 "Barriers to the career choice of engineering, medicine, or science among American women." Pp. 51–127 in Jacquelyn Mattfeld and Carol Van Aken (eds.),

Women and the Scientific Professions. Cambridge, Mass.: M.I.T. Press.

1968 "Transition to parenthood." *Journal of Marriage and the Family* 30:26–39.

1973a "Sexuality and gender roles." Lecture given in the Human Sexuality unit of the Year II Program in Psychiatry and Behavioral Sciences, The Johns Hopkins University School of Medicine, February 2. Revised version. Mimeographed.

1973b (ed.) *The Feminist Papers.* New York: Columbia University Press.

1977 "A biosocial perspective on parenting." *Daedalus* 106(Spring):1–31.

Rowbotham, Sheila
1972 *Women, Resistance and Revolution.* New York: Pantheon.

Rubin, Lillian Breslow
1976 *Worlds of Pain: Life in the Working-Class Family.* New York: Basic Books.

1979 *Women of a Certain Age: The Midlife Search for Self.* New York: Harper & Row.

Rubin, Zick
1973 *Liking and Loving.* New York: Holt.

Rugoff, Milton
1972 *Prudery and Passion.* New York: Putnam.

Russell, Bertrand
1929 *Marriage and Morals.*

Russell, Candyce Smith
1974 "Transition to parenthood: Problems and gratifications." *Journal of Marriage and the Family* 36(May):294.

Ryder, Norman
1973 "Contraceptive failure in the United States." *Family Planning Perspectives* 5(Summer):133–142.

Ryder, Norman, and Charles Westoff
1971 *Reproduction in the United States, 1965.* Princeton, N.J.: Princeton University Press.

Ryder, Robert G.
1970 "Dimensions of early marriage." *Family Process* 9(March):51–68.

1973 "Longitudinal data relating marriage satisfaction and having a child." *Journal of Marriage and the Family* 35:604–606.

Safa, Helen I.
1971 "The matrifocal family in the black ghetto: Sign of pathology or pattern of survival?" Pp. 35–59 in Charles O. Crawford (ed.), *Health and the Family: A Medical-Sociological Analysis.* New York: Macmillan.

Safilios-Rothschild, Constantina
1967 "A comparison of power structure and marital satisfaction in urban Greek and French families." *Journal of Marriage and the Family* 29:345–352.

1969 "Family sociology or wives' family sociology? A cross-cultural examination of decision making." *Journal of Marriage and the Family* 31:290–301.

1970 "The study of family power structure: A review 1960–1969." *Journal of Marriage and the Family* 32:539–552.

St. George, George
1973 *Our Soviet Sister.* Washington, D.C.: Luce.

Sanday, Peggy R.
1973 "Toward a theory of the status of women." *American Anthropologist* 75:1682–1700.

Satir, Virginia
1967 "Marriage as a statutory five-year renewable contract." Paper presented at the annual convention of the American Psychological Association, Washington, D.C., September 1.

Scanzoni, John
1965 "A note on the sufficiency of wife responses in family research." *Pacific Sociological Review* (Fall):109–115.

1970 *Opportunity and the Family.* New York: Free Press.

1972 *Sexual Bargaining: Power Politics in the American Marriage.* Englewood Cliffs, N.J.: Prentice-Hall.

1975a "Sex roles, economic factors, and marital solidarity in black and white marriages." *Journal of Marriage and the Family* 37:130–145.

1975b *Sex Roles, Life Styles, and Childbearing: Changing Patterns in Marriage and Family.* New York: Free Press.

1975c "Change in gender roles." Unpublished student study.

1977 *The Black Family in Modern Society: Patterns of Stability and Security.* Chicago: University of Chicago Press (enlarged edition).

1978 *Sex Roles, Women's Work, and Marital Conflict.* Lexington, Mass.: Lexington Books, D.C. Heath Co.

1979a "Strategies for changing male family roles: Research and practice implications." *The Family Coordinator* 28(October):435–442.

1979b "Social processes and power in families." In Wesley R. Burr, Reuben Hill, F. Ivan Nye, and Ira L. Reiss (eds.), *Contemporary Theories About the Family,* vol. 1. New York: The Free Press.

1979c "A historical perspective on husband-wife bargaining power and marital dissolution." Pp. 20–36 in Levinger and Moles (eds.).

1980 "Contemporary marriage types: A research note." *Journal of Family Issues* 1(March):125–140.

Scanzoni, Letha, and Virginia Ramey Mollenkott
1978 *Is the Homosexual My Neighbor? Another Christian View.* San Francisco: Harper & Row.

Schäfer, Siegrid
1977 "Sociosexual behavior in male and female homosexuals: A study in sex differences." *Archives of Sexual Behavior* 6(September):355–364.

Schelling, T. C., and M. H. Halperin
1961 *Strategy and Arms Control.* New York: Twentieth Century Fund.

Schlesinger, Yaffa
1977 "Sex roles and social change in the kibbutz." *Journal of Marriage and the Family* 39(November):771–779.

Schmidt, Gunter and Volkmar Sigusch
1970 "Sex differences in responses to psychosexual stimulation by films and slides." *The Journal of Sex Research* 6:268–283.

1972 "Changes in sexual behavior among

young males and females between 1960–1970." *Archives of Sexual Behavior* 2:27–45.

1973 "Women's sexual arousal." Pp. 117–143 in Joseph Zubin and John Money (eds.), *Contemporary Sexual Behavior: Critical Issues in the 1970s.* Baltimore: Johns Hopkins.

Schmidt, G., V. Sigusch, and S. Schafer
1973 "Responses to reading erotic stories: Male-female differences." *Archives of Sexual Behavior* 2(June):181–199.

Schneider, David
1968 *American Kinship: A Cultural Account.* Englewood Cliffs, N.J.: Prentice-Hall.

Schoenmaker, Adrian, and Davis Radosevich
1976 "Men nursing students: How they perceive their situation." *Nursing Outlook* 24(1976):298–303. Cited in *Signs* (Summer):1977, p. 831.

Schram, Rosalyn Weinman
1979 "Marital satisfaction over the family life cycle: A critique and proposal." *Journal of Marriage and the Family* 41(February):7–12.

Schulz, David A.
1969 *Coming Up Black.* Englewood Cliffs, N.J.: Prentice-Hall.

Scott, Hilda
1974 *Does Socialism Liberate Women?* Boston: Beacon Press.

Scott, Jean Pearson
1979 "Single rural elders: A comparison of dimensions of life satisfaction." *Alternative Lifestyles* 2(August)359–378.

Scott, John Finley
1965 "The American college sorority: Its role in class and ethnic endogamy." *American Sociological Review* 30:514–527.

Seaman, Barbara
1972 *Free and Female.* New York: Coward, McCann and Geoghegan.

Sears, Robert, Eleanor E. Maccoby, and Harry Levin
1957 *Patterns of Child Rearing.* Evanston, Ill.: Row, Peterson.

Sedugin, P.
1973 *New Soviet Legislation on Marriage and the Family.* Moscow: Progress Publishers.

Seeley, John R., R. Alexander Sim, and Elizabeth W. Loosley
1956 *Crestwood Heights.* New York: Basic Books.

Segal, Sheldon J.
1972 "Contraceptive research: A male chauvinist plot?" *Family Planning Perspectives* 4(July):21–25.

Seidenberg, Robert
1970 *Marriage between Equals.* First published as *Marriage in Life and Literature.* New York: Philosophical Library. Doubleday, Anchor Press edition, 1973.

Seltman, Charles
1956 *Women in Antiquity.* London: Thames and Hudson.

Shanas, Ethel
1972 "Adjustment to retirement: Substitution or accommodation?" in Frances Carp (ed.) *Retirement.* New York: Behavioral Publications.

Shannon, T. W.
1917 *Eugenics: The Laws of Sex Life and Heredity.*

Marietta, Ohio: Mullikin. Replica edition. Garden City, N.Y.: Doubleday, 1970.

Shedd, Charlie W.
1968 *The Stork Is Dead.* Waco, Tex.: Word.

Shenker, Israel
1976 "Smithsonian urges public to dig at the family tree." *New York Times* (June 17).

Sheppard, Harold, and Neal Herrick
1972 *Where Have All the Robots Gone? Worker Dissatisfaction in the '70s.* New York: Free Press.

Shideler, Mary McDermott
1971 "An amicable divorce." *The Christian Century* (May 5).

Shorter, Edward
1977 *The Making of the Modern Family.* New York: Basic Books.

Shulman, Norman
1975 "Life-cycle variations in patterns of close relationships." *Journal of Marriage and the Family* 37(November):813–821.

Sickels, Robert J.
1972 *Race, Marriage and the Law.* Albuquerque: Univ. of New Mexico Press.

Sidel, Ruth
1972 *Women and Child Care in China.* New York: Hill and Wang. Baltimore: Penguin.

SIECUS (Sex Information and Education Council of the U.S.)
1970 *Sexuality and Man.* New York: Scribner's Sons.

Siegel, Jacob S.
1979 "Prospective trends in the size and structure of the elderly population, impact of mortality trends, and some implications." Pp. 7–22 in *Current Population Reports*, Series P-23, no. 78 (January). Washington, D.C.: U.S. Bureau of the Census.

Siegel, Sidney, and Lawrence Fouraker
1960 *Bargaining and Group Decision Making.* New York: McGraw-Hill.

Silka, Linda, and Sara Kiesler
1977 "Couples who choose to remain childless." *Family Planning Perspectives* 9(January/February):16–25.

Silverman, Phyllis
1972 "Widowhood and preventive intervention." *The Family Coordinator* 21(January):95–102.

Silverstein, Arthur J.
1972–73 "Comment: Constitutional aspects of the homosexual's right to a marriage license." *Journal of Family Law* 12:607–634.

Simmel, Georg
1950 *The Sociology of Georg Simmel.* Translated and edited by Kurt H. Wolff. New York: Free Press.
1955 *Conflict and the Web of Group-Affiliations:* Translated by Kurt H. Wolff and Reinhard Bendix. New York: Free Press.

Simon, William, and John Gagnon
1969 "On psychosexual development." Pp. 733–752 in D. A. Goslin (ed.), *Handbook of Socialization Theory and Research.* Chicago: Rand McNally.

Simon, W., A. S. Berger, and J. H. Gagnon
1972 "Beyond anxiety and fantasy: The coital

experiences of college youth." *Journal of Youth and Adolescence* 1:203–222.

Simpson, Joanne
1973 "Meteorologist." *Annals of the New York Academy of Sciences* 208(March 15):41–46. (Special issue, "Successful women in the sciences: An analysis of determinants.")

Skipper, James K., Jr., and Gilbert Nass
1966 "Dating behavior: A framework for analysis and an illustration." *Journal of Marriage and the Family* 28(November):412–420.

Sklar, J., and B. Berkov
1974 "Abortion, illegitimacy and the American birth rate." *Science* 185:909. Also see summary, "Legal abortion reduces out-of-wedlock births." Research news report. *Family Planning Perspectives* 7(January-February), 1975:11–12.

Skolnick, Arlene
1973 *The Intimate Environment.* Boston: Little, Brown.

Slocum, Walter L.
1966 *Occupational Careers.* Chicago: Aldine.

Smith, Daniel Scott
1973 "The dating of the American sexual revolution: Evidence and interpretation." Pp. 321–335 in Michael Gordon (ed.), *The American Family in Social-Historical Perspective.* New York: St. Martin's.

Smith, Harold E.
1965 "Family interaction patterns of the aged: A review." Pp. 143–161 in Arnold Rose and Warren Peterson (eds.), *Older People and Their Social World.* Philadelphia: Davis.

Smith, James, and Lynn Smith
1970 "Co-marital sex and the sexual freedom movement." *Journal of Sex Research* 6(2):131–142
1974 (eds.), *Beyond Monogamy.* Baltimore: Johns Hopkins.

Smith, Lynn, and James Smith
1973 "Co-marital sex: the incorporation of extramarital sex into the marriage relationship." In J. Zubin and J. Money (eds.), *Critical Issues in Contemporary Sexual Behavior.* Baltimore: Johns Hopkins. (Reprinted in Smith and Smith, 1974.)

Sobol, Marion Gross
1974 "Commitment to work." Pp. 63–80 in Hoffman and Nye, 1974.

Spanier, Graham B., and Robert F. Casto
1979 "Adjustment to separation and divorce: A qualitative analysis." Pp. 211–227 in Levinger and Moles (eds.), 1979.

Spanier, Graham B., Robert A. Lewis, and Charles L. Cole.
1975 "Marital adjustment over the family life cycle: The issue of curvilinearity." *Journal of Marriage and the Family* 37(May):263–275.

Spanier, Graham, and William Sauer
1979 "An empirical evaluation of the family life cycle." *Journal of Marriage and the Family* 41(February):27–38.

Spiro, Melford E.
1965 *Children of the Kibbutz.* New York: Schocken.
1970 *Kibbutz: Venture in Utopia.* New York: Schocken.

Spreitzer, Elmer, and Lawrence Riley
1974 "Factors associated with singlehood." *Journal of Marriage and the Family* 36:533–542.

Sprey, Jetse
1971 "On the management of conflict in families." *Journal of Marriage and the Family* 33:722–732.

Stack, Carol B., Mina D. Caulfield, Valerie Estes, Susan Landes, Karen Larson, Pamela Johnson, Juliet Rake, and Judith Shirek.
1975 "Anthropology." *Signs* 1(Autumn):147–159.

Stafford, Rebecca, Elaine Backman, and Pamela diBona
1977 "The division of labor among cohabiting and married couples." *Journal of Marriage and the Family* 39(February):43–57.

Stannard, Una
1977 *Mrs. Man.* San Francisco: Germainbooks.

Staples, Robert (ed.)
1978 *The Black Family: Essays and Studies.* 2d edition. Belmont, Calif.: Wadsworth.

Staples, Robert
1973 "The black dating game." *Essence* (October):92–96. Reprinted in Staples, 1978. Pp. 64–67.

Stein, Peter
1976 *Single.* Englewood Cliffs, N.J.: Prentice-Hall.

Steinmann, Anne, D. J. Fox, R. Farkas.
1968 "Male and female perceptions of male sex roles." Pp. 421–422 in *Proceedings of the American Psychological Association.*

Steinmetz, Suzanne K.
1977 *The Cycle of Violence: Assertive, Aggressive, and Abusive Family Interaction.* New York: Praeger.
1978 "Violence between family members." *Marriage and Family Review*, vol. 1, no. 3(May/June) 1–16.

Steinmetz, Suzanne, and Murray Straus
1973 "The family as a cradle of violence." *Society* 10 (September-October):50–58.
1974 (eds.), *Violence in the Family.* New York: Dodd, Mead.

Stember, Charles H.
1966 *Jews in the Mind of America.* New York: Basic Books.

Stephens, William
1963 *The Family in Cross-Cultural Perspective.* New York: Holt.

Stevens, Evelyn P.
1973 "Marianismo: The other face of machismo in Latin America." In A. Pescatello (ed.), *Female and Male in Latin America.* Pittsburgh, Pa.: University of Pittsburgh Press.

Stevens, Joseph H., Jr., and Marilyn Mathews
1978 *Mother/Child, Father/Child Relationships.* Washington, D.C. National Association for the Education of Young Children.

Stinnett, Nick, Linda M. Carter, and James Montgomery
1972 "Older persons' perception of their marriages." *Journal of Marriage and the Family* 34:665–670.

Stoler, Ann
1977   "Class structure and female autonomy in rural Java." *Signs* 3(Autumn):74–89.

Stoller, Frederick
1970   "The intimate network of families as a new structure." Pp. 145–159 in Herbert Otto (ed.), *The Family in Search of a Future.* New York: Appleton-Century-Crofts.

Straus, Murray
1971   "Some social antecedents of physical punishment: A linkage theory interpretation." *Journal of Marriage and the Family* 33:658–663.
1973   "A general systems theory approach to a theory of violence between family members." *Social Science Information* 12:105–125.
1974   "Leveling, civility, and violence in the family." *Journal of Marriage and the Family* 36:13–29.
1977   "Sexual inequality, cultural norms, and wife-beating." Pp. 59–77 in Jane Roberts Chapman and Margaret Gates (eds.), *Women into Wives: The Legal and Economic Impact of Marriage.* Beverly Hills, Calif.: Sage.

Straus, Murray, Richard Gelles, and Suzanne Steinmetz
1980   *Behind Closed Doors: Violence in the American Family.* New York: Anchor/Doubleday.

Straus, Murray, and Gerald T. Hotaling
1980   *The Social Causes of Husband-Wife Violence.* Minneapolis: University of Minnesota Press.

Strauss, Anselm (ed.)
1956   *The Social Psychology of George Herbert Mead: Selected Writings of an American Pragmatist.* Chicago: University of Chicago Press.

Streib, Gordon F.
1978   "An alternative family form for older persons: Need and social context." *Family Coordinator* 27(October):413–420.

Streib, Gordon F. and Mary Anne Hilker
1980   "The Cooperative 'Family': An Alternative Lifestyle for the Elderly." *Alternative Lifestyles* 3(May):167–184.

Stryker, Sheldon
1964   "The interactional and situational approaches." Pp. 125–170 in Harold T. Christensen (ed.), *Handbook of Marriage and the Family.* Chicago: Rand McNally.

Stump, Al
1974   "Another oppressed minority is heard from." *TV Guide*, vol. 22, no. 30(July 27), Pp. 32–35.

Sullerot, Evelyne
1971   *Woman, Society and Change.* Translated from the French by Margaret Scotford Archer. New York: McGraw-Hill.

Sussman, Marvin B.
1966   "Theoretical bases for an urban kinship network system." Cleveland: Case-Western Reserve University. Mimeographed.

Sussman, Marvin B., and Lee Burchinal
1962   "Kin family network, unheralded structure in current conceptualization of family functioning." *Marriage and Family Living* 24:231–240.

Sussman, Marvin B., Judith N. Cates, and David T. Smith
1970   *The Family and Inheritance.* New York: Russell Sage.

Symonds, Carolyn
1971   "Sexual mate-swapping: Violation of norms and reconciliation of guilt." Pp. 81–109 in James Henslin (ed.), *Studies in the Sociology of Sex.* New York: Appleton-Century-Crofts.

Talmon, Yonina
1972   *Family and Community in the Kibbutz.* Cambridge, Mass.: Harvard University Press.

Tanner, Donna
1978   *The Lesbian Couple.* Lexington, Mass.: Lexington Books, D.C. Heath.

Targ, Dena
1979   "Toward a reassessment of women's experience at middle age." *The Family Coordinator* 28(July):377–382.

Tarvis, Carol, and Carole Offir
1977   *The Longest War: Sex Differences in Perspective.* New York: Harcourt Brace Jovanovich.

Taylor, Dalmas A.
1968   "The development of interpersonal relationships: Social penetration processes." *The Journal of Social Psychology* 75:79–90.

Taylor, Dalmas, Irwin Altman, and Richard Sorrentino
1969   "Interpersonal exchange as a function of rewards and costs and situational factors: Expectancy confirmation-disconfirmation." *Journal of Experimental Social Psychology* 5:324–339.

Taylor, Jeremy
1650   *The Rule and Exercises of Holy Living.*

Terman, L. M.
1938   *Psychological Factors in Marital Happiness.* New York: McGraw-Hill.

Thibaut, J. W., and H. H. Kelley
1959   *The Social Psychology of Groups.* New York: Wiley.

Thomas, W. I.
1923   *The Unadjusted Girl.* Boston: Little, Brown.
1928   *The Child in America.* New York: Knopf. Cited in Truzzi (ed.), 1971. Pp. 274–275.

Thompson, Linda, and Graham B. Spanier
1978   "Influence of parents, peers, and partners on the contraceptive use of college men and women." *Journal of Marriage and the Family* 40(August):481–492.

Tietze, Christopher
1973   "Two years' experience with a liberal abortion law: Its impact on fertility trends in New York City." *Family Planning Perspectives* 5(Winter):36–41.
1975   "The effect of legalization of abortion on population growth and public health." *Family Planning Perspectives* 7(May/June):123–127.
1979   "Unintended pregnancies in the United States, 1970–1972." *Family Planning Perspectives* 11(May/June):186–188.

Tiger, Lionel
1969 *Men in Groups*. New York: Random House.

Titus, Sandra L.
1976 "Family photographs and transition to parenthood." *Journal of Marriage and the Family* 38(August):525–530.

Toby, Jackson
1966 "Violence and the masculine ideal: Some qualitative data." Pp. 20–27 in Marvin Wolfgang (ed.), *Patterns of Violence: The Annals of the American Academy of Political and Social Science* 364(March).

Tomasson, R. F.
1970 *Sweden: Prototype of Modern Society*. New York: Random House.

Troll, Lillian
1971 "The family of later life: A decade review." *Journal of Marriage and the Family* 33 (May):263–290.

Trost, Jan
1975 "Married and unmarried cohabitation: The case of Sweden, with some comparisons." *Journal of Marriage and the Family* 37(August):677-682.

Truzzi, Marcello (ed.)
1971 *Sociology: The Classic Statements*. New York: Random House.

Turk, J. L., and N. W. Bell
1972 "Measuring power in families." *Journal of Marriage and the Family* 34:215–223.

Turner, Ralph H.
1970 *Family Interaction*. New York: Wiley

Twiss, Harold L. (ed.)
1978 *Homosexuality and the Christian faith: A symposium*. Valley Forge, Pa.: Judson Press.

Tyler, Alice Felt
1944 *Freedom's Ferment*. New York: Harper Torchbooks, 1962.

U.S. Bureau of the Census
1969 *Current Population Reports*. Series P-60, no. 64. October.
1970 *Current Population Reports*, Series P-60, no. 75. December.
1972 *Census of Population, 1970: Marital Status*. Final Report PC(2)-4C.
1972 *Current Population Reports*, Series P-23, no. 42. July.
1973 *Census of Population, 1970: Age at First Marriage*. Final Report PC(2)-4D.
1973 *Current Population Reports*, Series P-23, no. 46. July.
1973 *We the American Elderly*. June.
1974 *Current Population Reports*, Series P-23, no. 48. July.
1976 *Current Population Reports*, Series P-20, No. 297, "Number, Timing, and Duration of Marriages and Divorces in the United States: June, 1975." October.
1976 *Current Population Reports*, Series P-20, no. 298, "Population Characteristics: Daytime Care of Children: October, 1974, and February, 1975." October.
1977 *Current Population Reports*, Series P-20, no. 306, "Marital Status and Living Arrangements, March, 1976." January.
1977 *Current Population Reports*, Series P-20, no.

307, "Population Profile of the United States: 1976." April.
1977 *Current Population Reports*, Series P-20, no. 311, "Household and Family Characteristics: March, 1976." August.
1979 *Current Population Reports*, Series P-23, no. 80, "The Social and Economic Status of the Black Population in the United States: An Historical View, 1790–1978," June.
1979 *Current Population Reports*, Series P-60, no. 118. "Money Income in 1977 of Families and Persons in the United States."
1979 *Current Population Reports*, Series P-60, no. 119, "Characteristics of the Population below the Poverty Level: 1977." March.
1980 *Current Population Reports*, Series P-20, no. 349, "Marital Status and Living Arrangements: March, 1979."

U.S. Department of Health and Human Services: National Center for Health Statistics
1980 *Monthly Vital Statistics Report*, vol. 29, no. 1 Supplement (April 28). "Final Natality Statistics, 1978."

U.S. Department of Health, Education, and Welfare: National Center for Health Statistics
1973 National Center for Health Statistics, Series 21, no. 24. December. *100 Years of Marriage and Divorce Statistics, 1867–1967*.
1974 *Monthly Vital Statistics Report*, vol. 22, no. 13, "Annual Summary for the United States, 1973: Births, Deaths, Marriages, and Divorces."
1975 *Monthly Vital Statistics Report*, vol. 23, no. 12.
1979 *Monthly Vital Statistics Report*, vol. 27, no. 11, Final Natality Statistics, 1977."
1979 *Monthly Vital Statistics Report*, vol. 27, no. 13, "Annual Summary for the United States, 1978."
1979 *Monthly Vital Statistics Report*, vol. 28, no. 2, "Advance Report, Final Divorce Statistics, 1977."
1979 *Monthly Vital Statistics Report*, vol. 28, no. 4. "Final Marriage Statistics, 1977."
1980 *Advance Data*, no. 58. "Remarriages of Women 15-44 Years of Age Whose First Marriage Ended in Divorce: United States, 1976."
1980 *Vital Statistics of the United States, 1977*, vol. II, Section 5, "Life Tables."

U.S. Department of Health, Education, and Welfare: Social Security Administration
1978 "How Recent Changes in Social Security Affect You." February.

U.S. Department of Labor
1970 *Dual Careers: A Longitudinal Study of the Labor Market Experience of Women*, vol. 1. Manpower Research Monograph No. 21.
1973 *Dual Careers*, vol. 2. Manpower Research Monograph No. 21.
1973 *Manpower Report of the President*.

Van Buren, Abigail
1978 "Dear Abby" syndicated column. *Greensboro (N.C.) Record*, Oct. 25.

Varni, Charles A.
1973 "Contexts of conversion: The case of swinging." Pp. 166–181 in Roger W. Libby

and Robert N. Whitehurst (eds.), *Renovating Marriage*. Danville, Calif.: Consensus.

Vaughan, Denton, and Gerald Sparer
1974 "Ethnic group and welfare status of women sterilized in federally funded family planning programs, 1972." *Family Planning Perspectives* 6(Fall):224–229.

Vaughan, Diane
1979 "Uncoupling: The process of moving from one lifestyle to another." *Alternative Lifestyles* 2(November):415–442.

Veevers, J. E.
1972 "Factors in the incidence of childlessness in Canada: An analysis of census data." *Social Biology* 19:266–274.
1973a "Voluntarily childless wives: An exploratory study." *Sociology and Social Research* 57(April):356–366.
1973b "The child-free alternative: Rejection of the motherhood mystique." Pp. 183–199 in Maryles Stephenson (ed.), *Women in Canada*. Toronto: New Press.
1974 "The life style of voluntarily childless couples." In Lyle Larson (ed.), *The Canadian Family in Comparative Perspective*. Toronto: Prentice-Hall.

Vinick, Barbara
1978 "Remarriage in old age." *The Family Coordinator* 27(October):359–363.

Vogel, Ezra F.
1963 *Japan's New Middle Class*. Berkeley: Univ. of California Press.

Wallace, Michele
1979 *Black Macho and the Myth of the Superwoman*. New York: Dial Press.

Wallace, Walter L. (ed.)
1969 *Sociological Theory*. Chicago: Aldine.

Waller, Willard
1930 *The Old Love and the New*. Reprint edition. Carbondale: Southern Illinois University Press, 1967.
1932 *The Sociology of Teaching*. New York: Russell and Russell.
1937 "The rating-dating complex." *American Sociological Review* 2 (October): 727–735.
1951 *The Family*. Revised by Reuben Hill. New York: Dryden Press. (Original edition published in 1938.)

Walshok, Mary Lindenstein
1971 "The emergence of middle-class deviant subcultures: The case of swingers." *Social Problems* 18:488–495.
1973 "Sex role typing and feminine sexuality." Paper presented at the annual meetings of the American Sociological Association, New York, August 30.

Walstedt, Joyce Jennings
1978 "Reform of women's roles and family structures in the recent history of China." *Journal of Marriage and the Family* 40(May):379–392.

Walster, Elaine, and G. William Walster
1978 *A New Look At Love*. Reading, Mass.: Addison-Wesley.

Walster, Elaine, G. William Walster, and Ellen Berscheid
1978 *Equity: Theory and Research*. Boston: Allyn, Bacon.

Ware, Helen
1979 "Polygyny: Women's views in a transitional society, Nigeria, 1975." *Journal of Marriage and the Family* 41(February):185–195.

Washington, Joseph R.
1970 *Marriage in Black and White*. Boston: Beacon.

Watt, Ian
1957 *The Rise of the Novel*. Berkeley: University of California Press.

Weinberg, George
1972 *Society and the Healthy Homosexual*. New York: St. Martin's Doubleday Anchor Press edition, 1973.

Weinberg, Martin, and Colin Williams
1974 *Male Homosexuals*. New York: Oxford.
1975 "Gay baths and the social organization of impersonal sex." *Social Problems* 23(December):124–136.

Weisberg, D. Kelly
1975 "Alternative family structures and the law." *The Family Coordinator* 24(October):549–559.

Weiss, Robert S.
1975 *Marital Separation*. New York: Basic Books.
1979 "Issues in the adjudication of custody when parents separate." Pp. 324–336 in Levinger and Moles (eds).

Weisstein, Naomi
1971 "Psychology constructs and female, or the fantasy life of the male psychologist." Pp. 143–159 in Edith Hoshino Altback (ed.), *From Feminism to Liberation*. Cambridge, Mass.: Schenkman Publishing Co.

Weitz, Shirley
1977 *Sex Roles: Biological, Psychological, and Social Foundations*. New York: Oxford University Press.

Weitzman, Lenore J.
1974 "Legal regulation of marriage: Tradition and change." *California Law Review* 62(July/September):1169–1288.

Weitzman, Lenore J., and Ruth B. Dixon
1976 "Alimony: A quest for justice in changing times." Paper read at the annual meetings of the American Sociological Association, New York, August. Final version in *Family Law Quarterly*, Fall 1980 (in press).
1979 "Child Custody Awards: Legal Standards and Empirical Patterns for Child Custody, Support, and Visitation after Divorce." *UCD Law Review* 12 (Summer):473–521.

Weitzman, Lenore, Carol Dixon, Joyce Adair Bird, Neil McGinn, and Dena Robertson
1978 "Contracts for intimate relationships: A study of contracts before, within, and in lieu of legal marriage." *Alternative Lifestyles* 1(August):303–378.

Welter, Barbara
1966 "The cult of true womanhood: 1820-1860." *American Quarterly* 18:151–174.

Westoff, Charles F.
1972 "The modernization of U.S. contraceptive practice." *Family Planning Perspectives* 4(July):9–12.

1974a "Coital frequency and contraception." *Family Planning Perspectives* 6(Summer): 136–141.

1974b "The populations of the developed countries." *Scientific American* 231(September):109–120.

Westoff, Charles F., and others
1973 *Toward the End of Growth: Population in America.* Englewood Cliffs, N.J.: Prentice-Hall.

Westoff, Charles F., and Elise Jones
1977a "The secularization of U.S. Catholic birth control practices." *Family Planning Perspectives* 9(September/October):203–207.

1977b "Contraception and sterilization in the United States, 1965–1975." *Family Planning Perspectives* 9(July/August):153–157.

1978 "The end of 'Catholic' fertility." Paper presented at the annual meeting of the Population Association of America, Atlanta, April 12–15. Summarized in "Digest." *Family Planning Perspectives* 10(July/August): 240–241.

1979 "Patterns of aggregate and individual changes in contraceptive practice." *Vital and Health Statistics,* series 3, number 17. Department of Health, Education and Welfare.

Westoff, Charles, and James McCarthy
1979 "Sterilization in the United States." *Family Planning Perspectives* 11(May/June):147–152.

Westoff, C. F., R. G. Potter, and P. C. Sagi
1963 *The Third Child.* Princeton, N.J.: Princeton University Press.

Westoff, Charles F., and R. H. Potvin
1967 *College Women and Fertility Values.* Princeton, N.J.: Princeton University Press.

Westoff, Charles, and Norman Ryder
1977 *The Contraceptive Revolution.* Princeton, N.J.: Princeton University Press.

Westoff, Leslie Aldridge, and Charles F. Westoff
1971 *From Now to Zero: Fertility, Contraception, and Abortion in America.* Boston: Little, Brown.

Whelpton, P. K., A. A. Campbell, and J. E. Patterson
1966 *Fertility and Family Planning in the United States.* Princeton, N.J.: Princeton University Press.

White, Lynn
1979 "Sex differentials in the effect of remarriage on global happiness." *Journal of Marriage and the Family* 41(Nov.):869–876.

White, Mervin, and Carolyn Wells
1973 "Student attitudes toward alternate marriage forms." Pp. 280–295 in Roger Libby and Robert Whitehurst (eds.), *Renovating Marriage.* Danville, Calif.: Consensus Publishers.

White, Ralph
1966 "Misperception as a cause of two world wars." *Journal of Social Issues* 22:1–19.

Whitehead, Harriet
1976a "Review of *Woman's Evolution* by Evelyn Reed." *Signs* 1(Spring):746–748.
1976b "A reply." *Signs* 2(Winter):508–511.

Whitehurst, Robert
1974a "Sex role equality and changing meanings of cohabitation." Unpublished manuscript. University of Windsor.
1974b "Violence in husband-wife interaction." Pp. 75–82 in Steinmetz and Straus, 1974.

Williams, J. Allen, Jr., and Robert Stockton
1973 "Black family structures and functions: An empirical examination of some suggestions made by Billingsley." *Journal of Marriage and the Family* 33(February):39–49.

Williamson, Nancy E.
1976 *Sons or Daughters: A Cross-Cultural Survey of Parental Preferences.* Beverly Hills: Sage.

Wilson, Edward O.
1975 *Sociobiology: The New Synthesis.* Cambridge, Mass.: Belknap.

Wilson, Kenneth, Louis Zurcher, Diana Claire McAdams, and Russell L. Curtis.
1975 "Stepfathers and stepchildren: An exploratory analysis from two national surveys." *Journal of Marriage and the Family* 37(August):526–536.

Winch, Robert
1962 *Identification and Its Familial Determinants.* Indianapolis: Bobbs-Merrill.

Winch, Robert, and Margaret Gordon
1974 *Familial Structure and Function as Influence.* Lexington, Mass.: D. C. Heath, Lexington Books.

Winter, David
1973 *The Power Motive.* New York: Free Press.

Wirth, Louis
1938 "Urbanism as a way of life." *American Journal of Sociology* 44:1–24.

Wise, Daniel
1859 *The Young Lady's Counselor.* Cincinnati: Swormstedt and Poe.

Wollstonecraft, Mary
1792 *A Vindication of the Rights of Woman.* Reprint edition, edited by Charles W. Hagelman, Jr. New York: Norton, 1967.

Wood, Vivian, and Joan Robertson
1978 "Friendship and kinship interaction: Differential effect on the morale of the elderly." *Journal of Marriage and the Family* 40(May):367–375.

Woods, Richard
1978 *Another Kind of Love: Homosexuality and Spirituality.* Garden City, N.Y.: Doubleday Image Books.

Woolley, Persia
1978 "Shared Custody." *Family Advocate* 1(Summer):6–9, 33–34.

Worthy, Morgan, Albert Gary, and Gay Kahn
1969 "Self-disclosure as an exchange process." *Journal of Personality and Social Psychology* 13:59–63.

Wright, Gerald C., Jr. and Dorothy M. Stetson
1978 "The impact of no-fault divorce law reform on divorce in American states." *Journal of Marriage and the Family* 40(August):575–580.

Wu, Tson-Shien
1972 "The value of children or boy preference?" In Fawcett, 1972.

Yankelovich, Daniel
1974 "The meaning of work." Pp. 19–48 in

J. M. Rosow (ed.), *The Worker and the Job.* Englewood Cliffs, N.J.: Prentice-Hall.

Yllo, Kersti Alice
1978 "Nonmarital cohabitation: Beyond the college campus." *Alternative Lifestyles* 1(February):37–54.

Yoder, John Howard
1974 "Singleness in ethical and pastoral perspective." Mimeographed. Elkhart, Ind.: Associated Mennonite Biblical Seminaries.

Young, James, and Muriel Hamilton
1978 "Paternal behavior: Implications for child-rearing practice." Pp. 135–145 in Joseph Stevens, Jr. and Marilyn Mathews (eds.), *Mother/Child, Father/Child Relationships.* Washington, D.C.: National Association for the Education of Young Children, 1978.

Zablocki, Benjamin
1971 *The Joyful Community.* Baltimore: Penguin.

Zelnik, Melvin, and John F. Kantner
1977 "Sexual and contraceptive experience of young unmarried women in the United States, 1976 and 1971." *Family Planning Perspectives* 9(March/April):55–71.
1978 "Contraceptive patterns and premarital pregnancy among women aged 15-19 in 1976." *Family Planning Perspectives* 10(May/June):135–142.

Zetkin, Clara
1934 *Lenin on the Woman Question.* New York: International Publishers.

ACKNOWLEDGMENTS

Addison-Wesley Publishing Company, Inc.

Reprinted from *A New Look at Love* by Elaine Walster and G. William Walster, copyright © 1978, by permission of Addison-Wesley Publishing Company, Inc., Reading, Massachusetts.

The Art Institute of Chicago

Cover photograph of *America — Dawn* by Louise Nevelson. Photograph by Allan Mitchell.

Associated Press

Permission was granted by the Associated Press for "Woman Wins Award in Virginity Suit," "81-Year-Old Father Back into Diaper Routine," "Family Imprisons Woman 29 Years after Love Affair," "Finding Identical Twin Brother Alive 'Greatest Thing,' " "Number of Abortions Growing," "10-Year-Old Is Mother of Twins," "Love's Labor Lost and Found," "Jilted Husband Wins Suit over Stolen Wife," and "Lawyers: Repeal Marriage Tax Penalty."

Basic Books, Inc.

Excerpt from *Friends and Lovers* by Robert Brain reprinted by permission of Basic Books, Inc., © 1976 by Robert Brain.
Excerpt from *Divorce and Separation* by Arthur J. Norton and Paul C. Glick, reprinted by permission of Basic Books, Inc., © 1979 by the Society of Psychological Study of Social Issue.
Excerpt from *Fathers, Mothers, and Society* by Rhona Rapoport, Robert Rapoport, Ziona Strelitz, and Stephen Kew reprinted by permission of Basic Books, Inc., © 1977 by Rhona Rapoport, Robert Rapoport, and Ziona Strelitz.
Excerpt from *Worlds of Pain* by Lillian B. Rubin reprinted by permission of Basic Books, Inc., © 1976 by Lillian B. Rubin.

Beacon Press

From *Sunday's Women: A Report on Lesbian Life Today* by Sasha Gregory Lewis. Copyright © 1979 by Sasha Gregory Lewis. Reprinted by permission of Beacon Press.

California Law Review

Weitzman, Lenore J., "Legal Regulation of Marriage: Tradition and Change." Copyright © 1974, California Law Review, Inc., reprinted by permission.

The Dial Press

Excerpt from the book *The Future of Motherhood* by Jesse Bernard. Copyright © 1974 by Jesse Bernard. Reprinted by permission of The Dial Press.

Family Law Quarterly

Orthner, Dennis, and Ken Lewis, "Evidence of Single Father Competence in Childrearing." Reprinted by permission of Sanford H. Katz, editor in chief of *Family Law Quarterly*.

Family Planning Perspectives

Excerpt from "Anniversaries" reprinted with permission of *Family Planning Perspectives*, volume 11, number 1, 1979.
Excerpt from "Sexual and Contraceptive Knowledge, Attitudes, and Behavior of Male Adolescents," by Madelon F. Finkel and David J. Finkel reprinted with permission of *Family Planning Perspectives*, volume 7, number 6, 1975.

Excerpt from "Abortion in the United States, 1976-1977" by Jacqueline D. Forrest, Christopher Tietze, and Ellen Sullivan reprinted with permission of *Family Planning Perspectives*, volume 10, number 5, 1978.
Excerpt from "Contraceptive Failure in the United States" by Norman Ryder reprinted with permission of *Family Planning Perspectives*, volume 5, number 3, 1973.
Excerpt from "Coital Frequency and Contraception" by Charles F. Westoff reprinted by permission of *Family Planning Perspectives*, volume 6, number 3, 1974.
Excerpt from "The Secularization of U.S. Catholic Birth Control Practices" by Charles F. Westoff and Elise F. Jones reprinted by permission of *Family Planning Perscectives*, volume 9, number 5, 1977.
Excerpt from "Sexual and Contraceptive Experience of Young Unmarried Women in the United States" by Melvin Zelnick and John F. Kantner reprinted with permission of *Family Planning Perspectives*, volume 9, number 2, 1977.

Field Newspaper Syndicate

To Your Good Health by Paul G. Donohue, M.D. © 1980 Field Enterprises, Inc. Courtesy of Field Newspaper Syndicate.

G. K. Hall and Company

Chambers-Schiller, Lee, "The Single Woman: Family and Vocation among Nineteenth Century Reformers," in *Woman's Being Woman's Place*. Copyright © 1979 by G. K. Hall, and reprinted with the permission of G. K. Hall and Company, Boston.

Harper & Row, Publishers, Inc.

Brief excerpt from *Motivation and Personality*, 2nd edition, by Abraham H. Maslow. Copyright © 1970 by Abraham H. Maslow. From pp. 7-8, 179-180, 197-198 in *Woman of a Certain Age: The Mid-life Search for Self* by Lillian B. Rubin. Copyright © 1979 by Lillian B. Rubin.

Houghton Mifflin Company

From *Economics and the Public Purpose* by John Kenneth Galbraith, published by Houghton Mifflin Company. Copyright © 1973 by John Kenneth Galbraith. Reprinted by permission.
From *Living Together: A Guide to the Law for Unmarried Couples* by Barbara Hirsch, published by Houghton Mifflin Company. Copyright © 1976 by Barbara B. Hirsch. Reprinted by permission.
From *Unbought and Unbossed* by Shirley Chisholm, published by Houghton Mifflin Company. Copyright © 1970 by Shirley Chisholm. Reprinted by permission.

Macmillan Publishing Company

The Economics of Being a Woman by Dee Dee Ahern, with Betsy Bliss. Copyright © 1976 by Dee Dee Ahern and Betsy Bliss.

National Council on Family Relations

Berger, David G., and Morton G. Wegner, "The Ideology of Virginity," *Journal of Marriage and the Family*. Copyright © 1973 by the National Council on Family Relations. Reprinted by permission.
Christensen, Harold T., and Christina F. Gregg, "Changing Sex Norms in America and Scandinava," *Journal of Marriage and the*

A-3

ACKNOWLEDGMENTS

Stein and Day, Inc.

Excerpt from *Living in Step*, copyright © 1976 by Ruth Roosevelt and Jeanette Lofas. Reprinted with permission of Stein and Day Publishers.

University of Chicago Press

Reprinted from "Preface to Special Issue on Women and National Development," *Signs*, by permission of the University of Chicago Press, copyright 1977.
Reprinted from "Female Status and Premarital Sexual Codes," *American Journal of Sociology*, by permission of the University of Chicago Press, copyright 1966.
Reprinted from "Images of Women in Recent Chinese Fiction," *Signs*, by permission of the University of Chicago Press, copyright 1976.
Reprinted from "Nice Girl," *Signs*, by Greer Litton Fox, by permission of the University of Chicago Press, copyright 1977.
Reprinted from *The Black Extended Family* by Elmer and Joanne M. Martin by permission of the University of Chicago Press, copyright 1978.
Reprinted from *American Kinship* by David Schneider by permission of the University of Chicago Press, copyright 1968.
Reprinted from "Migrants and Women Who Wait," *Signs*, by permission of the University of Chicago Press, copyright 1977.

University of New Mexico Press

Excerpt from *Sex Roles in Law and Society* by Leo Kanowitz reprinted with permission of The University of New Mexico Press.

West Publishing Company, Inc.

Excerpt from *Sex-based Discrimination* by Kenneth Davidson, Ruth B. Ginsburg, and Herman H. Kay reprinted with permission of West Publishing Company, Inc.

NAME INDEX

SUBJECT INDEX